PATROLOGY

VOL. II
THE ANTE-NICENE LITERATURE
AFTER IRENAEUS

PATROLOGY

By

JOHANNES QUASTEN

PROFESSOR OF ANCIENT CHURCH HISTORY AND
CHRISTIAN ARCHAEOLOGY
THE CATHOLIC UNIVERSITY OF AMERICA
WASHINGTON D. C.

VOL. II

*The Ante-Nicene Literature
after Irenaeus*

MDCCCCLIII
THE NEWMAN PRESS
WESTMINSTER, MARYLAND

SPECTRUM PUBLISHERS
UTRECHT ANTWERP

5 1 7 6 4

TABLE OF CONTENTS

CHAPTER I

CHAPTER III

THE ROMANS

CHAPTER IV

CHAPTER V

The Other Writers of the West

CHAPTER I

THE ALEXANDRIANS

Towards 200 A.D., ecclesiastical literature not only shows signs of tremendous growth, it takes an entirely new turn. The writing of the second century had been conditioned by the struggle of the Church against her persecutors. The works of that period were characterized by defense and attack; they were apologetic and anti-heretical. But the enduring achievement of these early authors consisted in their service to Christian theology, for which they laid the foundation. While they were championing the faith with the weapons of the intellect, they prepared the way for the scientific study of revelation.

No Christian author had as yet attempted to consider the entire body of belief as a whole or make a systematic presentation of it. Even the accomplishment of St. Irenaeus, however great its merits, does not answer the question whether ecclesiastical literature should simply remain a weapon against enemies or become a tool of peaceful work within the Church's own borders. The deeper the new religion penetrated the ancient world, the more the need was felt for an exposition of its tenets that was orderly, comprehensive and exact. The more numerous the converts in educated circles, the greater the necessity to give such catechumens an instruction corresponding to their environment and to train teachers for that purpose. Thus were created the theological schools, the cradles of sacred science. They first arose in the Orient, where Christianity had its beginnings and widest extension, and the most famous, at Alexandria in Egypt, is also that about which we are best informed. This city, founded by Alexander the Great in 331 B.C., centre of a brilliant intellectual life long before Christianity made its appearance, was the birthplace of Hellenism; it was there that the commingling of Oriental, Egyptian, and Greek cultures had given rise to a new civilization. There, too, Jewish culture found a congenial soil. At Alexandria Greek thought exercised its strongest influence on the Hebrew mind. At Alexandria was created the work that constitutes the beginning of Jewish-Hellenistic literature, the Septuagint, and it was at Alexandria that lived the writer in whom that literature culminated, Philo. Firmly convinced that the teaching of the Old Testament could be combined with Greek speculation, his philosophy of religion embodies such a synthesis.

Studies: E. BREHIER, Les idées philosophiques et religieuses de Philon d'Alexandrie. Paris, 1908. — C. BIGG, The Origins of Christianity. Oxford, 1909. — P. D. SCOTT-MUNCRIEFF, Gnosticism and Early Christianity in Egypt: ChQ 69 (1909) 64–83; *idem,* Paganism and Christianity in Egypt. Cambridge, 1913. — K. VÖLKER, Alexandrien in der alten Kirche: Die Christl. Welt 27 (1913) 79 ff.; 102. — A. HECKEL, Die Kirche von Ägypten bis zum Nicaenum. Diss. Strasbourg, 1918. — E. BRECCIA, Alexandria ad Aegyptum. Milan, 1922. — L. CERFAUX, L'influence des mystères sur le Judaisme alexandrin avant Philon: Mus 37 (1924) 29–88. — H. J. BELL, Jews and Christians in Egypt. London, 1924. — E. BEVAN, History of Egypt. Oxford, 1927. — H. R. WILLOUGHBY, Pagan Regeneration. A Study of the Mystery Initiations in the Graeco-Roman World. Chicago, 1929. — J. HEINEMANN, Philos griechische und jüdische Bildung. Breslau, 1932. — F. C. BURKITT, Church and Gnosis. A Study of Christian Thought in the Second Century. Cambridge, 1932. — J. MUNCK, Untersuchungen über Klemens von Alexandria. Stuttgart, 1933, 180–185; 224–229. — E. BETHE, Tausend Jahre altgriechischen Lebens. Munich, 1933, 107–133. — L. ALLEVI, Ellenismo e Cristianesimo. Milan, 1934. — R. ARNOU, Platonisme des Pères: DTC 12 (1935) 2258–2392. — E. J. FOAKES JACKSON, A History of Church History. Cambridge, 1939, 39–55: Philo and Alexandrian Judaism. — A. D. NOCK, The Development of Paganism in the Roman Empire: Cambridge Ancient History 12. Cambridge, 1939, 409–448. — E. R. GOODENOUGH, An Introduction to Philo Judaeus. New Haven, 1940. — M. NILSSON, Problems of the History of Greek Religion in the Hellenistic and Roman Age: HThR 36 (1943) 251–275. — W. C. TILL, Die Gnosis in Ägypten: La parola del passato 12 (1949) 230–249. — W. SCHUBART, Alexandria: RACh 1, 271–283.

THE SCHOOL OF ALEXANDRIA

When Christianity entered the city at the end of the first century it came in close contact with all of these elements. As a result there sprang up that strong interest in problems of an abstract nature that led to the foundation of a theological school. The school of Alexandria is the oldest centre of sacred science in the history of Christianity. The environment in which it developed gave it its distinctive characteristics, predominant interest in the metaphysical investigation of the content of the faith, a leaning to the philosophy of Plato, and the allegorical interpretation of Sacred Scripture. It counted among its students and teachers such famous theologians as Clement, Origen, Dionysius, Pierius, Peter, Athanasius, Didymus and Cyril.

Studies: W. Bousset, Jüdisch-christlicher Schulbetrieb in Alexandria und Rom. Göttingen, 1915. — H. R. Nelz, Die theologischen Schulen der morgenländischen Kirchen während der sieben ersten christlichen Jahrhunderte in ihrer Bedeutung für die Ausbildung des Klerus. Diss. theol. Bonn, 1916. — J. Munck, *loc. cit.* — J. Salaverri, La Filosofía en la Escuela Alejandrina: Greg 15 (1934) 485-499. — P. Leturia, El primo esbozo de una universidad católica o la escuela catequética de Alejandria: RF 106 (1934) 297-314. — G. Bardy, Aux origines de l'école d'Alexandrie: RSR 27 (1937) 65-90; *idem,* Pour l'histoire de l'École d'Alexandrie: Vivre et Penser 2 (1942) 80-109. — R. Cadiou, Origen. His Life at Alexandria. Transl. by J. A. Southwell, St. Louis and London, 1944, 49-65. — P. Brezzi, La gnosi cristiana di Alessandria e le antiche scuole cristiane. 1950. — W. Jentsch, Urchristliches Erziehungsdenken. Die Paideia Kyriu im Rahmen der hellenistisch-jüdischen Umwelt (BFTh 45, 3). Gütersloh, 1951. — A. Knauber, Katechetenschule oder Schulkatechumenat?: TThZ 60 (1951) 243-266.

The allegorical method had been used for a long time by Greek philosophers in the interpretation of myths and fables about the gods as they appear in Homer and Hesiod. Xenophanes, Pythagoras, Plato, Antisthenes and others attemped thus to find a deep significance in such stories, the literal meaning of which was offensive. The Stoa, especially, adopted this system. The first Jewish representative of allegorical exegesis is the Alexandrian Aristobulus about the middle of the second century B.C. His Hellenistic education induced him to apply it to Greek poetry as well as to the Old Testament. The Epistle of Aristeas defends with the same weapon the food laws of the Old Dispensation. But it was above all Philo of Alexandria who employed allegory in the explanation of the Bible. To him the literal sense of Holy Scripture is only as the shadow to the body. The allegorical and deeper meaning represents the true reality. The Christian thinkers of Alexandria adopted this method because they were convinced that a literal interpretation is in many cases unworthy of God. Whereas Clement makes abundant use of it, Origen formed it into a system. Neither theology nor scriptural exegesis would have taken such magnificent initial strides without it. In the age of Clement and Origen and in the centre of Hellenistic learning, it had the great advantage of opening a vast field to nascent theology and of allowing the fertile contact of Greek philosophy and revelation. In addition, it contributed to the solution of the most significant problem posed for the early Church, i.e., the meaning to be given to the Old Testament. It had a legitimate authorized origin in St. Paul

(Gal. 4,24; 1 Cor. 9,9). However, the tendency to find prefigurations in every line of Scripture and to neglect the literal sense, was not without danger.

Studies: C. SIEGFRIED, Philo von Alexandrien als Ausleger des Alten Testamentes. Jena, 1875. — G. A. v. D. BERGH V. EYSINGA, Allegorische interpretatie. Amsterdam, 1904. — P. HEINISCH, Der Einfluß Philos auf die älteste christliche Exegese. Münster i.W., 1908. — A. B. HERSMAN, Studies in Greek Allegoric Interpretation. Chicago, 1906. — O. CASEL, De philosophorum Graecorum silentio mystico. Giessen, 1919, 42–50. — F. WEHRLI, Zur Geschichte der allegorischen Deutung Homers im Altertum. Leipzig, 1928. — E. STEIN, Allegorische Auslegung: Encycl. Judaica 2, 338–351; *idem*, Die allegorische Schriftauslegung des Philo aus Alexandrien. Giessen, 1929. — J. TATE, Cornutus and the Poets: CQ 23 (1929) 41–45; Plato and Allegorical Interpretation: *ibid.* 23 (1929) 142–154; 24 (1930) 1–10; On the History of Allegorism: *ibid.* 28 (1934) 105–114. — E. C. KNOWLTON, Notes on Early Allegory: Journal of Engl. and German Philology 29 (1930) 159–181. — J. L. KOOLE, Allegorische Schriftverklaring: Vox theologica 10 (1938) 14–22. — R. HINKS, Myth and Allegory in Ancient Art. London, 1939. — F. BÜCHSEL, ἀλληγορέω: Theol. Wörterbuch z. Neuen Test. 1, 260–264. — J. C. JOOSEN-J. H. WASZINK, Allegorese: RACh 1, 283–293. — H. DE LUBAC, Typologie et allégorisme: RSR 34 (1947) 180–226. — J. DANIÉLOU, Revue des revues: autour de l'exégèse spirituelle: Dieu vivant 8 (1947) 124 ff. — J. GUILLET, Les exégèses d'Alexandrie et d'Antioche: RSR 34 (1947) 257–302. — J. DANIÉLOU, Origène. Paris, 1948, 145–174; *idem*, Les divers sens de l'Écriture dans la tradition chrétienne primitive: ETL 24 (1948) 119–126. — W. J. BURGHARDT, On Early Christian Exegesis: TS 11 (1950) 78–116.

PANTAENUS

The first known rector of the school of Alexandria was Pantaenus. He was a Sicilian and became a convert to the Christian religion after having been a Stoic philosopher. Subsequently, according to Eusebius (*Hist. eccl.* 5,10,1), he made a missionary journey that brought him as far as India. Most probably about the year A.D. 180 he came to Alexandria and was soon appointed head of the school of catechumens in that city. In that position he became the teacher of Clement of Alexandria. He remained in charge of this institution until he died shortly before the year A.D. 200. Clement (*Strom.* 1,1,11) as well as Eusebius (*Hist. eccl.* 5,10) testifies that as an instructor he won universal acclaim and reputation. That's all the information we have about Pantaenus. If he composed any writings, none of them are left and known. The attempt to discover the literary work of Pantaenus or some of it in Clement of Alexandria must be pronounced unsuccessful. H. I. Marrou thinks that he is the author of the *Epistle to Diognetus* (cf. vol. I, p. 248 f).

Texts: MG 5, 1327–1332. — A. v. HARNACK, Geschichte der altchristl. Literatur 1, 291–296.

Studies: TH. ZAHN, Forschungen zur Geschichte des neutestamentl. Kanons 3. Erlangen, 1884, 156–176. — J. MUNCK, Untersuchungen über Klemens von Alexandria. Stuttgart, 1933, 151–204. — G. BARDY, Aux origines de l'école d'Alexandrie: RSR 27 (1937) 65–90. — A. W. PARSONS, A Family of Philosophers at Athens and Alexandria: Hesperia Suppl. VIII (1950) (Studies Shear) 268–272. — H. I. MARROU, A Diognète. Introduction, édition critique, traduction et commentaire (SCH 33). Paris, 1941, 266 ff.

CLEMENT OF ALEXANDRIA

Titus Flavius Clemens was born about the year A.D. 150. He was the son of pagan parents. It seems that Athens was his native city and that he received his first training there. Nothing is known about the date, the occasion and the motives for his conversion. After he became a Christian he made extensive travels to Southern Italy, Syria and Palestine. His purpose was to seek instruction from the most famous Christian teachers. He remarks himself that he 'was privileged to hear discourses of blessed and truly remarkable men' (*Strom.* 1,1,11). But what was of the greatest importance for his scholarly education was that his journeying brought him in the end to Alexandria. Pantaenus' lectures had such attraction for him that he settled down there and made that city his second home. Of his teacher Pantaenus he states:

> When I came upon the last [teacher]—he was the first in power—having tracked him out concealed in Egypt, I found rest. He, the true, the Sicilian bee gathering the spoil of the flowers of the prophetic and apostolic meadow, engendered in the souls of his hearers a deathless element of knowledge (ANF).

He became the pupil, associate and assistant of Pantaenus and finally succeeded him as head of the school of catechumens. It is not possible to ascertain when he fell heir to his master's position, most probably about 200 A.D. Two or three years later the persecution of Septimius Severus forced him to leave Egypt. He took refuge in Cappadocia with his pupil, Alexander, later bishop of Jerusalem. There he died shortly before 215 A.D. without having seen Egypt again.

Studies: F. R. M. HITCHCOCK, Clement of Alexandria. London, 1899. — E. BUONAIUTI, Clemente Alessandrino e la cultura classica: Rivista storico-crit. di scienze teolog. 1 (1905) 393–412. — E. DE FAYE, Clément d'Alexandrie. 2nd ed. Paris, 1906. — A. DE LA BARRE, DTC 3 (1908) 137–199. — J. PATRICK, Clement of Alexandria. Edinburgh, 1914. — R. B. TOLLINTON, Clement of Alexandria. A Study in Christian Liberalism. London, 1914. — H. EIBL, Die Stellung des Klemens v. Alexandrien zur griechischen Bildung: Zeitschrift f. Philosophie 164 (1917) 33–59. — H. KOCH, War Klemens von Alexandrien Priester?: ZNW 20 (1921) 43–48. — J. ZELLINGER, Klemens von Al. und die Erscheinungsformen spätantiken Lebens: Gelbe Hefte 1 (1924) 28–44. — F. PRAT, Projets littéraires de Clément d'Alexandrie: RSR 15 (1925) 234–257. — R. B. TOLLINTON, Alexandrine Teaching on the Universe. New York, 1932. — J. MUNCK, Untersuchungen über Klemens von Alexandria. Stuttgart, 1933. — J. BARDY, Aux origines de l'école d'Alexandrie: RSR (1933) 430–450. — A. PHYTRAKES, Αἱ κοινωνικαὶ ἰδέαι Κλήμεντος τοῦ 'Αλεξανδρέως. Athens, 1935. — G. LAZZATI, Introduzione allo studio di Clemente Alessandrino. Milan, 1939. — H. POHLENZ, Klemens von Alexandria und sein hellenisches Christentum: NGWG Philol.-histor. Klasse 3 (1943) 103–180. — J. CHAMPONIER, Naissance de l'humanisme chrétien: Bulletin de l'Association G. Budé. N.S. 3 (1947) 58–96. — M. PUGLIESI, L'apologetica greca e Clemente Alessandrino. Diss. Catania, 1947. — R. WILDE, The Treatment of the Jews in the Greek Christian Writers of the First Three Centuries (PSt 81). Washington, 1949, 169–180. — G. CATALFAMO, S. Clemente Alessandrino. Brescia, 1951.

I. HIS WRITINGS

Although we know very little of Clement's life, we gain a clear picture of his personality from his writings, which show the hand of a master planner and for the first time brought Christian doctrine face to face with the ideas and achievements of the time. For this reason he must be called the pioneer of Christian scholarship. His literary work proves that he was a man of comprehensive education extending to philosophy, poetry, archaeology, mythology and literature. He did not, it is true, always go back to the original sources but in many instances used anthologies and florilegia. But his knowledge of early Christian literature, of the Bible as well as of all post-apostolic and heretical works, is complete. He alludes to the Old Testament in 1500 passages and to the New in 2000. He is also well versed in the classics, from which he quotes no fewer than 360 passages.

Clement knew very well that the Church could not avoid

competition with pagan philosophy and literature if she was to fulfill her duty towards mankind and live up to her task as teacher of the nations. His Hellenistic education enabled him to make of the Christian faith a system of thought with a scientific foundation. We owe it above all to him if scholarly thinking and research are recognized in the Church. He proved that the faith and philosophy, Gospel and secular learning, are not enemies but belong together. All secular learning serves theology. Christianity is the crown and glory of all the truths that are found in the various philosophical doctrines.

Editions: MG 8–9. — O. STÄHLIN, GCS 12 (2nd ed. 1939), 15 (2nd ed. 1939), 17 (1909), 39, 1–2 Index (1934/36).

Translations: English: W. WILSON, ANL 4, 12, 22, 24 (1867–1872); ANF 2 (1887). — *French:* A. E. DE GENOUDE, Les Pères de l'église 4, 5 (1839). — *German:* O. STÄHLIN, BKV³ 7 (1934), 8 (1934), 17 (1936), 19 (1937), 20 (1938). — *Dutch:* H. U. MEY-BOOM, (Oudchristelijke geschriften, dl. 8–19). Leiden, 1912–1915.

Selections: English: R. M. JONES, Selections from the Writings of Clement of Alexandria. London, 1909. — *French:* G. BARDY, Clément d'Alexandrie (Les moralistes chrétiens). Paris, 1926. — *Spanish translation:* G. BARDY, Clemente de Alejandria. Trad. por J. GUASP DELGADO. Madrid, 1930. — *German:* Th. RÜTHER, Gott ruft die Seele. Auslese aus Clemens von Alexandrien (Dokumente der Religion 9). Pader-born, 1923.

Of his writings, three form a kind of trilogy and give reliable information about his theological position and his theological system. They are his *Protrepticus*, his *Paedagogus* and his *Stromata*.

1. *The Exhortation*

The first of these writings, the *Exhortation to the Greeks* (Προτρεπτικὸς πρὸς "Ελληνας) is an 'address aiming at conversion.' Its purpose is to convince the worshippers of the gods of the folly and worthlessness of pagan beliefs, to point out the shameless features of obscure mysteries and to induce them to accept the only true religion, the teaching of the Logos of the world, who after being announced by the prophets, has appeared as Christ. He promises a life which leads to the fulfilment of the deepest human longing because it gives redemption and immortality. Clement defines this address at the end of his work as follows:

What then is the address I give you? I urge you to be
saved. This Christ desires. In one word, He freely bestows
life on you. And who is He? Briefly learn. The Word of
truth, the Word of incorruption that generates man by
bringing him back to the truth—the goad that urges to
salvation—He who expels destruction and pursues death—He
who builds up the temple of God in men that He may cause
God to take up His abode in men (*Protrept.* 11,117, 3–4, ANF).

As far as the content goes, the *Exhortation to the Greeks* is closely
related to the early Christian apologies with their familiar
polemic against the ancient mythology and their defense of the
greater antiquity of the Old Testament. Clement knew these
writings and made use of them. Like them he takes his proofs
against pagan religion and worship from Greek popular philosophy. However, if we compare these with the *Exhortation*, it
becomes evident that Clement does not deem it necessary any
longer to defend Christianity against the false accusations and
calumnies to which it was exposed at the beginning. There is
another definite advance in Clement's treatise because he combines with his polemic a superior conviction, a calm assurance
of the educative function of the Logos throughout the history of
mankind. He praises with poetic power and in glowing words
the sublimity of the revelation of the Logos and the marvellous
gift of divine grace which fulfills all human desire.

According to its literary form the *Exhortation* must be classified
with the *Protreptikoi* or Exhortations intended to encourage men
to come to a certain decision and to inspire them for a lofty
goal, for instance, for the study of philosophy. Aristotle, Epicurus
and the Stoics Cleanthes, Chrysippus and Poseidonius wrote a
Protrepticus. Cicero's *Hortensius*, which St. Augustine read before
his conversion, belongs to the same class. Thus Clement intends
to fill his readers with enthusiasm for the only true philosophy,
the Christian religion.

Editions: O. Stählin, GCS 12 (1936) 3–86. — G. W. Butterworth, Clement of
Alexandria with an English translation (LCL). London-New York, 1919, 2–263. —
Q. Cataudella, Protreptico ai Greci, testo, trad., comm. (Corona Patrum Sal. Ser.
graec. 3). Turin, 1940. — C. Mondésert, Clément d'Alexandrie, Le Protreptique.
Introduction, text, translation. 2nd ed. (SCH 2). Paris, 1949.

Translations: English: W. Wilson, ANL 4; ANF 2, 171–206. — G. W. Butterworth, *loc. cit.* — *French:* C. MONDÉSERT, *loc. cit.* — *German:* O. STÄHLIN, BKV³ 7 (1934) 71–199. — *Italian:* Q. CATAUDELLA, *loc. cit.* — *Dutch:* H. U. MEYBOOM, De vermaning tot de Grieken (Oudchristelijke geschriften, deel 8). Leiden, 1911.

Studies: G. BUTTERWORTH, Clement of Alexandria's Protrepticus and the Phaedrus of Plato: CQ 10 (1916) 198–205. — M. R. JAMES, Protrept. 44: JThSt 21 (1920) 337 ff. — A. J. FESTUGIÈRE, Εἰς ἄνθρωπον ὑποφέρεσθαι (Protr. 9, 186, 2): RSPT 20 (1931) 476–482. — J. JACKSON, Minutiae Clementinae: JThSt 32 (1931) 357–370; 394–407. — A. J. FESTUGIÈRE, 'Tomber dans l'homme' (Protr. 9, 83, 2): RSPT 26 (1937) 41–42. — P. WINDHORST, Χερσὶν ἡπλωμέναις (Protr. 1): De difficilioris cuiusdem textus apud Clem. Alex. forma primigenia: RSR (1939) 496–497. — L. ALFONSI, In Clementis Alexandrini Προτρεπτικὸν πρὸς "Ελληνας criticae annotatiunculae quattuor: Aevum (1942) 83–86; *idem,* L'elemento artistico nel Protreptico di Clemente Alessandrino: SC (1945) 205–216; *idem,* Il Protreptico di Clemente Alessandrino e l'Epistola a Diogneto: Aevum (1946) 100–108.

For Clement's description of *pagan mysteries* E. BRATKE, Die Stellung des Klemens Alexandrinus zum antiken Mysterienwesen: ThStKr 60 (1887) 647–708. — C. HONTOIR, Comment Clément d'Alexandrie a connu les Mystères d'Eleusis: Le Musée Belge 9 (1905) 180 ff. — H. WALTERSCHEID, Die Nachrichten des Clemens Alexandrinus über die griechischen Mysterien. Diss. Bonn, 1921. — S. A. SIMON, Clemens Alexandrinus es a mysteriumok (Clement of Alexandria and the mysteries). Budapest, 1938. — K. MRAS, Die in den neuen Διηγήσεις zu Kallimachos' Aitia erwähnten Kultbilder der samischen Hera: RhM (1938) 277–284. — H. RAHNER, Griechische Mythen in christlicher Deutung. Zürich, 1945, 21–72.

2. The Tutor

The *Tutor* (Παιδαγωγός), which consists of three books, presents the immediate continuation of the *Exhortation*. It addresses those who followed the advice given in Clement's first treatise and accepted the Christian faith. The Logos now comes forward as tutor in order to instruct these converts how to conduct their lives. The first book is of a more general character and discusses the educational task of the divine Logos as instructor: 'His aim is to improve the soul, not to teach, and to train it up to a virtuous, not to an intellectual life' (*Paed.* I, 1,1,4). Clement states that 'pedagogy is a training of children' (*ibid.* 1,5,12,1) and then raises the question who those are that Scripture calls 'children' (παῖδες). They are not, as the Gnostics claim, only those who live on a lower level of Christian faith whereas the Gnostics alone are perfect Christians. All those who are redeemed and reborn by baptism are children of God: 'Being baptized, we are illuminated; illuminated we become sons; being made sons, we are made perfect; being made perfect, we are made immortal' (*ibid.* 1,6,26,1). The basic principal by which the Logos educates His children is love, whereas the education of the Old Dispensation is based on fear. However, the Saviour administers not only mild but also stringent medicines because God is at the same time good and just and a successful tutor reconciles goodness with punishment. Righteousness and love do not exclude each other in God. Clement refers here to the heretical doctrine of the Marcionites that the God of the Old Testament is not the same as that of the New. Fear is good if it protects against sin:

The bitter roots of fear arrest the eating sores of our sins. Wherefore also fear is salutary, if bitter. Sick, we truly stand in the need of the Saviour; having wandered, of one to guide us; blind, of one to lead us to light; thirsty, of the fountain of life of which whosoever partakes shall no longer thirst (John 4,13–14); dead, we need life; sheep, we need a shepherd; we who are children need a tutor while universal humanity stands in need of Jesus... You may learn if you will the crowning wisdom of the all-holy Shepherd and Tutor, of the omnipotent and paternal Word, when He figuratively represents Himself as the Shepherd of the sheep. And He is the Tutor of the children. He says therefore by Ezechiel directing His discourse to the elders and setting before them a salutary description of His wise solicitude: 'And that which is lame I will bind up, and that which is sick I will heal, and that which has wandered I will turn back; and I will feed them on my holy mountain' (Ez. 34,14,16). Such are the promises of the good Shepherd.

Feed us, the children, as sheep. Yea, Master, fill us with righteousness. Thine own pasture; yea, O Tutor, feed us on Thy holy mountain the Church, which towers aloft, which is above the clouds, which touches heaven (*ibid.* 1,9,83,2–84,3 ANF).

With the beginning of the second book the treatise turns to the problems of daily life. Whereas the first deals with the general principles of ethics, the second and third present a kind of casuistry for all spheres of life: eating, drinking, homes and furniture, music and dancing, recreation and amusements, bathing and anointings, behaviour and marital life. These chapters give an interesting description of daily life in the city of

Alexandria with its luxury, debauchery and vices. Clement speaks here with a frankness which is surprising and at times repulsive. The author warns his Christians against indulging in such a life and gives a moral code of Christian behaviour in such surroundings. However, Clement does not demand that the Christian should abstain from all refinements of culture nor does he wish him to renounce the world and take the vow of poverty. The decisive point is the attitude of the soul. As long as the Christian keeps his heart independent and free from attachment to the goods of this world there is no reason why he should withdraw from his fellows. It is more important that the cultural life of the city should be imbued with the Christian spirit. The *Tutor* ends with a hymn to Christ the Saviour. There have been doubts about the authenticity of this hymn. However, there is every reason to believe that Clement himself is the author of it. The imagery corresponds exactly to that of the *Tutor*. Perhaps it represents the official prayer of praise of the School of Alexandria (cf. vol. I, p. 158 f).

Editions: O. STÄHLIN, GCS 12 (1936) 87–340. — A. BOATTI, T. Fl. Clemens Alexandrinus, Il Pedagogo, Testo, introd. trad. (Corona Patrum Sales. Ser. graec. 2). Turin, 1937.

Translations: English: W. WILSON, ANL 4 (1868); ANF 2 (1885) 209–296. — *German:* O. STÄHLIN, BKV³ 7 (1934) 204–297; 8 (1934) 7–223. — *Italian:* A. MAZZI, Il Pedagogo. Verona, 1917. — E. NERO, Il Pedagogo di Clemente Alessandrino (Classici cristiani). Siena, 1928. — A. BOATTI, *loc. cit.* — *Dutch:* H. U. MEYBOOM, Clemens van Alex., De paedagoog of opvoeder (Oudchrist. geschriften, dl. 9–11). Leiden, 1912.

Studies: F. J. WINTER, Die Ethik des Klemens von Alexandrien. Leipzig, 1882. — K. ERNESTI, Die Ethik des T. Flavius Klemens von Alexandrien oder die erste zusammenhängende Begründung der christlichen Sittenlehre. Paderborn, 1900. — W. CAPITAINE, Die Moral des Klemens von Alexandrien. Paderborn, 1903. — W. WAGNER, Der Christ und die Welt nach Klemens von Alexandrien. Göttingen, 1903. — C. SCLAFERT, Propos rassurants d'un vieux pédagogue. Un éducateur optimiste, Clément d'Alexandrie: ETL 175 (1923) 532–556. — U. v. WILAMOWITZ-MOELLENDORFF, Lesefrüchte (examination of Clem. Paed. II): Hermes (1929) 458 ff. — F. WAGNER, Der Sittlichkeitsbegriff in der Heiligen Schrift und der altchristlichen Ethik. Münster, 1931, 121–142. — J. STELZENBERGER, Die Beziehungen der frühchristlichen Sittenlehre zur Ethik der Stoa. Munich, 1933, 166–170; 226–231. — A. DECKER, Kenntnis und Pflege des Körpers bei Klemens von Alexandrien. Innsbruck, 1936. — J. STROUX, Paed. I: Phil (1933) 222–240. — E. C. EVANS, The Study of Physiognomy in the Second Century A.D.: TP (1941) 96–108. — F. QUATEMBER, Die christliche Lebenshaltung des Klemens von Alexandrien nach seinem Paedagogus. Vienna, 1946. — N. S. GEORGESCU, Doctrina morală dupa Clemens Alexandrinus. Bukarest, 1933. — R. A. GAUTHIER, Magnanimité. L'idéal de la grandeur dans la philosophie paienne et dans la théologie chrétienne. Paris, 1951.

The authorities that Clement consulted for his *Tutor* are, besides the Old and the New Testament, which form the main source, the philosophical writings of the Greeks. There are references to Plato and Plutarch's moral treatises. In addition, the influence of Stoic ethics can be seen, although it remains very difficult to name the specific works upon which he depends. Many passages are almost identical with some in the Stoic thinker C. Musonius Rufus. However, whatever is borrowed in this way is combined with Christian ideas to such a degree that a Christian theory of life emerges.

3. *The Stromata or Carpets* (Στρωματεῖς)

At the end of the introduction to his *Tutor* Clement remarks:
Eagerly desiring then to perfect us by a gradation conducive to salvation, suited for efficacious discipline, a beautiful arrangement is observed by the all-benignant Word who first exhorts, then trains, and finally teaches (1,1,3,3 ANF).

From these words it appears that Clement intended to compose as the third part of his trilogy a volume entitled the *Teacher* (Διδάσκαλος). Clement had not the gifts for writing such a book, which demands a strictly logical arrangement. The two previous works show that he was not a systematic theologian and unable to dominate great masses of material. Thus he abandoned his plan and chose the literary form of the Stromata or 'Carpets,' which was more suited to his genius, allowing him, as it did, to bring in splendid and extensive discussions of details in a light, entertaining style. The name, *Carpets*, is similar to others used at the time, like *The Meadow, The Banquets, The Honeycomb.* Such titles indicated a genre favored by philosophers of the day, in which they could discuss most varied questions without strict order or plan and pass from one problem to another without systematic treatment, the different topics being woven together like colors in a carpet.

Clement's *Stromata* consists of eight books. The most important subject is the relation of the Christian religion to secular learning, especially of the Christian faith to Greek philosophy. In his first book Clement defends philosophy against the objection that it is of no value to Christians. He answers that philosophy is given by God and was granted to the Greeks by divine providence in the same way as the Law to the Jews. But it can render important service to the Christian, too, if he wishes to attain knowledge (γνῶσις) of the content of his faith:

> Accordingly, before the advent of the Lord, philosophy was necessary to the Greeks for righteousness. And now it becomes conducive to piety, being a kind of preparatory training to those who attain to faith through demonstration. 'For thy foot,' it is said, 'will not stumble,' if thou refer what is good, whether belonging to the Greeks or to us, to Providence. For God is the cause of all good things; but of some primarily, as of the Old and New Testament, and of others by consequence, as philosophy... Perchance, too, philosophy was given to the Greeks directly and primarily, till the Lord should call the Greeks. For this was 'a schoolmaster to bring' the Hellenic mind, as the Law the Hebrews, 'to Christ.' Philosophy, therefore, was a preparation, paving the way for him who is perfect in Christ (*Strom.* 1,5,28 ANL).

Thus Clement goes far beyond Justin Martyr, who speaks of the seeds of the Logos to be found in the philosophy of the Greeks. He compares it to the Old Testament in so far as it trained mankind for the coming of Christ. On the other hand, Clement is anxious to stress the fact that philosophy can never take the place of divine revelation. It can only prepare for the acceptance of the faith. Thus, in the second book, he defends faith against the philosophers:

> Faith, which the Greeks disparage deeming it futile and barbarous, is a voluntary preconception, the assent of piety— 'the subject of things hoped for, the evidence of things not seen' according to the divine apostle. Without faith it is impossible to please God (*Strom.* 2,2,8,4 ANF).

The knowledge of God can be attained only through faith and faith is the foundation of all knowledge. If germs of divine truth can be found in different philosophical doctrines, it is because the Greeks derived many tenets from the prophets of the Old Testament. Clement goes to great length in proving that even Plato, in framing his laws, was an imitator of Moses, and that the Greeks borrowed from the barbarians, i.e., the Jews and Christians. The other books deal with the refutation of the Gnosis and its false religious and moral principles. The author draws a magnificent picture of the true Gnosis and its relation to faith, as a counterpart to the false Gnosis. Moral perfection, consisting of chastity and love of God, is the mark of the ideal, in striking contrast to the heretical Gnostic. At the end of the seventh book Clement finds that he has not yet answered all questions that seem to him important for the daily life of the Christians and their religious knowledge. He therefore promises another part and is willing to make a new beginning (*Strom.* 7,18,111,4). However, the so-called eighth book of the *Stromata* does not appear to be a continuation of the seventh but a collection of sketches and studies used in the other sections of the work. It seems therefore that they were not intended for publication but that they were issued after his death against his intention. Evidently he died before he could fulfill his promise.

Editions: O. STÄHLIN, GCS 15 (1939) Books 1–6; 17 (1909) 3–102, Books 7–8. — C. MONDÉSERT-M. CASTER, Clément d'Alexandrie, Stromates I (SCH 30). Paris, 1951. — The seventh book was edited by F. J. A. HORT and J. B. MAYOR, Clement of Alexandria, Miscellanies, Book VII. The Greek text with introduction, translation and notes. London-New York, 1902.

Translations: English: W. WILSON, ANL 4 (1868), 12 (1869), ANF 2 (1885) 299–567. — Book 7: F. J. A. HORT and J. B. MAYOR, *loc. cit.* — *German:* O. STÄHLIN, BKV³ 17 (1936) Books 1–3; 19 (1937) Books 4–6; 20 (1938) Book 7 and Index. — C. A. BERNOULLI und L. FRUECHTEL, Klemens von Al., Die Teppiche (Stromateis), deutscher Text nach der Übersetzung von J. OVERBECK. Basel, 1936. — *French:* C. MONDÉSERT, *loc. cit.* — *Dutch:* H. U. MEYBOOM, Clemens van Alexandrie, De tapijten of vlechtwerken (Oudchrist. geschriften, dl. 12–19). Leiden, 1912.

Studies: C. HEUSSI, Die Stromateis des Clemens Alexandrinus und ihr Verhältnis zum Protreptikos und Paedagogos: Zeitschr. wiss. Theol. 45 (1902) 465–512. — C. DE WEDEL, Symbola ad Clementis Alex. Stromatum librum VIII interpretandum. Diss. Berlin, 1905. — W. ERNST, De Clementis Alex. Stromatum libro VIII qui fertur. Diss. Göttingen, 1910. — J. P. POSTGATE, On the Text of the Stromates of Clement of Alexandria: CQ (1914) 237–247. — J. P. ARENDZEN, Strom. III 5, 50: JThSt 20 (1919) 236 ff. — A. SMITH, 'Ἀπαρέμφατος dans Strom. IV 25, 156: JThSt 21 (1920) 319–332. — A. S. FERGUSON, On a Fragment of Gorgias (Strom. I 11, 51): CPh (1921) 284–287. — F. H. COLSON, Strom. IV 25, 198: JThSt 22 (1921) 156 ff. — U. VON WILAMOWITZ-MOELLENDORFF, Lesefrüchte (critical exam. and commentary to Strom. IV): Hermes (1929)458 ff.—C. L. PRESTIGE, Clement of Alexandria, Stromata, 2, 8 and the meaning of *hypostasis:* JThSt 30 (1929) 270–272. — E. PETERSON, Zur Textkritik des Clemens Alexandrinus und Euagrios (Strom. 1, 28): ThLZ (1931).

69–70. — C. Del Grande, Brevi note al testo del primo Stromate di Clemente Alessandrino: Rivista Indo-Greca-Italia di filologia (1934) 152–158. — J. Levy, Héracles fut-il roi d'Argos? (Strom. I, 21, 105): REAN (1935) 5–8. — K. Rahner, De termino aliquo in theologia Clementis Alexandrini qui aequivalet nostro conceptui entis supernaturalis (Strom. VII, 3, 18, 2): Greg 18 (1937) 426–431. — K. Prümm, Glaube und Erkenntnis im zweiten Buch der Stromata des Klemens von Alexandrien: Schol 12 (1937) 17–57. — J. Vergote, Clément d'Alexandrie et l'écriture égyptienne. Essai d'interprétation de Stromates V 4, 20–21: Mus (1939) 199–221; idem, Chronique d'Egypte. 1941, 21–38. — G. Ogg, A Note on Stromateis I 144, 1–146, 4: JThSt (1945) 59–63. — L. Fruechtel, Beiträge zu Clemens Alexandrinus (Strom. I, 7): Würzburger Jahrbücher für Altertumswissenschaft 2 (1947) 148–151.

4. Excerpta ex Theodoto and Eclogae propheticae

The same holds true of these two works which follow the Stromata in the tradition of the manuscripts. They are not excerpts made by someone else of the lost parts of the Stromata, as Zahn thought, but excerpts from Gnostic writings like those of the Valentinian Gnostic Theodotus (cf. vol. I, p. 265 f) and preliminary studies of Clement. It is very difficult to separate the excerpts of Gnostic sources from the words of Clement himself.

Editions: O. Stählin, GCS 17 (1909) 103–133 Excerpta; 135–155 Eclogae. — R. P. Casey, The Excerpta ex Theodoto of Clement of Alexandria, edited with translation and notes (Studies and Documents 1). London, 1934. — F. Sagnard, Extraits de Théodote, texte grec, trad. et notes (SCH 23). Paris, 1948.

Translations: English: R. P. Casey, loc. cit. — French: F. Sagnard, loc. cit.

Studies: G. Heinrici, Die Valentinianische Gnosis und die Heilige Schrift. Berlin, 1871, 88–127: Die Exzerpte aus Theodot und der Didaskalia anatolike. — A. Hilgenfeld, Die Ketzergeschichte des Urchristentums. Leipzig, 1884, 505–516. — G. Quispel, The Original Doctrine of Valentine: VC 1 (1947) 43–73. — A. J. Festugière, Notes sur les Extraits de Théodote de Clément d'Alexandrie et sur les fragments de Valentine: VC 3 (1949) 193–207.

5. Quis dives salvetur? (Τίς ὁ σωζόμενος πλούσιος;)

The little work Who is the Rich Man that is saved? is a homily on Mark 10,17–31, which however seems not to be a sermon delivered in a public service. It shows how Clement tried to overcome the difficulties which resulted among his hearers from a literal interpretation of the commandments of the Gospel. The Paedagogus indicates that Clement had well-to-do people among his listeners. This homily presupposes the same. Clement is of the opinion that the commandment of the Lord 'Go, sell whatsoever thou hast and give to the poor' cannot be understood in the sense that wealth as such excludes one from the kingdom of heaven. It is not necessary to get rid of all one owns in order to be saved. Clement interprets the words of the Lord as an exhortation to keep the heart from any desire for money and make it free of any inordinate attachment thereto. If every Christian gave up his possessions there would be no possibility of supporting the poor. The attitude of the soul is decisive, not the fact that one is needy or affluent. We must relinquish the passion, not riches. Sin, not wealth, excludes from the kingdom of heaven. At the end Clement tells the legend of the Apostle John and the youth who had fallen among the robbers in order to prove that even the greatest sinner can be saved if he does real penance.

Editions: O. Stählin, GCS 17 (1909) 157–191. Separate edition: O. Stählin, Quis dives salvetur. Leipzig, 1908. — G. W. Butterworth, LCL (1919) 270–367.

Translations: English: W. Wilson, ANL 22, 2 (1871); ANF 2 (1885) 591–604. — P.M. Barnard, A Homily of Clement of Alexandria entitled Who is the Rich Man that is being saved? (SPCK). London-New York, 1901. — G. W. Butterworth, *loc. cit.* — *German:* O. Stählin, BKV³ 8 (1934) 227–280. — *Dutch:* H. U. Meyboom, Welke rijke zal zalig worden? (Oudchrist. geschriften, dl. 18). Leiden, 1912.

Studies: F. X. Funk, Clemens von Alexandrien über Familie und Eigentum: ThQ 53 (1871) 427–449. — L. Paul, Welcher Reiche wird selig werden?: Zeitschr. f. wiss. Theologie 44 (1901) 504–544. — Markgraf, Klemens von Alexandrien als asketi-scher Schriftsteller in seiner Stellung zu den natürlichen Lebensgütern: ZKG 22 (1901) 487–515. — O. Schilling, Reichtum und Eigentum in der altkirchlichen Literatur. Freiburg i.B., 1908, 40–47. — E. J. Bruck, Ethics versus Law: Traditio 1 (1944) 97–121. — S. Giet, La doctrine de l'appropriation des biens chez quelques-uns des Pères: RSR (1948) 55–91.

2. LOST WRITINGS

1. The most important of the lost works is his commentary on the writings of the Old and the New Testament, entitled *Hypotyposeis* ('Υποτυπώσεις), i.e., outlines or sketches. It comprised eight books. Eusebius (*Hist. eccl.* 6,14,1) states that Clement included even an interpretation of writings whose canonicity was doubtful: 'And in the *Hypotyposeis*, to speak briefly, he has given concise explanations of all the Canonical Scriptures, not passing over even the disputed writings, I mean the Epistle of Jude and the remaining Catholic Epistles, and the Epistle of

Barnabas, and the Apocalypse known as Peter's (LCL). There are only a few short excerpts preserved in Greek. Eusebius has the greatest number of them. Others can be found in the commentaries of Pseudo-Oikomenius and in the *Pratum spirituale* of John Moschus. A longer passage survives in an old Latin translation which goes back to Cassiodorus (ca. 540). It contains explanations of the first Epistle of Peter, the Epistle of Jude and the first and second Epistles of John and is entitled *Adumbrationes Clementis Alexandrini in epistolas canonicas*. All these fragments make it certain that the *Hypotyposeis* did not give a running exposition of the entire text but an allegorical interpretation of selected verses. According to Eusebius (*Hist. eccl.* 5,11,2; 6,13,3), Clement mentioned his teacher Pantaenus in this work. But it remains doubtful how far his views were based on the lectures of his professor. Photius had still the entire text of the *Hypotyposeis* and he passes a severe judgment on it:

> In some places he [Clement] holds firmly to the correct doctrine; elsewhere he is carried away by strange and impious notions. He asserts the eternity of matter, excogitates a theory of ideas from the words of Holy Scripture, and reduces the Son to a mere creature. He relates fabulous stories of metempsychosis and of many worlds before Adam. Concerning the formation of Eve from Adam he teaches things blasphemous and scurrilous, and anti-scriptural. He imagines that the angels had intercourse with women and begot children of them, also that the Logos did not become man in reality but only in appearance. It even seems that he has a fabulous notion of two Logoi of the Father, of which the inferior one appeared to men (*Bibl. Cod.* 109).

For this reason Photius doubts the authenticity of the *Hypotyposeis*. At any rate, the heretical doctrines explain perhaps why the work is not preserved.

Edition: O. STÄHLIN, GCS 17 (1909) 195–202.

Translation: English: W. WILSON, ANL 24 (1872); ANF 2 (1885) 571–577.

Studies: G. MERCATI, Un frammento delle Ipotiposi (Studi e Testi 12). Rome, 1904. — A. v. HARNACK, SAB (1904) 901–908. — TH. ZAHN, NKZ 16 (1905) 415–419. — H. A. ECHLE, The Baptism of the Apostles. A Fragment of Clement of Alexandria's Lost Work Ὑποτυπώσεις in the Pratum Spirituale of John Moschus: Traditio 3 (1945) 365–368.

2. We know from Eusebius (*Hist. eccl.* 6,13,9) that Clement had also composed a book *On the Pasch* in which 'he professes that he was compelled by his companions to commit to writing traditions that he had heard from the elders of olden time, for the benefit of those that should come after; and he mentions in it Melito and Irenaeus and some others, whose accounts also of the matter he has set down' (LCL). Only a few short quotations of this writing are preserved.

Fragments: O. STÄHLIN, GCS 17 (1909) 216-218.

3. Another work, of which we possess but one fragment, is his *Ecclesiastical Canon or Against the Judaizers*, which he had dedicated to Alexander, the bishop of Jerusalem (Euseb., *Hist. eccl.* 6,13,3).

Fragment: O. STÄHLIN, *loc. cit.* 218 f.

Studies: W. C. VAN UNNIK, Opmerkingen over het karakter van het verloren werk van Clemens Alexandrinus Canon ecclesiasticus: Nederlandsch archief voor Kerkgeschiedenis 33 (1941) 49-61. — C. MONDÉSERT, A propos du signe du Temple: RSR 36 (1949) 580-584.

4. Anastasius Sinaites reproduces a passage from the first part of a work *On Providence*. Several other fragments are extant which indicate that it gave philosophical definitions. It is not mentioned by Eusebius nor any of the other early ecclesiastical authors. The authenticity remains, therefore, doubtful.

Fragments: O. STÄHLIN, GCS 17, 219-221.

5. However, Eusebius knows of another production by Clement with the title *Exhortation to Endurance or To the Recently Baptized*. It is possible that a fragment in a manuscript of the Escorial entitled *Exhortations of Clement* is from this lost work.

Fragment: O. STÄHLIN, GCS 17, 211-223. — G. W. BUTTERWORTH, LCL (1919) 370-377.

Translations: English: J. PATRICK, Clement of Alexandria. Edinburgh, 1914, 183-185. — G. W. BUTTERWORTH, *loc. cit.*

6. Nothing is preserved nor otherwise known of two other writings which Eusebius (*Hist. eccl.* 6,13,3) attributes to Clement: *Discourses on Fasting* and *On Slander*.

7. Palladius (*Hist. Laus.* 139) is the only source which mentions Clement as the author of a work *On the Prophet Amos*.

8. We do not have any letters of Clement. But the *Sacra Parallela* 311, 312 and 313 (ed. Holl) contains three sentences ascribed to letters of Clement, two of them from his Letter 21.

Fragments: O. STÄHLIN, GCS 17, 223 ff.
For *other fragments*, cf. J. THACKERAY, A Papyrus Scrap of Patristic Writing: JThSt 30 (1929) 179–180. — L. FRUECHTEL, Neue Zeugnisse zu Clemens Alexandrinus: ZNW 36 (1937) 81–90; *idem,* Nachweisungen zu Fragmentsammlungen II: PhW (1936) 1439; *idem,* Clemens Alexandrinus und Albinus: PhW (1937) 591–592; *idem,* Isidoros von Pelusion als Benutzer des Clemens Alexandrinus und anderer Quellen: PhW (1938) 61–64; *idem,* Clemens Alexandrinus und Theodoretos von Kyrrhos: PhW (1939) 765–766. — H. FLEISCH, Fragments de Clément d'Alexandrie conservés en arabe: Mélanges de l'Université Saint Joseph, Beyrouth, 27 (1947/48) 63–71.
For *relations to other Christian authors:* A. BELTRAMI, Clemente Alessandrino nell' Ottavio di Minucio Felice: Rivista di Filosofia (1919) 366–380. — J. R. M. HITCH-COCK, Did Clement of Alexandria know the Didache?: JThSt 24 (1923) 397–401. — E. RAPISARDA, Clemente fonte di Arnobio. Turin, 1939. — J. E. L. OULTON, Clement of Alexandria and the Didache: JThSt 41 (1940) 177–179. — Q. CATAUDELLA, Minucio Felice e Clemente Alessandrino: Studi Italiani di Filologia Classica 17 (1940) 271–281. — W. DEN BOER, Clément d'Alexandrie et Minuce Félix: Mnem 11 (1943) 161–190. — L. ALFONSI, Il Protreptico di Clemente Alessandrino e l'Epistola a Diogneto: Aevum (1946) 100–108.

TEXT TRADITION

The original of all the manuscripts of the *Protrepticus* and *Paedagogus* is the Arethas Codex of the Bibliothèque Nationale (*Codex Paris. graec.* 451), which was copied by Baanes at the request of Archbishop Arethas of Caesarea in Cappadocia in 914. Unfortunately forty folia have been lost. Thus the first ten chapters of the *Paedagogus* and the two hymns at the end are lacking. However they can be supplied from two copies of the Arethas Codex made while it was still complete. These are *Codex Mutin.* III. D. 7 and *Codex Laur.* V 24 of which *Codex Mutin.* is the more faithful.

The text of the *Stromata,* the *Excerpta ex Theodoto* and the *Eclogae propheticae* is preserved in a manuscript of the eleventh century, *Codex Laur.* V 3. The other manuscript containing these works, *Codex Paris. Suppl. gr.* 250, is only a copy of the *Laur.*

The first edition of the *Quis dives salvetur* was made from *Codex Vatic. gr.* 623. However this merely reproduces *Codex Scorial.* Ω-III-19 of the eleventh or twelfth century.

The text of the Latin fragment of the *Hypotyposeis,* the *Adum-*

brationes Clementis Alexandrini, is supplied by three independent manuscripts, *Codex Laudun.* 96 of the ninth, *Berol. Phill.* 1665 (now No. 45) of the thirteenth and *Vatic. lat.* 6154 of the sixteenth century.

3. ASPECTS OF CLEMENT'S THEOLOGY

The work of Clement of Alexandria is epoch-making and it is no exaggeration to praise him as the founder of speculative theology. If we compare him to his contemporary, Irenaeus of Lyons, it is evident that he represents an altogether different type of ecclesiastical teacher. Irenaeus was the man of tradition, who derived his doctrine from the apostolic preaching and regarded every influence from the environing culture and philosophy as a danger to the faith. Clement was the courageous and successful pioneer of a school that purposed to protect and deepen faith by making use of philosophy. He saw, it is true, the great danger of a Hellenization of Christianity, as did Irenaeus, and, with him, fought against the false and heretical Gnosis. But Clement's distinction is that he did not remain merely negative in his attitude but over against the false Gnosis set up a true and Christian Gnosis, which placed in the service of the faith the treasure of truth to be found in the various systems of philosophy. Whereas the Gnostic heretics taught that faith and knowledge cannot be reconciled because they are contradictions, Clement endeavors to prove that they are akin to each other and that a harmony of faith (*Pistis*) and knowledge (*Gnosis*) produces the perfect Christian and the true Gnostic. The beginning and foundation of philosophy is faith. It is, moreover, of the greatest importance to any Christian who wishes to penetrate the content of his faith by reason. At the same time philosophy proves that the attacks of the enemies against the Christian religion are without foundation:

> The Hellenic philosophy does not, by its approach, make the truth more powerful; but by rendering powerless the assault of sophistry against it, and frustrating the treacherous plots laid against the truth, is said to be the proper fence and wall of the vineyard (*Strom.* 1,20,100).

Clement expresses most appositely the relation between faith and knowledge. At times, it is true, he goes too far by attributing to Greek philosophy an almost supranatural and justifying role, but he regards faith as fundamentally more important than knowledge: 'Faith is something superior to knowledge and is its criterion' (*Strom.* 2,4,15).

Studies: C. BIGG, The Christian Platonists of Alexandria. Oxford, 1886. — F. L. CLARK, Citations of Plato in Clement of Alexandria: TP 33 (1902) XII–XX. — E. DE FAYE, De l'originalité de la philosophie chrétienne de Clément d'Alexandrie: Annales de l'École des Hautes Études de Gand (1919/20) 1–20. — R. P. CASEY, Clement of Alexandria and the Beginnings of Christian Platonism: HThR 18 (1925) 39–101. — J. MEIERT, Der Platonismus bei Clemens Alexandrinus. Tübingen, 1928. Cf. J. LEBRETON, RSR 19 (1929) 370 f. — R. E. WITT, The Hellenism of Clement of Alexandria: CQ 25 (1931) 195–204. — TH. CAMELOT, Clément d'Alexandrie et l'utilisation de la philosophie grecque: RSR 21 (1931) 541–569; *idem,* Les idées de Clément d'Alexandrie sur l'utilisation des sciences de la littérature et de la philosophie profanes: RSR 21 (1931) 38–66; 541–569. — E. MOLLAND, Clement of Alexandria on the Origin of Greek Philosophy: SO 25 (1936) 57–85. — K. PRÜMM, Christentum als Neuheitserlebnis. Freiburg i.B., 1939, 193–196. — P. J. SCHMIDT, Clemens von Alexandria in seinem Verhältnis zur griechischen Religion und Philosophie. Diss. Vienna, 1939. — A. SAITTA, Note sul problema della φιλία in Aristotele e nello stoicismo: Annali della Scuola Normale Superiore di Pisa (1939) 68–73. — E. ELORDUY, La fisica estoica absorbida por la filosofia cristiana: So 16 (1948) 195–198. — A. C. OUTLER, The Platonism of Clement of Alexandria: JR (1940) 217–239. — J. MOINGT, La gnose de Clément d'Alexandrie dans ses rapports avec la foi et la philosophie: RSR 37 (1950) 195–251. — K. REINHARDT, Heraklits Lehre vom Feuer (in Clement's interpretation): Hermes (1942) 1–27. — H. A. BLAIR, Two Reactions to Gnosticism: ChQ 152 (1951) 141–158. For other *pagan sources,* see: W. GEMOLL, Xenophon bei Clemens Alexandrinus: Hermes (1918) 105–107. — K. HUBERT, Zur indirekten Überlieferung der Tischgespräche Plutarchs: Hermes (1938) 307–328. — C. WENDEL, Zum Hieroglyphen-Buche Chairemons: Hermes (1940) 227–229. — S. MARIOTTI, Nuove testimonianze ed echi dell' Aristotele giovanile: Atene e Roma (1940) 48–60. — L. FRUECHTEL, Die Penketier bei Kallimachos: PhW (1941) 189–190. — Q. CATAUDELLA, Democrito fr. 55B 30 Vorsokr.: Atene e Roma (1941) 73–81.

1. *The Doctrine of the Logos*

Clement attempted to set up a theological system with the idea of the Logos as its beginning and basis. All his thinking and reasoning are dominated by this idea. Thus he stands on the same ground as St. Justin, the philosopher, but he has advanced far beyond him. Clement's idea of the Logos is more concrete and fertile. He made it into the highest principle for the religious explanation of the world. The Logos is the creator of the universe. He is the one who manifested God in the Law of the Old Testament, in the philosophy of the Greeks and finally

3

in the fullness of time in His incarnation. He forms with the Father and the Holy Ghost the divine trinity. It is through the Logos that we can recognize God because the Father cannot be named:

> Since the first principle of everything is difficult to find out, the absolutely first and oldest principle, which is the cause of all other things being and having been, is difficult to exhibit. For how can that be expressed which is neither genus, nor difference, nor species, nor individual, nor number; nay more, is neither an event, nor that to which an event happens? No one can rightly express Him wholly. For on account of His greatness He is ranked as the All, and is the Father of the universe. Nor are any parts to be predicated of Him. For the One is indivisible; wherefore also it is infinite, not considered with reference to its being without dimensions, and not having a limit. And therefore it is without form and name. And if we name it, we do not do so properly, terming it either the One, or the Good, or Mind, or Absolute Being, or Father, or God, or Creator, or Lord. We speak not as supplying His name; but for want we use good names, in order that the mind may have these as points of support, so as not to err in other respects. For each one by itself does not express God; but all together are indicative of the power of the Omnipotent. For predicatives are expressed either from what belongs to things themselves or from their mutual relation. But none of these are admissible in reference to God. Nor any more is He apprehended by the science of demonstration. For it depends on primary and better known principles. But there is nothing antecedent to the Unbegotten. It remains that we understand then the Unknown by divine grace and by the Word alone that proceeds from Him (*Strom.* 5,12,82 ANF).

The Logos is, as divine reason, essentially the teacher of the world and the lawgiver of mankind. But Clement knows Him also as the saviour of the human race and the founder of a new life which begins with faith, proceeds to knowledge and contemplation and leads through love and charity to immortality and deification. Christ as the incarnate Logos is God and man, and it is through Him that we have risen to divine life. Thus he speaks of Christ as the sun of justice:

Hail, O light! For in us, buried in darkness, shut up in the shadow of death, light has shone forth from heaven, purer than the sun, sweeter than life here below. That light is eternal life; and whatever partakes of it lives. But night fears the light, and hiding itself in terror, gives place to the day of the Lord. Sleepless light is now over all, and the west has given credence to the east. For this was the meaning of the new creation. For 'the Sun of Righteousness' who drives His chariot over all, pervades equally all humanity, like 'His Father, who makes His sun rise on all men' and distils on them the dew of the truth. He has changed sunset into sunrise, and through the cross brought death to life; and having wrenched man from destruction, He has raised him to the skies, transplanting mortality into immortality and translating earth to heaven,—He, the husbandman of God, having bestowed on us the truly great, divine, and inalienable inheritance of the Father, deifying man by heavenly teaching, putting His laws into our minds and writing on our hearts (*Protrept.* 11,88,114 ANF).

Thus the idea of the Logos is the centre of Clement's theological system and of all his religious thinking. However, the supreme idea in Christian thought is not the idea of the Logos but the idea of God. For this reason Clement failed in his attempt to create a scientific theology.

Studies: V. ERMONI, The Christology of Clement of Alexandria: JThSt 5 (1904) 123 ff. — R. P. CASEY, Clement and the Two Divine Logoi: JThSt 25 (1923) 43–56. — T. RÜTHER, Die Leiblichkeit Christi nach Clemens von Alexandrien: ThQ 107 (1926) 231–254. — F. J. DÖLGER, Sonne und Sonnenstrahl als Gleichnis in der Logostheologie des christlichen Altertums: AC 1 (1929) 271–290. — J. D. FRANGOULIS, Der Begriff des Geistes bei Clemens Alexandrinus. Leipzig, 1936. — J. QUASTEN, Der Gute Hirte in hellenistischer und frühchristlicher Logostheologie: Heilige Überlieferung, Festgabe für I. Herwegen hrsg. v. O. Casel. Münster i.W., 1938, 51–58. — B. PADE, Λόγος Θεός. Untersuchungen zur Logos-Christologie des Titus Flavius Clemens von Alexandrien. Rome, 1939. — M. PELLEGRINO, La catechesi cristologica di S. Clemente Alessandrino. Milan, 1940. — F. J. DÖLGER, Χαῖρε ἱερὸν φῶς als antike Lichtbegrüßung bei Nikarchos und Jesus als heiliges Licht bei Klemens von Alexandrien: AC 6 (1941) 147–151. — J. LEBRETON, La théologie de la Trinité chez Clément d'Alexandrie: RSR 34 (1947) 55–76; 142–179. — G. KRETSCHMAR, Jesus Christus in der Theologie des Klemens von Alexandrien. Diss. Heidelberg, 1950. — H. A. WOLFSON, Clement of Alexandria on the Generation of the Logos: Church History 20 (1951) 3–11.

2. *Ecclesiology*

Clement is firmly convinced that there is only one universal Church as there is only one God the Father, one divine Word and one Holy Spirit. He calls this Church the virgin mother who feeds her children with the milk of the divine Word:

> O wondrous mystery! One is the Father of all, one also the Logos of all, and the Holy Spirit is one and the same everywhere and there in only one Virgin Mother; I love to call her the Church. This mother alone had no milk, because she alone did not become woman, but she is both virgin and mother, being undefiled as a virgin and loving as a mother; and calling her children to her she nurses them with holy milk, the Logos for the children (*Paed.* 1,6,42,1).

In another passage he remarks: 'The Mother draws the children to herself and we seek our Mother, the Church' (*Paed.* 1,5,21,1). In the final chapter of the *Paedagogus* Clement calls the Church the spouse and mother of the Tutor. She is the school in which hers pouse Jesus is the teacher (*ibid.*, 3,12,98,1). He then continues:

> O graduates of His blessed tutorship! Let us [by our presence] make complete the fair countenance of the Church, and let us as children run to our good Mother. And when we have become hearers of the Word, let us extol the blessed dispensation by which man is brought up and sanctified as a child of God, and being trained on earth attains to citizenship in heaven and there receives his Father, whom he learns to know on earth (*Paed.* 3,12,99,1).

This Church differs in its unity and in its antiquity from the heresies:

> Such being the case, it is evident, from the high antiquity and perfect truth of the Church, that these later heresies, and those yet subsequent to them in time, were new inventions falsified [from the truth].
>
> From what has been said, then, it is my opinion, that the true Church, that which is really ancient, is one, and that in it those who according to God's purpose are just, are enrolled. For from the very reason that God is one, and the Lord one, that which is in the highest degree honorable is lauded in consequence of its singleness, being an imitation of the one first principle. In the nature of the One, then, is

associated in a joint heritage the one Church, which they strive to cut asunder into many sects.

Therefore, in substance and idea, in origin, in pre-eminence, we say that the ancient and Catholic Church is alone collecting as it does into the unity of the one faith those already ordained, whom God predestinated knowing before the foundation of the world that they would be righteous. But the pre-eminence of the Church, as the principle of union, is in its oneness, in this surpassing all things else and having nothing like or equal to itself (*Strom.* 7,17,107 ANF).

Clement knows that the great obstacle for the conversion of pagans and Jews to the Christian religion is the fact that Christianity is divided by heretical sects:

First then they make this objection to us saying that they ought not to believe on account of the discord of the sects. For the truth is warped when some teach one set of dogmas, others another.

To whom we say that among you Jews and among the most famous of the philosophers among the Greeks very many sects have sprung up. And yet you do not say that one ought to hesitate to philosophize or to be a follower of the Jews because of the want of agreement of the sects among you between themselves. And then, that heresies should be sown among the truth as 'tares among the wheat' was foretold by the Lord; and what was predicted to take place could not but happen. And the cause of this is that everything that is beautiful is always shadowed by its caricature. If one then violate his engagements and go aside from the confession which he makes before us, are we not to stick to the truth because he has belied his profession? But as the good man must not prove false or fail to ratify what he has promised although others violate their engagements, so also are we bound in no way to transgress the rule of the Church. And especially the confession, which deals with the essential articles of the faith, is observed by us, but disregarded by the heretics (*Strom.* 7,15,89 f ANF).

The last sentences of this passage indicate that Clement knew a symbol in which the essential articles of faith were collected. Clement is firmly convinced of the divine inspiration of the

Scriptures: 'He who believes the divine Scriptures with sure judgment receives in the voice of God, who bestowed the Scripture, a demonstration that cannot be impugned' (*Strom.* 2,2,9).

But he warns against the misuse of Scripture by heretics:

And if those also who follow heresies venture to avail themselves of the prophetic Scriptures, in the first place they will not make use of all the Scriptures, and then they will not quote them entire, nor as the body and texture of prophecy prescribe. But selecting ambiguous expressions, they wrest them to their own opinions, gathering a few expressions here and there, not looking to the sense, but making use in the mere words. For in almost all the quotations they make, you will find that they attend to the names alone while they alter the meanings, neither knowing as they affirm, nor using the quotations they adduce, according to their true nature. But the truth is not found by changing the meanings, for so people subvert all true teaching, but in the consideration of what perfectly belongs to and becomes the Sovereign God, and establishing each one of the points demonstrated in the Scriptures again from similar Scriptures. Neither then do they want to turn to the truth being ashamed to abandon the claims of self-love; nor are they able to manage their opinions by doing violence to the Scriptures (*Strom.* 7,16,96 ANF).

Studies: H. SEESEMANN, Das Paulusverständnis des Clemens Alexandrinus: ThStKr 107 (1936) 312–346; *idem*, De Chester-Beatty Papyrus 46 und der Paulustext des Clemens Alexandrinus: ZNW 36 (1937) 90–97. — H. WAITZ, Neue Untersuchungen über die sog. judenchristl. Evangelien: ZNW (1937) 60–81. — E. MOLLAND, The Conception of the Gospel in the Alexandrian Theology. Oslo, 1938. — F. BURI, Clemens Alexandrinus und der paulinische Freiheitsbegriff. Zürich, 1939. — C. M. EDSMAN, Schöpferwille und Geburt Jac. 1, 18. Eine Studie zur altchristlichen Kosmologie: ZNW (1939) 11–44. — W. DEN BOER, De allegorese in het werk van Clemens Alexandrinus. Diss. Leiden, 1940. — C. C. TARELLI, A Note on Luke 12, 15: JThSt (1940) 260–262. — K. F. EVANS-PROSSER, On the Supposed Early Death of John the Apostle: ExpT 54 (1942/43) 138. — C. MONDÉSERT, Clément d'Alexandrie. Introduction a l'étude de sa pensée religieuse à partir de l'Écriture. Paris, 1944. — TH. CAMELOT, Clément d'Alexandrie et l'Écriture: RBibl (1946) 242–248. — W. DEN BOER, Hermeneutic Problems in Early Christian Literature: VC 1 (1947) 150–167. — J. RUWET, Clément d'Alexandrie: Canon d'Écritures et Apocryphes: Bibl 29 (1948) 240–268. — W. J. BURGHARDT, On Early Christian Exegesis: TS 11 (1950) 78–116.

The hierarchy of the Church, consisting of the three grades, the episcopacy, the priesthood and the deaconate, is according to Clement an imitation of the hierarchy of the angels:

> According to my opinion the grades here in the Church of bishops, priests and deacons are imitations of the angelic glory and of that economy which, the Scriptures say, awaits those who following the footsteps of the apostles, have lived in perfection of righteousness according to the Gospel (*Strom.* 6,13,107 ANF).

This attempt to describe specifically the hierarchical order of angels marks something new in the development of theology. The theory also of their cognition is definitely advanced and lays the foundation for the opinions of St. Augustine. From the fact that they carry our prayers to God, Clement concludes that they know the thoughts of men. He teaches, too, that they have no senses, that they know instantaneously, fast as thought, without the senses as intermediary. His concept, therefore, of the spirituality and bodilessness of the angels is high, much higher than St. Justin's.

Studies: F. ANDRES, Die Engel- und Dämonenlehre des Klemens von Alexandrien: RQ 34 (1926) 13–37, 129–140, 307–329. — J. C. PLUMPE, Mater Ecclesia. An Inquiry into the Concept of the Church as Mother in Early Christianity (SCA 5). Washington, 1943, 63–69. — G. BARDY, La Théologie de l'Église de saint Irénée au concile de Nicée (Unam sanctam 14). Paris, 1947, 115–128.

3. Baptism

Although the teaching of the Logos occupies the centre of Clement's theological doctrine, he does not fail to pay attention to the *mysterion*, to the sacrament. In fact, Logos and *mysterion* are the two poles around which his christology and ecclesiology move.

Baptism is for him a rebirth and a regeneration:

> For thus he wishes us to be converted and to become as children acknowledging him who is truly our father, regenerated by water; and this is a different begetting than that in creation (*Strom.* 3,12,87).

> Listen to the Saviour: I regenerated you, unhappily born by the world to death. I set you free, I healed you, I redeemed you. I will give you life that is unending, eternal, supernatural. I will show you the face of God, the good

father. Call no one on earth your father. . . . For you I fought
with death and paid your death which you owed for your
past sins and your unbelief towards God (*Quis div. salv.* 23,1).
It is hardly possible to give a better explanation of the adoption
as children of God which takes place in the sacrament of regeneration. Clement uses also the terms seal (σφραγίς), illumination,
bath, perfection and mystery for baptism. In his *Paedagogus*
(1,6,26) he describes its effects in the following words:

> Being baptized, we are illuminated; illuminated, we
> become sons; being made sons, we are made perfect; being
> made perfect, we are made immortal. 'I,' says He,' have said
> that you are gods and all sons of the Highest' (Ps. 81,6).
> This work is variously called grace, illumination, and per-
> fection, and bath: bath, by which we cleanse away our
> sins; grace, by which the penalties accruing to transgressions
> are remitted; and illumination, by which that holy light
> of salvation is beheld, that is, by which we see God clearly.
> Now we call that perfect which wants nothing. For what
> is yet wanting to him who knows God? For it were truly
> monstrous that that which is not complete should be called
> a gift of God's grace (ANF).

Studies: C. CASPARI, Hat die alexandrinische Kirche zur Zeit des Clemens ein Tauf-
bekenntnis besessen?: Zeitschrift f. kirchl. Wissenschaft 7 (1886) 352–375. — A. v.
HARNACK, Die Terminologie der Wiedergeburt und verwandter Erlebnisse in der
ältesten Kirche (TU 42, 3). Leipzig, 1920, 97–143. — A. OEPKE, Urchristentum und
Kindertaufe: ZNW 29 (1930) 81–111. — F. J. DÖLGER, Das Lösen der Schuhriemen
in der Taufsymbolik des Klemens von Alexandrien: AC 5 (1936) 87–95. — H. A.
ECHLE, The Baptism of the Apostles: Traditio 3 (1945) 365–368; *idem*, The Terminology of the Sacrament of Regeneration according to Clement of Alexandria. Diss.
Washington, 1949; *idem*, Sacramental Initiation as a Christian Mystery-Initiation
according to Clement of Alexandria: Vom christlichen Mysterium. Gesammelte
Arbeiten zum Gedächtnis Odo Casels. Düsseldorf, 1951, 54–64.

4. *Eucharist*

There is a passage in *Strom.* 7,3, which indicates that Clement
did not believe in sacrifices:

> We rightly do not sacrifice to God, who, needing nothing,
> supplies all men with all things; but we glorify Him who
> gave Himself in sacrifice for us, we also sacrificing our-
> selves. . . For in our salvation alone God delights (ANF).

However, it would be incorrect to draw the conclusion from these words that Clement does not know the Eucharist as the sacrifice of the New Dispensation. In the passage quoted he speaks of the *pagan* rites, because he continues:

> We do not therefore, and with reason too, offer sacrifice to Him who is not overcome by pleasures, inasmuch as the fumes of the smoke stop far beneath and do not even reach the thickest clouds; but those they reach are far from them. The Deity neither is then in want of aught, nor loves pleasure or gain or money, being full and supplying all things to everything that has received being and has wants. And neither by sacrifices nor offerings, nor on the other hand by glory and honour, is the Deity won over; nor is He influenced by any such things; but He appears only to excellent and good men who will never betray justice for threatened fear nor by the promise of considerable gifts (*Strom.* 7,3,14–15 ANF).

The pagan bloody sacrifices did not correspond to the Christian concept of God and therefore the Christians regarded them as unworthy of Him. Clement is here in full agreement with the Greek Apologists, who repudiate bloody offerings for the same reason. But he knows of a sacrifice of the Church:

> The sacrifice of the Church is the word breathing as incense from holy souls, the sacrifice and the whole mind being at the same time unveiled to God (*Strom.* 7,6,32 ANF).

From this passage it might appear that Clement knows of no eucharistic sacrifice by the Church but only an inner, moral immolation of the soul. However, such an interpretation would not do justice to him. In his polemic against the pagan and Jewish concept he wishes to emphasize the spiritual character of the offering, its essential difference from all others. But this spiritual character does not exclude the symbolical oblation of gifts as it occurs in the liturgy. Clement knows such a ceremony very well. He mentions in *Strom.* 1,19,96 that there are heretical sects which substitute bread and water: 'The Scripture manifestly applying the terms bread and water to nothing else but to those heresies, which employ bread and water in the oblation, not according to the canon of the Church. For there are those who celebrate the Eucharist with mere water' (ANF). The wording of this passage presupposes that Clement is acquainted with an oblation (προσφορά) concerned with physical objects. He speaks of a canon of the Church (κανόνα τῆς ἐκκλησίας) and of a celebration of the Eucharist. He condemns the use of water as against this canon of the Church, which demands bread and wine, as he himself indicates *Strom.* 4,25: 'Melchisedek, king of Salem, priest of the most high God, who gave bread and wine, furnishing consecrated food for a type of the Eucharist' (ANF). Thus he recognizes in the Eucharist a sacrifice, but he sees it also as the food for believers:

'Eat ye my flesh,' He says, 'and drink my blood' (John 5,53). Such is the suitable food which the Lord ministers, and He offers His flesh and pours forth His blood, and nothing is wanting for the children's growth. O amazing mystery! We are enjoined to cast off the old and carnal corruption, as also the old nutriment, receiving in exchange another regimen, that of Christ, receiving Him if possible, to hide Him within; and that, enshrining the Saviour in our souls, we may correct the affections of our flesh.

But you are not inclined to understand it thus, but perchance more generally. Hear it also in the following way. The flesh figuratively represents to us the Holy Spirit; for the flesh was created by Him. The blood points out to us the Word, for as rich blood the Word has been infused into life; and the union of both is the Lord, the food of babes—the Lord who is Spirit and Word (*Paed.* 1,6,42,3–43,2 ANF).

In the first part of this passage Clement speaks of the Eucharist as the new food by which we receive Christ and enshrine Him in our souls. In the second part he offers an allegorical explanation for those who would not understand his literal interpretation. But the most important passage occurs in his *Paedagogus* 2,2,19,4–20,1:

The blood of the Lord is twofold. For there is the blood of His flesh, by which we are redeemed from corruption; and the spiritual, that by which we are anointed. And to drink the blood of Jesus, is to become partaker of the Lord's immortality; the Spirit being the energetic principle of the Word, as the blood is of the flesh.

Accordingly, as wine is blended with water, so is the

Spirit with man. And the one, the mixture of wine and water, nourishes to faith; while the other, the Spirit, conducts to immortality.

And the mixture of both—of the drink and of the Word— is called Eucharist, renowned and glorious grace; and they who by faith partake of it are sanctified both in body and soul (ANF).

Clement distinguishes here clearly between the human and the Eucharistic blood of Christ. The latter he calls the mixture of the drink and the Logos. The reception of this Eucharistic blood has a sanctifying effect on body and soul of man.

Texts: J. Quasten, Monumenta Eucharistica. Bonn, 1937, 348–349.

Studies: A. Scheiwiler, Die Elemente der Eucharistie (FLDG 3, 4). Mainz, 1903, 56–66. — F. Wieland, Der vorirenäische Opferbegriff. Munich, 1900, 106–121. —J. Brinktrine, Der Messopferbegriff in den ersten zwei Jahrhunderten (FThSt 21). Freiburg i.B., 1918, 105–110. — P. Batiffol, L'Eucharistie. La présence réelle et la transsubstantiation. 9th ed. Paris, 1930, 248–261. — F. R. M. Hitchcock, Holy Communion and Creed in Clement of Alexandria: ChQ 129 (1939) 57–70.

5. *Sins and Penance*

According to Clement, the sin of Adam consisted in his refusal to be educated by God and has been inherited by all human beings not through generation but through the bad example given by the first man (*Adumbr. in Jud.* 11; *Strom.* 3,16,100; *Protrept.* 2,3). Clement is convinced that only a personal act can stain the soul. His conception resulted most likely from a reaction to the Gnostics, who held evil matter responsible for wrong. With reference to God's punishments, he holds, following Plato, that they have only a purgative character:

Plato says beautifully: 'For all who suffer punishment are in reality treated well, for they are benefited since the spirit of those who are justly punished is improved.' And if those who are corrected receive good at the hands of justice, and, according to Plato, what is just is acknowledged to be good, fear itself does good, and has been found to be men's good (*Paed.* 1,8,67 ANF).

However, he mentions nowhere that he applies this interpretation even to hell.

Clement agrees with Hermas (cf. vol. I, pp. 97–99) that there

should be only one penance in the life of a Christian, that
preceding baptism, but that God, out of mercy for human
weakness, has granted a second, which can be obtained only
once:

> He who has received the forgiveness of sins ought to sin
> no more. For in addition to the first and only repentance
> from sins (this is from the previous sins in the first and
> heathen life—I mean that in ignorance), there is forth-
> with proposed to those who have been called, the repent-
> ance which cleanses the seat of the soul from transgressions,
> that faith may be established. And the Lord, knowing the
> heart, and foreknowing the future, foresaw both the fickle-
> ness of man and the craft and subtlety of the devil from the
> first, from the beginning; how that, envying man for the
> forgiveness of sins, he would present to the servants of God
> certain causes of sins, skilfully working mischief, that they
> might fall together with himself. Accordingly, being very
> merciful, He has vouchsafed, in the case of those who,
> though in faith, fall into any transgression, a second repent-
> ance, so that should any one be tempted after his calling,
> overcome by force and fraud, he may receive still a repent-
> ance not to be repented of. 'For if we sin wilfully after that
> we have received the knowledge of the truth, there remains
> no more sacrifice for sins, but a certain fearful looking-for
> of judgment and fiery indignation, which shall devour the
> adversaries' (Hebr. 10,26–27). But continual and successive
> repentings for sins differ nothing from the case of those who
> have not believed at all, except only in their consciousness
> that they do sin. And I know not which of the two is worst,
> whether the case of a man who sins knowingly, or of one
> who, after having repented of his sins, transgresses again
> (*Strom*. 2,13,56–57,4 ANF).

He then who from among the Gentiles and from that old
life has betaken himself to faith, has obtained forgiveness
of sins once. But he who has sinned after this, on his repentance, though he obtains pardon, ought to fear, as one no longer
washed to the forgiveness of sins. For not only must the
idols which he formerly held as gods, but the works also of
his former life be abandoned by him who has been 'born

again, not of blood, nor of the will of the flesh' (John 1,13) but in the Spirit; which consists in repenting by not giving way to the same fault. For frequent repentance and readiness to change easily from want of training, is the practice of sin again. The frequent asking of forgiveness then for those things in which we often transgress is the semblance of repentance, not repentance itself (*Strom.* 2,13,58–59,1 ANF). Clement distinguishes in these passages between voluntary and involuntary sins. He is of the opinion that of sins committed after baptism only those that are involuntary sins can be forgiven. Those who commit voluntary sins after baptism must fear the judgment of God. A complete break with God after baptism cannot be forgiven. It contradicts the early Christian idea of the inviolability of the baptismal seal. If the sin committed after baptism does not constitute a complete break with God on account of a certain lack of free decision, there exists the possibility of a second repentance. However, in reality Clement does not exclude any sin for its greatness from this second repentance. The story which he narrates at the end of his *Quis dives salvetur* of St. John and the youth who became the head of a gang of robbers is proof sufficient that all sins can be forgiven if there is not an obstacle in the soul of the sinner. Although Clement describes him as 'the fiercest, the bloodiest and the cruelest' St. John 'restored him to the Church, presenting in him a great example of true repentance and a great token of regeneration' (42,7,15). From all this it appears that Clement does not know of capital sins which could not be forgiven. Even the sin of apostasy seems to him to be forgivable because he prays that the heretics might return to the almighty God (*Strom.* 7,16,102,2). The unforgivable and 'voluntary' sin consists in man purposely turning away from God and refusing reconciliation and conversion.

Studies: T. Rüther, Die Lehre von der Erbsünde bei Clemens von Alexandrien (FThSt 28). Freiburg i.B., 1922. — J. Hering, Étude sur la doctrine de la chûte et de la préexistence des âmes chez Clément d'Alexandrie (BEHE 38). Paris, 1923. — H. Karpp, Probleme altchristlicher Anthropologie (BFTh 44, 3). Gütersloh, 1950, 92–130. — Gaudel, DTC 12, 329–332. — Th. Spacil, La dottrina del purgatorio in Clemente Alessandrino ed Origene: Bess (1919) 131–145. — J. Hoh, Die Busse bei Klemens von Alexandrien: ZkTh 56 (1932) 175–189; *idem,* Die kirchliche Busse im zweiten Jahrhundert. Breslau, 1932, 115–129. — B. Poschmann, Paenitentia secunda.

Die kirchliche Busse im ältesten Christentum bis Cyprian und Origenes (Theophaneia 1). Bonn, 1940, 229–260. — M. Schmaus, J. R. Geiselmann, H. Rahner, Handbuch der Dogmengeschichte, vol. 4, fasc. 3: B. Poschmann, Busse und letzte Ölung, Freiburg i. B., 1951, 32–34.

6. *Matrimony and Virginity*

Clement defends marriage against all attempts of the Gnostic sects to discredit and reject it. He not only recommends marriage for moral reasons, he goes so far as to regard it a duty for the welfare of the country, for the succession of children and for the perfection of the world:

> Therefore we must by all means marry, both for our country's sake, for the succession of children, and as far as we are concerned for the perfection of the world; since the poets also pity a marriage half-perfect and childless, but pronounce the fruitful one happy.

The purpose of marriage is the procreation of children, which is the duty of everyone who loves his country. But Clement elevates marriage to a much higher level, to an act of cooperation with the creator: 'Thus man becomes an image of God in so far as man cooperates in the creation of man' (*Paed.* 2,10,83,2). But the procreation of children is not the only purpose of marriage. The mutual love, and the assistance and help extended to each other unite them in a bond which is eternal:

> The virtue of man and woman is the same. For if the God of both is one, the master of both is also one; one Church, one temperance, one modesty; their food is common, marriage an equal yoke; respiration, sight, hearing, knowledge, hope, obedience, love all alike. And those whose life is common, have common graces and a common salvation; common to them are love and training (*Paed.* 1,4 ANF).

But the most beautiful concept of matrimony is found *Strom.* 3,10, 68, where Clement says: 'Who are the two ort hree gathered together in the name of Christ, in whose midst is the Lord? Are not they man, wife and child because man and wife are joined by God?' Thus Clement puts matrimony higher than a sexual union; it is a spiritual and religious union between husband and wife so that he avers: 'Sacred is the state of matrimony' (*Strom.* 3,12, 84). Even death does not dissolve this union.

completely and for this reason Clement is against any second marriage (*Strom.* 3,12,82).

Since Clement thus defended marriage against the heretical Gnostics, who rejected it and preached complete abstinence, the question arises how he regarded virginity. He himself was not married 'out of love for the Lord' (*Strom.* 3,7,59) and he says occasionally: 'We praise virginity and those to whom God has given this' (*Strom.* 3,1,4). He is convinced that 'he who remains single in order not to be separated from the service of the Lord will gain a heavenly glory' (*Strom.* 3,12,82). But when he compares matrimony and virginity he regards the married man as superior to the single. Carefully weighing the merits of both he feels obliged to remark:

> One is not really shown to be a man in the choice of single life; but he surpasses men, who, disciplined by marriage, procreation of children, and care for the house, without pleasure or pain, in his solicitude for the house has been inseparable from God's love, and withstood all temptation arising through children and wife and domestics and possessions. But he that has no family is in a great degree free of temptation. Caring then for himself alone, he is surpassed by him who is inferior, as far as his own personal salvation is concerned, but who is superior in the conduct of life (*Strom.* 7,12,70 anf 2,543).

Clement's opinion is unparalleled and might have been influenced by his strong defense of matrimony against the Gnostic attacks.

For Clement's *asceticism and mysticism*, cf.: G. W. BUTTERWORTH, The Deification of Man in Clement of Alexandria: JThSt 17 (1916) 157–169. — A. MÉNAGER, La doctrine spirituelle de Clément d'Alexandrie: VS 7 (1922) 407–430. — P. GUILLOUX, L'ascétisme de Clément d'Alexandrie: RAM 3 (1922) 282–300. — W. C. DE PAULEY, Man: The Image of God. A Study in Clement of Alexandria: ChQ 100 (1925) 96–121. — O. FALLER, Griechische Vergottung und christliche Vergöttlichung: Greg 6 (1925) 427–435. — P. DUDON, Le Gnostique de saint Clément d'Alexandrie. Opuscule inédit de Fénelon. Paris, 1930. — A. KOCH, Clemens von Alexandrien als Lehrer der Vollkommenheit: ZAM 7 (1932) 363–364. — H. PREISKER, Christentum und Ehe in den ersten drei Jahrhunderten. Berlin, 1927, 200–211. — J. M. TSERMOULAS, Die Bildersprache des Klemens von Alexandrien. Diss. Würzburg, 1934. — J. PASCHER, Studien zur Geschichte der ägyptischen Mystik. 2. Heft: Klemens von Alexandrien. Bamberg, 1934. — G. BARDY, La spiritualité de Clément d'Alexandrie: VS 39 (1934) 81–104, 129–145; *idem*, La vie spirituelle d'après les Pères des trois premiers siècles. Paris, 1935; *idem*, Apatheia: Dictionnaire de spirit. ascétique et mystique 1, 727–746. — J. D. PHRANKOULÈS, 'Η συμβολικὴ τῶν ἀριθμῶν παρὰ τῷ Κλήμεντι τῷ 'Αλεξανδρεῖ: Θεολογία 13 (1935) 5–21. — H. G. MARSH, The Use of μυστήριον in the Writings of Clement of Alexandria: JThSt 37 (1936) 64–80. — C. MONDÉSERT, Le symbolisme chez Clément d'Alexandrie: RSR 26 (1936) 158–180. — K. HEUSSI, Der Ursprung des Mönchtums. Tübingen, 1936, 40–44. — K. PRÜMM, *Mysterion* von Paulus bis Origenes: ZkTh 61 (1937) 391–425. — J. ZIEG-LER, Dulcedo Dei. Münster i.W., 1937, 62 f., 70–72. — J. GROSS, La divinisation du chrétien d'après les pères Grecs. Paris, 1938, 159–174. — D. PIRE, Sur l'emploi des termes Apatheia et Eleos dans les œuvres de Clément d'Alexandrie: RSPT 27 (1938) 427–431. — A. MAYER, Gottähnlichkeit als menschliche Vollendung, ein christliches Ideal in seiner Berührung mit Gnostizismus und griechischer Philosophie bei Klemens von Alexandrien: Nova et Vetera. Festschrift der Abtei Metten (1939) 44–64. — M. VILLER–K. RAHNER, Aszese und Mystik in der Väterzeit. Freiburg i.B., 1939, 60–71. — O. CASEL, Glaube, Gnosis und Mysterium: JL 15 (1941) 155–305. — G. BÉKÉS, De continua oratione Clementis Alexandrini doctrina (Studia Anselmiana 14). Rome, 1942. — A. MAYER, Das Gottesbild im Menschen nach Clemens von Alexandrien (Studia Anselmiana 15). Rome, 1942. Cf. J. DANIÉLOU, RSR 35 (1948) 601–603. — TH. CAMELOT, Foi et gnose. Introduction à l'étude de la connaissance mystique chez Clément d'Alexandrie. Paris, 1945. — G. BÉKÉS, Pura oratio apud Clementem Alexandrinum: Studia Benedictina (Studia Anselmiana 18/19). Rome, 1947, 157–172. — W. VÖLKER, Die Vollkommenheitslehre des Clemens Alexandrinus in ihren geschichtlichen Zusammenhängen: TZ 3 (1947) 15–40. — F. VAN DER GRINTEN, Die natürliche und übernatürliche Begründung des Tugendlebens bei Clemens von Alexandrien. Diss. Rome. Bonn, 1949. — TH. RÜTHER, Die sittliche Forderung der Apatheia in den beiden ersten christlichen Jahrhunderten und bei Klemens von Alexandrien (FThSt 63). Freiburg i.B., 1949. — E. E. MALONE, The Monk and the Martyr (SCA 12). Washington, 1950, 4–14. — W. VÖLKER, Der wahre Gnostiker nach Clemens Alexandrinus (TU 57). Leipzig, 1952.

For Clement's *language and style*, see: J. SCHAM, Der Optativgebrauch bei Klemens von Alexandrien in seiner sprach- und stilgeschichtlichen Bedeutung (FLDG 11, 4). Paderborn, 1913. — W. TELFER, 'Bees' in Clement of Alexandria: JThSt 28 (1927) 167. — J. BALOGH, 'Rerum dominis pietas semper amica': SJMS 4 (1929) 323–324. — H. MOSSBACHER, Präpositionen und Präpositionsadverbien unter besonderer Berücksichtigung der Infinitivkonstruktionen bei Klemens von Alexandrien. Ein Beitrag zur Geschichte des Attizismus. Diss. Erlangen, 1931. — E. TENGBLAD, Syntaktischstilistische Beiträge zur Kritik und Exegese des Klemens von Alexandrien. Lund, 1932. — J. TSERMOULAS, Die Bildersprache des Klemens von Alex. Diss. Würzburg, 1934. — H. G. MARSH, The Use of μυστήριον in the Writings of Clement of Alexandria: JThSt 37 (1936) 64–80. — C. MONDÉSERT, Le symbolisme chez Clément d'Alexandrie: RSR (1936) 158–180. — K. PRÜMM, *Mysterion* von Paulus bis Origenes: ZkTh 61 (1937) 391–425. — D. PIRE, Sur l'emploi des termes Apatheia et Eleos dans les œuvres de Clément d'Alexandrie: RSPT 27 (1938) 427–431. — P. VIELHAUER, Oikodome. Das Bild vom Bau in der christlichen Literatur vom Neuen Testament bis Clemens Alexandrinus. 1939. — M. G. MURPHY, Nature Allusions in the Works of Clement of Alexandria (PSt 65). Washington, 1941. — P. M. HERMANIUK, La parabole chez Clément d'Alexandrie. Définition et source: ETL 21 (1945) 5–60.

ORIGEN

The school of Alexandria reached its greatest importance
under Clement's successor, Origen, the outstanding teacher and
scholar of the early Church, a man of spotless character, encyclopaedic learning, and one of the most original thinkers the
world has ever seen. We have more biographical details about
him than about any of the previous theologians thanks to the
special interest which Eusebius, the historian, took in him.
A large part of the sixth book of his *Ecclesiastical History* deals
with Origen. Origen's more than one hundred letters would
have been the best source of information for an understanding
of his personality, but they have been lost. Fortunately, Eusebius
had collected these letters and he makes ample use of them in
the sketch of Origens' life. We would be even better informed if
the entire apology had survived which the presbyter Pamphilus
of Caesarea wrote in his defense. It comprised five books, to
which Eusebius added a sixth. Only the first has been preserved
in a not very reliable Latin translation by Rufinus. There is,
however, the Farewell Address which Gregory the Wonder-
worker composed on the occasion of his leaving Origen's circle,
a document as important for the personal history of Origen as
for his way of teaching. Finally St. Jerome mentions him in his
Who's Who of famous men (*De vir. ill.* 54,62), and in one of his
letters (*Epist.* 33) and Photius in his *Bibl. cod.* 118.

From these sources it appears that Origen was not a convert
from paganism but the child of a Christian home and the eldest
son of a large family. He was born in or about A.D. 185 most
probably at Alexandria. His father, Leonidas, who had given
him a careful education in Scripture and secular subjects, died
the death of a martyr in the persecution of Severus (A.D. 202),
and if his mother had not hidden Origen's clothes the youth,
in his passionate desire for martyrdom, would have joined his
father. His patrimony confiscated by the State, he maintained
himself and the family by teaching. The famous school for
catechumens at Alexandria had been broken up by the flight
of Clement, and Bishop Demetrius put in charge of it the young
Origen at the age of eighteen, a post he was to hold for many
years. He won a great number of pupils, who were attracted to

him not only by his teaching but also by his life, as Eusebius remarks: 'As was his speech, so was the manner of life that he displayed, and as his manner of life, so his speech, and it was especially for this reason that, with the cooperation of the divine power, he brought so many to share his zeal' (*Hist. eccl.* 6,3,7 LCL 19). Eusebius gives a vivid account of the asceticism practised by this *Adamantius*, 'Man of Steel,' as he calls him:

He persevered, as far as possible, in the most philosophic manner of life, at one time disciplining himself by fasting, at another measuring out the time for sleep, which he was careful to take, never on a couch, but on the floor. And above all he considered that those sayings of the Saviour in the Gospel ought to be kept which exhort us not to provide two coats nor to use shoes, nor, indeed, to be worn out with thoughts about the future (*Hist. eccl.* 6,3,9–10 LCL 21).

We learn, too, from this source that it was while he was instructing at Alexandria, i.e., about the year 202–3, that he emasculated himself, taking Matthew 19,12 in a too literal sense (*ibid.* 6,8,1–3).

The period of his life as an educator can be divided into two parts. The first, as head of the school at Alexandria, reaching from 203 to 231, was one of increasing success. He gained pupils even from heretical circles and from the pagan schools of philosophy. At first he taught the preparatory courses of dialectics, physics, mathematics, geometry and astronomy as well as Greek philosophy and speculative theology. When this became too much of a burden to him, he assigned to his pupil Heraclas the preparatory subjects, while he devoted himself to introducing the more advanced students to philosophy, theology and especially Holy Scripture. This busy schedule did not prevent him from attending the lectures of Ammonius Saccas, the famous founder of Neoplatonism. His influence can be seen in Origen's cosmology and psychology and in his method.

Origen's teaching at Alexandria was interrupted by several journeys. About the year 212 he went to Rome 'desiring to see the most ancient Church of the Romans' (Euseb., *Hist. eccl.* 6,14,10). This happened during the pontificate of Zephyrinus and he met there the most renowned theologian of the time, the Roman presbyter Hippolytus. Shortly before the year 215

we find him in Arabia, where he had gone in order to instruct
the Roman governor at the latter's own request. On another
occasion he travelled to Antioch, at the invitation of the mother
of the Emperor Alexander Severus, Julia Mamaea, who wished
to hear him. When Caracalla looted the city of Alexandria, closed
the schools and persecuted the teachers, Origen decided to go
to Palestine, about the year 216. The bishops of Caesarea,
Jerusalem and other Palestinian cities asked him to deliver some
sermons and to explain Scripture to their communities, which he
did, although not a priest. His own superior Demetrius at
Alexandria objected and blamed the Palestine hierarchy for
permitting a layman to preach in the presence of bishops, a
procedure which, according to him, was never heard of. Although the bishops of Palestine denied this, Origen obeyed his
superior's strict orders to return to Alexandria at once. However,
in order to avoid such difficulties for the future, Bishop Alexander
of Jerusalem and Theoctistus of Caesarea ordained Origen,
when, fifteen years later, he passed through Caesarea on his
way to Greece, where his bishop had sent him in order to refute
heretics. This but made the situation worse, because Demetrius
now took the view that according to canonical legislation, Origen
could not be admitted to the priesthood since he had castrated
himself. Eusebius most probably is more correct when he states
that Demetrius 'was overcome by human weakness when he saw
that Origen was prospering and a great man and distinguished
and famous in the sight of all' (*Hist. eccl.* 6,8,4 LCL 31). In any
case, Demetrius called a synod, which excommunicated Origen
from the Church of Alexandria. A second synod in the year 231
deprived him of the priesthood. After Demetrius' death (232)
he returned to Alexandria but his successor Heraclas, Origen's
former assistant, repeated the excommunication.

Origen left for Caesarea in Palestine and thus began the second
period of his life. The bishop of Caesarea ignored the censure
of his colleague at Alexandria and induced Origen to found a
new school of theology at Caesarea, over which he presided for
almost twenty years. It was here that Gregory the Wonder-
worker delivered his Farewell Address on the occasion of his
leaving Origen's circle. According to this valuable document
the course of instruction at Caesarea was practically the same

as at Alexandria. After an exhortation to philosophy, which formed the introduction, a preliminary course of instruction followed, preparing the student by means of continual mental training for scientific education. This latter consisted of logic and dialectic, natural science, geometry and astronomy, and finally ethics and theology. The course in ethics was by no means a rational discussion of moral problems only but gave a philosophy of life. Gregory informs us that Origen made his pupils read all the works of the ancient philosophers except those who denied the existence of God and divine providence.

About the year 244 he went again to Arabia, where he succeeded in curing Bishop Beryllus of Bostra of his monarchianism (Euseb. *Hist. eccl.* 6,33). During the Decian persecution he must have suffered great tortures because Eusebius remarks:

> The man's numerous letters contain both a true and accurate account of the nature and extent of that which he endured for the word of Christ, punishments as he lay in iron and in the recesses of his dungeon; and how, when for many days his feet were stretched four spaces in that instrument of torture, the stocks, he bore with a stout heart threats of fire and everything else that was inflicted by his enemies; and the kind of issue he had thereof, the judge eagerly striving with all his might on no account to put him to death; and what sort of sayings he left behind him after this, sayings full of help for those who need uplifting (*Hist. eccl.* 6,39,5 LCL 95).

He died at Tyre in A.D. 253 at the age of sixty-nine, his health broken by these sufferings.

It was Origen's destiny to be a sign of contradiction during his lifetime as well as after his death. There is hardly anyone who made so many friends or so many enemies. True, he committed errors, as we shall see, but no one can doubt but that he always wanted to be an orthodox and believing Christian. He states at the beginning of his main theological work: 'That alone is to be accepted as truth which differs in no respect from ecclesiastical and apostolic tradition' (*De princ.* praef. 2). He strove to follow that rule and sealed it with his blood at the end of his life.

Studies: B. F. WESTCOTT, Origenes: Dictionary of Christian Biography 4, 96–142. — G. BARDY, Origène: DTC 11, 1489–1565. — HAL KOCH, PWK 18, 1, 1036–1068. —

A. v. Harnack, Origenes: RGG 4, 780–787. — A. Antweiler, Origenes: LThK 7, 776–781.

E. R. Redepenning, Origenes. Eine Darstellung seines Lebens und seiner Lehre. Bonn, 1841/46, 2 vols. — E. Freppel, Origène. 2nd ed. Paris, 1875, 2 vols. — E. de Faye, Origène, sa vie, son œuvre, sa pensée. Paris, 1923/28, 3 vols. Cf. A. d'Alès, La doctrine d'Origène d'après un livre récent: RSR 20 (1930) 224–268. — G. Bardy, Les traditions juives dans l'œuvre d'Origène: RBibl 34 (1925) 217–252. — H. Koch, Zum Lebensgange des Origenes und Heraclas: ZNW 25 (1926) 278–282. — S. Martinelli, Origene e il mito di Attis: Mondo classico 4 (1931) 49–54. — G. Bardy, Origène. Paris, 1931. — R. Cadiou, Introduction au système d'Origène. Paris, 1932. — W. E. Barnes, The Third Century and its Greatest Christian, Origen: ExpT 44 (1932/33) 295–300. — R. Cadiou, La jeunesse d'Origène. Histoire de l'école d'Alexandrie au début du IIIe siècle. Paris, 1935. English translation by J. A. Southwell, Origen. His Life at Alexandria. St. Louis and London, 1944. — A. Goodier, Origen and his Generation: Month 169 (1937) 491–500. — F. Cavallera, Origène éducateur: BLE (1943) 61–75. — W. R. Inge, Origen (British Academy Annual Lectures on a Master Mind). London, 1946. — J. Lebreton, Origène: A. Fliche – V. Martin, Histoire de l'Église 2. Paris, 1946, 249–293. — J. Champonier, Naissance de l'humanisme chrétien: Bulletin de l'Asssociation G. Budé (1947) 58–96. — K. L. Schmidt, Origines statt Origenes: TZ (1947) 234–235. — G. L. Prestige, Fathers and Heretics. London, 1948, 43–66. — J. Daniélou, Origène. Paris, 1948. — E. Elorduy, Origenes, discipulo de Ammonio: Las Ciencias 12, 4 (1949) 897–912.
For terminology and style, see: J. Borst, Beiträge zur sprachlich-stilistischen Würdigung des Origenes. Diss. Münster, 1913. — R. Cadiou, Dictionnaires antiques dans l'œuvre d'Origène: REG (1932) 271–285. — K. Prümm, Mysterion von Paulus bis Origenes: ZkTh 61 (1937) 391–425. — E. Klostermann, Überkommene Definitionen im Werke des Origenes: ZNW 37 (1938) 52–61. — S. Laeuchli, Origen's Conception of Symbolon: AThR 34 (1952) 102–116.
For Origen's philosophy, see: C. Bigg, The Christian Platonists of Alexandria. 2nd ed. Oxford, 1913. — G. Rossi, Saggio sulla metafisica di Origine. Milan, 1929. — H. Koch, Pronoia und Paideusis. Studien über Origenes und sein Verhältnis zum Platonismus. Leipzig, 1932. — G. Bardy, Origène et l'aristotélisme: Mélanges G. Glotz. Paris, 1932, 75–83. — R. Arnou, Le thème néoplatonicien et la contemplation créatrice chez Origène et chez S. Augustin: Greg (1932) 124–136. — J. Stelzenberger, Die Beziehungen der frühchristlichen Sittenlehre zur Ethik der Stoa. Munich, 1933. — J. Murray, Origen, Augustine und Plotinus: Month 170 (1937) 107–117. — G. D. Kilpatrick, A Fragment of Musonius: CR (1949) 94.

If we compare his ideas with those of Clement of Alexandria, it seems at first that he did not share Clement's high regard for Greek philosophy. He never repeated Clement's dictum that Greek philosophy was a guide to Christ. In a letter addressed to the Gregory who delivered that fervent Farewell Address in his honor, Origen admonishes his former pupil to continue his studies of Holy Scripture and regard philosophy only as a preparatory subject: 'I beseech thee to draw from Greek philosophy such things as are capable of being encyclic or preparatory studies to Christianity, and from geometry and astronomy such things as will be useful for the exposition of Holy Scripture, in order that what the sons of the philosophers say about geometry and music and grammar and rhetoric and astronomy, that they are the handmaidens of philosophy, we may say of philosophy itself in relation to Christianity' (13,1 SPCK). Thus the importance of Holy Scripture is more emphasized by him than by Clement. However, Origen made the mistake of letting the philosophy of Plato influence his theology more than he thought. This led him to very serious dogmatic errors, especially the doctrine of the pre-existence of the human soul. The other pitfall in his system was his allegorical interpretation. It is not true that this method was for him only a means of eliminating the Old Testament, for which, on the contrary, he had the highest regard. But it is true that he thus introduced into exegesis a dangerous subjectivism leading to arbitrariness and error. So his doctrines were soon called in question. Disputes, which are known as 'Origenistic Controversies,' raged especially around the years 300, 400 and 550. In the first, Methodius of Philippi and Peter of Alexandria were his adversaries. Origen was defended by Pamphilus of Caesarea. The controversy remained in the literary field and there was no official ecclesiastical intervention. More serious was the dissension about 400 when Epiphanius of Salamis and Theophilus, the patriarch of Alexandria, attacked his doctrine. Epiphanius condemned him in a synod held near Constantinople and Pope Anastasius in a Paschal letter. Finally, the Emperor Justinian the First, in a council at Constantinople in 543, reached an agreement, which resulted in fifteen anathemas on some of Origen's doctrines and which was signed by Pope Vigilius (537–55) and all the patriarchs (ES 203–211).

Studies: G. Fritz, Origénisme: DTC 11, 1565–1588. — F. Diekamp, Die origenistischen Streitigkeiten im 6. Jahrhundert. Münster, 1899. — A. d'Alès, Origénisme: DAp 3, 1228–1258. — K. Holl, Die Zeitfolge des ersten origenistischen Streites: SAB (1916) 226–275. — A. Jülicher, Bemerkungen zu der Abhandlung Holls: Die Zeitfolge des ersten origenistischen Streites: SAB (1916) 256–275. — J. Lannoo, Version syriaque de dix anathèmes contre Origène: Mus (1930) 7–16. — C. C. Richardson, The Condemnation of Origen: Church History 6 (1937) 50–64. — M. Villain, Rufin d'Aquilée. La querelle autour d'Origène: RSR (1937) 5–37, 165–195. — E. v. Ivanka, Zur geistesgeschichtlichen Einordnung des Origenismus: BZ

44 (1951) 291–303. — F. X. Murphy, Rufinus of Aquileia (Studies in Mediaeval History. New Series 6). Washington, 1945, 59–81: Quarrel over Origen. — J. Leclercq, Origène au XIIe siècle: Irénikon 24 (1951) 425–439.

For Origen's *influence on later ecclesiastical writers*, see: R. Reitzenstein, Origenes und Hieronymus: ZNW 20 (1920) 90–93. — R. Cadiou, Origène et les 'reconnaissances clémentines': RSR (1930) 506–528. — J. Lebreton, Saint Cyprien et Origène: RSR (1930) 160–162. — G. Bardy, St. Jérome et ses maîtres hébreux: RB (1934) 145–164. — J. Daniélou, Origène et Maxime de Tyr: RSR (1947) 359–361. — B. Altaner, Augustinus und Origenes: HJG 70 (1951) 15–41.

1. HIS WRITINGS

The Origenistic Controversies caused most of the literary output of the great Alexandrian to disappear. The remains are mostly preserved, not in the original Greek, but in Latin translations. The complete list of his writings that Eusebius added to the biography of his friend and teacher Pamphilus was also lost. According to Jerome (*Adv. Ruf.* 2,22), who used it, the treatises numbered two thousand. Epiphanius (*Haer.* 64,63) estimates his literary productions at six thousand. We know only the titles of eight hundred, itemized in St. Jerome's Letter to Paula (*Epist.* 33). Origen would not have had the means for publication on so vast a scale if it had not been for his wealthy friends. Especially Ambrose, whom he converted from the Valentinian heresy, enabled him to engage in his literary activities by placing seven or more stenographers in his lecture room:

> Starting from that time Origen's commentaries on the divine Scriptures had their beginning, at the instigation of Ambrose, who not only plied him with innumerable verbal exhortations and encouragements, but also provided him unstintingly with what was necessary. For as he dictated there were ready at hand more than seven shorthand-writers, who relieved each other at fixed times, and as many copyists, as well as girls skilled in penmanship; for all of whom Ambrose supplied without stint the necessary means (Euseb., *Hist. eccl.* 6,23,1–2 LCL).

Editions: C. de la Rue, Paris, 1733–1759, 4 vols. Reprinted in MG 11–17. — C. H. E. Lommatzsch, Berlin, 1831–1848, 25 vols. — GCS, 12 vols. so far, Leipzig, 1899–1941, ed. by P. Koetschau, E. Klostermann, E. Preuschen, W. A. Baehrens and M. Rauer. — *Selections:* J. A. Robinson, The Philocalia of Origen. Cambridge, 1893.

Translations: English: F. Crombie, ANL 10, 23; ANF 4; A. Menzies, ANL additional volume; A. MENZIES–J. PATRICK, ANF 9. *Selections:* G. LEWIS, Origen. The Philocalia. Edinburgh, 1911. — R. B. TOLLINTON, Selections from the Commentaries and Homilies of Origen (SPCK). London, 1929. — *German:* P. KOETSCHAU, BKV[2] 48, 52, 53. *Selections:* H. U. v. BALTHASAR, Origenes: Geist und Feuer. Ein Aufbau aus seinen Schriften. Salzburg, 1938, 2nd ed. 1951. — *French:* L. DOUTRELEAU, SCH 7; P. FORTIER, SCH 16; A. MÉHAT, SCH 29. *Selections:* G. BARDY, Origène (Les moralistes chrétiens). Paris, 1931. — *Dutch:* H. U. MEYBOOM, Oudchristelijke geschriften in Nederlandsche vertaling, deel 31, 34–38. — Separate translations are listed with the individual works.

1. *Textual Criticism*

The greater part of his literary output is devoted to the Bible and for this reason he might be called the founder of biblical science. His *Hexapla* (or six-fold Bible) is the first attempt at establishing a critical text of the Old Testament. It was an immense task, to which Origen dedicated his whole life. He arranged in six parallel columns the Hebrew text of the Old Testament in Hebrew characters, the Hebrew text in Greek characters in order to fix the pronunciation, the Greek translation of Aquila, a Jew contemporary with Hadrian, the Greek translation of Symmachus, a Jew of the time of Septimius Severus, the Greek translation of the Septuagint, and lastly, that of the Jew Theodotion (about 180 A.D.). Origen's critical work consisted in marking the fifth column, the text of the Septuagint, with certain signs indicating its relation to the Hebrew original. Thus the *obelus* (÷) signified additions; the asterisk (※) *lacunae*, which were filled in from one of the other versions, usually Theodotion's. According to Eusebius, Origen published also an edition containing merely the four Greek interpretations, the so-called *Tetrapla*, most probably for those writings only for which no corresponding Hebrew text existed. He added in the part of the *Hexapla* devoted to the psalms three more renderings, increasing the columns to a total of nine, thus changing the *Hexapla* into an *Enneapla*. Of this colossal work only small fragments remain. It seems that the whole was never copied but remained for centuries at the disposal of scholars in the library of Caesarea. Jerome consulted it there and he remarks that this was the only exemplar he ever saw of it (*Commentarioli in Ps.*, ed. Morin 5). The fifth column containing the text of the Septuagint was multiplied many times. An almost completely preserved

Syriac version of it dates from the sixth century. However, it would be wrong to assume, as has been maintained, that this was the only part of Origen's work that was ever reproduced. The Italian scholar Giovanni Mercati discovered in a palimpsest of the Ambrosian Library at Milan fragments of a transcription of the *Hexapla* containing the psalms but with the first column omitted. Two vellum leaves found in the lumberroom of the Old Synagogue at Cairo and preserved in the Library of Cambridge (England) present the Hexapla text for Psalm XXII. In addition, some manuscripts of the Greek Old Testament and some Church Fathers preserve extracts.

Fragments: B. DE MONTFAUCON, Hexaplorum Origenis quae supersunt. Paris, 1713, 2 vols. — MG 15-16. — F. FIELD, Origenis Hexaplorum quae supersunt. Oxford, 1867/75, 2 vols. — E. KLOSTERMANN, Analecta zur Septuaginta, Hexapla und Patristik. Leipzig, 1894, 50-74. — G. MERCATI, Un palimpsesto Ambrosiano dei Salmi Esapli. Turin, 1896; *idem*, Note di letteratura biblica e cristiana antica (ST 5). Rome, 1901.

Studies: C. TAYLOR, Hexapla: Dictionary of Christian Biography 3, 14-23; *idem*, Hebrew-Greek Cairo Genizah Palimpsests from the Taylor-Schlechter Collection, including a fragment of the twenty-second Psalm according to Origen's Hexapla. Cambridge, 1900, 1-50. — H. B. SWETE, An Introduction to the Old Testament in Greek, 2nd ed. Cambridge, 1902, 59-76. — H. H. HOWORTH, The Hexapla and Tetrapla of Origen: Proceedings of the Society of Bibl. Archaeology 24 (1902) 147-172. — J. HALÉVY, L'origine de la transcription du texte hébreu en caractères grecs dans les Hexaples d'Origène: JA (1901) I 335-341. — A. RAHLFS, Studie über den griechischen Text des Buches Ruth: NGWG (1922) 47-163. — O. PRETZL, Der hexaplarische und tetraplarische Septuagintatext des Origenes in den Büchern Josua und Richter: BZ 30 (1930) 262-267. — B. H. STREETER, Origen and the Caesarean Text: JThSt (1935) 178-180. — H. M. ORLINSKY, The Columnar Order of the Hexapla: Jewish Quart. N.S. 27 (1936) 137-149. — O. PROCKSCH, Tetraplarische Studien: Zeitschrift für die alttestamentl. Wissenschaft 53 (1935) 240-269; 54 (1936) 61-90. — W. E. STAPLES, The Second Column of Origen's Hexapla: Journal of the American Oriental Society 59 (1939) 71-80. — H. DOERRIES, Zur Geschichte der Septuaginta im Jahrhundert Konstantins: ZNW (1940) 1-48, 57-110. — G. MERCATI, Nuove note (ST 95). 1941, 85-91, 139-150. — F. KENYON, Our Bible and the Ancient Manuscripts. New York, 1941, 57-60. — G. MERCATI, Note di letteratura biblica: Vivre et penser. Recherches d'exégèse et d'histoire I. Paris, 1941, 5-15.

2. *Exegetical Works*

Origen is the first scientific exegete of the Catholic Church. He wrote on all the books of the Old and New Testaments, and in three different literary forms: the scholia, which are brief explanations of difficult passages, the homilies and the commentaries.

1. *Scholia* (σχόλια, σημειώσεις, *excerpta, commaticum genus*)

According to St. Jerome (*Epist.* 33) Origen wrote scholia on Exodus, Leviticus, Isaias, Psalms 1–15, Ecclesiastes and the Gospel of St. John. Rufinus included some on Numbers in his translation of Origen's homilies on that book (Rufinus, *Interpr. hom. Orig. in Num. Prol.*). None has come down to us in its entirety. The work which C. Diobouniotis and A. Harnack edited as Origen's scholia to the Apocalypse of St. John cannot be regarded as such, since it combines longer or shorter notes to difficult passages of the Apocalypse from Clement of Alexandria, Irenaeus, and Origen. Some fragments of the scholia have been discovered in the *Catenae* and in the *Philocalia*, the anthology of Origen which St. Basil and St. Gregory Nazianzen prepared.

Bibliography: MG 12/13; 17, 9–370. — PITRA, Analecta sacra 2, 349–483; 3, 1–588. — J. A. CRAMER, Catenae Graecorum Patrum in Novum Testamentum. Oxford, 1838-1844, 8 vols. — C. DIOBOUNIOTIS und A. HARNACK, Der Scholienkommentar des Origenes zur Apokalypse Johannis (TU 38, 3). Leipzig, 1911. — C. H. TURNER, The Text of the Newly Discovered Scholia of Origen on the Apocalypse: JThSt (1912) 386–397. — A. DE BOYSSON, Avons nous un commentaire d'Origène sur l'Apocalypse?: RBibl 10 (1913) 555 ff. — C. H. TURNER, Origen, Scholia in Apocalypsin: JThSt 25 (1924) 1–16. — H. STRATHMANN, Origenes und die Johannesoffenbarung: NKZ 34 (1923) 228–236. — E. SKARD, Zum Scholienkommentar des Origenes zur Apokalypse Johannis: SO, fasc. 15/16 (1936) 204–208. — M. RICHARD, Une scolie d'Origène indument attribuée à Denys d'Alexandrie: RHE (1937) 44–46.

2. *Homilies* (ὁμιλίαι, *tractatus*)

The homilies are sermons on select chapters or passages of the Bible which he delivered in liturgical meetings. According to Socrates (*Hist. eccl.* 5,22) he preached on every Wednesday and Friday, but Origen's biographer, Pamphilus, reports that he did so almost every day. Thus he left discourses on nearly all the books of Scripture. However, only twenty on Jeremias and one on 1 Sam. 28,3–25 (the witch of Endor) are preserved in Greek. Recently fragments in the original language also of the concluding section of the thirty-fifth homily on Luke and his twenty-five on Matthew have been found. Sixteen on Genesis, thirteen on Exodus, sixteen on Leviticus, twenty-eight on Numbers, twenty-six on Joshua, nine on Judges and nine on the Psalms have survived in a Latin translation of Rufinus while two on the Canticle of Canticles, nine on Isaias, fourteen on

Jeremias, fourteen on Ezechiel and especially thirty-nine on the Gospel of St. Luke are extant in a Latin rendering of St. Jerome. Fragments of the twenty on Job are preserved in the Latin of St. Hilary of Poitiers and one on 1 Sam. 1–2 in that of an unknown author. There are also portions of Jeremias, Samuel 1–2, Kings 1–2, 1 Corinthians and Hebrews. Many excerpts in Greek and Latin can be identified in the *Catenae* and will be edited in the process of examining and editing this material. However, the total loss is immense. Out of 574 homilies only 20 have come down in the original Greek and of 388 homilies we do not have even a Latin version today. Nevertheless, the homilies at our disposal are of great value because they show their author in a new light, eager to derive from an explanation of Scriptures spiritual food for the edification of the faithful and the care of souls. These works thus belong to the history of Christian spirituality and mysticism rather than to biblical science. His contribution in this field was very much neglected until W. Völker and A. Lieske pointed out its hidden treasures. The outline, disposition and external form of these talks are simple and without any trace of rhetorical elaboration. The conversational tone is predominant, and the sermons surviving betray the marks of the spoken word as it was taken down by stenographers.

Editions: Homilies on Jeremias: E. KLOSTERMANN, GCS 6 (1901) 1–232. — Homilies on Genesis, Exodus and Leviticus: W. A. BAEHRENS, GCS 29 (1920) in Rufinus' translation. — Homilies on Numbers, Josua and Judges: W. A. BAEHRENS, GCS 30 (1921) in Rufinus' translation. — Homilies on Samuel I, the Canticle of Canticles, Isaias, Jeremias and Ezechiel: W. A. BAEHRENS, GCS 33 (1925) in the translations of Rufinus and Jerome. — Homilies on Luke, Greek fragments and the translation of Jerome: M. RAUER, GCS 35 (1941). — E. KLOSTERMANN, Eustathius von Antiochien und Gregor von Nyssa über die Hexe von Endor (KT 83). Bonn, 1913. — E. KLOSTERMANN, Ausgewählte Predigten I: Origenes Homilie X über den Propheten Jeremias, VII über Lukas, XXI über Josua (KT 4). 2nd ed. Bonn, 1914.

Translations: English: R. B. TOLLINTON, Selections from the Commentaries and Homilies of Origen (SPCK). London, 1929. — *French:* L. DOUTRELEAU, Homélies sur la Genèse, introd. de H. DE LUBAC (SCH 7). Paris, 1944. — P. FORTIER, Origène, Homélies sur l'Exode, notes de H. DE LUBAC (SCH 16). Paris, 1947. — A. MÉHAT, Origène, Homélies sur les Nombres (SCH 29). Paris, 1951. — *German:* F. A. WINTER, Origenes und die Predigt der drei ersten Jahrhunderte. Leipzig, 1893.

Studies: A table of contents of the homilies preserved will be found in: Dictionary of Christian Biography 4, 104–118. — F. BARTH, Prediger und Zuhörer im Zeitalter

des Origenes: Aus Schrift und Geschichte. Festschrift für Orelli. Basel, 1898, 24–58. —
W. A. Baehrens, Überlieferung und Textgeschichte der lateinisch erhaltenen Origenes-
homilien zum Alten Testament (TU 3. Reihe, 12, 1). Leipzig, 1916. — W. A. Baeh-
rens, Die neunte fragmentarische Jesaiashomilie des Origenes, eine Fälschung:
ThLZ 49 (1924) 263–264. — G. Bardy, Un prédicateur populaire au IIIe siècle:
RAp 45 (1927) 513–526, 679–698. — O. Dobiache-Rojdestvensky, Le Codex
Q. v. I. 6–10 de la bibliothèque publique de Léningrad (two homilies of Origen):
Speculum (1930) 21–48. — M. Rauer, Form und Überlieferung der Lukas-Homilien
des Origenes (TU 47, 3). Leipzig, 1933. — A. Vogliano, Frammenti di due omelie di
Origene: BNJ 15 (1939) 130–136. — G. Morin, Les homélies latines sur Matthieu
attribuées à Origène: RB (1942) 3–11. — A. Meunier, Hieronymus' vertaalwijze in
Origenes' Jeremiashomelieën. Thèse. Louvain, 1943. — F. X. Murphy, Rufinus of
Aquileia. His Life and His Works. Washington, 1945, 111–112, 213–217. — M. Stenzel, Das erste Samuelbuch in den lateinisch erhaltenen Origeneshomilien zum Alten Testament: Zeitschrift für die alttestamentl. Wissenschaft 61 (1945–48) 30–43. —
R. M. Grant, More Fragments of Origen?: VC (1948) 243–247; idem, New Fragments of the Homilies of Origen: VC 2 (1948) 161–162. — P. Courcelle, Fragments
patristiques de Fleury-sur Loire: Mélanges Grat. Paris, 1949, II, 145–157 (Fragments
of homilies on Leviticus). — S. Läuchli, Eine alte Spur von Joh. VIII, 1–11: TZ
6 (1950) 151.

3. *Commentaries* (τόμοι, *volumina*)

If the homilies served the purpose of popular edification, the
commentaries were written in order to give a scientific exegesis.
They are a strange mixture of philological, textual, historical,
etymological notes and theological and philosophical observations. The author's main interest is not the literal but the
mystical sense, which he finds by applying the allegorical method.
Although he thus fell into many errors of interpretation, his
grasp of the inner meaning of the biblical books shows that he
possessed in abundance the gift of spiritual penetration, which
many of the later ecclesiastical writers lack. Unfortunately, of
these lengthy commentaries there is even less extant than of the
homilies. None of them has survived complete.

a) Of the *Commentary on St. Matthew*, which he composed in
twenty-five books at Caesarea after the year 244, there are only
eight preserved in Greek, namely, 10–17, which deal with
Matthew 13,36 to 22,33. An anonymous translation supplies
a much greater portion, namely, the section which forms the
commentary to Matthew 16,13 to 27,65 (*Commentariorum in
Matth. series*).

Editions: E. Klostermann, GCS 38 (1933) 1–299 Latin translation; 40 (1935) 1–703
Greek text; 41 (1941) Fragments and Indices.

Translation: English: J. PATRICK, ANF 4, 409–512.

Studies: E. KLOSTERMANN, Zur Matthaeuserklärung des Origenes und des Petrus von Laodicea: ZNW (1911) 287 f. — H. SMITH, Catenae Fragments of Origen's Commentary on Matthew: JThSt 17 (1916) 101 ff. — J. P. ARENDZEN, Origen, In Matt. 1, 14, 16 (Divorce): JThSt 20 (1919) 237 ff. — E. KLOSTERMANN und E. BENZ, Zur Überlieferung der Matthäuserklärung des Origenes (TU 47, 2). Leipzig, 1932. — E. KLOSTERMANN, ZNW (1932) 312 (in Mt. ser. 89). — R. DEVREESSE, Pro Theodoro (in Matth. 8, 6 sqq.): RBibl (1932) 261–263. — A. SOUTER, The Anonymous Latin Translation of Origen on S. Matthew XXII, 34 to the end and Old Latin Ms. 9 of the Gospels: JThSt (1934) 63–66. — V. G. TASKER, The Text of St. Matthew used by Origen in his Commentary on St. Matthew: JThSt (1937) 60–64. — J. REUSS, Origenes-Fragmente in Matthaeuskatenen: Bibl 20 (1939) 401–414. — E. KLOSTERMANN, Formen der exegetischen Arbeiten des Origenes: ThLZ 72 (1947) 203–208. — K. W. KIM, The Matthean Text of Origen in his Commentary on Matthew: JBL (1949) 125–139.

b) We have also in Greek eight books of his *Commentary on the Gospel of St. John,* which comprised at least thirty-two and which he dedicated to his friend Ambrose. The first four volumes were most probably written at Alexandria between 226 and 229, the fifth perhaps during the voyage in the East in 230–231, the sixth was interrupted by his exile in the subsequent year, and the rest was composed at Caesarea. The work is of great importance for a study of Origen the mystic, and his concept of the inner life.

Editions: A. E. BROOKE, The Commentary of Origen on St. John's Gospel. The text revised with a critical introduction. Cambridge, 1896, 2 vols. — E. PREUSCHEN, GCS 10 (1903) 1–574.

Translation: English: A. MENZIES, Origen's Commentary on the Gospel of John, ANF 9, 297–408.

Studies: P. KOETSCHAU, Beiträge zur Textkritik von Origenes' Johanneskommentar (TU 28, 2). Leipzig, 1905. — J. J. MAYDIEU, La procession du Logos d'après le Commentaire d'Origène sur l'Evangile de saint Jean: BLE (1934) 3–16, 49–70. — R. V. G. TASKER, The Text of the Fourth Gospel used by Origen in his Commentary on John: JThSt (1936) 146–155.

c) Origen composed also a *Commentary on the Epistle to the Romans* in fifteen books. Of the Greek original only fragments remain in a papyrus found in Toura near Cairo in 1941, in the *Philocalia,* in St. Basil, in the *Catenae* and in a Bible manuscript which E. v. d. Goltz discovered on Mount Athos. We have a very free Latin translation of this work by Rufinus, which counts only ten books and substitutes a Latin version of the Epistle to the Romans for the Greek text which Origen used. It seems that this commentary was composed before that on St. Matthew, most probably before the year 244.

Editions: MG 14. — O. BAUERNFEIND, Der Römerbrieftext des Origenes nach dem Codex 184 B 64 des Athosklosters Lawra, untersucht und herausgegeben (TU 44, 3). Leipzig, 1923.

Translation: A. H. WRATISLAV, Exegesis of Romans VIII, 18–25: Journal of Sacred Literature 3rd ser. 12 (1860/61) 410–420.

Studies: A. RAMSBOTHAM, The Commentary of Origen on the Epistle to the Romans: JThSt 13 (1912) 209–224, 357–368; 14 (1913) 10–22: Greek fragments from the catenae. — G. WILBRAND, Ambrosius und der Kommentar des Origenes zum Römerbriefe: BiZ 8 (1910) 26–32. — G. BARDY, Le texte de l'épître aux Romains dans le commentaire d'Origène-Rufin: RBibl (1920) 229–241. — O. BAUERNFEIND, *loc. cit.* — K. STAAB, Neue Fragmente aus dem Kommentar des Origenes zum Römerbrief: BiZ 18 (1928) 72–83: Fifteen hitherto unknown fragments in *Cod. Vindob. gr.* 166, *saec.* XIV. — C. VERFAILLIE, La doctrine de la justification dans Origène d'après son commentaire de l'épître aux Romains. Strasbourg, 1926. — F. X. MURPHY, Rufinus of Aquileia. Washington, 1945, 192–194. — O. CULLMANN, Die neuesten Papyrusfunde von Origenestexten und gnostischen Schriften: TZ 5 (1949) 153–157. — J. SCHERER, Une leçon méconnue de Cor. 12, 19 et son interprétation marcionite: The Journal of Juristic Papyrology 4 (1950) 229–233.

d) Of the numerous elucidations of the Old Testament which Origen compiled we have only a part of his *Commentary on the Canticle of Canticles*, books 1–4, in a Latin rendering of Rufinus from the year 410. Origen seems to have written the first five books at Athens about the year 240, while the other five were composed shortly afterwards at Caesarea (Euseb., *Hist.eccl.*6,32,2). St. Jerome, who translated two homilies on the Canticle of Canticles into Latin, regarded this commentary as the most important exegetical work of the great Alexandrian. In the preface to his translation he states: *Origenes cum in caeteris libris omnes vicerit, in Cantico canticorum ipse se vicit.* The allegorical interpretation of Origen sees in Solomon a figure of Christ. While in the two discourses surviving in the version of Jerome the Church is predominantly regarded as his bride, throughout the commentary, translated by Rufinus, it is above all the individual Christian soul that is regarded as the spouse of Christ.

Edition: W. A. BAEHRENS, GCS 33 (1925).

Translation: English: R. B. TOLLINTON, Selections from the Commentaries and Homilies of Origen. London, 1929 (excerpts).

Studies: W. RIEDEL, Die Auslegung des Hohen Liedes in der jüdischen Gemeinde und der griechischen Kirche. Leipzig, 1898, 52–66. — M. FAULHABER, Hohelied-, Proverbien- und Prediger-Katenen: Theol. Studien der Leo-Gesellschaft 4 (1902) 38f., 46 f.—L. M. MELIKSET-BEKOV, Commentaire d'Origène sur le Cantique des Cantiques de Salomon dans une version vieille-arménienne: Bull. Inst. caucasian hist. et arch. Tiflis, 1926, 4, 10–14. — L. WELSERHEIMB, Das Kirchenbild der griechischen Väterkommentare zum Hohen Liede: ZkTh 70 (1949) 393–449. — A. DE BROUWER, Note critique sur un passage du commentaire d'Origène sur le Cantique: RB (1949) 202–203.

4. Lost Commentaries

Origen also composed thirteen books on Genesis, forty-six on forty-one psalms, thirty on Isaias, five that Eusebius knew of (*Hist. eccl.* 6,24,2) on Lamentations, twenty-five on Ezechiel, at least the twenty-five on the minor prophets mentioned by Eusebius (*ibid.* 6,32,2), fifteen on Luke, five on Galatians, three on Ephesians, besides others on Philippians, Colossians, Thessalonians, Hebrews, Titus and Philemon. Of all these only small fragments have survived in *Catenae*, biblical manuscripts and quotations by later ecclesiastical authors. Out of 291 commentaries 275 have been lost in Greek and very little is preserved in Latin. Fragments of the Greek text of a commentary on the Books of Kings were found in Toura in 1941. A commentary on Job attributed to Origen and extant in a Latin translation in three books is not authentic.

Fragments: MG 11–14. — E. KLOSTERMANN, GCS 6 (1901) 233–279 Lamentations; 281–304 Samuel and Kings.

Studies: C. H. TURNER, Notes on the Text of Origen's Commentary on I Corinthians: JThSt 10 (1908/9) 270–276. — G. RIETZ, De Origenis prologis in Psalterium questiones selectae. Diss. Jena, 1914. — A. WAGNER, Die Erklärung des 118. Psalmes durch Origenes. Linz, 1916–1921. — A. HARNACK, Der kirchengeschichtliche Ertrag der exegetischen Arbeiten des Origenes (TU 42, 3–4). Leipzig, 1919. — R. DRAGUET, Un commentaire grec arien sur Job: RHE 20 (1924) 38–65. — P. GLAUE, Ein Bruchstück des Origenes über Genesis 1, 28 (Mitteilungen aus der Papyrussammlung der Gießener Universitätsbibliothek II). Giessen, 1928. — W. SCHUBART, Christliche Predigten aus Ägypten: Mitteilungen des Deutschen Instituts für ägyptische Altertumskunde. Cairo, 1930, 93–105 (Gen. 1, 28). — R. DEVREESSE, Anciens commentateurs grecs de l'Octateuque: Origène: RBibl (1935) 166–191. — R. CADIOU, Commentaires inédits des Psaumes. Étude sur les textes d'Origène contenus dans le ms. Vindobonensis 8. Paris, 1936. — H. U. VON BALTHASAR, Die Hiera des Evagrius (and the commentaries attributed to Origen): ZkTh (1939) 86–106, 181–206. — F. X. MURPHY, Rufinus of Aquileia. Washington, 1945, 186–191: Commentaries on the Heptateuch.

3. Apologetical Works

The most important apologetical treatise of Origen is his *Against Celsus* in eight books (Κατὰ Κέλσου, *Contra Celsum*). It is a refutation of the *True Discourse* (᾽Αληθὴς λόγος) which the pagan philosopher Celsus directed against the Christians about the year 178. Celsus' work has been lost but it could be almost entirely rewritten from the quotations of Origen, which amount to three quarters of its text. The aim of Celsus was to convert the Christians by shaming them out of their religion. He does not repeat the popular calumnies. He had studied his subject, had read the Bible and many Christian books. He knows the difference between the Gnostic sects and the main body of the Church. He is a resourceful opponent, who shows great skill and misses nothing that could be said against the faith. It is first attacked from the Jewish point of view in a dialogue in which a Jew sets forth his objections to Jesus Christ. Then Celsus comes forward on his own account with a wholesale attack on both the Jewish and the Christian beliefs. He mocks at the idea of a Messias and sees in Jesus an imposter and magician. As a Platonic philosopher he asserts the striking superiority of the worship and philosophy of the Greeks. He applies severe criticism to the Gospel, especially to all that concerns the resurrection of Christ, and declares that the apostles and their successors had invented this superstition. He does not reject everything Christianity teaches. He approves, for instance, of its ethics and the doctrine of the Logos. He is willing to let Christianity live on the condition that the Christians abandon their political and religious isolation and subordinate themselves to the common religion of Rome. His chief anxiety springs from the fact that they create a schism in the State weakening the Empire by division. Thus he closes with an exhortation to the Christians 'to help the king and to labour with him in the maintenance of justice, to fight for him, and if he requires it, to fight under him or lead any army along with him, to take office in the government of the country, if that is required for the maintenance of the laws and the support of religion' (8,73–75 ANF).

It seems that the *True Discourse* did not make much of an impression on those to whom it was addressed. Christian writers

contemporary with Celsus never allude to it. About 246 A.D.
Ambrose, Origen's friend, asked his teacher to answer it lest
some of the shrewd statements of Celsus might do harm. Origen
who till then had never heard either of the work nor of its author
was at first not at all convinced that this would be the right
way of refuting Celsus:

When false witnesses testified against our Lord and Saviour
Jesus Christ, He remained silent; and when unfounded
charges were brought against Him, he returned no answer, believing that His whole life and conduct among the Jews were a
better refutation than any answer to the false testimony, or
than any formal defense against the accusations. And I
know not, my pious Ambrose, why you wished me to write
a reply to the false charges brought by Celsus against the
Christians and to his accusations directed against the faith
of the Churches in his treatise; as if the facts themselves
did not furnish a manifest refutation and the doctrine a
better answer than any writing, seeing it both disposes of
false statements and does not leave to the accusations any
credibility or validity (*Contra Cels.*, Preface 1 ANF).

For I do not know in what rank to place him who has
need of arguments written in books in answer to charges of
Celsus against the Christians, in order to prevent him from
being shaken in his faith and to confirm him in it. But
nevertheless, since in the multitude of those who are considered believers some such persons might be found as would
have their faith shaken and overthrown by the writings
of Celsus, but who might be preserved by a reply to them
of such nature as to refute his statements and to exhibit
the truth, we have deemed it right to yield to your injunction
and to furnish an answer to the treatise which you sent us,
but which I do not think that any one, although only a
short way advanced in philosophy, will allow to be a 'True
Discourse,' as Celsus has entitled it (*ibid.* 4, ANF).

This book has been composed not for those who are
thorough believers, but for such as are either wholly
unacquainted with the Christian faith or for those who,
as the apostle terms them (Rom. 14,1) are 'weak in the
faith' (*ibid.* 6 ANF).

With these words Origen indicates for whom and for what reason he undertook this refutation when he was over sixty years of age (Euseb., *Hist. eccl.* 6,36,1). His method is to follow the arguments of Celsus from point to point so that here and there his answer to a criticism appears not too convincing and sometimes narrow-minded. However, the overall impression is of deep religious conviction and a personality that combines faith and knowledge to a degree to put his pagan opponent in the shadow, and that wins over the reader by its calm and dignified tone. Celsus, as a true Greek, proud of the achievements of Hellenic philosophy 'and with an appearance of fairness, does not reproach Christianity because of its origin among barbarians, but gives the latter credit for their ability in discovering such doctrines. To this, however, he adds the statement that the Greeks are more skilful than any others in judging, establishing and reducing to practice the discoveries of barbarous nations' (*Contra Cels.* 1,2 ANF). Origen answers him as follows:

The Gospel has a demonstration of its own, more divine than any established by Grecian dialectics. And this diviner method is called by the apostle the 'manifestation of the Spirit and of power': of 'the Spirit,' on account of the prophecies which are sufficient to produce faith in any one who reads them, especially in those things which relate to Christ; and of 'power,' because of the signs and wonders which have been performed as can be proved both on many other grounds and on this, that traces of them are still preserved among those who regulate their lives by the precepts of the Gospel (*ibid.*).

The divinity of Christ is evident not only from the wonders which He produced (2,48) and from the prophecies which He fulfilled (1,50) but also from the power of the Holy Spirit operating in the Christians:

And there are still preserved among Christians traces of that Holy Spirit which appeared in the form of a dove. They expel evil spirits and perform many cures and foresee certain events, according to the will of the Logos. And although Celsus or the Jew whom he has introduced may treat with mockery what I am going to say, I shall say it nevertheless—that many have been converted to Christianity as if against their will, some sort of spirit having suddenly transformed their minds from a hatred of the doctrine to a readiness to die in its defense (1,46 ANF).

The belief in Christ and the Christian doctrine presupposes grace:

The word of God (1 Cor. 2,4) declares that the preaching, although in itself true and most worthy of belief, is not sufficient to reach the human heart, unless a certain power be imparted to the speaker from God and a grace appear upon his words; and it is only by the divine agency that this takes place in those who speak effectually. The prophet says in the sixty-seventh Psalm that 'the Lord will give word with great power to them who preach.' If then it should be granted that the same doctrines are found among the Greeks as in our own Scriptures, yet they do not possess the same power of attracting and disposing the souls of men to follow them (6,2 ANF).

It is especially interesting to note Origen's answer to Celsus regarding the attitude towards the civil ruler. Since the structure of Roman government was intimately connected with the pagan religion, naturally Christians kept very reserved on everything of a political nature. Whereas Celsus stresses the law and the authority of the secular power, Origen emphasizes that obedience to its commands can be exacted only if they are not in contradiction to Divine Law. Whereas Celsus appears to be a fervent patriot, Origen impresses the reader as a cosmopolitan, to whom the history of nations and empires is the history of the guidance of mankind by God. In his reply to Celsus on these matters Origen shows the influence of Plato, whose principle it was that the goal of the State must not be increase in power but the spread of civilization and culture.

Thus Origen refuses to seek the favor of civil rulers:

Celsus remarks: 'What harm is there in gaining the favour of the rulers of the earth, whether of a nature different from ours, or human princes and kings? For these have gained their dignity through the instrumentality of gods' (8,63 ANF).

There is One whose favour we should seek and to whom we ought to pray that He would be gracious to us—the Most High God, whose favor is gained by piety and the

practice of every virtue. And if he would have us to seek
the favor of others after the Most High God, let him consider
that, as the motion of the shadow follows that of the body
which casts it, so in like manner it follows, that when we
have the favor of God, we have also the good will of all
angels and spirits who are friends of God (8,64 ANF).

Moreover, we are to despise ingratiating ourselves with
kings or any other men, not only if their favor is to be won
by murders, licentiousness or deeds of cruelty, but even if
it involves impiety toward God or any servile expressions
of flattery and obsequiousness, which things are unworthy
of brave and high-principled men who aim at joining with
their other virtues that highest of virtues, patience and
fortitude. But whilst we do nothing which is contrary to
the law and word of God, we are not so mad as to stir
up against us the wrath of kings and princes, which will
bring upon us sufferings and tortures or even death. For
we read: 'Let every soul be subject unto the higher powers.
For there is no power but of God: the powers that be, are
ordained of God. Whosoever therefore resisteth the power,
resisteth the ordinance of God' (Rom. 13,1,2) (8,65 ANF).

The treatise *Against Celsus* is an important source for the history
of religion. In it we see the struggle between paganism and
Christianity as in a mirror. The value of this greatest apology
of the primitive Church is heightened by the fact that here we
have highly cultivated men as the representatives of the two
worlds. The work earned the admiration of scholars in early
Christian times. Eusebius was so convinced of the force of
Origen's refutation that he thought the author had answered
the heresies of all centuries to come (*Adv. Hierocl.* 1). This may
be an exaggeration but Origen's contribution remains a monument to his erudition.

Edition: P. KOETSCHAU, GCS 2–3 (1899).

Translations: English: F. CROMBIE, ANL 10, 23; ANF 4, 395–669. Books VII and
VIII were translated by W. H. CAIRNS. — H. CHADWICK, Cambridge, 1953. —
German: P. KOETSCHAU, BKV² 52–53 (1926/27). — *Dutch:* H. U. MEYBOOM, Ori-
genes, Tegen Celsus (Oudchr. geschriften, dl. 34–37). Leiden, 1924.

Studies: P. KOETSCHAU, Die Textüberlieferung der Bücher des Origenes gegen
Celsus in den Handschriften dieses Werkes und der Philocalia. Prolegomena zu einer

kritischen Ausgabe (TU 6, 1). Leipzig, 1889. — F. WALLIS, On the MSS of Origenes C. Celsum: CR 3 (1888/9) 392–398. — J. A. ROBINSON, On the Text of Origen against Celsus: The Journal of Philology 18 (1890) 288–296. — P. WENDLAND, GGA (1899) 276–304. — P. KOETSCHAU, Kritische Bemerkungen zu meiner Ausgabe von Origenes' Exhortatio, Contra Celsum, De oratione. Entgegnung auf die von P. Wendland in den GGA 1899, Nr. 4 veröffentlichte Kritik. Leipzig, 1899. — P. WENDLAND, GGA (1899) 613–622. — E. PREUSCHEN, PhW (1899) 1185–1193, 1220–1224. — P. KOETSCHAU, Bibelzitate bei Origenes: Zeitschr. f. wiss. Theologie 43 (1900) 321–377. — F. A. WINTER, Über den Wert der direkten und indirekten Überlieferung von Origenes' Büchern Contra Celsum 1–2. Burghausen, 1903/4. — The discussion about the critical text will receive new light from the newly discovered fragments of Contra Celsum. Cf. O. GUÉRAUD, Note préliminaire sur les papyrus d'Origène découverts à Toura: RHR 131 (1946) 85–108. — O. CULLMANN, Die neuesten Papyrusfunde von Origenestexten und gnostischen Schriften: TZ 5 (1949) 153–157. L. ROUGIER, Celse ou le conflit de la civilisation antique et du Christianisme primitif. Paris, 1925. — A. MIURA STANGE, Celsus und Origenes. Das Gemeinsame ihrer Weltanschauung nach den acht Büchern des Origenes gegen Celsus. Giessen, 1926. — G. BARDY, Origène et la magie: RSR 18 (1928) 126–142. — TH. HOPFNER, Origenes, Contra Celsum VI 21–34, 38: Charisteria A. Rzach. Reichenberg, 1930, 86–98. — G. MASSART, La funzione penale dello stato nella concezione di Origine: Rivista Internationale di Filosofia del Diritto 11 (1931) 1–17; idem, Società e stato nel cristianesimo primitivo. La concezione di Origene. Padova, 1932. — P. DE LABRIOLLE, Celse et Origène: RH 159 (1932) 1–44. — F. J. DÖLGER, Origenes über die Beurteilung des Ehebruchs in der Stoischen Philosophie: AC 4 (1934) 284–287. — G. KRÜGER, Die Rechtsstellung der vorkonstantinischen Kirche. Giessen, 1935, 69–83. — F. J. DÖLGER, Θεοῦ φωνή: Die Gottes-Stimme bei Ignatius von Antiochien, Kelsos und Origenes: AC 5 (1936) 218–223. — G. MERCATI, Opere minore 4 (ST 79). Vatican City, 1937, 89–97. — F. CAVALLERA, La doctrine d'Origène sur les rapports du christianisme et de la société civile: BLE (1937) 30–39. — Q. CATAUDELLA, Trace della sofistica nella polemica celso-origeniana: Rendiconti dell' Istituto Lombardo di scienze e lettere 70 (1937) 185–201. — W. BARCLAY, Church and State in the Apologists: ExpT 49 (1937/38) 360–362. — R. BADER, Der 'Αληθὴς Λόγος des Kelsos. Stuttgart, 1940. — A. WIFSTRAND, Kelsos' stridskrift mot kristendomen: Svensk teol. Kvartalskrift 18 (1942) 1–18. — H. CHADWICK, Origen, Celsus and the Stoa: JThSt (1947) 34–49; idem, Origen, Celsus, and the Resurrection of the Body: HThR 41 (1948) 83–102. — F. J. DÖLGER, Asklepios als Gegensatz zu Christus bei Kelsos: AC 6 (1950) 250–257. — W. DEN BOER, Gynaeconitis: VC 4 (1950) 61–64.

4. Dogmatic Writings

1. First Principles (Περὶ ἀρχῶν, De principiis)

Origen's most important production is his First Principles, the first Christian system of theology and the first manual of dogma. As such it stands in majestic isolation in the history of the early Church. He wrote it at Alexandria between the years 220 and 230. All we have of the Greek text are several fragments in the

Philocalia and in two edicts of the Emperor Justinian I. However, it has survived entire in a free rendering of Rufinus, who evidently tampered with it by expurgating dubious passages here and there. A literal translation, which St. Jerome undertook, had the same fate as the original.

The work consists of four books, the content of which could be summarized under the headings: God, World, Freedom, Revelation. The title 'bases' or 'principles' reveals the scope of the whole. Origen intended to deal in this treatise with the fundamental doctrines of the Christian faith. The introduction, which precedes the first book, makes this quite clear. The source of all religious truth is the teaching of Christ and his apostles (τὸ κήρυγμα). Thus the preface and the whole work begins:

All who believe and are assured that grace and truth were obtained through Jesus Christ, and who know Christ to be the truth, agreeably to his own declaration, 'I am the truth' (John 14,6), derive the knowledge (γνῶσις) which incites men to a good and happy life from no other source than from the very words and teaching of Christ. And by words of Christ we do not mean those only which he spoke when he became man and tabernacled in the flesh, for before that time, Christ, the Word of God, was in Moses and the prophets. For without the Word of God, how could they have been able to prophesy of Christ? And were it not our purpose to confine the present treatise within the limits of all attainable brevity, it would not be difficult to show, in proof of this statement, out of the Holy Scriptures, how Moses or the prophets both spoke and performed all they did through being filled with the Spirit of Christ... Moreover, after his ascension into heaven he spoke in His apostles, as is shown by Paul in these words: 'Or do you seek a proof of Christ who speaks in me' (2 Cor. 13,3).

Since many, however, of those who profess to believe in Christ differ from each other, not only in small and trifling matters, but also on subjects of the highest importance,... it seems on that account necessary first of all to fix a definite limit and to lay down an unmistakable rule regarding each one of these, and then to pass to the investigation of other points... as the teaching of the Church, transmitted in

orderly succession from the apostles, and remaining in the
Churches to the present day, is still preserved, that alone is
to be accepted as truth which differs in no respect from
ecclesiastical and apostolical tradition (Preface 1–2 ANF).

Here Origen clearly indicates that Scripture and tradition are
the sources of Christian doctrine and he points to the rule of
faith which contains the basic teaching of the apostles. However,
they did not give any reasons for these truths nor did they
present any account of their interrelations. In addition, there
remain a number of questions unanswered regarding the origin
of the human soul, of the angels, of Satan, etc. There lies the
task of sacred theology:

> Now it ought to be known that the holy apostles, in
> preaching the faith of Christ, delivered themselves with the
> utmost clearness on certain points which they believed to
> be necessary to everyone, even to those who seemed to be
> somewhat dull in the investigation of divine knowledge;
> leaving, however, the grounds of their statements to be
> examined into by those who should deserve the excellent
> gifts of the Spirit, and who especially by means of the Holy
> Spirit Himself, should obtain the gift of language, of wisdom
> and of knowledge: while on other subjects they merely
> stated the fact that things were so, keeping silence as to the
> manner or origin of their existence; clearly in order that
> the more zealous of their successors, who should be lovers
> of wisdom, might have a subject of exercise on which to
> display the fruit of their talents,—those persons I mean who
> should prepare themselves to be fit and worthy receivers
> of wisdom (Preface 3 ANF).

With these words Origen points to the two elements of all
theology, tradition and progress, positive and speculative theology. Christian doctrine, far from being sterile and stagnant,
shows a development and follows the natural laws of growth
and life:

> Every one, therefore, must make use of elements and
> foundations of this sort, according to the precept, 'Enlighten
> yourselves with the light of knowledge' (Os. 10,12), if he
> would desire to form a connected series and body of truths
> agreeable to the reason of all these things, that by clear

and necessary statements he may ascertain the truth regarding each individual topic, and form, as we have said, one body of doctrine, by means of illustrations and arguments,— either those which he has discovered in Holy Scripture, or which he has deduced by closely tracing out the consequences and following a correct method (Preface 10 ANF).

After this statement of the task of theology in general and of his own work in particular, Origen presents in the four books a theology, a cosmology, an anthropology and a teleology.

1. The first book deals with the supernatural world, with the oneness and spirituality of God, with the hierarchy of the three divine persons and their characteristic relations towards created life, the Father acting upon all beings, the Word upon reasonable beings or souls, the Holy Spirit upon beings who are both reasonable and sanctified. There follow discussions of the origin, essence and fall of the angels.

2. The second book treats the material world, the creation of man as a result of the defection of the angels, man as a fallen spirit enclosed in a material body, the transgression of Adam and redemption by the incarnate Logos, the doctrine of the resurrection, the last judgment and afterlife.

3. The union of body and soul gives the latter the opportunity for struggle and victory. In this contest men are helped by angels and hindered by demons, but they retain their free will. Thus the third book, examining the extension of free will and responsibility, gives an outline of moral theology.

4. The fourth book presents a recapitulation of the fundamental doctrines with some additions, and discusses Holy Scripture as the source of faith, its inspiration and its threefold meaning:

The way, then, as it appears to us, in which we ought to deal with the Scriptures and exact from them their meaning is the following, which has been ascertained from the Scriptures themselves. By Solomon in the Proverbs we find some such rule as this enjoined respecting the divine doctrines of Scripture: 'And do thou portray them in a threefold manner, in counsel and knowledge, to answer words of the truth to them who propose them to thee' (Proverbs 22, 20,21) The individual ought then to portray the ideas of Holy Scripture in a threefold manner upon his own soul in order that the simple man may be edified by the *flesh* as it were of the Scripture, for so we name the obvious sense, while he who has ascended a certain way [may be edified] by the *soul*, as it were. The perfect man again [may receive edification] from the spiritual law, which has a shadow of good things to come. For as a man consists of body, soul and spirit, so in the same way does Scripture, which has been arranged to be given by God for the salvation of men (4,1,11 ANF).

This earliest synthesis of ecclesiastical doctrine has had a far-reaching effect and influence on the development of Christian thought. We cannot be surprised that a pioneer attempt had its shortcomings in form as well as in content. It suffers from repetitions and a lack of coordination. The author is nowhere in a hurry to come to a head. As he goes along he touches upon all the questions that he regards as important. Thus the composition of the book is much too lax for modern tastes. However, it would be a mistake to compare his work with later scientific treatments of theology or modern manuals of dogma. The main defect, as we shall see later, is the predominant influence of Platonic philosophy. In justice to its author we must realize the number of difficulties he faced in this first effort to coordinate the various elements in the deposit of faith and mold them into a complete system. Thus it can be easily understood that he relied for the solution of many questions on Greek philosophy. The fact that he based his speculations on passages from Scripture allegorically interpreted indicates that even in these theories he did not want to depart from biblical truth or the teaching of the Church. Despite its defects the *De principiis* was epoch-making in the history of Christianity.

Edition: P. KOETSCHAU, GCS 22 (1913).

Translations: English: F. CROMBIE, ANL 10; ANF 4, 237–382. — G. W. BUTTER-WORTH, Origen on First Principles, being Koetschau's text of the De principiis, translated into English with notes (SPCK). London, 1936. — *Dutch:* H. U. MEYBOOM, Oudchr. geschriften, dl. 31. Leiden, 1921. — *German:* C. F. SCHNITZER, Origenes über die Grundlehren der Glaubenswissenschaft. Wiederherstellungsversuch in deutscher Übersetzung. Stuttgart, 1835. — *Modern Greek:* A. HIPPOLYTOS, Νέα Σιών. 1923, 306 ff. — *Russian:* N. PETROVA, Origenes, De principiis. Riga, 1936.

Studies: G. BARDY, Les citations bibliques d'Origène dans le De principiis: RBibl 16

(1919) 106–136. — K. Mueller, Zu den Auszügen des Hieronymus (ad Avitum) aus
des Origenes Περὶ ἀρχῶν: SAB (1919) 616–631; idem, Über die ang. Auszüge des
Gregor von Nyssa aus Περὶ ἀρχῶν: SAB (1919) 640–681. — G. Bardy, Recherches
sur l'histoire du texte et des versions latines du 'De principiis' d'Origène. Paris, 1933.
— M. Richard, RHE (1937) 794–796. — B. Steidle, Neue Untersuchungen zu
Origenes' Περὶ ἀρχῶν: ZNW (1941) 239–243. — F. X. Murphy, Rufinus of
Aquileia. Washington, 1945, 82–110. — H. Jonas, Origenes' Peri archon – ein
System patristischer Gnosis: TZ 4 (1948) 101–119. — J. F. Bonnefoy, Origène, théo-
ricien de la methode théologique: Mélanges F. Cavallera, Toulouse, 1948, 87–145:
analyse du De principiis.

2. Discussion with Heraclides

Among a number of papyri found at Toura near Cairo in 1941
is a codex of about the end of the sixth century containing the
text of a discussion between Origen and Heraclides. The exact
title reads: Ὠριγένους διάλεκτοι πρὸς Ἡρακλείδαν καὶ τοὺς σὺν αὐτῷ
ἐπισκόπους. Even without this title, the vocabulary, style and
doctrine of the document testify to Origen's authorship. It is
not a literary dialogue but the complete record of an actual
discussion, something unique, as A.D. Nock remarks, not only
among Origen's writings but in early Christian literature and in
ancient literature as a whole outside Augustine. The opinions of
Heraclides regarding the Trinitarian question had worried his
brother bishops. Thus Origen was called in to straighten out the
situation. The meeting, which was entirely informal and not
judicial, took place in a church in Arabia in the presence of the
bishops and the people about the year 245. Origen seems to be
in full possession of his authority as a teacher. It was not the first
time he had held such a conference. We know of interviews of
his with Beryllus and the Valentinian Candidus. Stenographers
took a record of the proceedings. The style has all the vivacious
character of an actual conversation, which speaks for the high
fidelity of the recording.

The introduction mentions that the bishops who were present
made inquiries regarding the faith of bishop Heraclides until he
himself confessed before all that which he believed. After everyone had made his remarks and raised his questions, Heraclides
began to speak. Here the recording sets in. The first part of it
has three subdivisions: Origen interrogates Heraclides; he then
develops his own idea regarding the relations between the Father
and the Son; finally he points with great delicacy to the attitude

one should take in such difficult doctrinal questions. The cross-examination of Heraclides indicates that he was suspected of modalism. The second part of the discussion consists of questions asked by others who were present and of Origen's answers.

It appears that Heraclides did not like Origen's formula 'two gods' (δύο θεοί) as the only clear expression of the distinction between the Father and the Son. There was too much danger of polytheism involved. Origen remarks in the discussion: 'Since our brethren are scandalised, that there are two gods, this subject deserves to be treated with care.' He refers to Scripture in order to show in what sense two can be one. Adam and Eve were two, but only one flesh (Gen. 2,24). He mentions St. Paul who, speaking about the union between the just man and God, states: 'He who is joined to the Lord, is one spirit with Him' (1 Cor. 6,17). Finally he introduces Christ himself as a witness because He said: 'I and My Father are one.' In the first example, the unity consisted of 'flesh'; in the second of 'spirit'; but in the third of 'God.' Thus Origen states: 'Our Lord and Saviour is in His relation to the Father and God of the universe not one flesh, nor one spirit, but what is much higher than flesh and spirit, one God.' He declares that such an interpretation of Christ's word enables the theologian to defend the duality of God against monarchism and the unity against the impious doctrine of the Jews, who deny the divinity of Christ. It is important to note that Origen regards here the divinity as the element of unity between Christ and the Father. In his *Contra Celsum* (8,12) he adduces the same text of John 10,30, as proof for the unity existing between Christ and His Father, but speaks only of 'a unity of thought and identity of will.' The interrogation of Heraclides ends with the following agreement:

Origen said: Is not the Father God?

Heraclides answered: Yes.

Origen said: Is not the Son another (ἕτερος) than the Father?

Heraclides answered: How could he be simultaneously Son and Father?

Origen said: Is not the Son who is another than the Father, also God Himself?

Heraclides answered: He is also God Himself.

Origen said: Do not therefore the two Gods become one?

Heraclides said: Yes.

Origen said: We confess therefore two Gods?

Heraclides answered: Yes but the power is one (δύναμις μία ἐστίν).

In other words the formula δύο θεοί and δύναμις μία is for both sides acceptable. It is the same as the formula of later theology: Two persons but one nature.

Among the questions raised by others in the second part of the discussion is that of Dionysius, whether the soul and the blood of man are identical. Origen distinguishes in his answer between the physical blood and a blood of the interior man (164,9). The latter is identical with the soul. In the death of the just, this blood-soul separates from the body and enters the company of Christ even before the resurrection.

The end of the discussion deals with the immortality of the soul. Bishop Philippus is the one who asks this question. Origen replies that the soul is on the one hand immortal, on the other mortal, depending entirely on the three different kinds of death. The first is the death to sin (Rom. 6,2). The one who is dead to sin, lives to God. The second is the death to God (Ezech. 18,4). The one who is dead to God, lives to sin. The third, that which is commonly understood by the word, is natural death. To this last the soul is not subject; though those in sin desire it, they cannot find it (Apoc. 9,6). But the soul is subject to the first and the second kind of death, and may thus be called mortal with respect to either. However, this type of death man can escape.

Edition: J. SCHERER, Entretien d'Origène avec Héraclide et les évêques ses collègues sur le père, le fils, et l'âme (Publications de la Société Fouad I de Papyrologie, Textes et documents IX). Cairo. 1949.

Studies: O. GUÉRAUD, Papyrus découverts à Toura en 1941: Comptes rendus de l'Académie des Inscriptions et Belles-Lettres (1946) 367–369; *idem*, Note préliminaire sur les papyrus d'Origène découverts à Toura: RHR 131 (1946) 85–108. — E. KLOSTERMANN, ThLZ 73 (1948) 47. — O. CULLMANN, Die neuesten Papyrusfunde von Origenestexten und gnostischen Schriften: TZ 5 (1949) 153–157. — L. FRUECHTEL, Das neuentdeckte Streitgespräch des Origenes mit Herakleidas und Genossen: ThLZ 75 (1950) 504–506. — H. CHADWICK, I Thess. 3, 3 σαίνεσαθὶ: JThSt N.S. 1 (1950) 156–158. — J. CREHAN, The Dialectos of Origen and John 20, 17: TS 11 (1950) 368–373. — B. CAPELLE, L'Entretien d'Origène avec Héraclide: Journal of Ecclesiastical History 2 (1951) 143–157. — A. D. NOCK, American Journal of Archaeology 55 (1951) 283–284. — H. C. PUECH, Les nouveaux écrits d'Origène et de Didyme découverts à Toura: RHPR 31 (1951) 293–329.

3. On the Resurrection (Περὶ ἀναστάσεως, De resurrectione)

In his work *First Principles* Origen remarks (2,10,1): 'We ought first to consider the nature of the resurrection, that we may know what that body is which shall come either to punishment or to rest or to happiness; which question in other treatises which we have composed regarding the resurrection we have discussed at greater length, and have shown what our opinions are regarding it' (ANF). Eusebius mentions two volumes *On the Resurrection* (*Hist. eccl.* 6,24,2). The list of St. Jerome names *De resurrectione libros II* but adds *et alios de resurrectione dialogos II*. It seems that later these were both combined into one. That would explain why Jerome (*Contra Joh. Hier.* 25) speaks of a fourth book of Origen *On the Resurrection*. The essay of which Origen speaks in *First Principles* must have been written at Alexandria before 230, if not earlier. Only fragments of all these works survive in Pamphilus (*Apol. pro Orig.* 7), Methodius of Philippi (*De resurr.*) and Jerome (*Contra Joh. Hier.* 25–26). From Methodius we learn that Origen rejected the idea of a material identity of the risen, with the human, body and its parts.

Fragments: MG 11, 91–100. — For Origen's doctrine of the resurrection, see W. L. KNOX, H. CHADWICK, below p. 91.

4. Miscellaneous (Στρωματεῖς, Carpets)

Another work which has been lost except for small fragments is his *Stromateis* or *Miscellanies* 'which he composed in ten books in the same city (of Alexandria) before his removal, as is shown by the annotations in his own hand in front of the tomes' (Euseb., *Hist. eccl.* 6,24,3). The title indicates, as in the case of Clement of Alexandria, a variety of subjects discussed in no particular order. This squares with St. Jerome's remark (*Epist.* 70,4) that in this study Origen compared Christian doctrine with the teaching of ancient philosophers like Plato, Aristotle, Numenius and Cornutus.

Fragments: MG 11, 99–108. — I. A. CRAMER, Catena in Acta ss. apostolorum. Oxford, 1838, 10. — E. v. D. GOLTZ, Eine textkritische Arbeit des 10. bzw. 6. Jahrhunderts. Leipzig, 1899, 96–98.

5. *Practical Writings*

1. *On Prayer* (Περὶ εὐχῆς, *De oratione*)

A gem among the writings of Origen is his work *On Prayer*, which he composed at the suggestion of his friend Ambrose and his wife or sister Tatiana in the years 233–34. The text is extant in a codex of the fourteenth century at Cambridge (*Codex Cantabrig. Colleg. S. Trinitatis* B.8. 10 *saec.* XIV), while a fifteenth-century manuscript at Paris contains a fragment.

The treatise consists of two parts. The first (ch. 3–17) deals with prayer in general and the second (ch. 18–30) deals with the 'Our Father' in particular. An appendix (ch. 31–33), which makes additions to the first section, deals with the attitude of body and soul, gestures, the place and the direction of prayer, and finally the different kinds. At the end Origen begs Ambrose and Tatiana to be content with the present writing for the time being until he could offer something better, more beautiful and more precise. Apparently Origen was never able to fulfil this promise.

The treatise reveals more clearly than any of his other writings the depth and warmth of Origen's religious life. Certain fundamental views, which he stresses in this work, are very valuable for an analysis of his theological system.

It is the oldest scientific discussion of Christian prayer in existence.

The introduction opens with the statement that what is impossible for human nature becomes possible by the grace of God and the assistance of Christ and the Holy Ghost. Such is the case with prayer. After discussing the name and the meaning of the biblical term for it, *euche* (εὐχή) and *proseuche* (προσευχῆ) (ch. 3–4), the author gives in ch. 5 an answer to Ambrose's question about the use and the necessity of petition. Its opponents claim that God knows our needs without our asking. Moreover, it is senseless, since God has predestined everything. To this objection Origen answers by pointing to the free will which God has given to every human being and which He coordinated with His eternal plan. Passages from Scripture prove that the soul lifts itself up and is given a vision of divine beauty and majesty. Repeated conversation with God has a sanctifying effect on one's

entire existence. The utility and advantage of prayer is, therefore, that it enables us to enter into a union (ἀνακραθῆναι) with
the spirit of the Lord, which fills heaven and earth. Its real
purpose is not to influence God but to share in His life, to com-
municate with heaven. The best example is given by Christ, our
High Priest. He offers up our homage together with that of the
angels and the souls of the deceased, especially the guardian
angels, who carry our invocations to God. Prayer fortifies the
soul against temptations and drives evil spirits away. For this
reason we should engage in it at certain times during the day.
In fact, our entire life should be a prayer. The author admonishes
those who long for a spiritual being in Christ not to ask for small
and worldly things in their intercourse with God but for great
and heavenly values. Commenting on 1 Tim. 2,1, he gives Scriptural examples for the four kinds of prayer, petition (δέησις),
adoration (προσευχῆ), supplication (ἔντευξις), and thanksgiving
(εὐχαριστία). Treating of adoration he remarks that it should be
directed to God the Father only, but to none of the created
beings, not even to Christ. Christ Himself taught us to adore the
Father. We should pray in the name of Jesus. We should adore
the Father through the Son in the Holy Ghost but only God
the Father is entitled to accept adoration. Origen gives as reason
for this peculiar opinion that one should not pray to someone
who prays himself, if one wants to pray correctly. He who refused
to be called 'good' because only God is to be thus called, would
certainly have refused to be adored. And if Christ terms Christians his brothers, He makes it clear that He wishes them to adore
the Father, not Him, the Brother: 'Let us pray therefore to God
through Him and let us speak all in the same way without any
division in the form of prayer. Or are we not divided, if some
pray to the Father, the others to the Son? Those simple-minded
who thoughtlessly and inconsiderately pray to the Son with the
Father or without the Father, commit a sin of ignorance' (16,1).
Origen remained alone in this theory, which most probably
stems from a subordinationist concept of the Logos and an
exaggerated monotheism.

The second part gives a commentary on the 'Our Father,'
the oldest which we possess. After an introduction, which discusses the difference in the texts of Matthew and Luke and the

proper way of speaking to God, he gives a beautiful interpretation of the opening address 'Our Father, who art in heaven.'
He points out that the Old Testament does not know the name
'Father' for God in the Christian sense of a steady and changeless
adoption. Only those who have received this spirit of adoption
and prove that they are children and images of God by their
actions can recite the prayer rightly. Our entire life should say:
'Our Father who art in heaven,' because our conduct should be
heavenly, not worldly.

The advice which he gives in the first part of his treatise, not
to ask for things of this earth but for supernatural treasures,
explains his interpretation of the fourth petition: 'Since some
are of the opinion that this must be understood as if we should
ask for the bread for our body, it will be worth it to refute their
wrong idea and find out the truth about *the daily bread*. One ought
to answer such people how it is possible that He, who demands
that one ought to pray for heavenly and great things, forgot
His own teaching, according to their opinion, and ordered them
to ask the Father for a worldly and small cause' (27,1). He derives
the word ἐπιούσιος (Matthew 6,11; Luke 11,3) from οὐσία,
substance, and regards the ἄρτος ἐπιούσιος as a heavenly food
which nourishes the substance of the soul, making it healthy and
strong. The food is the Logos, who calls himself 'the bread of life.'

In speaking about attitudes during prayer, Origen states that
all worship should be directed towards the East, in order to
indicate that the soul is looking towards the dawn of the true
light, the sun of justice and of salvation, Christ (32).

Throughout the treatise Origen stresses the predisposition of
the soul. The effects of prayer depend on interior preparation.
First, there cannot be any true worship unless the war against
sin is waged in order to cleanse the heart. Secondly, this fight
against everything that defiles is intimately connected with a
continuous battling to free the spirit of disordered affections,
with a struggle against all passions (πάθη). Commenting on
Matthew 5,22 Origen makes it clear that only those who are
entirely reconciled with their neighbours are able to converse
with God. Thirdly, we must turn away from all disturbing
impressions and thoughts, whether they have their cause in the
surrounding world or in ourselves. Only after such detachment

is it possible to approach the Almighty. The better the soul is thus prepared the sooner its petitions will be answered by God and the more will it benefit from the colloquy with Him. However, even after such steps are taken, prayer remains a gift of the Holy Spirit, who prays in us and leads us in prayer.

The ideas of this treatise had a far-reaching effect in the history of spirituality. Origen's writings were read by the early monks of Egypt and the oldest monastic rules show his influence especially in their treatment of prayer and compunction.

Edition: P. KOETSCHAU, GCS 3 (1899) 297-403.

Translations: English: J. J. O'MEARA, ACW 19 (1953). — *French:* G. BARDY, Origène, De la prière. Exhortation au martyre. Paris, 1931. — *German:* P. KOETSCHAU, BKV² 48 (1926) 7-148. — *Dutch:* H. U. MEYBOOM, Origenes, Over het gebed (Oudchr. geschriften, dl. 38). Leiden, 1926.

Studies: F. H. CHASE, The Lord's Prayer in the Early Church (TSt 1, 3). Cambridge, 1891. — P. KOETSCHAU, GCS 2 (1899) LXXV-XC. — E. V. D. GOLTZ, Das Gebet in der ältesten Christenheit. Leipzig, 1901, 266-278. — D. GENET, L'enseignement d'Origène sur la prière. Thèse. Cahors, 1903. — O. DIBELIUS, Das Vaterunser. Umrisse zu einer Geschichte des Gebetes in der alten und mittleren Kirche. Giessen, 1903, 33-45. — L. CIGANOTTO, Della preghiera. Saggio di ascetica Origeniana ricavato dal libro: De oratione': Bess II 9 (1905) 2, 193-204, 299-307; II 10 (1906) 1, 137-150; III 1 (1906) 2, 52-70; III 2 (1907) 1, 46-62. — H. KOCH, Kennt Origenes Gebetsstufen?: ThQ 87 (1905) 592-596. —J. LEBRETON, Les origines du dogme de la Trinité. Paris, 1910, 22-24. — G. WALTHER, Untersuchungen zur Geschichte der griechischen Vaterunserexegese (TU 40, 3). Leipzig, 1914, 4-22. — H. POPE, Origen's Treatise on Prayer: AER 60 (1919) 533-549. — A. DALE, Origen on 'Our Daily, Bread': ExpT 16 (1918) 13-24. — A. d'ALÈS, À propos d'Origène, De oratione cap. XXVIII: RSR 13 (1923) 556-558. — F. J. DÖLGER, Sol Salutis (LF 4/5). Münster i.W., 1925, 165-170. — J. JUNGMANN, Die Stellung Christi im liturgischen Gebet (LF 7/8). Münster i.W., 1925, 137-141. — B. F. M. XIBERTA, La doctrina de Origenes sobre el sacramento de la Penitencia: Reseña Eclesiástica 18 (1926) 237-246, 309-318: De oratione 28, 10. — W. VÖLKER, Das Vollkommenheitsideal des Origenes (BHTh 7). Tübingen, 1931, 197-215. — J. E. L. OULTON, A Variant Reading in 1 Cor. 7, 5 (De oratione 2, 2): Hermathema 72 (1948) 20. — K. W. KIM, Origen's Text of John in his On Prayer, Commentary on Matthew, and Against Celsus: JThSt N.S. 1 (1950) 74-84.

2. *Exhortation to Martyrdom* (Εἰς μαρτύριον προτρεπτικός, *Exhortatio ad martyrium*)

This is the title which manuscripts and editions give to Origen's work *On Martyrdom* (Περὶ μαρτυρίου), as Pamphilus (*Apol. pro Orig.* 8) and Eusebius (*Hist. eccl.* 6,28) and St. Jerome (*De*

6

vir. ill. 56) call it for short. He composed it at the beginning of
the persecution of Maximinus Thrax in 235 at Caesarea in
Palestine. In fact, the treatise is addressed to Ambrose and Protectus, a deacon and a priest respectively, of the Christian community of that city. It deals with a topic dear all his life to
the heart of its author. Eusebius reports about his early youth:

> When the flame of persecution was kindled to a fierce
> blaze and countless numbers were being wreathed with the
> crown of martyrdom, Origen's soul was possessed with such
> a passion for martyrdom, while he was still quite a boy,
> that he was all eagerness to come to close quarters with
> danger and to leap forward and rush into conflict. In fact,
> it were but a very little step and the end of his life was at
> hand, had not the divine and heavenly Providence, acting
> for the general good through his mother, stood in the way
> of his zeal. She, at all events, at first had recourse to verbal
> entreaties, bidding him spare a mother's feeling; then, when
> he learnt that his father had been captured and was kept
> in prison and his whole being was set on the desire for
> martyrdom, perceiving that his purpose was more resolute
> than ever, she hid all his clothes, and so laid upon him the
> necessity of remaining at home. And since nothing else
> remained for him to do, and a zeal, intense beyond his years,
> suffered him not to be quiet, he sent to his father a letter on
> martyrdom most strongly urging him on, in which he
> advised him in these very words, saying: 'Take care not to
> change thy mind on our account' (*Hist. eccl.* 6,2,2–6 LCL).

That was Origen's first 'exhortation to martyrdom.' The book
which he wrote on this subject in 235 shows that he had lost
nothing of his enthusiasm. However, in chapters 45 and 46, he
mentions, not without purpose, that this desire for martyrdom
was not shared by all. There were some who regarded it as a
matter of indifference if a Christian sacrificed to the demons or
directed his invocation to God under another name than the
correct one. There were others who thought it no crime to agree
to the sacrifice which the pagan authorities demanded, since it
would be enough 'to believe in your heart.' It was for such circles
that Origen wrote his treatise.

The introduction of the work reminds one of a homily. The

author quotes Isaias 28,9–11 and applies these biblical words to the two addressees, Ambrose and Protectus. Their faith has been tried and proved to be loyal. They are admonished to remain steadfast in tribulations, because after a short time of suffering their reward will be eternal (ch. 1–2). Martyrdom is a duty of every true Christian because all who love God wish to be united with Him (ch. 3–4). Only those can enter eternal happiness who courageously confess the faith (ch. 5).

The second part warns against apostasy and idolatry. To deny the true God and to venerate false gods is the greatest sin (ch. 6), because it is senseless to adore creatures instead of the creator (ch. 7). God intends to save souls from idolatry (ch. 8–9). Those who commit this crime enter into a union with the idols and will be punished severely after death (ch. 10).

The third part contains the real exhortation to martyrdom (ch. 11). Only those will be saved who take the cross upon themselves with Christ (ch. 12–13). The reward will be greater in proportion to the earthly possessions left behind (ch. 14–16). Since we renounced the pagan deities when we were catechumens, we are not permitted to break our promise (ch. 17). The conduct of the martyrs will be judged by the whole world (ch. 18). For this reason we must take every kind of martyrdom upon ourselves in order not to be numbered with the fallen angels (ch. 19–21).

The fourth part gives Scriptural examples of perseverance and endurance: Eleazar (ch. 22) and the seven sons with their heroic mother of which the second Book of the Maccabeans reports (ch. 23–27).

The fifth part deals with the necessity, the essence and the kinds of martyrdom. The Christians are obliged to suffer such a death in order to repay God for all the benefits He bestowed upon them (ch. 28–29). Sins committed after the reception of the baptism of water can only be forgiven by the baptism of blood (ch. 30). The souls of those who withstand all temptations of the evil one (ch. 32) and give their lives for God as a pure oblation, not only enter eternal bliss (ch. 31) but can procure forgiveness for all who pray to them (ch. 30). As God extended His help to the three youths in the fiery furnace and to Daniel in the lions' den, so His support will not be lacking to the martyrs (ch. 33).

But not only God the Father, Christ, too, demands this sacrifice. If we deny Him, He will deny us in heaven (ch. 34–35). On the other hand, He will lead the confessors of the faith to paradise (ch. 36) because only those who hate the world shall be heirs of the kingdom of heaven (ch. 37, 39). They will bestow blessing on their children, whom they have left behind here on earth (ch. 38). On the other hand, whosoever denies the Son, denies God the Father also (ch. 40); but if we follow the example of Christ and offer up our life, His consolation will be with us (ch. 41–42). For this reason the Christians are urged to be ready for martyrdom (ch. 43–44).

Chapters 45 and 46 deal with a side issue, the veneration of the demons and the question with what name to invoke God. The last part of the essay summarizes the exhortations and admonitions for courageous perseverance under duress and danger, emphasizing the duty of every Christian to stand the test in times of persecution (ch. 47–49). There is one consolation: God will take vengeance for their blood, but they by their sufferings will elevate themselves and redeem others (ch. 50). In conclusion the author hopes that his work will be of use to his two friends or, since they are ready to acquire the crown, that it may prove superfluous.

The treatise *On Martyrdom* is the best commentary on Origen's conduct as a youth and as an old man who died in consequence of tortures suffered for the name of Christ. It reveals his courage, his loyalty to the faith and his undying love for his Saviour. The principles which he laid down in this writing governed his own life. Beyond this the work has great importance as an historical source for the persecution of Maximinus Thrax.

The text is preserved in three manuscripts, the *Codex Basiliensis* No. 31 (A III 9) *saec.* XVI, the *Codex Parisinus Suppl. gr.* No. 616a. 1339 and *Codex Venetus Marcianus* No. 45 *saec.* XIV.

Edition: P. Koetschau, GCS 2 (1899) 1–47.

Translations: English: J. J. O'Meara, ACW 19 (1953). — *French:* G. Bardy, Origène, De la prière. Exhortation au martyre. Paris, 1931. — *German:* P. Koetschau, BKV² 48 (1926). — *Dutch:* H. U. Meyboom, Origenes, Opwekking tot het martelaarschap (Oudchr. geschriften, dl. 38). Leiden, 1926.

Studies: P. Koetschau, GCS 2, IX–XXII. — M. Metcalfe, Origen's Exhortation to Martyrdom and 4 Maccabees: JThSt 22 (1921) 268 f. — V. G. Tasker, The Quotations from the Synoptic Gospels in Origen's Exhortation to Martyrdom: JThSt 36 (1935) 60–65. — E. E. MALONE, The Monk and the Martyr (SCA 12). Washington, 1950, 14–19.

3. On Easter (Περὶ πάσχα)

The same codex, found at Toura in 1941, that contains the *Discussion with Heraclides*, also preserves fragments of a treatise of Origen *On Easter* of which very little was hitherto known. It is to be hoped that an edition of it will be soon available.

4. Letters

At the end of his list, Jerome cites four different collections of Origen's correspondence then extant in Caesarea. One of them counted nine volumes and must be that which Eusebius (*Hist. eccl.* 6,36,3) edited and which contained more than one hundred epistles. Of all this only two letters have survived complete.

a) The *Philocalia* contains in chapter thirteen a communication which Origen addressed to his former pupil Gregory Thaumaturgos. It was written apparently between 238 and 243 while Origen was in Nicomedia. In paternal words the teacher admonishes his former student 'to draw from Greek philosophy such things as are capable of being made general or preparatory studies to Christianity' (1). As the Jews took the vessels of gold and silver from the Egyptians for the decoration of the Holy of Holies, thus the Christians should take over the treasures of the mind from the Greeks and use them in the service of the true God (2). Origen is honest enough to admit that this procedure can be dangerous: 'Having learned by experience, I would assure thee that he is rare who takes the useful things of Egypt, and comes out of it and fashions the things for the worship of God, but there is many a brother of the Edomite Ader. These latter are they who from some Greek liaison beget heretical notions' (3 SPCK). The letter ends with an ardent admonition, not to relax in the reading of the Scriptures:

But do thou, sir my son, first and foremost attend to the reading of the Holy Scriptures, yea attend. For we need great attention in reading the Scriptures that we may not speak or think too rashly about them. And, attending to the reading of the divine oracles with a closeness faithful and well-pleasing to God, knock at its closed places, and they shall be opened unto thee by the porter of whom Jesus said, 'To him the porter openeth'(Matth. 7,7, John 10,3). And attending to the divine reading, seek rightly and with unwavering faith in God for the mind of the divine letters, hidden from most. Be not content with knocking and seeking; for most essential is the prayer to understand divine things (4 spck).

b) The second letter, the complete text of which still survives, is addressed to Julius Africanus and is in answer to one from him to Origen, which is also preserved. Origen had made use of the incident of Susanna in a disputation. Julius Africanus had called attention to the fact that this is not found in the Hebrew text of the Book of Daniel and that there are reasons of language and style as well as plays upon words which make it quite clear that it did not belong originally to the Book of Daniel and therefore cannot be regarded as canonical. Origen in his reply defends with a great display of erudition and scholarship the canonicity of this story as well as that of the narrative of Bel and the Dragon, the prayers of Azarias and the hymn of praise of the three youths in the fiery furnace. All these passages are in the Septuagint as well as Theodotion's version. Moreover, the Church defines the canon of the Old Testament and it would be well to remember the words: 'Thou shalt not remove the ancient landmarks which thy fathers have set' (Prov. 22,28).

This epistle was written about the year 240 in the house of his friend Ambrose at Nicomedia: 'My lord and dear brother Ambrose who has written this at my dictation and has, in looking over it, corrected as he pleased, salutes you' (15 anf).

c) Several other letters of Origen, which have been lost, are known to us from the sixth book of the *Ecclesiastical History* of Eusebius, among them one to the Emperor Philippus Arabs and another to his wife Severa. Eusebius mentions several to Pope Fabianus (236–250), in which, according to St. Jerome (*Epist.* 84, 10), Origen regretted that his writings contained passages not in agreement with the ecclesiastical doctrine.

Editions: MG 11, 88–92; 11, 48–85. — P. Koetschau, Des Gregorios Thaumaturgos Dankrede an Origenes (SQ 9). Freiburg, 1894, 40–44. — W. Reichardt, Die Briefe des Sextus Julius Africanus an Aristides und Origenes (TU 34, 3). Leipzig, 1909.

Translations: English: F. CROMBIE, ANL 10; ANF 4, 386–392: Letter to Africanus; 393–394: Letter to Gregory Thaumaturgos. — M. METCALFE, Gregory Thaumaturgos Address to Origen (SPCK). London-New York, 1920, 89–93: Origen's Letter to Gregory. — *Dutch:* H. U. MEYBOOM, Oudchristelijke geschriften, dl. 38. Leiden, 1926: Letters to Africanus and Gregory.

Studies: J. DRÄSEKE, Der Brief des Origenes an Gregorios von Neocäsarea: Jahrbücher für protestant. Theologie 7 (1881) 102–126. — A. v. HARNACK, Die Sammlung der Briefe des Origenes und sein Briefwechsel mit Julius Africanus: SAB (1925) 41 ff. — U. VON WILAMOWITZ-MOELLENDORFF, Der Brief des Origenes an Gregorios: Hermes (1928) 369 ff.

2. ASPECTS OF ORIGEN'S THEOLOGY

Origen did not repeat Clement of Alexandria's mistake of basing his theology on the doctrine of the Logos as the source of all knowledge. He proceeds from the supreme and highest Christian idea, from God. His greatest theological work, *First Principles*, begins with the statement that God is a spirit, that God is light (*De princ.* 1,1,1). God alone is unbegotten (ἀγέννητος). He is free of all matter:

God, therefore, is not to be thought of as being either a body or as existing in a body, but as an uncompounded intellectual nature (*simplex intellectualis natura*), admitting within Himself no addition of any kind; so that He cannot be believed to have within Him a greater and a less, but is such that He is in all parts μονάς, and so to speak, ἑνάς, and is the mind and source from which all intellectual nature or mind takes its beginning (*De princ.* 1,1,6 ANF).

This absolute principle of the world is at the same time personally active as its creator, sustainer and ruler.

God the Father is as an absolute being incomprehensible. He becomes comprehensible through the Logos, who is Christ, the *figura expressa substantiae et subsistentiae Dei* (*De princ.* 1,2,8; *Contra Cels.* 7,17). He can be recognized through his creatures, too, as the sun through its rays:

Our eyes frequently cannot look upon the nature of the light itself—that is, upon the substance of the sun: but when we behold his splendour or his rays pouring in, perhaps, through windows or some small openings to admit the light, we can reflect how great is the supply and source of the light of the body. So, in like manner, the works of

Divine Providence and the plan of this whole world are a sort of rays, as it were, of the nature of God, in comparison with His real substance and being. As, therefore, our understanding is unable of itself to behold God Himself as He is, it knows the Father of the world from the beauty of His works and the comeliness of His creatures (*De princ.* 1,1,6 ANF).

Origen is very anxious to avoid assigning any anthropomorphical features to the divinity. He defends the changeless character of God especially against the pantheistic and dualistic concepts of the Stoics, Gnostics and Manicheans. In answer to Celsus, who accused the Christians of attributing change to God, he states:

Now it appears to me that the fitting answer has been returned to these objections, when I have related what is called in Scripture the 'condescension' of God to human affairs; for which purpose He did not need to undergo a transformation, as Celsus thinks we assert, nor a change from good to evil, nor from virtue to vice, nor from happiness to misery, nor from best to worst. For, continuing unchangeable in His essence, He condescends to human affairs by the economy of His providence. We show, accordingly, that the Holy Scriptures represent God as unchangeable, both by such words as 'Thou art the same,' and 'I change not' (Ps. 101,27; Mal. 3,6); whereas the gods of Epicurus, being composed of atoms, and as far as their structure is concerned, capable of dissolution, endeavour to throw off the atoms which contain the elements of destruction. Nay, even the god of the Stoics, as being corporeal, at one time has his whole essence composed of the guiding principle when the conflagration of the world takes place; and at another, when a rearrangement of things occurs, he again becomes partly material. For even the Stoics were unable distinctly to comprehend the natural idea of God, as of being altogether incorruptible and simple, and uncompounded and indivisible (*Contra Cels.* 4,14 ANF).

1. *Trinity*

Origen is quite familiar with the term *trinity* (τριάς) (*In Joh.*

10,39,270; 6,33,166; *In Jes. hom.* 1,4,1). He refutes and rejects the modalistic negation of the distinction of the three divine persons. That he teaches subordinationism has been both affirmed and denied; St. Jerome does not hesitate to accuse him of doing so, while Gregory Thaumaturgos and St. Athanasius clear him of all suspicion. Modern authors like Régnon and Prat also acquit him.

According to Origen, the Son proceeds from the Father not by a process of division, but in the same way as the will proceeds from reason:

> For if the Son do all those things which the Father does, then, in virtue of the Son doing all things like the Father, is the image of the Father formed in the Son, who is born of Him, like an act of His will proceeding from the mind. And I am therefore of opinion that the will of the Father ought alone to be sufficient for the existence of that which He wishes to exist. For in the exercise of His will He employs no other way than that which is made known by the counsel of His will. And thus also the existence (*subsistentia*) of the Son is generated by Him. For this point must above all others be maintained by those who allow nothing to be unbegotten, i.e., unborn, save God the Father only... As an act of the will proceeds from the understanding, and neither cuts off any part nor is separated or divided from it, so after some such fashion is the Father to be supposed as having begotten the Son, His own image; namely, so that, as He is Himself invisible by nature, He also begat an image that was invisible. For the Son is the Word, and therefore we are not to understand that anything in Him is cognizable by the senses. He is wisdom, and in wisdom there can be no suspicion of anything corporeal. He is the true light, which enlightens every man that cometh into this world; but he has nothing in common with the light of this sun. Our Saviour, therefore, is the image of the invisible God, inasmuch as compared with the Father Himself He is the truth: and as compared with us, to whom He reveals the Father, He is the image by which we come to the knowledge of the Father, whom no one knows save the Son, and he to whom the Son is pleased to reveal Him (*De princ.* 1,2,6 ANF).

Thus Origen makes it quite clear that the Son proceeds from the Father not by division but by a spiritual act. Since everything is eternal in God, this generating act is eternal also: *aeterna ac sempiterna generatio* (*In Jer.* 9,4; *De princ.* 1,2,4). For the same reason the Son has no beginning. There is no time that He was not: οὐκ ἔστιν ὅτε οὐκ ἦν (*De princ.* 1,2,9f; 2; 4,4,1; *In Rom.* 1,5). It almost sounds as if Origen anticipated the refutation of the Arian heresy which claimed exactly the opposite: There was a time that He was not, ἦν ὅτε οὐκ ἦν. The same is true regarding the sonship of Christ. He is not *per adoptionem spiritus filius, sed natura filius* (*De princ.* 1,2,4). The relation of the Son to the Father is, therefore, that of the unity of substance. It is in this connection that Origen coins the word which became famous in the Christological controversies and at the Council of Nicaea (325), ὁμοούσιος:

> What else are we to suppose the eternal light is but God the Father, who never so was that, while He was the light, His splendor (Hebr. 1,3) was not present with Him? Light without splendor is unthinkable. But if this is true, there is never a time when the Son was not the Son. He will be, however, not, as we have described the eternal light, unborn (lest we seem to introduce two principles of light), but, as it were, the splendor of the unbegotten light, with that very light as His beginning and source, born of it indeed, but there was not a time when He was not.

> Thus Wisdom, too, since it proceeds from God, is generated out of the divine substance itself. Under the figure of a bodily outflow, nevertheless, it, too, is thus called 'a sort of clean and pure outflow of omnipotent glory' (Wisd. 7,25). Both these similes manifestly show the community of substance between Son and Father. For an outflow seems ὁμοούσιος, i.e., of one substance with that body of which it is the outflow or exhalation (*In Hebr.* frg. 24,359).

Thus Origen's doctrine of the Logos represents a remarkable advance in the development of theology and had a far-reaching influence on ecclesiastical teaching.

Two trains of thought, however, become evident upon closer examination of his theology of the Logos. The one emphasizes the divinity of the Logos, whereas the other calls Him 'second God,' δεύτερος θεός (*Contra Cels.* 5,39; *In Joh.* 6,39,202). Only the

Father is αὐτόθεος and ἁπλῶς ἀγαθός, the primal goodness; the Son is the image of goodness, εἰκὼν ἀγαθότητος (*Contra Cels.* 5,39; *De princ.* 1,2,13). Origen states: 'We who say that the visible world is under the government of Him who created all things, do thereby declare that the Son is not mightier than the Father, but inferior to Him' (*Contra Cels.* 8,15). The Son and the Holy Spirit are to Origen intermediaries between the Father and creatures:

> As for us, who believe the Saviour when He said: 'The Father, who has sent Me, is greater than I,' and who for that reason did not allow that the word 'good' should be applied to Himself in its full, true and perfect sense, but attributed it to the Father and gave Him thanks, condemning him who would glorify the Son to excess—we say that the Saviour and the Holy Spirit are without comparison and are very much superior to all things that are made, but also that the Father is even more above them than they are themselves above creatures even the highest (*In Joh.* 13,25).

From this and similar passages it can be easily understood why Origen has been accused of subordinationism. It is quite evident that he presupposes an hierarchical order in the Trinity and regards the Holy Spirit as ranking even below the Son (*De princ.* praef. 4).

Studies: T. DE RÉGNON, Études de théologie positive sur la Sainte Trinité. Première série, deuxième série. Paris, 1892; troisième série. Paris, 1898. — A. AALL, Der Logos. Geschichte seiner Entwicklung in der griechischen Philosophie und der christlichen Literatur 2. Leipzig, 1899, 427–445. — W. FAIRWEATHER, Origen and Greek Patristic Theology. New York, 1901. — F. PRAT, Origène, le théologien et l'exégète. 3rd ed. Paris, 1907. — G. BARDY, La règle de foi d'Origène: RSR 9 (1919) 162–196. — J. LEBRETON, Le désaccord de la foi populaire et de la théologie savante dans l'Église chrétienne du III siècle: RHE 19 (1923) 501–506; 20 (1924) 16–23; *idem*, Les origines du dogme de la Trinité, vol. 1, Paris, 1927; 2, Paris, 1928. — A. D'ALÈS, La doctrine d'Origène: RSR 20 (1930) 224–268. — A. EHRHARD, Die Kirche der Märtyrer. Munich, 1932, 292–300. — R. CADIOU, Introduction au systeme d'Origène. Paris, 1932. — J. J. MAYDIEU, La procession du Logos d'après le Commentaire d'Origène sur l'Évangile de saint Jean: BLE 35 (1934) 3–16, 49–70. — C. W. LOWRY, Origen as Trinitarian: JThSt 37 (1936) 225–240; *idem*, Did Origen style the Son a κτίσμα?: JThSt 39 (1938) 39–42. — A. LIESKE, Die Theologie der Logosmystik bei Origenes. Münster, 1938.

2. *Christology*

It is interesting to see how Origen combines his doctrine of the

Logos with that of the incarnate Jesus of the Gospels. He introduces the concept of the soul of Jesus and regards this pre-existent
soul as the connecting link between the infinite Logos and the
finite body of Christ:

> This substance of a soul, then, being intermediate between
> God and the flesh—it being impossible for the nature of God
> to intermingle with a body without an intermediate instru-
> ment—the God-man (θεάνθρωπος), is born, as we have said,
> that substance being the intermediary to whose nature it was
> not contrary to assume a body. But neither, on the other
> hand, was it opposed to the nature of that soul, as a rational
> existence, to receive God, into whom, as stated above, as
> into the Word, and the Wisdom, and the Truth, it had al-
> ready wholly entered. And therefore deservedly is it also
> called, along with the flesh which it had assumed, the Son
> of God, and the Power of God, the Christ, and the Wisdom
> of God, either because it was wholly in the Son of God, or
> because it received the Son of God wholly into itself (De
> princ. 2,6,3 ANF).

Origen is the first to use the designation God-man, θεάνθρωπος
(In Ez. hom. 3,3), which was to remain in the terminology of
Christian theology. Regarding the Incarnation he states that the
flesh into which this soul of Christ entered was ex incontaminata
virgine assumpta et casta sancti spiritus operatione formata (In Rom. 3,8).
By its union with the Logos Christ's soul was incapable of sin:

> That the nature, indeed, of His soul was the same as that
> of all others cannot be doubted, otherwise it could not be
> called a soul were it not truly one. But since the power of
> choosing good and evil is within the reach of all, this soul
> which belonged to Christ elected to love righteousness, so
> that in proportion to the immensity of its love it clung to it
> unchangeably and inseparably, so that firmness of purpose,
> and immensity of affection, and inextinguishable warmth of
> love, destroyed all susceptibility for alteration and change;
> and that which formerly depended upon the will was
> changed by the power of long custom into nature; and so
> we must believe that there existed in Christ a human and
> rational soul, without supposing that it had any feeling or
> possibility of sin (De princ. 2,6,5 ANF).

The union of the two natures in Christ is an extremely intimate one, 'for the soul and the body of Jesus formed, after the *oikonomia*, one being with the Logos of God' (*Contra Cels.* 2,9). Thus Origen teaches the *communicatio idiomatum*, i.e., the interchange of attributes. Though Christ be designated by a name which connotes His divinity, human attributes can be predicated of Him and *vice versa*:

> The Son of God, through whom all things were created, is named Jesus Christ and the Son of man. For the Son of God also is said to have died—in reference, namely, to that nature which could admit of death; and He is called the Son of man, who is announced as about to come in the glory of God the Father, with the holy angels. And for this reason, throughout the whole of Scripture, not only is the divine nature spoken of in human words, but the human nature is adorned by appellations of divine dignity (*De princ.* 2,6,3 ANF).

It remains Origen's merit to have given to Greek Christology the scientific terms, *physis, hypostasis, ousia, homousios, theanthropos*.

Studies: H. SCHULTZ, Die Christologie des Origenes im Zusammenhange seiner Weltanschauung: Jahrbücher für protestantische Theologie 1 (1875) 193–247, 362–424. — J. RIVIÈRE, Le dogme de la rédemption. Louvain, 1931, 165–212; *idem*, Théologie du sacrifice rédempteur: BLE (1944) 3–12. — J. BARBEL, Christos Angelos (Theophaneia 3). Bonn, 1941, 97–107.

3. *Mariology*

The historian Sozomen reports (*Hist. eccl.* 7,32 EG 866) that Origen used the title θεοτόκος for Mary, although we cannot be surprised that it is not found in the wreckage of his works. This title had been employed in the School of Alexandria for a long period to express Mary's divine motherhood, when in the first half of the fifth century it was attacked and defended in the Nestorian controversies and defined in the Council of Ephesus (431).

But Origen teaches Mary's universal motherhood also: 'No one may understand the meaning of the Gospel [of St. John], if he has not rested on the breast of Jesus and received Mary from Jesus, to be his mother also' (*In Joh.* 1,6).

Studies: J. ERNST, Origenes und die geistige Mutterschaft Marias: ZkTh (1923)

617–621. — A. AGIUS, The Blessed Virgin in Origen and St. Ambrose: Downside Review 50 (1932) 126–137. — C. VAGAGGINI, Maria nelle opere di Origene (Orientalia Christiana Analecta 131). Rome, 1942. — J. C. PLUMPE, Some Little-known Early Witnesses to Mary's virginitas in partu: TS (1948) 567–577.

4. Ecclesiology

Origen defines the Church as the *coetus populi christiani* (*In Ez. hom.* 1,11) or *coetus omnium sanctorum* (*In Cant.* 1) as *credentium plebs* (*In Ex. hom.* 9,3), but she is at the same time the mystical body of Christ. As the soul dwells in the body, thus the Logos lives in the Church as in His body. He is the principle of her life:

> We say that the Holy Scriptures declare the body of Christ, animated by the Son of God, to be the whole Church of God, and the members of this body—considered as a whole—to consist of those who are believers; since, as a soul vivifies and moves the body, which of itself has not the natural power of motion like a living being, so the Word, arousing and moving the whole body, the Church, to befitting action, awakens, moreover, each individual member belonging to the Church, so that they do nothing apart from the Word (*Contra Cels.* 6,48 ANF).

Origen is the first to declare the Church to be the city of God here on earth (*In Jer. hom.* 9,2; *In Jos. hom.* 8,7), existing for the time being side by side with the secular state. As such she has ecumenical character and her laws 'are in harmony with the established constitution in all countries' (*Contra Cels.* 4,22). The Church is at the present a state within a state but the power of the Logos working in her will result in overcoming the secular state:

> Our belief is, that the Word shall prevail over the entire rational creation, and change every soul into His own perfection; in which state every one, by the mere exercise of his power, will choose what he desires, and obtain what he chooses (*Contra Cels.* 8,72 ANF).

Enlightened by the Logos the Church becomes the world of worlds (κόσμος τοῦ κόσμου, *In Joh.* 6,59,301,304).

There can be no salvation without this Church. Thus he states: *Extra hanc domum, id est ecclesiam, nemo salvatur* (*In Jos. hom.* 3,5). The doctrines and laws which Christ brought down to mankind are only to be found in the Church, like His blood shed for our salvation (*ibid.*). For this reason there can be no faith outside of this Church. The faith of the heretics is no *fides*, but arbitrary *credulitas* (*In Rom.* 10,5).

Studies: E. GÖLLER, Die Bischofswahl bei Origenes: Ehrengabe f. J.G.H. zu Sachsen. hrsg. v. F. Fessler. Freiburg i.B., 1920, 603–616. — J. T. SHOTWELL and L. R. LOOMIS, The See of Peter. New York, 1927, 87–91, 314–322. — E. MERSCH, Le corps mystique du Christ. 2nd ed. Louvain, 1936, 282–305. — J. HODŽEGA, Die Lehre des Origenes über den Primat Petri und die Orthodoxen: ThGl 29 (1937) 431–440. — H. RAHNER, Mysterium Lunae. Ein Beitrag zur Kirchentheologie der Väterzeit: ZkTh (1939) 311–349, 428–442. — R. P. C. HANSON, Origen's Doctrine of Tradition: JThSt (1948) 17–27. — G. BARDY, La Théologie de l'Église de saint Irénée au concile de Nicée. Paris, 1947, 128–165. — J. LUDWIG, Die Primatworte Mt. 16, 18. 19 in der altkirchl. Exegese. Münster, 1952, 37–44.

5. *Baptism and Original Sin*

Origen testifies to original sin and infant baptism. Every human being is born in sin and for this reason it is apostolic tradition to baptize the newly born:

> If you like to hear what other saints have felt in regard to physical birth, listen to David when he says, I was conceived, so it runs, in iniquity and in sin my mother hath borne me (Ps. 50,7), proving that every soul which is born in the flesh is tainted with the stain of iniquity and sin. This is the reason for that saying which we have already quoted above, No man is clean from sin, not even if his life be one day long (Job 14,4). To these, as a further point, may be added an inquiry into the reason for which, while the church's baptism is given for the remission of sin, it is the custom of the Church that baptism be administered even to infants. Certainly, if there were nothing in infants that required remission and called for lenient treatment, the grace of baptism would seem unnecessary (*In Lev. hom.* 8,3 SPCK).

> The Church has received from the apostles the custom of administering baptism even to infants. For those who have been entrusted with the secrets of the divine mysteries, knew very well that all are tainted with the stain of original sin, which must be washed off by water and the spirit (*In Rom. com.* 5,9 EH 249).

Studies: GAUDEL, DTC 12, 332–339 (original sin). — A. v. HARNACK, Die Terminologie der Wiedergeburt und verwandter Erlebnisse in der ältesten Kirche (TU 42, 3).

Leipzig, 1918. — H. Rahner, Taufe und geistliches Leben bei Origenes: ZAM 7 (1932) 205–222. — C. M. Edsman, Le baptême de feu. Leipzig-Uppsala, 1940, 1–15. — Ph. M. Menoud, Le baptême des enfants dans l'Église ancienne: Verbum Caro 2 (1948) 15–26. — G. Burke, Des Origenes Lehre vom Urstand des Menschen: ZkTh 72 (1950) 1–39. — F. Lovsky, L' Église ancienne baptisait–elle les enfants?: Foi et Vie 48 (1950) 109–138. — I. J. von Almen, L' Église primitive et le baptême des enfants: Verbum Caro 4 (1950) 43–47.

6. *Penance and Forgiveness of Sins*

Origen stresses on different occasions that strictly speaking there is only one forgiveness of sins, that of baptism, because the Christian religion gives the power and grace to overcome sinful passions (*Exh. ad mart.* 30). However, there are a number of means to obtain remission even of sins committed after baptism. Origen lists seven of them: martyrdom, almsgiving, forgiving those who trespass against us, conversion of a sinner (according to Jac. 5,20), charity (according to Luke 7,47) and finally:

> dura et laboriosa per poenitentiam remissio peccatorum, cum lavat peccator in lacrimis stratum suum et fiunt ei lacrimae suae panes die et nocte, et cum non erubescit sacerdoti domini indicare peccatum suum et quaerere medicinam (*In Lev. hom.* 2,4).

In other words, Origen knows of a remission of sins to be obtained through penance and by a confession of sins before a priest. The latter decides whether the sins should be confessed in public or not:

> But observe carefully to whom you confess your sins; put the physician to the test, in order to know whether he is weak with the weak, and a mourner with those that mourn. Should he consider your disease to be of such a nature that it must be made known to, and cured in the presence of the assembled congregation, follow the advice of the experienced physician (*In Ps. hom.* 37,2,5).

However, the question remains, whether Origen regarded all sins as forgivable. There is a passage in his treatise *On Prayer* which seems to testify to the contrary and to indicate that he holds capital sins to be unpardonable:

> There are some, who, I know not how, arrogate to themselves a power exceeding that of the priests (ἱερατικὴ τάξις), presumably because they know nothing of sacerdotal science;

they boast that they can forgive the sins of idolatry, adultery, and fornication, as if their prayer over such criminals could pardon mortal sins (De orat. 28).

Here, however, Origen does not affirm that such sins cannot be remitted at all, but that they cannot be pardoned by prayer alone, without the previous performance, on the part of the sinner, of a public, long-lasting penance of excommunication. It is true, the priest has not the power of forgiving a capital sin by his prayer. But that does not mean that he is unable to pardon such after he is convinced that God has forgiven the sinner who submitted to public penance. Origen makes this quite clear on another occasion, where he expressly states that every sin can be forgiven:

> The Christians mourn as dead those who have committed licentiousness or any other sin, because they are lost and dead to God. But if they give sufficient evidence of a sincere change of heart, they are received back into the fold at some future time (after a greater interval than in the case of those who were admitted at first) as though they were risen from the dead (Contra Cels. 3,50; EH 253).

Studies: B. POSCHMANN, Die Sündenvergebung bei Origenes. Breslau, 1912. — B. F. M. XIBERTA, La doctrina de Origenes sobre el sacramento de la Penitencia: Reseña Eclesiástica 18 (1926) 237–246, 309–318. — C. VERFAILLIE, La doctrine de la justification dans Origène. Strasbourg, 1926. — P. GALTIER, Les péchés 'incurables' d'Origène: Greg 10 (1929) 177–209. — C. FRIES, Zur Willensfreiheit bei Origenes: AGP (1930) 92–101. — F. J. DÖLGER, Origenes über die Beurteilung des Ehebruchs in der Stoischen Philosophie: AC 4 (1934) 284–287. — M. WALDMANN, Synteresis oder Syneidesis? Ein Beitrag zur Lehre vom Gewissen: ThQ (1938) 332–371. — B. POSCHMANN, Paenitentia secunda. Die kirchliche Busse im ältesten Christentum bis Cyprian und Origenes. Bonn, 1940, 425–480. — G. H. JOYCE, Private Penance in the Early Church: JThSt 42 (1941) 18–42. — E. F. LATKO, Origen's Concept of Penance. Québec Univ. Laval, 1949. Cf. TEICHTWEITER, ThQ 130 (1950) 373–375. — K. RAHNER, La doctrine d'Origène sur la pénitence: RSR 37 (1950) 47–97, 252–286. B. POSCHMANN, Busse und letzte Ölung (SCHMAUS c.s., Dogmengeschichte, vol 4). Freiburg i.B. 1951, 34–39.

7. Eucharist

In his Contra Celsum Origen remarks (8,33):

> We give thanks to the Creator of all, and, along with thanksgiving and prayer (μετ' εὐχαριστίας καὶ εὐχῆς) for the blessings we have received, we also eat the bread presented to us; and this bread becomes by prayer a sacred body, which sanctifies those who sincerely partake of it.

While Origen calls here the eucharistic bread 'a sacred body,' there are other passages in which he definitely speaks of the Eucharist as the body of the Lord:

> You who are wont to assist at the Divine Mysteries, know how, when you receive the body of the Lord, you take reverent care, lest any particle of it should fall to the ground and a portion of the consecrated gift (*consecrati muneris*) escape you. You consider it a crime—and rightly so—if any particle thereof fall down through negligence (*In Ex. hom.* 13,3 EP 490).

He is convinced of the sacrificial and expiatory character of the Eucharist and mentions a real altar: 'You see how the altars are no longer sprinkled with the blood of oxen, but consecrated by the precious blood of Christ' (*In Jesu Nave* 2,1). It is true, there are other passages in the writings of Origen, in which 'the body and blood' of the Lord in the Eucharist are interpreted allegorically as the teaching of Christ by which our souls are nourished:

> That bread which God the Word (*deus verbum*) owns to be His body, is the Word which nourishes the soul, the Word which proceeds from God the Word (*verbum de deo verbo procedens*), and that bread from heavenly bread which is placed upon the table, of which it is written: Thou hast prepared a table before me, against them that afflict me (Ps. 22,5). And that drink which God the Word owns to be His blood, is the Word which saturates and inebriates the hearts of those that drink it, the drink in that cup, of which it is said: How goodly is thy inebriating chalice (Ps. 22)... Not that visible bread which He held in His hands, did the Divine Logos call His body, but the word, in the mystery of which the bread was to be broken. Not that visible drink did He call His blood, but the word, in the mystery of which this drink was to be poured out. For the body of the Divine Logos or His blood, what else can they be than the word which nourishes and the word which gladdens the hearts? (*In Matth. ser.* 85).

However, such passages do not exclude the literal interpretation which he gives on other occasions. He expressly states that the blood of Christ can be drunk in a twofold manner, namely 'sacramentally' (*sacramentorum ritu*), and 'when we receive His life-giving words' (*In Num. hom.* 16,9). Moreover, he describes the literal interpretation of Holy Communion as the one commonly held in the Church (κοινοτέρα), but says it is the conception of simple souls (*In Matth.* 11,14), whereas the symbolical interpretation is more worthy of God and is held by the learned (*In Joh.* 32,24; *In Matth.* 86).

Texts: J. QUASTEN, Monumenta eucharistica. Bonn, 1935–1937, 349/352.

Studies: See bibliography J. QUASTEN, *loc. cit.* — E. KLOSTERMANN, Eine Stelle des Origenes (In Matth. ser. 85): ThStKr 103 (1931) 195–198. — F. R. M. HITCHCOCK, Holy Communion and Creed in Origen: ChQ (1941) 216–239. — O. CASEL, Glaube, Gnosis und Mysterium: JL 15 (1941) 164–195. — L. GRIMMELT, Die Eucharistiefeier nach den Werken des Origenes. Eine liturgiegeschichtliche Untersuchung. Diss. Münster, 1942.

8. *Eschatology*

There is nothing more typical of Origen's theological speculation than his doctrine of the Apokatastasis (ἀποκατάστασις), or universal restoration of all things in their original, purely spiritual state. It is a grand vision, according to which the souls of those who have committed sins here on earth will be submitted to a purifying fire after death, whereas the good ones will enter paradise, i.e., a kind of a school in which God will solve all problems of the world. Origen does not know any eternal fire or punishment of hell. All sinners will be saved, even the demons and Satan himself will be purified by the Logos. When this has been achieved, Christ's second coming and the resurrection of all men, not in material, but in spiritual bodies, will follow, and God will be all in all:

> The end of the world, then, and the final consummation, will take place when everyone shall be subjected to punishment for his sins; a time which God alone knows, when He will bestow on each one what he deserves. We think, indeed, that the goodness of God, through His Christ, may recall all His creatures to one end, even His enemies being conquered and subdued. For thus says Holy Scripture: 'The Lord said to My Lord, Sit Thou at My right hand, until I make Thine enemies Thy footstool (Ps. 109,1)' (*De princ.* 1,6,1 ANF).

> Stronger than all evils in the soul is the Word, and the healing power that dwells in Him; and this healing He applies, according to the will of God, to every man. The

consummation of all things is the destruction of evil, although as to the question whether it shall arise again, it is beyond our present purpose to say (*Contra Cels.* 8,72 ANF).

But when things have begun to hasten to that consummation that all may be one, as the Father is one with the Son, it may be understood as a rational inference, that where all are one, there will no longer be any diversity. The last enemy, moreover, who is called death, is said on this account to be destroyed, that there may not be anything left of a mournful kind when death does not exist, nor anything that is adverse when there is no enemy. The destruction of the last enemy, indeed, is to be understood, not as if its substance, which was formed by God, is to perish, but because its mind and hostile will, which came not from God, but from itself, are to be destroyed. Its destruction, therefore, will not be its nonexistence, but its ceasing to be an enemy and death. For nothing is impossible to the Omnipotent, nor is anything incapable of restoration to its Creator. For He made all things that they might exist, and those things which were made for existence cannot cease to be... Finally, our flesh is supposed by ignorant men and unbelievers to be destroyed after death, in such a degree that it retains no relic at all of its former substance. We, however, who believe in its resurrection, understand that a change only has been produced by death, but that its substance certainly remains; and that by the will of its Creator, and at the time appointed, it will be restored to life; and that a second time a change will take place in it, so that what at first was flesh [formed] out of earthly soil, and was afterwards dissolved by death, and again reduced to dust and ashes, will be again raised from the earth, and shall after this, according to the merits of the indwelling soul, advance to the glory of a spiritual body.

Into this condition, then, we are to suppose that all this bodily substance of ours will be brought, when all things shall be re-established in a state of unity, and when God shall be all in all. And this result must be understood as being brought about, not suddenly, but slowly and gradually, seeing that the process of amendment and correction will take place imperceptibly in the individual instances during the lapse of countless and unmeasured ages, some outstripping others, and tending by a swifter course towards perfection, while others again follow close at hand, and some again a long way behind; and thus, through the numerous and uncounted orders of progressive beings who are being reconciled to God from a state of enmity, the last enemy is finally reached, who is called death, so that he also may be destroyed, and no longer be an enemy. When, therefore, all rational souls shall have been restored to a condition of this kind, then the nature of this body of ours will undergo a change into the glory of a spiritual body (*De princ.* 3,4–6 ANF).

I am of the opinion that the expression, by which God is said to be 'all in all,' means that He is 'all' in each individual person. Now He will be 'all' in each individual in this way: when all with any rational understanding, cleansed from the dregs of every sort of vice, and with every cloud of wickedness completely swept away, can either feel, or understand, or think, will be wholly God; and when it will no longer behold or retain anything else than God, but when God will be the measure and standard of all its movements; and thus God will be 'all,' for there will no longer be any distinction of good and evil, seeing evil nowhere exists; for God is all things, and to Him no evil is near: nor will there be any longer a desire to eat from the tree of the knowledge of good and evil on the part of him who is always in the possession of good, and to whom God is all. So then, when the end has been restored to the beginning, and the termination of things compared with their commencement, that condition of things will be re-established in which rational nature was placed, when it had no need to eat of the tree of the knowledge of good and evil; so that when all feeling of wickedness has been removed, and the individual has been purified and cleansed, He who alone is the one good God becomes to him 'all,' and that not in the case of a few individuals, or of a considerable number, but He Himself is 'all in all.' And when death shall no longer anywhere exist, nor the sting of death, nor any evil at all, then verily God will be 'all in all' (*De princ.* 3,6,3 ANF).

However, this universal restoration (ἀποκατάστασις) is not to be regarded as the end of the world, but as a passing phase. Influenced by Plato, Origen taught that before this world came into existence there were other worlds and after this comes to an end there will be others in unlimited succession. Apostasy from God and return to God follow each other again and again:

> But this is the objection which they generally raise: they say, 'If the world had its beginning in time, what was God doing before the world began? For it is at once impious and absurd to say that the nature of God is inactive and immovable, or to suppose that goodness at one time did not exercise its power.' Such is the objection which they are accustomed to make to our statement that this world had its beginning at a certain time, and that, agreeably to our belief in Scripture, we can calculate the years of its past duration. To these propositions I consider that none of the heretics can easily return an answer that will be in conformity with the nature of their opinions. But we can give a logical answer in accordance with the standard of religion, when we say that not then for the first time did God begin to work when He made this visible world; but as after its destruction there will be another world, so also we believe that others existed before the present came into being... There were ages before our own and there will be others after it. It is not, however, to be supposed that several worlds existed at once, but that, after the end of this present world, others will take their beginning (*De princ.* 3,5,3 ANF).

Origen derived, as these passages show, the last conclusion from his concept of the created spirit whose free will enables it to apostatise from good and turn to evil whenever it wishes to do so. Such a relapse of the spirits makes a new corporeal world necessary and thus one world follows the other and the creation of the world becomes an eternal act.

Studies: L. ATZBERGER, Geschichte der christlichen Eschatologie. Freiburg, 1896, 409 ff., 451 ff. — G. ANRICH, Klemens und Origenes als Begründer der Lehre vom Fegfeuer: Theologische Abhandlungen. Festgabe f. H. J. Holtzmann. Tübingen, 1902, 95–120. — W. STOHMANN, Überblick über die Geschichte des Gedankens der Ewigen Wiederkunft mit besonderer Berücksichtigung der 'Palingenesis aller Dinge'. Diss. Munich, 1917. — TH. SPACIL, La dottrina del purgatorio in Clemente Alessandrino ed in Origene: Bess (1919) 131–145. — H. MEYER, Die Lehre von der ewigen Wiederkunft aller Dinge. 1922, 359–380. — G. ROSSI, La dottrina della creazione in

Origene: SC 20 (1921) 339–357, 427–435. — O. Procksch, Wiederkehr und Wieder-geburt: Das Erbe M. Luthers. Ihmels-Festschrift hrsg. R. Jelke, Leipzig, 1928, 1–18. — G. Rossi, Saggi sulla metafisica di Origene. Milan, 1929. — R. Arnou, Le thème néo-platonicien de la contemplation créatrice chez Origène et chez saint Augustin: Greg 13 (1932) 124–136. — R. B. Tollinton, Alexandrine Teaching on the Universe. New York, 1932. — W. L. Knox, Origen's Conception of the Resurrection Body: JThSt (1938) 247–248. — H. Chadwick, Origen, Celsus, and the Resurrection of the Body: HThR 41 (1948) 83–102. — C. Lenz, Apokatastasis: RACh 1, 510–516.

9. *The Pre-existence of Souls*

Origen's doctrine of the pre-existence of souls is intimately connected with his idea of a universal restoration (ἀποκατάστασις). The present visible world was preceded by another. The pre-existent human souls are spirits who fell away from God in the preceding world and are therefore now enclosed in material bodies. The sins committed by the soul in the preceding world explain the different measure of graces which God bestows on every one and the diversity of men here on earth. It is interesting to see how Origen fits this doctrine into his etymology of the word psyche (ψυχή), which he derives from ψύχεσθαι, 'to grow cold.'

We have therefore to see if, perchance, as we have said is declared by the name itself, it was called ψυχή, i.e., *anima*, because it has waxed cold from the fervor of just things and from participation in the divine fire, and yet has not lost the power of restoring itself to that condition of fervor in which it was at the beginning. Whence the prophet also appears to point out some such state of things by the words: 'Return, O my soul, unto thy rest' (Ps. 114,7). From all this it appears to be made out, that the understanding (νοῦς), falling away from its status and dignity, was made or named soul; and that, if repaired and corrected, it returns to the condition of the understanding (νοῦς).

Now, if this be the case, it seems to me that this very decay and falling away of the understanding (νοῦς) is not the same in all, but that this conversion into a soul is carried to a greater or less degree in different instances, and that certain understandings retain something even of their former vigor, and others again either nothing or a very small amount. Whence some are found from the very commencement of their lives to be of more active intellect, others again of a slower habit of mind, and some are born wholly obtuse, and altogether incapable of instruction (*De princ.* 2,9,3–4 ANF).

Is it not more in conformity with reason, that every soul, for certain mysterious reasons (I speak now according to the opinion of Pythagoras, and Plato, and Empedocles, whom Celsus frequently names), is introduced into a body, and introduced according to its deserts and former actions? (*Contra Cels.* 1,32 ANF)

Studies: W. SCHÜLER, Seele bei Origenes und Plotin: Zeitschrift für Theologie u. Kirche 10 (1900) 167–188. — F. RÜSCHE, Das Seelenpneuma. Seine Entwicklung von der Hauchseele zur Geistseele. Paderborn, 1933. — H. D. SIMONIN, La prédestination d'après les Pères grecs: DTC 12, 2822–2828. — C. M. EDSMAN, Schöpferwille und Geburt Jac. 1, 18. Eine Studie zur altchristlichen Kosmologie: ZNW (1939) 11–44. — H. RAHNER, Das Menschenbild bei Origenes: Eranos-Jahrbuch 15 (1947) 197–248. — H. KARPP, Probleme altchristlicher Anthropologie. Gütersloh, 1950, 186–229.

10. *The Doctrine of Scriptural Senses*

The Bible was to Origen not only a dogmatic or moral treatise but something far more living, far more elevated, the reflection of the invisible world. His first principle is that the Bible is the Word of God, not a dead word imprisoned in the past, but a living word addressed immediately to the man of today. His second principle is that the Old Testament is illuminated by the New, just as the New only discloses its profundity once it is illuminated by the Old. The bond between the two is determined by allegory. Origen is convinced that the understanding of Scripture is a grace:

Then there is the doctrine that the Scriptures were composed through the Spirit of God and that they have not only that meaning which is obvious, but also another which is hidden from the majority of readers. For the contents of Scripture are the outward forms of certain mysteries and the images of divine things. On this point the entire Church is unanimous, that while the whole law is spiritual, the inspired meaning is not recognized by all, but only by those who are gifted with the grace of the Holy Spirit in the word of wisdom and knowledge (*De princ.*, praef. 8 SPCK).

On another occasion he distinguishes three senses of Scripture, historical, mystical and moral, corresponding to the three parts of man, body, soul and spirit, and the three degrees of perfection (cf. above, p. 60). The mystical sense gives the collective and universal meaning of the mystery; the moral gives its interior and individual meaning.

Since he defends a strict verbal inspiration of Scripture (*In Psalm.* 1; *In Jer. hom.* 21,2), he uses symbolic interpretation at times as an easy escape from embarrassments occasioned by the proper literal sense (*De princ.* 4,16). He goes so far as to affirm that in Scripture 'all has a spiritual meaning, but not everything has a literal meaning' (*De princ.* 4,3,5). We have here the point of departure for all the exaggerations of medieval allegorism. Thus it is by reason of the Philonian impact on his thought that Origen occasionally denies the reality of the letter, in a manner indefensible, that he sees a spiritual sense in each and every passage of Scripture, and that some of his symbolistic techniques become fantastic.

Studies: See the bibliography on allegory above, p. 4. — E. KLOSTERMANN, Origeniana: Neutestamentliche Studien Georg Heinrici dargebracht. Leipzig, 1914, 245–251. — E. VON DOBSCHÜTZ, Vom vierfachen Schriftsinn: Harnack-Ehrung. Leipzig, 1921, 1–13. — H. U. MEYBOOM, Het Schrift-gebruik van Origenes: Nieuwe Theol. Stud. 5 (1922) 24–30. — W. VÖLKER, Paulus bei Origenes: ThStKr 102 (1930) 258–279; *idem*, Das Abraham-Bild bei Philo, Origenes und Ambrosius: ThStKr 103 (1931) 199–207. — H. RAHNER, Le début d'une doctrine des cinq sens spirituels chez Origène: RAM 13 (1932) 113–145. — R. P. C. HANSON, Origen's Interpretation of Scripture Exemplified from his Philocalia: Hermathena 63 (1944) 47–58. — W. DEN BOER, Hermeneutic Problems in Early Christian Literature: VC 1 (1947) 150–167. — J. DANIÉLOU, L'unité des deux Testaments dans l'œuvre d'Origène: RSR (1948) 27–56; *idem*, Origène. Paris, 1948. — H. DE LUBAC, Histoire et esprit. L'intelligence de l'Écriture d'après Origène. Paris, 1950. — R. BULTMANN, Ursprung und Sinn der Typologie als hermeneutischer Methode: Pro regno et sanctuario. Studies in honor of G. van der Leeuw. Nijkerk, 1950, 89–100. — H. C. PUECH, Origène et l'exégèse trinitaire du Psaume 50, 12–14: Aux sources de la tradition chrétienne. Mélanges M. Goguel. Paris, 1950, 180–194. — J. DANIÉLOU, Sacramentum futuri. Études sur les origines de la typologie biblique. Paris, 1950. — J. L. McKENZIE, A Chapter in the History of Spiritual Exegesis: TS 12 (1951) 365–381.

For Origen's *canon of the Bible*, see J. B. COLON, En lisant la Philocalie d'Origène. À propos du canon des livres saints: RSR (1940) 1–27. — H. WAITZ, Neue Untersuchungen über die sog. judenchristlichen Evangelien: ZNW (1937) 60–81. — J. RUWET, Les Antilegomena dans les œuvres d'Origène: Bibl (1942) 18–42; (1943) 15–58. — G. BARDY, Saint Jérome et l'Évangile selon les Hébreux (quoted by Origen): Mélanges des sciences religieuses 3 (1946) 5–36.

For Origen's *doctrine of inspiration:* A. ZÖLLIG, Die Inspirationslehre des Origenes. Freiburg, 1902. — C. M. JACOBS, The Authority of Holy Scripture in the Early Church: Theological Studies dedicated to H. E. Jacobs. Philadelphia, 1924, 195–233.

3. THE MYSTICISM OF ORIGEN

Going through Origen's spiritual thoughts frequently reminds one of the language and ideas of St. Bernard of Clairvaux and St. Teresa of Avila. He is in fact one of the great mystics of the Church. Unfortunately, this side of Origen's teaching and writing had been very much neglected and began only recently to attract attention. We shall not be able to do justice to his teaching and personality without a study of his mysticism and piety, because these are the ethical forces behind his life and doctrine.

1. *Notion of Perfection*

For Origen's notion of perfection, it is interesting to note what he says in *De princ.* 3,6,1:

> By saying 'to the image of God He created him' and omitting the mention of 'the likeness,' he indicates nothing else but that man received the dignity of 'the image' at his creation, but the perfection of 'the likeness' was reserved for his consummation, that is, that he should acquire it by his personal efforts through the imitation of God; so that, while the possibility of reaching perfection was given him in the beginning by the dignity of 'the image,' he might by performing works himself achieve the perfect 'likeness' in the end (ANF).

From this passage it appears that to Origen the highest good is 'to become as like to God as possible.' In order to achieve this goal we need the grace of God as well as our own efforts. The best way to the ideal of perfection is the imitation of Christ. As not all his disciples were called to be apostles, so not all men are invited to undertake the imitation of Him:

> In a proper sense, it is true, all those who believe in Christ are the brethren of Christ. Properly speaking, however, only they are His brethren who are perfect, and who imitate Him, like him who said, 'be you imitators of me as I am of Christ' (1 Cor. 11,1) (*In Matth. comm. ser.* 73).

Here we have again the distinction between the common faithful and the chosen souls, the educated, that we found in Clement of Alexandria, Origen's teacher. On other occasions he compares those who have this special vocation with the disciples of Christ and the rest of men with the multitudes that listened to Him:

It was the purpose of the evangelists to display by means
of the Gospel narrative the distinction among those who
come to Jesus. Some of them are the multitudes and are not
called disciples: others are the disciples and superior to the
multitudes... Thus it is written, when the multitudes were
below, but the disciples were able to come unto Jesus who
had gone up to the mountain where the multitudes could
not come, that seeing the multitudes He went up into the
mountain: and when He had sat down, His disciples came
unto Him: and He opened His mouth and taught them
saying, Blessed are the poor in spirit, and so on (Matth.
5,1–3). Again, in another place, when the multitudes needed
healing, it is said, Great multitudes followed Him and He
healed them (Matth. 12,15). But we do not find any healing
mentioned in connection with the disciples, since if a man
is already a disciple of Jesus, he is in sound health, and being
well he has need of Jesus not as a physician but in his other
offices... Thus among those who come to the name of Jesus,
they who know the mysteries of the kingdom of heaven
would be called disciples, those to whom such knowledge
(*gnosis*) was not given would be called multitudes, who
would be counted less than disciples. Observe carefully that
it was to the disciples He said, Unto you it is given to know
the mysteries of the kingdom of heaven, but in regard to the
multitudes, To them it is not given (*In Matth. comm.* 11,4
SPCK).

2. *Self-knowledge*

The first step for those who have chosen to imitate Christ and
arrive at perfection is to acquire self-knowledge. It is absolutely
necessary to discover what we have to do and what to avoid, what
to improve and what to preserve:

Our remarks must be regarded as addressed by the Word
of God to the soul which is in a state of progress, but has not
yet climbed to the height of perfection. By virtue of its progress it is described as beautiful, but to secure its arrival at
perfection there is need that warning be addressed to it. For
unless it acquires self-knowledge in the way we have detailed
above, and carefully practises itself in the word of God and

the divine law, its fate will be to gather on these points the views of the various teachers, and to follow after men whose words have no excellence, no prompting of the Holy Spirit... It is as if He [God] speaks to the soul already within, already in its place among the mysteries. Yet because it is careless about self-knowledge, about inquiring what it is, what it should do and how, and what leave undone, to this soul it is said, Go thy way forth, like one sent forth by the master for this fault of sloth. So great a danger is it for the soul to neglect the knowledge and understanding of itself (*In Cant.* 2,143–145 SPCK).

3. *The Battle against Sin*

The result of this self-knowledge and examination of conscience will be to recognize that we have to take up arms against sin, which prevents us from reaching perfection. This presupposes the battle against the passions (πάθη) and the world as the causes of sin. The goal is the complete freedom from passions, the ἀπάθεια, the total destruction of the πάθη. In order to reach it, there must be a perpetual mortification of the flesh. This leads to a renunciation of marriage, not that Origen rejected it, but only that he recommends the celibate life and the vow of chastity for the true imitator of Christ:

And if we offer to Him our chastity, that is, our body's chastity, we receive from Him chastity of the spirit... This is the vow of the Nazarene, which is above every other vow. For when we offer a son or a daughter, or cattle or an estate, all this is exterior to us. To offer oneself to God and to please Him, not by the labor of another but by one's own labor, this is the most perfect and eminent of all vows; and he who does this is an imitator of Christ (*In Num. hom.* 24,2).

Origen praises Christ as the one who brought virginity into the world; he sees in it the model of perfection, which consists in *castitas et pudicitia et virginitas* (*In Cant.* 2,155).

However, the imitator of Christ must also practise detachment from his relatives, from all worldly ambition, and property. Only this will enable him *vacare deo*, to make room for God in his heart (*In Ex. hom.* 8,4,226,2f), without which no interior ascent is possible.

4. Ascetical Exercises

Such complete detachment from the world can be acquired only by the life-long exercise of asceticism. Frequent vigils should break the power of the body (*In Ex. hom.* 13,5; *In Jos. hom.* 15,3), severe fasting force it down (Ps. 34,13), continual study day and night of Holy Scripture help in concentrating on divine things (*In Gen. hom.* 10,3). Origen appears here as a forerunner of monasticism. This holds true also for his emphasis on the virtue of humility. In his homilies he demands that the one who wishes to be perfect should feel like the last of all (*In Jer. hom.* 8,4), and declares that pride is the root of every sin and evil, the cause of Lucifer's fall (*In Ez. hom.* 9,2).

5. The Beginnings of the Mystical Ascent

In his *Homily to Numbers 27* Origen draws an interesting picture of the steps leading to the interior ascent. The journey begins with the departure from the world and its confusion and wickedness. The first advance is made as soon as it is realized that man on earth lives only in transit. After this preparation he has to fight against the devil and the demons in order to acquire virtue. The time of progress is always a time of danger, and thus with the arrival at the Red Sea the temptations within begin. After passing successfully through these, the soul is not free yet, because new trials have to be faced. These are the inward sufferings of the soul, which accompany every step higher. Origen for this reason refers on many occasions to the necessity of such temptations.

> Therefore if the Son of God, Himself God, was made man for you and is tempted, you, a man by nature, have no right to be aggrieved if you happen to be tempted. And if in temptation you imitate Him who was tempted for you and overcame every temptation, your hope then lies with Him who was once a man but has now ceased to be a man... For if He who once was man, after He had been tempted and the devil departed from Him till the time of His death, on arising from the dead shall die no more, whereas every man is subject to death; he consequently who dies no more is no longer man but God. And if He who once was man is God, you too must be like Him, for we shall be like Him and

we shall see Him as He is. You too must become a god in
Christ Jesus, to whom be the glory and the dominion for
ever and ever (*In Luc. hom.* 29 SPCK).

However, the more the conflicts and battles multiply, the more
consolations are granted to the soul. A deep longing for heavenly
things and for Christ enters it, enabling it to pass through all
tribulations. Moreover, it receives the gift of visions, about which
Origen speaks with such clearness that he must have realized
their purpose and value from his own experience. They consist of
illuminations in prayer and reading of the Scripture, which reveal
divine mysteries. There is a steady increase of such spiritual favors, the higher the spirit climbs, until it reaches Mount Tabor:

> Yet not all who have sight are illuminated by Christ in
> equal measure; each has illumination in proportion as he
> has capacity to receive the power of the light. The eyes of our
> body do not receive the light of the sun in equal measure,
> but the higher the levels to which one climbs, the more lofty
> the view point from which one watches the vista of the sun-
> rise, the larger is one's sense of the power of the sun's light
> and heat. So it is also with our spirit; the higher and the
> further it goes in its approach to Christ, the more nearly it
> exposes itself to the glory of His light, the more finely and
> splendidly is it illuminated by His radiance... And if a
> man be even so advanced as to be able to go up with Him
> to the mount, as Peter and James and John, he shall have the
> illumination not only of the light of Christ but even of the
> very Father's voice (*In Gen. hom.* 1,7 SPCK).

The purpose of such visions is to fortify the soul against future
affliction: *ut animae post haec pati possint acerbitatem tribulationum et
tentationum (In Cant.* 2,171). They are the oases in the desert of
suffering and temptation. Origen does not fail to caution against
paying too much attention to such experiences of sweetness. Even
they can be used by the devil: *cavendum est et sollicite agendum, ut
scienter discernas visionum genus (In Num. hom.* 27,11).

6. *The Mystical Union with the Logos*

The next step is the mystical union of the soul with the Logos.
Origen uses two symbols for this state. He first speaks of the birth
of Christ in the heart of man and His growing in the soul of the

pious (*In Cant. comm.* prol. 85; *In Jer. hom.* 14,10). But he prefers
to express the relation existing between the soul and the Logos
in the form of a mystical marriage:

Let us bring in the soul whose every desire it is to be joined
in fellowship with the Word of God and to enter into the
mysteries of His wisdom and knowledge, as into the chamber
of a heavenly bridegroom. Unto this soul His gifts by way
of dowry have been already given. For just as the dowry of
the church was the books of the law and of the prophets, so
to the soul the law of nature, the reasonable mind, the freedom of the will, must be accounted as marriage gifts. Regard
the teaching of her earliest training as coming down to her
from guides and teachers, bearing these gifts for her dowry.
But since she does not find in them the full and complete
satisfaction of her longing and her love, she prays that her
clear and virgin mind may have the light of the illumination
and the intercourse of the very Word of God. For when the
mind is filled with divine knowledge and understanding
through no agency of man or of angel, then may the mind
believe that it receives the very kisses of the Word of God.
For these and similar kisses suppose the soul to say in prayer
to God, Let Him kiss me with the kisses of His mouth. For
so long as the soul was unable to receive the full and substantial teaching of the very Word of God, she had the kisses
of his friends, knowledge, that is, from the lips of teachers.
But when she begins of her own accord to see things hidden,
to disentangle intricacies, to solve what is complicated, to
expound parables and riddles and the words of the wise
upon correct lines of interpretation, then may the soul believe she has now received the very kisses of her lover, that is,
the Word of God. Kisses, the writer says, in the plural, that
we may understand that the bringing of each particular
hidden meaning into light is a kiss of the Word of God
bestowed upon the perfect soul... Possibly it was upon this
principle the prophetic and perfect mind used to say, I
opened my mouth and drew in my breath (Ps. 118,131). By
the mouth of the lover we understand to be meant the power
whereby He enlightens the mind. Addressing as it were some
word of love to her, supposing she be worthy to receive the

visitation of such excellence, He explains to her all unknown and hidden things. This is the truer, closer, holier kiss which is said to be given by the lover, the Word of God, to His beloved, the pure and perfect soul (*In Cant.* 1 spck).

Origen mentions the *spiritalis amplexus* (*ibid.* 1,2) and the *vulnus amoris* (*In Cant. comm.* prol. 67,7) in this wedding of the Logos and the soul. It is especially interesting that his mysticism of the Logos is interwoven with a deep mysticism of the Cross and the Crucified (*In Joh. comm.* 2,8). The perfect have to follow Christ even in His suffering and in His cross. The real disciple of the Saviour is the martyr, as Origen proved in his *Exhortatio ad martyrium.* For those who want to imitate Christ and cannot undergo true martyrdom, there remains the spiritual death of mortification and renunciation. Both martyr and ascetic have one and the same ideal, the perfection of Christ. Many of Origen's beliefs were adopted by the early monastic writers and his influence in the development of the later monastic life was of great and lasting importance.

Studies: K. KNELLER, Mystisches bei Origenes: Stimmen der Zeit 67 (1904) 238–240. — J. LEBRETON, Les degrés de la connaissance religieuse d'après Origène: RSR 12 (1922) 265–296. — W. BOUSSET, Apophtegmata. Studien zur Geschichte des ältesten Mönchtums. Tübingen, 1923, 287–355. — H. LEWY, Sobria ebrietas. Giessen, 1929, 119–128. — W. VÖLKER, Das Vollkommenheitsideal des Origenes (BHTh 7). Tübingen, 1931. — G. BARDY, La spiritualité d'Origène: VS 31 (1932) 80–106.— R. CADIOU, Introduction au système d'Origène. Paris, 1932. — H. KOCH, Pronoia und Paideusis. Studien zu Origenes und sein Verhältnis zum Platonismus. Berlin, 1932. — J. STELZENBERGER, Die Beziehungen der frühchristlichen Sittenlehre zur Ethik der Stoa. Munich, 1933. — SESTON, Remarques sur le rôle de la pensée d'Origène dans les origines du monachisme: RHR 108 (1933) 197–213. — K. RAHNER, Cœur de Jésus chez Origène?: RAM 15 (1934) 171–174. — S. MARSILI, Giovanni Cassiano ed Evagrio Pontico (Studia Anselmiana 5). Rome, 1935, 150–158. — H. RAHNER, Die Gottesgeburt. Die Lehre der Kirchenväter von der Geburt Christi im Herzen der Gläubigen: ZkTh 59 (1935) 351–358. — R. CADIOU, La jeunesse d'Origène. Paris, 1935. English translation by J. A. SOUTHWELL, Origen. His Life at Alexandria. St. Louis-London, 1944. — K. HEUSSI, Der Ursprung des Mönchtums. Tübingen, 1936, 44–49. — H. U. VON BALTHASAR, Le mystérion d'Origène: RSR 26 (1936) 513–562; 27 (1937) 34–64. — K. PRÜMM, *Mysterion* von Paulus bis Origenes: ZkTh 61 (1937) 391–425. — H. DE LUBAC, Textes alexandrines et bouddhiques: RSR (1937) 336–351. — A. LIESKE, Die Theologie der Logosmystik bei Origenes. Münster i.W., 1938. — M. VILLER-K. RAHNER, Aszese und Mystik in der Väterzeit. Freiburg i.B., 1939, 72–80. — H. RAHNER, Flumina a ventre Christi. Die patristische Auslegung von Joh. 7, 37–38: Bibl (1941) 269–302, 367–403. — O. CASEL, Glaube, Gnosis und Mysterium: JL 15 (1941) 155–305. — I. HAUSHERR, Penthos. La doctrine de la componction dans l'orient chrétien. Rome, 1944. — S. BETTENCOURT, Doctrina ascetica Origenis (Studia Anselmiana 16). Rome, 1945. — W. VÖLKER, Die Vollkommenheitslehre des Clemens Alexandrinus (compared with Origen): TZ 3 (1947) 15-40. — J. DANIÉLOU, Origène. Paris, 1948. — J. LEBRETON, La source et le caractère de la mystique d'Origène: AB 67 (1949) 55-62. — H. JONAS, Die origenistische Spekulation und die Mystik: TZ 5 (1949) 24-45. — F. J. DÖLGER, Christus als himmlischer Eros und Seelenbräutigam bei Origenes: AC 6 (1950) 273-275. — F. BERTRAND, Mystique de Jésus chez Origène. Paris, 1951.

AMMONIUS

Ammonius, who seems to have been a contemporary of Origen, wrote a *Harmony between Moses and Jesus*. Eusebius (*Hist. eccl.* 6,19,10) mistakenly identified him with the Neo-Platonist Ammonius Saccas and St. Jerome (*De vir. ill.* 55) repeats the error. The treatise was probably composed in order to prove the unity of the Old and the New Testament, which many Gnostic sects denied. Possibly, Ammonius is the same as 'Ammonius the Alexandrian,' whom Eusebius mentions in his letter to Carpianus as the author of a Diatessaron or harmony of the gospels built on the text of Matthew. St. Jerome (*De vir. ill.* 55) is convinced of this identification.

Studies: A. v. HARNACK, Geschichte der altchristl. Literatur 1, 406 f.; 2, 2, 81-83. — For the *harmony of the gospels*, see J. W. BURGON, The Last Twelve Verses of the Gospel according to S. Mark. Oxford and London, 1871, 125-132, 295-312. — F. H. A. SCRIVENER, A Plain Introduction to the Criticism of the New Testament. Cambridge, 1883, 56-60. — TH. ZAHN, Forschungen zur Geschichte des neutestamentlichen Kanons 1. Erlangen, 1881, 31-34. — G. H. GWILLIAM, The Ammonian Sections, Eusebian Canons and Harmonizing Tables in the Syriac Tetraevangelium (Studia biblica et ecclesiastica 2). Oxford, 1890, 241-272. — TH. ZAHN, Der Exeget Ammonius: ZKG 38 (1920) 1-22.

DIONYSIUS OF ALEXANDRIA

The most remarkable of Origen's pupils was Dionysius of Alexandria. Upon Origen's departure from that city, Heraclas followed him as head of the catechetical school and subsequently, upon the death of Demetrius, became bishop of Alexandria. His successor in both posts was Dionysius (248-265). His parents were pagans and well-to-do. He was, it seems, led to the Christian faith by his extensive reading and search for truth, since he remarks in one of his letters:

But as for me, I read both the compositions and the traditions of the heretics, polluting my soul for a little with their abominable thoughts, yet all the while deriving this advantage from them, that I could refute them for myself and loathed them far more. And indeed a certain brother, one of the presbyters, attempted to dissuade and frighten me from becoming involved in the mire of their wickedness, for he said that I should injure my soul; and said truly, as I perceived. But a vision sent by God came and strengthened me, and a word of command was given me, saying expressly: 'Read all things that may come to thy hand. For thou art able to sift and prove each matter; which thing was originally the cause of thy faith' (Euseb. *Hist. eccl.* 7,7,1–3 LCL).

As bishop of the Egyptian metropolis, the persecution of Decius forced him to flee. He returned to Alexandria after the Emperor's death but during the reign of Valerian was exiled to Libya, and later to the Mareotis in Egypt. After his restoration, new troubles occurred, civil war and pestilence broke out, and other calamities befell him. He died during the synod of Antioch (264–65) of the illness that prevented him from attending.

Posterity has given him the name 'Dionysius the Great' for his courage and steadfastness in the struggles and troubles of his life. He was an important ecclesiastic, whose influence reached far beyond the borders of his own diocese. Moreover, he is the author of a great number of writings which deal with practical as well as doctrinal questions. His letters show that he took an active part in all the great dogmatic controversies of his time.

Unfortunately, only small fragments remain of his numerous works. Most of them are preserved by Eusebius, who dedicated to him almost the entire seventh book of his *Ecclesiastical History*.

Editions: MG 10. — C. L. Feltoe, Διονυσίου Λείψανα. The Letters and Other Remains of Dionysius of Alexandria (CPT). Cambridge, 1904. — F. C. Conybeare, Newly discovered Letters of Dionysius of Alexandria to the Popes Stephen and Xystus: The English Historical Review 25 (1910) 111–114.

Translations: English: S. D. F. Salmond, ANL 20, 161–266; ANF 6, 81–120. — C. L. Feltoe, St. Dionysius of Alexandria, Letters and Treatises (SPCK). London, 1918. — F. C. Conybeare, *loc. cit.* (from an Armenian codex).

Studies: B. F. Westcott, Dionysius of Alexandria: Dictionary of Christian Biography 1, 850–852. — F. Dittrich, Dionysius der Große von Alexandrien. Freiburg i.B.,

1867. — P. Morize, Denys d'Alexandrie. Paris, 1881. — T. Panaitescu, Das Leben und die literarische Tätigkeit des hl. Dionysius von Alexandrien. Bucarest, 1905 (Rumanian). — J. Burel, Denys d'Alexandrie. Sa vie, son temps, ses œuvres. Paris, 1910. — C. Papadopulos, Ὁ ἅγιος Διονύσιος ὁ Μέγας. Alexandria, 1918. — P. S. Miller, Studies in Dionysius the Great of Alexandria. Diss. Erlangen, 1933. — M. Athenagoras, Διονύσιος ὁ μέγας ἐπίσκοπος Ἀλεξανδρείας: EPh 33 (1934) 161–193, 443–462. — H. G. Opitz, Studies presented to K. Lake. London, 1937, 41–53.

HIS WRITINGS

1. On Nature (Περὶ φύσεως)

In this work Dionysius refutes, in the form of a letter addressed to his son Timothy, the Epicurean materialism based on the atomism of Democritus and demonstrates the Christian doctrine of creation. The fragments preserved by Eusebius in his *Preparation for the Gospel* (14,23–27) show that Dionysius had a good knowledge of Greek philosophy and was a very able writer. He testifies in a very convincing way to the order in the universe and divine providence against the materialistic explanation of the world.

Edition: Feltoe 127–164.

Translations: English: S. D. F. Salmond, ANL 20; ANF 6, 84–91. — C. L. Feltoe, St. Dionysius of Alexandria. London, 1918, 91–101. — *German:* G. Roch, Die Schrift des alexandrinischen Bischofs Dionysius des Großen 'Über die Natur', eine altchristliche Widerlegung der Atomistik Demokrits und Epikurs. Diss. Leipzig, 1882.

2. On Promises (Περὶ ἐπαγγελιῶν)

Eusebius reports the occasion and contents of the two books *On Promises*:

The occasion was supplied him [Dionysius] by the teaching of Nepos, a bishop of those in Egypt, that the promises which had been made to the saints in the divine Scriptures should be interpreted after a more Jewish fashion, and his assumption that there will be a kind of millenium on this earth devoted to bodily indulgence. Thinking, for example, to establish his own peculiar opinion from the Apocalypse of John, he composed a certain book on the subject and entitled it *Refutation of the Allegorists*. Dionysius attacked him in the books *On Promises*, in the first of which he sets out the view that he himself held with regard to the doctrine, and in the second treats of the Apocalypse of John (*Hist. eccl.* 7,14, 1–3 LCL).

The bishop Nepos mentioned here was the head of the diocese of Arsinoe. He had made use of the Apocalypse of St. John for his chiliastic views, refusing Origen's allegorical interpretation. This book had great success, even after Nepos' death, so that 'schisms and defections of whole churches had taken place' (*ibid.* 7). Dionysius therefore went to Arsinoe and held a discussion of the chiliastic question:

> I called together the presbyters and teachers of the breth-ren in the villages and I urged them to hold the examination of the question publicly. And they brought me this book [of Nepos] as some invincible weapon and rampart. I sat with them and for three successive days from morn till night attempted to correct what had been written...

In the end, Coracion, the pastor and leader of this movement, consented no longer to adhere to it, since he had been convinced by the arguments against it. However, Dionysius found it neces-sary after his return to Alexandria to follow up this discussion with his two books *On Promises* in order to counteract any further influence of Nepos' book. It is interesting to note that in his refutation he denies that the apostle John is the author of the Apocalypse:

> That, then, he [the author of the Apocalypse] was cer-tainly named John and that this book is by one John, I will not gainsay; for I fully allow that it is the work of some holy and inspired person. But I should not readily agree that he was the apostle, the son of Zebedee, the brother of James, whose are the Gospel entitled *According to John* and the *Catholic Epistle*. For I form my judgment from the character of each and from the nature of the language and from what is known as the general construction of the book, that [the John therein mentioned] is not the same. For the evangelist nowhere adds his name, nor yet proclaims himself, through-out either the Gospel or the Epistle (Euseb., *Hist. eccl.* 7,24,6–8 LCL).

Edition: FELTOE 106–126.

Translations: English: S. D. F. SALMOND, ANL 20; ANF 6, 81–84. — FELTOE. London, 1918, 82–91.

Studies: F. H. Colson, Two Examples of Literary and Rhetorical Criticism in the Fathers (Dionysius on the Authorship of the Apocalypse): JThSt 25 (1924) 364–377. — H. Strathmann, Was soll die Offenbarung des Johannes im Neuen Testament? Dionysius von Alexandrien über die Offenbarung des Johannes. Gütersloh, 1947.

3. *Refutation and Apology* (Βιβλία ἐλέγχου καὶ ἀπολογίας)

This work in four books is addressed to his namesake at Rome, Pope Dionysius (259–268), as Eusebius (*Hist. eccl.* 7,26,1) informs us. The Roman pontiff had invited the bishop of Alexandria to explain himself regarding his belief in the trinitarian doctrine (Athanasius, *Ep. de sent. Dion.* 13). Dionysius answered with the *Refutation and Apology*, in which he demonstrated his orthodoxy. His explanations appear to have set at rest Roman scruples. Only fragments remain of this work in Eusebius (*Praep. ev.* 7; 9) and Athanasius (*De sententia Dionysii episc. Alex.*). With reference to the relation of the Father to the Son, which was the main point in the trinitarian controversy, Dionysius states in this letter:

There certainly was not a time when God was not the Father.

Neither, indeed, as though He had not brought forth these things, did God afterwards beget the Son, but because the Son has existence not from Himself, but from the Father.

Being the brightness of the eternal Light, He Himself also is absolutely eternal. For since light is always in existence, it is manifest that its brightness also exists, because light is perceived to exist from the fact that it shines, and it is impossible that light should not shine. And let us once more come to illustrations. If the sun exists, there is also a day; if nothing of this be manifest, it is impossible that the sun should be there. If then the sun were eternal, the day would never end; but now, for such is not really the state of the case, the day begins with the beginning of the sun, and ends with its ending. But God is the eternal Light, which has neither had a beginning nor shall ever fail. Therefore the eternal brightness shines forth before Him, and co-exists with Him, in that, existing without a beginning, and always begotten, He always shines before Him; and He is that Wisdom which says, 'I was that wherein He delighted, and I was daily His delight before His face at all times' (Prov. 8,30).

Since, therefore, the Father is eternal, the Son also is

eternal, Light from Light. For where there is the begetter,
there is also the offspring. And if there is no offspring, how
and of what can He be the begetter? But both are, and always are. Since then God is the Light, Christ is the Brightness. And since He is a Spirit—for, says He, 'God is a Spirit'
(John 4,24)—fittingly again is Christ called Breath; for 'He,'
saith He, 'is the breath of God's power' (Wisd. 7,25).

Moreover, the Son alone, always co-existing with the
Father, and filled with Him who is, Himself also is, since He
is of the Father (ANF).

Eusebius mentions (*Hist. eccl.* 7,26,2) that Dionysius dedicated
a work *On Temptations* to a certain Euphranor, but of this we
know only the title.

Edition: FELTOE 165–198.

Translations: English: S. D. F. SALMOND, ANL 10; ANF 6, 92–94. — FELTOE, London, 1918, 101–107.

4. *Letters*

His letters were an important source for the history of his life
and times. For this reason Eusebius makes frequent use of them
in his *Ecclesiastical History.* There are only two extant in their
entirety. Of the others only fragments have survived. However,
even they indicate the author's far-reaching influence and great
variety of interests.

a. The Letter to Novatian. The Roman schism of Novatian occasioned several of Dionysius' letters, in which he pleaded with
Novatian and his adherents to return to the flock and asked the
authorities for a mild decision in the case of those who had fallen
away during the persecution of Decius. A short letter addressed
to Novatian, the antipope, is completely preserved and deserves
to be quoted:

Dionysius to Novatian a brother, greeting.

If thou wast led on unwillingly, as thou sayest, thou wilt
prove it by retiring willingly. For a man ought to suffer
anything and everything rather than divide the Church of
God, and it were not less glorious to incur martyrdom to
avoid schism than to avoid idolatry, nay, in my opinion it
were more so. For in the one case a man is a martyr for the
sake of his own single soul but in the other for the sake of

the whole Church. And if thou wert even now to persuade or compel the brethren to come to one mind, thy recovery will be greater than thy fall, and the one will not be reckoned, while the other will be praised. But if they obey thee not and thou hast no power, by all means save thine own soul. I pray thou mayest fare well and cleave to peace in the Lord (Euseb., *Hist. eccl.* 6,45 LCL).

Edition: FELTOE 59–62.

Translations: English: S. D. F. SALMOND, ANL 10; ANF 6, 97 — FELTOE 50.

b. The Letter to Basilides. The other epistle which has survived in its entirety is one of his letters to Basilides, bishop of the Pentapolis. It answers several questions which the bishop had addressed to Dionysius regarding the duration of Lent and the physical conditions required for the reception of the Eucharist. It is preserved in the collection of *Canonical Epistles* of the Greek Church that forms one of the sources of oriental Canon Law.

Edition: FELTOE 91–105.

Translations: English: S. D. F. SALMOND, ANL 10; ANF 6, 94–96. — FELTOE, 76–82.

c. The Letter to Fabius. This letter addressed to Fabius, the bishop of Antioch, although preserved only in an excerpt by Eusebius, is of special interest for the history of penance and the Eucharist. Dionysius deals with the vexed problem of forgiveness after apostasy during persecution. In the course of his letter he tells the following:

But this one example that happened amongst us I shall set forth for thee. There was a certain Serapion amongst us, an old man and a believer, who lived blamelessly for a long time, but in the trial fell. This man oftentimes besought [absolution], and no one paid him heed. For indeed he had sacrificed. And, falling sick, he continued for three successive days speechless and unconscious; but on the fourth day he rallied a little, and calling his grandson to him, he said: 'How long, my child, do ye hold me back? Haste ye, I pray, and grant me a speedy release; do thou summon me one of the presbyters.' And having said this he again became speechless. The boy ran for the presbyter. But it was night, and he was unwell and could not come. Yet since I had given an order that those who were departing this life, if they besought it, and especially if they had made supplication before, should be absolved, that they might depart in hope, he gave the little boy a small portion of the eucharist, bidding him soak it and let it fall in drops down into the old man's mouth. Back came the boy with it, and when he was near, before he entered, Serapion revived again and said, 'Hast thou come, child? The presbyter could not come, but do thou quickly what he bade thee, and let me depart.' The boy soaked it and at the same time poured it into his mouth, and when he had swallowed a little he straightway gave up the ghost. Was it not plain that he was preserved and remained until he obtained release, that, with his sin blotted out, he might be acknowledged for all the good deeds he had done? (Euseb., *Hist. eccl.* 6,44,2–6 LCL).

Edition: FELTOE 59–62.

Translations: English: S. D. F. SALMOND, ANL 10; ANF 6, 97–101. — FELTOE 35–43.

Studies: F. J. DÖLGER, ΙΧΘΥΣ II. Münster, 1922, 528 sq. — P. BATIFFOL, L'Eucharistie. La présence réelle et la transsubstantiation. 9th ed. Paris, 1930, 285–289. — J. QUASTEN, Monumenta eucharistica et liturgica vetustissima. Bonn, 1935/37, 353. — G. DEL TON, L'episodio eucaristico di Serapione narrato da Dionizi Alessandrino: SC (1942) 37–47.

d. Festal Letters ('Επιστολαὶ ἑορταστικαί). Up to the ninth century it was a custom among the bishops of Alexandria to send every year to all the Churches of Egypt an announcement of the date of Easter and the beginning of the preceding fast. This took the form of a pastoral epistle exhorting the congregation to observe the Lenten and the Easter season carefully. Dionysius of Alexandria is the first bishop known to have sent such a letter (Euseb., *Hist. eccl.* 7,20):

Dionysius, in addition to the letters of his that were mentioned, composed at that time also the festal letters which are still extant, in which he gives utterance to words specially suited to a solemn occasion with reference to the festival of the Pascha. Of these he addressed one to Glavius, another to Domitius and Didymus, in which also he sets forth a canon based on a cycle of eight years, proving that it is not proper to celebrate the festival of the Pascha at any other time than after the vernal equinox (LCL).

However, of these letters only fragments remain. They indicate that beyond their direct purpose Dionysius took the occasion also to discuss important ecclesiastical questions of the time.

Edition: FELTOE 64–91.

Translation: English: FELTOE 63–76.

Studies: F. NAU, Le comput pascal de la Didascalie et Denys d'Alexandrie: Revue Bleue (1914) 423–425. — W. TILL, Osterbrief und Predigt in achmim. Dialekt. Leipzig, 1931.
For *unauthentic writings*, cf.: F. DITTRICH, *loc. cit.* 123–127. — N. BONWETSCH, Der Brief des Dionysius von Alexandrien an Paulus von Samosata: NGWG Phil. hist. Klasse (1909) 103–122. — E. SCHWARTZ, SAB 1927, 3. Heft. — M. RICHARD, Une scolie d'Origène indûment attribuée à Denys d'Alexandrie: RHE 33 (1937) 44–46.

THEOGNOSTUS

Theognostus was most probably the successor to Dionysius the Great as head of the school of Alexandria, which he directed from ca. 265 to 282. While Eusebius and St. Jerome do not mention him, Photius (*Bibl. cod.* 106) outlines his work, the *Hypotyposeis* ('Υποτυπώσεις), and links his ideas with Origen's:

Read the work by Theognostus of Alexandria, entitled *The Outlines of the Blessed Theognostus of Alexandria, Interpreter of the Scriptures*, in seven books. In the first book he treats of the Father, and endeavours to show that He is the creator of the universe, in opposition to those who make matter coeternal with God; in the second, he employs arguments to prove that it is necessary that the Father should have a Son; and when he says Son, he demonstrates that He is a creation, and has charge of beings endowed with reason. Like Origen, he says other similar things of the Son, being either led astray by the same impiety, or (one might say) eager to exert himself in his defence, putting forward these arguments by way of rhetorical exercise, not as the expression of his real opinion; or, lastly, he may allow himself to depart a little from the truth in view of the feeble condition of his hearer, who is perhaps entirely ignorant of the mysteries of the Christian faith and incapable of receiving the true doctrine, and because he thinks that any knowledge of the Son would be more profitable to the hearer than never to have heard of Him and complete ignorance of Him. In

oral discussion it would not appear absurd or blameworthy
to use incorrect language, for such discussions are generally
carried on according to the judgment and opinion and
energy of the disputant; but in written discourse, which is
to be set forth as a law for all, if any one puts forward the
above defence of blasphemy to exculpate himself, his justification is a feeble one. As in the second book, so in the
third, in treating of the Holy Spirit, the author introduces
arguments by which he endeavours to show the existence of
the Holy Spirit, but in other respects talks as much nonsense
as Origen in his *Principles*. In the fourth book, he talks
similar nonsense about angels and demons, attributing re-
fined bodies to them. In the fifth and sixth, he relates how the
Saviour became incarnate, and attempts, after his manner,
to show that the incarnation of the Son was possible. Here,
also, he trifles greatly, especially when he ventures to say
that we imagine the Son to be confined now to this place,
now to that, but that in energy alone he is not restricted. In
the seventh book, entitled 'On God's Creation,' he discusses
other matters in a greater spirit of piety—especially at the
end of the work concerning the Son.

His style is vigorous and free from superfluities. He uses
beautiful language as in ordinary Attic, in such a manner
that he does not sacrifice its dignity for the sake of clearness
and accuracy (SPCK).

From Photius' description, it is quite clear that the work of
Theognostus was a kind of a dogmatic summa which followed
the doctrine of Origen and especially his subordinationism. Except for a small fragment of the second book, which Diekamp
discovered in a Venetian manuscript of the fourteenth century,
nothing survives of the *Hypotyposeis*.

Editions: Fragments of the Hypotyposes in MG 10, 235–242. — M. J. Routh, Reliquiae sacrae, 2nd ed. 3, Oxford, 1846, 405–422 has a larger collection. — F. Diekamp, Ein neues Fragment aus den Hypotyposen des Alexandriners Theognostus:
ThQ 84 (1902) 481–494.

Translation: English: S. D. F. Salmond, ANF 6, 155 f.

Studies: A. v. Harnack, Die Hypotyposen des Theognost (TU 24, 3). Leipzig, 1903,
73–92. — L. B. Radford, Three Teachers of Alexandria: Theognostus, Pierius and
Peter. Cambridge, 1908.

PIERIUS

Pierius, who succeeded Theognostus in the headship of the school of Alexandria, was, according to Eusebius (*Hist. eccl.* 7,32,27) 'noted for his life of extreme poverty and for his learning in philosophy. He was exceedingly well practised in the deeper study of divine things and in expositions thereof, as well as in public discourses in church' (LCL). St. Jerome gives even more information about him:

> Pierius, presbyter of the church at Alexandria, in the reign of Carus and Diocletian, at the time when Theonas ruled as bishop in the same church, taught the people with great success and attained such elegance of language and published so many treatises on all sorts of subjects (which are still extant) that he was called Origen Junior. He was remarkable for his self-discipline, devoted to voluntary poverty and thoroughly acquainted with the dialectic art. After the persecution, he passed the rest of his life at Rome. There is extant a long treatise of his *On the Prophet Hosea,* which from internal evidence appears to have been delivered on the vigil of Passover (*De vir. ill.* 76 LNPF).

Jerome's report that he passed the rest of his life at Rome does not contradict other testimonies that he suffered for his faith at Alexandria; Photius, for instance, says: 'According to some, he suffered martyrdom; according to others, he spent the rest of his life at Rome after the time of the persecution' (*Bibl. cod.* 119). Most probably, both statements are true. He suffered, but did not die, in the persecution of Diocletian. Since he wrote about the life of Pamphilus, who died 309, he must have lived at least to that year.

HIS WORKS

In the passage quoted above, St. Jerome mentions 'many treatises on all sorts of subjects,' and names especially the long treatise *On the Prophet Osee.* By the term, treatise (*tractatus*), Jerome apparently means sermon, since he states that the treatise *On the Prophet Osee* was delivered on the vigil of Easter. Photius read a work of Pierius containing twelve *logoi,* and, as the *Homily on Osee* is mentioned among them, this word, too, refers to orations or homilies:

Read a work by Pierius the presbyter, who is said to have
suffered martyrdom with his brother Isidore, and to have
been the teacher of the martyr Pamphilus in theology and
head of the catechetical school at Alexandria. The volume
contains twelve *logoi*. The style is clear and brilliant, and so
to say, spontaneous; there is nothing elaborate about it, but
as it were unpremeditated, it flows along evenly, smoothly
and gently. The work is distinguished by a wealth of argumentation. It contains much that is foreign to the present
institutions of the Church, but is possibly in accordance with
older regulations. In regard to the Father and the Son his
statements are orthodox, except that he asserts that there are
two substances and two natures, using these terms (as is clear
from what follows and precedes the passage) in the sense of
hypostasis, not in the sense given by the adherents of Arius.
But in regard to the Holy Ghost his views are dangerous and
impious; for he declares that His glory was less than that of
the Father and the Son. There is a passage in the treatise
entitled *On St. Luke's Gospel*, from which it can be shown that
the honour and dishonour of the image is the honour and
dishonour of the prototype. It is hinted, in agreement with
Origen's absurd idea, that souls have a pre-existence. In his
oration *On Easter and the prophet Hosea*, the author discusses
the Cherubim made by Moses and Jacob's pillar; he admits
that they were made, but talks nonsense about their being
providentially granted, as if they were nothing, or something
else; for he says that they did not exhibit any sort of form,
but absurdly asserts that they only had wings of a kind (*Bibl.
cod.* 119 SPCK).

St. Jerome mentions the Homily *On the Prophet Osee* twice.
While he remarks in *De vir. ill.* (76) that it was delivered *in vigilia
paschae*, he says in the preface to his *Commentary on Osee*, that
Pierius preached it *die vigiliarum dominicae passionis*. These quotations agree with Photius, who speaks about a logos *On Easter
and on the Prophet Osee*. It was a long homily held before Easter
and dealt with the introduction to Osee, since Philip Sidetes calls
this sermon *On the Beginning of Osee* (Εἰς τὴν ἀρχὴν τοῦ ᾿Ωσηέ).
The same Philip mentions three other works of Pierius *On the
Gospel of Luke*, *On the Mother of God* and *The Life of St. Pamphilus*

(Εἰς τὸ κατὰ Λουκᾶν, Περὶ τῆς θεοτόκου, Εἰς τὸν βίον τοῦ ἁγίου Παμφίλου). Most probably the first two belong to the same group of sermons and the last might have been a eulogy on his pupil, the martyr Pamphilus.

Editions: M. J. ROUTH, Reliquiae sacrae, 2nd ed. 3, 423–435. — MG 10, 241–246: Fragments of his sermons. — Additions were made by C. DE BOOR, Neue Fragmente des Papias, Hegesippus und Pierius in bisher unbekannten Exzerpten aus der Kirchengeschichte des Philippus Sidetes (TU 5, 2). Leipzig, 1888, 165–184.

Translation: English: S. D. F. SALMOND, ANF 6, 157.

Studies: A. v. HARNACK, Geschichte der altchristl. Literatur 1, 439–441; 2, 2, 66–69. — L. B. RADFORD, Three Teachers of Alexandria: Theognostus, Pierius and Peter. A Study in the Early History of Origenism and Anti-Origenism. Cambridge, 1908. — G. FRITZ, DTC 12, 1744–1746. — J. QUASTEN, LThK 8 (1936) 267.

PETER OF ALEXANDRIA

Peter became bishop of Alexandria about the year 300, most probably after having been head of the school of that city. He left his diocese during the persecution of Diocletian and died a martyr about the year 311. Eusebius has the highest praise for him:

> After Theonas had given his utmost service for nineteen years, Peter succeeded to the episcopate of the Alexandrians, and he too was especially prominent for twelve entire years; he ruled the church for less than three entire years before the persecution, and for the remainder of his days practised a life of severer discipline, and cared in no hidden manner for the general good of the churches. For this reason, therefore, in the ninth year of the persecution he was beheaded, and so adorned with the crown of martyrdom (Euseb., *Hist. eccl.* 7,32,31 LCL).

During his absence, Meletius, bishop of Lycopolis, invaded his church and the dioceses of four other bishops who were taken prisoners in the persecution, assuming all episcopal rights such as ordination, etc. In a synod held at Alexandria in 305 or 306 Peter deposed the usurper 'after having been convicted of many crimes, especially of having sacrificed to the gods' (Athanasius, *Apol. c. Arianos* 59). Thereupon Meletius started the so-called Meletian Schism, which lasted for centuries. He made himself a champion of rigorism and set up 'the church of the martyrs.' Not even the

Council of Nicaea succeeded in reconciling this faction. Arius, who was himself a Meletian, found among the adherents of the sect his most enthusiastic followers.

HIS WRITINGS

Eusebius does not say anything about Peter's writings, most probably because Peter was an anti-Origenist. Unfortunately, only small fragments are all that remain of his letters and theological treatises.

Editions: M. J. ROUTH, Reliquiae sacrae, 2nd ed. 4, 21–82. — MG 18, 449–522. — J. B. PITRA, Analecta sacra 4, 187–195, 425–430. — C. SCHMIDT, Fragmente einer Schrift des Märtyrerbischofs Petrus von Alexandrien (TU, 20, 4b). Leipzig, 1901. — W. E. CRUM, Texts attributed to Peter of Alexandria, edited and translated: JThSt 4 (1902/3) 387–397. – PO 1, 383–400; 3, 353–361: Biographical fragments.

Translations: English: J. B. H. HAWKINS, ANL 14; ANF 6, 261–283. — W. E. CRUM, *loc. cit.* — *German:* C. SCHMIDT, *loc. cit.*

Studies: A. v. HARNACK, Geschichte der altchristl. Literatur 1, 443–449; 2, 2, 71–75. — J. M. HEER, Ein neues Fragment der Didaskalie des Märtyrerbischofs Petros von Alexandrien: OC 2 (1902) 344–351. — G. MERCATI, Un preteso scritto di S. Pietro, vescovo d'Alessandria e martire, sulla bestemmia e Filone l'istoriografo: Rivista storico-critica delle scienze teol. 1 (1905) 162–180. — L. B. RADFORD, Three Teachers of Alexandria: Theognostus, Pierius and Peter. A Study in the Early History of Origenism and Anti-Origenism. Cambridge, 1908. — E. SCHWARTZ, Codex Vaticanus graec. 1431, 1927, 98 n. 4 and 5 (New Fragments in Timoth. Aelurus). — A. ZIKRI, Un fragment copte inédit sur le patriarche Pierre d'Alexandrie: Annales du service des antiquités d'Égypte 29 (1929) 71–75. — FRITZ, DTC 12, 1802–1804. — KETTLER, PWK 19, 2, 1281–1288. — J. LEFORT, St. Athanase, écrivain copte: Mus 46 (1933) 31 (a coptic homily). — O. H. E. BURMESTER, Mus 1932, 50 f., 68 f. (fragments of a coptic homily). — M. RICHARD, Pierre Ier d'Alexandrie et l'unique hypostase du Christ: Mélanges de science religieuse (1946), 357–358. — W. TELFER, St. Peter of Alexandria and Arius: AB 67 (1949) 117–130.

1. *On the Godhead* (Περὶ θεότητος)

The Acts of the Council of Ephesus (431) contain three quotations from Peter's work *On the Godhead*. They indicate that it was written in defense of the true divinity of Christ against subordinationism. 'The Word was made flesh,' one of the fragments states, 'and was found in fashion as a man but yet He was not left without His divinity.'

2. *On the Advent of Our Saviour* (Περὶ τῆς σωτῆρος ἡμῶν ἐπιδημίας)

Leontius of Byzantium quotes a passage from Peter's *On the Advent of Our Saviour* which emphasizes the two natures in Christ:

These things and the like, and all the signs which He showed, and His miracles, prove that He is God made man. Both things therefore are demonstrated, that He was God by nature, and that He was man by nature (Leont., *Contra Nestor. et Eutych.* 1 ANF).

It is possible that this treatise is identical with that *On the Godhead*.

3. *On the Soul* (Περὶ ψυχῆς)

The same Leontius quotes in his work *Against the Monophysites* two passages from the first book of a writing of Peter directed against the Origenistic doctrine of the soul's pre-existence and its imprisonment in the body for a sin formerly committed. The author states 'that man was not formed by a conjunction of the body with a certain pre-existent type. For if the earth, at the bidding of the Creator, brought forth the other animals endowed with life, much rather did the dust, which God took from the earth, receive a vital energy from the will and operation of God.' The doctrine of the pre-existence of souls 'comes from the philosophy of the Greeks; it is foreign to those who wish to live piously in Christ.' From all this it appears that Peter wrote a treatise on this subject consisting of at least two books and directed against one of the basic principles of Origen's system.

4. *On the Resurrection* (Περὶ ἀναστάσεως)

There are seven Syriac fragments extant of his work *On the Resurrection*. This, too, was most probably a refutation of Origen, stressing, as it does, the identity of the body in the resurrection with that of the present life, a doctrine that Origen denied.

5. *On Penance* (Περὶ μετανοίας)

Of Peter's lost disquisition *On Penance*, usually called the *Canonical Epistle*, the law collection of the Eastern Church has preserved fourteen canons. The opening clause of the first of these, 'Since the fourth passover of the persecution is at hand,' dates the work to the year 306 A.D. and indicates, in all likelihood, that it was the Easter letter. The prescriptions concern those who are doing penance for having denied the faith during the persecution, and the apostates are divided into several classes. For those who yielded only after grievous torments and dreadful afflictions, the time past should suffice for penance and they should be admitted to communion. Those who lapsed without torture should do penance for another year, while those who, submitted neither to the rack nor to imprisonment, spontaneously apostatized, must do penance for four more years. The canons mention, furthermore, those who escaped by fraud either by procuring false certificates or by sending pagan friends in their stead, and also those who sent in their place their Christian slaves. They disapprove of those who went out to the authorities and sought martyrdom because they acted imprudently and in opposition to the example of the Lord and the apostles. But in none of the canons is the reconciliation postponed to the day of death, as it had been previously (cf. above, p. 107).

Editions: P. A. DE LAGARDE, Reliquiae iuris eccles. antiquissimae. Leipzig, 1856, 63–73: Greek text; 99–117: Syriac text. — J. B. PITRA, Iuris eccles. Graecorum historia et monumenta 1. Rome, 1864, 551–561.

Translations: English: J. B. HAWKINS, ANL 14; ANF 6, 269–279.

Studies: E. SCHWARTZ, NGWG, Philol.-hist. Klasse (1905) 166–175. — J. LEBRETON, in: J. Lebreton and J. Zeiller, The History of the Primitive Church. London, 1948, vol. 4, 906–908.

6. *On Easter* (Περὶ τοῦ πάσχα).

We know from the fragment of an Alexandrian Chronicon that Peter dedicated a treatise *On Easter* to a certain Tricenius. It is possible that this, too, was an Easter letter addressed to an Egyptian bishop of that name. In some of the manuscripts containing his work *On Penance*, the fourteenth canon is followed by another, entitled: 'From the treatise *On Easter* by the same.' It deals with fasting on the fourth and the sixth day of the week.

7. *The Letter to the Alexandrians on Meletius*

There is a brief letter extant in which Peter warned the faithful of his diocese against Meletius. It must have been written shortly after the beginning of the persecution, and is of great importance for the history of the Meletian Schism:

Peter, to the brethren beloved and established in the faith of God, peace in the Lord. Since I have found out that Meletius acts in no way for the common good—for neither is he contented with the letter of the most holy bishops and martyrs—but, invading my parish, hath assumed so much to himself as to endeavour to separate from my authority the priests, and those who had been entrusted with visiting the needy; and, giving proof of his desire for preeminence, has ordained in the prison several unto himself; now, take ye heed to this, and hold no communion with him, until I meet him in company with some wise and discreet men, and see what the designs are which he has thought upon. Fare ye well (ANF).

The 'letter of the most holy bishops and martyrs' referred to here was that written by the four Egyptian bishops Hesychius, Pachomius, Theodorus and Phileas, and addressed to Meletius, in which they protested vehemently against the ordinations which Meletius had held in their churches. This document is also preserved; its text, together with the above epistle of Peter, was discovered in an old manuscript of the Chapter of Verona by Scipio Maffei.

Editions: S. MAFFEI, Osservazioni Letterarie 3. Verona, 1738, 11–18. – MG 18, 509–510.

Translation: English: J. B. HAWKINS, ANL 14; ANF 6, 280.

Studies: P. BATIFFOL, BZ 10 (1910) 131 f. — E. SCHWARTZ, NGWG Phil.-Hist. Klasse (1905) 175 ff. — For the *Meletian Schism,* see: H. I. BELL, Jews and Christians in Egypt. Oxford, 1924, 38–99. — K. HOLL, Die Bedeutung der neuveröffentlichten meletianischen Urkunden für die Kirchengeschichte: SAB (1925) 18–31; *idem,* Gesammelte Aufsätze zur Kirchengeschichte. Tübingen, 1928, vol. 2, 283–297. — CRUM, Journal of Aegyptian Archaeology 13, 1–6. — AMANN, DTC 10, 531–536. — F. J. DÖLGER, Klingeln, Tanz und Händeklatschen im Gottesdienst der christlichen Meletianer in Ägypten: AC 4 (1934) 245–265. — F. H. KETTLER, Der meletianische Streit in Ägypten. Diss. Leipzig, 1934; *idem,* ZNW (1936) 155–193.

The *Acts of the Martyrdom of St. Peter of Alexandria* is extant in Greek, Latin, Syriac and Coptic versions. None of them represent an authentic report of his death, but all are later legends.

Editions: Greek: F. COMBEFIS, Illustrium Christi martyrum lecti triumphi. Paris, 1660, 189–221. — J. VITEAU, Passions des Saints Écaterine et Pierre d'Alexandrie, Barbara et Anysia. Paris, 1897. — *Latin:* MG 18, 451–466. — *Coptic:* H. HYVERNAT, Les actes des martyrs de l'Égypte. Paris, 1886–1887, vol. 1, 263 ff. — *Syriac:* P. BEDJAN, Acta martyrum et sanctorum 5, Paris, 1895, 543 ff.

Translations: English: J. B. HAWKINS, ANL 14; ANF 6, 261–268. — *French:* H. HYVERNAT, *loc. cit.* 247–283.

Studies: F. NAU, Les martyres de S. Léonce de Tripoli et de S. Pierre d'Alexandrie d'après les sources syriaques: AB 19 (1900) 9–13.

HESYCHIUS

It is interesting to know that during the fourth century the Churches of Egypt and Alexandria did not use Origen's redaction of the Septuagint but that of Hesychius (Jerome, *Praef. in Paral.; Adv. Ruf.* 2,27). Jerome criticizes the latter severely and accuses him of interpolations in the Book of Isaias (*Comm. in Is. ad* 58,11) and, on another occasion (*Praef. in Evang.*), he speaks of his false additions to the biblical text. The *Decretum Gelasianum* speaks of 'the gospels which Hesychius forged' and calls them 'apocryphal.'

Thus he must have made a revision of both the Septuagint and the Gospels, most probably about the year 300. From the fact that his edition was used at Alexandria and in Egypt it would appear that he was of Alexandrian origin. Whether he is the same Hesychius who with three other Egyptian bishops addressed a letter to Meletius and died as a martyr in the persecution of Diocletian (cf. above, p. 117), remains doubtful.

Studies: B. F. WESTCOTT and F. J. A. HORT, The New Testament in the Original Greek. Cambridge, 1881, Introduction 182–183. — W. BOUSSET, Textkritische Studien zum Neuen Testament (TU 11, 4). Leipzig, 1894, 74–110. — A. RAHLFS, Alter und Heimat der vatikanischen Bibelhandschrift: NGWG Phil.-hist. Klasse (1899). Heft 1, 72–79. — H. v. SODEN, Die Schriften des Neuen Testamentes in ihrer ältesten erreichbaren Textgestalt, 4 vols. Berlin, 1902/13, 995–1000, 1472–1478, 1672–1674. — A. RAHLFS, Septuaginta-Studien 2 (1907) 226–229; *idem,* Mitteilungen des Septuaginta-Unternehmens 3 (1918/26) 148. — H. LIETZMANN, PWK 8, 1327 f. — H. J. VOGELS, Handbuch der neutestamentlichen Textkritik. Münster, 1923. — J. GÖTTSBERGER, Einleitung in das Alte Testament. Freiburg i. B., 1928, 443. — F. G. KENYON, Hesychius and the Text of the New Testament: Mémorial Lagrange. Paris, 1940, 245–250; *idem,* Our Bible and the Ancient Manuscripts. New York, 1941, 60, 77. Kenyon is of the opinion that the revision of the text of the New Testament made in Egypt at about the beginning of the fourth century may have been by Bishop Hesychius, 'but the only evidence we have about Hesychius in connection with the New Testament (that of Jerome) does not support this identification'.

APPENDIX

THE APOSTOLIC CHURCH ORDER

The Apostolic Church Order is a very valuable source of ecclesiastical law dating most probably from the beginning of the fourth century. The author and the place of origin are unknown. It seems to have been composed in Egypt, although there are some who think that it came from Syria. J. W. Bickell was the first to publish the Greek original in 1843. He gave it the name 'Apostolic Church Order.' We have reasons to believe that its real title was *Ecclesiastical Canons of the Holy Apostles.*

Addressed to 'the Sons and Daughters,' the small treatise claims to be written at the command of the Lord by the twelve apostles. The first half of it contains moral precepts (4–14), the second canonical legislation (15–29). The moral precepts are set forth by means of a description of two ways, that of good and that of evil. This first part is only an adaptation of the corresponding section of the *Didache* (1–4) to the more developed ecclesiastical situation of the fourth century. The second part issues regulations for the election of a bishop, priests, readers, deacons and widows. One of the reasons why Egypt is supposed to be the country of provenance is the high authority in which the Apostolic Church Order was held there.

Only one manuscript contains the entire text of the Greek original, *Codex Vindobonensis hist. gr. olim* 45, *nunc* 7, *saec.* XII. An excerpt from the first part is extant in *Codex Mosquensis bibl. S. Synodi* 124, *saec.* X and three later codices. In addition, Latin, Syriac, Coptic, Arabic and Ethiopic versions testify to the reputation that the Apostolic Church Order enjoyed.

Editions: Greek: J. W. BICKEL, Geschichte des Kirchenrechts 1. Giessen, 1843, 107–132. — P. A. DE LAGARDE, Reliquiae iuris ecclesiasticae antiquissimae graece. Leipzig, 1856, 74–79. — J. B. PITRA, Iuris ecclesiastici Graecorum historia et monumenta 1. Rome, 1864, 75–88. — TH. SCHERMANN, Die allgemeine Kirchenordnung, frühchristliche Liturgien und kirchliche Überlieferung, vol. 1 (StGKA 3. Ergänzungsband). Paderborn, 1914, 12–34. — *Syriac:* A. P. DE LAGARDE, *loc. cit.* 19–23: Ch. 3–14. — A. BAUMSTARK, Στρωμάτιον ἀρχαιολογικόν. Mitteilungen dem internationalen Kongreß für christl. Archäologie zu Rom gew. vom Kollegium des deutschen Campo Santo. Rome, 1900, 15–31. — G. HORNER, The Statutes of the Apostles or Canones ecclesiastici. London, 1904 (gives an English translation of the Coptic-Sahidic version and the Arabic and Ethiopic text with an English translation). — E. HAULER,

Didascaliae apostolorum fragmenta Veronensia Latina. Accedunt canonum qui dicuntur apostolorum et Aegyptiorum reliquiae. Leipzig, 1900, fasc. 1, 92–101 (gives the fragment of the Latin version).

Translations: English: G. HORNER, *loc. cit.* — *German:* BAUMSTARK, *loc. cit.*

Studies: A. HARNACK, Die Lehre der zwölf Apostel (TU 2, 1–2). Leipzig, 1884/1893, 193–241; *idem,* Die Quellen der sog. Apostolischen Kirchenordnung (TU 2, 5). Leipzig, 1886. — F. X. FUNK, Didascaliae et Constitutiones Apostolorum. Paderborn, 1905, 2, Proleg. XLII–XLIV.

CHAPTER II

THE WRITERS OF ASIA MINOR,
SYRIA AND PALESTINE

Not only in Egypt was Origen's influence strongly felt, his ideas reached far beyond the borders of his native country. Asia Minor, Syria and Palestine became a battlefield of his friends and opponents. It is interesting to note that even his adversaries owe him more than they admit. A typical example is Methodius. Two schools became the centers of the controversy; the one, at Caesarea in Palestine, founded by Origen himself, carried on his work after his death; the other, at Antioch in Syria, was established in opposition to his allegorical interpretation of Scripture.

THE SCHOOL OF CAESAREA

Caesarea was privileged to become Origen's refuge after his exile from Egypt (232). The school which he founded there developed after his death into a shelter for his literary bequest. His works formed the basis of a library which the presbyter Pamphilus enlarged to a centre of scholarship and learning. As its head he carried on the tradition of the great Master. Here it was that Gregory Thaumaturgos and Eusebius of Caesarea received their training and that the Cappadocians, Basil the Great, Gregory of Nyssa, and Gregory of Nazianzus, were inspired by Alexandrian theology.

Studies: H. R. NELZ, Die theologischen Schulen der morgenländischen Kirchen. Bonn, 1916, 40–44. — R. CADIOU, La bibliothèque de Césarée et la formation des chaînes: RSR 16 (1936) 474–483. — A. KNAUBER, Katechetenschule oder Schulkatechumenat?: TThZ 60 (1951) 260–262.

THE SCHOOL OF ANTIOCH

The school of Antioch was founded by Lucian of Samosata (312) in direct opposition to the excesses and fantasies of the allegorical method of Origen. It gave careful attention to the text itself and led its pupils into the sphere of literal elucidation and historical and grammatical study of Scripture. The scholars in the two different seats of learning were themselves convinced of a deep-seated discord, a fundamental contradiction, in their respective approaches. At Antioch the object was to find in Holy Writ its most obvious meaning; at Caesarea or Alexandria the search was for the figures of Christ. The one side accused allegory of destroying the value of the Bible as a record of the past, of travestying it into mythological fable; the other dubbed 'carnal' all who clung to the letter. Still between the two there was no absolute opposition; there was even broad agreement on an entire traditional exegesis; but special emphasis fell on distinct points of view. For Origen discovers types not just in certain episodes, but in every detail of the inspired word. Each line is filled with mystery. On the other hand Antioch made it a fundamental principle to see figures of Christ just occasionally, not always, in the Old Testament. Where the resemblance was marked and the analogy clear, only there would it admit a foreshadowing of the Saviour. Types were the exception, not the rule; the Incarnation was everywhere prepared, but not everywhere prefigured.

In short, the diversity of method was a diversity of mind that had already made itself felt in Greek philosophy. Alexandria's idealism and speculative bent owed inspiration to Plato, Antioch's realism and empiricism to Aristotle; the former inclined to mysticism, the latter to rationalism.

The beginnings of the school of Antioch seem to have been very modest. It never could boast a head like Origen. Nevertheless, it was the cradle of great exegesis. It reached its peak under the direction of Diodorus of Tarsus at the end of the fourth century. St. John Chrysostom was its most famous student and Theodore of Mopsuestia its most extreme. Its rationalistic tendency led to its becoming the womb of heresy; Lucian, its founder, was the teacher of Arius.

Studies: H. KIHN, Die Bedeutung der antiochenischen Schule auf exegetischem Gebiet. Weissenburg, 1866. — J. PHILIP DE BARJEAU, L'école exégétique d'Antioche. Paris, 1898. — H. R. NELZ, Die theologischen Schulen der morgenländischen Kirchen. Bonn, 1916. — L. DENNEFELD, Der alttestamentliche Kanon der antiochenischen Schule. Freiburg i. B., 1909. — F. VIGOUROUX, École exégétique d'Antioche: Dictionnaire de la Bible 1, 683–687. — C. BAUER, Der Kanon des hl. Joh. Chrysostomus: ThQ 105 (1924) 258–271. — A. VACCARI, La teoria esegetica antiochena: Bibl 15 (1934) 93–101. — J. GUILLET, Les Exégèses d'Alexandrie et d'Antioche. Conflit ou malentendu?: RSR 34 (1947) 257–302. — G. BARDY, The Exegetical School of Antioch, in: A. Robert and A. Tricot, Guide to the Bible. English translation by E. P. ARBEZ and M. R. P. McGUIRE, vol. 1. Rome–Tournai–Paris, 1951, 460–462.

GREGORY THE WONDER-WORKER

Gregory the Wonder-Worker (Thaumaturgos) was born of a high-ranking pagan family at Neocaesarea in Pontus about the year 213. Apparently, he was originally called Theodore and received the name Gregory only at baptism. After studying rhetoric and law in his home town, he was on the point of setting out with his brother, Athenodorus, for Berytos in Phoenicia to complete his education, when he was invited to Caesarea in Palestine by his sister; her husband had been appointed the imperial governor of Palestine. While there, he attended some of Origen's lectures and this was the turning point in his life:

Like some spark kindled within my soul there was kindled and blazed forth my love both toward Him, most desirable of all for His beauty unspeakable, the Word holy and altogether lovely, and toward this man his friend and prophet. Deeply stricken by it, I was led to neglect all that seemed to concern me: affairs, studies, even my favourite law, home and kindred there, no less than those among whom I was sojourning. One thing only was dear and affected by me: philosophy and its teacher, this divine man (*Address to Origen*, 6 SPCK).

He and his brother remained in Caesarea five years (233–238) in order to take Origen's whole course, both embracing Christianity. On the eve of their departure, Gregory thanked Origen in an academic Farewell Address, which is preserved to us and is a valuable source of information for Origen's personal history and method of teaching (cf. above, p. 39). A few years later, Phaedimus, the bishop of Amasea, consecrated him the first bishop of his native city, Neocaesarea. Gregory preached the Gospel in town and in countryside with such zeal and success that at his death but a handful of pagans remained in all Pontus. He took part in the council of Antioch in 265 and died in the reign of Aurelian (270–275). The legends which soon afterwards grew up around the first bishop of the province procured for him the title Thaumaturgos or Wonder-Worker, but, at the same time, they testify to the striking personality of this disciple of a great master. The Cappadocian Fathers of the fourth century venerated him as the founder of the Church of Cappadocia. Gregory of Nyssa has left us his Life, and three other biographies, all mythical in character, have been preserved.

Gregory of Nyssa's *biography* is found: MG 46, 893–958. — The *Syriac biography* in: P. BEDJAN, Acta martyrum et sanctorum 6, Paris, 1896, 83–106. — *German translation* by V. RYSSEL, Eine syrische Lebensgeschichte des Gregorius Thaumaturgus: Theol. Zeitschrift aus der Schweiz 11 (1894). — P. KOETSCHAU, Zur Lebensgeschichte Gregors des Wundertäters: Zeitschr. für wiss. Theologie 41 (1898) 211–250 deals with the relations between the Greek and Syriac Life. — For a *Georgian version*, cf. G. PERADZE, Die altchristl. Literatur in der georgischen Überlieferung: OC (1930) 90 f. — For the *Latin biography*, see A. PONCELET, La Vie latine de St. Gregoire Thaumaturge: RSR 1 (1910) 132–160, 567–569. (There is also an Armenian Life, cf. Poncelet, 155 ff.) — W. TELFER, The Latin Life of St. Gregory Thaumaturgos: JThSt 31 (1930) 142–155, 354–363; *idem*, The cultus of St. Gregory Thaumaturgos: HThR 29 (1936) 225–344. — A. SOLOVIEW, Saint Grégoire, patron de Bosnie: Byz 19 (1949) 263–279.

HIS WRITINGS

Gregory was a man of action, not a writer, and whatever he did compose was for a practical purpose, mostly in connection with his pastoral labors. The following works are extant:

1. *The Panegyric to Origen* (Εἰς Ὠριγένην προσφωνητικὸς καὶ πανηγυρικὸς λόγος)

As mentioned above, this panegyric is an oration delivered by Gregory on leaving the school of Origen at Caesarea. It expresses with great tenderness of feeling as well as polish of style his sense of obligation to his revered guide. After an introduction (1–3), in which he declares himself unable to praise his teacher adequately, he thanks (3–15) first of all God, the giver of all good gifts, then his guardian angel, who had led him and his brother to Caesarea, and finally his great master, who filled his students with enthusiasm for sacred knowledge. In the course of his tribute of affectionate gratitude Gregory gives a very detailed and valuable description of Origen's method of instruction (cf. above, p. 39f). At the end, he expresses his regrets at leaving Caesarea (16–17) and asks for the blessing and prayers of his preceptor (18–19). The panegyric is an important document for the history of Christian education.

Editions: MG 10, 1049–1104. — P. KOETSCHAU, Des Gregorios Thaumaturgos Dankrede an Origenes (SQ 9). Freiburg, 1894.

Translations: English: S. D. F. SALMOND, ANL 20; ANF 6, 21–39. — M. METCALFE, Gregory Thaumaturgos Addres to Origen (SPCK). London-New York, 1920. — *German:* H. BOURIER, BKV² (1912). — *Russian:* N. J. SAGARDA, Petrograd, 1916.

Studies: V. RYSSEL, Gregorius Thaumaturgos. Sein Leben und seine Schriften. Leipzig, 1880. — C. WEYMAN, Zu Gregorios Thaumaturgos: Phil 55 (1896) 462–464. — A. BRINKMANN, Gregors des Thaumaturgen Panegyricus auf Origenes: RhM 56 (1901) 55–76.

2. *The Creed or Exposition of Faith* (Ἔκθεσις πίστεως)

Gregory composed a short Creed that, though restricted to the dogma of the Trinity, gives a very exact statement of it:

There is one God, the Father of the living Word, who is His subsistent Wisdom and Power and Eternal Image: perfect Begetter of the perfect Begotten, Father of the only-begotten Son. There is one Lord, Only of the Only, God of God, Image and Likeness of Deity, Efficient Word, Wisdom comprehensive of the constitution of all things, and Power formulative of the whole creation, true Son of true Father, Invisible of Invisible, and Incorruptible of Incorruptible, and Immortal of Immortal, and Eternal of Eternal. And there is one Holy Spirit, having His subsistence from God, and being made manifest by the Son, to wit to men: Image of the Son, Perfect Image of the Perfect; Life, the Cause of the living; Holy Fount; Sanctity, the Supplier, or Leader, of Sanctification; in whom is manifested God the Father, who is above all and in all, and God the Son, who is through all. There is a perfect Trinity, in glory and eternity and sovereignty, neither divided nor estranged. Wherefore there is nothing either created or in servitude in the Trinity; nor anything superinduced, as if at some former period it was non-existent, and at some later period it was introduced. And thus neither was the Son ever wanting to the Father, nor the Spirit to the Son; but without variation and without change, the same Trinity abideth ever (ANF, EP 611).

The Greek text of this Creed, besides being incorporated in Gregory of Nyssa's biography, is also extant in a large number of manuscripts; we have, in addition, a Latin version by Rufinus (*Hist. eccl.* 7,26) and a Syriac translation.

Editions: MG 10, 983–988. — C. P. CASPARI, Alte und neue Quellen zur Geschichte des Taufsymbols und der Glaubensregel. Christiania, 1879, 1–34 (gives the Greek text, two Latin translations and the Syriac version).

Translations: English: S. D. F. SALMOND, ANL 20; ANF 6, 7. — *German:* F. KATTEN-BUSCH, Das Apostolische Symbol 1. Leipzig, 1894, 338–342. — *French:* J. LEBRETON, in: A. Fliche-V. Martin, Histoire de l'Église, t. 2. Paris, 1946, 335–336.

Studies: C. P. CASPARI, *loc. cit.* — F. KATTENBUSCH, *loc. cit.* — L. FROIDEVAUX, Le symbole de saint Grégoire le Thaumaturge: RSR 19 (1929) 193–247.

3. *The so-called Canonical Epistle* (Ἐπιστολὴ κανονική)

The *Epistle*, addressed to some unknown bishop who had consulted the author, derives its name from the fact that it has been embodied in the collection of Canonical Epistles of the Greek Church. One of the most ancient treatises on casuistry, it was occasioned by the doubts and difficulties arising from the invasion of the Boradi and Goths, who, after the defeat of Decius (251), had devastated Pontus and Bithynia. The Christians of Pontus, whom the Goths had taken captive and then released, were vexed with scruples at having eaten pagan food. Women had been raped. Some of the Christians had made common cause with the barbarians, showing them the way, pointing out the houses worth pillaging, even enrolling among them and shaping their evil deeds. Gregory in his *Epistle* gives advice to his fellow-bishop regarding such delinquents. He shows himself firmly resolved to re-establish order and discipline but at the same time to be merciful, mild and tolerant. The last canon is especially interesting for the history of the penitential discipline; it enumerates the different classes of penitents:

> Weeping takes place without the gate of the oratory; and the offender standing there ought to implore the faithful as they enter to offer up prayer on his behalf. Listening to the word, again, takes place within the gate in the porch, where the offender ought to stand until the catechumens depart, and thereafter he should go forth. For let him hear the Scriptures and doctrine, it is said, and then be put forth, and reckoned unfit for the privilege of prayer. Prostration, again, is that one remain within the gate of the temple, and go forth along with the catechumens. Restoration is that one be associated with the faithful, and go not forth with the catechumens;

and last of all comes the participation in the holy mysteries (ANF).

Editions: MG 10, 1019–1048. — ROUTH, Reliquiae sacrae, 2nd ed. 3, 251–283.

Translations: English: S. D. F. SALMOND, ANL 20; ANF 6, 18–20.

Studies: RYSSEL, *loc. cit.* 15–16, 29–31. — J. DRÄSEKE, Der kanonische Brief des Gregorios von Neocaesarea: Jahrb. für prot. Theol. 7 (1881) 724–756; *idem,* Johannes Zonaras' Kommentar zum kanonischen Brief des Gregorios von Neocaesarea: Zeitschrift für wiss. Theol. 37 (1894) 246–260.

4. *The Metaphrase of Ecclesiastes* (Μετάφρασις εἰς τὸν ἐκκλησιαστὴν Σολομῶνος)

This is nothing more than a paraphrase of the Septuagint text of Ecclesiastes. Though assigned to Gregory of Nazianzus by almost all the manuscripts and printed among his works by Migne (MG 36,669f), yet it is regarded by both St. Jerome (*De vir. ill.* 65) and Rufinus (*Hist. eccl.* 7,25) as an authentic work of Gregory the Wonder-Worker.

Edition: MG 10, 987–1018.

Translations: English: S. D. F. SALMOND, ANL 20; ANF 6, 9–17.

Studies: RYSSEL, *loc. cit.* 27–29. — KOETSCHAU, *loc. cit.* XXIII.

5. *On the Impassibility and Passibility of God*

This treatise, addressed to a certain Theopompus, is extant in a Syriac translation only. It contains a philosophical dialogue between the author and the addressee about the incompatibility of suffering with the idea of God. God cannot be subject to suffering. However, He is free in His decisions. By His voluntary suffering the Son of God defeated death and proved his impassibility.

Editions: P. DE LAGARDE, Analecta Syriaca 46–64. — J. B. PITRA, Analecta sacra 4, 103–120, 363–376.

Translations: Latin: J. B. PITRA, *loc. cit.* — *German:* V. RYSSEL, Gregorius Thaumaturgos 71–99.

SPURIOUS WRITINGS

The treatise *To Philagrius on Consubstantiality*, preserved in Syriac, under Gregory's name, is of doubtful authenticity. Containing a brief exposition of the trinitarian doctrine, it is nothing but a translation of the Greek *Epistle to Euagrius* found among the works of Gregory of Nazianzus (MG 37,383–386) and of Gregory of Nyssa (MG 46, 1101–1108).

Also doubtful are the treatise *To Tatian On the Soul* and six homilies preserved in Armenian.

In his *Epistle* 210 Basil the Great refers to a *Dialogue with Aelianus* by Gregory Thaumaturgos, of which the Sabellians had made use for their own purpose. Nothing is extant of this dialogue today.

The same is true of various letters which St. Jerome mentions (*De vir.ill.* 65; *Epist.* 33,4).

Studies: W. BOUSSET, Apophtegmata. Tübingen, 1923, 340 f. (to Philagrius on consubstantiality). — F. J. DÖLGER, Sonnenscheibe und Sonnenstrahl in der Logos- und Geisttheologie des Gregorios Thaumaturgos: AC 6 (1940) 74–75. — M. JUGIE, Les homélies mariales attribuées à saint Grégoire le Thaumaturge: AB 43 (1925) 86–95. — C. MARTIN, Note sur deux homélies attribuées à saint Grégoire le Thaumaturge: RHE 24 (1928) 364–373. — EINARSON, CPh (1933) 129 f.: To Tatian On the Soul in a Syriac manuscript. — An edition of the treatise Περὶ τῆς τοῦ θεοῦ λόγου σαρκώσεως will be found in: E. SCHWARTZ, Acta Conciliorum oecumenicorum I 6, 146–151. — B. MARX, Procliana. 1940, 62 f.

FIRMILIAN OF CAESAREA

Firmilian, bishop of Caesarea in Cappadocia, was a contemporary of Gregory the Wonder-Worker, whom he met as a member of Origen's circle and whose regard for the Alexandrian teacher he shared: 'He displayed such esteem for Origen, that at one time he would summon him to his own parts for the benefit of the churches; at another, journey himself to Judaea, and spend some time with him for his own progress in divine knowledge' (Euseb., *Hist. eccl.*, 6,27). Both bishops attended the first two synods at Antioch that condemned the errors of Paul of Samosata. Firmilian died shortly after the second in 268. He was one of the outstanding prelates of his time. Of his writings there is extant only one letter, addressed to St. Cyprian of Carthage and dealing with the vexed question of the rebaptism of heretics. It represents the answer to a lost letter of Cyprian's on the same subject and was for this reason preserved in a Latin translation in the collection of the latter's epistles (*Epist.* 75). The original Greek is lost. The version shows all the peculiarities of Cyprian's Latin and was therefore most probably made by him. It seems to have been written about the year A.D. 256.

Firmilian assures Cyprian that he is in full agreement with his view that baptism conferred by heretics must be regarded as invalid; he criticizes Pope Stephen sharply and rejects his opinion with unusual vehemence and acerbity.

Edition: W. HARTEL, CSEL 3, 2 (1871) 810–827.

Translations: English: R. E. WALLIS, ANL 8; ANF 5, 390–397. — *German:* J. BAER, BKV 60 (1928). — *French:* L. BAYARD, S. Cyprien. Correspondance. Paris, 1925.

Studies: J. ERNST, Die Echtheit des Briefes Firmilians über den Ketzertaufstreit in neuer Beleuchtung: ZkTh 20 (1896) 364–367. — E. W. BENSON, Cyprian, His Life, His Times, His Work. London, 1897, 377–386. — F. LOOFS, Paulus von Samosata (TU 44, 5). Leipzig, 1924, 44, 56 f.

METHODIUS

One of the most distinguished adversaries of Origen was Methodius. As he is not mentioned in Eusebius' *Ecclesiastical History*, little is known of his life. According to F. Diekamp, he was most probably bishop of Philippi in Macedonia, but he must have spent a considerable period of his life in Lycia, so that for a long time he was thought to have been bishop of Olympus, a little town in Lycia. He died a martyr A.D. 311, evidently in Chalcis in Euboea.

Methodius was a highly educated man and an excellent theologian. He refuted Origen's doctrine of the pre-existence of the soul and his spiritualistic concept of the resurrection of the body. Unfortunately, of the great number of his treatises very few remain.

Editions: MG 18. — G. N. BONWETSCH, GCS 27 (1917). — A. VAILLANT, PO 22, 5 (1930).

Translations: English: W. R. CLARK, ANL 16, 1–230; ANF 6, 309–402. Other translations below.

Studies: G. SALMON, Methodius: Dictionary of Christian Biography 3, 909–911. — AMANN, DTC 10, 1606–1614. — G. N. BONWETSCH, Die Theologie des Methodius von Olympus. Berlin, 1903. — L. FENDT, Sünde und Buße in den Schriften des Methodius v. O.: Katholik (1905) I, 24–45. — E. BUONAIUTI, The Ethics and Eschatology of Methodius of Olympus: HThR 14 (1921) 255–266. — A. BIAMONTI, L'etica di Metodio di Olimpo: RSFR 3 (1922) 272–288; *idem,* L'escatologia di Metodio di Olimpo: RSFR 4 (1923) 182–202. — F. DIEKAMP, Über den Bischofssitz des hl. Märtyrers und Kirchenvaters Methodius: ThQ (1928) 285–308. Cf. A. VAILLANT PO 22, 5 (1930) 636. — J. FARGES, Les idées morales et religieuses de Méthode d'Olympe. Paris, 1929. — F. BOSTRÖM, Studier till den grekiska theologins fräsingslära med särskild hänsyn till Methodius av O. och Athanasius av Alex. Lund, 1932. Cf. RHE

(1933) 991–993. — E. MERSCH, Le corps mystique du Christ, 2nd ed. 1. Louvain, 1936, 276 f. — R. DEVREESSE, Anciens commentateurs grecs de l'Octateuque: Méthode d'Olympe: RBibl (1935) 166–191. — G. BARDY, La vie spirituelle d'après les Pères des trois premiers siècles. Paris 1935, 301–316. — F. BADURINA, Doctrina S. Methodii de Ol. de peccato originali. Rome, 1942. — H. CHADWICK, Origen, Celsus, and the Resurrection of the Body: HThR (1948) 82–102.

1. *The Banquet or On Virginity* (Συμπόσιον ἢ περὶ ἀγνείας)

A great reader of Plato, he loved to imitate his dialogues. *The Banquet* was evidently designed to be a Christian counterpart to the philosopher's. Ten virgins sing here the praises of virginity. All extol virginity as the perfect Christian life and the pre-eminent means of imitating Christ. At the end Thecla intones an enthusiastic hymn (of 24 verses) to Christ, the Bridegroom, and the Church, his Bride, in which the chorus of the virgins sings the refrain. It begins as follows:

> Thecla. From above, O virgins, the sound of a noise
>   that awakes the dead has come,
>   bidding us all to meet the Bridegroom
>   in white robes,
>   and with torches towards the east.
>   Arise, before the King enters within the gates.
>
> Chorus. I keep myself pure for Thee,
>   O Bridegroom,
>   and holding a lighted torch
>   I go to meet Thee.
>
> Thecla. Fleeing from the sorrowful happiness of mortals,
>   and having despised the luxuriant delights
>   of life and its love,
>   I desire to be protected
>   under Thy life-giving arms,
>   and to behold Thy beauty for ever,
>   O blessed One.
>
> Chorus. I keep myself pure for Thee,
>   O Bridegroom,
>   and holding a lighted torch
>   I go to meet Thee.
>
> Thecla. Leaving marriage and the beds of mortals
>   and my golden home for Thee, O King,
>   I have come in undefiled robes,

in order that I might enter with Thee
within Thy happy bridal chamber.

Chorus. I keep myself pure for Thee,
O Bridegroom, etc.

Thecla. Having escaped, O blessed One,
from the innumerable wiles of the serpent,
and moreover, from the flame of fire,
and from the mortal-destroying assaults
of wild beasts,
I await Thee from heaven.

Chorus. I keep myself pure for Thee,
O Bridegroom, etc.

Thecla. I forget my own country, O Lord,
through desire of Thy grace.
I forget also the company of virgins, my fellows,
the desire even of mother and of kindred,
for thou, O Christ, art all things to me.

Chorus. I keep myself pure for Thee,
O Bridegroom, etc.

Thecla. Giver of life art Thou, O Christ.
Hail, light that never sets,
receive this praise.
The company of virgins call upon Thee,
Perfect Flower, Love, Joy, Prudence, Wisdom, Word.

Chorus. I keep myself pure for Thee,
O Bridegroom, etc.

Thecla. With open gates,
O beauteously adorned Queen,
admit us within thy chambers.
O spotless, gloriously triumphant Bride,
breathing beauty,
we stand by Christ, robed as He is,
celebrating thy happy nuptials,
O youthful maiden.

Chorus. I keep myself pure for Thee,
O Bridegroom, etc.

(11,2,1–7 ANF).

This Queen, the Church, is adorned by both the blossoms of
virginity and the fruits of motherhood:

For the prophet's word compares the Church to a flower-covered and variegated meadow, adorned and crowned not only with the flowers of virginity, but also with those of child-bearing and of continence; for it is written: 'In embroidered garments with golden fringes the Queen takes her place to the right of the Bridegroom' (Ps. 44, 10 and 14) (*ibid.* 2,7,50).

We notice the influence of Irenaeus' doctrine of recapitulation (cf. vol. I, p. 295 ff), in the statement that, because the first Adam sinned, God undertook to re-create him in the Incarnation, but Methodius proposes a much more absolute and complete re-creation, and his ecclesiology is intimately connected with this idea of the second. The second Eve is to Irenaeus Mary, but to Methodius the Church:

Whence it was that the apostle directly referred to Christ the words that had been spoken of Adam. For thus will it be most certainly agreed that the Church is formed out of his bones and flesh; and it was for this cause that the Word, leaving His Father in heaven, came down to be 'joined to His wife' (Eph. 5,31); and slept in the trance of His passion, and willingly suffered death for her, that He might present the Church to Himself glorious and blameless, having cleansed her by the laver (Eph. 5, 26 –27), for the receiving of the spiritual and blessed seed, which is sown by Him who with whispers implants it in the depths of the mind; and is conceived and formed by the Church, as by a woman, so as to give birth and nourishment to virtue. For in this way, too, the command, 'Increase and multiply' (Gen. 1,18) is fully fulfilled, the Church increasing daily in greatness and beauty and multitude, by the union and communion of the Word, who now still comes down to us and falls into a trance by the memorial of his passion; for otherwise the Church could not conceive believers, and give them new birth by the laver of regeneration, unless Christ, emptying Himself for their sake, that He might be contained by them, as I said, through the recapitulation of His passion, should die again, coming down from heaven, and being 'joined to His wife,' the Church, should provide for a certain power being taken from His own side, so that all who are built up in Him should grow up, those who are born again by the laver, receiving of His bones and of His flesh, that is, of His Holiness and of His glory (3,8,70–72 ANF).

Reading such passages, we are surprised to learn that Methodius was one of Origen's adversaries, since the latter's *Commentary on the Canticle of Canticles* has the same ideas and the same allegory and follows the same mystical interpretation. In fact, it was only later that Methodius set out to refute the Alexandrian teacher. In his first writings he seems to have given great praise to him, because, according to St. Jerome (*Adv. Ruf.* 1,11), Pamphilus in his *Apology for Origen* reminds Methodius that formerly he had entertained a very high opinion of the great doctor.

The Banquet is the only writing of Methodius of which we have the complete Greek text. Of the other works we possess a more or less complete Slavonic rendering and some Greek fragments.

Edition: G. N. BONWETSCH, GCS 27 (1917) 1–141.

Translations: English: W. R. CLARK, ANL 16; ANF 6, 309–355. — *French:* J. FARGES, Méthode d'Olympe, Le banquet des dix vierges. Paris, 1932. — *Italian:* P. UBALDI, Turin, 1925, — *German:* L. FENDT, BKV² 2 (1911). — *Spanish:* B. VIZMANOS, Las Virgenes Cristianas. Madrid, 1949, 989–1088.

Studies: G. MERCATI, Emendazione a Metodio d'Olimpo (Simposio 11, p. 290): Didascaleion (1927) 2, 25–29. — P. HESELER, Zum Symposium des Methodius I: BNJ 6 (1928) 95–118. — J. MARTIN, Die Geschichte einer literarischen Form. 1931, 285 ff. — P. HESELER, Zum Symposium des Methodius II. Überlieferungs- und Textgeschichtliches: BNJ 10 (1933) 325–341. — M. MARGHERITIS, L'influenza di Platone sul pensiero e sull'arte di S. Metodio d'Olimpo: Studi dedicati alla memoria di Paolo Ubaldi. Milan, 1937, 401–412. — G. LAZZATI, La tecnica dialogica nel Simposio di Metodio d'Olimpo: *ibid.*, 117–124.

2. *The Treatise on Free Will* (Περὶ τοῦ αὐτεξουσίου)

The Slavonic version bears the title *On God, Matter and Free Will*, and this corresponds more to the contents. It aims to prove in the form of a dialogue that the free will of man is responsible for evil. The bad cannot be thought of as originating in God nor is it uncreated matter nor eternal like God. In the course of the discussion, Methodius rejects Origen's idea of an indefinite succession of worlds. It seems that the treatise is directed against the dualistic system of the Valentinians and other Gnostics. The greater part of the work is extant in Greek in fragments, and the whole text, except for a few lacunae, in the Slavonic version.

Furthermore, it is extensively quoted by Eznik of Kolb, the Armenian apologist of the fifth century, in his *Refutation of the Sects*, and thus large passages are preserved for us translated into his native language.

Editions: G. N. BONWETSCH, GCS 27 (1917) 143–206. — A. VAILLANT, Le De autexusio de Méthode d'Olympe, version slave et texte grec édit. et trad. en franç.: PO 22, 5, 631–889.

Translations: English: W. R. CLARK, ANL 16; ANF 6, 356–363. — *French:* A. VAILLANT, *loc. cit.* – J. FARGES, Méthode d'Olympe, Du libre arbitre. Paris, 1929. — *German:* G. N. BONWETSCH, *loc. cit.*

Studies: G. N. BONWETSCH, Die Theologie des Methodius 27–32. — F. J. DÖLGER, Ein Wahlspruch für wissenschaftlichen Redestreit bei Methodius von Philippi: AC 6 (1950) 133.

3. *On the Resurrection* ('Αγλαοφῶν ἢ περὶ ἀναστάσεως)

The original title was *Aglaophon or on the Resurrection* because this dialogue reports a discussion taking place in the house of the physician Aglaophon at Patara. It refutes in three books Origen's theory of resurrection in a spiritual body and defends the identity of the human body with the body of the resurrection:

I cannot endure the trifling of some who shamelessly do violence to Scripture, in order that their opinion, that the resurrection is without flesh, may find support; supposing rational bones and flesh, and in different ways changing it backwards and forwards by allegorizing (1,2 ANF).

Now the corruptible and mortal putting on immortality, what else is it but that which is 'sown in corruption and raised in incorruption' (1 Cor. 5,42),—for the soul is not corruptible or mortal; but this which is mortal and corrupting is of flesh,—in order that, 'as we have borne the image of the earthy, we shall also bear the image of the heavenly' (1 Cor. 15,49)? For the image of the earthy which we have borne is this, 'Dust thou art, and unto dust shalt thou return' (Gen. 3,19). But the image of the heavenly is the resurrection from the dead, and incorruption, in order that 'as Christ was raised from the dead by the glory of the Father, so we also should walk in newness of life' (Rom. 6,4). But if any one were to think that the earthy image is the flesh itself, but the heavenly image some other spiritual body besides the flesh; let him first consider that Christ, the heavenly man, when he appeared, bore the same form of limbs and the same image of flesh as ours, through which also He, who was not man, became man, that 'as in Adam all die, even so in Christ shall all be made alive' (1 Cor. 15,22). For if He bore flesh for any other reason than that of setting the flesh free, and raising it up, why did He bear flesh superfluously, as He purposed neither to save it, nor to raise it up. But the Son of God does nothing superfluously. He did not then take the form of a servant uselessly, but to raise it up and save it. For He truly was made man, and died, and not in mere appearance, but that He might truly be shown to be the first begotten from the dead, changing the earthy into the heavenly, and the mortal into the immortal (*De resurr.* 1,13 ANF).

In addition, Methodius refutes Origen's tenets about the pre-existence of the soul and the flesh as the spirit's prison, and also his ideas regarding the purpose and end of the world. In the beginning man was immortal in soul and body. Death and the separation of body from soul were caused by the envy of the devil only. It is the purpose of the redemption to unite that which has been unnaturally divided. For this reason man has to be remodelled:

It appears, then, as if an eminent craftsman were to cast over again a noble image, wrought by himself of gold or other material, and beautifully proportioned in all its members, upon his suddenly perceiving that it had been mutilated by some infamous man, who, too envious to endure the image being beautiful, spoiled it, and thus enjoyed the empty pleasure of indulged jealousy. For take notice, most wise Aglaophon, that, if the artificer wish that that upon which he has bestowed so much pains and care and labor, shall be quite free from injury, he will be impelled to melt it down, and restore it to its former condition... Now God's plan seems to me to have been the same as that which prevails among ourselves. For seeing man, His fairest work, corrupted by envious treachery, He could not endure, with His love for man, to leave him in such a condition, lest he should be for ever faulty, and bear the blame to eternity;

but dissolved him again into his original materials, in order that, by remodelling, all the blemishes in him might waste away and disappear. For the melting down of the statue in the former case corresponds to the death and dissolution of the body in the latter, and the remoulding of the material in the former, to the resurrection after death in the latter... For I call your attention to this, that, as I said, after man's transgression the Great Hand was not content to leave as a trophy of victory its own work, debased by the Evil One, who wickedly injured it from motives of envy; but moistened and reduced it to clay, as a potter breaks up a vessel, that by the remodelling of it all the blemishes and bruises in it may disappear, and it may be made afresh faultless and pleasing (*De resurr.* 1,6–7 ANF).

Although the dialogue suffers to a certain extent from lack of clear arrangement, the work as such is an important contribution to theology. The refutation of Origen's ideas is conducted on a high level and the speculations are no less lofty than those of his opponent. St. Jerome, not too well disposed on the whole towards Methodius, signalizes (*De vir. ill.* 33) this treatise as an *opus egregium.*

There are only fragments extant of the Greek text. Fortunately, Epiphanius incorporated an extensive and very important passage (1,20–2,8,10) into his *Panarion* (*Haer.* 64,12–62). The Slavonic version covers all three books but abbreviates the last two.

Edition: G. N. BONWETSCH, GCS 27 (1917) 217–424.

Translations: English: W. R. CLARK, ANL 16; ANF 6, 364–377. — *German:* G. N BONWETSCH, *loc. cit.,* gives the Slavonic version in German translation.

Studies: L. ATZBERGER, Geschichte der christlichen Eschatologie innerhalb der vor-nicänischen Zeit. Freiburg i.B., 1896, 484–490. — G. N. BONWETSCH, Die Theologie des Methodius 32–42. — J. R. M. HITCHCOCK, Loofs' Asiatic source (IQA) and Ps. Justin De resurrectione: ZNW (1937) 35–60. — H. CHADWICK, Origen, Celsus, and the Resurrection of the Body: HThR (1948) 82–102.

4. *On Life and Reasonable Actions*

This treatise appears in the Slavonic translation between the two dialogues *On Free Will* and *On the Resurrection.* The Greek original has been completely lost. The contents consist of an exhortation to be satisfied with what God has given us in this life and to put all our hope on the world to come.

Edition: G. N. BONWETSCH, GCS 27 (1917) 207–216: The old Slavic version in German translation.

5. *Exegetical Works*

After the dialogue *On the Resurrection* there follow in the Slavonic version three exegetical works. The first is addressed to two women, Frenope and Kilonia, and deals with *The Discrimination of Food and the Young Cow Mentioned In Leviticus* (read: *Numbers* 19). It is an allegorical interpretation of Old Testament laws regarding the different kinds of food and the red cow whose ashes were to be sprinkled on unclean persons. The second treatise, entitled *To Sistelius On Leprosy*, is a dialogue between Eubulius and Sistelius on the allegorical sense of Leviticus 13. There are some Greek fragments extant of this work besides the Slavonic version. The third treatise allegorizes Prov. 30,15 ff (the leech) and Ps. 18,2 'The heavens show forth the glory of God.'

Editions: G. N. BONWETSCH, GCS 27 (1917) 425–447: De cibis; 449–474: De lepra; 475–489: De sanguisuga; 491–500: De creatis.

6. *Against Porphyry*

St. Jerome mentions (*De vir. ill.* 83; *Epist.* 48,13; *Epist.* 70,3) on different occasions Methodius' *Books Against Porphyry* with great esteem. It is unfortunate that this work has been completely lost because Methodius was the first to refute the fifteen polemical books *Against the Christians* written by the Neo-Platonic philosopher Porphyry about the year A.D. 270.

Also lost are his works *On the Pythoness, On the Martyrs* and his *Commentaries on Genesis and on the Canticle of Canticles (De vir. ill.* 83).

Fragments: G. N. BONWETSCH, GCS 27 (1917) 501–507: Contra Porphyrium; 509–519: In Job; 520: De martyribus. — R. DEVREESSE, Anciens commentateurs grecs de l'Octateuque: RBibl (1935) 179: Commentary on Genesis.

Pseudo-Methodius: M. KMOSKO, Das Rätsel des Pseudomethodius: Byz 6 (1931) 273–296. — STOCKS, BNJ 15 (1939) 25–57.

SEXTUS JULIUS AFRICANUS

Sextus Julius Africanus was born at Jerusalem (Aelia Capitolina), not in Africa, as Bardenhewer and others thought. He served as an officer in the army of Septimius Severus and participated in his expedition against the principality of Edessa in the year 195. This was possibly the occasion of his good relationship with its Christian dynasty. From a papyrus fragment of the eighteenth book of his work *Kestoi* (*Oxyrh. Pap.* III No. 142,39ff), we know that he set up a library for the Emperor Alexander Severus at Rome 'in the Pantheon near the baths of Alexander.' At Alexandria in Egypt he attended the lectures of Heraclas and became one of Origen's friends. He lived later on in Emmaus (Nicopolis) in Palestine and died after 240. Although later tradition made him a bishop of Emmaus, he never held any ecclesiastical office. He dedicated himself more to secular than sacred sciences.

HIS WORKS

1. *Chronicles* (Χρονογραφίαι)

His *Chronicles* represent the first synchronistic history of the world. The events of the Bible and the Hellenistic and Jewish compendia are arranged with dates paralleled from the creation to 221 A.D., the fourth year of Elagabalus; 5500 years are counted to the birth of Christ. According to Julius Africanus the earth was to last in all 6000 years, and thus, 500 years after the birth of Christ, the Sabbath of the world, the millenium of Christ's Kingdom would begin. Apparently, therefore, the author had a chiliastic purpose in composing his work. He lacks the critical attitude towards his sources. The five books of the *Chronicles*, of which only fragments are preserved, became a mine of information for Eusebius and later historians.

Editions: Fragments MG 10, 63–94. — ROUTH, Reliquiae sacrae, 2nd ed. 2, 238–309; cf. 357–509.

Translations: S. D. F. SALMOND, ANL 9, 2; ANF 6, 130–138.

Studies: H. GELZER, Sextus Julius Africanus und die byzantinische Chronographie, 2 vols. Leipzig, 1880/98. — C. TRIEBER, Die Chronologie des Julius Afrikanus: NGWG Philol.-hist. Klasse (1880) 49–76. — AMANN, DTC 8, 1921–1925. — W. KROLL-J. SICKENBERGER, PWK 10, 116–125. — G. BARDY, Chronique d'histoire des origines chrétiennes: RAp (1933) 257–271. — C. WENDEL, Versuch einer Deutung der Hippolyt-Statue: ThStKr 108 (1937/38) 362–369. — J. J. KOTSONÈS, Ἰούλιος ὁ Ἀφρικανός, ὁ πρῶτος χριστιανὸς χρονόγραφος: Θεολογία 15 (1937) 227–238.

2. Kestoi (Κεστοί, *Embroideries*)

The *Kestoi* is an encyclopaedic work of twenty-four books dedicated to the Emperor Alexander Severus. The title *Embroideries* indicates the variety of subjects with which the author deals, ranging from military tactics to medicine, agriculture and magic. The large fragments that are preserved show that Julius Africanus was not only uncritical in his studies but also a believer in all kinds of superstition and magic.

Editions: J. R. VIEILLEFOND, Fragments des Cestes provenant de la collection des tacticiens grecs. Paris, 1932; *idem*, Un fragment inédit de Julius Africanus: REG (1933) 197–203. — B. P. GRENFELL and A. S. HUNT, The Oxyrhynchus Papyri 3. London, 1903, No. 412.

Studies: W. A. OLDFATHER and A. S. PEASE, On the Κεστοί of Julius Africanus: AJPh (1918) 405–406. — W. BAUER, Rechtgläubigkeit und Ketzerei im ältesten Christentum (BHT 10). Tübingen, 1934, 11 f., 162–167.

3. Two Letters

We know of two letters written by Julius Africanus. The one, addressed to Origen about the year A.D. 240, questions the authenticity of the history of Susanna. Here the author shows more sound judgment and critical sense than in his *Embroideries*. The entire text of this letter is extant (cf. above, p. 74). The other, preserved in fragments only, is his letter to Aristides, in which he tries to harmonize the various genealogies of Jesus in the gospels of Matthew and Luke.

Editions: W. REICHARDT, Die Briefe des Sextus Julius Africanus an Aristides und Origenes (TU 34, 3). Leipzig, 1909.

Translations: English: S. D. F. SALMOND, ANL 9, 2; ANF 6, 125–127: The Letter to Aristides. — F. CROMBIE, ANL 10; ANF 4, 385: The Letter to Origen. A translation of Origen's letter to Africanus: ANF 4, 386–392.

Studies: P. VOGT, Der Stammbaum Christi (Biblische Studien 12, 3). Freiburg i.B., 1907, 1–34. — A. HARNACK, Die Sammlung der Briefe des Origenes und sein Briefwechsel mit Julius Africanus: SAB 1925. — J. GRANGER, Julius Africanus and the Western Text: JThSt 35 (1934) 361–368. — E. H. BLAKENEY, Julius Africanus: A Letter to Origen: Theology 29 (1934) 164–169. — B. ALTANER, Augustinus und Julius Africanus: VC 4 (1950) 37–45.
Other Studies: K. BIHLMEYER, Die syrischen Kaiser zu Rom. Rottenburg 1916, 152–157. — A. HARNACK, Julius Africanus, der Bibliothekar des Kaisers Alexander Severus: Aufsätze F. Milkau gewidmet. Leipzig, 1921, 142–146. — J. GRANGER, Julius Africanus and the Library of the Pantheon: TJhSt 34 (1935) 157–161. —

R. McKenzie, A Note on Julius Africanus: CR (1933) 9. — J. Stroux, Zu Quintilian: Phil (1936) 222–237. — F. J. Dölger, Mein Herr und Sohn: AC 6 (1941) 66–67. — S. Björck, Apsyrtus, Julius Africanus et l'hippiatric grecque. Uppsala, 1944. — R. M. Grant, Patristica: VC 3 (1949) 225–229.

PAUL OF SAMOSATA AND MALCHION OF ANTIOCH

Paul, a native of Samosata, the capital of the Syrian province of Commagene, was governor and secretary of the treasury (*procurator ducenarius*) to Queen Zenobia of Palmyra and, from the year 260, bishop of Antioch. Eusebius (*Hist. eccl.* 7,27,2) informs us that soon after his consecration he 'espoused low and mean views as to Christ, contrary to the Church's teaching, namely, that He was in His nature an ordinary man.' Three synods were held at Antioch between the years 264–268 to deal with this heresy, the first two with no practical result. The third in 268 declared the teaching of Paul untenable and pronounced a sentence of deposition. The credit for the final conviction and condemnation belongs to the priest Malchion:

> In Aurelian's day a final synod of an exceedingly large number of bishops was assembled, and the leader of the heresy at Antioch, being unmasked and now clearly condemned of heterodoxy by all, was excommunicated from the Catholic Church under heaven. The person foremost in calling him to account and in utterly refuting his attempts at concealment was Malchion, a learned man, who also was head of a school of rhetoric, one of the Greek educational establishments at Antioch; and moreover, for the surpassing sincerity of his faith in Christ he had been deemed worthy of the priesthood of that community. In fact this man had stenographers take notes as he held a disputation with Paul which we know to be extant even to this day; and he alone of them all was able to unmask that crafty and deceitful person.

> The pastors, then, who had been assembled together, indited unanimously a single letter personally to Dionysius, bishop of Rome, and Maximus, of Alexandria, and sent it throughout all the provinces. In it they make manifest to all their zeal, and also the perverse heterodoxy of Paul, as well as the arguments and questions that they addressed to him;

and moreover, they describe the man's whole life and conduct (Euseb., *Hist. eccl.* 7,29,1–30,1 LCL).

Fragments of the debate between Paul and Malchion, taken from the stenographic records, are extant in Leontius of Byzantium, the Emperor Justinian and Peter the Deacon. According to St. Jerome (*De vir. ill.* 71) Malchion was also the author of the encyclical sent out by the bishops after the synod. Of this Eusebius (*ibid.*) quotes several passages, which, however, deal more with Paul's morals and character, copies of the minutes of the meeting having been attached to the letters. St. Hilary (*De synodis*, 81,86) and St. Basil (*Epist.* 52) say that the council which condemned Paul repudiated expressly the word ὁμοούσιος (*consubstantial*) as being unfit to describe the relation between Father and Son. But we do not know, in what sense Paul had made use of this term. Most probably he had given it a modalist interpretation, doing away with the difference of personality existing between the Father and the Son. He did not recognize three persons in God, but according to Leontius (*De sectis* 3,3) he merely 'gave the name of Father to God who created all things, that of Son, to him who was purely man, and that of the Spirit, to the grace which resided in the apostles.' Jesus was greater than Moses and the prophets, but he was not the Word. He was a man equal to us, though better in every respect. Thus the trinity which Paul recognized was only a trinity of names; clearly he shared the views of Monarchianism and his Christological ideas remind one of the modalist form of Adoptianism.

The so-called *Letter to Hymnaeus*, which six bishops are supposed to have sent to Paul before the synod of A.D. 268 took place, contains an extensive Creed and asks him to subscribe to this rule of faith. Although according to Eusebius (*Hist. eccl.* 7,30,2) the six bishops, whose names are given, participated in the council, the authenticity of this document remains doubtful. The same is true of five fragments of Paul's *Orations to Sabinus*, found in the florilegium *Doctrina Patrum de incarnatione Verbi*, compiled in the seventh century.

Fragments: MG 10, 247–260. — ROUTH, Reliquiae sacrae, 2nd ed. 3, 287–367. — F. DIEKAMP, Doctrina Patrum de incarnatione Verbi. Münster, 1907, 303–304. — H. J. LAWLOR, The Sayings of Paul of Samosata: TJhSt 19 (1917/18) 20–45, 115–120. *Studies:* P. GALTIER, L'ὁμοούσιος de Paul de Samosate: RSR 12 (1922) 30–45. —

F. Loofs, Paulus von Samosata (TU 44, 5). Leipzig, 1924. Cf. F. Diekamp, ThR 24 (1925) 205–209. P. Peeters, AB 43 (1925) 406–409. B. Capelle, RB 36 (1924) 366–369. E. Amann, RSR 15 (1925) 328–342. — A. Harnack, Die Reden Pauls von Samosata an Sabinus (Zenobia?) und seine Christologie: SAB (1924) 130–151. — J. Lebreton, Paul de Samosate et Origène: RAp 38 (1924) 193–202. — F. Loofs, ThLZ 50 (1925) 227–232. — E. Schwartz, Eine fingierte Korrespondenz mit Paulus dem Samosatener (SAM 3). Munich, 1927. — G. Bardy, Paul de Samosate (SSL 4) 2nd ed. Louvain, 1929. — E. Dumoutet, Paul de Samosate: RAp 51 (1930) 192–200. — R. L. P. Milburn, ὁ τῆς ἐκκλησίας οἶκος: JThSt (1945) 65–68. — G. Bardy, DTC 12, 46–51. — H. de Riedmatten, Les Actes du Procès de Paul de Samosate (Paradosis 6). Fribourg, 1952.

LUCIAN OF ANTIOCH

The founder of the theological school of Antioch was Lucian, born at Samosata. Eusebius (*Hist. eccl.* 9,6,3) gives the following description of him:

> Lucian, a most excellent man in every respect, of temperate life and well versed in sacred learning, a priest of the community at Antioch, was brought to the city of Nicomedia, where the emperor was then staying; and having made his defense before the ruler on behalf of the doctrine which he professed, he was committed to prison and put to death (LCL).

The ruler mentioned in this passage is the Emperor Maximinus Daia and the martyrdom took place Jan. 7, 312. Rufinus (*Hist. eccl.* 9,6) gives the text of the apology which he delivered before the pagan judge but its authenticity remains doubtful.

Lucian was not a prolific writer. Jerome refers to his 'small treatise on faith' (*De vir. ill.* 77) without indication of its contents. He was a Hebrew scholar and corrected the Greek version of the Old Testament from the original. This revision of the Septuagint was adopted by the greater number of the churches of Syria and Asia Minor from Antioch to Byzantium, and was highly esteemed (Jerome, *Praef. in Paral.*; *Adv. Ruf.* 2,27). Large fragments of it are extant in the writings of St. John Chrysostom and Theodoret. Lucian extended his textual criticism to the New Testament also, but limited it most probably to the four Gospels.

The school which he founded at Antioch stood in opposition to the allegorism of that of Alexandria. It dedicated itself to the task of interpreting the Scriptures literally. It produced biblical commentaries of lasting value and provided many of the later ecclesiastical authors with their exegetical training.

However, this school developed a peculiar theological trend. The oldest document we have about Lucian's teaching accuses him of being a successor to Paul of Samosata and the originator of the doctrine which soon became so notorious as Arianism. It is a letter written by bishop Alexander of Alexandria ten years after Lucian's death and sent to all the bishops of Egypt, Syria, Asia and Cappadocia. Theodoret (*Hist. eccl.* 1,4) quotes the following passage from it:

> You yourselves have been instructed by God; you are not unaware that this teaching, which is setting itself up again against the faith of the Church, is the doctrine of Ebion and Artemas; it is the perverse theology of Paul of Samosata, who was expelled from the church at Antioch by a conciliar sentence of bishops from all places; his successor Lucian remained for a long time excommunicated under three bishops; the dregs of the impiety of those heretics have been absorbed by these men who have arisen from nothing..., Arius, Achillas, and the whole band of their companions in malice.

In fact, Arius and the future upholders of his heresy were educated by Lucian at Antioch. Arius himself boasted of being a pupil of his, called himself a 'Lucianist,' and addressed Lucian's successor, Bishop Eusebius of Nicomedia, as 'Collucianist' (Epiphanius, *Haer.* 69,6; Theodoret, *Hist. eccl.* 1,4). All this indicates that Lucian was the father of Arianism. Thus this heresy had its roots not in Alexandria, where it was first taught, but at Antioch. The Adoptianism of Paul of Samosata survived, with modifications, in the teaching of Arius. It attacked the absolute Divinity of Christ, one of the most fundamental articles of the Christian faith.

Fragments: ROUTH, Reliquiae sacrae, 2nd ed. 4, 1–17. — MG 92, 689: Fragments of a letter.

Studies: A. HARNACK, Geschichte der altchristl. Literatur 1, 526–531; 2, 2, 138–146. — E. BUONAIUTI, Luciano Martire. La sua dottrina e la sua scuola: Riv. stor.-crit. delle scienze teol. 4 (1908) 830–837, 909–923; 5 (1909) 104–118. — F. LOOFS, Das Bekenntnis Lucians des Märtyrers: SAB (1915) 576–603. — G. BARDY, Le discours apologétique de S. Lucien d'Antioche (Rufinus, H.e. 9, 9): RHE 22 (1926) 487–512. — P. RIESSLER, Lucian von Samosata und die Heilige Schrift: ThQ 114 (1933) 64–72. — G. BARDY, Recherches sur saint Lucien d'Antioche et son école. Paris, 1936. — D. S. BALANOS, Actes de l'Académie d'Athènes 7 (1932) 306–311. — A. D'ALÈS, Autour de Lucien d'Antioche: Mélange Université Beyrouth 21 (1937) 185–199. —

H. Doerries, Zur Geschichte der Septuaginta im Jahrhundert Konstantins: ZNW (1940) 57–110. — G. Mercati, Di alcune testimonianze antiche sulle cure bibliche di San Luciano: Bibl (1943) 1–17; *idem*, Nuove note (ST 95). Vatican City, 1941, 137. — C. Lattey, The Antiochene Text: Scripture 4 (1951) 273–277. — B. Fischer, Lukian-Lesarten in der Vetus Latina der vier Königsbücher: SA 27/28 (1951) 169–177. — G. Bardy, DTC 9, 1024–1031.

DOROTHEUS OF ANTIOCH

Eusebius mentions another presbyter of Antioch, whom he met while Cyril was bishop of Antioch (ca. 280–303).

> During Cyril's episcopate we came to know Dorotheus, a learned man, who had been deemed worthy of the presbyterate at Antioch. In his zeal for all that is beautiful in divine things, he made so careful a study of the Hebrew tongue that he read with understanding the original Hebrew Scriptures. And he was by no means unacquainted with the most liberal studies and Greek primary education; but withal he was by nature a eunuch, having been so from his very birth, so that even the emperor, accounting this as a sort of miracle, took him into his friendship and honoured him with the charge of the purple-dye-works at Tyre. We heard him giving a measured exposition of the Scriptures in Church (Euseb., *Hist. eccl.* 7,32,2–4 LCL).

Eusebius does not mention any writings of this Dorotheus nor that he taught in the school of Antioch, although in modern times there has been a tendency to associate him with Lucian.

PAMPHILUS OF CAESAREA

Pamphilus, one of Origen's most enthusiastic followers, was the teacher of the first great Church historian, Eusebius of Caesarea, who used to call himself ὁ τοῦ Παμφίλου, the son of Pamphilus. Unfortunately, nothing is extant of the biography in three books that Eusebius wrote. But in his *Ecclesiastical History* (7,32,25) he says of him:

> In his day we came to know Pamphilus, a most eloquent man and a true philosopher in his mode of life, who had been deemed worthy of the presbyterate of that community. It would be no small undertaking to show the kind of man he was and whence he came. But of each particular of his life

and of the school that he established, as well as his contest in various confessions during the persecution, and the crown of martyrdom with which he was wreathed at the end of all, we have treated separately in a special work concerning him. Truly he was the most admirable of those of that city (LCL).

Born at Berytus in Phoenicia Pamphilus received his early training in his native town. He studied theology in the catechetical school of Alexandria under the direction of Pierius, the successor to Origen, who used to be called 'Origen Junior.' It was here that he received his high admiration of Origen. On returning to his own country, he settled at Caesarea in Palestine where Origen had taught in his later years. He was ordained by bishop Agapius and established a theological school in order to carry on the tradition of Origen. He was especially anxious to enlarge the library which Origen had founded and succeeded in acquiring a collection of valuable books that remained of the greatest importance for Christian literature and learning for centuries to come. Eusebius and Jerome owe their knowledge of earlier Christian literature to this library. Pamphilus copied with his own hand original manuscripts which he could not buy and he was helped by a staff of scribes. He trained Eusebius in transcribing, cataloguing and editing texts, and introduced him to studies of literary criticism and authenticity. Many of Origen's writings would have been lost, if he had not taken the greatest care in collecting and listing them, as Eusebius witnesses:

> We did record it in our account of the life of Pamphilus, that holy martyr of our day, in which, in showing the extent of Pamphilus' zeal for divine things, I quoted as evidence the lists in the library that he had brought together of the works of Origen and of other ecclesiastical writers; and from these anyone who pleases can gather the fullest knowledge of the works of Origen that have reached us (*Hist. eccl.* 6,32,3 LCL).

In the persecution of Maximinus Daia he was tortured and cast into prison in the year 307, where he remained until his execution on Feb. 16, 309 or 310.

1. *His Apology for Origen* (Ἀπολογία ὑπὲρ Ὠριγένους)

During his lengthy imprisonment he wrote a defence of Origen in five books. In this he was helped by his pupil Eusebius, who completed the work after Pamphilus' death by the addition of a sixth. Only the first book survives in a not too reliable Latin translation by Rufinus. Photius (*Bibl. cod.* 118) informs us that the *Apology* 'was addressed to those who were condemned to the mines for the sake of Christ, the chief of whom was Patermythius, who shortly after the death of Pamphilus ended his life at the stake with others,' in other words, to the martyrs of Palestine, most of whom opposed the theology of Origen. Pamphilus and Eusebius refuted the accusations made against their hero and defended his views with many passages quoted from his own works.

Editions: The first book of his Apology for Origen in Rufinus' translation: LOM-MATZSCH, Origenis Opera 24, 293–412. — MG 17, 521–616.

2. *His Copies of the Biblical Text*

Pamphilus deserves special credit for the numerous copies of the Bible that he made from the Hexapla of Origen. We owe it to him and Eusebius that the Septuagint as it appears in the revision of Origen was read in the Churches of Palestine and spread far beyond the borders of that country (Jerome, *Praef. in Paral.; Adv. Ruf.* 2,27). The history of the critical text of the Old and the New Testament is intimately connected with the names of Pamphilus and Eusebius and not a few of the extant manuscripts of the Bible go back to codices made by them.

Studies: A. v. HARNACK, Geschichte der altchristl. Literatur 1, 543–550. — G. BARDY, DTC 11, 1839–1841. — G. MERCATI, Nuove note (ST 95). Vatican City, 1941, 91.

THE DIALOGUE ON THE ORTHODOX FAITH

The dialogue *De recta in Deum fide* (Περὶ τῆς εἰς θεὸν ὀρθῆς πίστεως), extant in its Greek original as well as in a Latin translation by Rufinus, is of an unknown author, who was a contemporary of Methodius. It was attributed to Origen at an early date, the Greek manuscripts as well as Rufinus designating him as the author. However, the contents indicate clearly that it was composed by an opponent of Origen's doctrine and that the author used Methodius' *On Free Will* and *On the Resurrection* for his refutation of the adherents of Marcion, Bardesanes and Valentinus. It seems, therefore, that the dialogue *On the Orthodox Faith* did not appear before the year A.D. 300. It was written most probably in Syria. Since the defender of the orthodox faith in the dialogue has the name Adamantius, the treatise was wrongly attributed to Origen, also called Adamantius.

In the first part the disciples of Marcion, Megethius and Marcus, defend their master's ideas of two different Gods, one of the Jews and the other of the Christians and claim that their Gospel is alone authentic. The second part deals with the heresy of Bardesanes. Marinus, its representative, states that God cannot be called the creator of Satan or of evil, that the Logos did not take human flesh in the incarnation and that the body will not share in the resurrection. At the end, the pagan arbiter Eutropius declares himself convinced by Adamantius.

The author displays a good training in theology and philosophy and knows how to defend his faith effectively. But his dialogue is far from being a work of art and suffers from a lack of coordination and coherence.

Editions: MG 11. — W. H. VAN DE SANDE BAKHUYZEN, GCS 4 (1901).

Studies: F. J. A. HORT, Adamantius: Dictionary of Christian Biography 1 (1877) 39–41. — TH. ZAHN, Die Dialoge des 'Adamantius' mit den Gnostikern: ZKG 9 (1888) 193–239; *idem*, Geschichte des neutestamentl. Kanons 2, 2, 1892, 419–426. — A. v. HARNACK, Geschichte der altchristl. Literatur 1, 478–480; 2, 2, 149–151; *idem*, Marcion, 2nd ed. Leipzig, 1924, 56*–67*, 181*, 344*–348*. — P. BRANDHUBER, Die sekundären Lesarten bei 1 Kor. 15, 51. Ihre Verbreitung und ihre Entstehung: Bibl 18 (1937) 303–333: Dial. 5, 23. — F. X. MURPHY, Rufinus of Aquileia. Washington, 1945, 123–125.

APPENDIX

THE SYRIAC DIDASCALIA APOSTOLORUM

The *Didascalia*, or the *Catholic Teaching of the Twelve Apostles and Holy Disciples of Our Saviour*, is a Church Order, composed, according to recent investigations, in the first part, perhaps even the first decades, of the third century, for a community of Christian converts from paganism in the northern part of Syria. The work is modelled on the *Didache* (cf. vol. I, pp.29–39) and forms the main source of the first six books of the *Apostolic Constitutions*.

The unknown author of the *Didascalia* seems to have been of Jewish descent. A bishop with a considerable knowledge of medicine, he lacked special theological training. He makes ample use of Holy Scripture and borrows from the *Didache*, Hermas, Irenaeus, the *Gospel of Peter* and the *Acts of Paul*.

CONTENTS

The first chapters consist of admonitions, especially to husbands and wives. Warnings are issued against pagan literature and promiscuous bathing (1–2). There follow rules about the election and consecration of bishops, the ordination of priests and deacons and the instruction of catechumens (3). The rights and duties of a bishop are defined (4–9) with special emphasis on lenient treatment of the contrite sinner (5–7) and care for the poor (8). Cautions on false brethren and on testimony from a pagan against a Christian lead to regulations in regard to lawsuits (10–11). We get a good picture of the liturgical meetings and the places of worship:

> In your assemblies, in the holy Churches, after all good patterns form your gatherings, and arrange the places for the brethren carefully with all sobriety. Let a place be reserved for the presbyters in the midst of the eastern part of the house, and let the throne of the bishop be placed amongst them; let the presbyters sit with him; but also at the other eastern side of the house let the laymen sit; for thus it is required that the presbyters should sit at the eastern side of the house with the bishops, and afterwards the laymen, and next the women: that when ye stand to pray the rulers may stand first, afterwards the laymen, and then the women also, for towards the East it is required that ye should pray, as ye know that it is written, 'Give praise to God who rideth on the heavens of heavens towards the East' (Ps. 68). As for the deacons, let one of them stand constantly over the gifts of the Eucharist, and let another stand outside the door and look at those who come in; and afterwards when ye make offerings, let them serve together in the Church. And if a man be found sitting out of his place, let the deacon who is within reprove him, and make him get up and sit in the place that befits him (12 Gibson).

The Christian should not neglect attendance at the eucharistic service for work or shows (13). Regulations for widows (14–15), deacons and deaconesses (16), and Christian charity (17–18) are followed by an exhortation to bishops to take care of those who are persecuted or imprisoned for the name of Christ. It is obligatory that all believers should diligently comfort confessors with their goods (19). Since the faithful possess a sure hope of the resurrection, no one can have any excuse for shirking martyrdom (20). The regular fast days throughout the year are Wednesday and Friday (this is repeated from the *Didache*). But another fast also is set for the week preceeding Easter, lasting 'from Monday, fully six days, until the night after the Sabbath' (21). After a section which deals with the education of children (22), the author turns to the danger of heresies, 'Before everything beware of all odious heresies, and flee from them as from a burning fire, and from those who adhere to them.' Those who divide the flock by false teaching or schism will be condemned to eternal fire (23). God has left the synagogue and has come to the Church of the Gentiles, but Satan has done the same. He does not tempt the Jews any more, but he splits the one fold into sects. This had begun already at the time of the apostles (24), who, the context asserts (ch. 25), wrote the *Didascalia*: 'When therefore a danger arose that heresies should be in all the Church, we assembled together, the twelve apostles, in Jerusalem, and considered about what was to be. It pleased us all with one mind, to write this Catholic Didascalia, for the assurance of you all.' After returning to their congregations, the apostles confirmed the believers in the faith. 'Having decreed and established and confirmed with one mind, each one of us went out and departed to his first portion, confirming the Churches, because the things that had been predicted were fulfilled, and disguised wolves had come, and false Christs and lying prophets had appeared' (26).

The *Didascalia* contains little dogma, since it principally aims at moral instruction and canonical regulation for the maintenance of the constitution and order of the Church. Wherever it does enter into doctrinal discussions, it is in refutation of Gnosticism and Judaism. Nevertheless it supplies us with important information for the history of Christian life and practice. Thus it deals in all detail with the question of penance. It teaches against all rigoristic tendencies that every sin, even that of heresy, can be forgiven, except that against the Holy Spirit:

> Those who repent of error, shall be left in the Church; but
> those who hold fast the error and repent not, we cut off and
> appoint that they go out of the Church, and be separated
> from the believers, because they have heresies and they
> should have no communion with them either by word or by
> prayer; for these people are the enemies of the Church (25).

The writer explicitly numbers adultery and apostasy among
the offences that can be forgiven. Thus he admonishes the
bishops:

> Those who repent their sins heal and receive. For if thou
> receive not him who repents, because thou art merciless,
> thou sinnest against the Lord God, because thou dost not obey
> our Lord and God in acting as He acted; for even He did so
> to that woman who had sinned, her whom the elders placed
> before Him and left it to judgment at His hands and went
> away; He, the one who searcheth the hearts, asked her
> and said to her, 'Have the Elders condemned thee, my
> daughter?' She saith to Him, 'No, Lord.' And our Saviour
> said, 'Go, and return no more to this, neither do I condemn
> thee.' In this therefore let our Saviour and King and God
> be to you a sign, O bishops: be like Him that ye may be
> gentle and humble and merciful and clement (6 Gibson).

The author quotes the complete text of the prayer of Manasseh
and adds:

> Ye have heard, dear children. Like as Manasseh worshipped
> evil idols bitterly, and killed the righteous, and when he
> repented, the Lord forgave him, although there is no sin
> worse than the worship of idols, yet a place for repentance
> was given (*ibid.*).

Nothing even remotely indicates that after baptism there is
but one forgiveness of sins. We find a well developed liturgy of
public penance, a clear notion of its sacramental character, but
no private penance.

In the opinion of A. v. Harnack and E. Schwartz, the *Didascalia*, in its present form, contains passages directed against
Novatian, but these have been added later, and the work probably antedates that heresiarch. Be this as it may, we have still no
shred of proof that the original had any rigorism in respect to
public penance.

TEXT TRADITION

1. The Greek text is lost except for a few small fragments. But since it formed, as mentioned before, the main source of the first six books of the *Apostolic Constitutions*, most of it can be reconstructed.

2. The complete work has reached us in a Syriac translation. P.A. de Lagarde was the first to publish it in 1854 from a manuscript at Paris, *Codex Sangermanensis (Parisiensis) orient. 38, saec.* IX *vel* X. In 1903 Mrs. M. D. Gibson put out another recension from a Mesopotamian manuscript of the year 1036, discovered by J. R. Harris (*Codex Mesopotamicus* or *Harrisianus*); she lists also the variants of the *Sangermanensis*, of another *Codex Mesopotamicus* which contains only a fragment, of a *Codex Cantabrigiensis* and of a *Codex Musei Borgiani*. From all appearances the Syriac version must have been made shortly after the Greek work was composed.

3. An old Latin translation, comprising about three-eights of the whole, was published by E. Hauler in 1900 from a palimpsest of the Library of the Cathedral Chapter of Verona (*Codex Veronensis lat.* LV 53). It seems to date from the end of the fourth century.

4. The Syriac *Didascalia*, or rather its lost Greek original, is also the basis of the Arabic and the Ethiopic *Didascalia*.

Editions: P. A. DE LAGARDE, Didascalia apostolorum syriace. Leipzig, 1854. — E. HAULER, Didascaliae apostolorum fragmenta Veronensia latina. Leipzig, 1900. — M. GIBSON, Horae Semiticae I. The Didascalia Apostolorum in Syriac. London, 1903. — F. X. FUNK, Didascalia et Constitutiones Apostolorum I. Paderborn, 1905, 1–384.

Translations: English: M. GIBSON, Horae Semiticae II. The Didascalia apostolorum in English. London, 1903. — R. H. CONNOLLY, Didascalia apostolorum. The syriac version translated and accompanied by the Verona Latin fragments. Oxford, 1929. — J. M. HARDEN, The Ethiopic Didascalia translated (SPCK). London-New York, 1920. — *French:* F. NAU, La Didascalie des douze apôtres. 12th ed. Paris, 1912. — *German:* H. ACHELIS und J. FLEMMING, Die syrische Didascalia übersetzt und erklärt (TU 25, 2). Leipzig, 1904.

Studies: F. X. FUNK, Die Apostolischen Konstitutionen. Rottenburg, 1891; *idem,* La date de la Didascalie des apôtres: RHE 2 (1901) 798–809; *idem,* Kirchengeschichtliche Abhandlungen und Untersuchungen 3. Paderborn, 1907, 275–284. — A. HARNACK, Geschichte der altchristlichen Literatur 1, 515–518; 2, 2, 488–501. — E. SCHWARTZ, Bußstufen und Katechumenatsklassen. Strasbourg, 1911, 16–20. — H. ACHELIS und J. FLEMMING, *loc. cit.* 243–387. — P. A. PROKOSCHEV, Die Didascalia apostolorum und die ersten sechs Bücher der Apostolischen Konstitutionen. (Russian). Tomsk, 1913. — J. V. BARTLET, Fragments of the Didascalia in Greek: JThSt 18 (1917) 301 ff. — F. C. BURKITT, The Didascalia: JThSt 31 (1930) 258-265. — P. GALTIER, L'Église et la remission des péchés aux premiers siècles. Paris, 1932, 191 f. — J. QUASTEN, Monumenta eucharistica et liturgica vetustissima. Bonn, 1937, 34-36. — E. TIDNER, Sprachlicher Kommentar zur lateinischen Didascalia Apostolorum. Stockholm, 1938. — W. C. VAN UNNIK, De beteekenis van de Mozaische wet voor de kerk van Christus volgens de Syrische Didascalie: Nederlandsch Archief voor Kerkgeschiedenis 31 (1939) 65-100. — B. POSCHMANN, Paenitentia secunda. Bonn, 1940, 476-478. — J. V. BARTLETT, Church Life and Church Order during the First Four Centuries, with Special Reference to Early Eastern Church Orders. London, 1943. — G. GRAF, Geschichte der christlichen arabischen Literatur. Rome, 1944. vol. 1, 564-569. — P. GALTIER, La date de la Didascalie des apôtres: RHE 42 (1947) 315-351. — J. J. CUESTA, La penitencia medicinal desde la Didascalia apostolorum a S. Gregorio di Nisa: Revista Españ. Teol. 7 (1947) 337-344. — P. BEAUCAMP, Un évêque du IIIe siècle aux prises avec les pécheurs: son activité apostolique: BLE 69 (1949) 26-47. — K. RAHNER, Bußlehre und Bußpraxis der Didascalia Apostolorum: ZkTh 72 (1950) 257-281.

CHAPTER III

THE ROMANS

The pre-eminence of the Roman Church did not secure it a corresponding share in the development of thought throughout this period. It fostered no school like the famed oriental centers of scholarship—and that, too, despite the repeated intervention of the popes in the Alexandrian controversies and the preoccupation, mirrored in their letters, with all that concerned the whole Christian world. During this interval Rome gave birth to but one apology, the *Octavius* of Minucius Felix, which, however eloquent a defence of the faith, scarcely even alludes to its positive content, and produced only two divines worthy of mention, Hippolytus and Novatian, both anti-popes. Nevertheless, in the former, she could boast a savant comparable with Origen in breadth of learning and variety of scientific interests, and, in the latter, her first theologian to write in Latin. Moreover, it was in the Eternal City that originated two documents of no little significance, the *Muratorian Fragment*, the earliest known catalogue of the authentic books of the New Testament, and the *Apostolic Tradition* of Hippolytus, our richest source for the primitive liturgy of Christianity's center and for the inner life of the ancient Church.

THE BEGINNINGS OF LATIN CHRISTIAN LITERATURE AT ROME

The period under consideration sees the transition to Latin as the official language of the Roman Church. The letters of the pontiffs cease to be exclusively Greek. Pope Cornelius wrote seven epistles in Latin to Cyprian, of which two survive, and Pope Stephen, following the precedent thus set, one to the same correspondent, and of this, too, a fragment is preserved. More interesting still is the inauguration of a Latin theological literature. Whereas Hippolytus continues to use Greek, Novatian composes in cultured Latin. Furthermore, the latter's *De trinitate* quotes a Latin version of the Bible then already in existence. However, Christian Latin in Rome had its beginnings much further back than has been commonly believed, and its progress towards final

victory over its rival can, in reality, be divided into three distinct
stages.

The earliest phase of the transition occurred on the level of
ordinary conversation. When the faith was first preached at
Rome between the years 30 and 40 A.D., the mass of its population was not native but foreign; the primitive Christian community was, therefore, made up predominantly of easterners
Greek, under such circumstances the medium of everyday exchange, naturally became the official language of the Church and
of the liturgy. But that by around 150 A.D. this tongue was heard
less and less in the streets of the city and on the lips of its in-
habitants seems to follow from numerous indications in the
Shepherd of Hermas, published about that date. As a matter of fact
the change had then so far progressed as to render necessary the
first translation of the Bible into Latin. Proof of this is furnished
by the quotations from the Scriptures in a Latin version of
Clement's *Epistle to the Corinthians*, itself made in the middle of
the second century.

As to the second and third phases of the transition, they consist
respectively, in the shift of the official language and that of the
liturgy. The latter did not take place until the pontificate of
Damasus (366–384), though the former had been completed by
approximately 250 A.D. This is demonstrated by the epistles of
the Roman clergy during the vacancy after Fabianus' death
(250–51), by the letters of Popes Cornelius and Stephen, as well
as by Novatian's *De trinitate*.

Studies: A. HARNACK, Die Briefe des römischen Klerus aus der Zeit der Sedisvakanz
im Jahre 250: Theol. Abhandlungen Carl Weizsäcker gewidmet. Freiburg, 1892,
1–36. — G. MORIN, Sancti Clementis Romani ad Corinthios epistulae versio antiquissima (Anecdota Maredsolana 12). Maredsous, 1894. — G. LA PIANA, Il problema
della Chiesa latina in Roma. Rome, 1922. — A. HARNACK, Die Mission und Ausbreitung des Christentums. 4th ed., vol.2, Leipzig, 1924, 817–832. — G. LA PIANA, The
Roman Church at the End of the Second Century: HThR 18 (1925) 201 ff.; *idem*,
L'immigrazione a Roma nei primi secoli dell'Impero: RR 2 (1926) 485–547; 3 (1927)
36–75; *idem*, Foreign Groups in Rome During the First Centuries of the Empire:
HThR 20 (1927) 183 ff. — J. B. FREY, Les communautés juives à Rome aux premiers
temps de l'Église: RSR 20 (1930) 269 ff.; 21 (1931) 129 ff. — G. BARDY, La latinisa-
tion de l'Église d'Occident: Irénikon 14 (1937) 9–11, 113–130. — H. BARDON, Les
empereurs et les lettres latines d'Auguste à Hadrien. Paris, 1940. — M. MÜLLER, Der
Übergang von der griechischen zur lateinischen Sprache in der abendländischen
Kirche von Hermas bis Novatian. Diss. Rome, 1943. — TH. KLAUSER, Der Über-

gang der römischen Kirche von der griechischen zur lateinischen Liturgiesprache: Miscellanea G. Mercati, vol. 1, Rome, 1946, 467–482. — G. BARDY, La question des langues dans l'Église ancienne. Paris, 1948, 81–115. — C. MOHRMANN, Les origines de la latinité chrétienne à Rome: VC 3 (1949) 67–106, 163–183; *eadem*, Le Latin langue de la chrétienté occidentale: Aevum 24 (1950) 133 ff.; *eadem*, Quelques observations sur l'originalité de la littérature chrétienne: Rivista di Storia della Chiesa in Italia 4 (1950) 153 ff.; *eadem*, L'étude de la latinité chrétienne. État de la question, méthodes, résultats: Conférences de l'Institut de linguistique de l'Université de Paris 10 (1950/51) 125–141.

MINUCIUS FELIX

1. *The Octavius*

The only apology for Christianity written in Latin at Rome during the time of the persecutions is the dialogue *Octavius*. Preserved in a single manuscript, *Codex Parisinus* 1661, *saec.* IX, as the eighth book of Arnobius' *Against the Pagans*, it was actually composed by Minucius Felix, its true author, as Lactantius and Jerome testify. Lactantius gives the following information: 'Among the defenders of our cause known to me, Minucius Felix occupied a very distinguished rank at the bar. His book entitled Octavius shows what an excellent champion of the truth he might have been, if he had devoted himself entirely to this kind of study' (*Div. inst.* 5,1,21). Jerome refers to him on several occasions. In his *De viris illustribus* 58 we read: 'Minucius Felix, a distinguished advocate of Rome, wrote a dialogue representing a discussion between a Christian and a Gentile, which is entitled Octavius.'

The scene of the dialogue is Rome. Three persons participate in the discussion, the author, the lawyer Marcus Minucius Felix, and his two friends, the Christian Octavius and the pagan Caecilius. Octavius, of the same profession as Minucius Felix, had come from Africa on a visit. Caecilius seems to have been a native of Cirta in Numidia because he mentions Fronto, also of Cirta, as his countryman. It is doubtful whether the conversation ever took place. The author follows the pattern of Cicero's dialogues and uses this literary form in order to present the case of Christianity versus paganism, but it is not thereby necessarily implied that the characters taking part in it are fictitious.

It seems that the work was written in memory of Octavius, now no longer living because it opens with the author's recalling their intimate friendship. They were one in mind and one in heart. They had embraced the new faith together.

Our wills were tuned to perfect concert, whether of likes
or dislikes; you might have thought a single mind had been
parted in two. Thus he was at once sole confidant of my
affections, and my partner in wanderings from truth; and
when after the gloom had been dispelled I was emerging
from the depth of darkness into the light of wisdom and
truth, he did not reject me as a companion, but—all honor
to him—led the way. So, as my thoughts ranged over the
whole period of our association and familiarity, my attention
fastened above all else on that discourse of his, in which, by
sheer weight of argument, he converted Caecilius, who was
still immersed in superstitious vanities, to the true religion
(1 LCL).

The conversation took place on a walk to Ostia, the famous
resort of the Romans. They happen to pass a statue of Serapis
and Caecilius throws it a kiss. This incident starts the debate,
which is conducted on forensic lines with Caecilius acting as
prosecutor, Octavius speaking for the defense, and Minucius
presiding as arbiter in the conflict between the old faith and the
new (1–4).

Sitting down at the end of the mole, Caecilius opens the discussion with a passionate defense of paganism and a violent
attack against Christianity. As a philosopher of the Academy he
combines with a generally sceptical attitude an uncritical tenderness for tradition. His speech (5–13) may be summed up in three
statements:

a. In human affairs everything is doubtful, uncertain and in
suspense, a matter of probability rather than of truth. Man's intelligence is so limited that neither in the case of things above nor
of things below, is it given him to know. But if our audacious
eagerness still seeks to solve the riddles of the universe, there is no
need of a god and a creator. On the contrary, the disorder existing in the physical and moral world speaks against a divine providence. Lawless chance, tricky and haphazard, rules over all (5).

b. For this reason it is better to accept the teaching of our
elders, to maintain the beliefs handed down to us and to adore
the gods, whom from the cradle we were taught to revere. They
have advanced the bounds of the empire beyond the paths of the
sun and the confines of the ocean (6–7).

c. It is intolerable that any man should be so puffed up with pride and impious conceit of wisdom as to strive to abolish or undermine as do the Christians a religion, so ancient, so useful, and so salutary. They are atheists, conspirators who introduce everywhere a kind of worship of lust, a promiscuous 'brotherhood' and 'sisterhood,' by which ordinary fornication, under cover of a hallowed name, is perverted to incest. Their vain and foolish superstition makes an actual boast of crime. Their doctrines of one God, of a destruction of the world by fire, of immortality and resurrection of the flesh, of eternal reward and eternal damnation, are absurdities (5–13).

Octavius answers this violent attack in a calm and convincing tone, following his opponent step by step. His refutation is preceded by a few words of Minucius, who warns against all fascination of words and stresses the only purpose of the debate, the search for truth.

Octavius drives home the following points:

a. When Caecilius gave vent to feelings of indignation and regret that illiterate, poor and ignorant people like the Christians should discuss supernatural things, he should have remembered that all men, without distinction of age, sex, or rank are created with the capacity and power of reasoning and understanding. Discernment is not acquired by fortune, but implanted by nature. The rich, engrossed in business, have their eyes more often on gold than on heaven. It is the lowly that have pondered wisdom and handed on its teaching. Those who regard the design of this great universe not as the product of a divine intelligence, but a conglomeration of odds and ends fortuitously brought together, have neither mind, nor sense, nor even eyes. If we lift up our eyes to heaven and look at all things beneath, it is obvious, that there exists some deity, by whom all nature is inspired, moved, nourished and directed, and this supreme power cannot be divided, but must be one. God, it is true, cannot be seen by human eyes, because He is too bright for sight. Nevertheless, He exists, as does the sun, into which we cannot look either. Pagan poets and philosophers agree with the Christians on this point, so that we may call the Christians of today, philosophers, or the philosophers of old, Christians (14–19).

b. Therefore, charmed or captivated by our pet fables, we must not allow an ignorant tradition to mislead us. Pagan religion is a phantastic admixture of disgusting and immoral myths and mysteries. This superstition certainly did not give world-empire to the Romans. All that they hold, occupy and possess is the spoil of outrage. Their temples are all from loot taken in the ruin of cities. The Romans have grown great not by religion, but by unpunished sacrilege (20–27).

c. The accusations against the conduct and belief of the faithful are calumnies, which the demons have set afloat. The main doctrines of Christianity can be proved even from reason, as the pagan philosophers testify. The deportment of its adherents is their best apology. They do not preach great things, they live them (28–38).

After this masterly logic there was no need of an arbiter. Caecilius declares himself to be convinced on the principal points. Minor difficulties can be discussed later. Minucius is glad to be relieved from the invidious task of passing judgment. The dialogue ends: 'Thereupon we went our way cheerful and happy, Caecilius at having found belief, Octavius at having won a victory, I at the faith of the one and the victory of the other' (40).

This delightful defense of Christianity has always been admired for its nobility and elegance. The author displays remarkable impartiality towards the pagan point of view. Even in his refutation of the calumnies brought against the Christians he tries to avoid anything offensive. The setting of the dialogue, the charm of its presentation, its clearness of expression, its careful disposition of material, the absence of digressions—all these features contribute towards making it the finest of the early Christian apologies. Its finished style, its carefully balanced periods, its close attention to the classic norms of prose rhythm, strongly remind one of Cicero, and Cicero was undoubtedly the model. His *De natura deorum* not only furnished the framework but one passage (1,25–42) reappears verbatim in the *Octavius* as ch. 19. Other writings of the master were also exploited, particularly *De divinatione* and *De republica*. We find, in addition, numerous borrowings from Seneca. The ethics of the dialogue have much in common with the ideal of Stoic philosophy. Plato is quoted several times. There are reminiscences of Homer, Xenophon, Florus, Horace, Juvenal, Lucretius, Martial, Ovid, Sallust, Tibullus and Vergil. If we turn to Christian sources, we discover frequent resemblances to earlier apologists, for instance, Justin, Tatian, Athenagoras, Theophilus, but resemblances not strong enough to prove actual dependence. Not a single passage of Scripture is cited, in all likelihood because Minucius wanted principally to convince the educated pagan and such material would hardly appeal to him as evidence. For the same reason, probably, the dialogue contains very little that is characteristic of the revealed truth. The doctrine of God follows the Stoic concept. Monotheism and belief in immortality are the two poles around which the author's philosophy circles. Christianity is understood as ethics put into practice.

As for the date of its composition, it is of importance that the *Octavius* shows a close relation in ideas and expressions to Tertullian's *Apologeticum*, written about 197, and in some instances to his *Ad nationes*. This seems to be evidence of dependence of one upon the other. However, the vexed question of priority has created a long discussion among scholars, which is very far from being settled. Jerome (*De vir. ill.* 53; 58; *Epist.* 70,5) gives it to Tertullian but there are as many reasons in favor of the opposite theory.

Editions: C. HALM, CSEL 2 (1867) 1–71. — J. P. WALTZING, Minucius Felix, Octavius, recogn. Bruges, 1909 (with comm.). — A. SCHÖNE, M. Felix, Octavius. Leipzig, 1913. — G. RAUSCHEN, FP 8. Bonn, 1913. — A. VALMAGGI, Corpus script. lat. Paravianum 5. Turin, 1916. — T. FAHY, Octavius, with introduction and notes. Dublin-Belfast, 1919. — J. VAN WAGENINGEN, Min. Felix, Octavius, I Inleid. en tekst, II Aanteekeningen. Utrecht, 1923. — J. P. WALTZING, Octavius, iter. ed. Leipzig, 1926. — H. VON GEISAU, Minucius Felix, Octavius. Münster i.W., 1927. — J. MARTIN, FP 8. Bonn, 1930. — G. H. RENDALL, Minucius Felix with an English translation, based on the unfinished version by W. C. A. KERR (LCL). London-New York, 1931, 314–437. — A. D. SIMPSON, Minucii Felicis Octavius. Prolegomena, text and critical notes. New York, 1938. — M. PELLEGRINO, M. Minucii Felicis Octavius (Corpus script latin. Paravianum). Turin, 1950. — G. QUISPEL, Minucii Felicis Octavius, uitg. en van comment. voorzien (Griekse en Latijnse Schrijvers 61). Leiden, 1949.

Translations: English: R. JAMES, Minucius Felix, his Dialogue called Octavius. Oxford, 1636. — E. COMBE, The Octavius of Minucius Felix. London, 1703. — W. REEVES, The Octavius of Minucius Felix concerning the value of idols. London, 1709, II, 34–172. — D. DALRYMPLE, Octavius, a dialogue by M. Minucius Felix, Edinburgh, 1781. — R. E. WALLIS, ANL 13; ANF 4, 173–198. — J. H. FREESE, The Octavius translated (SPCK). London, 1919. — G. H. RENDALL, *loc. cit.* — R. ARBESMANN, FC 10 (1950) 321–402. — *German:* A. MÜLLER, BKV² 14 (1913). — *Dutch:* H. U. MEYBOOM, Oudchristl. geschriften, dl. 44. Leiden, 1929. — P. H. DAMSTÉ, M. Minucius Felix, Octavius (Hermeneus-serie 1). Amsterdam, 1936. — *French:* F. RECORD, Minucius Felix, Octavius, trad. précédée d'une étude. Paris, 1911. — J. P. WALT-ZING, L'Octavius de Minucius Felix, trad. littérale, 3rd ed. Louvain, 1914. — *Italian:* U. MORICCA, L'Ottavio, introd. e versione. Florence, 1918; 2nd ed. 1923. — D. BASSI, Minucio Felice L'Ottavio, introd. e trad. Milan, 1929. — U. MORICCA, L'Ottavio, testo e trad. Rome, 1933. — *Spanish:* S. DE DOMINGO, Colección Excelsa 2. Madrid, 1946.

Studies: Text Criticism: E. LOEFSTEDT, Annotationes criticae in Octavium: Eranos 6 (1906) 1–28. — V. CARLIER, Authenticité de deux passages de Min. Felix (Oct. 34, 5 et 35, 1): Musée Belge (1897) 176–185. — P. v. WINTERFELD, Zu Min. Felix: Phil (1904) 315–317. — J. P. WALTZING, Une interversion de deux feuillets dans l'Octavius (chap. 21–24) de Min. Felix: Musée Belge (1906) 83–100; *idem*, Minucius Felix. Cod. Parisinus 1661: Musée Belge (1907) 319–321. — R. NIHARD, Minucius Felix, Oct. 36, 7: Musée Belge (1910) 229–230. — P. H. DAMSTÉ, Ad Oct. 22, 6: Mnem (1911) 241. — P. L. CICERI, Di un luogo corrotto dell'Octavius (23, 6): RFIC (1913) 291–293. — F. DI CAPUA, Octavius 7, 4: Didaskaleion (1913) 175–179. — J. MARTIN, Zu Minucius Felix (Oct. 34, 1; 5, 5): WSt (1915) 478. — R. REITZENSTEIN, Philologische Kleinigkeiten: Hermes (1916) 609–623. — A. BELTRAMI, M. Minucio Felice, Oct. 14, 1: RFIC (1919) 271–273. — P. THOMAS, Ad Minucium Felicem 2; 48, 4; 24, 3: Mnem (1921) 63. — G. THÖRNELL, Min. Fel. Oct. 7, 2: Festskr. Per Persson. Uppsala, 1922, 383 f. — G. RÉVAY, 'Pistorum praecipuo'. Un passo difficile nell'Octavius di M. Minucio Felice: Didaskaleion 1 (1923) 3–22. — E. HEIKEL, Adversaria in Minucii Felicis Octavium: Eranos (1923) 17–37, 56–72, 130–150. — J. W. PH. BORLEFFS, Ad Minucii Felicis Oct. 22, 9: Mnem (1925) 209–210. — B. RYBA, Sigismund Gelenius et son édition d'Arnobe et de Minucius Felix: Listy Filologicke (1925) 13–23, 91–108, 222–236, 337–341. — TH. BIRT, Marginalien zu lateinischen Prosaikern. Zu Min. Felix, Oct. 8, 4; 14, 15; 34, 1: Phil (1927) 164–182. — C.FRIES, Ad Minuc. Fel. Octav. 34, 2: PhW 48 (1928) 350 f. — G. SÖRBORN-Y. ENGLUND, Ad Minucium Felicem (Oct. 4, 1–5, 10): Eranos (1929) 146–148. — W. H. SHEWRING, Une fin de phrase dans l'Octavius de Minucius Felix: RB 41 (1929) 367. — E. ORTH, Zu Minucius Felix 26, 6: PhW (1931) 1135–1136. — A. C. VEGA, Notas críticas a la edición Hanstein del Octavio de Minucio Felix: Religión y Cultura 17 (1932) 411–416. — A. KURFESS, Textkritisches zu Minucius Felix: WSt 56 (1938) 121–124. — K. PRINZ, Zu Minucius Felix: WSt 57 (1939) 138–147. — B. AXELSON, Textkritisches zu Florus, Minucius Felix und Arnobius. Lund, 1944, 20–39, 63. — A. KURFESS, Zu Minucius Felix 26, 6: Würzburger Jahrbücher für die Altertumswissenschaft 2 (1947) 193–194. — M. PELLEGRINO, Minucio Felice, Octavius 29, 3 Nec ille miserabilis: Aevum 21 (1947) 142–146. — D. KUIJPER, Minuciana: VC 6 (1952) 201–207. *For the sources of the Octavius:* E. BEHR, Der Oktavius des Minucius Felix in seinem Verhältnisse zu Ciceros Büchern 'De natura deorum'. Diss. Gera, 1870. — V. CAR-LIER, Min. Felix et Sénèque: Musée Belge (1897) 258–293. — F. KOTEK, Anklänge an Ciceros De natura deorum bei Minucius Felix und Tertullian. Progr. Vienna, 1901. — F. X. BURGER, Minucius Felix und Seneca. Munich, 1904. — P. SHOREY, Plato and Minucius Felix: CR (1904) 302–303. — J. P. WALTZING, Platon, source directe de Min. Felix: Musée Belge (1904) 424–428. — W. KROLL, Randbemerkungen: RhM (1905) 307–314. — A. KAROSI, Quibusnam scriptoribus non christianis Min. Felix in Octavio componendo usus sit. Budapest, 1909. — S. COLOMBO, Osservazioni sulla composizione letteraria e sulle fonti di M. Minucio Felice: Didaskaleion 3 (1914) 79-121; 4 (1915) 215-244. — W. A. BAEHRENS, Literarhistorische Beiträge III. Minucius Felix et Favorinus: Hermes (1915) 456-463. — A. BELTRAMI, Clemente Alessandrino nell' Ottavio di Minucio Felice: RFIC (1919) 366-380; (1920) 239-257. — G. DE SANCTIS, Minucio Felice e Lucio Vero: RFIC 55 (1927) 233-235. — M. GALDI, Quid Minucius Felix in Octavio conscribendo a Trogo seu Justino derivaverit: Rivista Indo-Greca-Italica di filologia (1932) 136-139. — G. LAZZATI, L'Aristotele perduto e gli scrittori cristiani. Milan, 1938, 62-66. — Q. CATAUDELLA, Minucio Felice e Clemente Alessandrino: Studi Italiani di Filologia Classica 17 (1940) 271-281. — B. AXELSON, Quod idola und Laktanz: Eranos (1941) 67-74. — W. DEN BOER, Clément d'Alexandrie et Minuce Félix: Mnem 11 (1943) 161-190. — J. TOMASELLI NICOLOSI, Pagine lucreziane nell' Octavius di Minucio Felice: Miscellanea di Studi di Letteratura cristiana antica 1 (1947) 67-78. — G. QUISPEL, A Jewish Source of Minucius Felix: VC 3 (1949) 113-122.

For its date: F. MANDÒ, De Minucii Felicis aetate. Florence, 1903. — F. RAMORINO, L'Apologetico di Tertulliano e l'Ottavio di Minucio: Atti del Congresso internazionale di scienze storiche, Roma 1903, vol. 11 (1904) 143-178. — W. BRIKINGA, De litterarische betrekking tusschen den Apologeticus van Tertullianus en den Octavius van Minucius Felix. Groningen, 1905. — F. RAMORINO, Minucio Felice e Tertulliano. Nota biografico-cronologica: Didaskaleion (1912) 125-137. — J. STIGLMAYR, Zur Priorität des 'Octavius' des Minucius Felix gegenüber dem 'Apologeticum' Tertullians: ZkTh 37 (1913) 221-243. — E. BUONAIUTI, Il culto d'Iside a Roma e la data dell' Ottavio: Athenaeum (1916) 91-93. — A. BELTRAMI, RFIC (1919) 366-380; (1920) 239-257; *idem*, Minucio (Octavius) – Cicerone (De natura deorum) – Clemente Alessandrino (Opere): Atti della R. Accademia delle Scienze di Torino 55 (1919/20)179-187. — TH. REINACH, Minucius Felix et Tertullien: RHR 83 (1921) 59-68. — J. P. WALTZING, Encore Minucius Felix et Tertullien: Musée Belge 25 (1921) 18 9-196. — J. W. PH. BORLEFFS, Quaeritur quae ratio intersit inter Minucii Felicis Octavium et Apologeticum Tertulliani: Musée Belge (1922) 229-249.— J. VAN WAGENINGEN, Minucius Felix et Tertullianus: Mnem 51 (1923) 223-228. — G. GOETZ, Die literarhistorische Stellung des Octavius von Minucius Felix: ZNW 23 (1924) 161-173. — W. A. BAEHRENS, Minucius Felix und Tertullians Apologeticum: ZNW 23 (1924) 110-122. — A. GUDEMAN, Minucius Felix und Tertullian: PhW 44 (1924) 90-92. — E. HINNISDAELS, Minucius Felix est-il antérieur à Tertullien?: Musée Belge 28 (1924) 29-34; *idem*, L'Octavius de M. Felix et l'Apologétique de Tertullien (Mémoires Acad. royale Belgique 19, 2). Brussels, 1924. — R. HEINZE, PhW (1925) 956-962. — S. COLOMBO, Tertulliano e Minucio Felice: Didaskaleion 2 (1925) 45-62. — J. W. PH. BORLEFFS, De Tertulliano et Minucio Felice. Groningen, 1925. — G. GOETZ, PhW (1926) 745-754. — A. GUDEMAN, Nochmals Minucius Felix und Tertullian: PhW 46 (1926) 1067-1071; *idem*, Minucius Felix est-il antérieur à Tertullien?: Phil 82 (1927) 353-359. — J. LORTZ, Tertullian als Apologet I. Münster i.W., 1927, 394 ff. — M. SCHUSTER, Zur Frage der Priorität Tertullians vor Minucius Felix: Mitteilung des Vereins klassischer Philologen in Wien (1927) 12-22. — H. V. M. DENNIS, The Date of the Octavius: AJPh 50 (1929) 185-193. — J. SCHMIDT, Minucius Felix oder Tertullian? Philologisch-historische Untersuchung der Prioritätsfrage des Octavius und des Apologeticum unter physiognomischer Universalperspektive. Diss. Leipzig, 1932. — G. KRÜGER, ThLZ (1933) 226. — M. SCHUSTER, WSt (1934) 163-167. — H. DILLER, In Sachen Tertullian-Minucius Felix: Phil 44

(1935) 98–114, 216–239. — Z. K. Vysoky, L'état des recherches récentes sur la chronologie des œuvres apologétiques de Tertullien et de l'Octavius de Minucius Listy Filologicke (1938) 110–123. — B. Axelson, Das Prioritätsproblem Tertullian-Minucius Felix. Lund, 1941. Cf. A. Klotz, PhW 63 (1943) 12–15. — E. Paratore, La questione Tertulliano-Minucio. Testimonianze esterne ed argomenti interni: RR 18 (1947) 132–159. — G. Quispel, A Jewish Source of Minucius Felix: VC 3 (1949) 113–122.

For style and language: E. Norden, De Minucii Felicis aetate et genere dicendi. Greifswald, 1897. — H. Bornecque, Les clausules métriques dans Min. Felix: Musée Belge (1903) 247–265. — G. Charlier, Le dialogue dans l'Octavius: Musée Belge (1906) 75–82. — P. Faider, De l'emploi insolite du comparatif dans Min. Felix (Oct. 24, 3) Musée Belge (1906) 287–292; *idem*, Le style de Minucius Felix. Le chiasme: Musée Belge (1906) 293–307. — J. P. Waltzing, Minucius et le Thesaurus linguae latinae Musée Belge (1906) 67–74. — L. Dalmasso, L'archaismo nell' Octavius: RFIC (1909) 7–37. — L. Valmaggi, Di alcune particolarità grammaticali di Min. Fel. RFIC (1910) 552–559. — F. di Capua, L'evoluzione della prosa metrica nei primi tre secoli d. C. e la data dell' Ottavio di Minucio: Didaskaleion (1913) 1–41. — J. van Wageningen, De siccandis umoribus (ad Min. Fel. Oct. II § 3): Mnem N.S. 49 (1921) 102–105. — G. Goetz, Die literarhistorische Stellung des Oktavius von Minucius Felix: ZNW 23 (1924) 161–170. — A. Delatte, La réalité du dialogue de l'Octavius: Serta Leodensia. Liège, 1930, 103–108. — H. Hagendahl, Methods of citation in post classical Latin prose: Eranos (1947) 114–128. — C. Mohrmann, Les éléments vulgaires du latin des chrétiens (réaction puriste chez Minucius Felix) VC 2 (1948) 89–101, 162–184. — G. Quispel, De wijsgerige en rhetorische achtergrond van de Octavius van Minucius Felix: Handelingen van het 21ste Nederland philologen-congres. Groningen, 1950, 27 ff. — J. P. Waltzing, Lexicon Minucianum Paris, 1910.

General Studies: H. Leclercq, DAL 11, 1388–1412. — H. Opitz, PWK 15, 1816–1820. — H. Dessau, Minucius Felix und Caecilius Natalis: Hermes (1905) 373–386 — J. P. Waltzing, Studia Minuciana. Paris, 1906. — G. B. Bertoldi, M. Minucio Felice e il suo Dialogo Ottavio. Rome, 1906. — A. Elter, Prolegomena zu Minucius Felix. Bonn, 1909. — J. van Wageningen, Minucius Felix: Theol. Tijdschr. 5 (1913) 463–467. — C. Synnerberg, Die neuesten Beiträge zur Minucius-Literatur. Helsingfors, 1914. — C. M. Buizer, Quid Minucius Felix in conscribendo dialogo Octavio sibi proposuerit. Diss. Amsterdam, 1915. — E. Hertlein, Antonius Julianus ein römischer Geschichtsschreiber? Ein Versuch zur Erklärung von Minucius Felix Octavius 33, 2 ss: Phil (1921) 174–193. — J. P. Waltzing, Le crime rituel reproché aux chrétiens du IIe siècle: Musée Belge (1925) 209–238. — H. J. Baylis, Minucius Felix and His Place among the Early Fathers of the Latin Church. London, 1928. — E. Magaldi Della controversia An homo Plautinae prosapiae: Didaskaleion 7 (1929) 41–52. — J. W. Ph. Borleffs, De Lactantio in Epitome Minucii imitatore: Mnem 57 (1929) 415–426. — B. Berge, Exegetische Bemerkungen zur Dämonenauffassung des Minucius Felix. Diss. Freiburg, 1929. — M. Schuster, Minucius Felix und die christlichen Popularphilosophen: WSt 52 (1934) 163–167. — J. Schnitzer, Minucio Felice e la cremazione: Religio (1934) 32–44. — J. Wotke, Der Octavius des Minucius Felix ein christlicher λόγος προτρεπτικός: WSt (1935) 110–128. — J. H. van Haeringen, Cirtensis Noster (Minuc. Fel. 9, 6): Mnem 3 (1935) 29–32. — J. J. de Jong Apologetiek en christendom in den Octavius van Minucius Felix. With a summary in

English. (Diss. Leiden). Maastricht, 1935. — R. Bentler, Philosophie und Apologe-tik bei Minucius Felix. Königsberg, 1936. — A. Kurfess, Zu Minucius Felix: ThGl 30 (1938) 546–552. — G. H. Rendall, Minucius Felix: ChQ 128 (1939) 128–133. — A. D. Simpson, Epicureans, Christians, atheists in the second Century: TP (1941) 372–381. — L. Alfonsi, Appunti sull' Octavius di Minucio Felice: SC (1942) 70–73. — M. Pellegrino, Studi su l'antica apologetica. Rome, 1947, 152 ff. — G. L. Ells-permann, The Attitude of the Early Christian Writers Toward Pagan Literature and Learning (PSt 82). Washington, 1949, 14–22. — G. Quispel, 'Anima naturaliter christiana': Latomus 10 (1951) 163–169.

2. *The De fato*

In his *Octavius*, Minucius Felix refers to a treatise *On Fate* which he intended to write later: 'But enough of Fate for the moment; we reserve it for a fuller and more complete discussion elsewhere' (36,2). If he did, it has been lost. Jerome (*De vir. ill.* 58) knows of a book *De fato vel contra mathematicos*, attributed to Minucius Felix, but he doubts its authenticity: 'Still another work passes current in his name, *On Fate or Against the Mathematicians*, but this, although it is the work of a talented man, does not seem to me to corre-spond in style with the above mentioned work [Octavius].'

Study: J. R. G. Préaux, A propos du De fato (?) de Minucius Felix: Latomus 9 (1950) 395–413.

HIPPOLYTUS OF ROME

When Origen visited the Christian community at Rome about the year 212, he heard in one of the churches a sermon *On the Praise of our Lord and Saviour*. The preacher was the Roman priest Hippolytus, who later became the first anti-pope and died as a martyr (235), to be venerated by the Church as a saint to the present day. There are many reasons for believing that he was not a native Roman nor of Latin origin at all. His astonishing know-ledge of Greek philosophy from its beginnings to his own times as well as his intimate acquaintance with Greek mystery cults, his entire mentality, in short, indicates that he came from the East. His theological attitude and the relation of his doctrine of the Logos to that of the Greek theologians prove his Hellenistic training and connection with Alexandria. He is Greek in ex-pression as well as in thought, is, in fact, the last Christian author of Rome to employ that language. His literary output is com-parable in volume to that of his contemporary Origen but not in depth and independence of thought. He is more concerned with practical questions than scholarly problems. His diversity of interests, however, is wider than that of the Alexandrian master and extends to fields which Origen never entered: He published anti-heretical treatises, a Chronicle, a Church Order and even religious poetry. Photius (*Bibl. cod.* 121) claims that Hippolytus in one of his lost writings declared himself a disciple of Irenaeus. In that event he certainly shared his master's zeal for the defence of the Catholic doctrine against the various heresies. However, in his violent attack on trinitarian modalism and patri-passionism as it was taught by Noetus, Cleomenes, Epigonus and Sabellius, he went too far and defended a theology of the Logos which had subordinationistic tendencies. When Pope Callistus relaxed the treatment of penitents who had been guilty of mortal sin, the austere and ambitious Hippolytus accused him of having departed from the tradition of the primitive Church by his leniency. Moreover, he charged Callistus with being a follower of Sabellius and a heretic and he and some of his adherents separated from the Church. He was elected bishop of Rome by a small but influential circle and thus became the first anti-pope. Even when Callistus was succeeded by Urban (223–230) and Urban by Pontianus (230–235), the schism continued until Maximinus Thrax exiled both Pontianus and Hippolytus to Sardinia, where a reconciliation seems to have taken place. Pontianus resigned on the 28th of September 235 in order to enable the Roman community to elect a successor. Hippolytus must have laid down his office and returned to the Church before or after his departure from Rome. The now united community elected Anteros (235–236). Pontianus and Hippolytus died soon on 'the island of death.' Their bodies were brought to Rome by Pope Fabian (236–250) and solemnly interred, Pope Pontianus in the papal crypt of San Callisto, Hippolytus in the cemetery of the Via Tiburtina, which still carries his name. The burial took place on the same day, the thirteenth of August 236 or 237, and it is on this date still that the Church commemorates Hippolytus as a martyr. The oldest list of martyrs, the *depositio martyrum*, of the year 354 gives for *idus Aug.*, *Ypoliti in Tiburtina et Pontiani in Callisti* (EH 544,7; 547,19). Pope Damasus honored the tomb of Hippolytus with an inscription, in which he remarks that he had been a follower of Novatian (sic) but that he became a martyr, after admonishing his adherents before his death to be reconciled to the Church (EH 590). The Lateran Museum in Rome preserves the famous statue of St. Hippolytus which, discovered A.D. 1551, must have stood in the subterranean cemetery where he was interred or in the basilica nearby. It bears every mark of having been executed during the third century. It was erected by his admirers. On the chair in which the saint is seated, his Paschal Table and a complete list of his works are engraved.

Studies: E. Amann, Hippolyte: DTC 6, 2487–2511. — I. Döllinger, Hippolytus und Kallistus. Regensburg, 1853. — K. J. Neumann, Hippolytus von Rom in seiner Stellung zu Staat und Welt. Leipzig, 1902. — G. P. Strinopulos, Hippolyts philosophische Anschauungen. Diss. Leipzig, 1903. — A. d'Alès, La théologie de saint Hippolyte. Paris, 1906. 2nd ed. 1929. — K. Müller, Kleine Beiträge zur alten Kirchengeschichte 7. Der Ursprung des Schismas zwischen Kallist und Hippolyt: ZNW 23 (1924) 231–234. — A. Donini, Ippolito di Roma. Polemiche teologiche e controversie disciplinari nella Chiesa di Roma. Rome, 1925. — A. Festugière, L'idéal relig. des Grecs et l'Évangile. Paris, 1932. — G. Bardy, La vie spirituelle d'après les Pères des trois premiers siècles. Paris, 1935, 149–159. — M. da Leonessa, S. Ippolito della Via Tiburtina. Studi storico critico. Rome, 1935. — E. Josi, Quattro frammenti del carme di Damaso in onore di S. Ippolito: RAC 13 (1936) 231–236. — G. Bovini, S. Ippolito della via Tiburtina. Esame e critica delle antiche testimonianze su Ippolito: RAC 19 (1942) 35–85; *idem*, Sant' Ippolito, dottore e martire del III secolo. Vatican City, 1943. — G. da Bra, Studio su S. Ippolito dottore. Rome, 1944. — G. Bardy, L'énigme d'Hippolyte: Mélanges de science religieuse 5 (1948) 53–88. — G. Oggioni, La questione di Ippolito: SC 78 (1950) 126–143. — B. de Gaiffier, Les oraisons de l'office de s. Hippolyte dans le Libellus oratorium de Vérone: RAM 25 (1949) 219–224.

For *Hippolytus' statue,* see: G. Morin, La liste épigraphique des travaux de saint Hippolyte au Musée du Latran: RB 7 (1900) 241–251. — A. d'Alès, Souvenir de S. Hippolyte: Et (1906) 330–348, 475–490. — C. Wendel, Versuch einer Deutung der Hippolyt-Statue: ThStKr 108 (1937/38) 362–369. — G. Bovini, La statua di Sant' Ippolito del Museo Lateranense: Bolletino della Commissione Archeologica comunale in Roma: 68 (1940) 109–128. — P. Nautin, Note sur le catalogue des œuvres d'Hippolyte: RSR 34 (1947) 99–107. — B. Capelle, Hippolyte de Rome: RTAM 17 (1950) 145–174.

I. HIS WORKS

The writings of Hippolytus suffered the same fate as those of Origen, though for other reasons. Of the great number of his publications, the Greek text of very little remains. The loss of the originals must be attributable not only to his heretical christology and schismatic position but much more to the fact that after his time the knowledge of Greek in Rome gradually disappeared. Fortunately, many of his works have survived complete and others in fragments in Latin, Syriac, Coptic, Arabic, Ethiopic, Armenian, Georgian and Slavonian versions. The volume and variety of oriental translations indicate that his name remained famous in the East; so much so that even many non-authentic treatises were attributed to him.

Editions: MG 10 and 16, 3. — G. N. BONWETSCH-H. ACHELIS, GCS 1 (1897); P. WENDLAND, GCS 26 (1916); A. BAUER-R. HELM, GCS 36 (1929).

Translations: English: J. H. MacMAHON and S. D. F. SALMOND, ANL 9, 2; ANF 5. — *French:* DE GENOUDE, Les Pères de l'Église. Paris, 1837–1843. — *German:* K. PREYSING, BKV² 40 (1922).

1. *The Philosophumena*

The most valuable of all his works is the *Philosophumena* or *Refutation of all Heresies*. The author himself calls it at the beginning of the first book Κατὰ πασῶν αἱρέσεων ἔλεγχος.

The entire treatise consists of ten books. Only the first four, dealing with the philosophy of the Greeks, are referred to by the writer himself (9,3) as the *Philosophumena* or *Exposition of Philosophical Tenets*, this name not applying to the rest. No list of his titles, neither Eusebius' (*Hist. eccl.* 6,22) nor St. Jerome's (*De vir. ill.* 61) nor that on his statue, mentions this, the principal study by Hippolytus. The first book has been known since 1701 but it was handed down as Origen's and always ascribed to him in the printed editions. Books 2 and 3 remain lost, but 4–10 were discovered by Minoides Mynas in 1842 in a Greek codex of the fourteenth century, which belonged then to Mt. Athos but is now in Paris. These were published (together with Book 1) for the first time at Oxford in 1851 by M. E. Miller, but as a composition of Origen's. It was not until 1859 that the *Philosophumena* was finally restored to Hippolytus, and that in the edition by L. Dunker and F. G. Schneidewind. In the proem and two other passages (10,32 and 10,30) the author refers to *Syntagma, Essence of the Universe,* and the *Chronicle* as previous monographs of his own— and all of these belong, we know, to Hippolytus. Thus his authorship was generally acknowledged until P. Nautin recently contested it without, it seems, convincing reasons.

The author depends for his material and method upon his

master, Irenaeus. The introduction describes the content, plan and division:

> We shall prove that they [the heretics] are atheists, both in opinion and their mode [of treating a question] and in fact, and whence it is that their attempted theories have accrued unto them, and that they have endeavoured to establish their tenets, taking nothing from the Holy Scriptures—nor is it from preserving the succession of any saint that they have hurried headlong into these opinions;—but that their doctrines have derived their origin from the wisdom of the Greeks, from the conclusions of those who have formed systems of philosophy, and from would-be mysteries and the vagaries of astrologers. It seems then advisable in the first instance to explain the opinions advanced by the philosophers of the Greeks and to prove to our readers that these are of greater antiquity than those [heresies], and more deserving of reverence in reference to their views respecting the divinity; in the next place to compare each heresy with the system of each speculator, so as to show that the earliest champion of the heresy availing himself of these attempted theories has turned them to advantage by appropriating their principles, and, impelled from these into worse, has constructed his own doctrine. The undertaking admittedly is full of labor, and is one requiring extended research. We shall not, however, be wanting in exertion... In the commencement, therefore, we shall declare who first among the Greeks pointed out the principles of natural philosophy. For from these especially have they furtively taken their views who have first propounded these theories, as we shall subsequently prove when we come to compare them one with another. Assigning to each of those who take the lead among philosophers their own peculiar tenets, we shall publicly exhibit these heresiarchs as naked and unseemly (Proem. ANF).

From this summary the entire plan of the work is quite evident. The author intends to show the unchristian character of the heresies by proving their dependence upon pagan philosophy. For this reason the *Refutation* consists of two parts. The first, comprising books 1–4, deals with the different pagan systems. Book One is a rather poor compendium of the history of Greek Philos-

ophy from Thales to Hesiod, using secondhand and unreliable
sources. Books Two and Three are lost, but they must have been
devoted to the mystery cults and mythologies of the Greeks and
barbarians. The fourth book discusses astrology and magic. The
second part of the treatise, books 5–9, refutes the heresies by
coupling each one of the 33 Gnostic sects with some philosophical
or pagan system previously mentioned. The tenth book, after
summing up the previous exposition, gives a chronology of Jewish
history and an exposition of the true doctrine. Books 5–9 have
more value than the others because here the author is more on
his own and shows more critical judgment. Although he depends
to a large extent on Irenaeus, *Adversus Haereses*, it is quite obvious
that he made use of various Gnostic works no longer extant. The
Refutation remains therefore one of the most important sources
for the history of Gnosticism. The author hints (9,12) that Pope
Callistus was dead when he composed his treatise. Thus it must
have been written after the year 222.

Editions: P. WENDLAND, GCS 26 (1916) 1–293. — E. MILLER, Origenis Philosophumena sive omnium haeresium refutatio, e codice Parisino nunc primum edidit,
Oxford, 1851. — L. DUNCKER et F. G. SCHNEIDEWIN, S. Hippolyti Episc. et Mart.
Refutationis omnium haeresium librorum decem quae supersunt, rec., latine vert.,
notas adiec. Göttingen, 1859. — MG 16.— P. CRUICE, Philosophumena sive haeresium omnium confutatio, opus Origeni adscriptum, e cod. Paris. rec. Paris, 1860. —
H. DIELS, Doxographi Graeci. Berlin, 1879, 551–576 (First book only).

Translations: English: J. H. MACMAHON, ANL 6; ANF 5, 9–153. — J. LEGGE, Philosophumena, or the Refutation of All the Heresies Formerly Attributed to Origen
but now to Hippolytus, translated (SPCK). London, 1921. — *French:* A. SIOUVILLE,
Philosophumena our réfutation de toutes les hérésies, trad. et notes (Coll. Les
textes du christianisme). Paris, 1928. — *German:* K. PREYSING, BKV² 40 (1922). —
Dutch: H. U. MEYBOOM, Hippolytus, Weerlegging van alle ketterijen (Oudchristl.
geschriften, dl. 23/24). Leiden, 1920.

Studies: C. C. J. BUNSEN, Hippolytus and His Age. London, 1852; 2nd ed. 1854,
4 vols. — C. WORDSWORTH, St. Hippolytus and the Church of Rome in the Early
Part of the Third Century. London, 1853. — J. DÖLLINGER, Hippolytus und Kal-
listus. Regensburg, 1853. — W. ELFE TAYLOR, Hippolytus and the Christian Church
of the Third Century. London, 1853. — G. VOLKMAR, Die Quellen der Ketzergeschichte bis zum Nicaenum. I: Hippolytus. Zürich, 1855. — J. B. LIGHTFOOT, The
Apostolic Fathers. Part I. London, 1890, 317–477: Hippolytus of Porticus. — G. SAL-
MON, The Cross-References in the 'Philosophumena': Hermathena 5 (1885) 389–402.
— H. STÄHELIN, Die gnostischen Quellen Hippolyts in seiner Hauptschrift gegen die
Häretiker (TU 6, 3). Leipzig, 1890, 1–108. — J. DRÄSEKE, Zur Refutatio omnium
haeresium des Hippolitus: Zeitschr. wiss. Theol. (1902) 263–289; *idem*, Noëtus und

die Noëtianer in des Hippolytus Refutatio IX, 6–10: *ibid.* (1903) 213–233; *idem*, Zur Frage der Eschatologie bei Hippolytus Refut. IX, 10: *ibid.* 49 (1906) 239–252. — A. D'ALÈS, Les livres II et III des Philosophumena: REG (1906) 1–9. — R. GAN-SCHINIETZ, Hippolytos' Capitel gegen die Magier, Ref. Haer. IV, 28–42 (TU 39, 2). Leipzig, 1913. — S. SCHNEIDER, St. Hippolytus on the Greek Mysteries: Rospr. Akademji 56 (1917) 329-377 (Polish). — K. MÜLLER, ZNW (1924) 231–234. — K. PREYSING, Hippolyt Philosophumena IX, 12, 16: ZkTh 50 (1926) 604–608. — LUK-MAN, Bogoslovni Vestnik (1927) 177–184. — G. REVEL, S. Ippolito ed i Philosophumena: Bilychnis (1929) I, 259–266. — C. M. EDSMAN, Schöpferwille und Geburt Jac 1, 18. Eine Studie zur altchristl. Kosmogonie: ZNW (1939) 11–44. — K. REIN-HARDT, Heraklits Lehre vom Feuer: Hermes (1942) 1–27. — G. DA BRA, I Filosofumeni sono di Ippolito? Rome, 1942. — J. FILLIOZAT, La doctrine des brâhmanes d'après saint Hippolyte: RHR 130 (1945) 59–91. — E. PETERSON, Le traitement de la rage par les Elkésaïtes d'après Hippolyte: RSR 34 (1947) 232–238. — P. NAUTIN, Hippolyte et Josippe. Contribution à l'histoire de la littérature chrétienne du 3e siècle. Paris, 1947. Cf. J. DANIÉLOU, RSR (1948) 596–598; G. BARDY, Mélanges de science religieuse (1948) 63–88; RICHARD, *ibid.* (1948) 294–308. — P. NAUTIN, RSR (1947) 100–107, 347–359. — G. QUISPEL, Note sur Basilide (citée par Hippolyte): VC 2 (1948) 115–116. — H. J. SCHOEPS, Theologie und Geschichte des Judenchristentums. Tübingen, 1949. — G. BARDY, 'Philosophie' et 'Philosophe' dans le vocabulaire chrétien des premiers siècles: RAM 25 (1949) 97–108. — J. DORESSE, Nouveaux aperçus historiques sur les gnostiques coptes. Ophites et Séthiens: Bulletin de l'Institut d'Egypte 31 (1948/49) 409–419. — P. NAUTIN, La controverse sur l'auteur de l'Elenchos: RHE 47 (1952) 5–43.

2. *The Syntagma or Against All Heresies* (Πρὸς ἁπάσας τὰς αἱρέσεις)

Long before his *Philosophumena* or *Refutation of all Heresies*, Hippolytus had composed a work called by Eusebius (*Hist. eccl.* 6,22) *Against All Heresies*, by St. Jerome (*De vir. ill.* 61) *Adversum omnes haereses*, but by Photius (*Bibl. cod.* 121) *Syntagma*, or to quote him exactly, 'Syntagma against thirty-two heresies of Hippolytus, the pupil of Irenaeus.' He gives the following description:

It begins with the Dositheans and goes down to the heresies of Noetus and the Noetians, which he says were refuted by Irenaeus in his lectures, of which the present work is a synopsis. The style is clear, and somewhat severe and free from redundancies, although it exhibits no tendency to atticism (*ibid.* SPCK).

This allusion is very valuable because the original is lost. However, it can be reconstructed from the extracts preserved. The catalogue of the thirty-two heresies with which Hippolytus dealt in the *Syntagma* can be assembled from later authors who went to him as a source. R. A. Lipsius proved that the list of false doctrines printed at the end of the *De praescriptione* (46–53) of Tertullian is only a summary of the above study and that Epiphanius in his *Panarion* and Philastrius in his *Liber de haeresibus* also made wide use of it. Thus it appears as if this smaller work had a greater influence on later generations than the *Philosophumena*. The *Syntagma* belongs to the earlier period of Hippolytus, when Zephyrinus was bishop of Rome (199–217). It is mentioned in the preface to his *Philosophumena* (1,20).

Edition: P. NAUTIN, Hippolyte: Contre les hérésies, fragment, étude et édition critique. Paris, 1949.

Studies: R. A. LIPSIUS, Zur Quellenkritik des Epiphanios. Vienna, 1865. — J. DRÄSEKE, Zum Syntagma des Hippolytos: Zeitschr. wiss. Theol. 46 (1903) 58–90. — C. MARTIN, Le Contra Noetum de saint Hippolyte fragment d'homélie ou finale du Syntagma?: RHE 37 (1941) 5–23.

3. *The Antichrist* (Περὶ τοῦ ἀντιχρίστου)

Of his dogmatic tracts only one has come down to us complete, that on antichrist, written about the year 200 and preserved in the Greek text. It is addressed to a certain Theophilus, whom the author calls 'my beloved brother.' Hippolytus, beginning with an outline of his work (ch. 5), states that he will deal with the following questions:

> What and of what manner the coming of antichrist is; on what occasion and at what time that impious one shall be revealed; whence and from what tribe he shall come; and what his name is, which is indicated by the number in the Scripture; and how he shall work error among the people, gathering them from the ends of the earth; and how he shall stir up tribulation and persecution against the saints; and how he shall glorify himself as God; and what his end shall be; and how the sudden appearing of the Lord shall be revealed from heaven; and what the conflagration of the whole world shall be; and what the glorious and heavenly kingdom of the saints is to be, when they reign together with Christ; and what the punishment of the wicked by fire (ANF).

Since many of his contemporaries regarded Rome as the empire of antichrist, the author makes it quite clear that Rome represents merely the fourth power in the vision of Daniel, and it is only later that antichrist will appear. Thus his coming is not imminent despite the new persecution of the Christians under Septimius Severus. This treatise is the most comprehensive discussion of the problem of antichrist in patristic literature. Hippolytus proves himself in some of his opinions a pupil of Irenaeus, although in others he differs with him considerably.

The authenticity of the work is established by the fact that Hippolytus calls it his own in his *Commentary on Daniel* (4,7,1; 13,1). The Greek text exists in three manuscripts. There are also an Old Slavonic and a Georgian version and fragments in Armenian.

Edition: H. ACHELIS, GCS 1, 2 (1897) 1–47.

Translations: English: S. D. F. SALMOND, ANL 9; ANF; 5, 204–209. — *German:* V. GRÖNE, BKV (1873).

Studies: H. ACHELIS, Hippolytstudien (TU NF 1, 4). Leipzig, 1897, 65 ff. — P. WENDLAND, Textkonstruktion der Schrift über den Antichrist: Hermes (1899) 412–427. — K. J. NEUMANN, Hippolytus von Rom in seiner Stellung zu Staat und Welt, Abt. I. Leipzig, 1902, 11–61.

4. *Exegetical Treatises*

Like his contemporary Origen, Hippolytus composed a great number of Commentaries on the Books of the Old and the New Testament. He also has this in common with the Alexandrian, that he follows the allegorical and typological method of interpretation, although there is quite a difference between Origen's mystical and Hippolytus' more jejune applications. But of all his exegetical treatises very little remains.

a. *The Commentary on Daniel*

The best preserved is that on Daniel. The entire text is extant in an Old Slavonic version and most of it in the original Greek in fragments. Composed about the year 204, it represents the earliest known exegetical treatise of the Christian Church that we possess. Quite a number of passages indicate that Hippolytus wrote it while still under the impression made by the persecution of Septimius Severus, which began in the year 202.

The Commentary is divided into four books. The author uses the Greek version of Theodotian as his text, including even the deuterocanonical sections. The first book deals with the story of Susanna. The author sees in her the prefiguration of the immaculate Bride of Christ, the Church, persecuted by two peoples, the Jews and the pagans:

> Susanna prefigured the Church and Joachim, her husband, Christ; and the garden, the calling of the saints, who are planted like fruitful trees in the Church. And Babylon is the world; and the two elders are set forth as a figure of the two peoples that plot against the Church—the one, namely, of the circumcision, and the other of the Gentiles. For the words, 'were appointed rulers of the people and judges' mean that in this world they exercise authority and rule, judging the righteous unrighteously... For how, indeed, can those who have been the enemies and corruptors of the Church judge righteously, or look up to heaven with pure heart, when they have become the slaves of the prince of this world?... for always the two peoples, being instigated by Satan working in them, strive to raise persecutions and afflictions against the Church, and seek how they may corrupt her, though they do not agree with each other (1,14–15 ANF)... The blessed Susanna, then, when she heard these words [of the elders], was troubled in her heart, and set a watch upon her mouth, not wishing to be defiled by the wicked elders. Now it is in our power also to apprehend the real meaning of all that befell Susanna. For you may find this also fulfilled in the present condition of the Church. For when the two peoples conspire to destroy any of the saints, they watch for a fit time, and enter the house of God, and seize some of them, and carry them off, and keep hold of them, saying, Come, consent with us, and worship our Gods; and if not, we will bear witness against you. And when they refuse, they drag them before the court, and accuse them of acting contrary to the decrees of Caesar, and condemn them to death (*ibid.* 20 ANF).

The second book explains the four kingdoms mentioned in Daniel 2 and 7 as the Babylonian, Persian, Greek and Roman Empires. The third deals with the all-important question of his day: the Christian and the State. In the fourth book (ch. 23) there appears for the first time in patristic literature December 25 as the date of the birth of Christ and March 25 as that of his death. The author states that Christ was born on Wednesday, December the 25th, in the forty-second year of the Emperor Augustus. The passage would be very valuable for the history of the feast of the Nativity but it seems to be an interpolation, though added very early.

Editions: G. N. BONWETSCH, GCS 1, 1 (1897) 1–340. — G. BARDY, Hippolyte, Commentaire sur Daniel, introd. de G. B., texte et trad. de M. LEFÈVRE (SCH 14). Paris, 1947.

Translations: English: S. D. F. SALMOND, ANL 9; ANF 5, 177–194. — *French:* M. LEFÈVRE, *loc. cit.* — *German:* G. N. BONWETSCH, *loc. cit.*

Studies: O. BARDENHEWER, Des hl. Hippolytus von Rom Kommentar zum Buche Daniel. Ein literärgeschichtl. Versuch. Freiburg i.B., 1877. — G. SALMON, The Commentary of Hippolytus on Daniel: Hermathena 8 (1893) 161–190. — E. BRATKE, Die Lebenszeit Christi im Danielkommentar des Hippolytus: Zeitschr. wiss. Theol. 35 (1892) 120–176; *idem,* Der Tag der Geburt Christi in der Ostertafel des Hippolytus: Jahrb. prot. Theol. 18 (1892) 439–456. — A. HILGENFELD, Die Zeiten der Geburt, des Lebens und des Leidens Jesu nach Hippolytus: Zeitschr. wiss. Theol. 35 (1892) 257–281. — E. BRATKE, Zur Frage nach dem Todesjahre Christi: ThStKr 65 (1892) 734–757. — A. HILGENFELD, Die Lebenszeit Jesu bei Hippolytus: Zeitschr. wiss. Theol. 36 (1893) 106–117. — G. N. BONWETSCH, Die Datierung der Geburt Christi in dem Danielkommentar Hippolyts: NGWG Phil. hist. Kl. (1895) 515–527; *idem,* Die handschriftliche Überlieferung des Danielkommentars Hippolyts: *ibid.* (1896) 16–42; *idem,* Studien zu den Kommentaren Hippolyts zum Buche Daniel und zum Hohenliede (TU NF 1, 2). Leipzig, 1897. — E. VIOLARD, Étude sur le 'Commentaire d'Hippolyte sur le livre de Daniel'. Montbéliard, 1903. — C. DIOBOUNIOTIS, Hippolyts Danielkommentar in Handschrift Nr. 573 des Meteoronklosters (TU 38, 1). Leipzig, 1911. — G. N. BONWETSCH, Hippolyts Danielkommentar, Buch I, 1–14: NGWG (1918) 313–317; (1919) 347–360. — R. EISLER, Κάστυ τοῦ γραμματέως im Danielkommentar des Hippolytus von Rom: OLZ (1930) 585–587. — G. OGG, Is A. D. 41 the date of the Crucifixion?: JThSt 43 (1942) 187–188. — P. ANDRIESSEN, À propos d'un agraphon cité par Hippolyte: VC 2 (1948) 248–249. — R. WILDE, The Treatment of the Jews in the Greek Christian Writers of the First Three Centuries (PSt 81). Washington, 1949, 159–168.

b. *The Commentary on the Canticle of Canticles*

The complete text is extant only in Georgian, but fragments exist in Greek, Slavonic, Armenian and Syriac. The Commentary, though it goes only to Canticle 3,7, in the Georgian version, may possibly, however, represent the entire treatise. This translation is preserved in a manuscript of the tenth century, but dates from a much earlier time. It is a literal rendering of an Armenian version, which came from the Greek original.

The tone of the Commentary is oratorical and several passages suggest that the author is speaking to a congregation. Thus it seems that the treatise consists of homilies. The interpretation is allegorical and reminds one of Origen's Commentary on the same biblical book. The King in the Canticle is Christ and the Church is His Bride. Hippolytus shares also with Origen the idea that occasionally the spouse in the Canticle stands for the God-loving soul; this allegory strongly influenced all later exegesis in the West and survived in the mysticism of the middle ages. St. Ambrose has made ample use of Hippolytus' work in his explanation of Psalm 118.

Editions: G. N. Bonwetsch, GCS 1, 1 (1897) 341–374. Greek fragment. The Armenian, Syriac and Slavic fragments in a German translation. — The original text of the Armenian and Syriac fragments in: J. B. Pitra, Analecta sacra 2, 232–235. — The Georgian version: N. Marr, Hippolyt, die Auslegung des Hohenliedes, der grusinische Text nach einer Handschrift des 10. Jahrhunderts, eine Übersetzung aus dem Armenischen, untersucht, übersetzt und hrsg. (Texte u. Untersuchungen in der armenisch-grusinischen Philologie III). St. Petersburg, 1901 (Russian). — G. N. Bonwetsch, Hippolyts Kommentar zum Hohenlied auf Grund von N. Marrs Ausgabe des grusinischen Textes herausgegeben (TU 23, 2c). Leipzig, 1902.

Translations: English: S. D. F. Salmond, ANL 9; ANF 5, 176. — *German:* G. N. Bonwetsch, *loc. cit.* — *Russian:* N. Marr, *loc. cit.*

Studies: G. N. Bonwetsch, Studien zu den Kommentaren zum Buche Daniel und Hohenliede (TU 16, 2). Leipzig, 1897. — W. Riedel, Die Auslegung des Hohenliedes in der jüdischen Gemeinde und der griechischen Kirche. Leipzig, 1897. — A. Sovic, Fragmentum commentarii anonymi in Canticum Canticorum: Bibl 2 (1921) 448–452. — R. P. Blake, ROC (1925/26) 225 ff. — J. A. Montgomery, in: The Song of Songs: a Symposium, ed. W. H. Schoff. Philadelphia, 1924, 21 ff. — L. Welsersheimb, Das Kirchenbild der griechischen Väterkommentare zum Hohen Lied: ZkTh 70 (1948) 400–404.

c. *On the Blessing of Jacob*

This Commentary on Genesis 49 is preserved in the Greek original as well as in an Armenian and a Georgian version. It served as a source for Ambrose's *De benedictionibus patriarcharum* and for the so-called *Tractatus Origenis de libris ss. scripturarum*, which seems rather to belong to Gregory of Eliberis.

d. *On the Blessing of Moses*

A Commentary on Deuteronomy 33, extant in an Armenian and a Georgian translation and in two small fragments of the Greek original.

Edition: L. Mariès, Hippolyte de Rome, Sur les bénédictions d'Isaac, de Jacob et de Moïse. Notes sur la tradition manuscrite, texte grec, versions arménienne et géorgienne (Coll. d'études anciennes). Paris, 1935.

Translations: German: G. N. BONWETSCH, Drei georgisch erhaltene Schriften von Hippolytus, der Segen Jakobs, der Segen Moses', die Erzählung von David und Goliath (TU 26, 1a). Leipzig, 1904.

Studies: O. BARDENHEWER, Neue exegetische Schriften des hl. Hippolytus: BiZ 3 (1905) 1–16. — C. DIOBOUNIOTIS und N. BEÏS, Hippolyts Schrift über die Segnungen Jakobs (TU 38, 1). Leipzig, 1911. — L. MARIÈS, Le Messie issu de Lévi chez saint Hippolyte: RSR 39/40 (1951/52) 381–396.

e. *The Story of David and Goliath*

It is a homily on 1 Kings 17 preserved in an Armenian and a Georgian version.

f. *On the Psalms*

The statue of Hippolytus mentions in the list of his writings a treatise on the Psalms (εἰς τοὺς ψαλμούς) and St. Jerome (*De vir. ill.* 61) knows of this work, which he calls *De psalmis*. However in his *Epist.* 112,20, he does not number Hippolytus among those who wrote a commentary on the entire Psalter, so it seems that he dealt only with a selection. Theodoret of Cyrus quotes three passages, one on Psalm 2,7, the other on Psalm 22,1 and the third on Psalm 23,7. This is all that remains of the Greek text. De Lagarde and Martin published an introduction to the Psalms by Hippolytus in a Syriac version. It differs very little from Origen's preface to the same book. Each studies the number of the psalms, their authors, their titles, and the different proofs for their authenticity. Each discusses what particular psalms are to be attributed to Moses, to David and to his assistant poets. From a reference which Origen makes to a passage of Hippolytus' Commentary, the authenticity of which is clearly established, it appears that Origen used the latter's work.

Editions: H. ACHELIS, GCS 1, 2 (1897) 127–153. — The Syriac text of the introduction, in: P. DE LAGARDE, Analecta Syriaca 83–87.

Translations: English: S. D. F. SALMOND, ANL 9; ANF 5, 170–172. — *German:* SCHULTESS, GCS 1, 2 (1897) 127–135.

Studies: H. ACHELIS, Hippolytstudien (TU NF 4). Leipzig, 1897. — G. FICKER, Studien zur Hippolytfrage. Leipzig, 1893, 107. — A. WAGNER, Die Erklärung des 118 Ps. durch Origenes (Progr. Gymnas. Seitenstetten). Linz, 1916/1921. — A. SOVIC, Bogoslovska Smotra (1925) 23–32 (Fragment). — H. E. W. TURNER, A Psalm Prologue contained in Ms. Bodl. Baroceianus: JThSt 41 (1940) 280–287.—E. SCHWARTZ, Zwei Predigten Hippolyts (SAM Philos.-hist. Abt. 1936, Heft 3). Munich, 1936.

The following exegetical writings are lost except for a few fragments: *The Six Days of Creation, What Followed the Six Days, The Blessing of Isaac, The Blessing of Balaam, Moses' Song, The Book of Ruth, Elkanah and Hannah, The Witch of Endor, Proverbs, Ecclesiastes, Part of Isaias, Parts of Ezechiel, Zacharias, Parts of Matthew, The Two Thieves, The Parable of the Talents, The Apocalypse.*

Fragments: H. ACHELIS, GCS 1, 2 (1897) 49–71 In Genesim; 85–119 In Pentateuchum; 82 Ex benedictionibus Balaam; 120 Ex interpretatione Ruth; 121–122 In Helcanam et Annam; 155–167 In Proverbia; 179 De Ecclesiaste; 180 In principium Isaiae; 183 In Ezechielen; 195–208 In Matthaeum; 211 De duobus latronibus; 213–227 In evangelium Johannis et de resurrectione Lazari; 209 De distributione talentorum.

Translations: English: S. D. F. SALMOND, ANL 9; ANF 5, 163–169 In Genesim; 163 In Hexaëmeron; 169 Ex benedictionibus Balaam; 172–176 In Proverbia; 176–177 In Isaiam; 194 In Matthaeum; In Lucam.

Studies: H. ACHELIS, Hippolytstudien 137–163. — C. MARTIN, Note sur l'homélie εἰς τὸν τετραήμερον Λάζαρον, attribuée à saint Hippolyte de Rome: RHE 22 (1926) 68–70. — P. BELET, Fragmentos desconocidos de Hipólito de Roma en la tradición copta (sobre Mateo 24, 15–34): Sefarad 6 (1946) 355–361. — M. L. CONCASTY, Le fonds Supplément grec du Département des manuscrits de la Bibliothèque Nationale de Paris: Byz 20 (1950) 21–26.

5. *Chronological Treatises*

a. *The Chronicle* (Χρονικῶν βίβλοι)

In 234 Hippolytus composed a chronicle of world history, which reaches from the creation to the year of its composition. He wrote it against any hasty expectations of the Day of Judgment and the millennium—a preoccupation of much Christian thought during the severe contemporary persecutions. In his anxiety to counteract this idea, Hippolytus takes the trouble to prove in three different ways that, when he wrote this *Chronicle,* only 5738 years could be counted since the beginning of the world. Consequently, its end, which would come only after six thousand years, was still far off. One of the most important parts of the book is the *Diamerismos* or 'Division' of the earth among the posterity of Noah (Gen. 10). Thanks to this very detailed section, the *Chronicle* was used again and again by later writers. Included was the *Stadiasmos,* or measurement in stadia, of the distance from Alexandria to Spain with a description of the harbors, the drinking water facilities, the shores of the Mediterranean and other valuable information for the captain of a ship, in other words, a kind of guide to navigation. Though this, like so many other things in the book, was probably taken from Hellenistic compendia, yet the main source of the work as a whole was the Bible. It owes some inspiration also to the *Chronicle* of Julius Africanus which appeared in A.D. 221 and to the chronological section of Clement of Alexandria's *Stromateis* (1,109 –136). The Greek original no longer exists save for a few fragments, one of considerable length found by A. Bauer in a Madrid manuscript of the tenth century, and another preserved in *Oxyrh. papyrus* No. 870 (Vol. 6,176) of the seventh. But, we have three independent Latin versions, the *Excerpta Barbari* and the two *Libri generationis*. Of the latter two, the first gives a rather faithful translation and employed an original apparently the same as that of the Armenian version edited by B. Sargisean.

Editions: A. BAUER-R. HELM, GCS 36 (1929) 45–227. Cf. K. MRAS, PhW 50 (1930) 769–772.

Studies: A. BAUER, Die Chronik des Hippolytos im Matritensis Graecus 121, nebst einer Abhandlung über den Stadiasmus Maris Magni von O. Cuntz (TU 29, 1). Leipzig, 1905; *idem,* Hippolytus von Rom, der Heilige und Geschichtsschreiber: Neue Jahrbücher für das klassische Altertum 33 (1914) 110–124. — D. SERRUYS, Un fragment sur papyrus de la Chronique d'Hippolyte de Rome: RPh 38 (1914) 26–31. — W. BANNIER, Ein Papyrusfragment aus der Chronik des Hippolytus: Phil 35 (1926) 123–127. Cf. R. P. BLAKE, ROC 25 (1926) 225–231. — G. OGG, The Computist of A.D. 243 and Hippolytus: JThSt 48 (1947) 206–207. — M. RICHARD, Comput et chronographie chez saint Hippolyte. Lille, 1950.

b. *The Determination of the Date of Easter*

The chair of the statue of Hippolytus contains, in the list of his works carved upon the back of it, a treatise entitled: *Determination of the Date of Easter* ('Απόδειξις χρόνων τοῦ πάσχα). It is evidently the same work as that mentioned by Eusebius in his *Ecclesiastical History* (6,22,1):

At that very time also Hippolytus, besides many other memoirs, composed the treatise *On Easter*, in which he sets forth a register of the times and puts forward a certain canon of a sixteen-year cycle for Easter, using the first year of the Emperor Alexander as a terminus in measuring his dates (LCL).

From this passage it appears that the work was written in the year A.D. 222. The Easter Tables carved on the side of the chair are taken from it and reach from 222 to 233. They represent the largest extant fragment. The intention of the author was to make the Church independent of the Jewish Calendar and to calculate scientifically the Easter full moon. He failed in the attempt, because as early as A.D. 237, his solution got out of harmony with the astronomical facts. This indicates that the famous statue must have been erected at least before that year. There are only brief passages of this work left in Greek and Syriac besides that on the chair. In order to correct Hippolytus' cycle, an anonymous author composed in the year 243 a work entitled *De pascha computus;* this is found among the writings of St. Cyprian (cf. below, p. 369f).

Fragments: A. HARNACK, Geschichte der altchristl. Literatur 1, 625 ff. — E.SCHWARTZ, Christliche und jüdische Ostertafeln (AGWG Phil.-histor. Kl. NF 8, 6). Berlin, 1906, 29–40. Cf. M. RICHARD, Comput et chronographie chez saint Hippolyte. Lille, 1950.

6. *Homilies*

Although most of the exegetical commentaries of Hippolytus are of homiletic character and written for the edification of the faithful, so that it is almost impossible to draw a line between the exegetical and homiletic works, there are some sermons which must be mentioned here.

a. *On the Passover* (Εἰς τὸ ἅγιον πάσχα)

Eusebius (*Hist. eccl.* 6,22,1) mentions two works of Hippolytus *On the Pasch.* One of them is his *Determination of the Date of Easter,* as explained above, the other was regarded as lost until Ch. Martin thought to have discovered it in 1926 among the sermons of Chrysostom (MG 59,735–746). Ten years later he published a large part of the work from a Grottaferrata palimpsest of the eighth or ninth century, *Codex Cryptoferratensis B. a.* LV, which attributes it even by name 'to Hippolytus, the bishop of Rome and martyr.' Thus the identification seemed to be beyond doubt. P. Nautin, however, has recently proven its theology definitely anti-Arian, stressing the undiminished Godhead and unimpaired manhood of Christ, though ascribing to the latter 'an ngelic nature.' Such considerations are foreign to the mind of Hippolytus. Furthermore, it lays special emphasis on the will of the Logos in the incarnation, whereas Hippolytus regards only the will of the Father. Finally, the doxology at the end praises Christ alone, while the great number of such formulas in Hippolytus never fail to mention the First Person also. All this points to the fourth century. Nevertheless the discovery of Ch. Martin remains important because of the unmistakable indications that Hippolytus served as principal source, and we are thus enabled to gain some idea of his lost *Homily on the Pasch*. The present sermon, as well as its third-century prototype, takes up Exodus 12,1–14. 43–49, the narrative of the institution of the Passover preparatory to Israel's deliverance, and shows clause by clause how the event foreshadows our redemption. It is a triumphal acclamation of the divine plan of salvation that becomes in form almost a hymn. Christ himself is the Passover and did not, consequently, partake of it. There follows a description of the descent into limbo and the victory of the Savior. It is also remarked that Easter falls on Nisan 14.

Edition: P. NAUTIN, Homélies Paschales I: Une homélie inspirée du traité sur la Pâque d'Hippolyte. Étude, édition et traduction (SCH 27). Paris, 1950.

Translations: French: P. NAUTIN, *loc. cit.* — *German:* O. CASEL, JL 14 (1938) 25–28 (excerpts).

Studies: C. MARTIN, Un περὶ τοῦ πάσχα de saint Hippolyte retrouvé?: RSR 16 (1926) 148–166. — A. EHRHARD, Überlieferung und Bestand der hagiographischen und homiletischen Literatur der griechischen Kirche, I. Teil. Die Überlieferung, I. Band (TU 50). Leipzig, 1936, 129–134. — C. MARTIN, Fragments palimpsestes d'un discours sur la Pâque attribué à saint Hippolyte de Rome (*Crypt.* B. a. LV): Annuaire de l'Institut de philologie et d'histoire orientales et slaves 6 (Mélanges F. Cumont). Brussels, 1936, 324–330; *idem,* Hippolyte de Rome et Proclus de Constantinople: RHE 33 (1937) 255–276. — K. PRÜMM, Mysterion und Verwandtes bei Hippolyt: ZkTh 63 (1939) 207–225. — R. H. CONNOLLY, New Attributions to Hippolytus: JThSt 46 (1944/45) 192–200. — H. DE LUBAC, L'arbre cosmique: Mélanges E. Podechard. Lyons, 1945, 191–198. — J. DANIÉLOU, Le symbolisme du jour de Pâques: Dieu Vivant 18 (1951) 45–56.

b. *On the Praise of the Lord Our Savior*

This homily, which Hippolytus delivered in the presence of Origen on his visit to Rome according to Jerome (*De vir. ill.* 61), is lost, and so far not even fragments of it have been recovered.

c. *Homily on the Heresy of Noetus* ('Ομιλία εἰς τὴν αἵρεσιν Νοήτου τινὸς)

There is a large fragment (*Cod. Vaticanus* 1431, *saec.* XII) with this title, but it seems to be incorrect to the extent that it calls itself a 'homily.' It is not a homily, but a part, perhaps the end, of an anti-heretical treatise. Photius in his description of the *Syntagma* (cf. above, p. 169) declares that this work concluded with an exposition of the heresy of Noetus. For this reason the opinion has been advanced that the so-called homily is the final section of that work, but the quotation is too long to fit into so brief a study. The fragment refutes the modalistic and patripassionistic monarchianism (EP 391–4)—a doctrine that, according to *Philosophumena* (1,7; 10,27), Noetus was the first to defend.

Editions: E. Schwartz, Zwei Predigten Hippolyts (SAM Phil.-hist. Abt. 1936, Heft 3). Munich, 1936. — MG 10, 817.

Translations: English: S. D. F. Salmond, ANL 9; ANF 5, 223–231.

Studies: J. Dräseke, Zum Syntagma des Hippolytos: Zeitschr. wiss. Theol. 46 (1903) 58–80. — C. H. Turner, The 'Blessed Presbyters' who condemned Noetus: JThSt 23 (1922) 28–35. — V. Machioro, L'eresia Noetiana. Naples, 1921. — E. Schwartz, *loc. cit.* — C. Martin, Le Contra Noetum de saint Hippolyte fragment d'homélie ou finale du Syntagma: RHE 37 (1941) 5–23. — S. Giet, Le texte du fragment contre Noët: RSR (1950) 315–322.

d. *Demonstration Against the Jews* ('Ομιλία πρὸς Ἰουδαίους ἀποδεικτικὴ)

There is a considerable fragment extant under this title blaming the Jews for their own misery and unhappiness; for their crimes against the Messias were the cause. The manuscripts attribute it to Hippolytus, but there is no ancient testimony to the effect that Hippolytus wrote a work *Against the Jews*.

7. *The Apostolic Tradition* ('Αποστολικὴ παράδοσις)

Among the writings of Hippolytus there is none which has attracted so much attention in our generation as his *Apostolic Tradition*. It is, with the exception of the *Didache*, the earliest and the most important of the ancient Christian Church Orders, providing as it does a rudimentary Sacramentary with set rules and forms for the ordination and functions of the various ranks of the hierarchy, the celebration of the Eucharist and the administration of baptism. The title of the work is inscribed on the chair of the third-century statue of Hippolytus, but it was regarded as lost until E. Schwarz claimed in 1910, and R. H. Connolly demonstrated in 1916, that the Latin text of the so-called Egyptian Church Order represents substantially the *Apostolic Tradition* of Hippolytus. The Egyptian Church Order was so named merely because it became known to the modern world first in Ethiopic and Coptic translations. The importance of this discovery is evident from the fact that it has provided a new foundation for the history of the Roman liturgy and has given us the richest source of information that we possess in any form for our knowledge of the constitution and life of the Church in the first three centuries. It was written about the year 215.

TEXT TRADITION

The original text of the *Apostolic Tradition* is lost but for a few small portions in later Greek documents, especially in the eighth book of the *Apostolic Constitutions* and its so-called *Epitome*. There are, however, Coptic, Arabic, Ethiopic and Latin translations. The combination of them enables us to get an adequate perception of its actual wording and the tenor of the entire document. The Latin version, most probably from the fourth century, was found in a palimpsest dating from the last quarter of the fifth century in the Library of the Cathedral Chapter of Verona. The rendering is pedantically literal and follows the construction and form of the Greek to such a degree that it is possible to reconstruct the original from it. However, it covers only a portion of the entire text. E. Hauler was the first to publish it in 1900.

Whereas in the West the *Apostolic Tradition* did not have any great influence and was soon forgotten together with his other works, this Church Order came to be accepted as typical in the East, especially in Egypt, so much so that the translations of it into Coptic, Ethiopic and Arabic played an important role in forming the liturgy as well as the Christian life and Canon Law of the Oriental Churches.

Of these oriental versions, the Sahidic alone is based directly on the Greek. It is preserved in a collection of laws, entitled *Egyptian Heptateuch*. It contains many transliterated Greek words, so that the original terms are obvious. Dating most probably from about the year 500, it was first published by P. de Lagarde in 1883. Of much less value is the Bohairic, made from an inferior Sahidic manuscript.

The Arabic was derived from the Sahidic, and not before the tenth century; yet, it has a certain value of its own, since it came from a copy not connected with the archetype of the known Sahidic codices. The Ethiopic was the first of all the versions of the *Apostolic Tradition* to be discovered. J. Ludolf edited portions of it in 1691. It is thrice-removed from the original, having been done from the Arabic, but contains some chapters not now found in the latter. Thus there must be an older Arabic form behind it, which in turn supposes an older Sahidic form. In these older forms the omissions that were made later to avoid conflicts with local usages had not yet occurred. Thus the Ethiopic is the only one of the Eastern translations that gives the text of the ordination prayers found in the Latin.

Editions: E. HAULER, Didascaliae apostolorum fragmenta Veronensia latina. Accedunt canonum qui dicuntur apostolorum et aegyptiorum reliquiae. Leipzig, 1900. — F. X. FUNK, Didascalia et Constitutiones Apostolorum. II. Testimonia et scripturae propinquae. Paderborn, 1905, 97–119. — TH. SCHERMANN, Die allgemeine Kirchenordnung, frühchristliche Liturgie und kirchliche Überlieferung. I. Die Allgemeine Kirchenordnung des zweiten Jahrhunderts (StGKA 3). Paderborn, 1914. — R. H. CONNOLLY, The So-called Egyptian Church Order and Derived Documents (Texts and Studies, 8, 4). Cambridge, 1916. — B. S. EASTON, The Apostolic Tradition of Hippolytus. Cambridge, 1924. — G. DIX, The Treatise on the Apostolic Tradition of St. Hippolytus of Rome. Historical Introduction, Textual Materials and Translation, with Apparatus Criticus and some Critical Notes. London, 1937. — B. BOTTE, Hippolyte de Rome, La Tradition Apostolique. Texte Latin, introduction, traduction et notes (SCH 11). Paris, 1946. — For the *Ethiopic version*, see: J. LUDOLF, Ad suam Historiam Aethiopicam Commentarius. Frankfurt, 1691. — H. DUENSING, Der äthiopische Text der Kirchenordnung, nach acht Handschriften herausgegeben und übersetzt (AGWG Phil.-hist. Kl. 3, 32). Göttingen, 1946. — For the *Ethiopie, Arabic and Bohairic versions*, see: G. HORNER, The Statutes of the Apostles or Canones ecclesiastici. London, 1904.

Translations: English: CONNOLLY, *loc. cit.* — B. S. EASTON, *loc. cit.* — G. DIX, *loc. cit.* — *French:* B. BOTTE, *loc. cit.* — *German:* E. HENNECKE, Neutestamentliche Apokryphen, 2nd ed. Tübingen, 1924, 569–583. — E. JUNGKLAUS, Die Gemeinde Hippolyts, dargestellt nach seiner Kirchenordnung. Leipzig, 1928. — *Anonymus*, Die apostolische Überlieferung des hl. Hippolytus. Klosterneuburg, 1932. — H. DUENSING, *loc. cit.* — A. M. SCHNEIDER, Stimmen aus der Frühzeit der Kirche. Cologne, 1948, 101–103.

Studies: H. ACHELIS, Die ältesten Quellen des orientalischen Kirchenrechts. 1. Buch: Die Canones Hippolyti (TU 6, 4). Leipzig, 1891; *idem*, Hippolytus im Kirchenrecht: ZKG 15 (1895) 1–43; *idem*, Hippolytstudien (TU NF 1, 4). Leipzig, 1897. — F. X.

Funk, Die Symbolstücke in der ägyptischen Kirchenordnung und den Kanones Hippolyts: ThQ (1899) 161–187. — G. Morin, L'origine des Canons d'Hippolyte: RB 7 (1900) 241–246. — A. Baumstark, Die nichtgriechischen Paralleltexte zum achten Buche der Apostolischen Konstitutionen: OC 1 (1901) 98–137. — J. A. Maclean, The Ancient Church Orders (The Cambridge Handbooks of Liturgical Study). Cambridge, 1910. — E. Schwartz, Über die pseudoapostolischen Kirchenordnungen (Schriften der wissenschaftlichen Gesellschaft in Straßburg 6). Strasbourg, 1910. — Th. Schermann, Ein Weiheritual der römischen Kirche am Schlusse des ersten Jahrhunderts. Munich, 1913; idem, Die allgemeine Kirchenordnung, frühchristliche Liturgie und kirchliche Überlieferung (StGKA 3. Ergänzungsband, Teil 1–3). Paderborn, 1914. — A. Wilmart, Le texte latin de la Paradosis de saint Hippolyte: RSR 9 (1916) 62–71; idem, Un règlement écclésiastique du IIIe siècle. La 'Tradition apostolique' de saint Hippolyte: Revue du clergé français 96 (1918) 81–116. — E. Hennecke, Hippolyts Schrift 'Apostolische Überlieferung über Gnalengaben': Harnackehrung. Leipzig, 1921, 159–182. — R. Devreesse, La 'Tradition apostolique' de s. Hippolyte: La vie et les arts liturgiques 8 (1921/22) 11–18. — Vigourel, Autour de la 'Tradition apostolique', ibid. 8 (1922) 150–156. — R. H. Connolly, The Prologue to the Apostolic Tradition of Hippolytus: JThSt 22 (1921) 356–361. — E. Hennecke, Der Prolog zur 'Apostolischen Überlieferung' Hippolyts: ZNW 22 (1923) 144–146. — P. Galtier, La tradition apostolique d'Hippolyte: RSR 11 (1923) 511–527. — K. Müller, Kleine Beiträge zur Kirchengeschichte 6: Hippolyts Ἀποστολικὴ παράδοσις und die Canones Hippolyti: ZNW 23 (1924) 214–247. — A. Baumstark, Christus Jesus. Ein Alterskriterium römischer liturgischer Texte: StC 1 (1924/25) 44–55. — R. Lorentz, De Egyptische Kerkordening en Hippolytus van Rome. Leiden, 1929. — J. A. Jungmann, Beobachtungen zum Fortleben von Hippolyts 'Apostolischer Überlieferung' in Palladius und dem Pontificale Romanum: ZkTh 53 (1929) 579–585. — K. Müller, Noch einmal Hippolyts Ἀποστολικὴ παράδοσις: ZNW 28 (1929) 273–305. — P. O. Norwood, The Apostolic Tradition of Hippolytus: AThR 17 (1935) 15–18. — A. Hamel, Über das kirchenrechtliche Schrifttum Hippolyts: ZNW 36 (1937) 238–250. — H. Elfers, Die Kirchenordnung Hippolyts von Rom. Paderborn, 1938. — F. J. Foakes-Jackson, A History of Church History. Cambridge, 1939, 28–38: The Apostolic Tradition of Hippolytus and other Church Orders. — H. Engberding, Das angebliche Dokument römischer Liturgie aus dem Beginn des 3. Jahrhunderts: Miscellanea Liturgica in hon. L. C. Mohlberg 1 (1948) 47–71. — J. A. Jungmann, Missarum sollemnia. Vienna, 1948, I, 37–43. — C. C. Richardson, The Date and Setting of the Apostolic Tradition of Hippolytus: AThR 30 (1948) 38–44. — B. Botte, L'authenticité de la Tradition Apostolique de s. Hippolyte: RTAM 16 (1949) 177–185.— G. Dix, The Shape of the Liturgy. Westminster, 1949, 221–224.—J. H. Crehan, Early Christian Baptism and the Creed. London, 1950, 159–171: The Text of Hippolytus. — H. Elfers, Neue Untersuchungen über die Kirchenordnung Hippolyts von Rom: Abhandlungen über Theologie und Kirche. Festschrift f. Karl Adam, hrsg. v. M. Reding, Düsseldorf, 1952, 169–211. — O. Casel, Die Kirchenordnung Hippolyts on Rom: Archiv für Liturgiewissenschaft 2 (1952) 115–130.

DERIVED DOCUMENTS

The *Apostolic Tradition* is the source for a great number of later

Church Orders in the East. Thus we see clear signs of dependenc‹
on Hippolytus' work in the eighth book of the *Apostolic Consti*
tutions, compiled in Syria about 380 and the largest of the liturgi
cal-canonical collections that have come down to us from Christia‹
antiquity. There exists in addition an *Epitome* of this eighth boo›
which itself drew independently on the *Apostolic Tradition*. Th‹
title *Epitome* is misleading; it is not an abbreviation or conden
sation, but a series of excerpts. The author has in three or fou›
passages preferred to reproduce Hippolytus' own wording rathe›
than the adapted text of his immediate source. In some of th‹
manuscripts the *Epitome* is called *Constitutions through Hippolytus*
Its date and place of origin cannot be satisfactorily determined, bu
the excellence of its readings suggests that the extracts must hav‹
been made at a fairly early time after the *Apostolic Constitutions*

Editions: F. X. FUNK, Didascalia et Constitutiones Apostolorum, 2 vols. Paderborn
1905. — B. WIGAN, The Apostolic Constitutions Book VIII (Henry Bradshaw Society)
London, 1953. — *Liturgical selections:* J. QUASTEN, Monumenta eucharistica e
liturgica vetustissima. Bonn, 1935/37, 178–233. — H. LIETZMANN, KT 61. Bonn, 1910

Translations: English: J. DONALDSON, ANF 7, 391–505. — R. H. CRESSWELL, Th‹
Liturgy of the Eight Book of the 'Apostolic Constitutions', translated into Englis›
with Introduction and Notes (SPCK). London, 1900. — *German:* F. X. BOXLER
BKV. Kempten, 1874. — R. STORF, Griechische Liturgien übersetzt. Mit Einleitun
gen versehen von TH. SCHERMANN, BKV² 5 (1912) 17–79: Das achte Buch de›
Apostolischen Konstitutionen.

Studies: F. NAU, DTC 3, 1520–1537. — H. LECLERCQ, DAL 3, 2, 2732–2795. — F. X
FUNK, Die Apostolischen Konstitutionen, eine literarhistorische Untersuchung
Rottenburg a.N., 1891. — D. L. O'LEARY, The Apostolic Constitutions and Cognate
Documents with Special Reference to Their Liturgical Elements (SPCK). London,
1906. — A. BAUMSTARK, Ägyptischer oder antiochenischer Liturgietypus in AK
I–VII: OC 7 (1907); *idem*, Das eucharistische Hochgebet und die Literatur des
nachexilischen Judentums: ThGl 2 (1910) 353–370. — A. SPAGNOLO and C. H
TURNER, Fragment of a Latin Version of the Apostolic Constitutions: JThSt 13 (1912)
492–514. — A. SPAGNOLO, in: C. H. TURNER, Ecclesiae occidentalis monumenta
iuris antiquissima. I, 2, 1. Oxford, 1913, 32a–32nn. — C. H. TURNER, A Primitive
Edition of the Apostolic Constitutions and Canons: JThSt 15 (1914) 53–65. —
G. MERCATI, The MSS of the Apostolic Constitutions: JThSt 15 (1914) 453 ff. —
C. H. TURNER, The Apostolic Constitutions (the compiler Arian): JThSt 16 (1915)
54 ff. — W. BOUSSET, Eine jüdische Gebetssammlung im siebten Buch der aposto
lischen Konstitutionen: NGWG Phil.-hist. Kl. (1915) 449–479. — L. DUCHESNE,
Origines du culte chrétien. 5th ed. Paris, 1925, 57–66. — H. LIETZMANN, Messe und
Herrenmahl. Bonn, 1926, 122–136. — C. H. TURNER, The Apostolic Constitutions
(text. of Cod. Vat. 1506): JThSt 21 (1920) 160 ff.; *idem*, Notes on the 'Apostolic
Constitutions' III. The Text of the Eighth Book: JThSt 31 (1930) 128–141. — G.

MERCATI, Aegyptus 8 (1927) 40–42. — P. ANTOINE, ROC 28 (1931/32) 362–375. — G. PRADO, Una nueva recensión del himno Gloria in excelsis: EL 6 (1932) 481–486. — M. ATHENAGORAS, Νεώτεραι ἀπόψεις ἐπὶ τῆς Διδασκαλίας—Διδαχῆς καὶ τῶν Ἀποστολικῶν Διαταγῶν: EPh 32 (1933) 481–510. — E. R. GOODENOUGH, By Light, Light: The Mystic Gospel of Hellenistic Judaism. New Haven, 1935. — P. GALTIER, Imposition des mains et bénédictions du baptême: RSR 27 (1937) 464–466. — A. SPANIER, Die erste Benediktion des Achtzehngebetes (Const. Apost. 33–38): Monatsschrift für Geschichte und Wissenschaft des Judentums 45 (1937) 71–75. — G. MERCATI, Opere Minore 3 (ST 78). Vatican City, 1937, 338 f. (MSS ed. princeps); 4 (ST 79) 143–148 (Euchologia). — D. VAN DEN EYNDE, Baptême et confirmation d'après les Constitutions apostoliques VII 44, 3: RSR 27 (1937) 196–212. — G. DIX, The Shape of the Liturgy. Westminster, 1945, 477–480. — J. QUASTEN, The Blessing of the Baptismal Font in the Syrian Rite of the Fourth Century: TS 7 (1946) 309–313. — E. PETERSON, Henoch im jüdischen Gebet und jüdischer Kunst: Miscellanea L. Mohlberg I. Rome, 1948, 413–417. — J. N. D. KELLY, Early Christian Creeds. London, 1950, 186–187. — J. QUASTEN, Mysterium tremendum: Vom christlichen Mysterium. Gesammelte Arbeiten zum Gedächtnis von O. Casel. Düsseldorf, 1951, 71 f.

The so-called *Testament of Our Lord*, the last of the Church Orders proper, has made use of the *Apostolic Tradition* in a peculiar way. The author has added so much from two other sources that he provides a distinct and different work. However, recent investigations have shown that he reproduces Hippolytus more reliably than any one else and that he availed himself of an excellent codex of the *Apostolic Tradition*. Although the *Testament* was originally written in Greek, there is only a Syriac version extant, which I. Rahmani published with a Latin translation in 1899. It dates most probably from the fifth century and seems to have been composed in Syria.

Edition: I. E. RAHMANI, Testamentum Domini nostri Jesu Christi. Mainz, 1899 (with a Latin translation). — *Liturgical excerpts*, in: J. QUASTEN, Monumenta eucharistica et liturgica vetustissima. Bonn, 1935/37, 235–273.

Translations: English: J. COOPER–J. A. MACLEAN, The Testament of Our Lord Translated into English from the Syriac. London, 1902. — *French:* F. NAU, La version syriaque de l'Octateuque de Clément, trad. en français. Paris, 1913.

Studies: AMANN, DTC 15, 194–200. — H. LECLERCQ, DAL 11, 622–624. — W. H. KENT, The Syriac Testament of Our Lord: Dublin Review (1900) 245–274. — J. WORDSWORTH, The Testament of Our Lord: Internationale theologische Zeitschrift 8 (1900) 452–472. — J. P. ARENDZEN, A Syriac Text of the Testament of the Lord: JThSt 2 (1901) 401 ff. — J. PARISOT, Note sur la mystagogie du 'Testament du Seigneur': JA 9, 15 (1900) 377–380. — G. MORIN, Le testament du Seigneur: RB 17 (1900) 532–539. — F. X. FUNK, Das Testament unseres Herrn und die verwandten Schriften (FLD 2, 1/2). Mainz, 1901. — E. SCHWARTZ, Die pseudo-apostolischen

Kirchenordnungen. Strasbourg, 1910. — G. Leroux, Les églises syriennes à portes laterales et le Testamentum Domini: Mélanges Holleaux. Paris, 1913, 123 ff. — C. Schmidt, Gespräche Jesu mit seinen Jüngern nach seiner Auferstehung (TU 43). Leipzig, 1919, 157–166. — I. E. Rahmani, Les Liturgies Orientales et Occidentales. Beyrouth, 1929. — H. Selhorst, Die Platzordnung im Gläubigenraum der altchristlichen Kirche. Diss. Münster, 1931. — F. J. Dölger, Ne quis adulter! Christliche und heidnische Ächtung des Ehebruchs in der Kultsatzung: AC 3 (1932) 132–148. — O. H. E. Burmester, The Coptic and Arabic Versions of the Mystagogia: Muséon 46 (1933) 203–235. — A. Rücker, Forschungen und Funde: OC 31 (1934) 114 f. — G. Graf, Geschichte der christlichen arabischen Literatur I. Rome, 1944, 569–572. — J. N. D. Kelly, Early Christian Creeds. London, 1950, 90 f.

The *Canons of Hippolytus* are also based on the *Apostolic Tradition*. They were written probably in Syria about the year 500 and represent a comparatively late and unskillful redaction of Hippolytus' Church Order. Nothing remains of the original Greek, but an Arabic and an Ethiopic version are extant. It seems that the Arabic is a tertiary version, being a rendition of the Ethiopic rather than of the Greek.

Editions: D. Haneberg, Canones Hippolyti. Munich, 1870 (with a Latin translation). — H. Achelis, Die ältesten Quellen des orientalischen Kirchenrechts. Die Canones Hippolyti (TU 6, 4). Leipzig, 1891 (reprints 38sqq. a revised edition of this translation).

Translation: German: W. Riedel, Die Kirchenrechtsquellen des Patriarchats Alexandrien. Leipzig, 1900, 193–230.

Studies: C. J. Öhlander, Canones Hippolyti och besläkta de skrifter. Lund, 1911. — A. Maloy, L'onction des malades dans les canons d'Hippolyte et les documents apparentés: RSR 9 (1919) 222–229. — R. H. Connolly, The So-called Egyptian Church Order and Derived Documents. Cambridge, 1916, 50–134 The Egyptian Church Order in relation to Canones Hippolyti. — K. Müller, Hippolyts Ἀποστολικὴ παράδοσις und die Canones Hippolyti: ZNW 23 (1924) 214–247. — G. Dix, The Treatise on the Apostolic Tradition of St. Hippolytus of Rome. London, 1937, lxxvi–lxxxi. — G. Graf, Geschichte der christl. arabischen Literatur. I. Rome, 1944, 602–605.

CONTENTS

The contents of the *Apostolic Tradition* consists of three main parts.

I. The first contains a prologue, canons on the election and consecration of a bishop, the prayer for his consecration, the Eucharistic liturgy following thereon, and blessings of oil, cheese and olives. Then come laws and prayers for the ordination of priests and deacons; finally confessors, widows, readers, virgins, subdeacons and those who have the gift of healing are dealt with.

In the prologue the author explains the title of his treatise:

> And now, through the love which He had for all the saints (Eph. 1,15), having come to our most important topic, we turn to the subject of the Tradition which is proper for the Churches, in order that those who have been rightly instructed may hold fast to that tradition which has continued until now, and fully understanding it from exposition may stand the more firmly therein. This is now the more necessary because of that apostasy or error which was recently invented out of ignorance and because of certain ignorant men (Dix 1).

The passage indicates that Hippolytus intends to record only the forms and rites already traditional and customs already long established. He wishes to write them down in protest against innovations. Thus the liturgy described in this Church Order is of a much older date and all the more valuable. It is that of Rome most probably during the second half of the second century.

According to Hippolytus, the consecration of a bishop takes place on the Sunday after he has been chosen by all the people and in the most public manner possible. The neighboring bishops are to attend and the presbytery is to be present, together with the whole congregation. The bishops are to lay their hands upon the elected person, the presbytery standing by in silence. All are to keep silent, praying for the descent of the Holy Spirit. Then one bishop lays on his hand and prays:

> O God and Father of our Lord Jesus Christ, Father of mercies and God of all consolation, who dwellest on high yet has respect unto the lowly, who knowest all things before they come to pass, who didst give ordinances unto Thy Church by the Word of Thy grace, who didst foreordain from the beginning the race of the righteous from Abraham, instituting princes and priests and leaving not Thy sanctuary without ministers, who from the foundation of the world hast been pleased to be glorified in them whom Thou hast chosen, now pour forth that Power which is from Thee, of the princely Spirit which Thou didst deliver to Thy beloved Child Jesus Christ, which he bestowed on Thy holy Apostles who established the Church which hallows Thee in every

place to the endless glory and praise of Thy name. Thou, Father, who knowest the hearts, grant upon this Thy servant whom Thou hast chosen for the episcopate, to feed Thy holy flock, to present before Thy eyes the primacy of the priesthood, that he may serve Thee blamelessly by night and by day, that he may unceasingly propitiate Thy countenance and offer to Thee the gifts of Thy holy Church, and that by the high priestly Spirit he may have authority to forgive sins according to Thy command, to assign lots according to Thy bidding, to loose every bond according to the authority Thou gavest to the Apostles and that he may please Thee by meekness and purity of heart, offering to Thee an odour of sweetness through Thy Child Jesus Christ our Lord, through Whom to Thee be glory, power and honour, to the Father and to the Son with the Holy Spirit, now and for ever and ever. Amen (Dix 3).

The Apostolic succession is stressed in this prayer and the authority to remit sins. The mentioning of the latter indicates that Hippolytus did not question this power of forgiveness, although he opposed Callistus for having absolved from grave offences. The liturgy of the mass following the consecration of a bishop contains the oldest Canon or Eucharistic prayer which we possess. It is very brief and purely christological. The only topic is the work of Christ. There is no Sanctus but an epiclesis:

The Lord be with you.

And with thy spirit.

Lift up your hearts.

We have them in the Lord.

Let us give thanks to the Lord.

That is proper and right.

We thank Thee God through Thy beloved servant Jesus Christ whom Thou hast sent in the latter times to be our Saviour and Redeemer and the messenger of Thy counsel, the Logos who went out from Thee, through whom Thou hast created all things, whom Thou wast pleased to send out from heaven into the womb of the Virgin, and in her body He became incarnate and was shown to be Thy Son born of the Holy Ghost and of the Virgin. In order to fulfil Thy will and to make ready for Thee a holy people, He spread out His

hands when He suffered in order that He might free from
sufferings those who have reached faith in Thee.

And when He gave himself over to voluntary suffering, in
order to destroy death, and to break the bonds of the devil,
and to tread down hell, and to illuminate the righteous, and
to set up the boundary stone, and to reveal the Resurrection,
He took bread, gave thanks, and said: 'Take, eat, this is my
body which is broken for you.' In the same manner also the
cup, and said: 'This is my blood which is poured out for you.
As often as you do this you keep my memory.'

When we remember His death and His resurrection in this
way, we bring to Thee the bread and the cup, and give
thanks to Thee, because Thou hast thought us worthy to
stand before Thee and to serve Thee as priests.

And we beseech Thee that Thou wouldst send down Thy
Holy Spirit on the sacrifice of the church. Unite them, and
grant to all the saints who partake in the sacrifice, that they
may be filled with the Holy Spirit, that they may be strengthened in faith in the truth, in order that we may praise and
laud Thee through Thy servant, Jesus Christ, through whom
praise and honour be to Thee in Thy holy church now and
forever more. Amen (Dix 4).

These prayers indicate that the liturgy, in contrast to the practice in St. Justin's day, was passing from improvisation to set
form. Whereas Justin testifies that the bishop 'sends up to heaven
prayers and thanksgiving to the best of his ability' (cf. vol.I, p.
217), Hippolytus provides a definite wording. However, there was
nothing obligatory about this formula, as Hippolytus makes quite
clear that the celebrant still had the right to compose his own:

And the bishop shall give thanks according to the afore-
said models. It is not altogether necessary for him to recite
the very same words which we gave before as if he had to
study them in order to say them by heart in his thanksgiving
to God; but let each one pray according to his own ability.
If indeed he is able to pray suitably with a grand and elevated prayer, this is a good thing. But if on the other hand
he should pray and recite a prayer according to a fixed form,
no one shall prevent him. Only let his prayer be correct and
right [in doctrine] (Dix 10).

It is interesting to note that the Arabic and Ethiopic leave out the *not* at the beginning of this passage and read 'It is altogether necessary for him to recite the very same words.' Thus, when these versions were made, the liturgy was fixed, so that no possibility of improvisation remained. At the time of Hippolytus it still existed.

Studies: W. H. FRERE, Early Ordination Services: JThSt 16 (1915) 323–369. — C. H. TURNER, The Ordination Prayer for a Presbyter in the Church Order of Hippolytus: JThSt 16 (1915) 542 ff. — J. V. BARTLET, The Ordination Prayers in the Ancient Church Order: JThSt 17 (1916) 248 ff. — A. NAIRNE, The Prayer for the Consecration of a Bishop in the Church Order of Hippolytus: JThSt 17 (1916) 598 ff. — P. BATIFFOL, Une prétendue anaphore apostolique: RBibl 13 (1916) 23–32. — R. H. CONNOLLY, The Ordination Prayers of Hippolytus: JThSt 18 (1917) 55 ff; *idem*, An Ancient Prayer in the Mediaeval Euchologia: JThSt 19 (1918) 132–144. — S. SALAVILLE, Un texte romain du Canon de la Messe au début du IIIe siècle: EO 21 (1921) 79–85. — R. DEVREESSE, La prière eucharistique de saint Hippolyte: La vie et les arts liturgiques 8 (1921/22) 393–397, 448–453. — R. H. CONNOLLY, On the Meaning of 'Epiclesis': Downside Review (1923) 28–43; *idem*, On the Meaning of ἐπίκλησις: a Reply: JThSt 25 (1924) 337–364. — J. B. THIBAUT, La liturgie romaine. Paris, 1924, 57–80. — H. LIETZMANN, Messe und Herrenmahl (Arbeiten zur Kirchengeschichte 8). Bonn, 1926, 174–186. — J. QUASTEN, Monumenta eucharistica et liturgica vetustissima. Bonn, 1935/37, 26–31. — O. CULLMANN, La signification de la sainte Cène dans le christianisme primitif: RHPR 16 (1936) 1–22. — A. ARNOLD, Der Ursprung des christlichen Abendmahles (FThSt 45). Freiburg, 1937. — W. H. FRERE, The Anaphora or Great Eucharistic Prayer. London, 1938. — R. H. CONNOLLY, The Eucharistic Prayer of Hippolytus: JThSt 39 (1938) 350–369. — B. BOTTE, Le rituel d'ordination des Statuta Ecclesiae antiqua: RTAM (1939) 223–241. — H. D. SIMONIN, La prière de la consécration épiscopale dans la Tradition apostolique d'Hippolyte de Rome, trad. et comm.: VS 60 (1939) 65–86. — G. ELLARD, Bread in the Form of a Penny: TS 4 (1943) 319–346. — G. V. JOURDAN, Agape or Lord's Supper. A Study of Certain Passages in the Canons of Hippolytus: Hermathena 64 (1944) 32–43. — A. J. OTTERBEIN, The Diaconate According to the Apostolic Tradition of Hippolytus and Derived Documents. Diss. Washington, 1945. — B. BOTTE, L'épiclèse de l'anaphore d'Hippolyte: RTAM 14 (1947) 241–251. — C. C. RICHARDSON, The So-called Epiclesis in Hippolytus: HThR (1947) 101–108. — N. A. DAHL, Anamnesis. Mémoire et commémoration dans le christianisme primitif: Studia Theologica 1 (1947) 69–95. — J. A. JUNGMANN, Missarum sollemnia. Eine genetische Erklärung der römischen Messe. Vienna, 1948, 1, 37–43. — D. VAN DEN EYNDE, Nouvelle trace de la 'Traditio apostolica' d'Hippolyte dans la liturgie romaine: Miscellanea Mohlberg I. Rome, 1948, 407–411. — C. C. RICHARDSON, A Note on the Epicleses in Hippolytus and the 'Testamentum Domini': RTAM 15 (1948) 357–359. — A. GRILLMEIER, Der Gottessohn im Totenreich: ZkTh 71 (1949) 1–53, 184–203. — C. CALLEWAERT, Histoire positive du Canon romain. Une épiclèse à Rome?: Sacris Erudiri 2 (1949) 95–110. — E. C. RATCLIFF, The Sanctus and the Pattern of the Early Anaphora I: Journal of Ecclesiastical History 1 (1950) 29–36, 125–134. — C. A. BOUMAN, Variants in the Introduction to the Eucharistic Prayer: VC 4 (1950) 94–115.

II. Whereas the first part of the *Apostolic Tradition* deals with the hierarchy, the second gives rules for the laity. There we find legislation regarding new converts, crafts and professions forbidden to Christians, catechumens, baptism, confirmation and First Holy Communion. The description of baptism given here is invaluable because it provides us with the first Roman Creed (cf. vol. I, p. 26 f).

> And when he who is to be baptised goes down to the water, let him who baptises lay hand on him saying thus:
> Dost thou believe in God the Father Almighty? And he who is being baptised shall say: I believe. Let him forthwith baptise him once, having his hand laid upon his head.
> And after this let him say:
> Dost thou believe in Christ Jesus, the Son of God,
> Who was born of the Holy Spirit and the Virgin Mary,
> Who was crucified in the days of Pontius Pilate,
> And died and was buried
> And He rose the third day living from the dead
> And ascended into heaven,
> And sat down at the right hand of the Father,
> And will come to judge the living and the dead?
> And when he says: I believe, let him baptise the second time.
> And again let him say:
> Dost thou believe in the Holy Spirit in the Holy Church
> And the resurrection of the flesh?
> And he who is being baptised shall say: I believe.
> And so let him baptise him the third time.
> And afterwards when he comes up from the water he shall be anointed by the presbyter with the Oil of Thanksgiving saying:
> I anoint thee with holy oil in the Name of Jesus Christ.
> And so each one drying himself with a towel they shall now put on their clothes, and after this let them be together in the assembly [Church] (Dix 21, 12–20).

The administration of the sacrament is here divided up between the three questions addressed to the candidate. Each time he answers he is immersed in the water. There is no indication that the minister of the sacrament recites a special formula while baptising. We have the same custom in Tertullian (*De baptismo*

2,1, *De corona* 3), in Ambrose (*De sacramentis* 2,7,20) and the Church of Rome kept it for a long time, because the *Gelasian Sacramentary* (ed. Wilson p. 86) testifies to the procedure. The passage of the *Traditio Apostolica* quoted above is very instructive for the origin and history of the Creed.

After the description of baptism follows that of the rite of confirmation:

And the Bishop shall lay his hand upon them invoking and saying:

O Lord God, who didst count these Thy servants worthy of deserving the forgiveness of sins by the laver of regeneration, make them worthy to be filled with Thy Holy Spirit and send upon them Thy grace, that they may serve Thee according to Thy will; for to Thee is the glory, to the Father and to the Son with the Holy Ghost in the holy Church, both now and ever and world without end. Amen.

After this, pouring the consecrated oil from his hand and laying his hand on his head, he shall say:

I anoint thee with holy oil in God the Father Almighty and Christ Jesus and the Holy Ghost.

And sealing him on the forehead, he shall give him the kiss of peace and say:

The Lord be with you.

And he who has been sealed shall say:

And with thy spirit.

And so he shall do to each one severally.

Thenceforward they shall pray together with all the people. But they shall not previously pray with the faithful before they have undergone all these things.

And after the prayers, let them give the kiss of peace (Dix 22).

This description of confirmation demonstrates that it was conferred by an act clearly distinct from baptism. The candidates' reception into the community of the faithful was followed by the First Holy Communion service or the Paschal Mass, which is interesting for its special features. The deacons bring to the bishop bread together with three chalices, the first containing water and wine, the second a mixture of milk and honey, and the third, water only. At the Communion, the newly-baptised receive first the Eucharistic Bread. Immediately afterwards the three chalices are presented to them in the following order: first, the chalice of water, symbolizing the interior cleaning which had been effected in baptism; secondly, the chalice containing a measure of milk mixed with honey; and finally, the chalice with the consecrated wine:

And then let the oblation at once be brought by the deacons to the bishop, and he shall eucharistize first the bread into the presentation which the Greek calls the anti-type of the Flesh of Christ; and the cup mixed with wine for the antitype which the Greek calls the likeness of the Blood which was shed for all who have believed in Him; and milk and honey mingled together in fulfilment of the promise which was made to the Fathers, wherein He said, I will give you a land flowing with milk and honey; which Christ indeed gave, even His Flesh, whereby they who believe are nourished like little children, making the bitterness of the human heart sweet by the sweetness of His Word; water also for an oblation for a sign of the laver, that the inner man, which is psychic, may receive the same rites as the body.

And the bishop shall give an explanation concerning all these things to them who receive.

And, when he breaks the Bread, in distributing to each a fragment he shall say:

The Bread of Heaven in Christ Jesus.

And he who receives shall answer: Amen.

And the presbyters—but if there are not enough of them the deacons also—shall hold the cups and stand by in good order and with reverence: first he that holdeth the water, second he who holds the milk, third he who holds the wine. And they who partake shall taste of each cup thrice, he who gives it saying:

In God the Father Almighty;

and he who receives shall say: Amen.

And in the Lord Jesus Christ;

and he shall say: Amen.

And in the Holy Spirit and in the Holy Church;

and he shall say: Amen.

So shall it be done to each one (Dix 23).

Texts: J. Quasten, Monumenta eucharistica et liturgica vetustissima. Bonn, 1935, 31–33.

Studies: P. Galtier, La consignation à Carthage et à Rome: RSR 2 (1911) 350–383; *idem*, La consignation dans les églises d'Occident: RHE 13 (1912) 257–301; *idem*, Onction et confirmation: RHE 13 (1912) 467–476. — R. H. Connolly, On the Text of the Baptismal Creed of Hippolytus: JThSt 25 (1924) 131–139. — B. Capelle, Le symbole romain au second siècle: RB 39 (1927) 33–45; *idem*, Les origines du symbole romain: RTAM 2 (1930) 5–20; *idem*, L'introduction du catéchumenat à Rome: RTAM 5 (1933) 129–154. — D. van den Eynde, Baptême et Confirmation: RSR 27 (1937) 196 ff. — F. X. Steinmetzer, Empfangen vom Heiligen Geiste. Eine Auseinandersetzung mit der Antike. Prague, 1938. — H. J. Carpenter, The Birth from the Holy Spirit and the Virgin in the old Roman Creed: JThSt 40 (1939) 31–36. — D. van den Eynde, Notes sur les rites postbaptismaux dans les Églises d'Occident: Antonianum 14 (1939) 257–276. — B. Welte, Die postbaptismale Salbung, ihr symbolischer Gehalt und ihre sakramentale Zugehörigkeit nach den Zeugnissen der alten Kirche (FThSt 51). Freiburg i.B., 1939. — H. Elfers, Gehört die Salbung mit Chrisma im ältesten abendländischen Initiationsritus zur Taufe oder zur Firmung?: ThGl 34 (1942) 334–341. — G. Dix, The Theology of Confirmation in Relation to Baptism. Westminster, 1946. — R. H. Connolly, The Theology of Confirmation in Relation to Baptism: Clergy Review 27 (1947) 282–284. — W. C. van Unnik, Les cheveux défaits des femmes baptisées. Un rite de baptême dans l'ordre ecclés. d'Hippolyte: VC 1 (1947) 77–100. — P. Nautin, Je crois à l'Esprit dans la saint Église pour la résurrection de la chair. Paris, 1947. — Ph. M. Menoud, Le baptême des enfants dans l'Église ancienne: Verbum Caro 2 (1948) 15–26. — J. N. D. Kelly, Early Christian Creeds. Oxford, 1950, 113–119. — J. H. Crehan, Early Christian Baptism and the Creed. London, 1950, passim. — B. Botte, Note sur le symbole baptismal de saint Hippolyte: Mélanges De Ghellinck 1 (1951) 189–200.

III. The third part of the *Apostolic Tradition* deals with various Church observances. There is a description of the Sunday Eucharist. Rules for fasting, for the Agape and for the service of the blessing of the lamp are given. The 'times at which it is right to pray' are discussed; daily communion at home and care in handling the holy Eucharist there are recommended. The account of the Agape distinguishes clearly between the consecrated bread of the Eucharist and the blessed bread of the Eulogy: 'this is blessed bread, but it is not the Eucharist as is the Body of the Lord' (26). There follow regulations for burial, for morning prayers and catechetical instruction. At the end we find an exposition of the hours for spiritual reading, prayer and the sign of the cross. The epilogue makes reference to the title of the work: 'I counsel that these things be observed by all who rightly understand. For upon all who hearken to the Apostolic Tradition and keep it, no heretic will prevail to deceive' (38).

II.   LOST WRITINGS

We know of several other treatises no longer extant.

a.   *On the Universe, against the Greeks and Plato*

Under this title Hippolytus refers to a work of his at the end of the *Philosophumena* (10,32). The list on his statue cites it as *Against the Greeks and Plato and on the Universe*. It seems to be the same study that Jerome has in mind when he states in his *Epist.* 70,4 that Hippolytus wrote *contra gentes*. Photius speaks (*Bibl. cod.* 48) of an '*On the Universe*, elsewhere called *On the Cause of the Universe* and *On the Nature of the Universe*,' which must be identical with this treatise. He describes it as follows:

> It consists of two little treatises, in which the author shows that Plato contradicts himself. He also refutes Alcinous, whose views on the soul, matter and the Resurrection are false and absurd, and introduces his own opinion on the subject. He proves that the Jewish nation is far older than the Greek. He thinks that man is a compound of fire, earth, and water, and also of spirit, which he calls soul. Of the spirit he speaks as follows: Taking the chief part of this, he moulded it together with the body, and opened a passage for it through every joint and limb. The spirit, thus moulded together with the body and pervading it throughout, is formed in the likeness of the visible body, but its nature is colder, compared with the three other substances of which the body is compounded. These views are not in harmony with Jewish ideas of human physiology, and are below the customary standard of his other writings. He also gives a summary account of the creation of the world. Of Christ the true God he speaks like ourselves, openly giving him the name of God, and describing, in language to which no objection can be taken, His indescribable generation from the Father (SPCK).

Discussing the authorship Photius remarks that, in the copy which he read, the treatise was attributed to Josephus. However, he found a marginal note to the effect that it was not by Josephus, but by one Gaius, a presbyter of Rome, the writer of *The Labyrinth*. *The Labyrinth* is another title for the *Philosophumena* of Hippolytus (cf. *Philos.* 10,5). Thus the gloss was correct in ascribing *On the Universe* and *The Labyrinth* to the same man, a presbyter of Rome, but mistaken in calling him Gaius. He is Hippolytus, and the description of the contents of *On the Universe*, as Photius gives it, fits exactly the longer title of the book at the end of the *Philosophumena* and on the statue.

The work was written before 225. The text is lost except for a fragment of considerable length in the *Sacra Parallela* of St. John Damascene. It contains an interesting description of Hades.

Edition: K. Holl, Fragmente vornicänischer Kirchenväter aus den Sacra Parallela (TU 20, 2). Leipzig, 1899, 137–143.

Translations: English: S. D. F. Salmond, ANL 9; ANF 5, 221–223.

Studies: E. Schürer, Geschichte des jüdischen Volkes im Zeitalter Jesu Christi. 3rd ed. vol. 1. Leipzig, 1901, 90 f. — C. Martin, RSR (1926) 148–166. — H. Cherniss, The so-called Fragment of Hippolytus περὶ ᾅδου: CPh (1929) 346–350. — J. Vergote, Zwei koptische Fragmente einer unbekannten patristischen Schrift: OCP 4 (1938) 47–64.

b. *Against the Heresy of Artemon*

In a further confusion of the Roman presbyter Gaius with Hippolytus, the writer of the marginal note in Photius (*Bibl. cod.* 48) attributes to the former what is probably another work of the latter, *Against the Heresy of Artemon*. Theodoret (*Haer. fab.* 2,5) refers to it as 'The Little Labyrinth,' and this implies a comparison with a greater *Labyrinth*, the proper name, as indicated above, of the *Philosophumena*. Eusebius (*Hist. eccl.* 5,28) cites several passages from a treatise, *Against the Heresy of Artemon*, but does not mention any author. It was apparently composed after the *Philosophumena* since the latter makes no mention of Artemon. The passages quoted by Eusebius (5,28) are all that remains.

Studies: E. Schwartz, Zwei Predigten Hippolyts. Munich, 1936, 49–51. — H. Schöne, Ein Einbruch der antiken Logik und Textkritik in die altchristliche Theologie: Pisciculi. Festschrift Fr. J. Dölger darg. Münster, 1939, 252–265. — R. H. Connolly, Eusebius, H. E. V, 28: JThSt 49 (1948) 73–79.

c. *On the Resurrection*

According to Jerome (*De vir. ill.* 61) Hippolytus composed a work *On the Resurrection* and the list on his statue speaks of a treatise *On God and the Resurrection of the Flesh*. Theodoret of Cyrus has preserved two fragments of the Greek original and Anastasius

Sinaita one. The Excerpts in Syriac give the name *The Sermon on the Resurrection to the Empress Mamea* and attribute it to 'St. Hippolytus, Bishop and Martyr.' The treatise evidently contained answers to questions which the Empress had addressed to him concerning the doctrine of the resurrection.

Edition: H. ACHELIS, GCS 1, 2 (1897) 249–253.

Translations: S. D. F. SALMOND, ANL 9; ANF 5, 238 (fragment).

Study: H. ACHELIS, Hippolytstudien, 189–193.

d. *Exhortation to Severina*

The statue of Hippolytus lists also an *Exhortation to Severina,* of which nothing survives.

e. *Against Marcion*

Eusebius (*Hist. eccl.* 6,22) and Jerome (*De vir. ill.* 61) know of a work by Hippolytus *Against Marcion.* The list on the statue does not mention it, but does have a title *On Good and the Source of Evil.* Since Marcion's doctrine dealt largely with the origin of good and evil, it is possible that Eusebius and Jerome have this study in mind. The treatise is entirely lost.

f. *On the Gospel of John and the Apocalypse* (Ὑπὲρ τοῦ κατὰ Ἰωάννην εὐαγγελίου καὶ ἀποκαλύψεως)

This is another title in the list on the statue. The Syrian Ebedjesu (*Cat. libr. omn. eccl.* 7) knows of it and calls it *Apologia pro apocalypsi et evangelio Joannis apostoli et evangelistae.* It was evidently directed against the Alogoi, who denied the doctrine of the Logos. Their leader Gaius rejected the Gospel of St. John and the Apocalypse for this reason. It seems that Epiphanius (*Haer.* 51) uses Hippolytus' treatise for his description of the Alogoi.

g. *Against Gaius*

According to Ebedjesu (*Cat.* 7) again, Hippolytus wrote a special work *Against Gaius* (Κεφάλεια κατὰ Γαΐου). There are five fragments extant in Dionysius Bar Salibi (1171), all of which deal with texts from the Apocalypse. It appears therefore that this treatise was also composed in defense of that book. Gaius rejects several of its passages for eschatological reasons, and Hippolytus defends them from other biblical sources.

14

Editions: J. Gwynn, Hippolytus and his 'Heads against Caius': Hermathena 6 (1888) 397–418. (Syriac text with an English translation). — A. Harnack, Die Gwynnschen Caius- und Hippolytus-Fragmente (TU 6, 3). Leipzig, 1890, 121–133 (gives a German translation of Gwynn's English version). — Th. Zahn, Geschichte des neu-testamentl. Kanons 2, 2. Erlangen, 1892, 973–991 (offers a German translation from the Syriac text). — H. Achelis, GCS 1, 2 (1897) 239–247. (German translation of all seven fragments from the Syriac). Cf. H. Achelis, Hippolytstudien 184–188.

III. THE THEOLOGY OF HIPPOLYTUS OF ROME

In the preceding pages Hippolytus was compared on several occasions to his contemporary Origen. His immense literary output and his predilection for exegetical studies remind one indeed of the great Alexandrian. Tradition holds that he was a disciple of Irenaeus and he certainly imitated his master in his efforts to refute the heretics. Thus he is in more than one respect a connecting link between Catholic controversialists like Irenaeus and Catholic scholars like Origen. As far as we know he never attempted to form a theological system as the latter did. He is less interested in scientific problems and theological speculations than in practical questions. He was a brilliant writer; although he at times made extravagant use of rhetorical devices. Yet he was without that depth which we admire in Origen. His knowledge of philosophy must be characterized as superficial. Whereas the Greek Apologists, especially St. Justin and more so the Alexandrians like Clement and Origen, intended to build a bridge between Hellenistic thought and Christian faith, acknowledging the germs of truth in it, Hippolytus looked upon philosophy as the source of heresies. Yet he borrowed much more from Greek philosophy than Irenaeus. Of lasting influence, however, were his canonical and polemical writings, especially his *Apostolic Tradition*.

1. *Christology*

In his christological doctrine Hippolytus thought in the terms of apologists like Justin, Athenagoras, Theophilus and Tertullian. He defines the relation of the Logos to the Father in a subordinationist way as they did. Moreover, his subordinationism is worse than theirs. He not only distinguishes between the Word internal or immanent in God (λόγος ἐνδιάθετος) and the Word emitted or uttered by God (λόγος προφορικός) as Theophilus did,

ιε describes the generation of the Word as a progressive development in three periods and teaches that the Logos appeared as a
person only later, at the time and in the way determined by the
Father:

God, subsisting alone, and having nothing contemporaneous with Himself, determined to create the world. And
conceiving the world in mind, and willing and uttering the
Word, He made it; and straightway it appeared, formed as
it had pleased Him. For us, then, it is sufficient simply to
know that there was nothing contemporaneous with God.
Beside Him there was nothing; but He, while existing alone,
yet existed in plurality. For He was neither without reason,
nor wisdom, nor power, nor counsel. All things were in Him,
and He was the All. When He willed, and as He willed, He
manifested His Word in the times determined by Him, and
by Him He made all things. When He wills, He does; and
when He thinks, He executes; and when He speaks, He
manifests; when He fashions, He contrives in wisdom. For
all things that are made He forms by reason and wisdom—
creating them in reason, and arranging them in wisdom. He
made them, then, as He pleased, for He was God. And as
the Author, the fellow-Counsellor, and Framer of the things
that are in formation, He begat the Word; and as He bears
this Word in Himself, and that, too, as [yet] invisible to the
world which is created. He makes Him visible; [and] uttering the voice first, and begetting Him as Light of Light, He
set Him forth to the world as its Lord, [and] His own mind;
and whereas He was visible formerly to Himself alone, and
invisible to the world which is made, He makes Him visible
in order that the world might see Him in His manifestation,
and be capable of being saved.

And thus there appeared another beside Himself. But
when I say *another* (ἕτερος), I do not mean that there are
two Gods, but that it is only light from light, or as water from
a fountain, or as a ray from the sun. For there is but one
power, which is from the All, from whom cometh this Power,
the Word. And this is the mind (λόγος) which came forth
into the world, and was manifested as the Son (παῖς) of God.
All things, then, are by Him and He alone is of the Father.

Who then adduces a multitude of Gods brought in, time after
time? For all are shut up, however unwillingly, to admit this
fact, that the All runs up into one (*Contra Noet.* 10–11, ANF).

The time before and after the creation are the first two phases
in the evolution of the World. The third is the Incarnation, which
makes the Logos the *perfect Son* (υἱὸς τέλειος):

What Son of His own, then, did God send through the
flesh but the Word, Whom he addressed as Son because He
was to become such (or be begotten) in the future? And He
takes the common name for tender affection among men in
being called the Son. For neither was the Lord, prior to the
incarnation and when by Himself, yet perfect Son, although
He was perfect Word, only-begotten. Nor could the flesh
subsist by itself apart from the Word, because it has its subsistence in the Word. Thus, then, one perfect Son of God
was manifested (*Contra Noet.* 15 ANF).

Thus Hippolytus went beyond the apologists, associating not
only the creation of the world but also the incarnation with the
generation of the Logos. Evidently, he did not realize that this
development of the Word in distinct phases introduced into the
divine essence a growth, progression incompatible with its immutability. Another error consisted in the fact that Hippolytus
regarded the generation of the Word as a free act like creation
and maintained that God could have made any man a God, if
he had desired to do so:

Man is neither God nor angel; make no mistake. If He
had willed to make thee God He could have done so: thou
hast the example of the Word; but willing to make thee
man, He made thee thus (*Philos.* 10,33,7 EP 398).

Thus Pope Callistus was correct in dubbing Hippolytus and
his adherents ditheists or worshippers of two gods, although Hippolytus resented this accusation bitterly (*Philos.* 9,12,4, EH 231).

2. *Soteriology*

Whereas the christology of Hippolytus shows the influence of the
apologists and suffers from its shortcomings, his soteriology follows
the sound doctrine of Irenaeus, especially his theory of recapitulation. He explains on several occasions that the Logos took
the flesh of Adam in order to renew mankind (*De antichr.* 4 ANF):

For whereas the Word of God was without flesh, He took upon Himself the holy flesh by the holy Virgin, and prepared a robe which He wove for Himself, like a bridegroom, in the sufferings of the cross, in order that by uniting His own power with our mortal body, and by mixing the incorruptible with the corruptible, and the strong with the weak, He might save perishing man.

In taking the flesh of Adam, the Logos restored immortality to man:

Let us believe then, dear brethren, according to the tradition of the apostles, that God the Word came down from heaven, [and entered] into the holy Virgin Mary, in order that, taking the flesh from her, and assuming also a human— by which I mean rational—soul, and becoming thus all that man is with the exception of sin, He might save fallen man, and confer immortality on men who believe in His name (*Contra Noet.* 17 ANF).

The doctrine of recapitulation as taught by Irenaeus is evident in the soteriology of Hippolytus. Thus he says on one occasion:

This Logos we know to have received a body from a virgin, and to have remodelled the old man by a new creation. And we believe the Logos to have passed through every period in this life, in order that He Himself might serve as a law for every age, and that, by being present [amongst] us, He might exhibit His own manhood as an aim for all men. And that by Himself in person He might prove that God made nothing evil, and that man possesses the capacity of self-determination, inasmuch as he is able to will and not to will, and is endued with power to do both. This man we know to have been made out of the compound of our humanity. For if He were not of the same nature with ourselves, in vain does He ordain that we should imitate the Teacher. For if that Man happened to be of a different substance from us, why does He lay injunctions similar to those He has received on myself, who am born weak; and how is this the act of one that is good and just? In order, however, that He might not be supposed to be different from us, He even underwent toil, and was willing to endure hunger, and did not refuse to feel thirst, and sunk into the quietude of slumber. He did not protest against His Passion, but became obedient unto death, and manifested His resurrection (*Philos.* 10,33 ANF).

Thus the redeemer is truly man, who by a new creation remodelled the old man. But He is also 'God above all,' who regenerated the old man:

For Christ is the God above all, and He has arranged to wash away sin from human beings, rendering regenerate the old man. And God called man His likeness from the beginning, and has evinced in a figure His love towards thee. And provided thou obeyest His solemn injunctions, and becomest a faithful follower of Him who is good, thou shalt resemble Him, inasmuch as thou shalt have honour conferred upon thee by Him. For the Deity does not diminish aught of the dignity of His divine perfection; He makes thee even God unto His glory (*ibid.* 34 ANF).

Here Hippolytus following Irenaeus understands the redemption as a deification of mankind.

Studies: K. PREYSING, Δίθεοί ἐστε: ZkTh 50 (1926) 604–608. — G. JOUASSARD, Le premier-né de la Vierge chez saint Irénée et saint Hippolyte: RSR (1932) 509–532; (1933) 25–37. — H. RAHNER, Hippolyt von Rom als Zeuge für den Ausdruck θεοτόχος: ZkTh 59 (1935) 73–81; idem, Probleme der Hippolytüberlieferung: ZhTh 60 (1936) 577–590. — F. J. DÖLGER, Zum Theotokos-Namen: AC 5 (1936) 152. — B. CAPELLE, Le logos, Fils de Dieu, dans la théologie d'Hippolyte: RTAM 9 (1937) 109–124. — H. RAHNER, Flumina de ventre Christi: Bibl (1941) 269–302, 367–403. — J. BARBEL, Christos Angelos (Theophaneia 3). Bonn, 1941, 68–70. — E. LENGELING, Das Heilswerk des Logos-Christos beim hl. Hippolyt von Rom. Rome, 1947.

3. *The Church*

The ecclesiology of Hippolytus has two aspects, a hierarchical and a spiritual. With regard to the former, he has much in common with Irenaeus. Throughout his refutation of heresy, he purposes to prove the Church the bearer of truth and the apostolic succession of the bishops the guarantee of her teaching.

Although he was a disciple of Irenaeus, who speaks so clearly of the Church's motherhood (*Adv. Haer.* 3,38,1; 5,20,2), it is surprising that in his works there is no mention whatever of the title *Mother Church*. Thus he follows the early Roman tradition and not the Eastern concept. This is all the more striking, if he was born and educated in the East. There are numerous references in his works to the Church as the Bride and Spouse of Christ (cf. above, p. 172, 174); in his interpretation of Apocalypse 12,1–6, which he gives in *De antichr.* 61, the Woman clothed with the sun is, indeed, the Church but the 'man-child' that she is in labor with is not the faithful, but the Logos, and the word *Mother* is not used at all.

He went astray with regard to the spiritual aspect of the Church, conceiving of a society composed too exclusively of the just (*In Dan.* 1,17,5–7), and making no room for those who, though repentant, had erred gravely in faith and morals. His whole life was a protest against 'opening the gates' too widely; as Adam was expelled from the garden after he had eaten the forbidden fruit, so the man who plunges into sin is deprived of the Holy Spirit, driven out of the new Eden, the Church, and reduced to an earthly state (*ibid.*).

On another occasion he sees the Church as a ship sailing towards the East and the heavenly paradise, guided by Christ, its pilot:

> The sea is the world, in which the Church is set, like a ship tossed in the deep, but not destroyed, for she has with her the skilled Pilot, Christ. And she bears in her midst also the trophy [which is erected] over death; for she carries with her the cross of the Lord. For her prow is the east, and her stern is the west, and her hold is the south, and her tillers are the two Testaments; and the ropes that stretch around her are the love of Christ, which binds the Church; and the net which she bears with her is the laver of regeneration which renews the believing. As a splendid sail, the Spirit from heaven is present, by whom those who believe are sealed; she has also anchors of iron accompanying her, i.e., the holy commandments of Christ Himself, which are strong as iron. She has also mariners on the right and on the left, assessors like the holy angels, by whom the Church is always governed and defended. The ladder in her leading up to the sailyard is an emblem of the Passion of Christ, which brings the faithful to the ascent of heaven. And the topsails aloft upon the yard are the company of prophets, martyrs and apostles, who have entered into their rest in the kingdom of Christ (*De antichr.* 59 ANF).

It is very interesting to observe how much stress Hippolytus lays on the security of the voyage; 'strong as iron' are the anchors, the commandments of Christ, and he who breaks them does so to his own peril.

It was another symbol, the ark of Noe, that played an important role in the controversy with Pope Callistus over the remission of sins. In fact, it is in this disagreement that Hippolytus' concept of the Church appears clearly as a 'society of saints who live in righteousness,' as the κλῆσις τῶν ἁγίων (*In Dan.* 1,17).

Studies: A. HAMEL, Der Kirchenbegriff Hippolyts. Diss. Bonn, 1929. — G. BARDY, La théologie de l'Église de saint Irénée au concile de Nicée. Paris, 1947, 98–111. — H. RAHNER, Navicula Petri: ZkTh 69 (1947) 1 ff. — M. KUPPENS, Notes dogmatiques sur l'épiscopat: Revue éccl. Liège 36 (1949) 355–367; (1950) 9–26, 80–93. — E. PETERSON, Das Schiff als Symbol der Kirche: TZ 6 (1950) 77 ff. — A. HAMEL, Die Kirche bei Hippolyt von Rom (BFTh 2. r. 49). Gütersloh, 1951.

4. *The Remission of Sins*

In his *Philosophumena* (9,12) he says, among other charges against Callistus:

The impostor Callistus, having ventured on such opinions [sc. regarding the Logos] established a school in antagonism to the Church [i.e. that of Hippolytus], adopting the foregoing system of instruction. And he first invented the device of conniving with men in regard of their indulgence in sensual pleasures, saying that all had their sins forgiven by himself. For he who is in the habit of attending the congregation of any one else, and is called a Christian, should he commit any transgression, the sin, they say, is not reckoned unto him, provided only he hurries off and attaches himself to the school of Callistus. And many persons were gratified with his regulation, as being stricken in conscience, and at the same time having been rejected by numerous sects; while also some of them, in accordance with our condemnatory sentence, had been by us forcibly ejected from the Church [i.e. that of Hippolytus]. Now such disciples as these passed over to these followers of Callistus, and served to crowd his school. This one propounded the opinion that, if a bishop was guilty of any sin, if even a sin unto death, he ought not to be deposed. About the time of this man, bishops, priests, and deacons, who had twice married and thrice married, began to be allowed to retain their place among the clergy. If also, however, any one in holy orders married, Callistus permitted such a one to continue in holy orders as if he had not sinned... he asserted that likewise the parable of the tares is uttered in reference to this one: 'Let the tares grow along with the wheat' (Math. 13,30), or in other words, let those who in the Church are guilty of sin remain in it. But also he affirmed that the ark of Noe was made for a symbol of the Church, in which were both dogs and wolves and ravens and all things clean and unclean; and so he alleges that the case should stand in like manner with the Church... He permitted females, if they were unwedded and burned with passion at an age at all events unbecoming, or if they were not disposed to overturn their own dignity through a legal marriage, that they might have whomsoever they would choose as a bedfellow, whether slave or free, and that a woman, though not legally married, might consider such a companion as a husband. Whence women, reputed believers, began to resort to drugs for producing sterility, and to gird themselves round, so as to expel what was being conceived on account of their not wishing to have a child either by a slave or by any paltry fellow, for the sake of their family and excessive wealth. Behold, into how great impiety that lawless one has proceeded, by inculcating adultery and murder at the same time! And withal, after such audacious acts, they, lost to all shame, attempt to call themselves a Catholic Church (ANF).

The bitterness and passion of these accusations make it difficult to distinguish between fact disguised by malicious misinterpretation and out-and-out falsehood. According to Tertullian (*De pudicitia* 1,6) an edict of the 'Pontifex maximus' pardoned adultery and fornication after penance, but whether Hippolytus here opposes this decision remains doubtful. He is trying to explain why the 'school of Callistus' had such great attraction and the number of his own followers remained very small; he gives as a reason what he calls the laxity of his antagonist in contrast to, and disagreement with, his own sterner principles. If this viewpoint is kept in mind, then the passage deals not with the disciplinary question of proper expiation of wrongs committed, nor of absolution thereafter, but with alleged disregard of sins by Pope Callistus and his failure to enforce ecclesiastical sanctions. The Pontiff is accused of receiving all, even the greatest offenders, into his 'school,' and of appealing in support of his conduct to the parable of the tares among the wheat and the figure of clean and unclean animals placed by Noe in the ark. Hippolytus demands, in other words, greater severity in cases of impurity, of guilty bishops, in the admission to orders of men who had married more than once, and, he denies the validity of marriages between free women and slaves. But nowhere is anything said against the power of the Church to absolve from sin after submission to penance, while, on the other hand, the *Apostolic Tradition* positively recognizes its authority, to do so. The prayer for the consecration of a bishop quoted there reads:

> Grant upon this Thy servant whom Thou hast chosen for the episcopate... that by the high priestly Spirit he may have authority 'to forgive sins' (*facultatem remittendi peccata*) according to Thy command, 'to assign lots' according to Thy bidding, to 'loose every bond' (*solvendi omne vinculum iniquitatis*) according to the authority Thou gavest to the Apostles (Dix 3).

According to this text the authority to absolve has no restriction. If Hippolytus presents this prayer as an apostolic tradition, he must have acknowledged this ecclesiastical power.

It is extremely difficult to say what Hippolytus means when he states: 'He was the first to pardon sins of impurity.' Since he intends thus to stigmatize his opponent, his charge must be taken with great caution, as is amply demonstrated by his narrow reaction to, and mean distortion of, one of the greatest achievements of Callistus' pontificate. The Roman Empire placed an insurmountable barrier between slave and free, stringently forbidding any marriage between them. Already prohibited by the Julian and Papian laws, such weddings were declared null and void by the Emperor Marcus and Commodus and reduced to the level of concubinage. It was an epoch-making advance when Callistus defied the popular prejudices of his day and granted ecclesiastical sanction to these unions for Christians. By giving her blessing in such cases, the Church broke down the barrier between the classes and treated their respective members as equals. She thus took a tremendous stride forward in the direction of the abolition of human bondage, and Callistus' startling innovation in the ancient marriage customs stands as a striking testimony to the social progress promoted by the Church in the Roman Empire. The injustice and bitter unfairness of Hippolytus can be gauged from the fact that all he sees in this enlightened act is an opportunity, based on the abuses inevitably connected with all such advances, to level at Callistus a venomous charge of teaching adultery and murder.

Studies: See the bibliography to Tertullian's *De pudicitia*, below, p. 314. — E. ROLFFS, Das Indulgenzedikt des römischen Bischofs Kallist (TU 11). Leipzig, 1894. — K. PREYSING, Zwei offizielle Entscheidungen des römischen Stuhles um die Wende des 2. Jahrhunderts: ZkTh 41 (1917) 595 ff.; 42 (1918) 177–186; 43 (1919) 358–362. — P. GALTIER, L'Église et la rémission des péchés, Paris, 1932, 141–183; *idem*, RHE (1927) 465–488; (1928) 41–51. — A. DONINI, Ippolito di Roma. Rome, 1925, 185 ff.; *idem* RR (1925) 56–71. — K. PREYSING, ZkTh 50 (1926) 143–150. — J. HOH, Die kirchliche Busse im 2. Jahrhundert. Breslau, 1932, 58–63. — B. POSCHMANN, Paenitentia secunda. Bonn, 1940, 348–367.

THE MURATORIAN FRAGMENT

There is another document attributed to Hippolytus of Rome, the so-called *Muratorian Fragment*. It contains the oldest extant list of the New Testament writings accepted as inspired and hence has the greatest importance for the history of the canon. It was discovered and published by L. A. Muratori in 1740 from a manuscript of the eighth century in the Ambrosian Library at Milan; its Latin is clumsy and its spelling bad. Four fragments of the same text were found in codices of the eleventh and twelfth centuries at Montecassino, whereas that of the Ambrosian Library had originally come from the ancient monastery of Bobbio. Mutilated at beginning and end, it commences in the middle of a sentence about the Gospel of Mark and comprises 85 lines altogether. Not only are the various books enumerated but their apostolic origin is demonstrated and other details regarding the authorship and canonicity are added, especially with reference to the Gospel of St. John. After the Gospels, the list gives the Acts of the Apostles, thirteen Epistles of St. Paul, the Epistles of St. John and St. Jude, and two Apocalypses, that of John and that

of Peter. The Epistle to the Hebrews, and the Epistles of St. James
and St. Peter are not mentioned. Other Epistles of St. Paul, such
as that to the Laodiceans and the Alexandrians, are stigmatized
as heretical: 'Moreover there is in circulation an Epistle to the
Laodiceans, another to the Alexandrians forged under the name
of Paul, looking toward the heresy of Marcion, and several others
which cannot be received into the Catholic Church: for gall
should not be mixed with honey' (3). It is interesting that in this
oldest canon of the New Testament the Book of Wisdom 'written
by the friends of Solomon' is also cited. The *Apocalypse of Peter* (cf.
vol. I, p. 144 ff) is mentioned after that of John but with a
certain reservation: 'though some amongst us will not have this
read in the Church,' indicating that opposition to it existed. The
Shepherd of Hermas (cf. vol. I, p. 92 ff) is recommended for private
reading but not accepted as inspired, since it belongs to the post-
apostolic period: 'But the *Shepherd* did Hermas write very recently
in our times in the city of Rome, while his brother, Bishop Pius,
sat in the chair of the Church of Rome. And therefore it ought
also to be read; but it cannot be publicly read in the Church to
the people, either among the prophets as their number is complete, or among the Apostles, to the end of time' (4). At the end
several other heretical works are rejected: 'Of [the writing of]
Arsinous, called also Valentinus, or of Miltiades, we receive
nothing at all. Those, too, who wrote the new Book of Psalms for
Marcion, together with Basilides and the founder of the Asian
Cataphrygians [are rejected]' (4).

The passage dealing with the *Shepherd of Hermas* indicates that
the *Muratorian Canon* was compiled shortly after Pius ruled the
Church of Rome (142–155), most probably before the end of the
second century. It is generally allowed that it emanated from
Rome, as indeed the mention of 'the city' suggests. However, it
cannot be considered an official document involving the responsibility of the Roman Church, as A. v. Harnack maintained.
H. Koch has shown that there are too many reasons against such
an opinion.

It is still a disputed point whether our fragment was originally
Greek or Latin. J. B. Lightfoot with many others held for the
former and regarded the work as only rather an unskilful but
literal translation greatly corrupted in the course of transmission.

He argued that the literature of the Roman Church was still Greek, as we see from the example of Hippolytus, and that the whole cast and connexion of sentences are Greek. Recent investigations by C. Mohrmann have demonstrated though, that the transition in language had begun in the Christian community of Rome about the middle of the second century and that Latin versions of the Old Testament were already in existence at that time. Nevertheless, the possibility of a Greek original remains, because the pun on words *fel enim cum melle misceri non congruit* is hardly a proof to the contrary.

In the absence of any definite evidence we cannot attribute the fragment to any particular individual with certainty. J. B. Lightfoot has strongly advocated the authorship of Hippolytus of Rome. Th. H. Robinson, Th. Zahn, N. Bonwetsch, M. J. Lagrange hold the same opinion. As far as time is concerned, it would be one of his earliest works and we can ascribe it to him with a greater probability than to any other whose name has been suggested, e.g. Clement of Alexandria, Melito of Sardes and Polycrates of Ephesus.

Editions: L. A. MURATORI, Antiquitates Italicae medii aevi 3. Milan, 1740, 851–854. — S. P. TREGELLES, Canon Muratorianus. The Earliest Catalogue of the Books of the New Testament. Oxford, 1867, 8. — E. S. BUCHANAN, The Codex Muratorianus: JThSt 9 (1907) 537–545. — G. RAUSCHEN, Monumenta minora saeculi secundi (FP 3) 2nd ed. Bonn, 1914, 24–34. — H. LIETZMANN, Das Muratorische Fragment und die monarchianischen Prologe zu den Evangelien (KT 1) 4th ed. Bonn, 1933. — A. SCHAEFER–M. MEINERTZ, Einleitung in das Neue Testament, 5th ed. Paderborn, 1949, Anhang II, 410–414.

Translations: English: ANL 9, 2, 159 ff. — B. J. KIDD, Documents Illustrative of the History of the Church, vol 1 (SPCK). London-New York, 1938, 166–168. — *German:* E. HENNECKE, Neutestamentliche Apokryphen, 2nd ed. Tübingen, 1924, 135 f.

Studies: J. B. LIGHTFOOT, The Apostolic Fathers, Part I, vol. 2. London and New York, 1890, 405–413. — A. HARNACK, Exzerpte aus dem Muratorischen Fragment (saec. XI et XII): ThLZ (1898) 131–134; *idem*, Zum Muratorischen Fragment (TU 20, 3). Leipzig, 1900. — TH. ZAHN, Geschichte des neutest. Kanons 2, 1. Erlangen, 1890, 1–143. — TH. H. ROBINSON, The Authorship of the Muratorian Canon: The Expositor, Ser. 7, vol. 1 (1906) 481–495. — C. ERBES, Die Zeit des Muratorischen Fragmentes: ZKG 35 (1914) 331–362. — TH. ZAHN, Miscellanea: II. Hippolytus, der Verfasser des Muratorischen Kanons: NKZ 33 (1922) 417–436. — G. N. BONWETSCH, Hippolytisches: NGWG (1923) 27 ff, 63 f. — A. v. HARNACK, ZNW (1925) 1–16; (1926) 154–160; *idem*, Über den Verfasser und den literarischen Charakter des Muratorischen Fragments: ZNW (1925) 1–16. — M. J. LAGRANGE, L'auteur du Canon de Muratori: RBibl 35 (1926) 83–88; *idem*, Le canon d'Hippolyte et le fragment de Muratori: RBibl 42 (1933) 161–186; *idem*, Histoire anc. du Canon du Nouveau Testament. Paris, 1933, 66–84. — A. Donini, Il Canone Muratoriano: Ricerche religiose 2 (1926) 127–138. — S. Ritter, Il frammento Muratoriano: RAC (1926) 215–268. — H. Koch, Zu A. v. Harnacks Beweis für den amtlichen römischen Ursprung des Muratorischen Fragments: ZNW 25 (1926) 154–160. — G. Roethe, Zur Geschichte der römischen Synoden im 3. und 4. Jahrhundert. 1937, 112–114. — Faure, Z. syst. Theol. 19, 143–149. — H. Leclercq, DAL 12, 543–560. — J. Schmidt, LThK 7, 382 f. — M. Meinertz, Einleitung in das Neue Testament, 5th ed. Paderborn, 1949, 336–338.

THE OLD PROLOGUES TO THE GOSPELS AND THE EPISTLES OF ST. PAUL

Many manuscripts of the Vulgate contain prologues to the different biblical books with information about the author of each, its importance and characteristics, sometimes also its occasion and history. The writers of these introductions, also called *praefationes* or *argumenta*, are generally unknown and the majority of them late. However, three groups deserve mention here.

1. *The Anti-Marcionite Prologues to the Gospels*

The most ancient prologues to the Gospels were compiled by an anti-Marcionite, and must be assigned to a period shortly after the Marcionite crisis, approximately to the years between 160 and 180, according to D. de Bruyne and A. v. Harnack. They were composed probably at Rome, originally in Greek, but translated in Africa at the end of the third century for a new edition of the older Latin Gospels. Inasmuch as they show the tradition of the early Church concerning the authors of the Gospels, they have great historical interest. Unfortunately, the foreword to Matthew has been lost—apparently at a very early date —, only that to Luke, which is the longest, has been preserved in the original Greek, but those to Mark and John, together with Luke, have come down in Latin. Recently these opinions of De Bruyne and Harnack have been questioned by E. Gutwenger; as he points out, they take for granted that all three prologues come from the same pen. But the disproportion in length and in content, the difference in coloring and atmosphere make it difficult indeed to accept their assumption. We must rather conclude, therefore, that the origin and date of each introduction have to be investigated separately.

Editions: D. DE BRUYNE, Les plus ancients prologues latins des Évangiles: RB 40 (1928) 193–214. — A. v. HARNACK, Die ältesten Evangelien-Prologe und die Bildung des Neuen Testamentes: SAB Phil.-histor. Klasse 24 (1928) 322–341. — K. TH. SCHÄFER, Einleitung in das Neue Testament. Bonn, 1938, 2*.

Studies: D. DE BRUYNE, *loc. cit.* Cf. M. J. LAGRANGE, RBibl (1929) 115–121. — D. DE BRUYNE, RB 1929, Bull. 2 n. 22. — A. v. HARNACK, *loc. cit.* — B. W. BACON, The Anti-Marcionite Prologue to John: JBL 49 (1930) 43–54. — R. EISLER, La ponctuation du prologue antimarcionite à l'Évangile selon Jean: RPh 4 (1930) 350–371. — W. F. HOWARD, The Anti-Marcionite Prologues to the Gospels: ExpT 47 (1935/36) 534–538. — E. GUTWENGER, The Anti-Marcionite Prologues: TS 7 (1946) 393–409.

2. *The Monarchian Prologues to the Gospels*

There is a series of longer prologues to the Gospels, the so-called Monarchian prologues, which used to be assigned to the first half of the third century. According to P. Corssen they were written at Rome about thirty years after the *Muratorian Fragment* in Monarchian circles. Their original language was Latin although they used Greek sources. Corssen held that they constituted another proof for the Monarchian character of the official Roman teaching at the date mentioned above. However, his idea of the Monarchian origin never seemed very convincing and was abandoned after J. Chapman and E. Ch. Babut connected them rather with Spain. They are now thought to have been composed at the end of the fourth or beginning of the fifth century by some Priscillianist.

Editions: J. WORDSWORTH–H. J. WHITE, Novum Testamentum Domini Nostri Jesu Christi, Latine. Oxford, 1898, 15–17, 171–173, 269–271, 485–487. — H. LIETZMANN, Das Muratorische Fragment und die monarchianischen Prologe zu den Evangelien (KT 1) 4th ed. Bonn, 1933, 12–16.

Translation: *German:* E. HENNECKE, Neutestamentliche Apokryphen, 2nd ed. Tübingen, 1924, 136–137.

Studies: E. v. DOBSCHÜTZ, Studien zur Textkritik der Vulgata. Leipzig, 1894, 65–119. — P. CORSSEN, Monarchianische Prologe zu den vier Evangelien (TU 15, 1). Leipzig, 1896. — J. CHAPMAN, Notes on the Early History of the Vulgate Gospels. Oxford, 1908, 217–288. – E. CH. BABUT, Priscillien et le Priscillianisme: BEHE 169 (Paris, 1909) 294-308. — K. VOLLERS-E. v. DOBSCHÜTZ, Ein spanisch-arabisches Evangelienfragment: ZDMG 56 (1902) 633–648. — F. LOOFS, Theophilus von Antiochien Adv. Marcionem und die andern theologischen Quellen bei Irenaeus (TU 46, 2). Leipzig, 1930, 158 note 1, 161 note 2. — A. BAUMSTARK, Liturgischer Nachhall der 'monarchianischen' Evangelienprologe: JL 12 (1932) 194–197. — A. DOLD, Zentralblatt für Bibliothekswissenschaft (1935) 125 ff. — F. TAESCHNER, Die monarchianischen

Prologe zu den vier Evangelien in der spanisch-arabischen Bibelübersetzung de Isaak-Velasquez nach der Münchener Handschrift Cod. arab. 238: OC 7 (1935 80–99.

3. The Prologues to the Epistles of St. Paul

The short prologues to the writings of St. Paul were not mad up by the same individual. According to D. de Bruyne, those t the Pastoral Letters were furnished by the Roman author of th oldest Gospel forewords (a conclusion that, of course, has to b modified to meet the above-mentioned objections of Gutwenger) while those to the other Epistles (with the exception of Hebrews the introduction to which was added much later) were compose by Marcion or one of his collaborators.

Editions: D. DE BRUYNE, Prologues bibliques d'origine marcionite: RB 24 (1907 1–16. — P. CORSSEN, Zur Überlieferungsgeschichte des Römerbriefes: ZNW 8 (1909 1–45, 97–102. — K. TH. SCHÄFER, Einleitung in das Neue Testament. Bonn, 1938, 1*

Studies: D. DE BRUYNE, *loc. cit.* — P. CORSSEN, *loc. cit.* — W. MUNDLE, Die Herkunf der marcionistischen Prologe zu den paulinischen Briefen: ZNW (1925) 56–77. — A. V. HARNACK, Der marcionistische Ursprung der ältesten Vulgata-Prologe zu de Paulusbriefen: ZNW (1925) 204–217; (1926) 160–162. — D. DE BRUYNE, RB (1925 Bull. I, 187–188. — M. J. LAGRANGE, Les prologues pretendus marcionites: RBibl 3! (1935) 161–173. — G. BARDY, La question des langues dans l'Église ancienne. Paris 1948, 105 f.

NOVATIAN

The theology of the Logos represented by Hippolytus escaped formal condemnation. In the next generation it was openly pro fessed by the Roman priest Novatian. According to the historiar Philostorgius (*Hist. eccl.* 8,15) he was of Phrygian origin, but thi: testimony remains doubtful. In a letter addressed to Bishop Fabiu: of Antioch, Pope Cornelius states that he was baptised whil seriously ill and never received confirmation:

The occasion of his acceptance of the faith was Satan, who resorted to him and dwelt in him for a long time. While he was being healed by the exorcists he fell into a grievou sickness, and, as he was considered to be all but dead, re ceived baptism by infusion on the very bed in which he lay, i indeed one may say that such a man has received it. Nor yet indeed did he obtain the other things, when he recovered from his sickness, of which one should partake according to

the rule of the Church, or the sealing by the bishop. And as
he did not obtain these, how could he obtain the Holy
Spirit? (Euseb., *Hist. eccl.* 6,43,14–15 LCL, EH 254–6)

Nevertheless, his bishop ordained him but not without heavy
opposition:

> He was deemed worthy of the presbyterate through the
> favor of the bishop, who laid his hand on him to confer that
> order, meeting the opposition of all the clergy and many lay
> persons as well—since one who has received baptism by in-
> fusion on his bed owing to sickness, might not be ordained
> to an order (*ibid.* 6,43,17).

Although Cornelius brands 'his craftiness and duplicity, his
perjuries and falsehoods, his unsociability and wolf-like friendship' and goes so far as to call him a 'treacherous and malicious
wild beast' (*ibid.* 6,43,6), he must have been eminently well-
qualified, because about the year 250, he occupied a leading
position among the clergy of Rome. In the correspondence of St.
Cyprian we find two letters (*Epist.* 30,36) addressed to the bishop
of Carthage in answer to questions about apostates (*lapsi*) and
written during the long vacancy of the Apostolic See which preceded the election of Cornelius. Although sent in the name of the
'presbyters and deacons abiding at Rome,' they were composed
by Novatian, as Cyprian testifies (*Epist.* 4,5) in regard to the first,
and as contents and style prove for the second. Both are outstanding for their careful, elaborate and brilliant style and for
the moderation and far-sightedness of their author. Epistle 30
makes it clear that the Church of Rome agrees fully with the
bishop of Carthage regarding the maintenance of ecclesiastical
discipline in the case of those who apostatised during the persecution, but does not wish to settle the question of their reconciliation until a new bishop is elected. Only in case of imminent
death should absolution be given:

> Desiring to maintain the moderation of this middle course
> in these matters, we for a long time, and indeed many of us,
> and, moreover, with some of the bishops who are near to us
> and within reach, and some whom, placed afar off, the heat
> of the persecution had driven out from other provinces, have
> thought that nothing new was to be done before the appoint-
> ment of a bishop; but we believe that the care of the lapsed

must be moderately dealt with, so that, in the meantime, whilst the grant of a bishop is withheld from us by God, the cause of such as are able to bear the delays of postponement should be kept in suspense; but of such as impending death does not suffer to bear the delay, having repented and professed a detestation of their deeds with frequency; if with tears, if with groans, if with weeping they have betrayed the signs of a grieving and truly penitent spirit, when there remains, as far as man can tell, no hope of living; so then, finally, such cautious and careful help should be ministered, God Himself knowing what He will do with such, and in what way He will examine the balance of His judgment; while we, however, take anxious care that neither ungodly men should praise our smooth facility, nor truly penitent men accuse our severity as cruel (30,8 ANF).

It seems that Novatian had hoped to become bishop of Rome. When Cornelius was chosen in March of 251 and showed leniency in the question of the reconciliation of the lapsed, Novatian, reversing his former stand, demanded that apostates should be forever excommunicated and set himself up as the champion of exclusive rigorism. He sought out three bishops 'in a small and very insignificant part of Italy... When they arrived, inasmuch as they were too simple, as we said before, for the unscrupulous devices of the wicked, they were shut up by certain disorderly men like himself, and at the tenth hour, when they were drunk, and sick with the aftereffects, he forcibly compelled them to make him a bishop by a counterfeit and vain laying on of hands, an office that he assumed by crafty treachery since it did not fall to his lot' (Euseb., *Hist. eccl.* 6,43,9, LCL). Thus the Novatian schism, it seems, did not arise from doctrinal, but from personal differences. Novatian had originally no special views on penance. But once the schism was organized, it was inevitably bound to take up an attitude and principles opposed to those of Cornelius on this burning question. Novatianism became an important sect. In vain did Bishop Dionysius of Alexandria address a personal letter to Novatian to return to the Church (see above, p. 106). Novatian's party found a footing as far as Spain in the West and Syria in the East and lasted for several centuries. Eusebius reports (*Hist. eccl.* 6,43,1) that in the east the followers of Novatian 'styled themselves Puritans (καθαροί).' They were excommunicated by a synod held at Rome, which settled the question of the lapsed:

> Whereupon a very large synod assembled at Rome, of sixty bishops and a still greater number of presbyters and deacons, while in the rest of the provinces the pastors in their several regions individually considered the question as to what was to be done. It was unanimously decreed that Novatus [read: Novatian], together with the partners of his arrogance, and those who decided to agree with the man's brother-hating and most inhuman opinion, should be considered as strangers to the Church, but such of the brethren as had fallen into the misfortune should be treated and restored with the medicines of repentance (Euseb., *Hist. eccl.* 6,43,2 LCL).

Nothing is known about Novatian's later personal history. Indications in his writings date them during the persecution either of Gallus or Valerian, when he was separated from his disciples at Rome. Socrates (*Hist. eccl.* 4,28) is the first to report that he died as a victim of Valerian's persecution. Eulogius, Bishop of Alexandria, saw at the end of the sixth century acts of the martyrdom of Novatian, which he describes as a fictitious composition of no value. However, in the Martyrology of Jerome, a Novatian, without further title, is named among the Roman martyrs on June 29. Moreover, in the summer of 1932 a richly decorated tomb was found in a newly discovered anonymous cemetery near St. Lawrence in Rome. The inscription, painted in red letters and in a good state of preservation, reads:

NOVATIANO BEATISSIMO

MARTYRI GAUDENTIUS DIAC

Thus it is the authentic grave of a Novatian venerated as a martyr to whom the deacon Gaudentius dedicated the artistic improvements. There is reason to suppose that we have here the burial place of our heretic, although it remains strange that Novatian is not given the title of bishop in the inscription.

Novatian was a vigorous personality, wanting in strength of

character, but a man of great talents and learning. He was well
trained in Stoic philosophy (Cyprian, *Epist.* 55,24) and a master
of rhetoric; he shows the influence of Vergil in his style. Since
almost everything we know of him comes from his adversaries, it
must be taken with a certain caution. Fabian must have had his
reasons why he ordained him against strong opposition. The
author of the treatise *Ad Novatianum* states (ch. 1) that he could
have been 'a precious vessel' if he had remained in the Church.
Even his adversary, Bishop Cornelius, in his letter to Bishop
Fabius of Antioch (Euseb., *Hist. eccl.* 6,43), calls him a 'marvellous
fellow,' 'this highly distinguished person' (7), 'this master of
doctrine, this champion of the Church's discipline' (8), 'this
vindicator of the Gospel' (11). Of course Cornelius intends this
sarcastically, but it shows, nevertheless, Novatian's reputation.
That he speaks of Novatian as 'enamoured of a different philosophy' is interesting (16). In fact, Novatian seems to have been a
Christian Stoic. His works betray the influence of that philosophy
on several occasions. He was the first theologian of Rome to
publish in Latin and he is thus one of the founders of Roman
theology. He writes a cultivated idiom in a careful and elaborate,
but always clear and calm style.

Studies: E. Amann, Novatien et novatianisme: DTC 11, 815–849. — H. Koch, PWK
17, 1138–1156. — V. Ammundsen, Novatianus og Novatianismen. Copenhagen,
1901. — Fr. Torm, En kritisk Fremstilling af Novatianus' liv og Forfattervirks-
omhed. Copenhagen, 1901. — J. O. Anderson, Novatian. Copenhagen, 1901. —
H. Jordan, Die Theologie der neuentdeckten Predigten Novatians. Leipzig, 1902. —
A. d'Alès, Le corpus de Novatien: RSR 10 (1919) 293 f. — H. Koch, Cyprianische
Untersuchungen. Bonn, 1926, 117–131, 270–275, 475 f, 485. — F. J. Dölger, Die
Taufe des Novatian: AC 2 (1930) 258–267. — A. Baumstark, Die Evangelienzitate
Novatians und das Diatessaron: OC 27 (1930) 1–14. — J. Stelzenberger, Die Be-
ziehungen der frühchristlichen Sittenlehre zur Ethik der Stoa. Munich, 1933, 262–
264, 465–467. — H. Koch, Novaziano, Cipriano e Plinio il Giovane: Religio 11
(1935) 321–332; *idem*, Il martire Novaziano: Religio 14 (1938) 192–198. — F. J.
Dölger, Zum Oikiskos des Novatianus. Klausnerhäuschen oder Versteck?: AC 6
(1940) 61–64. — A. Ferrua, Novaziano martire: CC (1944) 4, 232–239.
For the *inscription*, see: E. Josi, Cimitero al viale Regina Margherita: RAC 10
(1933) 213–217. — P. Styger, Die römischen Katakomben. Berlin, 1933, 194 ff. —
L. C. Mohlberg, Osservazioni storico-critiche sulla iscrizione tombale di Nova-
ziano: EL 51 (1937) 242–249. — D. van den Eynde, L'inscription sépulcrale de
Novatien: RHE 33 (1937) 792–794. — J. P. Kirsch, The Catacombs of Rome.
Rome, 1946, 101 f.

I. HIS WRITINGS

According to Jerome, Novatian 'wrote *On the Passover, On the Sabbath, On Circumcision, On the Priesthood, On Prayer, On the Food of the Jews, On Zeal, On Attalus,* and many others, especially, a great volume *On the Trinity*' (*De vir. ill.* 70). Two of these titles survive among the works of Tertullian; two others not listed above have been discovered in the literary remains of Cyprian.

1. *On the Trinity (De trinitate)*

This study was probably written well before 250 and is the first great Latin contribution to theology to appear in Rome. Jerome's remark that it is 'a sort of epitome of the work of Tertullian' (*De vir. ill.* 70), evidently alludes to *Adversus Praxean*, a defence of the doctrine of the trinity, but he is greatly mistaken and considerably underrates Novatian. Composed in poetical prose, outstanding in form and content, it is the most valuable and most extensive of Novatian's productions and the cause of his high reputation as a divine. In completeness, wealth of biblical proof and influence on succeeding times, it would stand comparison with Origen's *First Principles*, except for the fact that the sober theology of the West falls much below the wide range of Alexandrian speculation. It sums up in classic fashion the doctrine of the trinity, as developed by Theophilus of Antioch, Irenaeus, Hippolytus and Tertullian, but by no means lacks originality or independence. In fact, the treatment of the subject is much more exact and systematic, much more complete and extensive than that of any prior attempt.

Although the word Trinity (*trinitas*) does not occur, the entire work deals with that dogma. The old Roman Symbol providing the basis, it thus takes the form of an exposition of the three chief articles of the Creed. The introduction to the first chapter on God the creator reveals the influence of Stoic philosophy in its enthusiastic description of the universe:

> The rule of truth requires that we believe, first, in God the Father and Lord Almighty, that is to say, the most perfect Founder of all things. He made the sky, poised above in its lofty height, the solid mass of earth laid out beneath, the seas flowing freely in every direction; and He furnished all these, in full abundance and order, with their peculiar and suitable

agencies. In the firmament of heaven He set the sun, aroused at each day's dawn to give light with his beams; the brilliant sphere of the moon, waxing to fullness with her monthly phases, to relieve the gloom of night; and the glittering stars, shining with rays of varying degrees of intensity. It is by His will that they run their courses according to the laws of their orbits, to mark for mankind days, months, years, and seasons, and to be for signs and other useful purposes. On the earth, too, He reared the mountains with their towering crests, hollowed out the deep valleys, levelled the plains, and appointed the different species of animals, to supply the various needs of man... In the sea, again, wonderful as it is in its extent and its usefulness to man, He fashions living creatures of all sorts, some of moderate, some of enormous size... Even this was not enough; the roaring billows and currents of waters might have encroached upon a domain which is not theirs, at the expense of its human possessor. But God has set them their bounds which they cannot pass, and when the roaring surge and the waters foaming from the deep trough of the sea reach the shores, they must draw back again. They cannot pass the limits allowed to them, but obey the fixed laws of their being, teaching men the better to observe God's laws by the example of obedience which the very elements provide (SPCK).

The rest of the first chapter deals with the creation of man and of the spiritual powers. Chapters 2–8 discuss the essence of God and his attributes.

The second part, comprising chapters 9–28, is a defense of the two natures and their union in Christ, the Son of God and the Son of man, promised in the Old Testament and revealed in the New, against Docetism, Ebionitism, Adoptianism, Modalism and Patripassionism.

The third part treats briefly of the Holy Spirit (ch. 29), his gifts to the Bride of Christ, the Church, and his work in the Church.

The fourth part, consisting of chapters 30 and 31, demonstrates the unity of the godhead and aims to prove that the divinity of the Son does not impair it. The last chapter sums up the eternal relationship of the Son to the Father against the different heresies.

Nothing in the entire treatise indicates that it came out after Novatian broke with the Church of Rome, and Cyprian in his work *De unitate ecclesiae* seems acquainted with it. It must, there-fore, have been written before the Decian persecution.

The text of *De trinitate* survived among the works of Tertullian. Since the manuscripts have been lost, the published editions of Mesnart-Gagneius (Paris 1545), Gelenius (Bales 1550) and Pamelius (Antwerp 1579) are the only witnesses.

Editions: ML 3, 861–970. — W. Y. FAUSSET, Novatiani Romanae urbis presbyteri De Trinitate liber (Cambridge Patristic Texts). Cambridge, 1909.

Translations: English: R. E. WALLIS, ANL 13, 293–395; ANF 5, 611–644.—H. MOORE, The Treatise of Novatian on the Trinity (SPCK). London, 1919.

Studies: TH. HERMANN, Das Verhältnis von Novatianus De Trinitate zu Tertullians Adversus Praxean. Marburg, 1918. — R. GANSZYNIEC, Animadversiones criticae in Novatiani De Trinitate: Eos 25 (1922) 10–23; 28 (1925) 124; 31 (1928) 296, 304, 368, 438, 452, 473, 484, 494, 536, 552–556; 32 (1929) passim. — M. KRIEBEL, Studien zur älteren Entwicklung der abendländischen Trinitätslehre bei Tertullian und Novatian. Diss. Marburg, 1932.

2. On Jewish Foods (De cibis Judaicis)

This is one of three works against the Jews mentioned by Jerome (*De vir. ill.* 70), *On Circumcision, On the Sabbath,* and *On Jewish Foods,* all in the form of letters to the brethren. It alone survives, but its introduction alludes to the others as issued earlier: 'But how perverse are the Jews, and remote from the under-standing of their law, I have fully shown, as I believe, in two former letters, wherein it was absolutely proved that they are ignorant of what is the true circumcision, and what the true Sabbath; and their ever increasing blindness is confuted in this present epistle, wherein I have briefly discoursed concerning their meats' (1 ANF). Then Novatian endeavours to prove that the food laws, as well as all the other prescriptions of the Old Testament, must be understood spiritually according to St. Paul (Rom. 7,14). To call some animals clean and others unclean would mean that God the creator, after He had blessed all as good, subsequently reprobated some of them. Such a contradiction cannot be attributed to Him, and for this reason the appropriate and spiritual application must be restored. Novatian gives an interesting history of human food:

To begin from the beginning of things, whence it behooves
me to begin; the only food for the first men was fruit and the
produce of the trees. For afterwards, man's sin transferred
his need from the fruit-trees to the produce of the earth,
when the very attitude of his body attested the condition of
his conscience. For although innocence raised men up towards the heavens to pluck their food from the trees so long
as they had a good conscience, yet sin, when committed, bent
men down to the earth and to the ground to gather its grain.
Moreover, afterwards the use of flesh was added, the divine
favor supplying for human necessities the kinds of meats
generally fitting for suitable occasions. For while a more
tender meat was needed to nourish men who were both
tender and unskilled; it was still a food not prepared without
toil, doubtless for their advantage, lest they should again
find a pleasure in sinning, if the labor imposed upon sin did
not exhort innocence. And since now it was no more a paradise to be tended, but a whole world to be cultivated, the
more robust food of flesh is offered to men, that for the advantage of culture something more might be added to the
vigor of the human body. All these things, as I have said,
were by grace and by divine arrangement (2 ANF).
  If the Law distinguishes between clean and unclean animals,
it is no reflection on these creatures of God.
    It is the characters and doings, and wills of men that are
symbolised in the animals. They are clean if they chew the
cud; that is, if they ever have in their mouth as food the
divine precepts. They divide the hoof, if with the firm step
of innocency, they tread the ways of righteousness, and of
every virtue of life... Thus in the animals, by the law, as it
were a certain mirror of human life is established, wherein
men may consider the images of penalties: so that everything
which is vicious as committed against nature, in men, may
be the more condemned, when even those things, although
naturally ordained in brutes, are in them blamed (3).
  If the law forbids swine to be eaten, it reproves a filthy and
dirty life that delights in the garbage of vice and places its
supreme good not in generosity of mind but in the flesh alone.
If it banns the weasel, it reproves theft. The hawk, the kite and

he eagle symbolise plunderers and violent people who live by crime, the sparrow intemperance, the owl those who fly from the light of truth, the swan the proud with high neck, the bat those who seek the darkness of night as well as of error, etc. Another reason for prohibiting so many kinds of flesh to the Jews was that they might be restrained to the service of one God, after they had dared to prefer the vilest meats of the Egyptians to the divine banquets of manna and the juicy fare of their enemies and masters to liberty. 'Moderation is always found to be approximate to religion, nay so to speak, rather related and akin to it; for luxury is inimical to holiness' (4 ANF). 'But now Christ, the end of the law, has come, disclosing all the obscurities of the law... For the illustrious Master, and the heavenly Teacher, and the ordainer of the perfect truth, has come, under whom at length it is rightly said (Tit. 1,15): *To the pure all things are pure*' (5). The true and holy meat must now be understood allegorically, as the true faith, an unspotted conscience and an innocent soul. However, the abrogation of the Old Testament does not mean that luxury is permitted to the Christians or that fasting and continence should not be observed anymore. 'Nothing has so restrained intemperance as the Gospel nor has any one given such strict laws against gluttony as Christ, who is said to have pronounced even the poor blessed, and the hungering and thirsting happy' (6 ANF). In the last chapter Novatian warns especially against eating that which has been offered to idols:

> As far as pertains to God's creation, every creature is clean. But when it has been offered to demons, it is polluted so long as it is offered to the idols; and as soon as this is done, it belongs no longer to God, but to the idol. And when this creature is taken for food, it nourishes the person who so takes it for the demon, not for God, by making him a fellow guest with the idol, not with Christ (7 ANF).

Novatian's solution of the regulations in Leviticus resembles that found in the *Epistle of Barnabas* (cf. vol. I, p. 85 ff) in the first half of the second century. Long before this time Philo of Alexandria, the contemporary of Jesus Christ, had interpreted the animals as symbols of human passions (*De plantatione* 43) and Ps.-Aristeas, a Hellenised Jew, had explained the Old Testament precepts to the Greeks in the same way. But no one prior to

16

Novatian had given such extensive treatment to the topic, and he thus paved the way for the wholesale allegorization that prevailed in the art and literature of the Middle Ages.

In this treatise the author shows himself well acquainted with Seneca and Vergil, whose imagery and phraseology have influenced him, as can be proved from a number of passages. Thus he reminds one of Seneca's condemnation of those who drank too early in the morning (*Epist.* 122,6) when he rebukes Christians 'whose vices have come to even that pitch, that while fasting they drink early in the morning, not thinking it Christian to drink after meat, unless the wine poured into their empty and unoccupied veins should have gone down directly after sleep; for they seem to have less relish of what they drink if food be mingled with the wine' (6 ANF).

There is no indication of the schism throughout the treatise. The introduction suggests that it was written during an enforced absence from the community, most probably during the persecution of Gallus and Volusianus of the year 253:

> Nothing, most holy brethren, holds me bound with such bonds, nothing stirs and arouses me with such a stimulus of care and anxiety, as the fear lest you should think that any disadvantage is suffered by you by reason of my absence; and this I strive to remedy, in laboring to show myself present with you by frequent letters. Although, therefore, the duty which I owe, and the charge I have undertaken, and the very ministerial office imposed upon me, require of me this necessity of writing letters, yet you still further enhance it, by stirring me up to write through means of your continual communications. And inclined although I am to those periodical expressions of love you urge me the more by showing that you stand fast continually in the Gospel (1 ANF).

The *captatio benevolentiae* at the end of this passage appears also in the address which precedes the letter in the manuscripts: 'to the people steadfast in the gospel' (*plebi in evangelio perstanti*).

TEXT TRADITION

The text of *De cibis Judaicis* was available only in the same old editions of Tertullian as preserve *De trinitate* until in 1893 a manuscript was discovered in the library of St. Petersburg containing our treatise together with Latin versions of the Epistle of St. James, the *Epistle of Barnabas* and the writings of Filaster. The edition of Landgraf and Weyman is based on this *Codex Petropolit., saec.* IX; *Codex* 1351 of the Library of St. Geneviève at Paris, discovered by A. Wilmart, is but a copy made in the 15th century of the above.

Editions: ML 3, 953. — G. LANDGRAF und C. WEYMAN, Novatians Epistula de cibis Iudaicis: Archiv für lateinische Lexikographie und Grammatik 11, 2 (1898) 221–249.

Translations: English: E. WALLIS, ANL 13; ANF 5, 645–650.

Studies: C. WEYMAN, Novatian und Seneca über den Frühtrunk: Phil 52 (1893) 728–730. — A. WILMART, Un manuscrit du De cibis et des œuvres de Lucifer: RB (1921) 124–135.

3. *On Shows (De spectaculis)*

In this writing, found among the works of St. Cyprian, Novatian condemns attendance at public shows and warns those who are not ashamed to justify going to such plays by Scriptural quotations. The mother of all such displays is idolatry, which is forbidden to Christians (ch. 1–3). The author gives a vivid description of the different kinds of pagan amusements and the cruelty, perversities, vices and absurdities they defend and propagate (ch. 4–8). 'The Christian has nobler exhibitions, if he wishes for them. He has true and profitable pleasures, if he will recollect himself' (9). It shows Novatian trained in Stoic philosophy and Christian faith when he refers his readers at the end to the beauty of the world (cf. *De trinitate* 1, above, p. 217 f) and to the worthy spectacles provided by Holy Writ:

He has the beauty of the world to look upon and to admire. He may gaze upon the sun's rising, and again on its setting, as it brings round in their mutual changes days and nights; the moon's orb, designating in its waxings and wanings the courses of the seasons; the troops of shining stars and those which glitter from on high with extreme mobility, —their members divided through the changes of the entire year, and the days themselves with the nights distributed into hourly periods; the heavy mass of the earth balanced by the mountains, and the flowing rivers with their sources; the expanse of the seas, with their waves and shores... Let these, I say, and other divine works, be the exhibitions for faithful Christians. What theatre built by human hands could ever be compared to such works as these (9 ANF)?

Let the faithful Christian, I say, devote himself to the Sacred Scriptures, and there he shall find worthy exhibitions for his faith. He will see God establishing His world and making not only the other animals, but that marvellous and better fabric of man. He will gaze upon the world in its delightfulness, righteous shipwrecks, the rewards of the good, and the punishment of the impious, seas drained dry by a people, and again from the rock seas spread out by a people... He will behold in some cases faith struggling with the flame, wild beasts overcome by devotion and soothed into gentleness. He will look also upon souls brought back even from death... And in all these things he will see a still greater exhibition—that devil who had triumphed over the whole world lying prostrate under the feet of Christ. How honorable is this exhibition, brethren... This is a spectacle which is beheld even when sight is lost. This is an exhibition which is given by neither praetor nor consul, but by Him who is alone and above all things (10 ANF).

This work shows again the inspiration of Tertullian, who had a tract with the same title; it also borrows from Cyprian's *Ad Donatum*.

Editions: W. Hartel, CSEL 3, 3 (1871) 1–13. — A. Boulanger, Tertullien, De spectaculis, suivi de Pseudo-Cyprien, De spectaculis. Paris, 1933.

Translations: English: R. E. Wallis, ANL 3; ANF 5, 575–578.

Studies: J. Haussleiter, Zwei strittige Schriften Cyprian's: De spectaculis und De bono pudicitiae: ThLB 13 (1892) 431 ff. — C. Weyman, Über die dem Cyprianus beigelegten Schriften de spectaculis und de bono pudicitiae: HJG 13 (1892) 737–748; 14 (1893) 330 f. — E. Wölfflin, Cyprianus De spectaculis: Archiv für lateinische Lexikographie und Grammatik 8 (1893) 1–22; 9 (1894) 319. — A. Demmler, Über den Verfasser der unter Cyprians Namen überlieferten Traktate 'De bono pudicitiae' und 'De spectaculis'. Diss. Tübingen, 1894. — H. von Soden, Die cyprianische Briefsammlung. Leipzig, 1904, 211–213. — H. Koch, Zum novatianischen Schrifttum: ZKG 38 (1920) 90–95; *idem*, Codex Parisinus 1658 e lo scritto pseudo-ciprianeo (novazianeo) De spectaculis: Religio 12 (1936) 245–265. — B. Melin, Studia in Corpus Cyprianeum. Uppsala, 1946, 67–122.

4. *On the Advantage of Modesty* (*De bono pudicitiae*)

The introduction to this excellent work (ch. 1–2) has much in common with that to the treatise *On Jewish Foods*. Here, too, the author speaks of being absent from his flock, with whom he keeps in touch by letters: 'By my letters I try to make myself present to you, addressing you in faith, in my usual manner, by the exhortations that I send you' (1) and he admonishes them to remain steadfast in the Gospel: 'I call upon you, therefore, to be established in the power of the root of the Gospel, and to stand always armed against all assaults of the devil' (*ibid.*). He exhorts his readers to chastity (ch. 2), which is fitting for those who are temples of the Lord, members of Christ and habitations of the Holy Spirit. He contrasts (ch. 3) this virtue with its enemy, immodesty. Whereas the one is the dignity of the body, the ornament of morality, the sacredness of the sexes, the bond of modesty, the source of purity, the peacefulness of the home and crown of concord and mother of innocence, the other is the foe of continency, the perilous madness of lust, the destruction of a good conscience, the mother of impenitence and the disgrace of one's race. There are three degrees of chastity, virginity, continence and faithfulness to the marriage bond (ch. 4). The last was ordained with the creation of man and renewed by Christ and his apostles (ch. 5–6). But 'virginity and continency are beyond all law, there is nothing in the laws of matrimony which pertains to virginity; for by its loftiness it transcends them all... Virginity places itself on an equality with angels; moreover, if we investigate, it even excels them, because struggling in the flesh it gains the victory even against a nature which angels have not' (ch. 7). Glorious examples of chastity are Joseph in Egypt (ch. 8) and Susanna (ch. 9). Both of them withstood all temptations and received their reward (ch. 10). But the greatest reward is the fact, that 'to have vanquished pleasure is the greatest pleasure; nor is there any greater victory than that which is gained over one's own desires... He who gets rid of desires has got rid of fears also; for from desires come fears. He who overcomes desires, triumphs over sin; he who overcomes desires shows that the mischief of the human family lies prostrate under his feet; he who has overcome desires, has given to himself perpetual peace; he who has overcome desires, restores to himself liberty—a most difficult matter even for noble natures' (ch. 11 ANF). At the end (ch. 12–14) the dangers to this virtue and the means of protecting it are discussed.

The entire treatise is dependent on Tertullian's *De virginibus velandis, De cultu feminarum* and *De pudicitia* as well as on Cyprian's *De habitu virginum*.

Edition: W. HARTEL, CSEL 3, 3 (1871) 13–25.

Translations: English: R. E. WALLIS, ANL 3; ANF 5, 587–592.

Studies: S. MATZINGER, Des hl. Thascius C. Cyprianus Tractat 'De bono pudicitiae'. Diss. Nürnberg, 1892. — J. HAUSSLEITER, *loc. cit.* — C. WEYMAN, *loc. cit.* — A. DEMM-LER, *loc. cit.* — H. VON SODEN, *loc. cit.* 213 f. — J. MARTIN, Zu Novatians 'De bono pudicitiae': Wochenschrift f. kl. Phil. 30 (1919) 239 ff. — B. MELIN, *loc. cit.*

5. *Epistles*

Regarding the two letters (*Epist.* 30,36) which Novatian addressed to Cyprian of Carthage, see above p. 213, B. Melin has recently shown that *Epist.* 31 is most probably also of Novatian's pen. Addressed to Cyprian by Moses, Maximus, Nicostratus and the other Roman confessors in answer to his letter (*Epist.* 28), it proves that Cyprian's gentle reproof of their former implied regret at his retreat during the persecution had been effective. In the case of the lapsed, the judgment of Cyprian is acquiesced in.

Editions: Epistula 30: W. HARTEL, CSEL 3, 2 (1871) 549–556; Epistula 31: *ibidem* 557–564; Epistula 36: *ibidem* 572–579. — L. BAYARD, St. Cyprien, Correspondance, texte établi et trad. Paris, 1925, I, 71–77, 89–92.

Translations: English: H. CAREY, Library of Fathers 17. Oxford, 1844, 62–68, 68–74, 79–82. — R. E. WALLIS, ANL 8; ANF 5, 307–308, 308–311, 311. — *German:* J. BAER, BKV² 60 (1928) 90–98, 99–106, 114–118. — *French:* L. BAYARD, *loc. cit.*

Studies: A. HARNACK, Die Briefe des römischen Klerus aus der Zeit der Sedisvakanz im J. 250: Theol. Abhandlungen für C. v. Weizsäcker. Freiburg, 1892, 1–36. — H. KOCH, Zu Novatians Ep. 30: ZNW 34 (1935) 303–306. — B. MELIN, *loc. cit.* — M. BÉVENOT, A Bishop is responsible to God alone: RSR 39/40 (1951/52) 397–415. — C. B. DALY, Novatian and Tertullian: Irish Theological Quarterly 19 (1952) 33–43.

II. THE THEOLOGY OF NOVATIAN

The work *On the Trinity* established Novatian's reputation as a theologian. Avoiding every trace of Platonism, he makes use of the Stoic and Aristotelian syllogistic and dialectic method, which his Monarchian opponents also employed. This proves to be very successful, especially in connection with his copious and well-selected quotations from Scripture, which give the work the advantage of great certainty and power of conviction. It brings the development of the trinitarian doctrine to a certain conclusion for the pre-Augustinian period, and reads like a manual of Western christology.

Novatian follows in his trinitarian doctrine the road entered upon by Justin, Theophilus, Irenaeus, Hippolytus and especially Tertullian. Thus he asserts like his predecessors that the Logos was indeed always with the Father, but that He was only sent forth by Him at a definite period of time for the purpose of creating the world:

> The Son, then, since He is begotten of the Father, is always in the Father. When I say 'always,' I do not maintain that He is unborn, but that He is born. Yet He Who is born before all time must be said to have always existed in the Father; for a date in time cannot be fixed for Him Who is before all time. He is eternally in the Father; otherwise the Father were not always Father. At the same time, the Father is antecedent to Him, for the Father must be of necessity before the Son, as Father, inasmuch as He Who knows not an origin must of necessity exist before Him Who has an origin. Of necessity, too, the Son must be less than the Father, for He knows Himself to be in the Father; He has an origin, in that He is born, and through the Father, in some mysterious manner, although He has an origin, as born, He is germane (vicinus) to Him, in the matter of His birth, seeing that He is born of the Father, Who alone has no origin. He, then, at such time as the Father willed, proceeded from the Father; and He Who was in the Father, because He was of the Father, was thereafter with the Father, because He proceeded from the Father, being none other than the Divine Personal Substance. Whose name is the Word, through Whom all things were made, and without Whom nothing was made. For all things are after Him, since they are through Him, and of course He is before all things (but after the Father), seeing that all things were made through Him. He proceeded from the Father at Whose will all things were made, God, assuredly, proceeding from God, constituting

the Second Person after the Father, as Son, yet not robbing
the Father of the unity of the Godhead (*De Trin.* 31 SPCK)
Novatian intends to take the middle road between the two
opposing tendencies of Monarchianism, the dynamistic or adop-
tianistic form which regarded Christ as a man filled with divine
power or given divine dignity afterwards, and the modalistic or
patripassionistic form to which Christ is nothing more than another sort of manifestation of the Father Himself. He is so concerned with stressing the unity of the Godhead that he does not
even dare to use the term *trinitas* (τριάς), which Theophilus,
Hippolytus, Tertullian employ. For the same reason he repeats
their mistake, making the Son subordinate to the Father:

> As He receives sanctification from the Father, it follows
> that He is not the Father but the Son. For if He had been
> the Father He would have given, not received, sanctification.
> On the contrary, He maintains that He has received sancti-
> fication from the Father, and the proof which He gives by
> this receiving of sanctification that He is less than the Father,
> demonstrates that He is the Son, not the Father. Further, He
> asserts that He has been sent by the Father. So the Lord
> Christ came, because He was sent in obedience; a proof that
> He is not the Father, but the Son, Who certainly would have
> been the sender, not the sent, had He been the Father. But
> it was not the Father Who was sent; had it been so, His
> being sent would prove that the Father was in subjection to
> another God (*ibid.* 27 SPCK).

Christ remains forever subject to His Father. He is His messenger, *the angel of great counsel:*

> The only intelligible explanation is, that He [Christ] is
> both angel and God. Such a description cannot be appro-
> priate and suitable to the Father, Who is God only; but it
> can be appropriately applied to Christ, Who has been de-
> clared to be not God only, but also an angel. It is obvious,
> therefore, that it was not the Father Who spoke to Hagar in
> the present passage (Gen. 21,17) but Christ; since He is not
> only God, but One to Whom the title of angel is also ap-
> propriate, by virtue of His being made 'the angel of great
> counsel'—angel, as declaring the inmost purpose in the
> bosom of the Father, as John declares (John 1,18). For

seeing that John says this Person, Who reveals the inmost purpose of the Father, was made flesh, so that He might be able to declare this purpose, it follows that Christ is not man only, but also angel; and He is shown in the Scriptures to be not angel only, but God also. Such is our Christian belief. Otherwise if we refuse to acknowledge that it was Christ Who spoke to Hagar in this passage, we must either make an angel God, or reckon God the Father among the angels (*ibid.* 18 SPCK).

Christ is the servant of the Father whose commands He always obeys:

It is, accordingly, part of the same truth, that He [Christ] does nothing of His own will, and makes nothing of His own counsel, and comes not from Himself, but obeys every command and injunction of the Father. His birth proves Him to be the Son, yet His devoted obedience declares that He is the minister of the will of the Father, from Whom He has His Being. And so, while He renders due submission to the Father in all things, though He is God as well as minister, yet by His obedience He shows that the Father, from Whom He drew His origin, is One God (*ibid.* 31).

Novatian is so afraid of being accused of ditheism that he goes even beyond the subordinationism of his predecessors. He thinks he can maintain the unity of the Godhead better by understanding the Logos as a temporary and passing personal manifestation of the Father, to whom, at the end, He will return all authority, and to whom He will go back like a wave receding:

Hence all things are placed under His feet, and delivered to Him who is God, and the Son acknowledges that all things are in subjection to Him as a gift from the Father; thus He refers back to the Father the entire authority of the Godhead. The Father is shown to be the One God, true and eternal; from Him alone this power of Divinity issues, and though it is transmitted to the Son and centred upon Him it runs its course back to the Father, through their community of Substance. The Son is shown to be God, since Divinity is manifestly delivered and granted to Him; yet none the less, the Father is proved to be the One God, while step by step that same Majesty and Divinity, like a billow returning upon itself, sent forth again from the Son Himself, returns and finds its way back to the Father Who gave it (*ibid.*).

As the Son is less than the Father, so the Holy Spirit is less than the Son:

> The Paraclete did receive his message from Christ. But if He received it from Christ, then Christ is greater than the Paraclete, since the Paraclete would not receive from Christ unless He were less than Christ. This inferiority of the Paraclete at once proves that Christ, from Whom He received His message, is God. Here, then, is a strong testimony to the Divinity of Christ, when we find that the Paraclete is less than He, and takes of Him the message which He delivers to the world (*ibid.* 18 SPCK).

Novatian's treatment of the personality of the Holy Spirit is very brief and lacking in preciseness. He does not describe the relations of the Holy Spirit to the Father and the Son, as he does for the two latter, although Tertullian, whom he follows, makes at least an attempt at it (*Adv. Prax.* 4 and 8). It is significant that he calls the Son *secundam post patrem personam* (10) but fails to call the Holy Spirit *tertiam personam*, which Tertullian had done (*Adv. Prax.* 11).

Nevertheless, Novatian has valuable statements on the connection between the Holy Spirit and the Church; that, long ago promised, and duly bestowed on the proper occasions, He was already operating in the prophets temporarily, whereas He wrought in the apostles permanently:

> So it is one and the same Spirit, Who is in the prophets to meet a particular situation, in the apostles at all times. In other words, He is in the one, not so as to be in them always, in the other, so as to abide in them always; in the one, as doled out in moderation, in the other as poured forth in His entirety; in the one, as sparingly given, in the other, as generously granted, and yet not granted before the resurrection of the Lord, but bestowed through the resurrection of Christ... And as the Lord was presently to go away into heaven, He could not but give the Paraclete to His disciples, or He would most unaccountably have left them in the position of wards, and forsaken them without any to be their advocate and guardian. For it is He Who strengthened their

souls and minds, Who clearly brought out for them the mysteries of the gospel, Who threw light within them upon divine
things, by Whom they were made strong to fear neither
bonds nor imprisonment for the name of the Lord; nay,
more, they trampled under foot the very powers and the
torments of the world, only because they were ready-armed
and fortified through Him, since they possessed within themselves the gifts which this same Spirit distributes and assigns,
like ornaments to the Church, the Bride of Christ (29 SPCK).

He makes the Church perfect and complete by these gifts and
keeps her uncorrupted and inviolate in the sanctity of perpetual
virginity and truth:

He it is Who appoints the prophets in the Church, in-
structs the teachers, distributes the tongues, performs acts
of power and of healing, works miracles, bestows the dis-
cernings of spirits, assigns governments, suggests counsels,
and sets in their right places and due order all other gifts of
grace. Thus does He make the Church of the Lord perfect
and complete, in all places and in all things. He gives in
apostles due witness to Christ, shows in martyrs the unyield-
ing faith of religion, locks in the breast of virgins the marvellous continence of sealed chastity, guards in the rest of mankind the laws of the Lord's doctrine, uncorrupted and
untainted; He destroys heretics, corrects the wayward, con-
vinces unbelievers, reveals impostors, and corrects the
wicked; He keeps the Church uncorrupted and inviolate in
the sanctity of perpetual virginity and truth (29 SPCK).

From Christ, upon whom the Holy Spirit descended in His
baptism, we receive Him:

In Christ alone He dwelt fully and entirely, not crippled
in any measure or portion, but in all His overflowing abundance dispensed and sent forth, so that the rest of mankind
can enjoy what I will call a first sip of grace, issuing from
Christ. For the source of the Holy Spirit in the entirety of
His Being ever remains in Christ, in order that from Him
might issue streams of gifts and works, because the Holy
Spirit dwells in Him in rich affluence (*ibid.*).

The Holy Spirit brings about our new birth in baptism:

He it is Who brings about the second birth, from water.

Thus He is, as it were, the seed of a divine generation, the consecrator of a heavenly birth, the pledge of the promised inheritance, the written bond, so to speak, of eternal salvation, to make us the temple of God and perfect us as His home... He is given us to dwell in our bodies, and to bring about our sanctification; to advance our bodies, by this operation of His, to eternal life and to the resurrection of immortality, while He accustoms them in Himself to be mingled with heavenly powers, and to be associated with the divine eternity of the Holy Spirit. For in Him, and through Him, our bodies are instructed to progress to immortality, through learning the discipline of temperance in accordance with His decrees. For it is He who 'lusteth against the flesh' because 'the flesh is contrary to him' (Gal. 5,17); it is He Who restrains insatiable lusts, breaks unbridled desires, quenches unlawful passions; Who overcomes fiery assaults, hurls back the hordes of drunkenness, drives off the hosts of avarice, turns to flight the armies of debauch; Who joins men together in love, and knits them together in affection; Who drives off sects, explains the rule of truth, vanquishes heretics, casts forth the wicked beyond the doors, and guards the gospels (*ibid.*).

Since Novatian's work *On the Trinity* is the first theological treatise of Roman origin to be written in Latin, its terminology and precise dogmatic formulae are of special interest, influencing, as they have, Latin thought to an important degree and enabling the West to meet the Greeks on equal terms in the christological controversy.

Christ is *Deus* and *homo* (11), He is *dei filius* (9) and has *auctoritas divinitatis* (31) and there is no *inaequalitas* or *dissonantia divinitatis* (31) between Him and the Father. The sharp distinction which he makes between the humanity and divinity in Christ do not prevent him from using the following expressions for the unity of the two natures in Christ: *Concretio permixta* (11), *in unam foederasse concordiam* (13), *ex verbi et carnis coniunctione concretus* (14), *utrumque in Christo confoederatum, coniunctum, connexum* (16), *deum et hominem sociasse* (16), *divinitatis et humilitatis concordia* (16), *concordia terrenorum atque caelestium* (18), *deum homini et hominem deo copulare* (18), *connexione et permixtione sociata* (19), *et utroque connexum, contextum atque concretum* (19), *in eadem utriusque substantiae concordia* (19), *foederis confibulatione sociatum* (19), *societatis concordia* (22), *concordiae unitatem cum personarum tamen distinctione* (22). These citations indicate that Novatian not only adopted Tertullian's expressions for the union and separation of the two natures, but coined new ones of his own and assigned a wider meaning to Tertullian's terminology. While adopting from the latter the formulae: *una substantia, tres personae—ex substantia dei—semper apud patrem—duae substantiae—una persona*, he himself introduced the verbs *incarnari* and *se exinanire*. Thus he speaks of the *verbum dei incarnatum* (24) and influenced by Phil. 2,6–11, he employs for the birth of Christ *quo tempore se etiam exinanivit* (22) and *dum in nativitatem secundum carnem se exinanisse monstratur* (22). He first brought into Christian usage *praedestinatio*, destined to play so important a role in the history of theology. He shares with Tertullian the concept of the divine economy, translating the Greek term οἰκονομία by *dispositio*, and with Cyprian the earliest use of *praefigurare* (14; 23), not found in Tertullian.

Studies: A. D'ALÈS, Novatien. Étude sur la théologie romaine au milieu du IIIe siècle. Paris, 1925. — A. HARNACK, Lehrbuch der Dogmengeschichte. 5th ed. vol. 1. Tübingen, 1931, 632–634. — M. KRIEBEL, Studien zur älteren Entwicklung der abendländischen Trinitätslehre bei Tertullian und Novatian. Diss. Marburg, 1932. — G. KEILBACH, Divinitas Filii eiusque Patri subordinatio in Novatiani libro De Trinitate: Bogoslovska Smotra 21 (1933) 193–224. — R. FAVRE, La communication des idiomes dans l'ancienne tradition latine: BLE 37 (1936) 130–145. — J. BARBEL, Christos Angelos (Theophaneia 3). Bonn, 1941, 80–94. — J. GEWIESS, Zum altkirchlichen Verständnis der Kenosisstelle (Phil. 2, 5–11): ThQ 128 (1948) 463–487.
For *language and style:* H. JORDAN, Rhythmische Prosa in der altchristlichen lateinischen Literatur. Leipzig, 1905, 38–74: Die Novatian zugeschriebenen Schriften. — H. KOCH, Zum Ablativgebrauch bei Cyprian von Karthago und andern Schriftstellern (Novatian): RhM (1929) 427–432; *idem*, La lingua e lo stilo di Novaziano: Religio 13 (1937) 278–294. — M. M. MÜLLER, Der Übergang von der griechischen zur lateinischen Sprache in der abendländischen Kirche von Hermas bis Novatian. Diss. Rome, 1943. — C. MOHRMANN, Les origines de la latinité chrétienne à Rome: VC 3 (1949) 67–106, 163–183.

PAPAL LETTERS OF THE THIRD CENTURY

1. *Callistus*

From Hippolytus of Rome (*Philos.*, 9,12) we know that Callistus (217–222) excommunicated Sabellius 'as not entertaining orthodox opinions,' and made several doctrinal statements and disciplinary decisions. Whether any of these acts was performed by a written document, we do not know for certain. Hippolytus attributes the following teaching to him:

> The Logos is the Son himself, the Father himself. There is one and the same indivisible spirit, though denominated by a different title. The Father is not one person and the Son another, they are one and the same; and all things are full of the Divine Spirit, above and below. The Spirit, which became incarnate in the virgin, is not different from the Father, but one and the same. Hence Scripture says: 'Do you not believe that I am in the Father, and the Father in me?' (John 14,11). That which is seen, which is man, is the Son, whereas the Spirit which dwells in the Son is the Father. I will not profess belief in two Gods, Father and Son, but in one. For the Father who rested in the Son himself, having taken unto himself our flesh, raised it to the nature of Deity in uniting it to himself and made it one with himself, so that the names of Father and Son apply to one and the same God, and that this person being one, cannot be two; thus the Father suffered with the Son, for we must not say that the Father suffered (*Philos.* 9,12,16–19).

We cannot determine how much of this statement can be taken without reserve as the doctrinal position of Callistus. Hippolytus' antagonism is so heated that we dare not rely on what he says of Callistus in the absence of any other testimony.

In his *De pudicitia* (1,6) Tertullian makes the following complaint 'The Sovereign Pontiff, that is the bishop of bishops, issues an edict: I remit the sins of adultery and fornication to those who have done penance.' For a long time Callistus was held to be the author of this 'peremptory edict,' as Tertullian calls it. G. B. de Rossi first ascribed it to him and A. v. Harnack's support gained such universal recognition for the view that the 'peremptory edict' came simply to be called the 'edict of Callistus.' The basis of the identification was the charge directed against the Pope by Hippolytus in his *Philosophumena* (9,12). However, in 1914, G. Esser demonstrated that this accusation has nothing to do with the 'peremptory edict' mentioned by Tertullian. Moreover, K. Adam in 1917 advanced the opinion that the decree which Tertullian has in mind originated not in Rome but in Africa. The words *Pontifex Maximus* and *episcopus episcoporum* which Tertullian uses do not refer to any Roman, but to an African bishop, most probably Agrippinus of Carthage. G. Bardy, K. Preysing, A. Ehrhard, especially P. Galtier, and others have adopted this idea; B. Poschmann has given it his full support. On the other hand, the attribution to Callistus has been defended again by H. Koch, A. v. Harnack, P. Batiffol, E. Goeller, J. Hoh, D. van den Eynde, E. Caspar, B. J. Kidd, W. Koehler, J. Haller, K. Müller, and H. Stoeckius. The reasons against identifying the object of Hippolytus' opposition with the 'peremptory edict' have been given above (cf. p. 204 f). The titles *Pontifex Maximus* and *episcopus episcoporum* do not prove the authorship of a Roman bishop. It must be remembered that *Pontifex Maximus* was no special name for the bishop of Rome at that time, but a purely pagan distinction reserved for the emperor alone. Tertullian applies it sarcastically to his adversary because he had arrogated to himself the power of an emperor. Thus it could quite possibly designate the bishop of Carthage, Agrippinus. The same can be said of *episcopus episcoporum*. There is no sufficient reason to assume that the bishop of Rome is meant. Cyprian uses the term ironically for an arrogant layman in the Church of Carthage (*Epist.* 66,3). D. Franses and A. de Vellico have tried to mediate in this controversy by suggesting that Tertullian refers to an edict of Callistus as well as of Agrippinus, the latter finding it necessary to specialize the more general decree of the former.

Studies: See the bibliography to Tertullian's De pudicitia, below, p. 314.

2. *Pontianus* (230–235)

He was successor to Urbanus (222–230). According to Jerome (*Epist.* 33,5) he approved in a synod held at Rome (231 or 232) the deposition of Origen by Demetrius of Alexandria. It may be assumed that he informed Demetrius of this decision by a letter, especially since Demetrius had addressed one to him in this dispute (*Hist. eccl.* 6,8,4; Jerome, *De vir. ill.* 54).

Studies: I. DÖLLINGER, Hippolyt und Kallistus. Regensburg, 1853, 68 ff. — J. T. SHOTWELL and L. R. LOOMIS, The See of Peter. New York, 1927, 312 ff.

3. *Fabianus* (236–250)

Cyprian reports (*Epist.* 59,10) that Fabian gave his written approval to the condemnation of Bishop Priatus of Lambese by a Numidian synod.

4. *Cornelius* (251–253)

The pontificate of Cornelius is, though short, important for the history of the penitential discipline and the schism of Novatian. Most of his letters deal with these two questions. In his difficulties he found a loyal supporter in Cyprian of Carthage, to whom he sent not less than seven epistles, and in whose correspondence two have survived, as *Epist.* 49 and 50, the other five being lost. Written in a rather vulgar Latin, the first of the two extant communications informs Cyprian of the solemn return of the Roman Confessors 'who had been circumvented and almost deceived and alienated from the Church by the craft and malice of that wily and subtle man' Novatian. Cornelius quotes as theirs the following words significant for the history of the monarchical hierarchy:

> We know that Cornelius is bishop of the most holy Catholic Church elected by Almighty God, and by Christ our Lord. We confess our error; we have suffered imposture; we were deceived by captious perfidy and loquacity. For although we seemed, as it were, to have held a kind of communion with a man who was a schismatic and a heretic, yet our mind was always sincere in the Church. For we are not ignorant that there is one God; that there is one Christ the Lord, whom we have confessed, and one Holy Spirit; and that in the Catholic Church there ought to be one bishop (*Epist.* 49,2 ANF).

The second letter, a short warning to Cyprian, describes the kind of leaders and protectors that Novatian had joined to his side and sent to Africa.

Eusebius (*Hist. eccl.* 6,43,3–4) knows of three epistles of Cornelius' to Bishop Fabius of Antioch. Written in Greek, the first of them dealt with the schism of Novatian, 'telling the facts concerning the Roman Synod, and what was decreed by them of Italy and Africa and the regions thereabout' (*ibid.* 6,43,3), the second 'on the resolutions of the synod' and the third 'on the doings of Novatian' (*ibid.* 4). In the last, from which Eusebius quotes at length (cf. above, p. 215 f), Cornelius gives a repulsive picture of Novatian's life and character in order to warn the bishop of Antioch, who was tempted to favor the schismatic. However, critical examination shows up many of the charges as untrustworthy, based seemingly on malicious gossip. Another letter in the same vein to Bishop Dionysius of Alexandria (Euseb., *Hist. eccl.* 6,46,3) no longer exists. Socrates (*Hist. eccl.* 4,28) mentions a circular to all the Churches, in which were justified from Scripture the decisions in the vexed question of apostates.

Editions: P. Coustant, Epistolae Romanorum Pontificum 1. Paris, 1721, 125–206. — M. J. Routh, Reliquiae Sacrae, 2nd ed. 3 (1846) 11–89. — G. D. Mansi, SS. Conc. Coll. 1, 805–832. — ML 3, 675–848. — G. Mercati, D'alcuni nuovi sussidi per la critica del testo di S. Cipriano. Rome, 1899, 72–86.

Studies: C. P. Caspari, Ungedruckte Quellen zur Geschichte des Taufsymbols und der Glaubensregel 3. Kristiania, 1875, 439–441. — A. Harnack, Geschichte der altchristlichen Literatur 1, 650–652. — B. J. Kidd, History of the Church to A.D. 461. Oxford, 1922/25, 1, 442–454. — J. T. Shotwell and L. R. Loomis, *loc. cit.* 348–389. — E. Caspar, Geschichte des Papsttums 1. Tübingen, 1930, 66–70. — G. Mercati, Opere minore 2 (TS 77). Vatican City, 1937, 226–240. — G. Roethe, Zur Geschichte der römischen Synoden im 3. und 4. Jahrhundert. 1937. — J. Zeiller, in: A. Fliche et V. Martin, Histoire de l'Église 2. Paris, 1946, 409–413.

5. *Lucius* (253–254)

It is only through Cyprian (*Epist.* 68,5) that we learn of letters which Lucius addressed to the bishop of Carthage on the procedure to be followed in the reconciliation of apostates.

6. *Stephen* (254–257)

Stephen wrote two epistles in the controversy about the validity of baptism conferred by heretics. The first to the Church of Asia Minor threatened to excommunicate the bishops of Cilicia, Cappadocia, Galatia and the neighboring provinces for rebaptizing heretics (Euseb., *Hist. eccl.* 7,5,4; Cyprian, *Epist.* 75,25). The second to Cyprian in 256 dealt with the same question. The African hierarchy under the guidance of Cyprian held the sacrament invalid, if administered by dissidents, and insisted upon reconferring it upon converts. Stephen repudiates this stand in the strongest terms as erroneous and against the faith, and his antagonist quotes one sentence that he particularly resented:

If anyone, therefore, come to you from any heresy whatever, let nothing be innovated which has not been handed down, to wit, that hands be imposed on him for repentance; since the heretics themselves, in their own proper character, do not baptize such as come to them from one another, but only admit them to communion (Cyprian, *Epist.* 74,1 ANF).

A controversy has arisen over the meaning of the words *nihil innovetur nisi quod traditum est.* However, quite obviously Stephen wants to say, 'Nothing new should be introduced but tradition should be followed.' To rebaptize heretics would, in his opinion, constitute a departure. Cyprian is roused at being called an innovator, as his own words in answer to Stephen's statement indicate:

He [Stephen] forbade one coming from any heresy to be baptized in the Church; that is, he judged the baptism of all heretics to be just and lawful, and although special heresies have special baptisms and different sins, he, holding communion with the baptism of all, gathered up the sins of all, heaped together into his own bosom. And he charged that nothing should be innovated except what had been handed down; as if he were an innovator, who, holding the unity, claims for the one Church one baptism; and not manifestly he who, forgetful of unity, adopts the lies and the contagion of a profane immersion. Let nothing be innovated, says he, except what has been handed down. Whence is that tradition? (*ibid.* 2 ANF).

As this answer makes evident, Stephen here is not giving his own opinion but citing an ancient principle of the Roman Church as decisive of the issue. He warns Cyprian against making any changes. We know that Eusebius understood the letter in exactly the same way, since he gives the following account of this incident:

Cyprian, pastor of the community of Carthage, was the first of those of his day to consider that they [the heretics] ought not to be admitted otherwise than by having been first cleansed from their error by baptism. But Stephen, thinking that they ought not to make any innovation contrary to the tradition that had prevailed from the beginning, was full of indignation thereat (*Hist. eccl.* 7,3,1 LCL).

Thus it had been an ecclesiastical custom from the beginning to receive heretics back into the Church without a new baptism. The principle cited by Stephen is important for the history of the doctrine of tradition in the Church of Rome. Novatian seems also to have it in mind, when he states in the epistle addressed to Cyprian in the name of the Roman presbytery: *Nihil innovandum putavimus* (Cyprian, *Epist.* 30, 8; cf. above, p. 213 f).

According to Eusebius (*Hist. eccl.* 7,5,2) Stephen directed a letter to the communities of Syria and Arabia; a passage of one to him from Dionysius of Alexandria speaks of 'the Syrias as a whole and Arabia, which you constantly help and to which you have now written.' From these words it appears that the Pope had given financial support to these communities and that his missive was nothing more than an accompanying note.

Edition: P. COUSTANT, Epistolae Romanorum Pontificum 1. Paris, 1721, 209–256.

Studies: A. HARNACK, *loc. cit.* 656–658; *idem,* Über verlorene Briefe und Aktenstücke, die sich aus der Cyprianischen Briefsammlung ermitteln lassen. Leipzig, 1902, 13–15. — G. BARDY, L'autorité du Siège Romain et les controverses du 3e siècle: RSR (1924) 255 ff. — B. J. KIDD, *loc. cit.* 464–474. — J. T. SHOTWELL and L. R. LOOMIS, *loc. cit.* 391–423. — F. J. DÖLGER, Nihil innovetur nisi quod traditum est: AC 1 (1929) 79–80.

7. Sixtus II (257–258)

In the short reign of Sixtus II relations between Rome and the African and the Asiatic bishops became friendlier again. There is a small fragment of a letter extant in Armenian which he addressed to Dionysius of Alexandria, indicating, though, that he shared the views of his predecessor and considered the baptism administered by heretics to be valid. Rufinus attributed to this Pope the so-called *Sayings of Sextus,* confusing him with the Pythagorean philosopher Sextus (cf. vol. I, p. 170 f).

Editions: F. C. CONYBEARE, The English Historical Review 25 (1910) 158 f. — P. COUSTANT, *loc. cit.* 255–270.

Studies: A. HARNACK, Geschichte der altchristl. Literatur 1, 658. — J. T. SHOTWELL and L. R. LOOMIS, *loc. cit.* 420–428.

8. Dionysius (259–268)

Dionysius wrote two epistles to his namesake, Dionysius of Alexandria, on Sabellianism and Subordinationism. The Alex-

andrian prelate in a communication sent to certain bishops of the
Pentapolis called Ammon and Euphranor, condemned the heresy
of Sabellius, which was very popular in that section, insisting on
the distinctness of the Son from the Father. Some Christians of
the Pentapolis or Alexandria objected to the strong expressions
he used in that letter, because, very much akin to the language
of Origen, they seemed to favor the subordination of the Son to
the Father. For this reason 'they went to Rome without asking
him, so as to learn from him how he had written; and they spoke
against him in the presence of his namesake Dionysius the Bishop
of Rome' (Athanasius, *Ep. de sent. Dion.* 13). The Pope, 'upon
hearing it, wrote simultaneously against the partisans of Sabellius
and against those who held the very opinions for uttering which
Arius was cast out of the Church; calling it an equal and opposite
impiety to hold with Sabellius or with those who say that the
Word of God is a thing made and formed and originated. And he
wrote also to Dionysius to inform him of what they had said
about him' (*ibid.* LNPF). A very valuable passage of the first letter
(the Pope despatched this after the condemnation by a synod of
Rome in 262 of both Sabellianism and Subordinationism), is
quoted by Athanasius, *De decretis Nic. syn.* 26, and thus preserved,
whereas the rest of the letter is lost. Without mentioning the name
of Dionysius, the Pontiff refers to 'some among you' and defends
the trinitarian doctrine against the two opposing heresies in a
statement outstanding for its preciseness and clearness:

Next, I may reasonably turn to those who divide and cut
to pieces and destroy that most sacred doctrine of the Church
of God, the Divine Monarchy, making it as it were three
powers and partive subsistences and godheads. I am told
that some among you who are catechists and teachers of the
Divine Word, take the lead in this tenet, who are diametri-
cally opposed, so to speak, to Sabellius' opinions; for he blas-
phemously says that the Son is the Father, and the Father
the Son, but they in some sort preach three Gods, as dividing
the sacred Monad into three subsistences foreign to each
other and utterly separate. For it must needs be that with
the God of the Universe, the Divine Word is united, and the
Holy Ghost must repose and habitate in God; thus in one
as in a summit, I mean the God of the Universe, must the

Divine Triad be gathered up and brought together...

Equally must one censure those who hold the Son to be a work, and consider that the Lord has come into being, as one of things which really came to be; whereas the divine oracles witness to a generation suitable to Him and becoming, but not to any fashioning or making. A blasphemy then is it, not ordinary, but the highest, to say that the Lord is in any sort a handiwork. For if He came to be Son, once He was not; but He was always, if (that is) He be in the Father, as He says Himself, and if the Christ be Word and Wisdom and Power (which, as ye know, divine Scripture says), and these attributes be powers of God. If then the Son came into being, once these attributes were not; consequently there was a time, when God was without them; which is most absurd...

Neither then may we divide into three Godheads the wonderful and divine Monad; nor disparage with the name of 'work' the dignity and exceeding majesty of the Lord; but we must believe in God the Father Almighty, and in Christ Jesus His Son, and in the Holy Ghost, and hold that to the God of the universe the Word is united. For 'I,' says He, 'and the Father are one;' and 'I in the Father and the Father in me.' For thus both the Divine Triad, and the holy preaching of the Monarchy, will be preserved (Athan. *De decr.* 26 LNPF).

To the second letter in which the bishop of Rome informed Dionysius of Alexandria of the accusations made against him, and asked for an explanation, the latter answered with a *Refutation and Apology*, which seems to have satisfied the former (cf. above, p. 105).

From St. Basil (*Epist.* 70) we know that this Pope sent a consolatory epistle to the Church of Caesarea. It accompanied a contribution to ransom members of the Christian community from captivity when in the time of Gallienus the Scythians ravaged Cappadocia and the neighboring countries.

Editions: P. COUSTANT, *loc. cit.* 269–292. — M. J. ROUTH, Reliquiae sacrae, 2nd ed. 3, 369–403. — G. D. MANSI, SS. Conc. Coll. 1, 1003 ff. — ML 5, 99–136.— The fragment of the synodical letter to Dionysius of Alexandria: C. L. FELTOE, Διονυσίου Λείψανα. Cambridge, 1904, 176–182; cf. 168–170.

Studies: C. P. CASPARI, *loc. cit.* 3, 445–447. — H. HAGEMANN, Die römische Kirch und ihr Einfluß auf Disziplin und Dogma in den ersten drei Jahrhunderten. Freibur, i.B., 1864, 432–453. — P. PAPE, Die Synoden von Antiochien. Berlin, 1903, 264 269. — A. HARNACK, *loc. cit.* 1, 409–427. — B. J. KIDD, *loc. cit.* 1, 484–504. — J. T SHOTWELL and L. R. LOOMIS, *loc. cit.* 429–438.

9. *Felix* (269–274)

The records of the first session of the Council of Ephesus hel on June 22, 431, contain an extract of a letter of Pope Felix t Bishop Maximus of Alexandria (265–282) and his clergy, whicl treats the divinity and perfect humanity of Christ, and reads a follows:

> As regards the incarnation of the Logos and our faith, w believe in our Lord Jesus Christ, born of the Virgin Mary that He is Himself the eternal Son and Word of God and no man adopted by God to be another beside Him. Nor did th Son of God adopt a man to be another beside Himself, bu being perfect God, He became at the same time also perfe man, incarnate from the Virgin.

The same passage was cited as a statement of Felix by Cyril c Alexandria in his *Apologia* as well as by others. In addition, tw Syriac fragments on the nature of Christ purport to come from document by Felix, the shorter beginning with the text read a the Council of Ephesus. But the letter from which the Council o Ephesus and the smaller Syriac fragment quote has been prove a forgery, made by Apollinaris or one of his followers at the be ginning of the fifth century.

Editions: P. COUSTANT, *loc. cit.* 291–298. — H. LIETZMANN, Apollinaris von Laodice und seine Schule 1. Tübingen, 1904, 162, 318–321. — J. FLEMMING und H. LIETZ MANN, Apollinaristische Schriften syrisch (Abh. der Kgl. Gesellschaft der Wiss. z Göttingen, Phil.-histor. Kl. N.F. 7, 4). Berlin, 1904, 55–56. — I. RUCKER, Flori legium Edessenum anonymum (SAB 1933, 5. Heft). Munich, 1933, 3*.

Studies: C. P. CASPARI, *loc. cit.* 111–123. — J. T. SHOTWELL and L. R. LOOMIS, *loc. ci* 439–441. For the date of the Papal Letters of the third century, see: C. H. TURNEF Papal Chronology of the Third Century: JThSt 17 (1915/16) 338–353.

CHAPTER IV

THE AFRICANS

Although the Church of Africa had a comparatively late beginning, its contribution to early Christian literature and theology is far greater than Rome's. It gave to Latin Christianity the most original thinker of the ante-Nicene period, Tertullian, besides the martyr bishop, Cyprian, and two lay divines, Arnobius and Lactantius.

According to tradition Africa was evangelized from Rome, though we have no real information about the foundation of its Church. It is, however, a fact that the Christians of the province at an early time looked to that city for leadership. Their most frequent communications were with the capital and they were deeply concerned with all that occurred there. Every intellectual movement, every disciplinary, ritual, or literary event in Rome found its echo at once in Carthage. The best witness to this intimate relation is the writings of the African authors.

There is reason to believe that in Africa as in Rome the gospel was in the beginning preached in Greek. Four of Tertullian's works, for instance, were published first in that tongue, *De spectaculis*, *De baptismo*, *De virginibus velandis*, *De corona militis*, and one of them was not issued in Latin at all, *De exstasi*. He seems also to have composed *Passio Perpetuae et Felicitatis* (cf. vol. I, pp. 181 ff), which appeared in both languages. In this we notice (13) that Perpetua has a conversation with the bishop Optatus and the priest Aspasius in Greek.

Studies: P. CAGNAT, L'armée romaine d'Afrique et l'occupation militaire de l'Afrique sous les empereurs. Paris, 1892. — E. MERCER, La population indigène de l'Afrique sous la domination romaine, vandale et byzantine: Recueil Soc. archéol. de Constantine 30 (1895/96) 127 ff. — P. MONCEAUX, Histoire littéraire de l'Afrique chrétienne I. Paris, 1901. — G. BOISSIER, L'Afrique romaine, 2nd ed. Paris, 1901. English translat. 1912, 314–326. — H. LECLERCQ, L'Afrique chrétienne, 2 vols. Paris, 1904; *idem*, Afrique (langues parlées en): DAL 1 (1907) 747–754. — F. CABROL, Afrique I. Liturgie antenicéenne: DAL 1 (1907) 592–619. — W. C. BISHOP, The African Rite: JThSt 13 (1911/12) 250–277. — J. MESNAGE, L'Afrique chrétienne. Paris, 1912; *idem*, Le christianisme en Afrique, 3 vols. Paris, 1915. — A. HARNACK, Mission und Ausbreitung des Christentums. 4th ed. Leipzig, 1924, 1, 887–919. — E. BUONAIUTI, Il cristianesimo nell' Africa Romana. Bari, 1928. — T. R. S. BROUGHTON, The Romanization of Africa Proconsularis. Baltimore, 1929. — G. BARDY,

L'Afrique chrétienne. Paris, 1930. — C. CECCHELLI, Africa Christiana: Africa Romana. Rome, 1936. — J. QUASTEN, Vetus superstitio et nova religio: HThR 33 (1940) 253–266. — A. M. SCHNEIDER, Afrika: RACH 1, 174–178. — G. BARDY, La question des langues dans l'Église ancienne. Paris, 1948, 52–72. — W. M. GREEN, Augustine's Use of Punic: Semitic and Oriental Studies 11 (1951) 179–190.

THE FIRST LATIN VERSIONS OF THE BIBLE

The oldest dated Latin document of Christian Africa is the *Acts of the Martyrs of Scilli* (cf. vol. I, p. 178 f), who were sentenced to death on July 17, 180. This work furnishes us with the earliest evidence for a translation of part of the New Testament. Arraigned before the tribunal of the proconsul Saturninus at Carthage, the saints declared that they had with them *libri et epistulae Pauli, viri justi*. It is hard to believe that people of such lowly condition knew Greek. Some years later, Tertullian testifies to the existence of a version of the whole Bible (*Adv. Prax.* 5; *De monog.* 11). This had no official character, and he criticizes it on several occasions. About 250, however, the Church of Africa apparently did have a Latin edition of the entire Scriptures recognized as authentic, as shown by Cyprian's adherence to it throughout his works. In fact, his two collections of excerpts from the sacred writings, *Ad Fortunatum* and *Ad Quirinum*, together with the early fourth century anonymous excerpts from the prophets *Prophetiae ex omnibus libris collectae*, constitute the best witness to its text.

Studies: J. WORDSWORTH, W. SANDAY, H. J. WHITE, Old-Latin Biblical Texts, 6 vols. Oxford, 1883–1911. — H. VON SODEN, Das lateinische Neue Testament in Afrika (TU 3, 3). Leipzig, 1909. — D. DE BRUYNE, Quelques documents nouveaux pour l'histoire du texte africain des Évangiles. Maredsous, 1910. — B. CAPELLE, Le Psautier latin en Afrique. Rome, 1913. — A. DOLD, Konstanzer altlateinische Propheten- und Evangelienbruchstücke mit Glossen. Beuron, 1923. — A. D'ALÈS, Vetus romana: Bibl (1923) 56–90. — TH. ZAHN, Ein Kompendium der biblischen Prophetie aus der afrikanischen Kirche um 305–325: Oriental Studies in Comm. of Paul Haupt. Baltimore, 1926, 52–63 Latin text and comments. — A. ALLGEIER, Die altlateinischen Psalterien. Freiburg, 1928. — A. V. BILLEN, The Old-Latin Texts of the Heptateuch. Cambridge, 1927. — K. TH. SCHÄFER, Untersuchungen zur Geschichte der lateinischen Übersetzung des Hebräerbriefes (RQ Suppl.–Heft 23). Freiburg, 1929. — F. STUMMER, Einführung in die lateinische Bibel. Paderborn, 1928, 4–76. — W. SÜSS, Das Problem der lateinischen Bibelsprache: Historische Vierteljahrschrift 27 (1932) 1–39. — G. J. D. AALDERS, Tertullianus' citaten uit de Evangeliën en de oudlatijnsche Bijbelvertalingen. Amsterdam, 1932. — D. DE BRUYNE,

.es anciennes traductions latines des Machabées (Anecdota Maredsolana 4). Mared-
.ous, 1932. — M. MATZKOW, De vocabulis quibusdam Italae et Vulgatae christianis
quaestiones lexicographae. Berlin, 1933.—J. E. STEINMÜLLER, The Pre-Jerome Latin
Version of the Bible: Homil. and Past. Review 36 (1935/36) 1037–1041.—G. BARDY,
'rénikon 14 (1937) 3–20, 113–130. — H. SCHNEIDER, Die altlateinischen biblischen
.antica. Beuron, 1938. — A. JÜLICHER, Itala. Das Neue Testament in altlateinischer
Überlieferung nach den Handschriften herausgegeben. I: Matthäus-Evangelium.
Berlin, 1938; II: Marcus-Evangelium. Berlin, 1940. — H. SCHNEIDER, Der altlatei-
nische Palimpsest-Psalter in Cod. Vat. Lat. 5359: Bibl 19 (1938) 361–382. — A.
DOLD, Die altlateinischen Proverbientexte im Cod. 25.2.36 von St. Paul in Kärnten:
Bibl 19 (1938) 241–259; idem, Neue St. Galler vorhieronymische Prophetenfragen.
Beuron, 1940. — J. P. SCHILDENBERGER, Die altlateinischen Texte des Proverbien-
buches I. Beuron, 1941. — K. TH. SCHÄFER, Die Überlieferung des altlateinischen
Galater-Briefes. Freiburg i. B., 1939. — G. MERCATI, Nuove note di letteratura biblica
e cristiana antica (ST 95). Vatican City, 1941, 95–134: Frammenti d'Is. e Paralip.
I. — B. BISCHOFF, Neue Materialien zum Bestand und zur Geschichte der alt-
ateinischen Bibelübersetzungen: Miscellanea G. Mercati I (ST 121) 407–436. —
R. WEBER, Les anc. versions lat. du 2e livre Paralipomenon. Rome, 1945. — H.
ROST, Die Bibel in den ersten Jahrhunderten. Westheim bei Augsburg, 1946, 81–
05, 124–182. — B. FISCHER, Vetus Latina. Die Reste der altlateinischen Bibel
nach Petrus Sabatier neu gesammelt und hrsg. von der Erzabtei Beuron. I Ver-
eichnis der Sigel. Beuron, 1949; II Genesis. Beuron, 1951. — M. STENZEL, Zum
Wortschatz der NTL Vulgata: VC 6 (1952) 20–27.

In the *Passio Perpetuae et Felicitatis* (12) the angels intone the
Sanctus in Greek. Tertullian in *De spectaculis* (25, 5) blames those
who go to the public shows for their profanation of prayer formulas like εἰς αἰῶνας ἀπ' αἰῶνος. These are perhaps indications that
originally the services were held in that language. However, it
seems that long before Rome had adopted Latin as a liturgical
tongue, Africa had already made the change.

The writers of Africa during this period testify to the hard
struggle which the Church had to wage against the enemy from
without in bloody persecutions and the enemy from within in
heretical controversies. From the *Acts of the Martyrs of Scilli*,
through Tertullian's *Apologeticum, Ad nationes, Ad Scapulam,* and
Cyprian's *De lapsis* and his own martyrdom, down to Arnobius'
Ad nationes and Lactantius' *De mortibus persecutorum* we are
conscious always of the pagan attack. It may not be accidental
that the aphorism *Semen est sanguis Christianorum* originated with an
African (Tert. *Apol.* 50, 13). The rapid spread of Christianity in
this country was purchased at the exorbitant price of numerous
martyrdoms.

Even more serious was the offensive from within. We see the greatest of the African authors fighting against the different Gnostic sects, the Valentinians and the followers of Marcion (cf. vol. I, pp. 268–272), only to witness at the end his own fall into Montanism. We cannot fail to be impressed by Cyprian's deep concern for the unity of the Church in his struggle against the schisms of Novatian and Felicissimus, yet we find him on the brink of a split with Rome in the bitter controversy with Pope Stephen over the validity of heretical baptism.

Finally, the African writers testify better than all other Christian authors of the West to the great difference between Greek and Latin Christendom, a difference which will increase in the centuries to come but which already looms large at this early period. The comparison between the first great theologians of both sides will show this immediately. Whereas Clement of Alexandria and Origen are anxious to put in relief the meta-physical content of the gospel and to prove the faith the only true philosophy and far above the Hellenistic systems, Tertullian and Cyprian set great store by the Christian way of life against the background of pagan vice. The Alexandrians stress the objective value of redemption, based on the incarnation of the Logos, which filled mankind with divine power; the Africans focus their attention on the subjective side of salvation, i.e., what remains to be done by the individual, on faith in action, i.e., the Christian's fight against sin and practice of virtue. These different points of view correspond to the natural bent of the Eastern and the Western mind.

TERTULLIAN

Quintus Septimius Florens Tertullianus, a native of Carthage, was born about 155 A.D. His father was a centurion of the pro-consular cohort. Both of his parents were pagans. He was an expert in law and gained a reputation for himself as an advocate at Rome. Most probably he is to be identified with the jurist Tertullianus, of whose writings the digests of the *Corpus Civilis* include a few excerpts. After his conversion about 193, he settled in Carthage, and enlisted at once all his knowledge of law, litera-ture, and philosophy on the side of the Christian faith. According to Jerome (*De vir. ill.* 53), he became a priest. He never refers to his clerical status, but his unique position and his preponderant role of teacher could hardly be explained had he remained a layman. Between the years 195–220, he carried on his literary activity. The great number of writings which he composed during this time have had a lasting influence on Christian theology. About 207 he openly went over to the Montanists and became the head of a special sect within them, the so-called Tertullianists, which lasted at Carthage up to the time of St. Augustine. The year of his death is unknown. It must have been after 220 A.D.

Except for St. Augustine, Tertullian is the most important and original ecclesiastical author in Latin. With a profound knowledge of philosophy, law, Greek and Latin letters, Tertullian combines inexhaustible vigor, burning rhetoric, and biting satire. His attitude is uncompromising. Forever a fighter, he knew no relenting towards his enemies, whether pagans, Jews, heretics, or later on, Catholics. All his writings are polemic. He does not tell the reasons for his conversion. Evidently it was not a careful comparison of the various philosophical systems which led him to the faith, as was the case with St. Justin. It seems that the heroism of the Christians in times of persecution influenced him more than anything else, because he writes in one of his treatises: 'everyone in the face of such prodigious endurance feels himself, as it were, struck by some doubt, and ardently desires to find out what there is at the bottom of this matter; from the moment that he discovers the truth he forthwith embraces it himself' (*Ad Scapulam* 5). Truth was the great object of his defence of Christianity, and of his attack on paganism and heresy:

Veritas non erubescit
nisi solummodo abscondi

he states once. Of fiery temperament and burning energy he develops a fanatical passion for truth. In one of his works the word *veritas* occurs one hundred and sixty-two times. The whole problem of Christianity or paganism is to him identical with *vera vel falsa divinitas*. When Christ founded the new religion He did it in order to lead mankind *in agnitionem veritatis* (*Apol.* 21, 30). The Christian God is the *Deus verus*; those who find Him find the fullness of truth. *Veritas* is what the demons hate, what the pagans reject, and what the Christian suffers and dies for. *Veritas* separates the Christian from the pagan. In all these statements there is deep religious feeling, and an ardent longing for honesty. It is not right to represent Tertullian as a lawyer and rhetorician with a leaning towards sophism. Tertullian speaks from the heart. In his defence of the religious spirit he is adamant. 'It is the right of every individual,' says he, 'to choose his own religion' (*Ad Scapulam* 2). There can be no doubt that he was ready to die for his faith. In the last words of his *Apology* he gives expression to his passionate desire to suffer martyrdom. He is against flight in persecution. With this firmness of conviction he combines sincerity about himself. He knows his shortcomings; when he writes on patience he says he feels like an invalid talking about health, himself always sick with the fever of impatience. In fact, it is this impatience which robs him all too frequently of success. Although he knows that 'truth persuades by teaching, but does not teach by persuading' (*Adv. Val.* 1), he always tries to prove too much. Whenever he speaks, he acts like an advocate who is interested only in winning his case and annihilating his adversary. Thus in many instances he may silence, but he does not convince, his adversaries.

Studies: A. HAUCK, Tertullians Leben und Schriften. Erlangen, 1877.—J. M. FULLER, Dictionary of Christian Biography 4 (1887) 818–864. — E. NÖLDECHEN, Tertullian. Gotha, 1890. — P. MONCEAUX, Histoire littéraire de l'Afrique chrétienne depuis les origines jusqu'à l'invasion arabe. I Tertullien et les origines. Paris, 1901. — CH. GUIGNEBERT, Tertullien. Étude sur ses sentiments à l'égard de l'empire et de la société civile. Paris, 1901. — A. HARNACK, Die Chronologie der altchristlichen Literatur 2. Leipzig, 1904, 256 ff.—H. KOCH, War Tertullian Priester?: HJG 28 (1907) 95–103; *idem*, Tertullian und der römische Presbyter Florinus: ZNW 13 (1912) 59–83. — H. KELLNER, Tertullian als Historiker: ThQ 93 (1911) 319–321. — P. DE LABRIOLLE, Tertullien était-il prêtre?: Bull. d'anc. litt. et d'arch. chrét. 3 (1913) 161–177. — H. KOCH, Tertullians Laienstand: ZKG 35 (1914) 1–8. — O. HIRSCHFELD, Die Namen des Tertullianus: SAB (1915) 31. — H. KOCH, Tertullian und Cyprian als religiöse Persönlichkeiten: IKZ 10 (1920) 45–61. — F. RAMORINO, Tertulliano. Milan, 1923. — P. GUILLOUX, L'Évolution religieuse de Tertullien: RHE 19 (1923) 5–24, 141–156. — K. HOLL, Tertullian als Schriftsteller: Gesammelte Aufsätze zur Kirchengeschichte 3. Tübingen, 1928, 1–12. — L. BAYARD, Tertullien et St. Cyprien (Coll. des moralistes chrétiens). Paris, 1930. — H. KOCH, Nochmals: War Tertullian Priester?: ThStKr 10 (1931) 108–114. — S. L. GREENSLADE, Tertullien of Carthage: ExpT 44 (1932/33) 247–252. — A. EHRHARD, Die Kirche der Märtyrer. Munich, 1932, 359–367. — H. KOCH, Tertullianus: PWK 2. R. 5, 822–844. — V. NEMES, Tert. görög nüvelsége Pannonhalme. 1935. — A. D'ALÈS, Tertullien helléniste: REG (1937) 329–362. — L. CASTIGLIONI, Tertulliano. Milan, 1937. — Z. VYSOKY, Remarques sur les sources des œuvres de Tertullien. Prague, 1937; *idem*, L'état des recherches récentes sur la chronologie des œuvres apologétiques de Tertullien: Listy Filologicke (1938) 110–123. — M. S. ENSLIN, Puritan of Carthage: JR 27 (1947)

97-212. — M. M. Baney, Some Reflections of Life in North Africa in the Writings of Tertullian (PSt 80). Washington, 1948. — B. Nisters, Tertullian, seine Persönlichkeit und sein Schicksal (MBTh). Münster, 1950.

About *Tertullian and Montanism*, see: P. de Labriolle, La crise montaniste. Paris, 1913, 294 ff; *idem*, Les sources de l'histoire du montanisme. Texts grecs, latins, syriaques (Collectanea Friburgensia N.S. 15). Fribourg, 1913, 12 ff. — E. Buonaiuti, Il Cristianesimo nell'Africa Romana. Bari, 1928, 37 ff. — A. Fagitto, La diaspora catafrigia: Tertulliano e la 'Nuova Profezia'. Rome, 1924. — R. G. Smith, Tertullian and Montanism: Theology 46 (1943) 127-139.

For *Tertullian's influence on later writers*, see: A. Harnack, Über Tertullian in der Literatur der alten Kirche: SAB (1895) 545 ff. — H. Koch, Gelasius im kirchenpolitischen Dienste seiner Vorgänger: SAB (1935) 77-82. — A. d'Alès, Tertullien chez Bède: RSR (1937) 620. — J. Madoz, Vestigios de Tertuliano en la doctrina de la virginidad de Maria, en la carta Ad amicum aegrotum de viro perfecto: EE 18 (1944) 187-200. — Chr. Mohrmann, Saint Jérôme et saint Augustin sur Tertullien: VC 5 (1951) 111-112.

STYLE AND LANGUAGE

Tertullian has a style of his own. It is true that he followed the literary tradition of his age. His works present numerous examples of familiarity with the techniques of rhetoric. He is inspired by the 'Asianic' manner of Greek orators, which prefers short sentences to long periods and piles up questions followed by pointed answers in staccato fashion. He is fond of antithesis and balance and favors puns. But he shows a marked preference for uncommon forms of expression and he coined words and phrases such as no writer since Tacitus had been able to do. This fact, as well as his love for pregnant terseness, is responsible for a certain obscurity of thought in his works, and Vincent of Lerins' remark *Quot paene verba, tot sententiae*, is not without foundation.

Nevertheless the contribution of his artistic genius to the language of the early Church is of first importance. His works remain an outstanding source for our knowledge of Christian Latin. They contain a large number of new terms that have been adopted by subsequent theologians and have found a permanent place in the vocabulary of dogma. For this reason he has been called 'the creator of ecclesiastical Latin.' This, however, is an exaggeration and does not do justice to the profound and lasting influence of the oldest translations of the Bible, where many of the words which were thought to have been invented or adapted by Tertullian were first used, as recently proved for *sacramentum*

by A. Kolping. Even with this reservation, however, there still
remains enough that is Tertullian's own creation to secure him a
very prominent position in the history of Christian Latin.

Studies: A. Schmidt, De Latinitate Tertullianea, 2 vols. Erlangen, 1870/72; *idem*
Commentatio de nominum verbalium in tor et trix desinentium apud Tertullianum
vi ac copia. Erlangen, 1878. — H. Kellner, Über die sprachlichen Eigentümlich
keiten Tertullians: ThQ (1876) 229–251. — H. Hoppe, De sermone Tertulliane
questiones selectae. Thesis. Marburg, 1897. — G. R. Hauschild, Tertullian al
Wortbildner. Progr. Realschule Leipzig, 1876; *idem*, Die Grundsätze und Mittel de
Wortbildung bei Tertullian. Progr. Gymnasium Frankfurt a.M., 1881. — H. Hoppe
Syntax und Stil des Tertullian. Leipzig, 1903. — A. Engelbrecht, Lexikalische
und Biblisches aus Tertullian: WSt 27 (1905) 62–74; *idem*, Neue lexikalische un
semasiologische Beiträge aus Tertullian: WSt 28 (1906) 142–159. — H. Goelzer
Le style de Tertullien: Journal des Savants N.S. 5 (1907) 202 ff. — E. de Backer
Le sens classique du mot sacramentum dans les œuvres de Tertullien: Musée Belg
(1909) 147–155; *idem*, Sacramentum. Le mot et l'idée représentée par lui dan
les œuvres de Tertullien. Paris, 1911. — E. Löfstedt, Zur Sprache Tertullians
Lund, 1920. — J. P. Waltzing, La langue de Tertullien: Musée Belge 9 (1920
44–47. — E. Norden, Die antike Kunstprosa vom 6. Jahrh. v. Chr. bis in di
Zeit der Renaissance II, 4th ed. Leipzig–Berlin, 606–615. — F. C. Burkitt, D
Sanday's New Testament of Irenaeus with a note on Valentinian terms in Ire
naeus and Tertullian: JThSt 24 (1923) 56–67. — J. de Ghellinck, Pour l'histoir
du mot sacramentum I. Louvain, 1924. — S. W. J. Teeuwen, Sprachlicher Be
deutungswandel bei Tertullian (StGKA 14, 1). Paderborn, 1926. — S. Colombo
Concetto e forma nello stilo di Tertulliano: Didaskaleion (1926) I, 1–17. — H. Koch
Zum Ablativgebrauch bei Cyprian und andern Schriftstellern (Tertullian): RhM
NF 78 (1929) 427–432. — H. Wollmann, Defixus in morsus ursorum et spongia
retiariorum: Mitteilungen des Deutsch. Archäol. Instituts, Römische Abt. 45 (1930
227–233. — H. Rahner, Pompa diaboli. Ein Beitrag zur Bedeutungsgeschichte de
Wortes πομπή-pompa in der urchristlichen Taufliturgie: ZkTh 55 (1931) 239–273
— J. Schrijnen, Charakteristik des altchristl. Latein. Nijmegen, 1932. — H. Hoppe
Beiträge zur Sprache und Kritik Tertullians. Lund, 1932. — A. d'Alès, Tertullianea
Concutere, concussio, concussura, concussor: RSR 27 (1937) 97–99; *idem*
Ἐπερχόμενος ou οἰκονόμος?: RSR 27 (1937) 228–230. — H. Janssen, Kultur un
Sprache. Zur Geschichte der alten Kirche im Spiegel der Sprachentwicklung vo
Tertullian bis Cyprian (Latinitas Christianorum Primaeva 8). Nijmegen, 1938. -
C. Arpe, Substantia (in Tertullian): Phil 94 (1939) 65–78. — H. Pétré, L'exemplun
chez Tertullien. Dijon, 1940. — J. A. Demmel, Die Neubildungen auf -antia un
-entia bei Tertullian (Diss. Zürich). Immensee, 1944. — V. Morel, Disciplina, le mc
et l'idée représentée par lui dans les œuvres de Tertullien: RHE 40 (1944/45) 5–46
— E. Evans, Tertullian's Theological Terminology: ChQ 139 (1944/45) 56–77. —
E. Peterson, Christianus: Miscellanea Mercati 1 (ST 121). Vatican City, 1946
355–372. — J. H. Waszink, Pompa diaboli: VC 1 (1947) 13–41. — E. Skard
Vexillum virtutis: SO 25 (1947) 26–30. — H. Pétré, Caritas. Étude sur le vocabu
laire latin de la charité chrétienne (Spicilegium Sacrum Lovaniense 22). Louvain
1948. — A. Kolping, Sacramentum Tertullianeum I. Münster, 1948. — J. W. Ph

Borleffs, G. F. Diercks and E. Michiels, Un 'Lexicon Tertullianeum': Sacris Erudiri 2 (1949) 383–386. — Chr. Mohrmann, Le Latin langue de la chrétienté occidentale: Aevum 24 (1950) 133 ff; eadem, Quelques observations sur l'originalité de la litterature latine chrétienne: Rivista di Storia della Chiesa in Italia 4 1950) 153 ff.; eadem, MC 1, 3. Utrecht, 1951, LXXXVI–XCV. — W. Dürig, Disciplina. Eine Studie zur Bedeutung des Wortes in der Sprache der Liturgie und der Väter: Sacris Erudiri 4 (1952) 245–279.

I. WRITINGS

1. *Text Tradition*

At least six different collections of Tertullian's work must have existed from the beginning of the Middle Ages.

1. The *Corpus Trecense* is the smallest and most probably the oldest. Its chief representative is *Codex Trecensis* 523 (T), which Dom A. Wilmart discovered in 1916 in the library of Troyes. It contains five treatises more or less complete: *Adversus Judaeos, De carne Christi, De carnis resurrectione, De baptismo, De paenitentia.* Written in the twelfth century at Clairvaux, the *Codex Trecensis* rates in value highest of all. J. W. Ph. Borleffs has shown that the marginal notes in the edition of Tertullian by Martinus Mesnartius (Paris, 1545) contain a selection of its readings. Kroymann is of the opinion that the *Corpus Trecense* may even have begun with Vincent of Lerins (died 454) and that, at all events, it constituted the earliest attempt to restore the reputation of Tertullian's works.

2. The *Corpus Masburense* has come down in copies of a later date than the *Trecense*, though it must have originated as a collection prior to 494, the year in which the *Decretum Gelasianum* condemned all of Tertullian's writings. Its text is known to us through the edition of Sigismund Gelenius (Basel, 1550) based on the *Mesnartiana* and a *Codex Masburensis* no longer extant. The latter contained twelve treatises: *De carnis resurrectione, De praescriptione haereticorum, De monogamia, De testimonio animae, De anima, De spectaculis, De baptismo, Scorpiace, De idololatria, De pudicitia, De ieiunio, De oratione.*

3. The *Corpus Agobardinum*, preserved to us in the *Codex Agobardinus*, included originally twenty-one of Tertullian's works. Today, the manuscript *Codex Parisinus latinus* 1622, *saec.* IX, called

Agobardinus (A) after its first owner, Archbishop Agobard of Lyons (814–840), contains but thirteen: *Ad nationes, De praescriptione haereticorum, Scorpiace, De testimonio animae, De corona, De spectaculis, De idololatria* (incomplete), *De anima* (incomplete), *De oratione* (incomplete), *De cultu feminarum* (incomplete), *Ad uxorem, De exhortatione castitatis, De carne Christi* (to ch. 10). Despite its defects, this parchment manuscript remains a generally reliable source for the history of the text. The collection dates most probably from the same time as the *Corpus Masburense*.

4. The *Corpus Cluniacense* was most probably made later than the above three in Spain. It seems to go back to the middle of the sixth century and contains the largest assortment of Tertullian's works, including as it does twenty-seven treatises, among them even the anti-heretical writings, not found in any of the three other collections. The *Corpus Cluniacense* survives in a number of manuscripts, which are all derived from the lost *Codd. Cluniacenses*. The most outstanding is *Codex Montepessulanus* H 54, *saec.* XI (M) in the Bibliothèque Municipale of Montpellier. It includes *De patientia, De carne Christi, De resurrectione carnis, Adversus Praxean, Adversus Valentinianos, Adversus Marcionem, Apologeticum*. The *Codex Paterniacensis* 439, *saec.* XI (P), now at Schlettstadt, is related to the *Montepessulanus*, but much inferior in quality. It offers the text of *De patientia, De carne Christi, De resurrectione carnis, Adversus Praxean, Adversus Valentinianos, Adversus Iudaeos, De praescriptione haereticorum*, the non-authentic *Adversus omnes haereses, Adversus Hermogenem*. To the same group belong *Codex Florentinus Magliebechianus, Conventi soppressi* VI, 9, *saec.* XV (N), *Codex Florentinus Magliebechianus, Conv. soppr.* VI, 10, *saec.* XV (F), *Codex Vindobonensis* 4194, *saec.* XV (V), *Codex Leydensis latinus* 2, *saec.* XV (L), and a series of younger manuscripts from Italy, all derived from N or F. This group contains, in addition to treatises mentioned above, *De fuga, Ad Scapulam, De corona, Ad martyras, De paenitentia, De virginibus velandis, De cultu feminarum, De exhortatione castitatis, Ad uxorem, De monogamia, De pallio*.

5. Another *Corpus*, not related to any of the four, was unknown until recently. Gösta Claesson, a Swedish philologian, discovered in a manuscript of the Vatican Library, *Codex Ottobonianus latinus* 25, *saec.* XIV, a number of excerpts from Tertullian's *De pudicitia, De paenitentia, De patientia*, and *De spectaculis*. The readings

are in a number of places identical with *Codex Trecensis*, but else-where show such independence that a fifth corpus must have existed.

6. Finally, a most astonishing discovery has been made recently in the Netherlands. A. P. van Schilfgaarde and G. I. Lieftinck published a fragment of *De spectaculis* found in the archives of Keppel and now in the library of Leiden. This comes from a ninth-century manuscript, is thus older than any copy of Tertullian that we had so far, and exhibits a text not found in any corpus mentioned above. It was written near Cologne and may have belonged originally to the library of the cathedral. The most ancient catalogue (No. 833) of that cathedral lists a manuscript with several of Tertullian's treatises, though the name of the author is not given. It is possible that the Keppel fragment be-longs to this manuscript. Moreover, the catalogue of Cologne, together with a catalogue of the abbey of Corbie and a lost manu-script whose variants Pamelius used in his edition of Tertullian through the good offices of Johannes Clemens Anglus, prove that there was another corpus in existence.

Studies: See the 'praefationes' to CSEL 20, 47, 69 and 70. — A. KROYMANN, Zur Überlieferungsgeschichte des Tertulliantextes: RhM (1913) 128–152; *idem,* Das Tertullianfragment des Codex Parisinus 13047: RhM (1915) 358–367. — G. THÖR-NELL, Studia Tertullianea, 4 vols. Uppsala, 1918–1926. — A. WILMART, Un manu-scrit de Tertullien retrouvé: Comptes rendus de l'Académie des Inscriptions et Belles-Lettres (1920) 380–386. — J. W. PH. BORLEFFS, Zur Luxemburger Tertullianhand-schrift: Mnem 2 (1935) 299–308; *idem,* La valeur du Codex Trecensis de Tertullien pour la critique de texte dans le traité De Baptismo: VC 2 (1948) 185–200; *idem,* Un nouveau manuscrit de Tertullien: VC 5 (1951) 65–79. — CHR. MOHRMANN, MC, 1 ser. No. 3 (1951) XLI–LVIII. — E. DEKKERS, Note sur les fragments récemment découverts de Tertullien: Sacris Eruditi 4 (1952) 372–383.

Other manuscripts no longer extant are known to us through the oldest printed editions, which are also important for the history of the text.

The *editio princeps* by Beatus Rhenanus, published in 1521 at Basel (R), is based on *Codex Paterniacensis* (P) and a lost *Codex Hirsaugiensis*, which was related to the *Cluniacenses* and had former-ly belonged to the monastery of Hirsau in Wurtemberg. In a third edition, published at Paris in 1539, Rhenanus used in addition a *Codex Gorziensis* from the monastery of Gorce near

Metz. This codex, also related to the Cluniacenses group, has disappeared. The *editio princeps* comprised the treatises: *De patientia, De carne Christi, De resurrectione carnis, Adversus Praxean, Adversus Valentinianos, Adversus Iudaeos, De praescriptione haereticorum (Adversus omnes haereses), Adversus Hermogenem.*

The edition of M. Mesnartius (B), published in 1545 at Paris, adds the following works: *De trinitate* (of Novatian), *De testimonio animae, De anima, De spectaculis, De baptismo, Scorpiace, De idololatria, De pudicitia, De ieiunio, De cibis Iudaicis* (of Novatian), *De oratione.* These were taken from a manuscript for which the editor gives no name and no description. The text of *De baptismo* shows that it was inferior to the *Codex Trecensis*, from which, however, as mentioned above, some readings were added in the margin. Mesnartius used in addition *Codex Agobarlinus* and another unknown manuscript.

The edition (Gel.) of Sigismund Gelenius (Basel, 1550) bases its text on the Mesnartiana and a *Codex Masburensis*, as we have already pointed out.

The edition (Pam.) by Jacobus Pamelius (Antwerp, 1579) relies on those of Mesnartius and Gelenius. He also employed a *Codex Joannis Clementis Angli*, no longer extant, which contained *De spectaculis, De praescriptione haereticorum, De resurrectione carnis, De monogamia, De ieiunio, De pudicitia.*

The edition of Franciscus Junius (Jun.) published at Franeker in 1597 is no more than a reprint of the Pameliana. Of importance are its *Adnotationes* with many excellent emendations.

The edition (Rig.) by Nicolaus Rigaltius (Paris, 1634) rests on a collation of the Agobardinus to which Ph. Priorius added emendations in the second and the later reissues.

Editions: ML 1–2. — F. OEHLER, Q.S.F. Tertulliani opera omnia, ed. maior, vol. 1–3. Leipzig, 1851/54. Ed. minor, Leipzig, 1854. — A. REIFFERSCHEID–G. WISSOWA, CSEL 20 (1890); A. KROYMANN, CSEL 47 (1939); H. HOPPE, CSEL 69 (1939); A. KROYMANN, CSEL 70 (1942).

Translations: English: P. HOLMES and S. THELWALL, ANL 7, 11, 15, 18; ANF 3, 4. — *German:* H. KELLNER, BKV² 7 (1912); H. KELLNER–G. ESSER, BKV² 24 (1915). — *French:* A. DE GENOUDE, Les Pères de l'église. Paris, 1852. — *Dutch:* H. U. MEYBOOM, Oudchristel. geschriften, dl. 40–46. Leiden, 1929–1934. — *Spanish:* J. PELLICER DE OSSAU SALES Y TOBAR, Obras de Quinto Fl. Tertuliano. Barcelona, 1639. — *Italian:* L. BORGHINI, Rome, 1756.

2. The Apologetic Works of Tertullian

Of the apologetic works of Tertullian, the books *Ad nationes* and the *Apologeticum* are related to each other. Both of them were written in the year 197, and both treat of the same subject; however the *Apologeticum* represents the more finished form. For this reason, and for a number of definite allusions to the revolt of Albinus against Septimius Severus and the bloody battle at Lyons that followed on Feb. 19, 197, the *Ad nationes* must be regarded as composed before the *Apologeticum*.

1. To the Heathen (Ad nationes)

This treatise consists of two books, the first of which begins by showing that the juridical procedure against the Christians is not only unreasonable, but also contradicts all principles of justice. This lawlessness results from ignorance and from the fact that the pagans do not know what they condemn (ch. 1–6). In the following chapters (7–19) the author refutes the customary calumnies. He proves them untrue, but adds that, even if they were true, it would give pagans no right whatsoever to condemn the Christians, since they themselves commit worse crimes. While the first book remains on the defensive, the second is more aggressive. It contains a sharp criticism of pagan religion in general and of Roman belief in gods in particular. Tertullian draws here on Varro's *Rerum Divinarum Libri* XVI, in which the gods are divided into three classes, gods of the philosophers, gods of the poets and gods of the nations. Tertullian investigates the concept God, and proves that the pagan divinities are nothing but human inventions.

Editions: A. REIFFERSCHEID–G. WISSOWA, CSEL 20 (1890) 59–133. — J. W. PH. BORLEFFS, Ad nationes libri duo. Leiden, 1929.

Translations: English: P. HOLMES, ANL 11 416–506; ANF 3, 109–147. — *Dutch:* H. U. MEYBOOM, Tertullianus, Tegen de heidenen (Oudchristl. geschriften, dl. 42). Leiden, 1927. — *German:* M. HAIDENTHALLER, Tertullianus zweites Buch *Ad nationes* und *De testimonio animae*. Übertragung und Kommentar (StGKA 23, 1–2). Paderborn, 1942.

Studies: TH. BIRT, Marginalien zu lateinischen Prosaikern (Ad nat. 1,2; 4; 7; 10; 16): Phil (1927) 164–182. — J. W. PH. BORLEFFS, Observationes criticae ad Tertulliani Ad nationes libros: Mnem 56 (1928) 193–201, 225–242; 57 (1929) 1–51. — M. BALSAMO, Paralleli non ancora osservati tra l'Ad nationes e l'Apologeticum: Didaska-

leion, nuov. ser. 8 (1930), fasc. 1, 29–34. — L. Castiglioni, Ad Tertullianum adnotationes: Studi Ubaldi. Milan, 1937, 255–262. — J. H. Waszink, Tertullian ad nat.
2, 17, 14: Mnem 3, 11 (1943) 71–72.

2. Apology (Apologeticum)

The *Apologeticum* is the most important of all Tertullian's works.
It differs considerably from the book *Ad nationes*, although in
content it is similar. The *Apologeticum* has a plan, more unity than
the *Ad nationes*. The latter appears to be rather a collection of
materials than a finished composition, while the *Apologeticum*
definitely gives the impression of being inspired by the interior
need of the author and created by a personality that dominates
the material. The reasoning assumes a more juridical form while
the argumentation of the *Ad nationes* is philosophical and rhetori-
cal.The author shows greater restraint in the *Apology* than in the
Ad nationes, because the addressee is different in the two works. *Ad
nationes* is, as the title indicates, intended for the pagan world in
general, whereas the *Apologeticum* was directed to the Governors of
Roman provinces, whom he attacks but tries also to convince.
For this reason *Ad nationes* corresponds in type to the λόγος πρὸς
Ἕλληνας, while the *Apologeticum* represents that of the ἀπολογία.

CONTENT

Ignorance is the reason why the Christians are hated and
persecuted:

> Truth knows that she is a stranger on earth and easily finds
> enemies among men of another allegiance, but she knows
> that her race, home, hope, recompense, honor are in heaven.
> For one thing meanwhile she is eager—not to be condemned
> without being known. The laws are supreme in their own
> sphere: but what loss can they suffer if truth be heard?
> (1, 2).

The court procedure adopted by the authorities contravenes all
precedent and every principle of justice. Even the pagans cannot
give a plausible reason for their hatred of the name 'Christian.'
The value of all human legislation depends on its morality and
its end. Consequently, the Christian religion cannot be against the
decrees of the State. Moreover, an examination proves that only

wicked emperors made enactments against it: 'Such have ever been our persecutors; unjust, impious, infamous, whom even you yourself have been wont to condemn; and those whom such condemn, you have become accustomed to rehabilitate' (5, 5).

This fact throws light on the value of these statutes. Besides, history proves that laws can be and have been repealed. After his introduction, consisting of the first six chapters, Tertullian first deals briefly with the secret crimes (ch. 7–9) and then extensively with the public offences of which the Christians are accused. That they commit sacramental infanticide and indulge in Thyestaean banquets and incests has never been proved. Rumor alone, all this long time, is the authority for the crimes of the Christians' (7, 13). But the heathens have themselves been guilty of such enormities. More serious are the charges of contempt for the religion of the State (*intentatio laesae divinitatis*) and of high treason (*titulus laesae augustioris majestatis*). It is in the defence against these public crimes that Tertullian shows his skill as a jurist. The Christians, he states, do not participate in the veneration of the pagan gods, because they are nothing else than deceased human beings and their images are material and inanimate. It is no wonder that these divinities are mocked in the theatre and despised in the temple. But the Christians venerate the creator of the world, the only true God, who has revealed Himself in the Scriptures. It is therefore an injustice to accuse them of atheism, since the so-called gods of the pagans are no gods:

All this confession of theirs, their avowal that they are not gods, their response that there is no god but the one whose servants we are, is amply enough to repel the charge brought against us of treason, above all to the religion of Rome. If they definitely are not gods, then definitely it is not a religion; if it is not a religion because they definitely are no gods, then we are definitely not guilty of injuring religion. On the contrary, the taunt has recoiled upon you, who by your worship of a lie, by your neglect of the true religion and of the true God, and, more than that, by your assault upon it, commit against the true God the crime of real irreligion (24, 1–2 LCL).

And here Tertullian demands freedom of religion:

Look to it whether this also may form part of the accu-

sation of irreligion—to do away with freedom of religion, t
forbid a man choice of deity, so that I may not worship whom
I would, but am forced to worship whom I would not. N
one, not even a man, will wish to receive reluctant worship
Why, the Egyptians are allowed full freedom in their empty
superstition, to make gods of birds and beasts, and to con
demn to death any who may kill a god of that sort. Every
individual province, every city has its own gods... we, we
alone are forbidden a religion of our own. We injure the
Romans, we are reckoned not to be Romans, because we do
not worship the gods of the Romans. Happy it is that God i
the God of all, and that all of us are his, whether we would
wish it or not. But among you it is lawful to worship anything
at all, so long as it is not the true God!—as if he were no
rather God of all, whose we all are (24, 6–10 LCL).

Next Tertullian refutes the general belief that the Roman
rule the world because they venerate idols. Only the true God
entrusts universal domination to whom He chooses. It is no
stubbornness that prevents the Christians from worshipping the
State divinities but their realization that such homage is for
demons. Therefore, they may not sacrifice even for the welfare o
the emperor, especially since these pretended gods are powerless
to help him, and their refusal cannot be adjudged a crime. On
the contrary, they pray to the true God for the ruler. Here
Tertullian traces all authority to God:

For we, on behalf of the safety of the emperors, invoke the
eternal God, the true God, the living God, whom the
emperors themselves prefer to have propitious to them
beyond all other gods. They know who has given them the
empire; they know as men who has given them life; they
feel that he is God alone in whose power and no other's they
are, second to whom they stand, after whom they come first
before all gods and above all gods. Why not? Seeing that
they are above all men, and men at any rate live and so are
better than things. They reflect how far the strength of their
empire avails, and thus they understand God; against him
they cannot avail; so they know that it is through him that
they do avail. Let the emperor, as a last test, make war or
heaven, carry heaven captive in his triumph, set a guard or

heaven, lay taxes on heaven. He cannot. So he is great, because he is less than heaven. He himself belongs to him, whose is heaven and all creation. Thence comes the emperor, whence came the man before he was emperor; thence his power whence his spirit (30, 1–3 LCL).

In order to show that the Christians are not enemies of the State, nor of the human race, and that it is an injustice to class as unlawful their associations, Tertullian gives a delightful description of Christian worship:

We are a society with a common religious feeling, unity of discipline, a common bond of hope. We meet in gatherings and congregations to approach God in prayer, massing our forces to surround him. This violence pleases God. We pray also for the Emperors, for their ministers, and for those in authority, for the security of the world, for peace on earth, for postponement of the end. We meet to read the books of God, if anything in the nature of the times bids us look to the future or open our eyes to facts. In any case, with those holy words we feed our faith, we lift up our hope, we confirm our confidence; and no less we reinforce our teaching by inculcation of God's precepts. There is, besides exhortation in our gatherings, rebuke, divine censure. For judgment is passed and it carries great weight, as it must among men certain that God sees them; and it is a notable foretaste of judgement to come, if any man has so sinned as to be banished from all share in our prayer, our assembly, and all holy intercourse. Our presidents are elders of proved character, men who have reached the honor not for a price, but by character; for nothing that is God's goes for a price. Even if there is a chest of a sort, it is not made up of money paid in entrance fees as if religion were a matter of contract. Every man once a month brings some coin,—or whatever he likes, and only if he does wish, and if he can; for nobody is compelled; it is a voluntary offering. You might call them the trust funds of piety. For they are not spent upon banquets nor drinking parties nor thankless eating houses; but to feed the poor and to bury them, for boys and girls who lack property and parents, and then for slaves grown old, and shipwrecked mariners; and any who may be in mines, islands or prisons, provided that it is for the sake of God's love, become the pensioners of their confession. Such works of love (for so it is) put a mark upon us in the eyes of some. 'Look,' they say, 'how they love one another,' for themselves hate one another. 'And how they are ready to die for each other,' for themselves will be readier to kill each other (29, 1–7 LCL).

In the final section (46–50) Tertullian refutes the idea that Christianity is merely a new philosophy. It is far more than a speculation about human origins. It is divine revelation. It is truth manifested by God. For this reason it cannot be destroyed by its persecutors: 'Nothing whatever is accomplished by your cruelties, each more exquisite than the last. It is the bait which wins men for our school. We multiply whenever we are mown down by you; the blood of Christians is seed' (50, 13 LCL).

From some passages in Eusebius' *Ecclesiastical History* we learn that the *Apologeticum* was put into the Greek, most likely soon after its appearance. The translation, probably made in Palestine, disappeared not long afterwards but its existence indicates the importance of Tertullian's work. His *Apologeticum* is by common consent the masterpiece and the crown of all his writings.

TEXT TRADITION OF THE 'APOLOGETICUM'

The *Apologeticum*, on account of its great importance, boasts by far the largest number of manuscripts. It has a tradition of its own in so far as it appears often among Cyprian's, Lactantius' and Jerome's writings, but was originally excluded from the four collections mentioned above. However, it was later added to the *Codex Montepessulanus* and thus incorporated by later copyists into Tertullian's works. No less than thirty-six codices preserve its text and constitute the so-called *Vulgata recensio*. Two of them shall be mentioned here: *Codex Petropolitanus auct. lat.* I Q v. 40, *saec.* IX, formerly *Sangermanensis* (S), and *Codex Parisinus* 1623, *saec.* X (II), both of which have been used by Hoppe for his new edition in CSEL. But there is another text tradition which differs from the *Vulgata recensio* a great deal. It rests on a *Codex Fuldensis*, which has completely disappeared, and of which we know only that it contained the *Apologeticum* and the *Adversus Iudaeos*. However, it was seen at Fulda in the fall of 1584 by Franciscus

Iodius, who compared it with De la Barre's edition and re-
orded no less than 900 variants. This valuable collection of
eadings came later into the hands of Franciscus Junius. He
dded them as an appendix to the second part of his Tertullian,
rhich was just then in process of publication and appeared in
597 at Franeker. From this, they were reprinted by Waltzing in
Iusée Belge 16 (1912) 188 ff.

Hoppe found in the *Stadtbibliothek* of Bremen a manuscript
48, which reproduces on pp. 131–146 the beginning of Modius'
ollation, the variants to ch. 1–15. A. Souter discovered in the
antonsbibliothek of Zurich a *Codex Rhenaugiensis saec.* X that
ontained, among passages from other Latin authors, a fragment
f the *Apologeticum*, comprising ch. 38, 39 and 40 to the words
intos ad unum. It proved to be, if not a copy of the *Fuldensis*,
ertainly a witness to its text tradition. Thus we know that in the
enth century there were already two different groups of manu-
cripts, the one represented by the *Vulgata recensio*, the other by
ne *Fuldensis*.

The question is, how can this difference be explained? The
rst to answer it was Havercamp. In his edition of the *Apolo-
eticum* (Leiden 1718) he declared that the *Fuldensis* is the first and
ne *Vulgata recensio* the second edition of the *Apologeticum* and that
ne difference therefore goes back to the author, to Tertullian
imself. This theory was adopted by Oehler in 1854 and H.
chroers in 1914, was defended again by Thörnell in 1926 and
y Hoppe in 1939. The last-named reproduces in CSEL the
ulgata recensio and adds the variants of the *Fuldensis* below.
Iowever, this solution remains very doubtful. First of all, if
ertullian did publish a revision of his work, it is surprising that
e never speaks of it, as he does in the case of the *Adversus Marcio-
em;* secondly, it is even more surprising that nobody in Christian
ntiquity ever mentions the existence of two different versions.

For this reason an attempt was made to find another answer to
he difficult question. C. Callewaert in 1902 advanced the view
hat the *Fuldensis* preserves the authentic text but that an un-
nown scribe in Carolingian times normalized and simplified the
atin. In many cases he misunderstood Tertullian and changed
is meaning. This corruption created the *Vulgata recensio* and
ecame so popular that it supplanted the correct *Fuldensis*. A

9

critical edition of the *Apologeticum* must, therefore, be based on th
latter and the variants of the former must be treated wit
suspicion. J. P. Waltzing voiced the same opinion in 191ç
although in his later edition in 1929 he was rather cautious in h
use of the *Fuldensis*. G. Rauschen believed that both traditior
were subjected to normalization but is convinced that *Code
Fuldensis* offers the relatively purer text. Thus his edition in ⱷ
(Bonn, 1912) is eclectic, and Martin's edition (1930), whic
replaced that of Rauschen, adhered to this method.

E. Löfstedt in 1915 testified to the superiority of the *Fuldens*
and three years later again defended it. He was able to sho\
interpolations in the *Vulgata recensio* but he had to admit tha
even the text of the *Fuldensis* has been altered, especially in th
last part of the *Apologeticum*.

Editions: H. Hoppe, CSEL 69 (1939). —J. P. Waltzing, Tertullien, Apologétiqu
texte établi d'après le Codex Fuldensis. Liège-Paris, 1914. — S. Colombo, L'Apolᵉ
getico, ed. con introduzione, commento, apparato critico e appendice critica. Turiⁿ
1918. — A. Souter, Tertulliani Apologeticus, text of Oehler annotated with aⁱ
introduction by J. E. B. Mayor, with a translation by A. Souter. Cambridge, 1917.
G. Rauschen, FP 12. Bonn, 1919. — J. P. Waltzing, Tertullien, L'apologétique .
Texte établi d'après la double trad. manuscrite, apparat critique et trad. littéral
II: Comment. analytique, gramm. et hist. Liège-Paris, 1919; reprinted Paris, 193
— A. Souter, Tertullian, Apologeticus. Aberdeen, 1926. — S. Colombo, Tertulliᵃ
nus, Apologeticum, rec. praef. est, app. crit. et indic. instruxit (Corpus script. laⁱ
Paravianum 46). Turin, 1926. — G. Mazzoni, L'Apologetico di Tertulliano (I claⁱ
sici cristiani). Siena, 1928. — J. P. Waltzing et A. Severyns, Tertullien, Apolᵉ
gétique, texte établi et traduit. Paris, 1929. — T. R. Glover, Tertullian, Apologᵧ
De Spectaculis with an Englisch translation (LCL). London, 1931. — J. Martiⁿ
Tertullianus, Apologeticum, ed. et adnot. (FP 6). Bonn, 1933. — P. Henen, Indeⁿ
verborum quae Tertulliani Apologetico continentur. Louvain, 1910. — C. Beckeⁱ
Tertullian, Apologeticum. Lateinisch und deutsch. Munich, 1952.

Translations: English: H. Brown, Tertullian's Apology or Defense of the Christianⁿ
London, 1655. — C. Dodgson, Library of Fathers 10. Oxford, 1842, 1–106. — ⱷ
Thelwall, ANL 11, 53–140; ANF 3, 17–55. — A. Souter, *loc. cit.* — T. Ɽ
Glover, *loc. cit.* 3–227. — E. J. Daly, FC 10 (1950) 7–126. — *French:* J. P. Waltzin
et A. Severyns, *loc. cit.* — *Italian:* J. Giordani, Tertulliano, L'Apologetico, traᵈ
Brescia, 1935. — *Spanish:* P. Manero, Tertuliano, Apología contra los gentileⁿ
Zaragoza, 1644. — G. Prado, El Apologetico de Tertuliano (Colección Excelsa 7)
Madrid, 1943. — *German:* H. Kellner–G. Esser, BKV² 24 (1915). — C. Beckeⁱ
loc. cit. — *Dutch:* P. C. IJsseling, Tertullianus, Verdediging der Christeneⁿ
Nijkerk, 1909; *idem,* Tertullianus' Apologeticum, vertaald en toegelicht (Klassiekeⁿ
der Kerk). Amsterdam, 1947. — Chr. Mohrmann, Tertullianus, Apologeticum, eⁿ
andere geschriften uit Tertullianus' voormontanistischen tijd, ingeleid, vertaaↆ

n toegelicht (MC 1, 3). Utrecht-Brussels, 1951, 1–130. — *Polish:* J. SAJDAK, Apologetyk, z laciny tlumaczyl dal wstep i ojasbienia. Poznan, 1947. — *Modern Greek:* J. D. FRANCOULES, 'Ο άπολογητικός. Athens, 1936.

Text Critical Studies: J. P. WALTZING, Les trois principaux manuscrits de L'Apologétique de Tertullien: Musée Belge 16 (1912) 181–240. — C. CALLEWAERT, Le Codex Fuldensis, le meilleur manuscrit de l'Apologeticum de Tertullien: RHL 7 (1902) 322–353. — H. BÖHNER, Eine bisher nicht beachtete Hs. des Apologeticus Tertulians: ThLZ (1903) 645. — A. SOUTER, A Tenth-Century Fragment of Tertullian's Apology: JThSt 8 (1907) 297–300. — H. SCHROERS, Zur Textgeschichte und Erklärung von Tertullians Apologeticum (TU 60, 4). Leipzig, 1913. — G. RAUSCHEN, Prof. Heinrich Schroers und meine Ausgabe von Tertullians Apologeticum. Bonn, 1914. — C. CALLEWAERT, La valeur du Codex Fuldensis pour le rétablissement du texte de l'Apologeticum de Tertullien. Louvain, 1914. — J. P. WALTZING, Étude sur le Codex Fuldensis de l'Apologétique de Tertullien (Bibliothèque de la Fac. de philos. et lettr. de l'univ. de Liège, fasc. 21). Liège-Paris, 1914/17. — E. LÖFSTEDT, Tertulians Apologeticum textkritisch untersucht. Lund, 1915. — S. COLOMBO, Animadversiones criticae quaedam ad Tertulliani Apologetici textum: Didaskaleion 4 (1915) 55–96; *idem*, Per la critica del testo dell' Apologetico Tertullianeo: Didaskaleion 5 (1916) 1–36. — G. THÖRNELL, Kritische Studien zu Tertullians Apologeticum: Eranos 16 (1916) 82–161. — C. WEYMAN, Zu Tertullians Apologeticum: Hermes (1916) 309. — L. WOHLEB, Zu Tertullians Apologeticum: PhW 36 (1916) 539–544, 603–608, 636–640, 848–856, 1537–1538, 1568–1570, 1635–1639. — E. LÖFSTEDT, Kritische Bemerkungen zu Tertullians Apologeticum. Lund-Leipzig, 1918. — G. RAUSCHEN, Emendationes et adnotationes ad Tertulliani Apologeticum (FP 12). Bonn, 1919. — J. SCHRIJNEN, Ad Tertulliani Apologetici cap. VII, 11, 12: Mnem (1920) 260–263. — A. SOUTER, A Supposed Fragment of the Lost Codex Fuldensis of Tertullian: JThSt 22 (1921) 163 ff. — J. P. WALTZING, Pour l'étude de Tertullien. Introduction à l'Apologétique: Musée Belge (1921) 7–28. — A. MANCINI, Per la tradizione dell' Apologetico di Tertulliano: RFIC NS 4 (1926) 87–90. — G. THÖRNELL, Studia Tertullianea IV. De Tertulliani Apologetico bis edito. Uppsala, 1926. — G. PASQUALI, Per la storia del testo dell' Apologetico di Tertulliano: Studi Italiani di Filologia Classica 7 (1929) 13–57. — H. EMONDS, Zweite Auflage im Altertum. Leipzig, 1941, 137–187. — O. TESCARI, In Tertulliani Apologeticum 46, 14 adnotatiuncula: RAC 23/24 (1947/48) 349–352. — C. BECKER, *loc. cit.*, 285—316.

Other Studies: J. E. B. MAYOR, Tertullian's Apology: Journal of Philology 21 (1893) 259–295. — F. X. FUNK, Tertullien et l'Agape (Apol. 39): RHE (1904) 5–15; (1906) 2–25. — P. HENEN, L'Apologétique de Tertullien et le Thesaurus linguae latinae: Revue de l'Instruction publique en Belgique (1911) 1–9. — F. DI CAPUA, Tertulliano, Apologet. 47, 6: Didaskaleion 3 (1914) 65–68. — E. T. MERRILL, Tertullian on Pliny's persecution of Christians: AJPh (1918) 124–135. — A. VITALE, La storia della versione dei Settanta e l'antichità della Bibbia nell' Apologetico di Tertulliano: Musée Belge (1922) 62–72. — F. J. DÖLGER, Sonne und Sonnenstrahl als Gleichnis in der Logostheologie des christlichen Altertums (Apol. 21): AC 1 (1929) 271–290; *idem*, Vorbeter und Zeremoniar. Zu 'monitor' und 'praeire'. Ein Beitrag zu Tertullians Apologeticum 30, 4: AC 2 (1930) 241–251. — M. BALSAMO, Paralleli non ancora osservati tra l'ad Nationes e l'Apologetico di Tertulliano: Didaskaleion NS 8 (1930)

28–34. — J. W. Ph. Borleffs, Tertullian und Lukrez (Apol. 8): PhW 52 (1932) 350–352. — J. Carcopino, Survivances par substitution des sacrifices d'enfants dan l'Afrique romaine: RHR 106 (1932) 592–599. — F. J. Dölger, 'Sacramentum infanticidii': AC 4 (1934) 118–200. — G. Thörnell, Apol. 12, 8: Eranos (1934) 153–155; *idem*, Anulus pronubus. Der eiserne und der goldene Verlobungsring nach Plinius und Tertullianus (Apol. 6, 4, 6): AC 5 (1936) 188–200. — H. Emonds, Die Oligarchenrevolte zu Megara im Jahre 375 und der Philosoph Ichthyas bei Tertullian, Apol. 46, 16: RhM (1937) 180–191. — A. Bourgery, Le problème de l'Institutum Neronianum (invention de Tertullien): Latomus (1938) 106–111. — E. Bickel Fiunt, non nascuntur christiani (Apol. 18): Pisciculi, Festschrift für F. J. Dölger Münster, 1939, 54–61. — F. J. Dölger, Wenn der Tiber in die Stadtmauern steigt. . dann heißt es: Die Christen vor die Löwen (Apol. 40, 2): AC 6 (1940) 157–159. — L. Alfonsi, Tertulliano, Apol. 46, 15: Hommages J. Bidez-F. Cumont. Brussels 1949, 5–11. — J. Beran, De ordine missae secundum Tertulliani 'Apologeticum' Miscellanea L. C. Mohlberg 2. Rome, 1949, 7–32. — E. Griffe, Le christianisme en face de l'État romain. La base juridique des persécutions (chez Tertullien): BLE (1949) 129–145. — J. Zeiller, L'égalité et l'arbitraire dans les persécutions contre les chrétiens: AB 67 (1949) 49–54. — S. Oswiecimski, Ad litteras Romanas symbolae duae (Apol. 15): Eos 44, 1 (1950) 111–122. — R. M. Grant, Two Notes on Tertullian (Apol. 47, 6–7): VC 5 (1951) 6–7. — J. W. Ph. Borleffs, Institutum Neronianum: VC 6 (1952) 129–145.

3. *The Testimony of the Soul*

It was a commonplace of Hellenistic philosophers like Poseidonius, Philo, Chrysippus, Seneca and others to derive the knowledge of God from macrocosm and microcosm side by side, from the great universe and the little world of the human soul. Tertullian follows this example. In ch. 17 of his *Apologeticum* he writes:

> Would you have the proof from the works of his hands, so numerous and so great, which both contain you and sustain you, which minister at once to your enjoyment, and strike you with awe; or would you rather have it from the testimony of the soul itself? Though under the oppressive bondage of the body, though led astray by depraving customs, though enervated by lusts and passions, though in slavery to false gods, yet, whenever the soul comes to itself, as out of a surfeit, or a sleep, or a sickness, and attains something of its natural soundness, it speaks of God; using no other word, because this is the peculiar name of the true God. 'Great God!' 'Good God!' 'Which may God give!' are the words on every lip. It bears witness, too, that God is judge, exclaiming, 'God sees,' and 'I commend myself to

God,' and 'God will repay me.' O noble testimony of the soul by its very nature Christian! (17, 4–6 ANF).

This argument of the *Apologeticum*, the *testimonium animae naturaliter Christianae*, was expanded and treated in a special work entitled *The Testimony of the Soul* (*De testimonio animae*), written in the same year as the *Apologeticum* A.D. 197. The apologetic character of this treatise consisting of only six chapters is evident from the author's endeavour to use the soul not ruined by 'education' as a witness for the existence and attributes of God, for the life after death, and for the reward and punishment in the world beyond the grave. There is no need of philosophical reflexion and instruction, all these truths are present to the soul. Nature is the teacher of the soul to the effect that she is an image of God:

I call in a new testimony, yea, one which is better known than all literature, more discussed than all doctrine, more public than all publications, greater than the whole man— I mean all which is man's. Stand forth, O soul, whether you are divine and eternal substance, as most philosophers believe—if it be so, you will be the less likely to lie,—or whether you are the very opposite of divine, because indeed a mortal thing, as Epicurus alone thinks—in that case there will be the less temptation for you to speak falsely in this case: whether you are received from heaven, or sprung from earth, whether you are formed of numbers or of atoms; whether your existence begins with that of the body, or you are put into it at a later stage; from whatever source, and in what-ever way, you make man a rational being, in the highest degree capable of thought and knowledge—stand forth and give your witness. But I call you not as when, fashioned in schools, trained in libraries, fed in Attic academies and porticoes, you belch wisdom. I address you simple, rude, uncultured and untaught, such as they have you who have you only; that very thing of the road, the street, the work-shop, wholly. I want your inexperience, since in your small experience no one feels any confidence. I demand of you the things you bring with you into man, which you know either from yourself or from your author, whoever he may be (1 ANF).

In contrast to the Greek apologists Tertullian emphasizes the uselessness of recourse to philosophy. Nature pure and simple is a better witness to the truth than all learning. His expression *anima naturaliter christiana* does not designate any knowledge of God *a priori* since he states explicitly: 'You [the soul] are not, as I well know, Christian; for a man becomes a Christian, he is not born one' (ch. 1). The famous phrase means rather the spontaneous awareness of the Creator as derived immediately from the universe and from experience and as evidenced in the daily exclamations of the people. Thus common sense tells us of the existence of a Supreme Being. Critics differ in their judgment of this short treatise; to some it seems feeble, to others most precious — of all Tertullian's works, the deepest and possessing the widest appeal. The proofs for the existence of God may have their shortcomings, but the psychological demonstration wins conviction even from the modern reader.

Editions: A. Reifferscheid-G. Wissowa, CSEL 20 (1890) 134–143. — W. A. J. C. Scholte, Q.S.Fl. Tertulliani libellum De testimonio animae praefatione, translatione, adnot. instructum ed. (Diss. Utrecht). Amsterdam, 1934.

Translations: English: C. Dodgson, Library of Fathers 10. Oxford, 1842, 131–142 — S. Thelwall, ANL 11, 36–45; ANF 3, 175–179. — T. H. Bindley, On the Testimony of the Soul (SPCK). London, 1914. — R. Arbesmann, Tertullian, The Testimony of the Soul: FC 10 (1950) 131–143. — *German:* H. Kellner, BKV² (1912) — M. Haidenthaller, Tertullians zweites Buch Ad nationes und De testimonio animae. Paderborn, 1942. — *Dutch:* H. U. Meyboom, Over het getuigeni van de ziel (Oudchristl. geschriften, dl. 46). Leiden, 1930. — W. A. J. C. Scholte *loc. cit.* — *Spanish:* J. Pellicer de Ossau, Barcelona, 1639.

Studies: A. Miodoński, Tertullian de testimonio animae: Eos 5 (1904) 117. — L. Fuetscher, Die natürliche Gotteserkenntnis bei Tertullian: ZkTh (1927) 1–34, 217–251. — G. Lazzati, Il De natura deorum fonte del De testimonio animae di Tertulliano?: Atene e Roma (1939) 153–166. — G. Quispel, 'Anima naturaliter christiana': Eranos Jahrbuch 18 (1950) 173; *idem,* 'Anima naturaliter christiana': Latomus 10 (1951) 163–169; *idem,* Het getuigenis der ziel bij Tertullianus, Leiden, 1952.

4. *To Scapula*

'It is a fundamental human right, a privilege of nature, that every man should worship according to his own convictions: one man's religion neither harms nor helps another man. It... is certainly no part of religion to compel religion' (2). This manifesto for the freedom of worship is found in the open letter which

Tertullian addressed to Scapula, Proconsul (211–213) of Africa, who began to persecute the Christians and went so far as to expose them to wild beasts and burn them to death. It seems that Tertullian wrote it in 212, because he refers to the total eclipse of August 14, 212, as a sign of divine anger. Divided into five chapters, this courageous appeal stresses in the introduction (ch. 1) that it is not self-interest nor alarm about the persecutions, which causes the author to write, but the Christian's love of his enemies and concern for them. It is unreasonable and against the fundamental right of freedom of conscience to compel Christians to sacrifice. They are enemies to none, least of all to the Emperor of Rome, whom they know to be appointed by their God and so cannot but love and honor, and whose well-being, moreover, they must needs desire, together with that of the empire over which he reigns so long as the world shall stand—for so long as that shall Rome continue.

To the emperor, therefore, we render such reverential homage, as is lawful for us and good for him; regarding him as the human being next to God who from God has received all his power and is less than God alone... We therefore sacrifice for the emperor's safety, but to our God and his, and after the manner God has enjoined, in simple prayer. For God, Creator of the universe, has no need of odors and of blood. These things are the food of devils (ch. 2 ANF).

However, it cannot but distress the Christians that no State shall bear unpunished the guilt of shedding Christian blood. There are already signs of God's impending wrath. Here Tertullian anticipates a topic which Lactantius elaborated in his *The Deaths of the Persecutors* by pointing to the deaths of some provincial rulers, who in their last hours had painful memories of their sin in persecuting the followers of Christ (ch. 3). The fourth chapter opens with the striking warning: 'We who are without fear are not seeking to frighten you, but we would save all men if possible by warning them not to fight with God' (μὴ θεο-μαχεῖν, quoted in Greek from Acts 5, 39). The Proconsuls can always perform the duties of their charge and yet remember the claims of humanity. Scapula would act against his own instructions by wringing a denial from people who confess to be Christians. The last chapter warns him to spare himself, if not the poor Christians, to spare Carthage, if not himself. Cruelty will not succeed, it will only increase the number of the faithful:

> We have no master but God. He is before you, and cannot be hidden from you, but to Him you can do no injury. But those whom you regard as masters are only men, and one day they themselves must die. Yet this community will be undying, for be assured that just in the time of its seeming overthrow it is built up into greater power. For all who witness the noble patience of its martyrs, as struck with misgivings, are inflamed with desire to examine into the matter in question; and as soon as they come to know the truth, they straightway enroll themselves its disciples (5 ANF).

Edition: T. BINDLEY, Tertulliani De praescriptione haereticorum, Ad martyras, Ad Scapulam. Oxford, 1893.

Translations: English: C. DODGSON, Library of Fathers 10. Oxford, 1842, 142–149. — S. THELWALL, ANL 11; ANF 3, 105–108. — R. ARBESMANN, FC 10 (1950) 151–161. — *German:* H. KELLNER-G. ESSER, BKV² 24 (1915). — *Dutch:* H. U. MEYBOOM, Aan Scapula (Oudchristel. geschriften, dl. 43). Leiden, 1930. — *Spanish:* J. PELLICER DE OSSAU, Barcelona, 1639.

Studies: J. SCHMIDT, Ein Beitrag zur Chronologie der Schriften Tertullians und der Prokonsuln von Afrika: RhM NF 46 (1891) 77–98. — F. J. DÖLGER, Juppiter omnipotens (Ad Scap. 4): AC 6 (1940) 70–71. — A. QUACQUARELLI, La persecuzione secondo Tertulliano: Greg 31 (1950) 562–589.

5. *Against the Jews (Adversus Judaeos)*

This work was occasioned by a dispute held between a Christian and a Jewish proselyte; it lasted all day until evening, with the result that 'truth began to be overcast by a sort of cloud.' 'It was therefore our pleasure that that which, owing to the confused noise of disputation, could be less fully elucidated point by point, should be more carefully looked into, and that the pen should determine, for reading purposes, the questions handled' (1 ANF). The first eight chapters have for their purpose to show that, since Israel has departed from the Lord and rejected his grace, the Old Testament no longer has any force but must be interpreted spiritually. For this reason were the gentiles called (ch. 1). Law existed prior to Moses—that which God had given to all nations. The primordial statute was enacted for Adam and Eve in paradise and this was the womb of all positive divine precepts. Moreover, the code of the Jews, written on tablets of stone, came immeasurably after that which was unwritten, the law of nature. Consequently, the former is not necessary for salvation; circumcision (ch. 3), observance of the Sabbath (ch. 4), the ancient sacrifices (ch. 5), have been abolished and the ordinance of an eye for an eye has yielded to the rule of love. The giver of this new covenant, the priest of the new sacrifice, the observer of the eternal Sabbath has already appeared (ch. 6)—Christ, foretold by the prophets as the everlasting king of a universal kingdom (ch. 7). The time of His birth, of His passion and of Jerusalem's destruction was predicted by Daniel (ch. 8). The main source of this section is Justin's *Dialogue with Trypho.*

Chapters 9–14 continue with the proof that the Messianic oracles were fulfilled in Our Saviour. However, they are certainly spurious, merely an excerpt from Book III of Tertullian's own *Adversus Marcionem,* and represent a clumsy attempt to complete the work. The compiler has been identified by G. Quispel with the *frater* mentioned in *Adv. Marcionem* 1, 1, who later on apostatized; Tertullian had entrusted the second draught of *Adv. Marcionem* to him but had never gotten it back.

Edition: A. KROYMANN, CSEL 70 (1942) 251–331.

Translations: English: S. THELWALL, ANL 18, 201–258; ANF 3, 151–173. — *German:* H. KELLNER, BKV² 7 (1912). — *Dutch:* H. U. MEYBOOM, Tegen de Joden (Oudchristelijke geschriften, dl. 42). Leiden, 1924.

Studies: E. NÖLDECHEN, Tertullians Gegen die Juden auf Einheit, Echtheit, Entstehung geprüft (TU 12, 2). Leipzig, 1894. — J. M. EINSIEDLER, De Tertulliani adversus Judaeos libro. Diss. Würzburg, 1897. — M. AKERMANN, Über die Echtheit der letzteren Hälfte von Tertullians Adversus Judaeos. Lund, 1918. — H. KOCH, ThStKr (1929) 462–469. — A. L. WILLIAMS, Adversus Judaeos. A Bird's-Eye View of Christian 'Apologiae' until the Renaissance. Cambridge, 1935, 43–52. — L. BROU, Un passage de Tertullien (Adv. Judaeos 9) conservé dans un répons pour la fête de St. Jean-Baptiste: EL 52 (1938) 237–257. — B. CAPELLE, Bull. de théol. anc. et méd. 4 (1943) 8 f. — G. QUISPEL, De Bronnen van Tertullianus' Adversus Marcionem. Leiden, 1943, 61–79. Cf. J. BORLEFFS, VC 1 (1947) 195 f. — M. SIMON, Verus Israel. Étude sur les relations entre chrétiens et Juifs dans l'empire romain. Paris, 1948.

3. Controversial Treatises

1. The Prescription of Heretics

The treatise *De praescriptione haereticorum* exhibits more than all his other works Tertullian's profound knowledge of Roman Law.

It was supposed to finish the controversy between Catholics and
all heretics once and forever by advancing the technical argument
of the *praescriptio*, meaning a juridical objection with which the
defendant wishes to bar the suit in the form in which the plaintiff
enters it. This leads to a complete rejection of the case. It receives
its name from the fact that such an objection had to be made in
writing before (*prae-scribere*) the *intentio* in the *formula* of procedure.
The bone of contention between the Church and her antagonists
is the Scriptures. According to Tertullian, the opponent cannot
even use these in the discussion because there is a *praescriptio* that
excludes any such argument: he cannot employ the Bible for the
simple reason that the Bible is not his:

> We are therefore come to [the gist of] our position; for at
> this point we are aiming, and for this we were preparing in
> the preamble of our address which we have just completed
> [ch. 1–14]—so that we may now join issue on the contention
> to which our adversaries challenge us. They put forward the
> Scriptures, and by this insolence of theirs they at once influ-
> ence some. In the encounter itself, however, they weary the
> strong, they catch the weak, and dismiss waverers with a
> doubt. Accordingly, we oppose to them this step above all
> others, of not admitting them to any discussion of the
> Scriptures.
>
> If in these lie their resources, before they can use them, it
> ought to be clearly seen to whom belongs the possession of
> the Scriptures, that none may be admitted to the use thereof
> who has no title at all to the privilege (15 ANF).

The Apostle has sanctioned (1 Tim. 6, 3, 4; Tit. 3, 10) this
exclusion of heretics from the use of the Scriptures (ch. 16),
because they do not use, they only abuse them (ch. 17). Great
danger ensues to the weak in faith from any discussion out of
Holy Writ with such people and conviction never comes to the
dissident through such a process (ch. 18). The Bible belongs only
to those who have the rule of faith and the question is: 'From
what and through whom and when, and to whom, has been handed
down that rule, by which men become Christians? For wherever it shall be manifest that the true Christian rule and faith
shall be, there will likewise be the true Scriptures and expositions
thereof, and all the Christian traditions' (ch. 20 ANF). It is in ch.

21, as J. Stirnimann has shown, that Tertullian submits the two *praescriptiones* that deprive all heretical systems of their basis.

The first *praescriptio* is:

Christ sent the apostles as the preachers of the gospel and for this reason no others than those whom Christ appointed ought to be received as its preachers.

The second *praescriptio* is:

The apostles founded the churches, declared the gospel to them and empowered them to declare it to others. For this reason 'what that was which they preached—in other words, what it was which Christ revealed to them—can, as I must here likewise prescribe, properly be proved in no other way than by those very churches which the apostles founded in person... Whereas all doctrine must be prejudged as false which savours of contrariety to the truth of the churches and apostles of Christ and God' (ch. 21 ANF).

It still remains to be demonstrated that the Catholic doctrine has its origin in the tradition of the apostles. And here is the proof: 'We hold communion with the apostolic churches because our doctrine is in no respect different from theirs. This is our witness of truth' (ch. 21). These facts and their consequences constitute such a complete refutation of all heretical sects that strictly speaking it is not necessary to pay any further attention to the different controversies just as in a suit the plaintiff is rejected by the *praescriptio* of the defendant and any subsequent consideration of his plea is out of the question. However, Tertullian declares himself ready 'to give way for a while to the opposite side' (22) and thus he answers the objections, first, that the apostles were not safe transmitters of the truth in so far as they were ignorant of certain things or did not deliver all they knew to all (ch. 22–26), and secondly, that the Churches have been unfaithful in handing down the deposit of faith (ch. 27). It is presumptuous to believe that revelation had to wait for some heretic to set it free and that during the interval the gospel was corrupted. In all cases right must precede wrong and the earlier existence of the Church's doctrine is a mark of its purity (ch. 29). Christ's parable puts the sowing of the good seed before the useless tares, which indicates that that which was first delivered is of the Lord and is true while that is strange and false which was afterwards introduced. The principle of the priority of truth (*principalitas veritatis*) and the comparative lateness of falsehood (*posteritas mendacitatis*) stands against all heresies (ch. 31). The Church has never tolerated any alteration of the Scriptures, whereas the opposition has tampered with and mutilated Holy Writ (ch. 38). But little difference exists between dissent in matters of faith and rank heathenism; both pull down and destroy, both are born of Satan (ch. 40). The conduct of heretics is infamous, because they have lost all fear of God (ch. 41–44). A statement in the conclusion (ch. 44) implies that *De praescriptione* forms only a sort of general introduction to be followed in the near future by distinct treatments of the various errors: 'On the present occasion, indeed, our treatise has rather taken up a general position against heresies [showing that they must] all be refuted on definite, equitable, and necessary *praescriptiones*, without any comparison with the Scriptures. For the rest, if God in His grace permit, we shall prepare answers to certain of these heresies in separate treatises' (ANF).

De praescriptione haereticorum is by far the most finished, the most characteristic, and the most valuable of Tertullian's writings. The main ideas of this treatise have won for it enduring timeliness and admiration. Although it can be assigned no definite date, it was quite obviously written when the author was still on the best of terms with the Catholic Church, probably about the year 200 A.D.

A catalogue of thirty-two heresies added at the end of *De praescriptione* (ch. 46–53) is usually regarded as a mere summary of the *Syntagma* of Hippolytus. E. Schwartz is of the opinion, however, that this appendix represents an anti-Origenistic treatise, composed in Greek by Pope Zephyrinus or one of his priests and translated into Latin by Victorinus of Pettau (cf. below, p. 412).

Editions: A. KROYMANN, CSEL 70 (1942) 1–58. — E. PREUSCHEN, 2nd ed. Freiburg, 1914. — J. MARTIN, FP 4. Bonn, 1930. — J. N. BAKHUIZEN VAN DEN BRINK, Tertullianus Libri de praescriptione haereticorum, Adv. Praxean (Scriptores christiani primaevi 2). The Hague, 1946.

Translations: English: J. BETTY, Tertullian's Prescription against Heretics. Oxford, 1722. — C. DODGSON, Library of Fathers 10. Oxford, 1842, 434–480. — P. HOLMES, ANL 15, 1–54; ANF 3, 243–265. — T. H. BINDLEY, On the Testimony of the Soul and On the 'Prescription' of Heretics (SPCK). London-New York, 1914. — *German:* H. KELLNER-G. ESSER, BKV² 24 (1915). — *Dutch:* H. U. MEYBOOM, Tertullianus, De protestrede tegen de ketters (Oudchr. geschriften, dl. 43). Leiden, 1930. — CHR.

MOHRMANN, Het principiële voorbehoud tegen de ketters (Tert. Apol. etc): MC 1, 3. Utrecht, 1951, 131-182. — Italian: G. MAZZONI, De praescriptione haereticorum (I Classici cristiani). Siena, 1929. — J. GIORDANI, La prescrizione contro gli eretici. Brescia, 1935. — C. F. SAVIO, Della prescrizione degli eretici. Varallo, 1944.

Studies: P. DE LABRIOLLE, L'argument de préscription: RHL 11 (1908) 408-428, 497-514. — P. U. HÜNTEMANN, De praescriptione haereticorum libri analysis. Quaracchi, 1924. — H. KOCH, Tertullianisches: ThStKr (1929) 471-474. — F. J. DÖLGER, Die Sphragis der Mithrasmysterien. Eine Erläuterung zu Tertullian De praescriptione 40: AC 1 (1929) 88-91; idem, Sacramentum militiae (De praescr. 40): AC 2 (1930) 268-280. — F. CUMONT, La fin du monde selon les mages occidentaux: RHR 103 (1931) 31 ff. — A. D'ALÈS, Tertullianea (De praescr. 9, 1): RSR (1935) 593 ff. — A. VELLICO, La rivelazione e le sue fonti nel De praescriptione haereticorum di Tertulliano. Rome, 1935. — L. DE VITTE, L'argument de préscription et Tertullien (Collectanea Mechliniensia 3). Malines, 1936. — G. ZIMMERMANN, Die hermeneutischen Prinzipien Tertullians. Diss. Leipzig, 1937. — J. L. ALLIE, Nature de la préscription ou des préscriptions dans le De Praescriptione: Revue Univ. Ottawa 6 (1937) 211-225; 7 (1938) 16-28. — W. C. VAN UNNIK, De la règle d'or μήτε προσθεῖναι μήτε ἀφελεῖν dans l'histoire du canon (De praescr. 38): VC 3 (1949) 1-36. — J. STIRNIMANN, Die Praescriptio Tertullians im Lichte des römischen Rechtes und der Theologie (Paradosis 3). Fribourg, 1949.

2. Against Marcion

Adversus Marcionem is by far the longest of Tertullian's works and one of those 'separate treatises' against certain heresies which he promised at the end of his *De praescriptione*. It is of great importance because it forms the main source for our knowledge of the heresy of Marcion (cf. vol. I, pp. 268-272). Altogether it consists of five books, of which the first refutes the dualism existing according to Marcion between the God of the Old and the God of the New Testament and proves that the very concept of the Deity is incompatible with such a contrast. 'The Christian verity has distinctly declared this principle, 'God is not, if He is not one,' because we more properly believe that that has no existence which is not as it ought to be... That being which is the great Supreme, must needs be unique, by having no equal, and so not ceasing to be the great Supreme' (1, 3). Thus the Maker of the world is identical with the good God, as the second book demonstrates. The third deals with the Christology of Marcion. Against his claim that the Messias foretold under the Old Dispensation had not yet come, Tertullian shows that the Christ who appeared here on earth is no other than the Saviour proclaimed by the prophets, and sent by the Creator. The fourth and

fifth parts provide a critical commentary on the New Testament
of Marcion, proving that no contradictions exist between the Old
and the New Testament and that even the texts of Marcion's own
New Testament refute his heretical doctrines. Thus the fourth
section deals with his *Gospel* and the fifth with his *Apostolicon*.

The treatise had an interesting history, even in Tertullian's
times, as the opening words reveal:

> Whatever in times past we have wrought in opposition to
> Marcion, is from the present moment no longer to be ac-
> counted of. It is a new work which we are undertaking in
> lieu of the old one. My original tract, as too hurriedly
> composed, I had subsequently superseded by a fuller treatise.
> This latter I lost, before it was completely published, by the
> fraud of a person who was then a brother, but became after-
> wards an apostate. He, as it happened, had transcribed a
> portion of it, full of mistakes, and then published it. The
> necessity thus arose for an amended work; and the occasion
> of the new edition induced me to make a considerable
> addition to the treatise. This present text, therefore, of my
> work—which is the third as superseding the second, but
> henceforward to be considered the first instead of the third—
> renders a preface necessary to this issue of the tract itself that
> no reader may be perplexed, if he should by chance fall in
> with the various forms of it which are scattered about (1, 1
> ANF).

The treatise in its present form represents the third edition, the
first having been too superficial and the second stolen. Tertullian
states that in the last revision he made additions, which, according to J. Quispel, consist of Books IV and V. The work in its
earliest appearance probably comprised only Book I; the reissue,
supposed to treat the subject at greater length, seems to have
added Book II; the final redaction, in which the whole was
recast, expanded Book I into I and II and added Books IV and V.

Book III uses Justin's *Dialogue with Trypho* as the main source
and also Irenaeus' *Against the Heresies*. For Book IV Tertullian
employed Marcion's *Antitheses*, his edition of the New Testament,
and alongside it for comparison a Catholic text of it. Consequently, this section is very important for the history of the
biblical text. Harnack maintained that Tertullian had Latin

translations at his disposal, but the explicit citation (4, 9) of Greek terms from the *Antitheses* conclusively refutes this view at least for that work. J. Quispel goes farther and demonstrates that the biblical quotations, whether Marcionite or Catholic, were turned by Tertullian himself and do not depend on some previously existing version; the same holds true equally for Book V, dealing with Marcion's edition of St. Paul's Epistles. This does not exclude the possibility that Tertullian knew of an existing Catholic translation of the Bible and consulted it occasionally but his texts differ considerably from Cyprian's as well as the Vulgate.

The author supplies us with evidence (1, 15) that Book I was written in the fifteenth year of the Emperor Severus, i.e. 207 A.D. The others followed at short intervals except for the last, composed after *De resurrectione*, to which it refers (5, 10). Thus we arrive at the date of ca. 212, which fits in with the Montanism of certain passages (1, 29; 3, 24; 4, 22).

From Eusebius (*Hist. eccl.* 4, 24) we know that Theophilus of Antioch wrote an *Against Marcion* also, which has unfortunately been lost. Tertullian may have drawn on this work for Book II.

Edition: A. KROYMANN, CSEL 47 (1906) 290–650.

Translations: English: P. HOLMES, ANL 7; ANF 3, 271–474. — *Dutch:* H. U. MEYBOOM, Tegen Marcion (Oudchristel. geschriften, dl. 40/41). Leiden, 1927.

Studies: H. RÖNSCH, Das Neue Testament Tertullians. Leipzig. — A. BILL, Zur Erklärung und Textkritik des 1. Buches Tertullians adversus Marcionem (TU 38, 2). Leipzig, 1911. — P. DE LABRIOLLE, Tertullien a-t-il connu une version latine de la Bible?: Bull. d'ancienne Littérat. et d'Archéol. chrét. (1914) 210–213. — A. HARNACK, Tertullians Bibliothek christlicher Schriften: SAB (1914) 303–334. — F. H. COLSON, Tertullian on Luke VI. Two examples of literary and rhetorical criticism in the Fathers: JThSt 25 (1924) 364–377. — P. CORSSEN, Tertulliani Adversus Marcionem in librum quartum animadversiones: Mnem 51 (1923) 242–261, 390–411; 52 (1924) 225–249. — E. BOSSHARDT, Essai sur l'originalité et la probité de Tertullien dans son traité contre Marcion. Thèse. Fribourg, 1921. Cf. VON SODEN, ZKG (1924) 366. — A. HARNACK, Marcion. Das Evangelium vom fremden Gott. 2nd ed. (TU 45). Leipzig, 1924. — H. v. SODEN, Der lateinische Paulustext bei Marcion und Tertullian: Festgabe A. Jülicher. Tübingen, 1927, 229–281. — G. J. D. AALDERS, Tertullianus' citaten uit de Evangeliën en de oudlatijnsche Bijbelvertalingen. Amsterdam, 1932. — J. NAUMANN, Das Problem des Bösen in Tertullians zweitem Buch gegen Marcion: ZkTh 58 (1934) 311–363, 533–551. — A. D'ALÈS, Tertullien, IV Ad. Marcionem 21: RSR 26 (1936) 99–100, 585–586; 27 (1937) 228–230. — G. J. D. AALDERS, Tertullian's Quotations from St. Luke: Mnem 5 (1937) 241–282. — G. PFLIGERSDORFFER, De Tertulliani adversus Marcionem libri tertii argumento sententiarumque connexu. Diss. Vienna, 1939. — M. RIST, Pseudographic Refutations of

Marcionism: JR 22 (1942) 39–62. — J. H. Waszink, Mnem 3 (1935/36) 172; 11 (1943) 72–74; 13 (1947) 127–129. — G. Quispel, De bronnen van Tertullianus' Adversus Marcionem. Leiden, 1943; idem, Ad Tertulliani Adversus Marcionem librum observatio: VC 1 (1947) 42. — M. C. Tenney, The Quotations from Luke in Tertullian as Related to the Texts of the Second and Third Centuries: HS 56/57 (1947) 258–260. — R. M. Grant, Two Notes on Tertullian: VC 5 (1951) 114 f. (Adv. Marc. 1, 13). — A. J. B. Higgins, The Latin Text of Luke in Marcion and Tertullian: VC 5 (1951) 1–42. — M. Stengel, Zum Wortschatz der nt. Vulgata: VC 6 (1952) 20–27.

3. Against Hermogenes

Tertullian was not the first to write against the painter and Gnostic Hermogenes of Carthage, being preceded, according to Eusebius (*Hist. eccl.* 4, 24) by Theophilus of Antioch's *Against the Heresy of Hermogenes*. The latter, though no longer extant, was probably known to our author and served him as a source. Hermogenes thought matter eternal, making it equal to God and positing two Gods. According to Tertullian (1, 1) he derived his doctrine from pagan philosophy: 'Turning away from Christians to the philosophers, from the Church to the Academy and the Porch, he learned there from the Stoics how to place Matter on the same level with the Lord, just as if it too had existed ever both unborn and unmade, having no beginning at all nor end, out of which, according to him, the Lord afterwards created all things' (ANF). Tertullian refutes him in 45 chapters and in so doing gives a brilliant defense of the Christian teaching on creation. He argues (ch. 1–18) that the very concept of the deity cannot admit of the eternity of matter and, after a critical examination of Hermogenes' interpretation of Scripture (ch. 19–34), exposes the contradictions in his speculations regarding the essence and divine attributes of eternal matter (ch. 35–45). The opening words of the treatise refer to *De praescriptione*. Thus it was composed after A.D. 200. In his *De anima* Tertullian indicates several times that he published another work against Hermogenes about the origin of the soul, *De censu animae*, which is not preserved.

Edition: A. Kroymann, CSEL 47 (1906) 126–176.

Translations: English: P. Holmes, ANL 15, 55–118; ANF 3, 477–502. — *Dutch:* H. U. Meyboom, Tegen Hermogenes (Oudchristel. geschriften, dl. 43). Leiden, 1930.

Studies: E. Heintzel, Hermogenes, der Hauptvertreter des philosophischen Dualismus in der alten Kirche. Berlin, 1902. — W. C. van Unnik, De la règle d'or μήτε προσθεῖναι μήτε ἀφελεῖν dans l'histoire du canon: VC 3 (1949) 1–36.

4. *Against the Valentinians*

Adversus Valentinianos, a caustic comment on the tenets of that Gnostic sect, depends closely for its substance and arrangement on Book I of Irenaeus' *Adversus haereses*, but also owes something to Justin Martyr, Miltiades and Proculus:

> Nor shall we hear it said of us from any quarter, that we have of our own mind fashioned our own materials, since these have been already produced, both in respect of the opinions and their refutations, in carefully written volumes, by so many eminently holy and excellent men, not only those who have lived before us, but those also who were contemporary with the heresiarchs themselves: for instance Justin, philosopher and martyr; Miltiades, the sophist of the churches; Irenaeus, that very exact inquirer into all doctrines; our own Proculus, the model of chaste old age and Christian eloquence. All these it would be my desire closely to follow in every work of faith, even as in this particular one (5 ANF).

Most probably Tertullian has in mind lost anti-heretical writings of Justin, Miltiades and Proculus. The entire treatise consists of 39 chapters, of which the introduction (ch. 1–6) gives the impression of greater independence. Here the author exposes the esoteric character of the Valentinians, comparing the old Eleusinian mysteries and finding in both the same pride of the initiated and the same multiplication of sects. He refers (ch. 16) to his treatise *Against Hermogenes* and, indicating his intention later to write a more considerable work than the present one on the same subject, he calls this 'the very first weapon with which we are armed for our encounter' (ch. 3) and speaks of it as 'this little work wherein we merely undertake to propound this mystery' (ch. 6). 'I must postpone,' he says, 'all discussion and be content at present with the mere exposition... Let the reader regard it as the skirmish before the battle' (*ibid.*).

Edition: A. KROYMANN, CSEL 47 (1906) 177–212.

Translations: English: P. HOLMES, ANL 15, 119–162; ANF 3, 503–520. — *Dutch:* H. U. MEYBOOM, Tegen de aanhangers van Valentinus (Oudchristel. geschriften, dl. 42). Leiden, 1924.

Studies: F. J. DÖLGER, Unserer Taube Haus. Textkritik und Kommentar zu Tertul-

20

lian Adversus Valentinianos 2. 3: AC 2 (1930) 41–56. — A. D'ALÈS, Symbola (Ter tullien, Adv. Valent. 12): RSR 25 (1935) 496. — F. J. DÖLGER, Der Rhetor Philoso phus von Karthago und seine Stilübung über den tapferen Mann. Zu Tertullianus Adv. Valent. 8: AC 5 (1936) 272–274. — G. QUISPEL, De humor van Tertullianus Nederl. theol. Tijdschr. 2 (1948) 280–290.

5. On Baptism

De baptismo, extremely important for the history of the liturgy of initiation and the sacraments of baptism and confirmation, is not merely the earliest work on the subject, it is the only Ante-Nicene treatise on any of the sacraments. It may be classed with the anti-heretical writings, occasioned as it was, by the attacks of Carthage of a certain Quintilla, a member of the sect of Caius, who made rationalistic objections and 'carried away a great number with her most venomous doctrine, making it her first aim to destroy baptism' (ch. 1). Tertullian answers her in this small tract of twenty chapters, in which he speaks like a teacher to his catechumens: 'A treatise on this matter will not be superfluous; instructing both such as are just becoming formed in the faith, and those who, content with simple belief, do not investigate the grounds of tradition and carry an untried credible faith through inexperience' (ch. 1).

How could washing the body with water effect the cleaning of the soul and salvation from eternal death, was evidently one of the objections. Thus the first chapter begins with the exclamation: 'Happy sacrament of our water, in which the sins of our former blindness are washed away and we are set free for everlasting life!' and ends: 'We little fish, like our Fish ($IX\Theta\Upsilon\Sigma$), Jesus Christ, are born in water, and it is only by abiding in water that we are safe.' The fact that God uses such an everyday means should not be a stumbling-block to the carnal mind, because He chooses the lowly and unpretentious things for his purposes (ch. 2). Water, since the beginning of the world a preferred and life-giving element (ch. 3), was sanctified by the creator and chosen as a vehicle of His power (ch. 4). Here we learn incidentally that the consecration of the baptismal font was then practised in the Church of Africa:

> All waters, therefore, in virtue of the pristine privilege of their origin, do, after invocation of God, attain the sacramental power of sanctification; for the Spirit immediately

supervenes from the heavens, and rests over the waters, sanctifying them from Himself; and being thus sanctified, they imbibe at the same time the power of sanctifying (4 ANF).

Ever since the primeval hovering of the Spirit of God over the deep, water has been regarded as a symbol of purification and the dwelling-place of supernatural efficacy. Pagan rites, being but diabolical imitations of the sacrament, and even popular beliefs give testimony to this (ch. 5). Not the mere physical cleansing bestows grace but the sacred action united with the use of the trinitarian formula (ch. 6). Directly after baptism follows the anointing (ch. 7), then confirmation, in which the imposition of hands confers the Holy Spirit (ch. 8).

The passing through the Red Sea and the water from the rock (ch. 9) as well as the baptism of St. John (ch. 10) prefigured the Christian initiation. The author answers the objection that, because Christ did not personally administer the rite, it is, therefore, not necessary for salvation (ch. 11). He then deals with the problem: Since no one can attain eternal life without it, how is it that the apostles were saved, for we find none of them receiving it, except Paul? (ch. 12). It was not requisite before the resurrection of the Lord (ch. 13). St. Paul's assertion that he had not been sent to baptize (1 Cor. 1, 17) must be understood correctly (ch. 14). There is but one regeneration, that of the Church (ch. 15). The author denies here the validity of the heretics' ceremony without going into details because this point had already received a fuller discussion from him in Greek, as he remarks (15). There is one exception from the necessity of being baptized with water, and that is martyrdom, which he calls the 'second baptism,' the 'baptism of blood' (ch. 16). Thus he speaks of two baptisms, sent out by Christ 'from the wound of His pierced side, in order that they who believed in His blood might be bathed with the water; they who had been bathed in the water might also carry the stain of blood' (ibid.). The usual minister of baptism is the bishop; presbyters and deacons also have the right, but not without the ordinary's authority (ch. 17). Even laymen possess the power, 'for what is equally received can be equally given... Baptism which is equally a divine institution, can be administered by all... Let it suffice certainly to take advantage of the privilege in cases of necessity, if at any time circumstances

either of place or of time or of person compel it. For then the
boldness of the helper is welcomed, when the situation of the
endangered person is urgent, since he will be guilty of the loss of a
human creature, if he refrains from bestowing what he had free
liberty to confer' (*ibid.*). The sacrament is not rashly to be administered. The faith of the recipient must be examined carefully.
For this reason the author does not favor the baptism of infants:

And so, according to the circumstances and disposition,
and even the age, of each individual, the delay of baptism is
preferable; principally, however, in the case of little children.
For why is it necessary, if it is not so urgent, that the sponsors
likewise should be thrust into danger? Who both themselves,
by reason of mortality, may fail to fulfil their promises, and
may be disappointed by the development of an evil disposition? The Lord does indeed say, 'Forbid them not to come
unto me.' Let them 'come,' then, while they are growing up;
let them 'come' while they are learning whither to come; let
them become Christians when they have become able to
know Christ. Why does the innocent period of life hasten to
the 'remission of sins?' (ch. 18 ANF).

Easter and Pentecost are the liturgical dates for the ceremony,
but every time is apt. There might be a difference of solemnity,
but there is no distinction in grace (ch. 19). The last chapter deals
with the preparation for the reception of the sacrament (ch. 20).

The tract is free of every trace of Montanism and shows high
regard for ecclesiastical authority: 'Hostility to the bishop's
position begets schisms' (ch. 17). It must have been written in
Tertullian's early period, perhaps between 198 and 200 A.D.

Editions: A. REIFFERSCHEID-G. WISSOWA, CSEL 20 (1890) 201–218. — J. M. LUPTON,
De baptismo ed. with introduction and notes. Cambridge, 1908. — G. RAUSCHEN, FP
11. Bonn, 1916. — J. W. PH. BORLEFFS, De baptismo. Leiden, 1931. — A. D'ALÈS,
De baptismo, rec. not. ill. (Textus et Documenta, Series theolog. 10). Rome, 1933. —
J. W. PH. BORLEFFS, De patientia, de baptismo, de paenitentia, ed. (Scriptores
christiani primaevi 4). The Hague, 1948. — R. F. REFOULÉ-M. DROUZY, Traité du
baptême (SCH 35). Paris, 1952. — *Index:* J. W. PH. BORLEFFS, Index verborum quae
Tertulliani De Baptismo libello continentur: Mnem 59 (1931) 50–102.

Translations: English: C. DODGSON, Library of Fathers 10. Oxford, 1842, 255–280. —
S. THELWALL, ANL 11, 231–256; ANF 3, 669–679. — A. SOUTER, Tertullian's
Treatises Concerning Prayer, Concerning Baptism (SPCK). London, 1919. — *French:*
R. F. REFOULÉ-M. DROUZY, *loc. cit.* — *German:* H. KELLNER, BKV² 7 (1912). — *Dutch:*

H. U. Meyboom, Over het doopsel (Oudchristel. geschriften, dl. 46). Leiden, 1930. — Chr. Mohrmann, (Tert. Apol. etc.) M C 1, 3. Utrecht, 1951, 241–271.

Studies: E. Fruetsaert, De baptismo 5: RSR (1911) 462–466. — E. Amann, L'ange du baptême dans Tertullien: RSR (1921) 208–221. — K. Köhler, Das Agraphon bei Tertullian De bapt. 20: ThStKr (1922) 169 ff. — S. Eitrem, Tertullian De bapt. 5 'sanctified by drowning': CR (1924) 69. — A. d'Alès, Tertullien De baptismo 5: RSR (1924) 292. — A. D. Nock, Pagan Baptisms in Tertullien: JThSt 28 (1927) 289–290. — F. J. Dölger, Die Apollinarischen Spiele und das Fest Pelusia. Zu Tertullian De baptismo 5: AC 1 (1929) 150–155; *idem,* Die Taufe an den Apollinarischen und den Pelusischen Spielen: AC 1 (1929) 156–159; *idem,* Tertullian kein Zeuge für eine Taufe in den Mysterien von Eleusis: AC 1 (1929) 143–149; *idem,* Esietus. Der Ertrunkene oder der zum Osiris Gewordene. Ein sprachgeschichtlicher Beitrag zu Tertullian De baptismo 5: AC 1 (1929) 174–183; *idem,* Das erste Gebet der Täuflinge in der Gemeinschaft der Brüder: AC 2 (1930) 142–155; *idem,* Die Sünde in Blindheit und Unwissenheit. Ein Beitrag zu Tertullian De baptismo 1: AC 2 (1930) 222–226; *idem,* Tertullian über die Bluttaufe: AC 2 (1930) 117–141. — J. W. Ph. Borleffs, Mnem 59 (1931) 1–47; *idem,* Zu Tertullian de baptismo: PhW 51 (1931) 251–255. — F. J. Dölger, Zwei neue Textheilungsversuche zu Tertullian De baptismo 16, 2: AC 3 (1932) 216–219. — B. Leeming, A Note on a Reading in Tertullian's De baptismo: 'Credo quia non credunt': Greg 3 (1933) 423–431. — F. J. Dölger, Die Eingliederung des Taufsymbols in den Taufvollzug nach den Schriften Tertullians. Zu Tertullian De baptismo 2, 1: AC 4 (1934) 138–146. — G. Thörnell, Analecta critica: Eranos (1934) 153–155. — F. J. Dölger, Religiöse Waschung als Sühne für Meineid (De baptismo 5): AC 6 (1940) 73. — E. C. Ratcliff, The Relation of Confirmation to Baptism in the Early Roman and Byzantine Liturgies: Theology 49 (1946) 258–265, 290–295. — J. W. Ph. Borleffs, La valeur du Codex Trecensis de Tertullien pour la critique de texte dans le traité De baptismo: VC 2 (1948) 185–200. — P. Schepens, De baptismo 5: RSR (1948) 112–113. — Chr. Mohrmann, Tertullien, De baptismo 2, 2: VC 5 (1951) 49. — W. Bedard, The Symbolism of the Baptismal Font in Early Christian Thought. Diss. Washington, 1951. — F. X. Lukman, Das Anblasen des Teufels beim Taufgelöbnis: Festschrift f. R. Egger I. Klagenfurt, 1952, 343–346.

6. *Scorpiace*

Scorpiace, i.e. antidote against the Scorpion's sting, is the title of a small treatise of fifteen chapters, a defense of martyrdom against the Gnostics, who are compared to scorpions. They oppose the sacrifice of life as unnecessary and not demanded by God. However, it becomes the duty of every Christian, according to Tertullian, whenever there is no other way of avoiding participation in idolatry. Even in the Old Testament death had to be preferred to apostasy (ch. 2–4). It is a blasphemy to say with the Gnostics that such a view makes God out a murderer. Martyrdom is a rebirth and wins for the soul an everlasting existence.

There is an indication (ch. 1) that the treatise was written during a persecution, most probably that of Scapula in A.D. 213.

Edition: A. Reifferscheid-G. Wissowa, CSEL 20 (1890) 144-179.

Translations: English: S. Thelwall, ANL 11, 379-415; ANF 3, 633-648. — *German:* H. Kellner-G. Esser, BKV² 24 (1915). — *Dutch:* H. U. Meyboom, Tegen de schorpioensteek (Oudchristel. geschr., dl. 43). Leiden, 1930.

Studies: E. Buonaiuti, L'Antiscorpionico di Tertulliano: RR 3 (1927) 146-152. — J. H. Waszink, Tertullianea: Mnem 3 (1935/36) 165-174. — L. Castiglioni, Ad Tertullianum adnotationes: Studi Ubaldi. Milan, 1937, 256-260.

7. On the Flesh of Christ

The present treatise *De carne Christi* and the following *De resurrectione carnis* are intimately connected. Together they provide an irrefutable argument for the resurrection of the body. Rather than admit this dogma the heretics had denied the reality of Christ's flesh and thus revived the Docetic errors. Tertullian refers in *De resurrectione carnis* to the present tract and calls it *De carne Domini adversus quattuor haereses*—a more precise title, since he has in view four Gnostic sects, those of Marcion, Apelles, Basilides and Valentinus. In the first chapter he indicates his purpose in the following words: 'Let us examine our Lord's bodily substance, for about His spiritual nature all are agreed. It is His flesh that is in question. Its verity and quality are the points in dispute. Did it ever exist? whence was it derived? and of what kind was it? If I succeed in demonstrating it, we shall lay down a law for our own resurrection' (ANF). The entire treatise is devoted to answering these three questions. Thus he proves that Christ was really born, that His nativity was both possible and becoming, and that He truly lived and died in human flesh, thus refuting Marcion's Docetic ideas. His nature was not taken from the angels, though He is called the Angel of the Lord, nor from the stars, as Apelles maintained, nor from some spiritual substance, as Valentinus supposed, since He became exactly like us in all save only in sin, nor, on the other hand, derived from human seed; thus the flesh of the first Adam and that of the second Adam did not have an earthly father:

> As then the first Adam is thus introduced to us, it is a just inference that the second Adam likewise, as the apostle has told us, was formed by God into a quickening spirit out of

the ground—in other words, out of a flesh which was un-stained as yet by any human generation (17 ANF).

The author points out the dishonesty of the Gnostics who said that Christ obtained nothing at all from the Virgin, that He was born 'through' or 'in,' but not 'of' the Virgin. In defense of her true and real motherhood, he goes so far as to deny the *virginitas in partu* (23). He stresses the humaneness of Christ's body so strongly as to maintain that He was ugly:

His body did not reach even to human beauty, to say nothing of heavenly glory. Had the prophets given us no information whatever concerning his ignoble appearance, his very sufferings and the very contumely He endured bespeak it all (ch. 9 ANF).

There are passages of the Old Testament (Is. 52, 14; 53, 2) behind this opinion, shared by many of the Ante-Nicene Fathers. At the end of the treatise Tertullian announces the tract *De resurrectione carnis*: 'The resurrection, however, of our own flesh will have to be maintained in another little treatise, and so I bring to a close this present one, which serves as a general preface and which will pave the way now that it is plain what kind of body that was which rose again in Christ' (25). The date of composition for both treatises must be close to each other, perhaps between 210 and 212.

Edition: A. KROYMANN, CSEL 70 (1942) 189–250.

Translations: English: P. HOLMES, ANL 15, 163–214; ANF 3, 521–542. — *Dutch:* H. U. MEYBOOM, Over het lichaam van Christus (Oudchristel. geschriften, dl. 45). Leiden, 1930.

8. *The Resurrection of the Flesh*

The introduction (ch. 1–2) links all those who deny the resurrection of the flesh, the pagans, the Sadducees and the heretics and shows the inconsistency of their teaching. Right reason bears witness to this article of faith because the body was created by God, was redeemed by Christ, and must be judged together with the soul at the end (ch. 3–15). Objections are then refuted (16–17). All this serves only as a foundation: 'Thus far it has been my object by prefatory remarks to lay a foundation for the defense of all the Scriptures which promise a resurrection of the flesh' (ch. 18). Thus the real topic of the treatise is: The resurrection of the

body according to the Old and the New Testament (ch. 18–55).
The examination of the biblical passages is preceded by an
exposition of the proper interpretation of the figurative language
of the Scriptures. The last part (ch. 56–63) deals with the condition of the body after the resurrection, its integrity and its
identity with the present one. The closing sentences reveal his
leaning towards Montanism: 'He has accordingly now dispersed
all the perplexities of the past, and their self-chosen allegories and
parables, by the open and perspicuous explanation of the entire
mystery, through the new prophecy, which descends in copious
streams from the Paraclete' (63 ANF).

Edition: A. Kroymann, CSEL 47 (1906) 25–125.

Translations: English: P. Holmes, ANL 15, 215–332; ANF 3, 545–594. — A. Souter,
Concerning the Resurrection of the Flesh (SPCK). London, 1922.

Studies: L. Atzberger, Geschichte der christlichen Eschatologie innerhalb der vornicänischen Zeit. Freiburg, 1896, 317–329. — A. J. Mason, Tertullian and Purgatory:
JThSt 3 (1902) 598 ff. — M. Pohlenz, Die griechische Philosophie im Dienste der
christlichen Auferstehungslehre: Zeitschrift für wissenschaftl. Theologie 46 (1904)
241 ff. — J. Gewiess, Zum altkirchlichen Verständnis der Kenosisstelle (Phil. 2,
5–11): ThQ 128 (1948) 463–487: De resurr. carnis 6.

9. *Against Praxeas*

The last of the series of controversial writings is the treatise
Adversus Praxean, which Tertullian most probably wrote A.D. 213.
He had at that time joined the Montanists, since he accuses
Praxeas not only of Trinitarian heresy but also of opposition
to the new prophecy and makes him responsible for the condemnation of Montanus and his followers by the bishop of Rome,
despite an earlier approval:

> Praxeas was the first to import into Rome from Asia this
> kind of heretical pravity, a man in other respects of restless
> disposition, and above all inflated with the pride of con-
> fessorship simply and solely because he had to bear for a short
> time the annoyance of a prison; on which occasion, even 'if
> he had given his body to be burned, it would have profited
> him nothing' (1 Cor. 13, 3), not having the love of God,
> whose very gifts he has resisted and destroyed. For after the
> Bishop of Rome had acknowledged the prophetic gifts of
> Montanus, Prisca, and Maximilla, and in consequence of the

acknowledgement, had bestowed his peace on the churches of Asia and Phrygia, he by importunately urging false accusations against the prophets themselves and their churches, and insisting on the authority of the bishop's predecessors in the see, compelled him to recall the letter of peace which he had issued, as well as to desist from his purpose of acknowledging the gifts. By this Praxeas did a twofold service for the devil at Rome: he drove away prophecy, and he brought in heresy; he put to flight the Paraclete, and he crucified the Father (ch. 1 ANF).

Praxeas was, as the last words indicate, a Modalist or Patri-passian who so identified the Father with the Son that, according to him, 'the Father himself came down into the Virgin, was him-self born of her, himself suffered, indeed was himself Jesus Christ' (ch. 1). When his doctrine spread also in Carthage, Tertullian refuted him in this treatise, which represents the most important contribution to the doctrine of the Trinity in the Ante-Nicene period. Its terminology is clear, precise and apposite, its style vigorous and brilliant. The Council of Nicaea used not a few of its formulae and its influence on subsequent theologians cannot be overestimated. Hippolytus, Novatian (cf. above, p. 217), Dio-nysius of Alexandria and others are indebted to it. Augustine, in his great work *De Trinitate*, adopted the analogy between the Holy Trinity and the operations of the human soul found in the fifth chapter of Tertullian's treatise and devoted most of books 8–15 to an elaboration of it.

After the introductory chapter on Praxeas and his teaching, the author deals with the Catholic doctrine of the Trinity, some-times called the divine economy or dispensation (*oikonomia, dispositio*). In order to allay popular fears and prejudices, he draws a parallel with the theory of Roman Law which ac-knowledged several *imperatores* but only one *imperium;* that is, the State was ruled in virtue of one undivided power, but, since that sole authority could not be effectively exercised over so vast a territory, by an individual, the territory was divided but not the power, and each Emperor wielded that one power within an allotted area. Similarly, the divine monarchy is unimpaired in the Church's dogma. There follows a discussion of the generation of the Son, also called the Word and the Wisdom of God, with biblical quotations in proof of the plurality of divine persons. The testimony of the Gospel of John is adduced in order to refute the heretical interpretation of Scriptural passages by Praxeas. Finally, the writer treats of the Holy Ghost or Paraclete, as distinct from the Father and the Son. But this is only the frame of the treatise. Within the 31 chapters Tertullian develops completely the doctrine of the Trinity (this will be discussed later). There are striking passages like the following:

> Three, however, not in quality, but in sequence, not in substance, but in form, not in power, but in aspect; yet of one substance and one quality and one power, because there is one God from whom these sequences and forms and aspects are reckoned out in the name of the Father and the Son and the Holy Spirit (2).

He describes the relation existing between the Father and the Son as in no way destroying the Divine Monarchy, because it is not by division that the one differs from the other—but by distinction (9). He is the first of the Latin authors to use *trinitas* as the technical term (2 ff).

Unfortunately, in his defense of the distinction of the Divine persons, he did not escape the pitfalls of Subordinationism.

Editions: A. KROYMANN, CSEL 47 (1906) 227–289; *idem*, SQ 2, 8 (Tübingen, 1907). — E. EVANS, Q.S.Fl. Tertullianus, Treatise against Praxeas, edited and translated with introduction and commentary (SPCK). London, 1948.

Translations: English: P. HOLMES, ANL 15, 333–409; ANF 3, 597–627. — A. SOUTER, Tertullian, Against Praxeas (SPCK). London, 1920. — E. EVANS, *op. cit.* — *Dutch:* H. U. MEYBOOM, Tegen Praxeas (Oudchristel. geschriften, dl. 43). Leiden, 1930.

Studies: J. F. BETHUNE-BAKER, Tertullian's Use of substantia, natura and persona: JThSt 4 (1903) 440–442. — L. ROSENMEYER, Quaestiones Tertullianeae ad librum adversus Praxean pertinentes. Strasbourg, 1909. — G. ESSER, Wer war Praxeas? Progr. Bonn, 1910. — C. H. TURNER, Tertullianea I. Notes on the Adversus Praxean: JThSt 14 (1913) 556–564. — T. HERMANN, Das Verhältnis von Novatians De Trinitate zu Tertullians Adversus Praxean. Diss. Marburg, 1918. — G. BARDY, 'Praxean hesternum': RSR (1922) 361. — F. J. DÖLGER, Sonne und Sonnenstrahl als Gleichnis in der Logostheologie des christlichen Altertums: AC 1 (1929) 271–290. — J. BARBEL, Christos Angelos (Theophaneia 3). Bonn, 1941, 70–79. — TH. L. VERHOEVEN, Studiën over Tertullianus' Adversus Praxean, voornamelijk betrekking hebbend op Monarchia, Oikonomia, Probola, in verband met de Triniteit. (Diss. Utrecht). Amsterdam, 1948. — TH. CAMELOT, 'Spiritus a Deo et Filio': RSPT 33 (1949) 31–33. — TH. L. VERHOEVEN, Monarchia dans Tertullien, Adversus Praxean: VC 5 (1951) 43–48.

10. *On the Soul*

Except for his *Adversus Marcionem*, the treatise *De anima* is the largest of Tertullian's works. It belongs to the series of anti-heretical writings, because the author indicates at the beginning of the third chapter that only the contemporary errors compelled him to compose it. Thus it is misleading to call it 'the first Christian psychology.' It is not a scientific exposition but primarily a refutation of wrong doctrines as J. H. Waszink has sufficiently demonstrated. Tertullian regarded it as a continuation of his earlier work *De censu animae*, in which he defended the divine origin of the soul against Hermogenes, to which the opening sentence of *De anima* alludes. He states that after having dealt with Hermogenes concerning the origin of the soul, he now wishes to turn to the remaining questions, the discussion of which will force him to take up arms against philosophy. Thus in the preface (ch. 1–3) he avers that Socrates' declaration of personal immortality in Plato's *Phaedo* has no value. A discussion of the soul must resort to divine revelation and not to pagan thinkers, who are notorious for mixing true assertions with false arguments, and are therefore the 'patriarchs of heretics.' After this, the first part (ch. 4–22) is devoted to an examination of the basic qualities of the spiritual principle of the soul. Though sprung from the breath of God, it has a beginning in time and Plato's view is without foundation (4). To our surprise the idea of the Stoics that it has a material nature finds favor with the author: 'I call on the Stoics also to help me, who, while declaring almost in our own terms that the soul is a spiritual essence—in as much as breath and spirit are in their nature very near akin to each other—will yet have no difficulty in persuading us that the soul is a corporeal substance' (5). The contrary view of the Platonists is refuted and the corporeality demonstrated from the gospel. The invisibility, the shape and colour are studied and the unity defended in special chapters, which deal with the identity of soul and spirit, the mind as no more than a function thereof, the parts or 'powers' of the soul and many more questions concerning its homogeneity. The freedom of the will is stressed against the Valentinian doctrine of the immutability of human nature. The second part (23–37, 4) investigates the origin of the soul. After a refutation of heretical doctrines which stem from Plato's theory of oblivion, the inconsistency of this philosophical idea is demonstrated. The following chapters are the most important for Tertullian's anthropology. He refutes the notion that the soul pre-exists and is introduced after birth by proving the embryo to be an animate being. According to Tertullian soul and body come into existence simultaneously:

> How then is a living being conceived? Is the substance of both body and soul formed together at one and the same time? Or does one of them precede the other in natural formation? We indeed maintain that both are conceived, and formed, and perfected simultaneously, as well as born together; and that not a moment's interval occurs in their conception, so that a prior place can be assigned to either. Judge, in fact, of the incidents of man's earliest existence by those which occur to him at the very last. As death is defined to be nothing else than the separation of body and soul, life, which is the opposite of death, is susceptible of no other definition than the conjunction of body and soul. If the severance happens at one and the same time to both substances by means of death, so the law of their combination ought to assure us that it occurs simultaneously to the two substances of life. Now we allow that life begins with conception, because we contend that the soul begins from conception; life taking its commencement at the same moment and place that the soul does (27 ANF).

Tertullian distinguishes between the seed of the body and that of the soul and teaches that the act of generation reproduces the entire man, soul and body. Thus he speaks of a 'soul-producing seed which arises at once from the out-drip of the soul' (*ibid.*). The result is his heretical doctrine of traducianism, which denies the direct creation by God himself of each individual soul. There follows a refutation of the doctrine of transmigration as taught by Pythagoras, Plato and Empedocles and cognate heresies like that of Simon Magus and Carpocrates. At the end the author deals with the formation and state of the embryo. The third part (37, 5–58) answers further questions concerning the soul such as its growth, puberty and sin, sleep, dreams and death, finally, its fate after death. According to Tertullian all spirits are kept in Hades until the resurrection except those of the martyrs, to whom heaven is opened immediately. 'The sole key to unlock Paradise is your own life's blood' (55). On this occasion the author refers to the martyrdom of Perpetua, which took place on the 7th of March A.D. 202: 'How is it that the most heroic martyr Perpetua on the day of her passion saw only her fellow-martyrs there in the revelation which she received of Paradise, if it were not that the sword which guarded the entrance permitted none to go in thereat, except those who had died in Christ and not in Adam?' (*ibid.*) However, even the souls in Hades experience punishments and consolations in the interval between death and judgment, from the anticipation of certain gloom or glory.

Tertullian's most important source was *On the Soul* (Περὶ ψυχῆς) in four books by the physician Soranus of Ephesus, who thought the soul corporeal like the Stoics. Soranus, the most outstanding member of the so-called methodical school, lived at Rome at the beginning of the second century. In his work, no longer extant, he dealt not only with medicine, his profession, but showed a keen interest in etymology and in the refutation of contrary views of philosophers. Of these Plato is mentioned most frequently, and next the Stoics. Even Aristotle, who does not appear in any of the other works of Tertullian, is cited twelve times in *De anima*, whereas Heraclitus is mentioned seven and Democritus four. The most recent quotation comes from Arius Didymus of Alexandria, the court-philosopher of Augustus.

In the course of his exposition Tertullian professes the faith of the Montanists more than once and adopts their views (ch. 9, 45, 58). Thus the treatise *De anima* should be dated between the years A.D. 210–213.

Editions: A. REIFFERSCHEID-G. WISSOWA, CSEL 20 (1890). — J. H. WASZINK, Tertullianus, De anima ed. with a commentary. Amsterdam, 1947; *idem*, Index verborum et locutionum quae Tertulliani de anima libro continentur. Bonn, 1935.

Translations: English: P. HOLMES, ANL 15, 410–541; ANF 3, 181–235. — E. A. QUAIN, Tertullian, On the Soul: FC 10 (1950) 179–309. — *German:* H. KELLNER, BKV. Kempten, 1871. — J. H. WASZINK, Tertullianus, De anima mit Übersetzung und Kommentar. Amsterdam, 1933. — *Dutch:* H. U. MEYBOOM, Over de Ziel (Oudchristel. geschriften, dl. 45). Leiden, 1930. — *French:* M. DE GENOUDE, Œuvres de Tertullien 2. Paris, 1852, 1–115.

Studies: G. ESSER, Die Seelenlehre Tertullians. Paderborn, 1893. — A. BECK, Die Lehre des hl. Hilarius von Poitiers und Tertullians über die Entstehung der Seelen: PhJ 13 (1900) 42. — G. DE VRIES, Bijdrage tot de psychologie van Tertullianus.

Utrecht, 1929. — H. Koch, Tertullianeisches III, 7. Zur Lehre von Urstand und
Erlösung bei Tertullian: ThStKr 104 (1932) 127–160. — F. J. Dölger, 'Dogma' bei
Tertullian (De anima 33): AC 3 (1932) 80. — H. Karpp, Sorans vier Bücher Περὶ
ψυχῆς und Tertullians Schrift De anima: ZNW 33 (1934) 31–47. — F. J. Dölger,
Das Lebensrecht des ungeborenen Kindes und die Fruchtabtreibung in der Bewertung der heidnischen und christlichen Antike: AC 4 (1934) 32–37, 44 ff; idem, Tertullians Beurteilung der Machenschaften gegen das keimende Leben: AC 4 (1934)
281 f. — F. Seyr, Die Seelen- und Erkenntnislehre Tertullians und die Stoa: Commentationes Vindobonenses 3 (1937) 51–74. — J. H. Waszink, Tertullians eschato-
logische Deutung der Siebenzahl: Pisciculi. Münster, 1939, 276–278; idem, Tertullianea: Mnem 9 (1940) 129–137. — A. J. Festugière, La composition et l'esprit du
De Anima de Tertullien: RSPT 33 (1949) 129–161. — J. H. Waszink, Mors imma-
tura: VC 3 (1949) 107–112. — A. D. Nock, Tertullian and the ahori: VC 4 (1950)
129–141. — J. H. Waszink, The technique of the clausula in Tertullian's De anima:
VC 4 (1950) 212–245. — H. Karpp, Probleme altchristlicher Anthropologie. Gütersloh, 1951, 40–91.

4. *Disciplinary, Moral and Ascetical Works*

More than in his other writings Tertullian's deviation towards
Montanism becomes evident in his disciplinary treatises. Of his
pre-Montanistic period the following are extant:

1. *To the Martyrs*

The treatise *Ad Martyras* is one of his earliest works. Despite
its brevity (only 6 chapters) and simplicity of style, it has won the
sustained admiration of successive generations; the very spirit of
early Christian heroism breathes through and pervades it. Addressed to a number of confessors who were being kept in prison
soon to be condemned to death for the faith, it admonishes and
encourages them to steadfastness. The opening words call them
benedicti and *martyres designati*, the former clearly indicating that
they were still catechumens. The author reminds them of the
assistance received from *Domina mater ecclesia* and their fellow-
Christians and asks them to accept from him some contribution
to their spiritual sustenance. He not only wishes to take away the
fear of martyrdom, but to arouse in them a positive enthusiasm
by extolling it as the highest and most glorious of valiant deeds.
Death for Christ is not simply an indifferent acceptance of
suffering and stoic endurance, but the most arduous test of
strength and intrepidity, a struggle in the fullest sense of the word.
Tertullian chooses his most impressive images from the contests in

the arena and from phases of military life. Thus he says in the
first chapter: 'Not that I am specially entitled to exhort you; yet
not only the trainers and overseers, but even the unskilled, nay,
all who choose, without the slightest need for it, are wont to
animate from afar by their cries the most accomplished gladiators, and from the mere throng of onlookers useful suggestions
have sometimes come' (ABF). The second chapter heartens them
not to be alarmed at their separation from the world:

> For if we reflect that the world is more really the prison, we
> shall see that you have gone out of a prison rather than into
> one. The world has the greater darkness blinding men's
> hearts. The world imposes the more grievous fetters, binding
> men's very souls. The world breathes out the worst impuri-
> ties—human lusts. The world contains the larger number of
> criminals, even the whole human race... Then, last of all, it
> awaits the judgment, not of the proconsul, but of God.
> Wherefore, O blessed, you may regard yourselves as having
> been translated from a prison, to, we may say, a place of
> safety. It is full of darkness, but ye yourselves are light; it
> has bonds, but God has made you free (ANF).

The third chapter repeats the image of the contest to which the
martyrs are called and asks them to look upon the prison as a
training-ground:

> You are about to pass through a noble struggle, in which
> the living God acts the part of umpire, in which the Holy
> Ghost is your trainer, in which the prize is an eternal crown
> of angelic essence, citizenship in the heavens, glory ever-
> lasting. Therefore your Master, Jesus Christ, who has
> anointed you with His Spirit, and led you forth to the arena,
> has seen it good, before the day of conflict, to take you from a
> condition more pleasant in itself, and has imposed on you a
> harder treatment, that your strength might be greater. For
> the athletes, too, are set apart to a more stringent discipline,
> that they might have their physical powers built up. They
> are kept from luxury, from daintier meats, from more
> pleasant drinks; they are pressed, racked, worn out; the
> harder their labors in the preparatory training, the stronger
> is the hope of victory (3 ANF).

The following chapters (4–6) give examples of supreme suffering

and even the sacrifice of life for mere ambition and vanity or by
accidents and fate, whereas the martyrs suffer in the cause of
God. If the last sentence refers to the battle of Lyons, February 19
A.D. 197, in which Albinus was defeated, the treatise dates from
that year. Others think that Perpetua and Felicitas belonged to
the group here addressed. They were both catechumens and died
for the faith A.D. 202. The treatise would then belong to this
year. The *Passio Perpetuae et Felicitatis* (cf. vol. I, p. 181 ff) and *Ad
Martyras* have so much in common that Tertullian has been
presumed to be also the author of the former.

Edition: T. H. BINDLEY, Tertulliani De praescriptione haereticorum, Ad martyras
Ad Scapulam. Oxford, 1893.

Translations: English: C. DODGSON, Library of the Fathers 10. Oxford, 1842, 150–157
— S. THELWALL, ANL 11, 1–7, ANF 3, 693–696. — *German:* H. KELLNER, BKV
7 (1912). — *Dutch:* H. U. MEYBOOM, Aan de martelaren (Oudchristel. geschriften
dl. 43). Leiden, 1930. — CHR. MOHRMANN, (Tert. Apol. etc.) MC 1, 3. Utrecht
Brussels, 1941, 183–195. — *Spanish:* J. PELLICER DE OSSAU, Barcelona, 1639.

Studies: F. J. DÖLGER, Der Kampf mit dem Ägypter in der Perpetua-Vision. Da
Martyrium als Kampf mit dem Teufel: AC 3 (1932) 177–188. — H. v. CAMPEN
HAUSEN, Die Idee des Martyriums in der alten Kirche. Göttingen, 1936, 17–28. —
G. D. SCHLEGEL, The Ad martyras of Tertullian and the Circumstances of its Com-
position: Downside Review 63 (1945) 125–128. — Z. VYSOKY, The sources of the
treatise Ad martyras by Tertullian (Czech): Listy Filologicke 72 (1948) 156–166. —
E. E. MALONE, The Monk and the Martyr (SCA 12). Washington, 1950, 30–34.

2. *The Shows*

The treatise *De spectaculis* is a sweeping condemnation of all
public games in the circus, stadium or amphitheater, the ath-
letic contests and gladiatorial encounters. It consists of two
sections, the historical (ch. 4–13) and the ethical (ch. 14–30). In
the former, he demonstrates that no Christian may attend these
amusements; their origin, history, names, ceremonies and lo-
cations show them to be but another form of idolatry. Every be
liever has renounced them in his baptismal vows. In the latter, he
points out that, since they strongly incite the passions, they undermine all morality and are entirely out of keeping with the religion
of the Saviour. The last chapter paints in glowing colors a
picture of the greatest spectacle the world has ever witnessed, 'the
fast approaching advent of our Lord' and 'that last day of
judgment, with its everlasting issues; that day unlooked for by the

nations, the theme of their derision, when the world hoary with age, and all its many products, shall be consumed in one great flame' (30 ANF). The treatise is addressed to catechumens as is evident from the opening sentence: 'You Servants of God, about to draw near to God, that you may make solemn consecration of yourselves to Him, seek well to understand the condition of faith, the reasons of the Truth, the laws of Christian discipline, which forbid among other sins of the world the pleasures of the public shows' (ANF). Tertullian used as a source for the first part, which narrates the origin and history of the games, the works of Suetonius on this subject and perhaps Varro's *Libri rerum divinarum*, on which Suetonius had drawn. He wrote it in his pre-Montanistic period and evidently before *On Idolatry* and *On the Dress of Women*, because both of them refer to it (*De idol.* 13; *De cultu fem.* 1, 8). Except for an indication that a persecution was going on (ch. 27) while the author composed it, there is no further evidence for its exact date. However, the year A.D. 197 is more probable than A.D. 202. The author mentions (*De corona* 6) that he also prepared a Greek edition of *De spectaculis*.

Editions: A. REIFFERSCHEID-G. WISSOWA, CSEL 20 (1890) 1–29. — T. R. GLOVER, Tertullian (LCL). London-New York, 1931, 230–300. — A. BOULANGER, Tertullien, De spectaculis. Paris, 1933.

Translations: English: C. DODGSON, Library of Fathers 10. Oxford, 1842, 187–219. — S. THELWALL, ANL 11, 8–35; ANF 3, 79–91. — T. R. GLOVER, *loc. cit.* 231–301. — *German:* H. KELLNER, BKV² 7 (1912). — *Dutch:* H. U. MEYBOOM, Over de schouwspelen (Oudchristel. geschriften, dl. 46) Leiden, 1931. — CHR. MOHRMANN, De openbare spelen, MC 1, 3. Utrecht, 1951, 197–240.

Studies: E. NÖLDECHEN, Die Quellen Tertullians in seinem Buch von den Schauspielen: Philologus, Suppl.-Band 6, 2 (1894) 727–766; *idem*, Tertullian und das Spielwesen: Zeitschr. für wissensch. Theologie 37 (1894) 91–125; *idem*, Tertullian und der Agon: Neue Jahrbücher für deutsche Theologie 3 (1894) 206–226; *idem*, Tertullian und das Theater: ZKG 15 (1894/95) 161–203. — P. WOLF, Die Stellung der Christen zu den Schauspielen nach Tertullians Schrift De spectaculis. Diss. Vienna, 1897. — H. J. SOVERI, De ludorum memoria capita Tertullianea selecta. Helsingfors, 1912. — R. M. CHASE, Tertullian, De spectaculis: CJ 23 (1927) 107–120. — J. KÖHNE, Die Schrift Tertullians über die Schauspiele in kultur- und religionsgeschichtl. Bedeutung. Diss. Breslau, 1929. — J. BÜCHNER, Tertullian, De spectaculis. Kommentar. Würzburg, 1935. — E. WITTERS, Tertullien, De spectaculis. Index verborum omnium. Louvain, 1942. — J. LAMPAERT, Tertullianus' De spectaculis. Inleiding en commentaar. Louvain, 1943. — J. H. WASZINK, Varro, Livy and Tertullian on the History of Dramatic Art: VC 2 (1948) 224–242. — A. H. COURATIN, The Sanctus and the Pattern of the Early Anaphora (De spectacul. 25): Journal of

21

Ecclesiastical History 2 (1951) 19–23. — G. I. LIEFTINCK, Un fragment de 'D₁
spectaculis' de Tertullien provenant d'un manuscrit du neuvième siècle: VC
(1951) 193–203.

3. On the Dress of Women

The leading idea of *Ad Martyras* and *De·spectaculis* appears
again in Tertullian's *De cultu feminarum:* It is not sufficient to
renounce paganism at baptism, the religion of Christ must per-
vade our daily life. For this reason women are warned in this
tract not to be dominated by pagan fashion but to show modesty
in apparel. The two books of which it consists formed originally
two distinct works. The first had the title *De habitu muliebri,* the
second *De cultu feminarum.* The second is not a continuation of the
first but a new and more comprehensive treatment of the same
subject, which indicates that the author was not quite satisfied
with the first. The introductory chapter reminds the Christian
woman of the introduction of sin into the world through the first
woman. For this reason the only dress befitting the daughters of
Eve is the garb of penitence. Ornaments and cosmetics are of
diabolical origin, as the *Book of Henoch* proves (ch. 2). The author
devotes an entire chapter to the defense of the genuineness of this
apocryphal work (ch. 3). With the fourth chapter the author returns to his topic. He distinguishes between dress (*cultus*) and
make-up (*ornatus*) and accuses the first of ambition, the second of
prostitution (ch. 4). In dealing with the first (ch. 5–7) he condemns all ornaments like gold and silver, pearls and precious
stones. Rarity is the only cause which makes such things valuable.
The dyeing of garments is unnatural. 'That which He Himself
has not produced, is not pleasing to God, unless He was unable to
order sheep to be born with purple and sky-blue fleeces. If He was
able, then plainly He was unwilling and what God willed not, of
course ought not to be fashioned. Those things, then, are not the
best which are not from God, the author of nature. Thus they are
understood to be from the devil, for there is no other whose they
can be' (ch. 8). God's distribution must regulate our desires,
otherwise we become the prey of ambition which causes 'one deli-
cate neck to carry about it forests and islands and the slender lobs
of ears to exhaust a fortune' (ch. 9). Here the author breaks off
without having treated the second subject at all. The second book

deals with the same topic but in reversed order: it speaks first of the cosmetics (*ornatus*) and then of jewels and dress (*cultus*). The first chapter recommends modesty as the real Christian virtue: 'Since we are all the *temple of God*, modesty is the sacristan and priestess of that temple, who is to suffer nothing unclean or profane to be introduced into it, for fear that the God who inhabits it should be offended, and quite forsake the polluted abode.' This virtue does not permit women to change the work of the creator, the body, with paints and dyeing of the hair: 'They who rub their skin with medicaments, stain their cheeks with rouge, make their eyes prominent with soot, sin against Him. To them, I suppose, the plastic skill of God is displeasing. In their own persons, I suppose, they convict, they censure, the Artificer of all things' (ch. 5). After tracing the origin of the desire for jewelry and ornaments of gold and silver in the same way as in the first book, he persuades the Christian woman that her appearance should always distinguish her from pagans. The last chapter refers to the times and warns them to be ready for the hardships of persecution:

> Delicacies as tend by their softness and effeminacy to unman the manliness of the faith are to be discarded. Otherwise, I know not whether the wrist that has been wont to be surrounded with the palm leaf-like bracelet will endure till it grows into the numb hardness of its own chain! I know not whether the leg that has rejoiced in the anklet will suffer itself to be squeezed into the gyve! I fear the neck, beset with pearl and emerald nooses, will give no room to the broadsword! ...But Christians always, and now more than ever, pass their times not in gold but in iron. The stoles of martyrdom are being prepared; the angels who are to carry us are being awaited (ch. 13 ANF).

Although there are exaggerations in these works the second is by far milder in tone and more broad-minded in its opinions, the difference suggesting that it was composed considerably later. The first was written after Tertullian's treatise *De spectaculis*, as ch. 8 clearly states. Both books originated after *De oratione*, ch. 20 of which indicates as much. Montanistic ideas are completely absent.

Editions: A. KROYMANN, CSEL 70 (1942) 59–95. — J. MARRA, De cultu feminarum libri duo (Corpus script. lat. Paravianum 54). Turin, 1930. — W. Kok, De cultu feminarum, met vertaling en commentaar. Dokkum, 1934.

Translations: English: S. Thelwall, ANL, 11, 304–322; ANF 4, 14–25. — *German:* H. Kellner, BKV² 7 (1912). — *Dutch:* H. U. Meyboom, Over den opsmuk der vrouwen (Oudchristel. geschriften, dl. 46). Leiden, 1931. — W. Kok, *loc. cit.* — A. Ducheyne, Proeve van vertaling en commentaar van het eerste boek van De cultu feminarum, met enkele bemerkingen over Tertullianus' gedachtengang. Thèse de license Univ. de Gand, 1941. — *Spanish:* J. Pellicer de Ossau, Barcelona, 1639.

Studies: G. Cortellezzi, Il concetto della donna nelle opere di Tertulliano: Didaskaleion (1923) 1, 5–29; 2, 57–79; 3, 43–100. — U. Moricca, Degli ornamenti delle donne (Tert.): Bilychnis 21 (1923) 401. — M. Galdi, De Tertulliani 'de cultu feminarum' et Cypriani 'Ad virgines' libellis commentatio: Raccolta di scritti in onore di F. Ramorino. Milan, 1927, 539–567. — H. Koch, Tertullianisches: ThStKr 101 (1929) 469–471. — S. Seliga, Tertullianus et Cyprianus de feminarum moribus pravis: Munera philologica L. Cwiklinski oblata. Poznan, 1936, 262–269.

4. *Concerning Prayer*

The treatise *De oratione* from about A.D. 198–200 is addressed to catechumens. It begins with the idea that the New Testament has introduced a form of prayer unprecedented in the Old, in tenor and spirit, superior by its privacy, its faith and confidence in God, its brevity; all these characteristics appear in the Our Father, itself an epitome of the whole gospel. There follows (ch. 2–9) the earliest surviving exposition of the *Pater Noster* in any language. The author adds a number of practical counsels. Nobody should approach God without being reconciled to his brother and free from all anger and perturbation of mind (ch. 10–12). This requires above all true purity of heart, not the washing of hands, at least in all instances (ch. 13–14). The writer condemns the custom of taking off the cloak during services and of sitting down when the orations are ended (ch. 15–16), a posture scored as irreverent under the eye of the living God. He recommends that we worship with elevated hands and subdued voice (ch. 17), actions symbolizing modesty and humility. No one should exclude himself from the kiss of peace after devotions, not even one fasting, because it is the seal of prayer. An exception is made only for Good Friday, when all abstain from food as a religious observance (ch. 18). With reference to the days of stations (ch. 19) those who are not eating should not go to such extremes as to abstain from Holy Communion but should take it home and receive it there at the end of the fast (ch. 19).Tertullian discusses at great length whether virgins ought to be veiled in church and urges it strongly (ch. 20–22). It is customary to kneel on fast and station days and for the morning invocation, but this is not to be observed on Easter and Pentecost (ch. 23). Every place is suitable to pay one's homage to the Creator, if opportunity and necessity so render it (ch. 24). No special time is prescribed, but it would profit us greatly to recollect ourselves at the important intervals, the third, the sixth and the ninth hour. 'It becomes believers not to take food, and not to go to the bath, before interposing a prayer; for the refreshments and nourishments of the spirit are to be held prior to those of the flesh, and things heavenly prior to things earthly' (ch. 25). We should never receive or bid farewell to a guest without raising our thoughts to God with him. Every supplication might well end, in accordance with a laudable custom, with the Alleluia or a responsory psalm (ch. 26–27). The last two chapters (ch. 28–29) extol prayer as a spiritual sacrifice and praise its power and efficacy.

If we compare this work with Origen's on the same subject, we notice the total absence of philosophical preoccupations and Tertullian's predominantly practical bent. The latter is concerned with the interior and exterior discipline at prayer and addresses the Christian people in general rather than a select circle. His treatise is precious not for the depth of his ideas but as a spirited expression of the truly Christian conception of life.

Editions: A. REIFFERSCHEID-G. WISSOWA, CSEL 20 (1890) 180–200. — R. W. MUNCEY, Q.S.F. Tertulliani De oratione. Introduction and notes. London, 1926. — G. F. DIERCKS, Tertullianus, De oratione. Critische uitgave met prolegomena, vertaling en philologisch-exegetisch-liturgische commentaar. Bussum, 1947.

Translations: English: C. DODGSON, Library of the Fathers 10. Oxford, 1842, 298–321. — S. THELWALL, ANL 11, 178–204; ANF 3, 681–691. — A. SOUTER, Tertullian's Treatises Concerning Prayer, Concerning Baptism (SPCK). London-New York, 1919. — *German:* H. KELLNER, BKV² 7 (1912). — *Dutch:* H. U. MEYBOOM, Tertullianus, Over het gebed (Oudchristel. geschriften, dl. 46). Leiden, 1931. — G. F. DIERCKS, *loc. cit.*

Studies: W. HALLER, Das Herrengebet bei Tertullian: Zeitschr. für praktische Theologie 12 (1890) 327–354. — E. v. D. GOLTZ, Das Gebet in der ältesten Christenheit. Leipzig, 1901, 279–282. — G. LOESCHKE, Die Vaterunsererklärung des Theophilus von Antiochien. Eine Quellenuntersuchung zu den Vaterunsererklärungen des Tertullian, Cyprian, Chromatius und Hieronymus. Berlin, 1908. — J. MOFFAT, Tertullian on the Lord's Prayer: ExpT 18 (1919) 24–41. — F. J. Dölger, Das Niedersitzen nach dem Gebet. Ein Kommentar zu Tertullian, De oratione 16: AC 5 (1936) 116–137. — B. Simovic, Le pater chez quelques pères latins: France Franciscaine 21 (1938) 193–222, 245–264. — O. Schäfer, Das Vaterunser, das Gebet des Christen. Eine aszetische Studie nach Tertullian De oratione: ThGl 35 (1943) 1–6. — A. J. B. Higgins, Lead us not into temptation. Some Latin Variants: JThSt 46 (1945) 179–183. — E. Dekkers, Tertullianus en de geschiedenis der liturgie. Brussels-Amsterdam, 1947, 117–126. — H. Pétré, Les leçons du 'Panem nostrum quotidianum': RSR 38 (1951) Mélanges Lebreton, 63–79.

5. *Concerning Patience*

The treatise *De patientia* begins with the following admission:
> I fully confess unto the Lord God that it has been rash enough, if not even impudent, to have dared compose a treatise on patience, for practising which I am all unfit, being a man of no goodness... but to discuss that which is not given one to enjoy, will be, as it were, a solace; after the manner of invalids, who since they are without health, know not how to stop talking about its blessings. So I, most miserable, ever sick with the heats of impatience, must of necessity sigh after, and invoke, and persistently plead for that health of patience which I possess not (ch. 1 anf).

Patience has its origin and prototype in the Creator, who scatters over just and unjust equally the brightness of his light. Christ gives an even greater example in His incarnation and life, His sufferings and death. It is especially through obedience to God that we can attain this perfection. Impatience is the mother of all sins and the devil is its father. The virtue under discussion precedes and follows faith, which cannot exist without it. In daily life, it finds numerous occasions for exercise; for instance, in the loss of property, in provocations and insults, in bereavements and lapses. Impatience results most frequently from the lust of vengeance. We are bound in duty to suffer adversity, great or small, and the reward is happiness. Tertullian then praises the blessings of patience, which takes the lead in every species of salutary discipline, ministers to repentance and creates charity. It strengthens the body and enables it to bear with all constancy continence and martyrdom. Heroic examples appear in the Old and the New Testament, for instance, Isaias and Stephen. The value, the effects and the beauty of this virtue are beyond comparison. 'Where God is, there is His foster-child, namely patience. When God's Spirit descends, patience accompanies Him indivisibly' (ch. 15). The last chapter warns the reader that Christian patience differs radically from its pagan caricature, the stubborn perseverance in evil.

The treatise should be dated between the years A.D. 200–203. It paints the picture of the ideal Christian and, written in a pleasing and quiet style, remains an important source for the personality of the author. Cyprian made ample use of it in his *De bono patientiae*.

Editions: A. KROYMANN, CSEL 47 (1906) 1–24. — J. W. PH. BORLEFFS, Libri De patientia, De baptismo, De paenitentia (Scriptores christiani primaevi 4). The Hague, 1948.

Translations: English: C. DODGSON, Library of Fathers 10. Oxford, 1842, 327–348. — S. THELWALL, ANL 11, 205–230; ANF 3, 707–717. — *German:* H. KELLNER, BKV² 7 (1912). — *Dutch:* H. U. MEYBOOM, Over het geduld (Oudchristel. geschriften, dl. 46). Leiden, 1931. — CHR. MOHRMANN, MC 1, 3. Utrecht, 1951, 301–328. — *Spanish:* J. PELLICER DE OSSAU, Barcelona, 1639.

Studies: R. KADERSCHAFKA, Quae ratio et rerum materiae et generis dicendi intercedere videatur inter Cypriani libellum 'De bono patientiae' et Tertulliani librum 'De patientia'. Progr. Gymn. Pilsen, 1913. — M. L. CARLSON, Pagan Examples of Fortitude in the Latin Christian Apologists: CPh 43 (1948) 93–104. — J. W. PH. BORLEFFS, Een nieuw handschrift van Tertullianus: Handelingen van het 21e Nederl. Philologencongres. Groningen, 1950, 27.

6. *Concerning Repentance*

De paenitentia possesses exceptional importance for the history of ecclesiastical penance, especially since the author wrote it while still a Catholic. The eruption of the volcano mentioned in ch. 12 dates it to 203 A.D., because Mt. Vesuvius broke out that year. The treatise falls readily into two parts, the former of which deals with that penance to which the adult candidate for baptism is bound before its reception (ch. 4–6), the latter with a 'second' penance, which God in His mercy 'has set up in the vestibule, to open the door to such as knock, but only once, because this is already the second time' (ch. 7). This clearly testifies to the existence of a remission after the sacrament of initiation. If Tertullian insists that only one such opportunity is granted, he does so not on dogmatic grounds but as a matter of psychology and method, as the following excerpt makes quite evident:

So long, Lord Christ, may the blessings of learning or hearing concerning the discipline of repentance be granted to Thy servants, as it likewise behooves them, not to sin; in other words, may they thereafter [sc. after baptism] know nothing of repentance and require nothing of it. It is irksome to append mention of a second—nay, in that case, the last— hope; lest, by treating of a remedial repenting yet in reserve, we seem to be pointing to a yet further space for sinning. Far be it that any one so interpret our meaning, as if, because there is an opening for repenting, there were even now, on that account, an opening for sinning; and as if the redundance of celestial clemency constituted a license for human temerity. Let no one be less good because God is more so, by repeating his sin as often as he is forgiven. Otherwise be sure he will find an end of escaping, when he shall not find one of sinning. We have escaped once [sc. in baptism]; let us commit ourselves to perils no farther, even if we seem likely to escape a second time (ch. 7 ANF).

From this passage it appears that Tertullian, feeling responsible for the souls of his readers, hesitates to recommend this second penance for fear they might become guilty of presumption. On the other hand, he admonishes them not to go to the other extreme and despair:

If any do incur the debt of a second penance, his spirit is not to be forthwith cut down and undermined by despair. Let it by all means be irksome to sin again, but let not to repent again be irksome: irksome to imperil one's self again, but not to be again set free. Let no one be ashamed. Repeated sickness must have repeated medicine (ch. 7 ANF).

The second penance of which Tertullian speaks in this treatise is that followed by ecclesiastical reconciliation. To obtain this, it is necessary for the sinner to undergo the ἐξομολόγησις or public confession and disciplinary acts, of which ch. 9–12 treat.

The narrower, then, the sphere of action of this second and only remaining repentance, the more laborious is its probation; in order that it may not be exhibited in the conscience alone, but may likewise be carried out in some external act. This act, which is more usually expressed and commonly spoken of under a Greek name, is *exomologesis*, whereby we confess our sins to the Lord, not indeed as if He were ignorant of them, but inasmuch as by confession satisfaction is settled, of confession repentance is born; by repentance God is appeased. And thus *exomologesis* is a discipline for man's prostration and humiliation, enjoining a demeanor calculated to move mercy. With regard also to the very dress and food, it commands the penitent to lie in sackcloth and ashes, to cover his body in mourning, to lay his spirit low in sorrows, to exchange for severe treatment the sins which he has committed; moreover, to know no food and drink but such as is plain,—not for the stomach's sake, to wit, but the soul's; for the most part, however, to feed prayers on fastings, to groan, to weep and make outcries, unto the Lord your God; to bow before the feet of the presbyters, and kneel to God's dear ones; to enjoin on all the brethren to be ambassadors to bear his deprecatory supplication before God (ch. 9 ANF).

The mention of prostration before the presbyters indicates that this penance was an ecclesiastical institution. It ended with official absolution, because Tertullian asks those who 'shun this work, as being a public exposure of themselves, or else defer it from day to day': 'Is it better to be damned in secret than to be absolved in public?' The last chapter (12) pictures the eternal damnation in hell of those who abandon their own salvation by not using this second *planca salutis*. From these considerations it is evident that in this treatise the author had in mind the forgiveness of grave sins.

Editions: J. W. PH. BORLEFFS, Libri De patientia, De baptismo. De paenitentia (Scriptores christiani primaevi 4). The Hague, 1948. — E. PREUSCHEN, SQ 2, 2nd ed. Freiburg, 1910. — G. RAUSCHEN, FP 10. Bonn, 1915. — P. DE LABRIOLLE, De paenitentia, De pudicitia, texte et trad. Paris, 1906.

Translations: English: C. DODGSON, Library of Fathers 10. Oxford, 1842, 349–369. — S. THELWALL, ANL 11, 257–278; ANF 3, 657–666. — *German:* H. KELLNER, BKV² 7 (1912). — *Dutch:* H. U. MEYBOOM, Over de boete (Oudchristel. geschriften, dl. 46). Leiden, 1931. — CHR. MOHRMANN, MC 1, 3. Utrecht, 1951, 273–300. — *French:* P. DE LABRIOLLE, *loc. cit.*

Studies: G. ESSER, Die Bußschriften Tertullians De paenitentia und De pudicitia und das Indulgenzedikt des Papstes Kallistus. Bonn, 1905. — P. DE LABRIOLLE, Vestiges d'apocryphes dans le De paenitentia de Tertullien 12, 9: Bull. d'anc. littér. et d'arch. chrét. 1 (1911) 127–128. — A. D'ALÈS, L'Édit de Calliste. Paris, 1914, 136–171: Le

traité de Tertullien de paenitentia. — S. W. J. TEEUWEN, De voce 'paenitentia' apud
Tertullianum: Mnem 55 (1927) 410–419. — CHARTIER, L'excommunication ecclésiastique d'après les écrits de Tertullien: Antonianum (1935) 301 ff, 499 ff. — J.W.
PH. BORLEFFS, Observationes criticae in Tertulliani De paenitentia libellum: Mnem
60 (1932)41–106; *idem,* Index verborum quae Tertulliani de paenitentia libello continentur: Mnem 60 (1932) 254–316. — LUKMAN, Bogoslovni Vestnik (1939) 236–266.
— J. W. PH. BORLEFFS, Een nieuw handschrift van Tertullianus: Handelingen van
het 21e Nederl. Philologencongres. Groningen, 1950, 27. — For further studies, see
the bibliography on *De pudicitia.*

7. *To His Wife*

Tertullian wrote not less than three treatises on marriage and
remarriage, one as a Catholic, the next in his semi-Montanistic
period and the last after his final break with the Church. The
first, and by far the best, *Ad uxorem* was composed between the
years 200–206. Consisting of two books, it contains suggestions
which his wife is to follow after his departure from this world, and
which he bequeaths to her in the form of a spiritual legacy. He
admonishes her in the first book to remain a widow because there
are weighty reasons against, and no good excuses for her taking
another husband. The flesh, the world and the desire of posterity
should not induce a Christian to contract a second marriage because the servant of God is above all such necessities. The spirit
is stronger than the flesh, the things of earth should yield to the
things of heaven, and children are only a burden in view of the
strained times which are at hand, and constitute even a danger to
the faith in many cases. Let the faithful learn from the pagans.
They have a priesthood of widows and celibates and their
Pontifex maximus is not permitted to rewed. If God wills that a
woman·lose her partner by death, she should not attempt, by
taking another, to restore what God has put asunder. Such unions
are an obstacle to holiness, as the law of the Church indicates by
denying certain honors to those who have ventured into them.
Of course, none of these arguments is really convincing and thus
the author discusses in the second book the possibility that his
wife may not wish to stay single after his death. In that case he
begs her to make certain that she chooses a Christian. Marriages
between believers and unbelievers have been condemned by the
Apostle (1 Cor. 7, 12–14). They are a danger to faith and morals,
even if the infidel should be tolerant:

Among your 'pearls' count also the distinctive religious observances of your daily life. The more you attempt to conceal them, the more suspect they become and the more they arouse a pagan's curiosity. Do you think to escape notice when you make the sign of the Cross on your bed or on your body? Or when you blow away, with a puff of your breath, some unclean thing? Or when you get up, as you do even at night, to say your prayers? In all this will it not seem that you observe some magic ritual? Will not your husband know what it is you take in secret before eating any other food? If he recognizes it as bread, will he not believe it to be what it is rumored to be? Even if he has not heard these rumors, will he be so ingenuous as to accept the explanation which you give, without protest, without wondering whether it is really bread and not some magic charm. Suppose there are those who tolerate all this: yet they do so only to trample on and scoff at women who believe (2, 5 ACW 13).

There is an even greater risk for the Christian wife of having to take part in pagan rites on the holidays of demons and on the feasts of rulers. Women converted after marriage may be excused. It is quite a different thing, however, to wed a heathen and thus endanger one's religion. 'No marriage of this kind can turn out well: it is procured by the Evil One and damned by the Lord' (2, 7). The reason for such mixed unions is weakness of faith and passion for the riches and pleasures of this world. The author contrasts them with the happiness of two Christians:

How shall we ever be able adequately to describe the happiness of that marriage which the Church arranges, the Sacrifice strengthens, upon which the blessing sets a seal, at which angels are present as witnesses, and to which the Father gives His consent? For not even on earth do children marry properly and legally without their father's permission.

How beautiful, then, the marriage of two Christians, two who are one in hope, one in desire, one in the way of life they follow, one in the religion they practice. They are as brother and sister, both servants of the same Master. Nothing divides them, either in flesh or in spirit. They are, in very truth, two in one flesh; and where there is but one flesh there is also but one spirit. They pray together, they worship together, they fast together; instructing one another, encouraging one another, strengthening one another. Side by side they visit God's church and partake of God's banquet; side by side they face difficulties and persecution, share their consolations. They have no secrets from one another; they never shun each other's company; they never bring sorrow to each other's hearts... Psalms and hymns they sing to one another, striving to see which one of them will chant more beautifully the praises of their Lord. Hearing and seeing this, Christ rejoices. To such as these He gives His peace. Where there are two together, there also He is present, and where He is, there evil is not (2, 8 ACW 13).

Edition: A. KROYMANN, CSEL 70 (1942) 96–124.

Translations: English: C. DODGSON, Library of Fathers 10. Oxford, 1842, 409–431. — S. THELWALL, ANL 11, 279–303; ANF 4, 39–49. — W. P. LE SAINT, Treatises on Marriage and Remarriage (ACW 13). Westminster, Md., 1951, 10–36. — *German:* H. KELLNER, BKV² 7 (1912). — *Dutch:* H. U. MEYBOOM, Aan mijn echtgenoote (Oudchristel. geschriften, dl. 46). Leiden, 1931. — CHR. MOHRMANN, Aan mijn vrouw (MC 1, 3). Utrecht, 1951, 329–356.

Studies: H. KOCH, Zur Agapen-Frage (Tertullian, Ad uxor. 2, 4): ZNW (1915) 139–146. — H. PREISKER, Christentum und Ehe in den ersten drei Jahrhunderten. Berlin, 1927, 187–200.

8. *Exhortation to Chastity*

De exhortatione castitatis is addressed to one of Tertullian's friends who had recently lost his wife. The author, urging him not to rewed, takes up the problem of second marriage again, which he rejects as contrary to God's will and opposed by St. Paul (1 Cor. 7, 27, 28). Although he must admit that God tolerates such unions, he states that they are really nothing but a kind of fornication (9). His leaning to Montanism becomes evident. Whereas in the treatise *To His Wife* he praises the blessings of a Christian marriage, he now seems to regret that it was ever permitted and regards it as but legitimate debauchery. Instead, he now extols virginity and continence and even quotes the Montanistic visionary Prisca to this end: 'In like manner the holy prophetess Prisca declares that every holy minister will know how to administer things that are holy. 'For,' she says, 'continence effects the harmony of soul, and the pure see visions and, bowing down, hear

voices speaking clearly words salutary and secret' (10 ACW 13).
But there is no evidence that Tertullian had left the Church when
he wrote this treatise. Thus it must be dated between 204 and 212
A.D.

Edition: A. KROYMANN, CSEL 70 (1942) 125-152.

Translations: English: S. THELWALL, ANL 18, 1-20; ANF 4, 50-58. — W. P. LE
SAINT, Tertullian, Treatises on Marriage and Remarriage (ACW 13). Westminster,
Md., 1951, 42-64.—*German:* H. KELLNER, BKV² 7 (1912).—*Dutch:* H. U. MEYBOOM,
Over de vermaning tot kuischheid (Oudchristel. geschriften, dl. 46). Leiden, 1931.

9. *Monogamy*

De monogamia is of Tertullian's three treatises on marriage and
remarriage the most brilliant in style and most aggressive and
abusive in contents. The introduction (ch. 1) makes it quite clear
that he had thrown off the restraining influence of the Church
and definitely joined forces with the Montanists. This view,
according to him, represents the golden mean between the
heretical repudiation of the sacrament by the Gnostics and Catholic licentiousness in permitting repeated reception of it: 'The
former is blasphemy, the latter, wantonness; the former would
do away with the God of marriage, the latter would put Him to
the blush. We, however, who are deservedly called the *Spiritual*
because of the spiritual charisms which acknowledgedly are ours,
consider that continence is as worthy of veneration as freedom to
marry is worthy of respect, since both are according to the will of
the Creator. Continence honors the law of marriage, permission
to marry tempers it; the former is perfectly free, the latter is
subject to regulation; the former is a matter of free choice, the
latter is restricted within certain limits. We admit but one
marriage, just as we recognize but one God' (1 ACW 13). Thus he
now judges second marriage illicit and the next thing to adultery
(15). He defends his doctrine against the charge of innovation by
referring to the witness of the Paraclete (2-3), the evidence found
in the Old Testament (4-7), the Gospels (8-9), and the Epistles
of St. Paul (10-14). To repel the imputation of undue harshness he
argues that the pagan attitude against re-entering the wedded
state proves that weakness of the flesh is no excuse for such a step
(16-17).

The date of this treatise is most probably the year 217 A.D. because Tertullian states (ch. 3) that one hundred and sixty years have elapsed since St. Paul addressed his first Epistle to the Corinthians (57 A.D.).

Edition: F. OEHLER, Q.S.F. Tertulliani opera omnia, ed. maior 1, Leipzig, 1853, 761–787.

Translations: English: S. THELWALL, ANL 18, 21–55; ANF 4, 59–72. — W. P. LE SAINT, Tertullian, Treatises on Marriage and Remarriage (ACW 13). Westminster, Md., 1951, 70–108. — *German:* H. KELLNER-G. ESSER, BKV² 24 (1916). — *Dutch:* H. U. MEYBOOM, Leiden, 1930.

Studies: J. KÖHNE, Über die Mischehen in den ersten christlichen Zeiten: ThGl 23 (1931) 333–350; *idem,* Die kirchliche Eheschließungsformen in der Zeit Tertullians: ThGl 23 (1931) 645–654; *idem,* Die Ehe zwischen Christen und Heiden in den ersten christlichen Jahrhunderten. Paderborn, 1931. — J. DELAZER, De insolubilitate matrimonii iuxta Tertullianum: Antonianum 7 (1932) 441–464. — J. C. PLUMPE, Some Recommendations Regarding the Text of Tertullians 'De monogamia': TS 12 (1951) 557–559.

10. *Concerning the Veiling of Virgins*

De virginibus velandis deals with a topic which the author seems to have regarded as highly important. He demanded the veiling of virgins in *De oratione* (ch. 20–23) and again in *De cultu feminarum* (2, 7). The introduction of the present treatise indicates that he had previously written a Greek work with the same purpose: 'I will show in Latin also that it behooves our virgins to be veiled from the time that they have passed the turningpoint of their age and that this observance is exacted by truth, on which no one can impose prescription' (ANF).

After examining the question of custom and its gradual development, he points out that the contemporary etiquette, which required women to conceal their faces on various occasions, applied to the unmarried as well as the married. Since 1 Cor. 11, 5–16, contrary to what some Christians asserted, made no exception for the former, then Scripture, nature and good manners all demanded that the maiden should cover her head, and if she did so outside the Church, why not inside? The author gives an enthusiastic description of the continuous operation of the Paraclete:

> This law of faith being constant, the other succeeding points of discipline and conversation admit the novelty of correction; the grace of God, to wit, operating and advancing

to the end. For what kind of supposition is it, that, while the devil is always operating and adding daily to the ingenuities of iniquity, the work of God should either have ceased, or else have desisted from advancing? whereas why the Lord sent the Paraclete was, that, since human mediocrity was unable to take in all things at once, discipline should little by little be directed and ordained and carried on to perfection by that Vicar of the Lord, the Holy Spirit... What, then, is the Paraclete's administrative office but this: the direction of discipline, the revelation of the Scriptures, the reformation of the intellect, the advancement toward the 'better things?' (1 ANF 4)

Despite this reference to the Paraclete and the sarcastic criticisms of the clergy throughout the treatise, the break between the Montanists and the Catholics at Carthage had not taken place as yet. In the second chapter the author, after discussing the custom of the Eastern Churches, even stresses the unity of the Church: 'They and we have one faith, one God, the same Christ, the same hope, the same baptismal sacraments; let me say it once for all, we are one Church' (2 ANF 4). Thus the treatise must have been written before the year 207 A.D.

Edition: F. OEHLER, Q.S.F. Tertulliani opera omnia, ed. maior 1. Leipzig, 1853, 883–910.

Translations: English: S. THELWALL, ANL 18, 154–180; ANF 4, 27–37. — *Dutch:* H. U. MEYBOOM, Over de vraag, of de maagden zich moeten sluieren (Oudchristel. geschriften, dl. 46). Leiden, 1931.

11. *The Chaplet*

Although *De corona* is an occasional writing, it discusses one of the greatest problems, the participation of Christians in military service. The occasion was the following. When the Emperor Septimius Severus died on February 4, 211, his sons made a gift of money to the army, the so-called *donativum*. When it was distributed in the camp, the soldiers approached laurel-crowned, except for one of them, who had his head uncovered and carried the wreath in his hand. 'Accordingly all began to mark him out, jeering him at a distance, gnashing at him near at hand. The murmur is wafted to the tribune, when the person had just left the ranks. The tribune at once puts the question to him, Why are

you so different in your attire? He declared that he had no
liberty to wear the crown with the rest. Being urgently asked for
his reasons, he answered, I am a Christian... Then the case was
considered and voted on; the matter was remitted to a higher
tribunal; the offender was conducted to the prefects... and
crowned more worthily with the white crown of martyrdom, he
now awaits in prison the largess of Christ. Thereafter adverse
judgments began to be passed upon his conduct—whether on the
part of Christians I do not know, for those of the heathen are no
different—as if he were headstrong and rash, and too eager to
die, because, in being taken to task about a mere matter of dress,
he brought trouble on the bearers of the name [of Christ]... Now
as they put forth also the objection—But are we forbidden to be
crowned? I shall take this point up, as more suitable to be treated
of here, being the essence, in fact, of the present contention' (1
ANF 3). Thus the treatise is written in defense of the soldier in
order to show that the wearing of crowns was incompatible with
the Christian faith. The author resorts to an unwritten Christian
tradition to demonstrate that it is unnatural to put a chaplet on
the head. Moreover, this custom is of pagan origin and intimately
connected with idolatry. The Old and the New Testament do not
mention such a practice and, to be specific, the military wreath is
forbidden for the simple reason that warfare and army service
cannot be reconciled with the faith. The Christian knows only
one oath, the baptismal vow, he knows only one watchservice,
that for his King Christ. This is the camp of light; the other, the
camp of darkness. Tertullian takes most of his material from
Claudius Saturninus' work *De coronis*, to which he refers in ch. 7:
'Those who want additional information will find an ample
exposition of the subject in Claudius Saturninus, writer of
distinguished talent who treats this question also, for he has a
book on crowns, explaining their beginnings as well as causes, and
kinds and rites' (7 ANF 3).

De corona criticizes the Catholics for rejecting the Paraclete and
his prophecies and scoffs at the clergy: 'It is plain that as they
have rejected the prophecies of the Holy Spirit, they are also
purposing the refusal of martyrdom. So they murmur that a
peace so good and so long is endangered for them. Nor do I doubt
that some are already turning their back on the Scriptures, are

naking ready their luggage, are equipped for flight from city to
city; for that is all of the gospel they care to remember. I know,
oo, their pastors are lions in peace and deer in the fight' (1 *ibid.*).
The treatise is generally assigned to the year 211 A.D.

Editions: A. Kroymann, CSEL 70 (1942) 125–152. — J. Marra, Tertullianus, De
orona (Corpus script. lat. Paravianum 49). Turin, 1927.

Translations: English: C. Dodgson, Library of Fathers 10. Oxford, 1842, 158–184. —
». Thelwall, ANL 11, 333–355; ANF 3, 93–103. — *German:* H. Kellner-
J. Esser, BKV² 24 (1915). — *Dutch:* H. U. Meyboom, Over den lauwerkrans
ler soldaten (Oudchristel. geschriften, dl. 46). Leiden, 1931.

Studies: E. Vacandard, La question du service militaire chez les chrétiens des pre-
niers siècles. Paris, 1910, 127 ff. — P. Franchi de' Cavalieri, Note agiografiche,
'asc. 8 (ST 65). Vatican City, 1935, 357–386. — J. W. C. L. Schulte, Tertullianus
n de krijgsdienst: Onder eigen Vaandel 12 (1937) 71–89. — K. Baus, Der Kranz
n Antike und Christentum. Eine religionsgeschichtl. Untersuchung mit bes. Berück-
ichtigung Tertullians (Theophaneia 2). Bonn, 1940. — F. J. Dölger, Das Nach-
prechen der Formel beim Militärgebet am Jahres-Anfang. Zu Tertullians De corona
12: AC 6 (1941) 77. — H. R. Minn, Tertullian and War: Ev. Quarterly 13 (1941)
·02–213. — R. H. Bainton, The Early Church and War: HThR 39 (1946) 190 f. —
J. de Plinval, Tertullien et le scandale de la Couronne: Mélanges de Ghellinck.
Gembloux, 1951, 183–188. — E. A. Ryan, The Rejection of Military Service by the
Early Christians: TS 13 (1952) 1–32.

12. *Concerning Flight in Persecution*

A question touched upon in *De corona* receives a thorough
answer in *De fuga in persecutione:* Is the Christian permitted to take
refuge in flight during a persecution? *Ad uxorem*, 1, 3, Tertullian
stated: 'In time of persecution it is better to flee from place to
place, as we are permitted, than to be arrested and to deny the
faith under torture.' The same view prevails in *De patientia* 13. In
the present treatise, however, the author holds that such an
escape goes against the will of God; persecution comes from Him,
is designed by Him to strengthen the faith of the Christians,
although it cannot be denied that the devil has a part in it. If
some object and refer to Matthew 10, 23 'When they begin to
persecute you, flee from city to city,' Tertullian maintains that
this belongs especially to the persons of the apostles and to their
times and circumstances, but not to the present (6). Nor is it
permitted to escape molestation by money, because the reason is
the same, the fear of martyrdom. To ransom with money a man
whom Christ has ransomed with His blood, is unworthy of God

(12). The treatise is addressed to the author's friend Fabius and
announced in *De corona* (ch. 1). There is ample evidence for the
Montanist point of view (ch. 1; 11; 14). Thus it ought to be dated
in the year 212 A.D.

Editions: J. J. THIERRY, Tertullianus, De fuga in persecutione, met vertaling er
toel. Hilversum, 1941. — J. MARRA, Tertulliani De fuga in persecutione (Corpus
script. lat. Paravianum 59). Turin, 1933.

Translations: English: S. THELWALL, ANL 11, 356–378; ANF 4, 116–125. — *Dutch:*
H. U. MEYBOOM, Over de vlucht in de vervolging (Oudchristel. geschriften, dl.
43). Leiden, 1932.

Studies: L. CASTIGLIONI, Ad Tertullianum adnotationes: Studi Ubaldi. Milan, 1937,
260 ff. — J. H. WASZINK, Museum 1 (1943) 168–170.

13. *Concerning Idolatry*

Of the same time as *De corona* (211 A.D.) seems to be *De idololatria*, which again takes up the basic question: Is the Christian
permitted to serve in the army? But going far beyond this, it aims
to free the believer of everything that is in any way connected
with idolatry. Thus Tertullian condemns not only the makers and
worshippers of images (4) but any profession or art which he
regards as subservient to paganism. Thus astrologers, mathematicians, schoolmasters, professors of literature, are barred from
the Church, not to speak of trainers of gladiators, frankincense-
sellers, enchanters and magicians (8–11). Such a wholesale
exclusion creates two difficulties. First of all people will ask, 'How
am I to live?' The author answers that faith does not fear famine
and that since a Christian has learned to despise death, he
certainly does not hesitate to despise the necessities of human
maintenance (12). The second problem is, if teaching is not
lawful to Christians, no education will be possible. Here Tertullian makes the interesting concession, that teaching is forbidden, but learning permitted:

> Let us see, then, the necessity of literary erudition; let us
> reflect that partly it cannot be admitted, partly cannot be
> avoided. Learning literature is allowable for believers,
> rather than teaching; for the principle of learning and of
> teaching is different. If a believer teach literature, while he is
> teaching doubtless he commends, while he delivers he
> affirms, while he recalls he bears testimony to the praises of

idols interspersed therein... But when a believer learns these things, if he is already capable of understanding what idolatry is, he neither receives nor allows them; much more if he is not yet capable. Or, when he begins to understand, it behooves him first to understand what he has previously learned, that is, touching God and the faith. Therefore he will reject those things, and will not receive them; and will be as safe as one who from one who knows it not, knowingly accepts poison, but does not drink it. To him necessity is attributed as an excuse, because he has no other way to learn (10 ANF 3).

A sweeping condemnation of all forms of painting, modelling or sculpture (5) and of participation in national festivals follows (15). This leads to the question, what offices of the State a Christian may occupy. According to the author, no one can believe it possible to avoid idolatry in its many forms in any public position and for this reason no believer can enter upon one (18). Every member of the Church has forsworn the devil's pomps at baptism and he will be a happier magistrate in heaven for having avoided such honors here on earth. Tertullian declares the State the enemy of God: 'Let even this fact help to remind you that all the powers and dignities of this world are not only alien to, but enemies of God' (18). It can hardly surprise us that with such a view of the relation between the faith and the Empire he rejects military service outright: 'There is no agreement between the divine and the human oath, the standard of Christ and the standard of the devil, the camp of light and the camp of darkness. One soul cannot be due to two masters—God and Caesar' (19 ANF).

Edition: A. REIFFERSCHEID-G. WISSOWA, CSEL 20 (1890) 30–58.

Translations: English: C. DODGSON, Library of Fathers 10. Oxford, 1842, 220–252. — S. THELWALL, ANL 11, 141–177; ANF 3, 61–76. — *German:* H. KELLNER, BKV² 7 (1912). — *Dutch:* H. U. MEYBOOM, Over den afgodendienst (Oudchristel. geschriften, dl. 43). Leiden, 1930.

Studies: G. T. LANG, Tertullian and the Pagan Cults: TP (1913) XXXV ff. — J. L. SCHULTE, Het Heidendom bij Tertullianus. Diss. Leiden, 1923. — F. J. DÖLGER, Heidnische Begrüßung und christliche Verhöhnung des Heidentempels. Kultur- und religionsgeschichtl. Bemerkungen zu Tertullian De idololatria 11: AC 3 (1932) 192–203. — J. H. WASZINK, Tertullianea: Mnem 3 (1935/36) 171 ff. — G. L. ELLSPERMANN, The Attitude of the Early Christian Writers Toward Pagan Literature and Learning (PSt 82). Diss. Washington, 1949, 23–42.

14. *On Fasting*

The title of this treatise *De ieiunio adversus psychicos* indicates that the Montanist Tertullian directed it against the Catholics, i.e., the *psychici*, on the question of fasting, which had caused a passionate controversy between the two parties. The author violently attacks the Catholics, 'enthralled with voluptuousness and bursting with gluttony' (1), for rejecting the Montanist practices. The writer's faction was charged, it appears, with adding to the number of fast days, prolonging stations generally into the evening, keeping *xerophagies*, i.e., food unmoistened by meat, gravies, sauces or juicy fruits, touching nothing with a wine flavor, and abstaining from the bath on the occasion of such penitential observances (1). These were all condemned as novelties originating in heresy or pseudo-prophecy. Tertullian springs to the defence and arranges his argument like a lawyer's brief. From both the Old and the New Testament he demonstrates the necessity of fasting after Adam's disobedience and the advantages of abstinence, and he denies that there is anything new about this form of the stations (10). After refuting the accusation of heresy and pseudo-prophecy (11), he changes over to a virulent attack on the self-indulgence of the Catholics. He accuses them of 'furnishing cookshops in the prison to untrustworthy martyrs' (12) and of being more irreligious than the pagans (16). The treatise contains some of the lowest expressions Tertullian ever used. For the history of fasting it remains a valuable source of information.

Edition: A. REIFFERSCHEID-G. WISSOWA, CSEL 20 (1890) 274–297.

Translations: English: S. THELWALL, ANL 18, 123–153; ANF 4, 102–114. — *German:* H. KELLNER-G. ESSER, BKV² 24 (1915). — *Dutch:* H. U. MEYBOOM, Over de vasten tegen de Katholieken (Oudchristel. geschriften, dl. 46). Leiden, 1931.

Study: J. SCHÜMMER, Die altchristliche Fastenpraxis mit besonderer Berücksichtigung der Schriften Tertullians (LQF 27). Münster, 1933.

15. *On Modesty*

The treatise *De pudicitia* is no less violent than the preceding, but deals with a much more important subject, the power of the keys, which, according to the author's Montanistic concept of the Church, belongs not to the ecclesiastical hierarchy but to the spiritual, i.e. apostles and prophets. It represents chiefly a powerful polemic against the penitential discipline of the Catholic

Church of North Africa and specifically against an *edictum peremptorium* of a bishop whose name is not given. According to Tertullian this *pontifex maximus* and *episcopus episcoporum*, as he calls him, declares: 'I remit the sins of adultery and fornication to those who have done penance.' The question is, who was this bishop? Many identify him with Pope Callistus (217–222). No grounds for doubting this would exist, if Tertullian were pointing to the same case as caused the schism of Hippolytus, or if it were certain, that the precedent mentioned in *De pudicitia* could have been set only at Rome. Neither the former nor the latter can be established, as pointed out above (p. 234 f). The titles *pontifex maximus* and *episcopus episcoporum* do not prove the contrary, because they are employed ironically, like the others, *benignissimus Dei interpres, bonus pastor et benedictus papa*. Moreover, they were unknown at that time as specific designations of the bishop of Rome. Since Tertullian dubs his opponent *psychicus*, a name he often used for his fellow-Catholics at Carthage, we are justified in supposing that he refers to Bishop Agrippinus of that city (Cyprian, *Epist.* 71, 4). In addition, the situation differs entirely from that described by Hippolytus (cf. above, pp. 205 f). Finally, we have the following allusion (ch. 21):

> I now inquire into your opinion, to see from what source you usurp this right to 'the Church.' If, because the Lord has said to Peter, 'Upon this rock I will build My Church,' 'to thee have I given the keys of the heavenly kingdom,' or, 'Whatsoever thou shalt have bound or loosed in earth, shall be bound or loosed in the heavens,' you therefore presume that the power of binding and loosing has derived to you, that is, to every Church akin to Peter, what sort of man are you, subverting and wholly changing the manifest intention of the Lord, conferring this gift personally upon Peter? (ANF 4)

The words 'that is, to every Church akin to Peter' (*id est ad omnem ecclesiam Petri propinquam*) make sense only if they refer not solely to the bishop of Rome, but to that of *every* church related to Peter by faith or origin. This fits Carthage very well, founded as tradition holds, by Roman missionaries.

If we compare *De pudicitia* with Tertullian's earlier treatise *De paenitentia*, we notice the complete contradiction in which they stand to each other. In the history of penitential discipline *De pudicitia* is the first source to mention the three capital sins of idolatry, fornication and murder, which the author considers as 'unpardonable.' Thus he now introduces the distinction between *peccata remissibilia* and *irremissibilia* (2)—a distinction absent from *De paenitentia*. The Church, he argues, has no power to forgive such great iniquities after baptism, and even the intercession of the martyrs for the guilty cannot avail.

Editions: A. REIFFERSCHEID-G. WISSOWA, CSEL 20 (1890) 219–273. — E. PREUSCHEN, SQ 1, 2. Tübingen, 1910, 2nd ed. — P. DE LABRIOLLE, De paenitentia, De pudicitia. Texte et traduct. (Textes et documents, publ. par H. Hemmer et P. Lejay). Paris, 1906. — G. RAUSCHEN, FP 10. Bonn, 1915.

Translations: English: S. THELWALL, ANL 18, 56–122; ANF 4, 74–101. — *German:* H. KELLNER-G. ESSER, BKV² 24 (1915). — *Dutch:* H. U. MEYBOOM, Leiden, 1931. — *French:* P. DE LABRIOLLE, *loc. cit.*

Studies: E. ROLFFS, Das Indulgenzedikt des römischen Bischofs Callistus (TU 11, 3). Leipzig, 1893. — G. ESSER, Tertullian De pudicitia 21 und der Primat des römischen Bischofs: Katholik 92, 2 (1902) 193 ff; *idem,* Die Bußschriften Tertullians De paenitentia und De pudicitia und das Indulgenzedikt des Papstes Kallistus. Progr. Bonn, 1905; *idem,* Nochmals das Indulgenzedikt des Papstes Kallistus und die Bußschriften Tertullians: Katholik 87, 2 (1907) 184 ff, 297 ff; 88, 1 (1908) 12 ff, 93 ff; *idem,* Der Adressat der Schrift Tertullians 'De pudicitia' und der Verfasser des römischen Buß-edikts. Bonn, 1914. — F. X. FUNK, Das Indulgenzedikt des Papstes Kallistus: ThQ 88 (1906) 541 ff. — J. STUFLER, Zur Kontroverse über das Indulgenzedikt des Papstes Kallistus: ZkTh 32 (1908) 1 ff. — M. HAGUENIN, De pudicitia 6, 15: RSR (1911) 459 f. — A. D'ALÈS, L'Édit de Calliste. Paris, 1914. — K. PREYSING, Existenz und Inhalt des Bußedikts Kallists: ZkTh 43 (1919) 358 ff. — K. ADAM, Das sog. Bußedikt des Papstes Kallistus (Veröffentl. aus dem kirchenhistor. Seminar München 4, 5). Munich, 1917. — H. KOCH, Kallist und Tertullian. Ein Beitrag zur Geschichte der altchristl. Bußstreitigkeiten und des römischen Primats (SAH 1919, No. 22). Heidelberg, 1920. — A. D'ALÈS, RSR (1920) 254–257. — C. FIGGINI, Agrippino o Callisto?: SC VI, 3 (1924) 204–211. — D. FRANSES, Das 'Edictum Callisti' in der neueren Forschung: StC 1 (1924) 248–259. — G. BARDY, L'édit d'Agrippinus: RSR 4 (1924) 1–25. — A. DONINI, L'Editto di Agrippino: RR (1925) 56–71. — K. PREYSING, Römischer Ursprung des 'Edictum peremptorium': ZkTh 50 (1926) 143–150. — LUKMAN, Bogoslovni Vestnik (1926) 169–196. — P. BATIFFOL, Les origines de la pénitence (Études d'histoire et de théologie positive, Ie série), 7th ed. Paris, 1926, 78–105. — P. GALTIER, Le véritable édit de Calliste: RHE 23 (1927) 465–488. — A. HARNACK, Ecclesia Petri propinqua. Zur Geschichte der Anfänge des Primats des römischen Bischofs: SAB 28 (1927) 139–152. — K. ADAM, Neue Untersuchungen über die Ursprünge der kirchlichen Primatslehre: ThQ 109 (1928) 167–203. — F. CAVALLERA, La doctrine de la pénitence au IIIe siècle: BLE 30 (1929) 19–36; 31 (1930) 49–63. — H. KOCH, Cathedra Petri. Giessen, 1930, 5–32. — A. M. VELLICO, 'Episcopus episcoporum' in Tertulliani libro 'De pudicitia': Antonianum 5 (1930) 25–26. — E. GÖLLER, Papsttum und Bußgewalt in spätrömischer und frühmittelalterlicher Zeit: RQ 39 (1931) 77–85. — H. Koch, Zu Tertullian De pudicitia 21, 9 ff: ZNW (1932) 68–72. — A. Ehrhard, Die Kirche der Märtyrer. Munich, 1932, 359–366. — F. J. Dölger, Ne quis adulter! Zum Verständnis der scharfen Kritik Tertullians an dem Bußedikt des christlichen 'Pontifex Maximus': AC 3 (1932) 132–148. — W. Köhler, Omnis ecclesia Petri propinqua: ZNW 31 (1932) 60–67. — D. van den Eynde, Les normes de l'enseignement chrétien dans la littérature patristique des trois premiers siècles. Paris, 1933, 206. — B. Poschmann, Ecclesia principalis. Breslau, 1933, 10 f. — H. Koch, Nochmals zu Tertullian De pud. 21, 9 ff: ZNW (1934) 317–318. — A. d'Alès,Tertullianea. De pudicitia XXII, 9–10: RSR 26 (1936) 366–367; idem, Tertullianea. De pudicitia VI, 16: RSR 27 (1937) 230–231. — H. Stoeckius, Ecclesia Petri propria. Eine kirchengeschichtliche Untersuchung der Primatsfrage bei Tertullian: AKK 117 (1937) 24–126. — W. Koehler, Omnis ecclesia Petri propinqua (Tert. De pudicitia 21). Versuch einer religionsgeschichtlichen Deutung. Heidelberg, 1938. — A. D. Nock, A Feature of Roman Religion (De pud. 1): HThR 32 (1939) 83–96. — B. Altaner, Omnis ecclesia Petri propinqua: ThR 38 (1939) 129–138. — B. Poschmann, Paenitentia secunda. Bonn, 1940, 348–367. — P. Keseling, Aristoteles bei Tertullian (De pud. 1, 1): PhJ 57 (1947) 256–257. — A. Quacquarelli, Libertà, peccato e penitenza secondo Tertulliano: Rassegna di Scienze filosofiche 2 (1949) 16–37.

16. *Concerning the Pallium*

De pallio is the smallest of Tertullian's treatises, consisting only of six chapters. He wrote it in his own defense, when he was criticized for having substituted in everyday life the mantle or *pallium* for the *toga*. The latter, he reminds his fellow-citizens, introduced by the Romans after their victory over Carthage, symbolizes defeat and suppression, while the former had previously been worn by all ranks and conditions. Moreover, change is the universal law; to vary her attire is the stated function of all nature. The world alters, the earth alters, nations and rulers come and go. Animals, instead of garments, take off and on their form, their plumage, their skin, their color. Thus nobody can be surprised that man also changes. The history of dress is long, ever since its beginning after the Fall. It must, however, be admitted that the new is not always an improvement. If his fellow-citizens object to the Greek origin of the *pallium*, he finds this strange, because they always liked to imitate the Greeks, even in that which does not deserve to be imitated. And if they wish to criticize clothes, let them point their finger at what endangers modesty, at men who make themselves look like women, and at matrons whom one cannot tell from harlots. The *pallium* recommends itself for its simplicity and handiness. It is the garb of philosophers,

rhetoricians, sophists, physicians, poets, musicians and astrologers, grammarians. The author at this point lets the pallium
speak for itself. 'All that is liberal in studies is covered by my four
angles' (6). It is true, it is not the proper thing for the forum, the
election-ground, the senate-house, the praetorian residence and
the Roman knight. Thus it is excluded from the offices of the
State, but it has now received a much higher dignity, it has
become the vesture of the Christian: 'Joy pallium and exult! A
better philosophy has now deigned to honor thee, ever since thou
hast begun to be a Christian's vesture' (6). These are the closing
words of the treatise, which is full of wit, originality and sarcasm.
As to its date, great difference of opinion exists. *The triple power
of our present empire* (*praesentis imperii triplex virtus*) of ch. 2 is
inconclusive because it may refer to 193 A.D., when Didius
Julianus, Pescennius Niger and Septimius Severus divided the
authority, or to 209–211, when Severus and his two sons, An-
toninus and Geta, ruled jointly. The earlier of these is favored by
the complete absence of Montanistic views and the change of
dress would then have coincided with the writer's conversion.
However, the later fits better with a passage which describes the
soil as admirably cultivated all over the world and which speaks
of the eradication of all hostilities—a state of affairs most consistent with the peace ensuing upon Severus' ending of the bitter
strife among the various claimants to the throne.

Editions: G. MARRA, Tertulliano, De Pallio. Prima trad. ital. con testo critico e
comment. (Corpus script. lat. Paravianum 59). Turin, 1933. — A. GERLO, Tertullianus, De pallio. Critische uitgave met vertaling en commentaar. Wetteren, 1940. —
Q. CATAUDELLA, Il mantello di sagezza. De pallio. Testo crit. vers. e note. Genua,
1947.

Translations: English: S. THELWALL, ANL 18, 181–200; ANF 4, 5–12. — *Italian:*
G. MARRA, *loc. cit.* — Q. CATAUDELLA, *loc. cit.* — *German:* H. KELLNER, BKV² 7
(1912). — *Dutch:* H. U. MEYBOOM, Over den mantel (Oudchristel. geschriften, dl.
46). Leiden, 1931. — A. GERLO, *loc. cit.* — *Spanish:* E. DE UBANI, La Capa de Tertuliano. Madrid, 1631. — J. PELLICER DE OSSAU, Version parafrastica castellana de
Palio de Tertuliano. Barcelona, 1658.

Studies: M. ZAPPALA, L'ispirazione cristiana del De Pallio di Tertulliano: RR 1
(1925) 132 ff; *idem,* Le fonti del De Pallio: RR 1 (1925) 327–344. — D. S. ROBERT-
SON, Tertullian, De pallio IV: Proceedings of the Cambridge Philological Society
(1932) 151–153. — GUILLARD, La place du De pallio dans l'œuvre de Tertullien.
Paris, 1935. — L. CASTIGLIONI, Ad Tertullianum adnotationes: Studi Ubaldi.
Milan, 1937, 261 f. — A. GERLO, Textkritische nota's bij De pallio van Tertullianus:

RBPh (1939) 393–408. — C. ALBIZZATI, Il costume nel De pallio di Tertulliano: Athenaeum (1939) 138–149. — J. H. WASZINK, Mnem 3, 9 (1941) 131–137. — D. VAN BERCHEM, Un témoignage méconnu sur l'attitude des chrétiens à l'égard de l'empire, le De pallio de Tertullien: Bulletin de la Société des Études de Lettres (1943) 129–130; idem, Le De pallio de Tertullien et le conflit du christianisme et de l'empire: Museum Helveticum 1 (1944) 100–119. — J. M. VIS, Tertullianus' De Pallio tegen de achtergrond van zijn overige werken. Diss. Nijmegen, 1949.

2. LOST WRITINGS

These amount to a considerable number and, unfortunately, include all his works in Greek. Three of the latter have been mentioned above in connection with their Latin counterparts, *De spectaculis, De baptismo, De virginibus velandis*. A fourth was probably to be found in his *Concerning ecstasy*, which Jerome lists among the writings of the Montanistic period: 'Tertullian added to the six volumes which he wrote *On ecstasy* against the Church a seventh, directed especially against Apollonius, in which he attempts to defend all which Apollonius refuted' (*De vir. ill.* 40). Jerome gives it a Greek title, περὶ ἐκστάσεως. From the foregoing and two other passages (*ibid.* 24; 53), we see that to the original six books a seventh was added after Tertullian had read the attack on Montanism by Apollonius, the Asiatic bishop. Jerome gives the following account of this writer and his work:

Apollonius, an exceedingly talented man, wrote against Montanus, Prisca and Maximilla a notable and lengthy volume, in which he asserts that Montanus and his mad prophetesses died by hanging, and many other things, among which are the following concerning Prisca and Maximilla, 'if they denied that they have accepted gifts, let them confess that those who do accept are not prophets and I will prove by a thousand witnesses that they have received gifts, for it is by other fruits that prophets are shown to be prophets indeed. Tell me, does a prophet dye his hair? Does a prophet stain her eyelids with antimony? Is a prophet adorned with fine garments and precious stones? Does a prophet play with dice and tables? Does he accept usury? Let them respond whether this ought to be permitted or not, it will be my task to prove that they do these things' (*De vir. ill.* 40 LNPF 3).

Most probably Tertullian's seventh book answered these strange accusations, whereas the others dealt with his sect's prophecy and ecstasy. The whole was composed after his definite break with the Church, most probably about 213 A.D. Also lost are Tertullian's following Latin works:

1. *De spe fidelium*, in which he demonstrated that the Old Testament prophecies regarding the restoration of Judaea must be interpreted allegorically of Christ and the Church (*Adv. Marc.* 3,24). According to Jerome (*De vir. ill.* 18; *In Ez. comm.* ad 36, 1 ff; *In Is. comm.* 18 praef.) the chiliastic view was defended.

2. *De paradiso*, on questions concerning paradise (*Adv. Marc.* 5, 12; *De anim.* 55), voices the opinion that all souls, except those of the martyrs, will remain in Hades until the day of the Lord arrives.

3. *Adversus Apelleiacos*, against the adherents of Apelles, a follower of Marcion (cf. vol. I, p. 272 f), refutes their contention that not God, but a prominent angel, having the spirit, the power and the will of Christ, created this world, only to regret it afterwards (*De carne Christi* 8).

4. *De censu animae* (cf. above, p. 276).

5. *De fato*, announced in *De anima* 20, was to treat of fate and necessity, of Fortune and freedom of will, of the Lord God and His adversary, the devil, in their influence on the human intellect. This was actually written, as we know from a quotation of the African writer Fabius Planciades Fulgentius (*Exp. serm. antiqu.* 16). It seems also to have been used by the author (Ambrosiaster) of the tract *Quaestiones Veteris et Novi Testamenti* in *Quaestio* 115 (318–349 ed. A. Souter).

6. *Ad amicum philosophum.* According to Jerome (*Epist.* 22, 22; *Adv. Jovin.* 1, 13) Tertullian addressed in his early days a treatise on the troubles of married life (*De nuptiarum angustiis*) to a philosophic friend.

7. *De Aaron vestibus*, known to Jerome only from a list of Tertullian's writings (*Epist.* 64, 23).

8. *De carne et anima*, *De animae submissione*, and *De superstitione saeculi.* These titles are given in the table of contents of the *Codex Agobardinus* of the ninth century.

Non-authentic Writings

1. *De execrandis gentium diis.* Suarez found in a Vatican codex of the tenth century, along with Bede's *Chronicle* and other pieces,

this fragment of an apologetical treatise. The difference in style makes it impossible to attribute it to Tertullian, as the edition of Suarez did. The unknown author criticizes severely the pagan concepts of the deity and shows their unworthiness by the example of Jupiter.

Editions: ML, 2, 1115–1118. — E. BICKEL, Ps.-Tertullian, De execrandis gentium diis: RhM 76 (1927) 394–417.

Translations: English: S. THELWALL, ANL 18, 274–277; ANF 3, 149–150.

Study: H. KOCH, RhM 78 (1929) 220 ff.

2. *Adversus omnes haereses.* About this appendix to *De praescriptione*, cf. above, p. 272.

3. *Carmen adversus Marcionitas*, a poem of five books, dealing with the origin of the heresy (1), the intimate relation between the Old and the New Testaments against the dualism of Marcion (2–3), and his doctrine (4–5). Written in poor Latin most probably in Gaul before 325 A.D., it depends on Tertullian's treatise *Against Marcion*.

Editions: ML 2, 1051–1090. — M. MÜLLER, Untersuchungen zum Carmen adversus Marcionitas. Ochsenfurt, 1936, 7–38.

Translation: English: S. THELWALL, ANL 18, 318–384; ANF 4, 192–165.

Studies: A. OXÉ, Prolegomena de carmine Adv. Marcionitas. Diss. Leipzig, 1888. — H. WAITZ, Das pseudotertullianische Gedicht Adv. Marcionem. Darmstadt, 1901. — A. HARNACK, Geschichte der altchristl. Literatur 2, 2, 442–449. — Is. KOENIGS-DORFER, De carmine Adv. Marcionem, quod in Tertullianis libris traditur. Diss. Bayreuth, 1905.

4. *Passio SS. Perpetuae et Felicitatis* (cf. vol. I, p. 181 ff). The authorship of Tertullian remains doubtful.

5. *Carmen ad Flavium Felicem de resurrectione mortuorum et de iudicio Domini.* This poem consisting of more than 400 hexameters has been falsely attributed to Tertullian or to Cyprian. The real author is unknown. J. H. Waszink adduces good reasons for the end of the fifth or the beginning of the sixth century as its probable date.

Edition: J. H. WASZINK, Carmen ad Flavium Felicem de resurrectione mortuorum et de iudicio Domini (FP, Suppl. 1). Bonn, 1937.

3. ASPECTS OF TERTULLIAN'S THEOLOGY

Tertullian has been called the founder of Western theology and the father of our Christology. However, these are exaggerations, because he never created any system. In fact, he lacked the essential qualification, a balanced mind, which would enable him to arrange the different articles of faith in logical order and to assign to each of them its proper place. No one who reads his anti-heretical treatises will deny that he had speculative ability. But to dissolve apparent contradictions was not given him. Instead he created them. He had a predilection for the paradoxical. Although the sentence *Credo, quia absurdum* which has been attributed to him, does not occur in his writings, there are passages no less extraordinary for instance: 'The Son of God was crucified; I am not ashamed because men must needs be ashamed of it. And the Son of God died; it is by all means to be believed, because it is absurd' (*De carne Chr.* 5 ANF). Such abnormalities do not disturb him, because he is not concerned with building a bridge between religion and reason, but wants to emphasize that not even the apparent conflict between the facts of redemption and the human mind prevent him from believing in them. Thus he differs widely from the theologians of the school of Alexandria, especially from his younger contemporary Clement. He was not interested in bringing harmony between faith and philosophy. That explains perhaps why he never developed a theological system.

Studies: A. D'ALÈS, La théologie de Tertullien. Paris, 1905. — R. E. ROBERTS, The Theology of Tertullian. London, 1924. — J. LORTZ, Tertullian als Apologet (MBTh 9/10). Münster, 1927/28, 2 vols. — J. MORGAN, The importance of Tertullian in the Development of the Christian Dogma. London, 1928. — J. BERTON, Tertullien le schismatique. Paris, 1928. — TH. BRANDT, Tertullians Ethik. Gütersloh, 1929. — J. KLEIN, Tertullian. Christliches Bewußtsein und sittliche Forderungen (Diss. Bonn). Düsseldorf, 1940.

1. *Theology and Philosophy*

Whereas Clement of Alexandria greatly admired the thinkers of Greece and thought of them as playing the same role for the pagan as the Law for the Jew, Tertullian, by contrast, is convinced that philosophy and faith have nothing in common.

What indeed has Athens to do with Jerusalem? What concord is there between the Academy and the Church? what between heretics and Christians? Our instruction comes from the porch of Solomon, who himself taught that the Lord should be sought in simplicity of heart. Away with all attempts to produce a mottled Christianity of Stoic, Platonic and dialectic composition. We want no curious disputation after possessing Christ Jesus, no research after enjoying the gospel! With our faith we desire no further belief (*De praescr.* 7 ANF 3).

He speaks as if all human wisdom should be eliminated from the Church, because it 'pretends to know the truth, whilst it only corrupts it' (*ibid.*). 'Where is there any likeness between the Christian and the philosopher? between the disciple of Greece and of heaven? between the man whose object is fame, and whose object is life? between the talker and the doer? between the man who builds up and the man who pulls down? between the friend and the foe of error? between one who corrupts the truth, and the one who restores and teaches it?' (*Apol.* 46 ANF 3) Even Socrates, whom St. Justin called 'a Christian,' is only a 'corrupter of youth' (*ibid.*), not to speak of the 'miserable Aristotle' (*De praescr.* 7).

On the other hand, he has to admit that pagan speculation had caught glimpses of the truth: 'Of course, we shall not deny that philosophers have sometimes thought the same things as ourselves' (*De an.* 2), and it is especially Seneca, with whom he many times agrees: *Seneca saepe noster* (*De an.* 20). In fact, the influence of the Stoics on Tertullian is not to be underestimated. His concept of God, his notion of the soul and many of his moral principles testify to his dependence on their teaching. However, even where similarities exist between the doctrines of the Church and of pagan philosophers, he is careful to state that the latter stole such ideas from the Old Testament, which, as a source of revelation, belongs to the Christians. The ancient thinkers only distorted the God-given truths, and thus became responsible for the heresies; they are 'the patriarchs of heretics' (*De an.* 3). It is the same tendency that we notice twenty years later in the *Philosophumena* of Hippolytus of Rome, to blame all aberrations from the faith on heathen philosophy. We cannot be astonished that with such a distrust of the human intellect, he never tried to construct a theological system out of the isolated opinions which took shape in him in the course of his struggles with opponents.

Studies: C. DE L. SHORTT, The Influence of Philosophy on the Mind of Tertullian. London, 1933. — J. STELZENBERGER, Die Beziehungen der frühchristlichen Sittenlehre zur Ethik der Stoa. Munich, 1933. — F. J. DÖLGER, Die Bewertung von Mitleid und Barmherzigkeit bei Tertullianus: AC 5 (1936) 262–271. — J. H. Waszink, Traces of Aristotle's Lost Dialogues in Tertullian: VC 1 (1947) 137–149. — A. Labhardt, L'attitude de Tertullien vis-à-vis de la philosophie: RELA (1949) 73–74. — G. Bardy, 'Philosophie' et 'Philosophe' dans le vocabulaire chrétien des premiers siècles: RAM 25 (1949) 97–108. — A. Labhardt, Tertullien et la philosophie, ou la recherche d'une position pure: Museum Helveticum 7 (1950) 159 ff.

2. Theology and Law

As a lawyer Tertullian has much more confidence in law than in philosophy. Law and its genuine norms were what he demanded of those who carried on the persecution. Law inspired his great defense of the Church, his *Apologia* (p. 256 ff) and supplied his main argument against heresy, the 'praescriptio,' which according to him, made it unnecessary to enter into any controversy with dissidents because the burden of proof lay upon them as innovators: 'We *prescribe* against these falsifiers of our doctrine, and say to them that the only rule of truth is none other than that which comes from Christ, transmitted by his own companions, and it is easy to prove that these innovators are much later than they' (*Apol.* 47, 10). Law, too, suggested a great number of the concepts, figures and terms that he introduced into theology and that remain to the present day. Law permeated his representation of the relation between God and man. God is the giver of law (*De paen.* 1), the judge who administers law (*ibid.* 2). The gospel is the law of the Christians: *Lex proprie nostra, id est evangelium* (*De monog.* 8). Sin is a breach of this law. As such it is *culpa* or *reatus* and offends God (*De paen.* 3; 5; 7; 10; 11). To do good is to satisfy God (*satisfacere*) (*ibid.* 5; 6; 7), because God commanded it (*quia deus praecepit*) (*ibid.* 4). The fear of God, the lawgiver and judge, is the beginning of salvation (*ibid.* 4). *Timor fundamentum salutis est* (*De cultu fem.* 2, 1). God is satisfied by the merit of man (*De paen.* 2, 6). Here the author uses the law term *promereri*. The words *debt, satisfaction, guilt, compensation* occur frequently in his writings. He drew the distinction between counsel and precept, between *consilia* and *praecepta dominica*. Whereas Irenaeus conceived salvation as a divine economy (*Adv. haer.* 3, 24, 1), Tertullian speaks of a *salutaris disciplina* (*De pat.* 12), a discipline ordained of God through Christ.

Studies: K. H. Wirth, Der 'Verdienst'-Begriff in der christlichen Kirche nach seiner geschichtlichen Entwicklung dargestellt. I. Der 'Verdienst'-Begriff bei Tertullian.

Leipzig, 1892. Cf. H. Koch, ThR (1902) 274 ff. — A. Beck, Der Einfluß der römischen Rechtslehre auf die Formulierung des katholischen Dogmas bei Tertullian, insbesondere die Frage ob Tertullian Jurist gewesen sei. Diss. Heidelberg, 1923. — P. Vitton, I concetti giuridici nelle opere di Tertulliano. Rome, 1924. — A. Beck, Römisches Recht bei Tertullian und Cyprian. Eine Studie zur frühen Rechtsgeschichte (Schriften der Königsberger Gelehrten Gesellschaft 7, 2). Halle, 1930. — R. Höslinger, Die alte afrikanische Kirche im Lichte der Kirchenrechtsforschung nach der kulturhistorischen Methode. Vienna, 1935. — G. Gonella, La critica dell' autorità delle leggi secondo Tertulliano e Lattanzio: Rivista Internazionale di Filosofia del Diritto (1937) 23–37.

3. *The Rule of Faith*

The Creed, in which the teaching of the Church is summed up is for Tertullian not only a rule of faith (*regula fidei*), but also a law of faith (*lex fidei*) (*De praescr.* 14). He never gives us its precise wording. In *De virg. vel.* 1 he describes it as follows:

> The rule of faith, indeed, is altogether one, alone immovable and irreformable; the rule, to wit, of believing in one only God omnipotent, the Creator of the universe, and His Son Jesus Christ, born of the Virgin Mary, crucified under Pontius Pilate, raised again the third day from the dead, received in the heavens, sitting now at the right hand of the Father, destined to come to judge the living and the dead through the resurrection of the flesh (ANF 4).

The formula here presented is the freest of glosses and comments to be offered by Tertullian. On two other occasions, *Adv. Prax.* 2 and *De praescr.* 13, he refers to the rule of faith, the latter passage being the longer:

> Now the rule of faith is unquestionably that wherein our belief is affirmed that there is but one God, who is none other than the Creator of the world; it is He who produced all things out of nothing through His Word emitted before all things. This Word is called His Son. In the name of God He was seen under various forms by the patriarchs, was ever heard in the prophets and lastly descended by the Spirit and Power of God the Father into the Virgin Mary, became flesh in her womb, and being born of her, lived as Jesus Christ. Then He preached a new law and the new promise of the kingdom of heaven. He performed miracles, was crucified, and on the third day rose again; being raised to the heavens, He sat at the right hand of the Father; He sent in His place

the power of the Holy Spirit to guide believers. He will come in glory to take the saints to the enjoyment of life eternal and of the heavenly promises, and to condemn the wicked to everlasting fire, after the resurrection of both has taken place together with the restoration of their flesh.

This rule, as it will be proved, was taught by Christ, and raises among ourselves no other questions than those which heresies introduce and which make heretics (*De praescr.* 13). If we compare the above two quotations, *De virg. vel.* 1 and *De praescr.* 13 we see that the one does not mention the Holy Spirit, while the other does so clearly. *Adv. Prax.* 2 also introduces the third Person and ends, though without speaking of the resurrection of the flesh, in a brief Trinitarian creed: 'He sent forth, as He had promised, the Holy Spirit, the Paraclete, from the Father, the sanctifier of the faith of those who believe in the Father and the Son and the Holy Spirit.' Finally another passage in *De praescr.* 36 praises the faith which the Church of Rome has in common with the African: 'She acknowledges one Lord God, creator of the universe, and Christ Jesus, Son of God the creator from the Virgin Mary and the resurrection of the flesh.' This reads like *De virg. vel.* 1 above. Thus it seems as if Tertullian knew a Trinitarian formula as well as a Binitarian. With this exception, all these statements closely resemble one another in content and even wording, indicating an underlying creed-like summary of the faith that corresponds very nearly to the baptismal symbol quoted by Hippolytus of Rome in his *Apostolic Tradition* of A.D. 217 (cf. above, p. 191).

Studies: J. M. RESTREPO-JARAMILLO, Tertulliano y la doble fórmula simbólica: Greg 15 (1934) 3–58. — A. D'ALÈS, Tertullien. Symbolum: RSR 26 (1936) 468. — E. DEKKERS, Tertullianus en de geschiedenis der liturgie. Brussels-Amsterdam, 1947, 186–197. — J. H. CREHAN, Early Christian Baptism and the Creed. London, 1950, 89–110. — J. N. D. KELLY, Early Christian Creeds. Oxford, 1950, 82–88. — J. QUASTEN, Baptismal Creed and Baptismal Act: Mélanges de Ghellinck. Gembloux, 1951, 223–234.

4. *Trinity*

It is in the doctrine of the Trinity and the intimately connected Christology that Tertullian made the greatest contribution to theology. Some of his formulae and definitions are so precise and happy that they were adopted by the ecclesiastical terminology never to be discarded. It was mentioned above that Tertullian was the first to use the Latin word *trinitas* for the three divine persons. *De pud.* 21 speaks of a *Trinitas unius Divinitatis, Pater et Filius et Spiritus Sanctus.* However, it is in *Adv. Prax.*, that his doctrine of the trinity finds its best expression. He explains the compatibility between the unity and trinity of the Godhead by pointing to the oneness in substance and origin of the three: *tres unius substantiae et unius status et unius potestatis (De pud. 2).* The Son is 'of the substance of the Father': *Filium non aliunde deduco, sed de substantia Patris (ibid. 4).* The Spirit is 'from the Father through the Son': *Spiritum non aliunde deduco quam a Patre per Filium (ibid.).* Thus Tertullian states: 'I always affirm that there is one substance in three united together': *Ubique teneo unam substantiam in tribus cohaerentibus (ibid. 12).* In ch. 25 of *De pud.* he puts the relation of Father, Son and Paraclete in the following way: *Connexus Patris in Filio et Filii in Paracleto tres efficit cohaerentes, alterum e altero. Qui tres unum sunt, non unus.* Tertullian is the first to use the term *persona*, which became so famous in the subsequent development. He says of the Logos that he is 'another' than the Father 'in the sense of person, not of substance, for distinctiveness, not for division': *alium autem quomodo accipere debeas iam professus sum, personae non substantiae nomine, ad distinctionem non ad divisionem (Adv. Prax. 12).* The term *persona* is applied also to the Holy Spirit, whom Tertullian calls 'the third person':

If the plurality of the Trinity still offends you, as if it were not connected in simple unity, I ask you how it is possible for a Being who is merely and absolutely One and Singular, to speak in plural phrase, saying, 'Let us make man in our own image, and after our own likeness'; whereas He ought to have said, 'Let me make man in my own image, and after my own likeness,' as being a unique and singular Being? In the following passage, however, 'Behold the man is become as one of us,' He is either deceiving or amusing us in speaking plurally if He is the One only and singular. Or was it to the angels that He spoke, as the Jews interpret the passage, because these also acknowledge not the Son? Or was it because He was at once the Father, the Son, and the Spirit, that he spoke to Himself in plural terms, making Himself plural on

23

that very account? Nay, it was because He had already His
Son close at His side, as a second Person, His own Word, and
a third Person also, the Spirit in the Word, that He purposely
adopted the plural phrases 'Let us make' and 'in our image'
and 'become as one of us.' For with whom did He make man?
and to whom did He make him like? He was speaking with
the Son who was to put on human nature; and the Spirit
who was to sanctify man. With these did He then speak, in
the Unity of the Trinity, as with His ministers and witnesses
(*ibid.* 12 ANF 3).

However, Tertullian could not shake off entirely the influence
of subordinationism. The old distinction between the *Logos
endiathetos* and the *Logos prophorikos*, the Word internal or immanent in God and the Word emitted or uttered by God, which
misled the Greek apologists, made him regard the divine generation as taking place gradually. Although Wisdom and Word
are identical names for the second person in the Trinity, Tertullian distinguishes between a prior birth as Wisdom before the
creation, and a *nativitas perfecta* at the moment of creation, when
the Logos was sent forth and Wisdom became the Word: 'Hence
it was then that the Word itself received its manifestation and its
completion, namely sound and voice, when God said: *Let there be
light.* This is the perfect birth of the Word, when it proceeds from
God. It was first produced by Him for thought under the name of
Wisdom, *The Lord established me as the beginning of his ways* (Prov. 8,
22). Then He is generated for action: *When He made the heavens, I
was near Him* (Prov. 8, 27). Consequently, making the one of whom
He is the Son to be His Father by His procession, He became the
first-born, as generated before all, and only Son, as solely generated by God' (*Adv. Prax.* 7). Thus the Son as such is not eternal
(*Hermog.* 3 EP 321) although the Logos was *res et persona* even
before the creation of the world *per substantiae proprietatem* (*ibid.*).
The Father is the whole substance (*tota substantia est*) while the
Son is only an outflow and a portion of the whole (*derivatio totius
et portio*), as He Himself professes, *Because my Father is greater than I*
(John 14, 28). The analogies by which Tertullian tries to explain
the Godhead also indicate his subordinationist tendencies, especially when he states that the Son goes out from the Father as
the beam from the sun:

For God brought forth the Word, as also the Paraclete declares, as a root brings forth the ground shoot, and a spring the river and the sun its beam. For these manifestations also are emanations of the substances from which they proceed. I should not hesitate, indeed, to call the shoot the son of the root and the river son of the spring and the beam son of the sun, because every source is a parent and everything which issues from a source is an offspring—and especially the Word of God, who has actually received as His own peculiar designation the name of Son: yet the shoot is not shut off from the root nor the river from the spring nor the beam from the sun, anymore than the Word is separated from God. Following, therefore, the form of these analogies, I confess that I call God and His Word—the Father and His Son—two. For the root and the shoot are distinctly two things, but conjoined; and the spring and the river are also two manifestations, but undivided; so likewise the sun and the beam are two aspects, but they cohere. Everything which proceeds from something else must needs be second to that from which it proceeds, without being on that account separated. Where, however, there is a second, there must be two; and where there is a third, there must be three. Now the Spirit indeed is third from God and the Son; just as the fruit of the shoot is third from the root, or as the irrigation canal out of the river is third from the spring, or as the apex of the beam is third from the sun; nothing, however, is alien from that original source whence it derives its own properties... In like manner the Trinity, proceeding from the Father by intermingled and connected degrees, does not at all disturb the monarchy, while it guards the state of the economy (*Adv. Prax.* 8 ANF).

Studies: J. STIER, Die Gottes- und Logoslehre Tertullians. Göttingen, 1899. — K. ADAM, Die Lehre vom hl. Geiste bei Hermas und Tertullian: ThQ (1906) 36–61. — B. B. WARFIELD, Studies in Tertullian and Augustine. Oxford, 1930, 1–109: Tertullian and the beginnings of the doctrine of the Trinity. — M. KRIEBEL, Studien zur älteren Entwicklung der abendländischen Trinitätslehre bei Tertullian und Novatian. Diss. Marburg, 1932. — A. HANSON, Theophanies in the Old Testament and the Second Person of the Trinity : Hermathena 45 (1945) 67–73. — P. TH. CAMELOT, 'Spiritus a Deo et Filio' (Tertullien, Adv. Prax. 8): RSPT 33 (1949) 31–33. See the bibliography on *Adv. Praxean* (above, p. 286).

5. *Christology*

Tertullian's doctrine of the Trinity in spite of its shortcomings marks an important step forward. Some of his formulas are identical with those of the Council of Nicaea, held more than one hundred years later. Others have been adopted by tradition and later Councils. This holds true especially of his Christology, which has all the merits of his teaching on the Godhead and none of its defects. He clearly announces the two natures in the one person of Christ. There is no transformation of the divinity into the humanity, any more than a fusion or combination that would have made only one substance out of two:

> We see plainly the twofold state, which is not confounded, but conjoined in one person—Jesus, God and Man... so that the property of each nature is so wholly preserved that the Spirit on the one hand did all its own things in Jesus such as miracles, and mighty deeds and wonders; and the flesh, on the other hand, exhibited the affections which belong to it. It was hungry under the devil's temptation, thirsty with the Samaritan woman, wept over Lazarus, was troubled even unto death, and at last actually died. If, however, it was only some third thing, some composite essence formed out of the two substances, like the electrum, there would be no distinct proofs apparent of either nature. But by a transfer of functions, the Spirit would have done things to be done by the Flesh, and the Flesh such as are effected by the Spirit; or else such things as are suited neither to the Flesh nor to the Spirit, but confusedly of some third character. Nay more, on this supposition, either the Word underwent death, or the flesh did not die, if the Word had been converted into flesh; because either the flesh was immortal, or the Word was mortal. Forasmuch, however, as the two substances acted distinctly, each in its own character, there necessarily accrued to them severally their own operations and their own issues (*Adv. Prax.* 27 ANF 3).

We recognize in these statements the formula of the Council of Chalcedon (451 A.D.) of the two substances in one person.

Studies: J. JANSEN, De leer van den persoon en het werk van Christus bij Tertullianus (Akad. Proefschrift). Kampen, 1906. — J. RIVIÈRE, Tertullien et les droits du démon: RSR 6 (1926) 199–216; *idem*, Le dogme de la rédemption. Louvain, 1931, 146–164.—

R. FAVRE, La communication des idiomes dans l'ancienne tradition latine: BLE 17 (1936) 130–145.

6. *Mariology*

In his eagerness to defend the real humanity of Christ, Tertullian stresses the point that His body is not heavenly but really born of the very substance of Mary, *ex Maria*, to such a degree that he denies the virginity of Mary *in partu* and *post partum*. Thus he states 'Although she was a virgin when she conceived, she was a wife when she brought forth': *Virgo quantum a viro: non virgo quantum a partu* and *et si virgo concepit, in partu suo nupsit* (*De carne Chr.* 23). He understands the 'brethren of Jesus' as children of Mary according to the flesh (*ibid.*; cf. also *De carne Chr.* 7; *Adv. Marc.* 4, 19; *De monog.* 8; *De virg. vel.* 6). Tertullian's authority in this matter was later invoked by Helvidius. Jerome (*Adv. Helv.* 17) rejected it answering: 'As to Tertullian I have nothing else to say except that he was not a man of the Church.' The apparent hesitation of the earliest patristic writers to speak out clearly on this subject is owing to the same reason as led Tertullian to deny the *virginitas in partu* and *post partum*, namely, the heresy of the Docetes. The claim of a perduring virginity seemed to him a most welcome confirmation of their false belief that Christ had no real human body, that He was only apparently conceived and born. However, long before Origen had stated that 'Mary conceived and gave birth as a virgin' (*Com. in Levit. hom.* 8, 2), Irenaeus in his *Demonstration of the Apostolic Preaching* (ch. 54) written about A.D. 190, the apocryphal *Gospel of James* (18, 2–20, 1) from the middle of the second century (cf. vol. I, pp. 118 ff), the *Odes of Solomon* (19) from the first half of the second century (cf. vol. I, pp. 160, 163) and the *Ascension of Isaias* (11, 2–22) from the last decade of the first century testify to the traditional view.

Mary is to Tertullian the second Eve:

> For it was while Eve was yet a virgin, that the ensnaring word had crept into her ear which was to build the edifice of death. Into a virgin's soul, in like manner, must be introduced that Word of God which was to raise the fabric of life; so that what had been reduced to ruin by this sex, might by the selfsame sex be recovered to salvation. As Eve had believed the serpent, so Mary believed the angel. The de-

linquency which the one occasioned by believing, the other
by believing effaced. But (it will be said) Eve did not at the
devil's word conceive in her womb. Well, she at all events
conceived; for the devil's word afterwards became as seed to
her that she should conceive as an outcast, and bring forth
in sorrow. Indeed she gave birth to a fratricidal devil; while
Mary on the contrary bare one who was one day to secure
salvation to Israel (*De carne Chr.* 17 ANF 3).

Studies: H. Koch, Adhuc Virgo. Tübingen, 1929. Cf. RSR (1933) 509 ff; J. Lebon,
RTAM (1930) 129 ff. — H. Koch, Virgo Eva – Virgo Maria. Berlin, 1937, 8–17. Cf.
K. Adam, ThQ (1938) 171–189. — T. J. Motherway, The Creation of Eve in
Catholic Tradition: TS 1 (1940) 97–116. — J. C. Plumpe, Some Little-known Early
Witnesses to Mary's Virginitas in Partu: TS 9 (1948) 567–577.

7. *Ecclesiology*

Tertullian is the first to use 'mother' as a title of the Church. It
is an expression of dignity and affection, of reverence and love,
when he calls her *Domina mater ecclesia* (*Ad mart.* 1). On another
occasion, interpreting the Lord's Prayer to the catechumens, he
is anxious to show that the word 'Father' at the beginning
contains also an invocation of the Son and that a mother is also
to be understood: 'Not even the Mother, the Church, is passed by,
that is, if in the Son and Father is recognized the mother, by whom
the names of both father and son exist' (*De orat.* 2). In the closing
sentences of his treatise *On Baptism* he addresses the candidates
as follows: 'Therefore, ye blessed ones, whom the grace of God
awaits, when you come up from the most sacred bath of new
birth, and in the house of your Mother [*apud matrem*] for the first
time open your hands [to pray] with your brethren, ask the
Father, ask the Lord that to the grace [of baptism] a very special
gift may be added, the distribution of charismata' (*De bapt.* 20).
It is interesting that this concept stayed with Tertullian throughout his life, even during the Montanistic period. In his treatise *De
anima*, dating from the years between 210 and 212, he attempts to
show how the creation of Eve from the side of Adam prefigures
the birth of the Church from the wounded side of the Lord: 'As
Adam was a figure of Christ, Adam's sleep prefigured the death of
Christ, who was to sleep a mortal slumber, that from the wound
inflicted on His side might, in like manner [as Eve was formed], be

typified the Church, the true mother of the living' (*De an.* 43). Even in *De pudicitia*, most probably his last preserved work, he calls the Church a mother (5, 14).

The Church in *De praescriptione* is the repository of faith and the guardian of revelation; she alone inherits the truth and its records and alone possesses the Scriptures, to which heretics cannot legally appeal; she alone has the doctrine of the apostles and the legitimate succession from them and, consequently, she alone can teach the substance of their message. This concept of the author's orthodox period closely resembles Irenaeus' (cf. vol. I, p. 200). The more, however, that Tertullian leaned to Montanism, the more he came to regard the body of believers as a purely and exclusively spiritual group. 'Where there are three, that is, Father, Son, and Holy Spirit, there is the Church, which is a body of three' (*De bapt.* 6). *De exh. cast.* 7 is already out and out heresy: *Ubi tres, ecclesia est, licet laici* (cf. also *De fuga* 14). These expressions culminate in *De pudicitia* 21, 17, the clearest statement of the Montanistic notion:

> For the very Church itself is, properly and principally, the Spirit Himself, in whom is the Trinity of the One Divinity— Father, Son, and Holy Spirit. [The Spirit] combines that Church which the Lord has made to consist in 'three.' And thus, from that time forward, every number [of persons] who may have combined together into this faith is accounted 'a Church,' from the Author and Consecrator. And accordingly 'the Church,' it is true, will forgive sins: but [it will be] the Church of the Spirit, by means of a spiritual man; not the Church which consists of a number of bishops.

This is the new theory which for Tertullian replaces that of the apostolic succession. Here the Montanist idea, contrasting the organized with the spiritual church, has reached its ultimate logical conclusion. The Church of the Spirit and the Church of the bishops are now in total opposition.

Studies: J. KOLBERG, Verfassung, Kultus und Disziplin der christlichen Kirche nach den Schriften Tertullians. Braunsberg, 1886. — M. WINKLER, Der Traditionsbegriff des Urchristentums bei Tertullian. Munich, 1897. — E. MICHAUD, L'ecclésiologie de Tertullien: Kirchliche Zeitschrift (1905) 262–272. — H. KOCH, Tertullian und der Cölibat: ThQ (1906) 406–411. — K. ADAM, Der Kirchenbegriff Tertullians. Paderborn, 1907. — H. BRUDERS, Mt. XVI 19, XVIII 18 und Jo. XX 22, 23 in frühchristlicher Auslegung. Tertullian: ZkTh 34 (1910) 659–677. — K. KASTNER, Tertullian und die römische Primatfrage: Theol.-prakt. Quartalschrift 65 (1912) 77–83. — P. F. Preobrazensky, Tertullianus i Rim. Moskau, 1926. — J. T. Shotwell and L. R. Loomis, The See of Peter. New York, 1927, 84–87, 256–261, 286–295, 301–304. — E. Rolffs, Tertullian, der Vater des abendländischen Christentums. Ein Kämpfer für und gegen die römische Kirche. Berlin, 1930. — H. Koch, Priestertum und Lehrbefugnis bei Tertullian: ThStKr (1931) 95–108. — E. Altendorf, Einheit und Heiligkeit der Kirche. 1932, 11–43. — F. H. Hallock, Church and State in Tertullian: ChQ 119 (1934) 61–78. — E. Mersch, Le corps mystique du Christ. 2nd ed. Louvain, 1936, vol. 2, 11–15. — U. Gmelin, Auctoritas. Römischer Princeps und päpstl. Primat. 1931, 83–91. — J. N. Bakhuizen van den Brink, Kerk en traditie omstreeks het jaar 200: Nederl. Arch. Kerkgeschiedenis 29 (1937) 1–18. — G. Bardy, Le sacerdoce chrétien d'après Tertullien: VS 58 (1939) 109–124. — J. C. Plumpe, Ecclesia mater: TP (1939) 535–555. — V. Morel, Le développement de la 'disciplina' sous l'action du Saint-Esprit chez Tertullien: RHE 35 (1939) 243–265. — H. Rahner, Flumina de ventre Christi: Bibl (1941) 269–302, 367–403. — F. de Pauw, La justification des traditions non écrites chez Tertullien: ETL 19 (1942) 5–46. — J. C. Plumpe, Mater Ecclesia. An Inquiry into the Concept of the Church as Mother in Early Christianity (SCA 5). Washington, 1943, 45–62. — J. Quasten, Tertullian and 'traditio': Traditio 2 (1944) 481–484. — V. Morel, De ontwikkeling van de christelijke overlevering volgens Tertullianus. Bruges, 1946. — M. Maccarone, Vicarius Christi e Vicarius Petri nel periodo patristico: Rivista di Storia della Chiesa in Italia 2 (1948) 1–32. — J. Ludwig, Die Primatworte Mt 16, 18. 19 in der altkirchlichen Exegese. Münster i. W., 1952.

8. *Penance and the Power of the Keys*

Tertullian's teaching on penance exhibits the same shifts and contradictions as that on the Church. The difference between the two treatises *De paenitentia* and *De pudicitia* in that regard has been shown above (p. 313 f). He remains important for his account of the early penitential discipline and for his influence on later generations. He is the first author to give us a clear picture of the procedure and the forms which it acquired as time went on. He confirms what we know from the *Shepherd* of Hermas (cf. vol. I, p. 97 f) to have been the tradition, i.e., there is a second forgiveness after baptism, by which the sinner can recover the state of grace. It consists essentially in conversion and satisfaction. The latter demands, in addition to personal acts of atonement, a public confession, *exomologesis*, which is absolutely necessary.

In asking divine pardon the culprit is supported by the intercession of the Church—a factor that Tertullian does not fail to stress as essential in obtaining it. The final step is the reconciliation or ecclesiastical absolution conferred by the bishop (*De pud.* 18, 18; 14, 16), who also governs the excommunication. In

principle, every wrongdoer, even the greatest, was admitted to
this second remission. Not before he became a Montanist did
Tertullian restrict this opportunity to the *leviora peccata*. In *De
paenitentia*, written while he still remained a Catholic, he gives no
hint of any limitation on remission because of the heinousness of
certain crimes; he subjoins no list or catalogue of them. Instead,
he distinguishes only between 'corporeal and spiritual sins,' i.e.
between sins really committed and sins merely willed (ch. 3), and
regards both as equally subject to God's punishment; Christ had
pronounced an adulterer not only the man who actually invades
another's wedded rights, but likewise the man who infringes
them by the concupiscence of his gaze (*ibid.*). But all these trans-
gressions can be forgiven:

> To all sins, then, committed whether by flesh or spirit,
> whether by deed or will, the same God who has destined
> penalty by means of judgment, has withal engaged to grant
> pardon by means of repentance, saying to the people,
> 'Repent thee, and I will save thee' (Ezech. 18, 30, 32); and
> again, 'I live, saith the Lord, and I will have repentance
> rather than death' (Ezech. 33, 11). Repentance then is 'life'
> since it is preferred to 'death.' That repentance, O sinner,
> like myself, do you hasten so to embrace as a shipwrecked
> man the protection of some plank (*De paen.* 4 ANF 3).

This passage obviously excludes no sinner from the second
penance. 'The heavens and the angels who are there, are glad at
a man's repentance. Ho! you sinner, be of good cheer! you see,
where it is that there is joy at your return' (*ibid.* 8). Again, he
makes no reservations when he reminds his readers of the parables
of the lost drachma, the lost sheep and the prodigal son. Moreover, he refers to the Apocalypse of St. John and the letters to
the five communities, and mentions the offenses for which each
one of these is reproached. Speaking about Thyatira, he expressly
states that the members of that church are charged with 'fornication' and 'eating of meat sacrificed to idols,' and he continues:
'And yet the Spirit gives them all monitions to repentance, even
under comminations; but he would not utter comminations to
one unrepentant if he did not forgive the repentant' (*ibid.* 8).

Thus, when Tertullian composed this treatise, he must have
considered fornication and idolatry, not as incapable of, but, like

all other sins, subject to forgiveness. *De pudicitia* shows that his views have changed. It is especially fornication that he now asserts is unpardonable, but together with idolatry and murder. From the peculiar emphasis of this work, it has been inferred that previously the custom of the universal Church had refused absolution to all the above vices, but that henceforth his adversaries reserved only the last two and admitted the first to penance. But this conclusion has no basis in the sources. Tertullian's distinction between *peccata remissibilia* and *irremissibilia* confronts us with something entirely new, something without precedent in the primitive discipline. The so-called three capital sins appear here for the first time as a special group; they are not singled out in *De paenitentia* nor are they differentiated in the earlier literature. Consequently it cannot be maintained that before this they had been considered irremissible. *De pudicitia* proves only that in some communities a rigoristic tendency was gaining ground under the influence of Montanism, which claimed that homicide and apostasy could not be forgiven except in the hour of death, if at all. It is interesting to note in this treatise that the Catholics opposed to such trends arguments from Scripture. They pointed to the example of Christ, who pardoned all sorts of sins, even those of fornication and adultery. In rebuttal Tertullian held that the power thus exercised by the Saviour was purely personal and not transmitted in full to the Church:

> If, however, the Lord, by His deeds withal, issued any such proclamation in favor of sinners; as when He permitted contact even with His own body to the 'woman, a sinner,'—washing, as she did, His feet with tears, and wiping them with her hair, and inaugurating His sepulture with ointment; as when to the Samaritaness—not an adulteress by her now sixth marriage, but a prostitute—He showed (what He did show readily to anyone) who He was;—no benefit is hence conferred upon our adversaries, even if it had been to such as were already Christians that He in these several cases granted pardon. For we now affirm: This is lawful to the Lord alone (*De pud.* 11 ANF 4).

Thus Tertullian as a Montanist insists on the catchword *Solus Deus peccata dimittit* and, if the classical text, Matth. 16, 18, was cited against him, simply denied the Church the power of the keys. This authority, he argues, was given to Peter for himself not for the rest of the bishops:

> If, because the Lord has said to Peter, 'Upon this rock will I build My Church' (Matth. 16, 18) or 'Whatsoever thou shalt have bound or loosed on earth, shall be bound or loosed in the heavens' (Matth. 16, 19), you therefore presume that the power of binding and loosing has derived to you, that is, to every Church akin to Peter, what sort of man are you, subverting and wholly changing the manifest intention of the Lord, conferring, as that intention did, this gift personally upon Peter? 'On thee,' He says 'will I build my Church'; and 'I will give to thee the keys,' not to the Church; and 'Whatsoever thou shalt have loosed or bound,' not what they shall have loosed or bound... Hence the power of loosing and binding committed to Peter had nothing to do with the capital sins of believers... For in accordance with the person of Peter, it is to spiritual men that this power will correspondently appertain, either to an apostle or to a prophet (*De pud.* 21).

Thus the power of forgiving sins belongs to the *spiritalis homo* not to the hierarchy. The Montanism of this stand is obvious.

Studies: See the bibliography on *De paenitentia* (above, p. 301) and on *De pudicitia* (above, p. 314). — A. VANBECK, La pénitence dans Tertullien: RHL (1912) 350–369. — E. FRUETSAERT, La réconciliation ecclésiastique vers l'an 200: NRTh (1930) 379–391. — J. HOH, Die Buße bei Tertullian: ThGl 23 (1931) 625–638. — C. CHARTIER, L'excommunication ecclésiastique d'après les écrits de Tertullien: Antonianum 10 (1935) 301–344, 499–536. — K. RAHNER, Sünde als Gnadenverlust in der frühchristlichen Literatur. IV. Tertullian: ZkTh 60 (1936) 471–510. — B. POSCHMANN, Paenitentia secunda. Bonn, 1940, 270–348. — G. H. JOYCE, Private Penance in the Early Church: JThSt 42 (1941) 18–42. — C. B. DALY, The Sacrament of Penance in Tertullien: IER 69 (1947) 693–707, 815–821; 70 (1948) 731–746, 832–848. — C. B. DALY, Novatian and Tertullian: Irish Theological Quarterly 19 (1952) 33–43. — K. RAHNER, Zur Theologie der Buße bei Tertullian: Abhandlungen über Theologie und Kirche. Festschrift f. K. Adam, hrsg. v. M. REDING. Düsseldorf, 1952, 139–167.

9. *The Eucharist*

Tertullian speaks about the eucharist only occasionally. But these incidental utterances have been much discussed by theologians and variously interpreted. He uses the following terms: *eucharistia* (*De praescr.* 36), *eucharistiae sacramentum* (*De cor.* 3), *domi-*

nica sollemnia (*De fuga* 14), *convivium dominicum* (*Ad ux.* 2, 4), *convivium dei* (*Ad ux.* 2, 9), *coena dei* (*De spect.* 13) and *panis et calicis sacramentum* (*Adv. Marc.* 5, 8). Speaking about the effects of the three sacraments of baptism, confirmation and eucharist on the soul, Tertullian remarks: 'The flesh, indeed, is washed, in order that the soul may be cleansed; the flesh is anointed that the soul may be consecrated; the flesh is signed that the soul too may be fortified; the flesh is shadowed with the imposition of hands that the soul also may be illuminated by the Spirit; the flesh feeds on the body and blood of Christ, that the soul likewise may fatten on God' (*De resurr. carnis* 8). The same firm belief in the real presence that is evidenced in these words, that is horrified at hands that have made idols and receive the body of the Lord, also bewails that a Christian 'should apply to the Lord's body those hands which confer bodies on demons... Oh wickedness! Once did the Jews lay hands on Christ; these mangle His body daily. Oh hands to be cut off! ...What hands are more to be amputated than those in which scandal is done to the Lord's body?' (*De idol.* 7). The returning penitent is fed with the best food in the Father's house: *atque ita exinde opimitate dominici corporis vescitur* (*De pud.* 9).

Tertullian testifies also to the sacrificial character of the eucharist. Speaking of the difficulty experienced by some of receiving during a fast for fear of breaking it, he suggests that they first *stand at the altar* and *participate in the sacrifice* and then carry the sacred species home to be taken at the end of the fast:

Most think that they must not be present at the sacrificial prayers (*orationes sacrificiorum*) on the ground that their fast would be broken by reception of the Lord's body. Does the eucharist, then, abolish a service dedicated to God, or does it not rather bind it more to God? Will not your station be more solemn, if you also stand at God's altar? If you have received and preserved the Lord's body, both privileges are secure, your participation in the sacrifice (*participatio sacrificii*) and your performance of your duty (*De orat.* 19).

In this quotation we have also an early allusion to reservation. We find a similar reference in *Ad ux.* 2, 5, to some who, before they had eaten anything at all, partook of the consecrated morsel. From these passages it appears that Holy Communion privately in one's own house was not too unusual (cf. above, p. 303).

Tertullian attributes the consecration clearly to the words of the institution, for he states: 'The bread which Christ took and distributed to His disciples He made his body, saying (*dicendo*) *This is my body*' (*Adv. Marc.* 4, 40). But to this he immediately subjoins: *id est figura corporis mei*—an expression that has caused many discussions. The correct meaning seems to be: the body present under the symbol of bread. Tertullian is so convinced of the real presence that he accuses his Marcionite opponents of inconsistency for denying the reality of the crucified body of Christ and yet continuing the eucharistic service. If there was no real body on the cross, there cannot be any real body in the eucharist. The bread as *figura corporis* presupposes that Christ had a real body: *Figura autem non fuisset nisi veritatis esset corpus* (*ibid.*). The same idea is at the base of *Adv. Marc.* 3, 19: *Panem corpus suum appellans, ut et hinc iam eum intellegas corporis sui figuram pani dedisse. Adv. Marc.* 1, 14, he mentions the *panem, quo ipsum corpus suum repraesentat.* The verb *repraesentare* is used here in the sense of 'to make present,' not of 'to represent' (cf. *Adv. Marc.* 4, 22; *De resurr. carnis* 17). Thus the passage should be understood: 'He makes his own body present by means of bread.' Finally, *De orat.* 6 Tertullian states: *corpus eius in pane censetur,* when he discusses the meaning of the words 'Give us this day our daily bread.' The correct interpretation seems to be that Christ 'included his body in the category of bread' when he taught his disciples to pray for the daily bread.

Texts: J. Quasten, Monumenta eucharistica et liturgica vetustissima. Bonn, 1935/37, 354–355.

Studies: F. X. Dieringer, Die Abendmahlslehre Tertullians: Katholik 44 (1864) I 277–318. — C. Leimbach, Beiträge zur Abendmahlslehre Tertullians. Gotha, 1874. — P. Scharsch, Eine schwierige Stelle über die Eucharistie bei Tertullian (Adv. Marcionem 4, 40): Katholik 89 (1909) II 21–33. — B. Stakemeier, La dottrina di Tertulliano sul sacramento dell' Eucarestia: Rivista stor.-crit. delle scienze teol. (1909) 199 ff, 265 ff. — P. Batiffol, L'Eucharistie. La présence réelle et la transsubstantiation. 9th ed. Paris, 1930, 204–226. — F. J. Dölger, Sacramentum infanticidii: AC 4 (1934) 188–228; *idem,* Zu dominica sollemnia bei Tertullianus: AC 6 (1940) 108–117. — F. R. M. Hitchcock, Tertullian's Views on the Sacrament of the Lord's Supper: ChQ 134 (1942) 21–36. — E. Dekkers, Tertullianus en de geschiedenis der liturgie. Brussels-Amsterdam, 1947, 49–67.

10. *Eschatology*

Although the word *purgatory* does not occur in Tertullian's writings, there is no doubt that he knows of a penitential suffering of the soul after death:

> Even for this cause it is most fitting that the soul, without at all waiting for the flesh, should be punished for what it has done without the partnership of the flesh. So on the same principle, in return for the pious and kindly thoughts in which it shared not the help of the flesh, shall it without the flesh receive its consolation. Nay more, even in matters done through the flesh the soul is the first to conceive them, the first to arrange them, the first to authorize them, the first to precipitate them into acts. And even if it is sometimes unwilling to act, it is still the first to treat the object which it means to effect by help of the body. In no case, indeed, can an accomplished fact be prior to the mental conception thereof. It is therefore quite in keeping with this order of things, that that part of our nature should be the first to have the recompense and reward to which they are due on account of its priority. In short, inasmuch as we understand *the prison* pointed out in the Gospel to be Hades (Matth. 5, 25), and as we also interpret *the uttermost farthing* to mean the very smallest offense which has to be recompensed there before the resurrection, no one will hesitate to believe that the soul undergoes in Hades some compensatory discipline, without prejudice to the full process of the resurrection, when the recompense will be administered through the flesh besides (*De an.* 58 ANF, EP 352).

The martyrs are the only ones to be spared this suffering and waiting: 'No one, on becoming absent from the body, is at once a dweller in the presence of the Lord, except by the prerogative of martyrdom, he gains a lodging in Paradise, not in the lower regions' (*De resurr. carnis* 43). The others have to remain *apud inferos* up to the final judgment of the Last Day. However, the intercession of the living may give them relief and rest. Thus Tertullian speaks of the wife who prays for the husband after his death: 'To be sure, she prays for his soul. She asks that, during the interval, he may find rest (*refrigerium*) and that he may share in the first resurrection. She offers the sacrifice each year on the anniversary of his falling asleep' (*De monog.* 10 ACW).

Tertullian shares the chiliastic view that at the end of the present world the just will rise to reign a thousand years with Christ in the Jerusalem that will come from heaven:

> We do confess that a kingdom is promised to us upon the earth, although before heaven, only in another state of existence; inasmuch as it will be after the resurrection for a thousand years in the divinely-built city of Jerusalem... We say that this city has been provided by God for receiving the saints on their resurrection, and refreshing them with the abundance of all really spiritual blessings, as a recompense for those which in the world we have either despised or lost; since it is both just and God-worthy that his servants should have their joy in the place where they have also suffered affliction for his name's sake. Of the heavenly kingdom this is the process. After its thousand years are over, within which period is completed the resurrection of the saints, who rise sooner or later according to their deserts, there will ensue the destruction of the world and the conflagration of all things at the judgment: we shall then be changed in a moment into the substance of angels, even by the investiture of an incorruptible nature, and so be removed to that kingdom in heaven (*Adv. Marc.* 3, 24 ANF 3).

After the Day of Judgment the saints will be forever with God, the wicked condemned to eternal fire:

> When, therefore, the boundary and limit, that millennial interspace, has been passed when even the outward fashion of the world itself—which has been spread like a veil over the eternal economy, equally a thing of time—passes away, then the whole human race shall be raised again, to have its dues meted out according as it has merited in the period of good or evil, and thereafter to have these paid out through the immeasurable ages of eternity. Therefore after this there is neither death nor repeated resurrections, but we shall be the same that we are now, and still unchanged—the servants of God, ever with God, clothed upon with the proper substance of eternity; but the profane, and all who are not true worshippers of God, in like manner shall be consigned to the punishment of everlasting fire—that fire which from its very nature

indeed, directly ministers to their incorruptibility (*Apol.* 48 ANF 3).

Studies: L. ATZBERGER, Geschichte der christlichen Eschatologie innerhalb der vornicänischen Zeit. Freiburg, 1896, 291–331. — A. J. MASON, Tertullian and Purgatory: JThSt 3 (1902) 598–601. — J. DANIÉLOU, La typologie millénariste de la semaine: VC 2 (1948) 1–16.

CYPRIAN

The second African theologian, Cyprian of Carthage, was a personality totally different from Tertullian. He had nothing of the latter's intemperance nor of his dominating genius, but rather those noble qualities of heart that attract charity and gentleness, prudence and spirit of union; these Tertullian lacked. However, as a theologian Cyprian is entirely dependent on Tertullian, whose superiority as a writer he readily recognized. According to Jerome (*De vir. ill.* 53) 'he was accustomed never to pass a day without reading Tertullian and he frequently said to his secretary, *Hand me the master*, meaning by this, Tertullian.'

There are several valuable sources of information for his life. The most important and reliable are his treatises and his numerous letters. For the arrest, trials and martyrdom, we possess the *Acta Proconsularia Cypriani*, which are founded on official reports (cf. vol. I, p. 179). Finally, there is a *Vita Cypriani* extant in a great number of manuscripts, supposedly written by his deacon, Pontius, who shared his exile until the day of his death (Jerome, *De vir. ill.* 58). The first biography of which the history of early Christian literature knows, it has been found to be historically unreliable. The author, filled with admiration for his hero, has written a panegyric, in order 'that to posterity this incomparable and lofty pattern may be prolonged into immortal remembrance' (ch. 1). Thus his purpose is to edify.

Edition: W. HARTEL, CSEL 3, 3 (1871) XC–CX.

Translations: English: C. THORNTON, Library of Fathers 3 (1839). — R. E. WALLIS, The Life and Passion of Cyprian by Pontius the Deacon: ANL 8; ANF 5, 267–274. — *German:* A. HARNACK, Das Leben Cyprians von Pontius, die erste christliche Biographie (TU 39, 3). Leipzig, 1913. — J. BAER, BKV² 34 (1918).

Studies: A. HARNACK, *loc. cit.* — R. REITZENSTEIN, Die Nachrichten über den Tod Cyprians (SAH Phil.-hist. Kl. 1913, Abh. 14) 46–69. — L. BAYARD, Notes sur la Vita Cypriani et sur Lucianus: RPh (1914) 207–210. — P. CORSSEN, Das Martyrium des Bischofs Cyprian: ZNW 15 (1914) 221–233, 285–316; 16 (1915) 54–92, 198–230; 18 (1917) 118–139, 189–206; 19 (1918) 202–223, 249–272. — H. Dessau, Pontius, der Biograph Cyprians: Hermes 5 (1916) 65–72. — A. d'Alès, Le diacre Pontius: RSR 9 (1918) 319–378. — J. Martin, Die Vita et Passio Cypriani: HJG (1919) 674–712. — T. Sinko, De Cypriano a Gregori Nazianzeno laudato. Krakau, 1916. — H. Delehaye, Les passions des martyrs. Brussels, 1921, 82–104. — L. Wohleb, Cyprian de opere et eleemosynis: ZNW (1926) 270–278. — P. Franchi de Cavalieri, Note agiografiche (ST 49). Rome, 1928, 243 f.

Caecilius Cyprianus, with the cognomen Thascius, was born between 200 and 210 in Africa, most probably at Carthage, in a rich and highly cultivated pagan family. As an expert rhetorician and master of eloquence he won great fame in Carthage. Disgusted with the immorality of public and private life, with the corruption in government and administration, his soul, touched by grace, sought something higher. 'Under the influence of the priest Caecilius, from whom he received his surname, he became a Christian, and gave all his fortune to the poor' (Jerome, *De vir. ill.* 67). Shortly after his conversion he was raised to the priesthood and in A.D. 248 or the beginning of A.D. 249 he was elected bishop of Carthage 'by the voice of the people' but against the opposition of some elderly presbyters, amongst them a certain Novatus. He had not been in office more than about a year when the Decian persecution broke out (A.D. 250), which affected for the first time all the subjects of the Empire and compelled them to sacrifice. Cyprian found a safe place of refuge, from which he kept in touch with his flock and his clergy by frequent communications. Nevertheless, his flight was not approved by all. Shortly after Pope Fabian had been put to death, the presbyters and deacons conducting the Church of Rome during the vacancy sent news of his martyrdom and at the same time wrote a letter in which they expressed their surprise at the flight of the bishop of Carthage. Cyprian at once gave them a detailed account of his activities and the explanation of his decision to leave:

> I have thought it necessary to write this letter to you wherein I might give an account to you of my doings, my discipline, and my diligence; for as the Lord's commands teach, immediately the first burst of the disturbance arose, and the people with violent clamor repeatedly demanded me, I, taking into consideration not so much my own safety as the public peace of the brethren, withdrew for a while, lest

by my over-bold presence, the tumult which had begun
might be still further provoked. Nevertheless, although
absent in body, I was not wanting either in spirit, or in act,
or in my advice, so as to fail in any benefit that I could afford my brethren by my counsel (*Epist.* 20 ANF 5).

He accompanied this letter with copies of thirteen others
written to the clergy, the confessors and the communities, in
order to show that he had in no wise abandoned his pastoral
duties. The last items in this collection indicate the difficulties
which had meantime arisen at Carthage. The reconciliation of
those who had denied their Christian faith during the persecution
caused much dissension, which finally led to a schism. Some of
the confessors considered themselves authorities on religious
questions and demanded immediate reconciliation of the *lapsi,*
i.e., those who had in a greater or lesser degree compromised their
faith. When Cyprian refused to accede, the deacon Felicissimus
organized a group of his opponents among the confessors and
lapsed. And they were soon joined by five priests, who had voted
against his election to the episcopate. One of them, Novatus,
mentioned above, went to Rome and became a supporter of
Novatian against the new Pope Cornelius. Cyprian upon his
return to Carthage in the spring of A.D. 251, solemnly banned
Felicissimus and his adherents and published two pastoral letters,
which dealt with the backsliders (*De lapsis*) and the schism (*De
ecclesiae unitate*). Probably in May 251 A.D. a synod was held
which confirmed the principles laid down by Cyprian and approved the excommunication of his antagonists. It was decided
that all *lapsi,* without distinction, should be admitted to penance,
and in the hour of death, at least, reconciled to the Church. The
period of expiation should vary with the gravity of the case. A
devastating plague soon caused new sufferings and persecutions
for the Christians, who were held responsible for the wrath of the
gods. Cyprian's care for the sick and his charitable support of all
afflicted by the catastrophe did much to mitigate the enraged
pagans. Unfortunately, his last years were preoccupied by the
controversy over the baptism of heretics. In Carthage, the absolute repudiation of such rites seems to have been traditional.
Tertullian expressly calls them invalid in his treatise *De baptismo*
(cf. above, p. 279). This view was sanctioned by a great council of

the African and Numidian bishops called together by Agrippinus about A.D. 220, and reaffirmed, with Cyprian as president, by three synods of Carthage in A.D. 255 and 256. Pope Stephen (254–256), informed of the decision, answered in a sharp tone and warned against the introduction of novelties contrary to tradition (cf. above, p. 237 f), but Cyprian would not change his mind. The dispute soon became bitter and threatened to get dangerous, when the emperor Valerian promulgated an edict against the Christians. In the persecution that followed Pope Stephen died for the faith and Cyprian was banished to Curubis on August 30th, A.D. 257. A year later on the 14th of September, A.D. 258, he was beheaded not far from Carthage, the first African bishop to be a martyr.

Studies: E. W. BENSON, Cyprian. His Life, His Times, His Work. London, 1897. — W. MUIR, Cyprian. His Life and Teachings. London, 1898. — P. MONCEAUX, Le tombeau et le basilique de S. Cyprien à Carthage: Revue archéol. (1901) 181–200. — A. HARNACK, Cyprian als Enthusiast: ZNW (1902) 177–191. — P. MONCEAUX, Histoire littéraire de l'Afrique chrétienne depuis les origines jusqu'à l'invasion arabe II: Saint Cyprien et son temps. Paris, 1902. — J. A. FAULKNER, Cyprian the Churchman. Cincinnati, 1906. — E. DE LONGIS, Studio su Cecilio Cipriano. Benevento, 1909. — J. ERNST, Der Begriff des Martyriums bei Cyprian: HJG 34 (1913) 328–353. — P. MONCEAUX, Saint Cyprien, évêque de Carthage. Paris, 1914. — J. VÖGTLE, Die Schriften des hl. Cyprian als Erkenntnisquelle des römischen Rechts. Diss. Berlin, 1920. — H. KOCH, Cyprian in den Quaestiones Veteris et Novi Testamenti und beim Ambrosiaster: ZKG 45 (1926) 516–555; *idem,* Cyprianische Untersuchungen. Bonn, 1926. — A. D. NOCK, Conversion, Confession, and Martyrdom of St. Cyprian: JThSt 28 (1927) 411 ff. — S. COLOMBO, S. Cipriano di Cartagine. L'uomo e lo scrittore: Didaskaleion 6 (1928) 1–80. — H. KOCH, La sopravvivenza di Cipriano nell' antica letteratura cristiana: RR 6 (1930) 304–316, 492–501; 7 (1931) 122–132, 313–335; 8 (1932) 6–17, 317–337, 505–523; 9 (1933) 502–522. — W. D. NIVEN, Cyprian of Carthage: ExpT 44 (1932/33) 363–366. — D. D. SULLIVAN, The Life of the North Africans as Revealed in the Works of St. Cyprian (PSt 37). Washington, 1933. — B. BUSCH, Nova et Vetera. Festschrift Metten, 1939, 64–80. — G. NIEMER, Cyprian als Kritiker der spätrömischen Kultur und Bildner des Christentums: Deutsche Evang. Erziehung 49 (1939) 96–112, 146–159. — C. FAVEZ, La fuite de Saint Cyprien lors de la persécution de Décius: RELA 19 (1941) 191–201. — A. A. EHRHARDT, Cyprian, the Father of Western Christianity: ChQ 133 (1941/42) 178–196. — J. H. FICHTER, Saint Cecil Cyprian, Defender of the Faith. St. Louis, 1942. — E. HUMMEL, The Concept of Martyrdom according to St. Cyprian of Carthage (SCA 9). Washington, 1946. — J. LUDWIG, Der heilige Märtyrerbischof Cyprian von Karthago. Ein kulturgeschichtliches und theologisches Zeitbild aus der afrikanischen Kirche des 3. Jahrhunderts. Munich, 1951.

I. WRITINGS

Cyprian's literary activity was intimately connected with his life and times. All of his works are written for specific occasions and served practical purposes. He was a man of action, interested in the direction of souls rather than in theological speculation. He had neither Tertullian's depth and gift of expression nor his fiery passionateness. On the other hand, his practical wisdom avoids the exaggerations and provocations which did so much harm to the other. His language and style are clearer and more polished, and show a greater influence of the vocabulary and imagery of the Bible. But his admiration for Tertullian is evident from the fact that his treatises embody his master's best thoughts. In Christian antiquity, as in the Middle Ages, he was one of the most popular authors and his writings are extant in a great number of manuscripts.

Studies: For the *text tradition*, see: W. HARTEL, CSEL 3, 3 (1871) I–LXX. — J. WORDSWORTH, Old-Latin Biblical Texts. Nr. II. Oxford, 1886, App. 2, 123–132: Catalogue of Cyprian manuscripts at Oxford. — G. MERCATI, D'alcuni nuovi sussidi per la critica del testo di S. Cipriano. Rome, 1899. — W. SCHULTZ, Cyprianmanu-scripte in Madrid und im Escorial: ThLZ (1897) 179–180. — C. H. TURNER, The Original Order and Contents of Our Oldest MSS of St. Cyprian: JThSt 3 (1902) 282–285; *idem*, Our Oldest MSS of Cyprian II. The Turin and Milan Fragments: JThSt 3 (1902) 579–584. — H. L. RAMSAY, Our Oldest MSS of Cyprian III. The Contents and Order of the MSS: JThSt 3 (1902) 585–594. — C. H. TURNER, A Newly Discovered Leaf of a Fifth-century MS: JThSt 3 (1902) 576 ff. — H. L. RAMSAY, An Uncial Fragment of the Ad Donatum: JThSt 4 (1903) 86 ff. — H. VON SODEN, Die Cyprianische Briefsammlung (TU 25, 3). Leipzig, 1904, 247–265. — G. MERCATI, An Uncial MS of St. Cyprian: JThSt 7 (1906) 269–270. — R. REITZENSTEIN, Ein donatistisches Corpus cyprianischer Schriften: NGWG (1914) 85–92. — H. K. MENGIS, Ein donatistisches Corpus cyprianischer Briefe. Diss. Freiburg, 1916. — M. BÉVENOT, Note sur le ms. de Morimond contenant les œuvres de S. Cyprien: RB 49 (1937) 191–195. — A. C. LAWSON, The Shrewsbury MS of Cyprian and Bachiarius: JThSt 44 (1943) 56–58. — M. BÉVENOT, A New Cyprianic Fragment: BJR 28, 1 (1944) 76–82.

For *Cyprian's language and style*, see: E. W. WATSON, The Style and Language of St. Cyprian: Studia biblica et ecclesiastica 4 (1896) 189–324. — L. BAYARD, Le latin de saint Cyprien. Paris, 1902. — E. DE JONGE, Les clausules métriques dans saint Cyprien. Louvain, 1905. — J. B. POUKENS, *Sacramentum* dans les œuvres de s. Cyprien. Étude lexicographique: Bull. d'anc. litt. et d'arch. chrét. (1912) 214–288. — H. KOCH, Der Genetivus epexegeticus oder appositivus bei Cyprian: ZNW 13 (1912) 165–170. — L. BAYARD, Les clausules chez saint Cyprien et le cursus rythmique: RPh 48 (1924) 52–61. — H. KOCH, Zum Ablativgebrauch bei Cyprian von Karthago und andern Schriftstellern: RhM 78 (1929) 427–432. — P. C. KNOOK, De overgang van metrisch tot rythmisch proza bij Cyprianus en Hieronymus. Diss. Amsterdam, 1932. — O. GRASMUELLER, Koordinierende, subordinierende und fragende Partikeln bei St. Cyprian von Karthago. Diss. Erlangen, 1933. — B. BOTTE, Consummare (chez Cyprien): ALMA 12 (1937) 43–44. — H. HANSSEN, Kultur und Sprache. Zur Geschichte der alten Kirche im Spiegel der Sprachentwicklung von Tertullian bis Cyprian (Latinitas Christ. Primaeva 8). Nijmegen, 1938. — J. SCHRIJNEN und CHR. MOHRMANN, Studien zur Syntax der Briefe des hl. Cyprian. 2 vols. (Lat. Christ. Prim. 5/6). Nijmegen, 1936/37. — CHR. MOHRMANN, Woordspeling in de brieven van St. Cyprianus: Tijdschr. van taal en lett. 27 (1939) 163–175. — P. A. H. J. MERKX, Zur Syntax der Kasus und Tempora in den Traktaten des hl. Cyprian (Lat. Christ. Prim. 9). Nijmegen, 1939. — M. T. BALL, Nature and the Vocabulary of Nature in the Works of Saint Cyprian (PSt 75). Washington, 1946.

For *Cyprian's sources*, see: E. DE FAYE, Saint Cyprien et les influences qui l'ont formé: RTP 26 (1893) 105–116. — H. KOCH, Die Didache bei Cyprian: ZNW (1907) 69–70. — C. PASCAL, Sopra alcuni passi delle Met. Ovidiane imitati dai primi scrittori cristiani: RFIC (1909) 1–6. — S. COLOMBO, Osservazioni sui rapporti fra l'Octavius di M. Minucio Felice e alcuni opuscoli di Cipriano: Didaskaleion (1915) 215–244. — U. MORICCA, Di alcune probabili fonti d'un opusculo di S. Cipriano: Athenaeum (1917) 124–158. — H. KOCH, Cyprian und Seneca, in: Cyprianische Untersuchungen, Bonn, 1926, 286–313; Cyprian und Apuleius: *ibidem*, 314–333; *idem*, I rapporti di Cipriano con Ireneo ed altri scrittori greci: RR (1929) 137–163; *idem*, Ancora Cipriano e la letteratura cristiana greca: RR (1929) 523–637. — A. BECK, Römisches Recht bei Tertullian und Cyprian. Eine Studie zur frühen Kirchenrechtsgeschichte. Halle, 1930. — J. LEBRETON, Saint Cyprien et Origène: RSR 20 (1930) 160–162. — J. H. WASZINK, Eine Ennius-Reminiszenz: Mnem Ser. 3, 1 (1934) 232–233. — H. KOCH, Novaziano, Cipriano e Plinio il Giovane: Religio 11 (1935) 320–332. — G. L. ELLSPERMANN, The Attitude of the Early Christian Writers Toward Pagan Literature and Learning (PSt 82). Washington, 1949, 43–53.

Moreover, we possess three ancient lists of his works. The first is found in the *Vita* of Pontius, who in ch. 7 describes in the form of rhetorical questions the contents of twelve treatises in the same order as they appear in the oldest codices. The second catalog was published by Mommsen from a manuscript (No. 12266 s.X) in Philipps Library at Cheltenham dating from A.D. 359 and mentioning also a number of letters. The third is provided by a sermon of St. Augustine *De natale s. Cypriani* edited by G. Morin.

Studies: H. MOMMSEN, Zur lateinischen Stichometrie: Hermes 21 (1886) 142–156; 25 (1890) 636–638. — A. AMELLI, Miscellanea Cassinesi 1 (1897) Parte II, Fasc. 1. — W. SANDAY, The Cheltenham List of the Canonical Books of the Old and New Testament and of the Writings of Cyprian: Studia biblica et ecclesiastica 3 (Oxford, 1891) 217–325. — K. GOETZ, Geschichte der cyprianischen Literatur bis zur Zeit der ersten erhaltenen Handschriften. Diss. Marburg. Basel, 1891. — C. H. TURNER, Two Early Lists of St. Cyprian's Works: CR 6 (1892) 205–209; *idem*, Studies in Early Church History. Oxford, 1912, 263–265. — G. MORIN, Une liste des traités de saint Cyprien dans un sermon inédit de saint Augustin: Bull d'anc. litt. et d'archéol. chrét.

4 (1914) 16–22. — H. K. Mengis, Ein altes Verzeichnis cyprianischer Schriften: PhW 38 (1918) 326–336.

Edition: W. Hartel, CSEL 3, 1–3 (1868/71).

Translations: English: C. Thornton, Library of Fathers 3 (Oxford, 1839); H. Carey, *ibid.* 17 (1844). — R. E. Wallis, ANL 8 (1868), 13 (1869); ANF 5 (1886). — *German:* J. Baer: BKV² 34 (1918), 60 (1928). — *French:* A. de Genoude, Les Pères de l'Église. Paris, 1837–1843. — J. Boulet, St. Cyprien, évêque de Carthage et martyr. Avignon, 1923. — *Italian:* S. Colombo, Corona Patrum Salesiana. Series Latina 2. Turin, 1935. — *Spanish:* J. A. del Camino y Orella, Obras de San Cipriano. 2 vols. Valladolid, 1807.

I. *Treatises*

1. *To Donatus*

The *Ad Donatum* is the earliest of Cyprian's treatises. Addressed to his friend Donatus, it describes the marvellous effect of divine grace in his own conversion, which led him through the sacrament of regeneration from the corruption, violence and brutality of the pagan world and from the blindness, errors and passions of his own previous life to the peace and happiness of his Christian faith. It reminds one of the *Confessions* of St. Augustine, when Cyprian 'confesses' his own falls and at the same time the glory of God:

> I was entangled in the thousand errors of my previous life; I did not think I could get free of them, for I was so much the slave of my vices... and I had such complaisance in the evils which had become my constant companions. But the generating water washed me from the stains of my previous life, and a light from on high shone into my heart thus purified from its corruptions, and the Spirit coming from heaven changed me into a new man by a second birth. And immediately, in a wonderful way, I saw certitude take the place of doubt... You doubtless know and recognize with me what this death of vice and resurrection of virtue took away from me and brought to me in its place. You yourself know this and I do not boast of it. To praise oneself is a hateful bragging. Yet it may be not bragging but gratitude, to recall what is attributed, not to the virtue of man but to the blessing of God... From God, I say, comes all virtue. From God come our life and our power (ch. 3–4).

Written shortly after the author's baptism, which had probably occurred on the Easter Eve of 246, the treatise intends not only to justify Cyprian's own conversion but to invite others to take the same step. Every sinner was to feel heartened in considering from what an abyss Cyprian had been rescued. The style is wanting in simplicity, verbose and affected, and differs considerably from the 'more dignified and reticent eloquence' of his later works, as already St. Augustine observed (*De doctr. christ.* 4, 14, 31).

Editions: W. HARTEL, CSEL 3, 1 (1868) 3–16. — J. G. KRABINGER, Tübingen, 1859. — S. COLOMBO, Corona Patrum Salesiana. Series Latina 2. Turin, 1935. — J. N. BAKHUIZEN VAN DEN BRINK, Scriptores christiani primaevi 1. The Hague, 1946.

Translations: English: C. THORNTON, Library of Fathers 3. Oxford, 1839, 1–12. — R. E. WALLIS, ANL 8; ANF 5, 275–280. — J. C. PLUMPE, ACW 20 (1953). — *German:* J. BAER, BKV² 34 (1918). — *French:* J. BOULET, St. Cyprien, évêque de Carthage et martyr. Avignon, 1923. — L. BAYARD, Tertullien et saint Cyprien, Textes choisis. Paris, 1930. — *Italian:* S. COLOMBO, Corona Patrum Salesiana. Series Latina 2. Turin, 1935.

Studies: K. G. GOETZ, Der alte Anfang und die ursprüngliche Form von Cyprians Schrift ad Donatum (TU 19, 1c). Leipzig, 1899. Cf. C. WEYMAN, HJG 20 (1899) 500 f. — A. HARNACK, Geschichte der altchristlichen Literatur 2, 2, 338 f, 409. — H. L. RAMSAY, An Uncial Fragment of the Ad Donatum: JThSt 4 (1903) 86–89. — C. A. KNELLER, Sacramentum unitatis. Zu Cyprians Schrift ad Donatum: ZkTh 40 (1916) 676–703. — U. MORICCA, Athenaeum 5 (1917) 124 ff.

2. *The Dress of Virgins*

As a bishop concerned with the improvement of religious discipline, Cyprian addresses in *De habitu virginum* the virgins, 'the flower of ecclesiastical seed, the grace and ornament of spiritual endowment, a joyous disposition, the wholesome and uncorrupted work of praise and honor, God's image answering to the holiness of the Lord, the more illustrious portion of Christ's flock, the glorious fruitfulness of Mother Church' (3). He admonishes them concerning the dangers which beset those that have dedicated their virginity to Christ from the pagan world with its vanities and vices. The brides of Christ must dress plainly and avoid jewelry and cosmetics, which are only an invention of the demons. If they have wealth, they should use their riches not for such things, but for good purposes, as for the support of the poor. They are not permitted to attend boisterous wedding parties nor go to promiscuous bathing-places. In a brief epilogue, he exhorts them to hold fast what they have begun and to think of the great reward which awaits them. The treatise was in all probability written shortly after Cyprian's consecration as bishop of Carthage in A.D. 249. Its main source is Tertullian's *De cultu feminarum*. However, 'Cyprian has translated his master not only into an urbane Ciceronian diction, but into a wise urbanity of soul. Here speaks a great Christian teacher and father of his flock. Tertullian's disordered outbursts give place in Cyprian to a reasoned and effective art' (Rand, CAH 12, p. 602). Its style prompted Augustine to refer to it as a model for his young Christian orators (*De doctr. christ.* 4).

Editions: W. HARTEL, CSEL 3, 1 (1868) 185–205. — A. E. KEENAN, S. Thasci Caecilii Cypriani De habitu virginum (PSt 34). Washington, 1932. Cf. PhW (1936) 113–118.

Translations: English: C. THORNTON, Library of Fathers 3 (1839) 116–130. — R. E. WALLIS, ANL 8; ANF 5, 430–436. — A. E. KEENAN, *loc. cit.* — J. C. PLUMPE, ACW 20 (1953). — *German:* J. BAER, BKV² 34 (1918). — *French:* L. BAYARD, Tertullien et saint Cyprien. Paris, 1930. — J. BOULET, St. Cyprien, évêque de Carthage et martyr. Avignon, 1923. — *Italian:* S. COLOMBO, Corona Patrum Salesiana. Series Latina 2. Turin, 1935. — *Spanish:* F. DE B. VIZMANOS, Las vírgenes cristianas. Madrid, 1949, 649–666.

Studies: J. HAUSSLEITER, Commentationes Woelfflinianae. Leipzig, 1891, 377–389. — J. A. KNAAKE, Die Predigten des Tertullian und Cyprian: ThStKr 76 (1903) 608 ff. — E. W. WATSON, The De habitu virginum: JThSt 22 (1921) 361–367. — R. B. DONNA, Note on St. Cyprian's De habitu virginum. Its Source and Influence: Traditio 4 (1946) 399–407.

3. *Concerning the Lapsed*

De lapsis was written after Cyprian's return from his retirement during the Decian persecution in the spring of 251. After giving thanks to God for the restoration of peace, he praises the martyrs who have resisted the world, have afforded a glorious spectacle in the sight of God and have been an example to their brethren. However, his joy soon turns to gloom and sorrow because of the many brethren who had fallen away during the persecution. He speaks of those who had sacrificed to the gods even before they were forced to do so, of parents who had brought their children to participate in these rites and especially of those who, for blind love of their property, remained and denied the faith. No easy pardon can be granted them. He warns the confessors against interceding for such people. Leniency under these circumstances would merely prevent them from making due atonement. Those who became weak only after great tortures deserve more mercy. However all of those must submit to penance, even those who in some way or other had secured certificates of sacrifice without having polluted their hands with actual participation in such pagan worship (*libellatici*), because they have defiled their conscience. Cyprian's treatise was read at the council which met in Carthage in the spring of 251 and became the basis of a uniform course of action in the difficult question of the lapsed for the entire Church of North Africa.

Editions: W. HARTEL, CSEL 3, 1 (1868) 235–264. — J. MARTIN, FP 21. Bonn, 1930. Cf. H. KOCH, DLZ 51 (1930) 2458–2464. — S. COLOMBO, Corona Patrum Sales. Turin, 1935. — M. LAVARENNE, Sur ceux qui sont tombés pendant la persécution. Texte et trad. Clermont-Ferrand, 1940. — J. N. BAKHUIZEN VAN DEN BRINK, Script. christiani primaevi I. The Hague, 1946.

Translations: English: C. THORNTON, Library of Fathers 3 (1839) 153–176. — R. E. WALLIS, ANL 8; ANF 5, 437–447. — *German:* J. BAER, BKV² 34 (1918). — B. STEIDLE, Des Bischofs Cyprian Hirtenschreiben (Zeugen des Wortes). Freiburg i.B., 1939. — *French:* M. LAVARENNE, *loc. cit.* — *Italian:* S. COLOMBO, Corona Patrum Sales. Turin, 1935.

Studies: J. STUFLER, Die Behandlung der Gefallenen zur Zeit der decischen Verfolgung: ZkTh 31 (1907) 577–618; *idem*, Einige Bemerkungen zur Bußlehre Cyprians: ZkTh 33 (1909) 232–247. — A. D'ALÈS, La réconciliation des 'Lapsi' au temps de Dèce: RQH 91 (1912) 337–383. — B. POSCHMANN, Zur Bußfrage in der cyprianischen Zeit: ZkTh 37 (1913) 25–54, 244–265. — A. VANBECK, La pénitence dans St. Cyprien: RHL 18 (1913) 422–442. — H. KOCH, Cyprianische Untersuchungen. Bonn, 1926, 79–82, 211–285. — L. CASTIGLIONI, Cyprianea: Rendic. Reale Istit. Lombardo. Ser. 2, vol. 64 (1933) 1071–1080. — B. CAPELLE, L'absolution sacerdotale chez Cyprien: RTAM 7 (1935) 221–234. — M. C. CHARTIER, La discipline pénitentielle d'après les écrits de saint Cyprien: Antonianum 14 (1939) 17–42, 135–156. — B. POSCHMANN, Paenitentia secunda. Die kirchliche Buße im ältesten Christentums bis Cyprian und Origenes. Bonn, 1940, 368–424. — G. H. JOYCE, Private Penance in the Early Church: JThSt 42 (1941) 18–42. — J. H. TAYLOR, St. Cyprian and the Reconciliation of Apostates: TS 3 (1942) 27–46. — K. RAHNER, Die Busslehre des hl. Cyprian von Karthago: ZkTh 74 (1952) 252–276.

4. *The Unity of the Church*

De ecclesiae unitate had the most lasting influence of all Cyprian's works. It gives a key to his personality and to everything that he wrote, both books and letters. It seems that it was composed chiefly because of the schism of Novatian and only secondly because of that of Felicissimus at Carthage. The arguments adduced by J. Chapman, H. Koch and B. Poschmann that Cyprian could have had but the latter in view do not win conviction, as D. van den Eynde, O. Perler and M. Bévenot have shown. Thus it was not published before the author's return to Carthage but after it, most probably in May 251 at the time of the synod there. From his *Epist.* 54, 4, we learn that he sent it to the Roman confessors, while they were still on Novatian's side and against Cornelius as bishop of Rome. Their reconciliation took place not later than the end of 251.

The introduction explains that schisms and heresies are caused by the devil. They are even more dangerous than persecutions because they jeopardize the internal unity between believers, ruin the faith and corrupt the truth. Every Christian is obliged to remain in the Catholic Church and there is only one Church, that built upon Peter:

> The Lord speaks to Peter, saying, 'I say unto thee, that thou art Peter; and upon this rock I will build my Church, and the gates of hell shall not prevail against it...' (Matth. 16, 18). And although to all the apostles, after His resurrection, He gives an equal power, and says, 'As the Father hath sent me, even so send I you: Receive the Holy Ghost: Whose soever sins ye remit, they shall be remitted unto him; and whose soever sins ye retain, they shall be retained' (John 20, 21); yet, that He might set forth unity, He arranged by His authority the origin of that unity, as beginning from one. Assuredly the rest of the apostles were also the same as was Peter, endowed with a like partnership both of honor and power; but the beginning proceeds from unity that the Church of Christ might be manifested to be one... Does he who does not hold this unity of the Church think that he holds the faith? Does he who strives against and resists the Church trust that he is in the Church...? This unity we ought firmly to hold and assert, especially those of us that are bishops who preside in the Church, that we may also prove the episcopacy to be one and undivided... The episcopate is one, each part of which is held by each one for the whole. The Church also is one, which is spread abroad far and wide into a multitude by an increase of fruitfulness. As there are many rays of the sun, but one light; and many branches of a tree, but one strength based in its tenacious roots; and

since from one spring flow many streams, although the multitude seems diffused in the liberality of an overflowing abundance, yet the unity is still preserved in the source. Separate a ray of sun from its body of light, its unity does not allow a division of light; break a branch from the three— when broken it will not be able to bud; cut off the stream from its fountain, and that which is cut off dries up. Thus also the Church, shone over with the light of the Lord, sheds forth her rays over the whole world, yet it is one light which is everywhere diffused, nor is the unity of the body separated. Her fruitful abundance spreads her branches over the whole world. She broadly expands her rivers, liberally flowing, yet her head is one, her source one; and she is one mother, plentiful in the results of fruitfulness: from her womb we are born, by her milk we are nourished, by her spirit we are animated (4–5 ANF 5).

There is no salvation outside of this Church: 'He cannot have God for his Father, who has not the Church for his mother.' If any one could escape who was outside the ark of Noah, then he also may escape who shall be outside of the Church (5). He warns against heretics, who have left the one flock and founded their own organization. They deceive themselves by a wrong interpretation of the Lord's words, 'Wheresoever two or three are gathered in my name, there I am in the midst of them' (Matth. 18, 20). This passage can be understood correctly only in its context and those who quote the last words and put aside the former are corrupters of the gospel (12). He cannot be a martyr who is not in the Church. Even if such men are slain for the name of the Lord, the stain of heresy and schism is not washed away by blood. False teachers are far worse than the lapsed. We cannot be surprised that even confessors lose the faith because even their act of heroism does not make them immune to the snares of the devil, nor does it fortify them, still placed in the world, with perpetual security from temptation. Their deed is the beginning of glory, not the full deserving of the crown. If one has endured for Christ, he must be even more careful because the Adversary is more provoked. Let no one perish by the example of such, but let all who are separated from the Church return, because there are indications that the second coming of the Lord may be near.

The fourth chapter is preserved in a double version, one of them having 'additions,' which stress the primacy of Peter. These 'additions' have caused a long controversy on their origin. Fiercely denounced by Hartel, the editor of Cyprian's works in the CSEL, they came to be almost universally regarded as interpolations. Dom Chapman was the first to suggest another solution. He established the fact that the variations must not be ascribed to corruption of the text but to a recasting of it by Cyprian himself, who revised the original by making the 'additions.' This view has been firmly established by the subsequent investigations of D. van den Eynde, O. Perler and M. Bévenot, with, however, the important difference that they reverse the order of the two versions, making that with the 'additions' the earlier and the other the final form—which seems more probable.

Editions: W. HARTEL, CSEL 3, 1 (1868) 207–233. — E. H. BLAKENEY, Cyprianus, De unitate ecclesiae. Text and translation. London, 1929. — P. DE LABRIOLLE, Cyprien, De l'unité de l'Église catholique. Trad. et notes. Paris, 1942. — J. N. BAKHUIZEN VAN DEN BRINK, Scriptores christiani primaevi I. The Hague, 1946.

Translations: English: C. THORNTON, Library of Fathers 3 (1839) 131–152. — R. E. WALLIS, ANL 8; ANF 5, 421–429. — E. H. BLAKENEY, *loc. cit.* — *German:* J. BAER, BKV² 34 (1918). — B. STEIDLE, Des Bischofs Cyprian Hirtenschreiben. Feiburg i.B., 1939. — *French:* P. DE LABRIOLLE, *loc. cit.* — *Italian:* J. GIORDANI, S. Cipriano, L'unità della chiesa cattolica. Introd. e trad. Rome, 1930. — S. COLOMBO, Corona Patrum Sales. Ser. Lat. 2. Turin, 1935.

Studies: J. CHAPMAN, Les interpolations dans le traité de S. Cyprien sur l'unité de l'Église: RB 19 (1902) 246–254, 357–373; 20 (1903) 26–51. — E. WATSON, The Interpolations in Cyprian's De unitate ecclesiae: JThSt 5 (1904) 432–436. — J. CHAPMAN, JThSt 5 (1904) 634 ff. — H. KOCH, Cyprian und der römische Primat (TU 35, 1). Leipzig, 1910, 158–169; *idem*, Matrix et radix ecclesiae. Der Genetivus epexegeticus oder appositivus bei Cyprian: ZNW 13 (1912) 165 ff. — J. CHAPMAN, Prof. Hugo Koch on S. Cyprian: RB 27 (1910) 447–464. — J. ERNST, Cyprian und das Papsttum. Mainz, 1912, 4–19. — C. A. KNELLER, Cyprians Schrift von der Einheit der Kirche: ZkTh 36 (1912) 280–303; *idem*, Der hl. Cyprian und das Kennzeichen der Kirche: Stimmen aus Maria Laach. Ergänzungsheft 115 (1914) 31–71. — O. CASEL, Eine mißverstandene Stelle Cyprians (De unit. 4): RB 30 (1913) 413–420. — H. KOCH, Cyprianische Untersuchungen. Bonn, 1926, 83–131. — O. GRADENWITZ, Cipriano interpolante se stesso?: Zeitschrift der Savigny-Stiftung für Rechtsgeschichte. Romanistische Abteilung 50 (1930) 170–183. — D. VAN DEN EYNDE, La double édition du De unitate de S. Cyprien: RHE 29 (1933) 5–24. — J. LEBRETON, La double édition du De unitate de S. Cyprien: RSR (1934) 456–467. — O. PERLER, Zur Datierung der beiden Fassungen des vierten Kapitels De unitate ecclesiae: RQ 44 (1936) 1–44; *idem*, De catholicae ecclesiae unitate cap. 4–5. Die ursprünglichen Texte, ihre Überlieferung, ihre Datierung: RQ 44 (1936) 151–168; *idem*, Cyprians

Traktat De catholicae ecclesiae unitate in einer Freiburger Hs.: Zeitschrift für Schweizerische Kirchengeschichte 30 (1936) 49–57. — M. Bévenot, St. Cyprian's De unitate, Chap. 4, in the Light of the Manuscripts (Analecta Gregoriana 11). Rome, 1937. London, 1939. — C. Butler, Downside Review (1939) 452–468. — P. Schepens, Saint Cyprien, De unitate ecclesiae V: RSR 35 (1948) 288–289. — J. Ludwig, Der hl. Märtyrerbischof Cyprian von Karthago. Munich, 1951, 30–35.

5. *The Lord's Prayer*

De dominica oratione immediately follows *De unitate ecclesiae* in Pontius' list, and, besides, internal reasons also suggest that it was composed shortly afterwards. It may consequently be dated towards the end of 251 or the beginning of 252. Cyprian has made use of Tertullian's *De oratione*, but not to any great extent, the treatment being far deeper and more comprehensive. The interpretation of the Pater Noster, which in Tertullian forms only a fourth of the work, becomes the central and dominant theme (ch. 7–27) for Cyprian, who, it may be incidentally remarked, had a slightly different text. The introduction deals with prayer in general and points to the Our Father as the most excellent. It is far more effective than any other because God the Father is pleased to hear the words of His Son; so, whenever we say it, Christ becomes our advocate before the heavenly throne. Instructions follow on the discipline, quiet and modesty to be observed by those who address themselves to the Most High. It is interesting to note how the author's mind continues to be preoccupied with the idea of unity and how this writing re-echoes the preceding. At the beginning of his commentary, he says:

Before all things, the teacher of peace and the master of unity would not have prayer to be made single and individually, as for one who prays to pray for himself alone. For we say not 'My Father, which art in heaven,' nor 'Give me this day my daily bread'; nor does each one ask that only his own debt should be forgiven him; nor does he request for himself alone that he may not be led into temptation, and delivered from evil. Our prayer is public and common; and when we pray, we pray not for one, but for the whole people, because we the whole people are one. The God of peace and the teacher of concord, who taught unity, willed that one should thus pray for all, even as He Himself bore us all in one (8 ANF 5).

This exhortation to unity and concord reappears in several places. The Lord's Prayer constitutes for Cyprian as for Tertullian a compendium of the whole Christian faith (9), and the address, *Our Father*, is an expression of our adoption as children of God in baptism: 'The new man, born again and restored to his God by His grace, says 'Father,' in the first place because he has now begun to be a son' (9). The petition *Thy kingdom come* refers, according to the author, to the eschatological kingdom acquired by the blood and passion of Christ, in which those 'who first are His subjects in the world, may hereafter reign with Christ when He reigns' (13). The *daily bread* is Christ in the eucharist, 'the bread of those who are in union with His body. And we ask that this bread should be given to us daily, that we who are in Christ, and daily receive the eucharist for the food of salvation, may not, by the interposition of some heinous sin, by being prevented, as withheld and not communicating, from partaking of the heavenly bread, be separated from Christ's body' (18 ANF 5). The sixth petition is rendered *Et ne nos patiaris induci in tentationem* (25). The last chapters return to the thought of the introduction, enforcing earnestness and freedom from distractions. All carnal and worldly thoughts must pass away. 'For this reason also the priest, by way of preface before his prayer, prepares the minds of the brethren by saying, *Sursum corda*, that so upon the people's response, *Habemus ad Dominum*, he may be reminded that he himself ought to think of nothing but the Lord' (31 ANF). Prayers which are accompanied by fasting and almsgiving will ascend quickly to God, because He is a merciful hearer of petitions associated with good works (32-33). Cyprian next discusses the proper times, explains the custom of recollecting oneself at the third, sixth and ninth hours as in honor of the Trinity, and admonishes us to morning, evening and midnight devotions. He concludes with the idea that the true Christian perseveres in prayer day and night.

Edition: W. HARTEL, CSEL 3, 1 (1868) 265–294.

Translations: English: C. THORNTON, Library of Fathers 3 (1839) 177–198. — R. E. WALLIS, ANL 8; ANF 5, 447–457. — T. H. BINDLEY, St. Cyprian, On the Lord's Prayer (SPCK). London, 1898. — H. GEE, St. Cyprian, On the Lord's Prayer. London, 1904. — J. C. PLUMPE, ACW 20 (1953). — *German:* J. BAER, BVK² 34 (1918). — TH. MICHELS, S. Th. C. Cyprianus, Das Gebet des Herrn, in: Das Siegel.

Ein Jahrbuch katholischen Lebens. Leipzig, 1925, 53–75. — *Italian:* S. COLOMBO, Corona Patrum Sales. Turin, 1935.

Studies: J. SCHINDLER, Der hl. Cyprian über das Gebet des Herrn: Theol.-prakt. Quartalschr. 40 (1887) 285–289, 535–545, 809–812. — E. W. BENSON, Cyprian. His Life, his times, his work. London, 1897, 275–279: Table showing the verbal debts to Tertullian in Cyprian's treatise De dominica oratione. — E. V. D. GOLTZ, Das Gebet in der ältesten Christenheit. Leipzig, 1901, 279–287. — G. LOESCHKE, Die Vaterunsererklärung des Theophilus von Antiochien. Eine Quellenuntersuchung zu den Vaterunsererkl. des Tertullian, Cyprian, Chromatius und Hieronymus. Berlin, 1908. — J. MOFFAT, Cyprian on the Lord's Prayer: Expositor 18 (1919) 176–189. — H. KOCH, Cyprianische Untersuchungen. Bonn, 1926, 136–139. — L. CASTIGLIONI, *loc. cit.* — B. SIMOVIC, Le Pater chez quelques Pères latins. II: Saint Cyprien: La France franciscaine 21 (1938) 245–264. — H. JANSSEN, StC (1940) 273–286. — A. J. B. HIGGINS, Lead us not into Temptation. Some Latin Variants: JThSt (1945) 179–183. — H. BLAKENEY, Matthew VI, 13 (De dominica orat. 7): ExpT 57 (1945/46) 279.

6. *To Demetrianus*

Ad Demetrianum is a refutation of a certain Demetrianus who accused the Christians of being responsible for the recent calamities of war and pestilence, famine and drought. It was not the first time that these scourges were attributed to Christian infidelity to the gods of ancient Rome. Tertullian (*Apol.* 40; *Ad nat.* 1, 9; *Ad Scap.* 3) had to denounce the same charges. Nor was Cyprian the last to defend the Christians against such rumors. St. Augustine took up the question again and answered it fully in his *City of God*, after two other African writers, Arnobius (*Adv. nat.* 1) and Lactantius (*Div. inst.* 5, 4, 3), had found it necessary to oppose this slander. Cyprian begins with a reference to the aging of the world, which follows the law of deterioration and decay. It is only natural that the soil cannot produce as it used to do in the spring of creation. Thus it is not the fault of the Christians if the harvest is poor. But the real ills of the earth are due to the sins and immoral lives of the pagans. God has the right to punish the disobedience of mankind, because we are only His slaves. The crimes and idolatry of the pagans, moreover, and the cruel persecutions of the Christians, have challenged the Almighty and brought down His anger. There is only one solution, 'to make satisfaction to God and to emerge from the abyss of darkling superstition into the bright light of true religion' (25). The Christians are ready to show their enemies the way to eternal safety which is provided by the worship of the true Deity. 'We repay kindness for your hatred; and for the torments and penalties which are inflicted on us, we point out to you the ways of salvation. Believe and live, and do you who persecute us in time rejoice with us in eternity' (25).

The *Ad Demetrianum* is one of the most powerful and original of Cyprian's writings. Its apologetical tone and contents have much in common with Tertullian's *Apology* and *To Scapula* but its satire is even more telling. Lactantius (*Div. inst.* 5, 4) objects to the extensive use of proofs from Scripture, which would make no impression on Demetrianus, and thinks that the refutation should rather have been based on arguments and reason. This criticism, however, presupposes that Cyprian had in mind only to silence his opponent, whereas he had, seemingly, a further purpose. He wanted to strengthen Christians who were in danger of losing their faith on account of the pagan accusations. The date of composition remains uncertain, because the reference to the death of Decius and his children in ch. 17 is rather doubtful. Pontius lists it after *De dominica oratione*. Thus it is usually assigned to A.D. 252. H. Koch suggests that it should be put later.

Editions: W. HARTEL, CSEL 3, 1 (1868) 349–370. — S. COLOMBO, Corona Patrum Sales. Turin, 1935. — M. LAVARENNE, St. Cyprien, Contre Démétrien. Clermont-Ferrand, 1940.

Translations: C. THORNTON, Library of Fathers 3 (1839) 199–215. — R. E. WALLIS, ANL 8; ANF 5, 457–465. — *German:* J. BAER, BKV² 34 (1918). — *French:* M. LAVARENNE, *loc. cit.* — *Italian:* S. COLOMBO, *loc. cit.*

Studies: C. PASCAL, Lucrezio e Cipriano (Ad Dem. 3): RFIC (1903) 555–557. — F. MILLOSEVICH, L'Ad Demetrianum di S. Cipriano e la decadenza dell' Impero Romano, in: Annuario del R. Liceo T. Tasso. Salerno, 1925/26. — H. KOCH, Cyprianische Untersuchungen. Bonn, 1926, 140–145. — M. PELLEGRINO, *loc. cit.*

7. *On the Mortality*

The Decian persecution, which had taken such heavy toll of human lives, had just ended when a frightful plague spread new terror and dismay in 252. Death was a constant companion and to explain what it means to the believer was why Cyprian wrote his *De mortalitate* at this time. In nothing do the faithful differ more from the pagans than in the spirit with which they face life's end. This moment is to the Christian a release from conflict, a summons of Christ, the *arcessitio dominica*. It leads to immortality and eternal reward. Nobody who has faith will be afraid of that departure from this world to a better one:

We should consider, dearly beloved brethren, that we have renounced the world, and are in the meantime living here as guests and strangers. Let us greet the day which assigns each of us to his own home, which snatches us hence, and sets us free from the snares of the world, and restores us to paradise and the heavenly kingdom. Who that has been placed in foreign lands would not hasten to return to his own country? Who that is hastening to return to his friends would not eagerly desire a prosperous gale, that he might the sooner embrace those dear to him? We regard paradise as our country—we already begin to consider the patriarchs as our parents: why do we not hasten and run, that we may behold our country, that we may greet our parents? There are a great number of our dear ones awaiting us, and a dense crowd of parents, brothers, children, is longing for us, already assured of their own safety, and still solicitous for our salvation. To attain to their presence and their embrace, what a gladness both for them and for us in common! What a pleasure is there in the heavenly kingdom, without fear of death; how lofty and perpetual a happiness with eternity of living (26 ANF 5).

Therefore the brethren 'who have been freed from the world by the summons of the Lord should not be mourned, since we know that they are not lost, but sent before' (20). 'Let us show that this is what we believe, so that we may not mourn the death even of our dear ones, and, when the day of our own summons comes, without hesitation but with gladness we may come to the Lord at His call' (24). There are quite a number of conscious or unconscious borrowings from the Stoics, especially Cicero and Seneca, in this treatise; but it rises infinitely above Stoic resignation, it opens the gate of immortality and eternal happiness.

Editions: W. HARTEL, CSEL 3, 1 (1868) 295–314. — M. L. HANNAN, S. Th. C. Cypriani, De mortalitate, with a commentary and a translat. (PSt 36). Washington, 1933. — S. COLOMBO, Corona Patrum Salesiana. Series Latina 2. Turin, 1935. — L. PAUCHENNE, Epistola decima et De mortalitate liber. Texte annoté. Liège, 1936.

Translations: English: C. THORNTON, Library of Fathers 3 (1839) 216–230. — R. E. WALLIS, ANL 8; ANF 5, 469–475. — M. L. HANNAN, *loc. cit.* — *German:* J. BAER, BKV² 34 (1918). — A. HOELTZENBEIN, St. Cyprians Trostbüchlein über das Sterben. Leutersdorf, 1930. — A. M. SCHNEIDER, Stimmen aus der Frühzeit der Kirche. Cologne, 1948, 141–160. — *Italian:* S. COLOMBO, *loc. cit.*

Studies: W. Meyer, Fragmenta Burana. Berlin, 1901, 154 f.; *idem*, Gesammelte Abhandlungen zur mittellateinischen Rythmik. Berlin, 1905, 2, 243–249. — C. Pascal, Lucrezio e Cipriano: RFIC (1903) 555–557 (De mortalitate 16). — H. Koch, Cyprianische Untersuchungen. Bonn, 1926, 140–145. — A. C. Rush, Death and Burial in Christian Antiquity (SCA 1). Washington, 1941, 24–26, 57, 178, 215.

8. *Concerning Works and Almsgiving*

Of the same time as *De mortalitate* is Cyprian's treatise *De opere and eleemosynis*, which urges the practice of liberal giving. The devastating plague left many people impoverished and destitute. Here Christian charity found a wonderful opportunity for helping the needy, the sick and the dying. Cyprian reminds his 'beloved brethren' of all the graces they have received from God. They have been redeemed from sin by the blood of Christ. Moreover the divine mercy has provided a means of securing salvation a second time, if human weakness and frailty should cause them to fall into sin after baptism: 'As in the laver of saving water the fire of hell is extinguished, so by almsgiving and works of righteousness the flame is subdued. And because in baptism remission of sins is granted once for all, constant and ceaseless good works, following the likeness of baptism, once again bestow the mercy of God... those who after the grace of baptism, have become foul, may once more be cleansed' (2). Thus Cyprian teaches here the efficacy of good works for salvation. Since nobody can be 'without some wound of conscience,' everybody is bound to practise charity. There cannot be any excuse. Those who fear that by being generous they may diminish their wealth and may suffer from need and want in the future, should know that God takes care of those who support others. 'Neither let the consideration, dearest brethren, restrain and recall the Christians from good and righteous works, that any one should fancy that he could be excused for the benefit of his children since in spiritual expenditure we ought to think of Christ, who has declared that He receives them, and not prefer our fellow-servants, but the Lord, to our children' (16). 'If you truly love your children, if you show to them the full and paternal sweetness of love, you ought to be the more charitable, that by your righteous works you may commend your children to God' (18 ANF 5). Cyprian's treatise remained a favorite in Christian antiquity. The Acts of the General Council of Ephesus in 431 quote several passages, although a Greek translation of this writing is not known.

Editions: W. HARTEL, CSEL 3, 1 (1868) 371–394. — S. COLOMBO, Corona Patrum Sales. Series Latina 2. Turin, 1935.

Translations: English: C. THORNTON, Library of Fathers 3 (1839) 231–249. — R. E. WALLIS, ANL 13; ANF 5, 476–484. — *German:* J. BAER, BKV² 34 (1918). — *Italian:* S. COLOMBO, *loc. cit.*

Studies: E. WATSON, The De opere et eleemosynis of St. Cyprian: JThSt 2 (1901) 433–438. — L. WOHLEB, Cyprian de opere et eleemosynis: ZNW (1926) 270–278. — H. KOCH, Cyprianische Untersuchungen. Bonn, 1926, 145–148.

9. *The Advantage of Patience*

The treatise *De bono patientiae* is based on Tertullian's *De patientia*. A comparison of the two shows that the literary dependence is greater than in all the other of Cyprian's writings and especially evident in general outline and choice of illustrations. Yet the difference between the two authors in spirit and language remains quite obvious, as for instance in the description of Job. Against the Stoic quality of indifference Cyprian extols patience as a special distinction of the Christians, which they have in common with God. From Him the virtue begins. From Him its glory and its dignity take their rise, and whoever is gentle, and forbearing and meek, is an imitator of God the Father, who most longsufferingly endures even the profane temples and the images of earth, and the sacrilegious rites instituted by men in contempt of His majesty and honor (4–5). Moreover, patience is an imitation of Christ, who gave the best example of it by His life here on earth even to the very hour of His cross and passion (6–8).

The introduction indicates that the treatise represents a sermon. In his Epistle to Jubianus (73, 26), probably a bishop of Mauretania, Cyprian testifies that it was written down sometime about 256 in the troubled period of the baptismal controversy between the second and third African synods dealing with this question.

Editions: W. HARTEL, CSEL 3, 1 (1868) 395–415. — S. COLOMBO, Corona Patrum Sales. Series Latina 2. Turin, 1935.

Translations: English: C. THORNTON, Library of Fathers 3 (1839) 250–265. — R. E. WALLIS, ANL 13; ANF 5, 484–491. — J. C. PLUMPE, ACW 20 (1953). — *German:* J. BAER, BKV² 34 (1918). — *Italian:* S. COLOMBO, *loc. cit.*

Studies: C. ZIWSA, Über Entstehung und Zweck der Schrift Cyprians 'de bono patientiae': Festschrift für J. Vahlen. Berlin, 1900, 540–550. — R. KADERSCHAFKA, Quae ratio et rerum materiae et generis dicendi intercedere videatur inter Cypriani librum de bono patientiae et Tertulliani librum de patientia. Progr. Pilsen, 1912.—J. H. WAS-ZINK, Eine Ennius-Reminiszenz bei Cyprian?: Mnem Ser. 3, 1 (1934) 232–233.

10. *Jealousy and Envy*

The treatise *De zelo et livore* has been called a companion to *De bono patientiae*. In fact, Pontius lists it after the latter and thus it was thought to have been written in the course of the discussion relative to the baptism of heretics about A.D. 256 or the beginning of 257. In the Cheltenham list, however, it follows the *De unitate* and, according to H. Koch, it is indeed more closely associated with this and the *De lapsis*. Thus it is not the sacramental controversy that forms its background but the Carthaginian and Roman schisms. Koch suggests therefore the second half of 251 or 252 as the most probable date of composition.

'To be jealous of what you see to be good, and to be envious of those who are better than yourself, seems in the eyes of some people to be a slight and petty wrong' (1). However, the Lord warns us to be on our guard against Satan and it was by jealousy and envy that at the beginning of the world the devil himself fell and destroyed others. Since then, through the same vice, he robs man of the grace of immortality after he himself has lost that which he had previously been. 'Thenceforth envy rages on the earth, in that he who is about to perish by jealousy obeys the author of his ruin, imitating the devil in his jealousy; as it is written, 'But through envy of the devil death penetrated into the world' (Wisd. 2, 24). Therefore they who are on his side imitate him (4). These evil tendencies are the source of many other sins, of hatred, discord, ambition, avarice and disobedience, as illustrations from the Old Testament show. Moreover, they are the most dangerous enemies of the unity of the Church: 'By this the bond of the Lord's peace is broken; by this is violated brotherly charity; by this truth is adulterated, unity is divided; men plunge into heresies and schisms when priests are disparaged, when bishops are envied, when a man complains that he himself was not rather ordained, or disdains to suffer that another should be put over him' (6). There is only one medicine against such deathly sickness of the soul, to love your neighbour. 'Love those whom you previously hated, favor those whom you envied with unjust disparagements. Imitate good men, if you are able to follow them; but if you are not able to follow them, at least rejoice with them, and congratulate those who are better than you. Make yourself a sharer with them in united love; make yourself their associate in the alliance of charity and the bond of brotherhood' (17 ANF 5).

Editions: W. HARTEL, CSEL 3, 1 (1868). — S. COLOMBO, Corona Patrum Sales. Turin, 1935.

Translations: English: C. THORNTON, Library of Fathers 3 (1839) 266–277. — R. E. WALLIS, ANL 13, ANF 5, 491–496. — *German:* J. BAER, BKV² 34 (1918). — *Italian:* S. COLOMBO, *loc. cit.*

Studies: C. BRUNNER, Die Veranlassung zu Cyprians Schrift 'de zelo': Katholik 95, 2 (1915) 215 ff. — H. KOCH, Cyprianische Untersuchungen. Bonn, 1926, 132–136.

11. *Exhortation to Martyrdom, addressed to Fortunatus*

The treatise *Ad Fortunatum*, or, as some manuscripts render the title, *Ad Fortunatum de exhortatione martyrii*, is a compendium of Scripture, requested by a certain Fortunatus, to strengthen the Christians for a coming persecution. Texts are arranged under twelve headings. Thus Cyprian furnishes only material, not a finished exposition: 'But now I have sent you the very wool and the purple from the Lamb, by whom we were redeemed and quickened; which, when you have received, you will make into a coat for yourself according to your own will, so that you will rejoice in it as your own private and special garment. And you will exhibit to others also what we have sent, that they themselves may be able to finish it according to their own will' (3). The first headings deal with idolatry and the worship of the true God, the punishment of those who sacrifice to idols and God's anger against them (1–5). Being redeemed by the blood of Christ, we ought to prefer nothing to Him and never return to the world (7) but persevere in faith and virtue to the end (8). Persecutions arise in order to put the followers of Christ on trial (9) but they should not be feared because we are sure of the Lord's protection (10). They have been predicted (11), but also the reward and the crown which remains for the righteous and martyrs (12).

There is no doubt that the treatise refers to a persecution. Opinions differ, however, as to which, whether the Decian (250–51) or the Valerian (257), while H. Koch assigns it to the spring of 253, when Gallus' was imminent. Fortunatus seems to be the Bishop Fortunatus of Thuccabori, who participated in the African synod of September 256.

Edition: W. HARTEL, CSEL 3, 1 (1868) 315–347.

Translations: English: C. THORNTON, Library of Fathers 3 (1839) 278–301. — R. E. WALLIS, ANL 13; ANF 5, 496–507. — *German:* J. BAER, BKV² 34 (1918).

Studies: H. VON SODEN, Das lateinische Neue Testament zur Zeit Cyprians (TU 33). Leipzig, 1909, 19 f. — L. WOHLEB, Cyprian ad Fortunatum I: Woch. klass. Phil. 34 (1917) 378 ff. — C. A. KNELLER, ZkTh (1916) 676–703. — H. KOCH, Cyprianische Untersuchungen. Bonn, 1926, 149–183. — C. H. TURNER, Prolegomena to the Testimonia and Ad Fortunatum of St. Cyprian: JThSt 29 (1928) 113–136; 31 (1930) 225–246. — M. PELLEGRINO, Studi su l'antica apologetica. Rome, 1947.

12. *To Quirinus: Three Books of Testimonies*

Although *Ad Fortunatum* is of great value for the history of the oldest Latin versions of the Bible, there is no other work among Cyprian's writings of such importance for this question as *Ad Quirinum (Testimoniorum libri III)*, which consists of an abundance of Scriptural passages gathered under a number of headings. Addressed to Quirinus, whom the author calls 'his beloved son,' it counted originally two books only and was later increased by a third. Cyprian mentions in the introduction that he wants to afford only material for others and outlines his plan as follows: 'I have comprised in my undertaking two books of equally moderate length: one wherein I have endeavoured to show that the Jews, according to what had before been foretold, had departed from God, and had lost God's favor, which had been given them in past time, and had been promised them for the future; while the Christians had succeeded to their place, deserving well of the Lord by faith, and coming out of all nations and from the whole world. The second book likewise contains the mystery of Christ, that He has come who was announced according to Scriptures, and has done and perfected all those things whereby He was foretold as being able to be perceived and known' (1 ANF 5). Thus the first book is an apology against the Jews, whereas the second amounts to a compendium of christology. The arrangement is similar to that of the *Ad Fortunatum*. The first book has twenty-four headings, under which the Scripture texts are gathered, the second, thirty.

The third book has its own preface, which indicates that Cyprian complied with a further request of Quirinus when he composed it at a later time. It is a summary of the moral and disciplinary duties and a guide to the Christian virtues, consisting of one hundred and twenty theses followed by proofs from Scripture. Since the preface does not refer to the first and second books, it remains doubtful whether Cyprian combined the three, and it appears more probable that it was done later. No indications in the work enable us to assign it a definite date. However, Cyprian apparently made use of the third book when he wrote *De habitu virginum*. If that is the case, the time of composition would be before A.D. 249. There are also intrinsic reasons for suggesting so early a year. *Ad Quirinum* had a great and enduring influence on the teaching and preaching of the Church. Its Scripture texts were quoted again and again. Pseudo-Cyprian, *Adv. aleatores*, Commodianus, Lactantius, Firmicus Maternus, Lucifer of Calaris, Jerome, Pelagius, Augustine used them. The first explicit mention of the study is found in the Cheltenham list of 359.

Edition: W. HARTEL, CSEL 3, 1 (1868) 33–184.

Translations: English: CH. THORNTON, Library of Fathers 3, 21–115. — R. E. WALLIS, ANL 13; ANF 5, 507–557. — *German:* J. BAER, BKV² 34 (1918). — *French:* J. BOULET, St. Cyprien, évêque de Carthage et martyr. Avignon, 1923.

Studies: B. DOMBART, Über die Bedeutung Kommodians für die Textkritik der Testimonia Cyprians: Zeitschr. f. wissenschaftliche Theologie 22 (1879) 374–389. — G. MERCATI, D'alcuni nuovi sussidi per la critica del testo di S. Cipriano. Rome, 1899, 1–4, 48–67. — H. L. RAMSAY, On Early Insertions in the Third Book of St. Cyprian's Testimonia: JThSt 2 (1901) 276–288. — P. GLAUE, Zur Echtheit von Cyprians drittem Buch der Testimonia: ZNW 8 (1907) 274–289. — C. H. TURNER, Prolegomena to the Testimonia of St. Cyprian: JThSt 6 (1905) 62–87. — L. WOHLEB, Cyprians Spruchsammlung ad Quirinum: RQ 33 (1925) 22–38. — H. KOCH, Cyprianische Untersuchungen. Bonn, 1926, 183–210; *idem*, Das dritte Buch der Cyprianischen Testimonia in seinem zeitlichen Verhältnis zum ersten und zweiten: ZKG (1926) 1–9. — C. H. TURNER, Prolegomena to the Testimonia and Ad Fortunatum of St. Cyprian: JThSt 29 (1928) 113–136; 31 (1930) 225–246. — A. SOUTER, The Interpolations in S. Cyprian's Ad Quirinum: JThSt 34 (1933) 45–46. — N. J. HOMMES, Het Testimoniaalboek. Amsterdam, 1935, ch. 6. — A. L. WILLIAMS, Adversus Judaeos. Cambridge, 1935, 56–64.

13. *That the Idols are not Gods*

The small tract *Quod idola dii non sint* intends to demonstrate in

its first part (1–7) that the pagan deities are not gods but former
kings who, because of their royal memory, began to be worshipped
after their death. To preserve the features of the departed by an
image, their likenesses were carved out and men immolated
victims and celebrated festive days in their honor, as can be
proved from history. There is no reason for the close connection
between these religious practices and the glory of Rome. The
second part (8–9) shows that there is only one God, invisible and
incomprehensible. There follows an outline of christology, which
forms the third part.

Although St. Jerome (*Epist.* 70 *ad Magnum* 5) and St. Augustine
(*De bapt.* 6, 44, 87; *De unico bapt. adv. Petil.* 4) attribute this
treatise to Cyprian with enthusiastic comments, its authenticity
was long disputed. Pontius and the Cheltenham list do not
mention it, nor does Cyprian himself refer to it in any of his
writings. However, after H. Koch proved such evident traces of
Cyprian's manner in it, the generally accepted theory of its
spuriousness can hardly be maintained. He placed it among the
author's earliest efforts. Many of its ideas and expressions are
borrowed from Tertullian and Minucius Felix. Apparently, the
writer as a neophyte assembled quotations from the existing
Latin Apologies and summed up the arguments for the vanity of
idolatry and the supremacy of the one, true God. Perhaps these
excerpts were never intended for publication. The treatise has
nothing of the literary finish of the other works of Cyprian.

Edition: W. HARTEL, CSEL 3, 1 (1868) 17–31.

Translations: English: C. THORNTON, Library of Fathers 3 (1839) 13–20. — R. E.
WALLIS, ANL 8; ANF 5, 465–469.

Studies: A. MELARDI, San Cipriano di Cartagine. Contributo all'apologetica latina
del III secolo. Potenza, 1901. — L. BAYARD, Le Latin de St. Cyprien. Paris, 1902,
XXIX–XLV. — H. KOCH, Quod idola dii non sint: ein Werk Cyprians: Cypria-
nische Untersuchungen. Bonn, 1926, 1–78. — H. DILLER, In Sachen Tertullian-
Minucius Felix: Phil 90 (1935) 98–114, 216–239. — B. AXELSON, Quod idola und
Laktanz: Eranos 39 (1941) 67–74. — M. PELLEGRINO, Studi su l'antica apologetica.
Rome, 1947.

II. *Epistles*

These constitute an inexhaustible source for the history of a
most interesting period of the Church. They mirror the problems
and controversies of ecclesiastical administration around the

middle of the third century. They echo the words of great personalities like Cyprian, Novatian, Cornelius, Stephen, Firmilian of
Caesarea and others. They reveal the hopes and fears, the life
and death of the Christians in one of the most important ecclesiastical provinces. The assembling of these letters goes back to
antiquity and began practically when Cyprian arranged some
of his correspondence according to content and had copies sent to
different centres of Christianity and to his fellow-bishops. Other
collections were made for the purpose of edification. In modern
editions the corpus consists of eighty-one pieces; sixty-five from
Cyprian's pen, sixteen addressed to him or the clergy of Carthage. The latter group contains epistles from the presbytery of
Rome, from Novatian (cf. above, p. 213), from Pope Cornelius
(cf. above, p. 236), and others. Numbers 5–43 are from the time
of his retirement during the persecution of Decius (cf. above,
p. 341 f), among them twenty-seven addressed to his clergy and
people. His exchange with Popes Cornelius and Lucius consists of
44–61, 64, 66, twelve of them (44–55) concerning the schism of
Novatian. The letters 67–75, written during the pontificate of
Stephen (254–257), deal with the baptismal controversy, and
78–81 were sent from his last exile. The remainder, 1–4, 62, 63,
65, all by Cyprian himself, cannot be arranged with reference to
any of these chronological series because they lack any allusion to
times or conditions. The first emphasizes the decision of an
African synod that a cleric is not permitted to act as guardian or
as executor. The second discusses the question whether it could be
tolerated that a Christian actor, who resigned from his profession,
give instruction in the histrionic art. The third deals with a
deacon who greatly offended his bishop. The fourth takes action
against the abuses of the *syneisaktoi* (cf. vol. I, p. 59, 156). Letter
62, addressed to eight Numidian bishops, accompanied a contribution collected at Carthage for the redemption of Christians of
both sexes held as prisoners by the barbarians. Epistle 63 amounts
to a treatise, and is sometimes entitled *On the Sacrament of the Cup
of the Lord (De sacramento calicis domini)*. It rejects the peculiar
custom of using water in the Lord's supper, instead of wine
mixed with water, which had developed in some of the Christian
communities. Item 65 warns the congregation of Assurae
not to allow their former bishop Fortunatianus, who had sacri-

ficed to the idols during the persecution, to return to his office. The collection is by no means complete, as mention is made of other letters no longer preserved. None of those extant is dated, but all, except two (8 and 33) give the address. Only one manuscript contains the entire eighty-one epistles, *Codex Taurinensis.*

This corpus is not only an important source for the history of the Church and of Canon Law but also an outstanding monument of Christian Latin. Whereas his treatises are more affected by stylistic devices, his missives reproduce the conversational Latin of the educated believer of the third century. Here the spoken word of the man of action is recorded, while his writings testify to the brilliant style of the ecclesiastical author and former professor of rhetoric, well acquainted with Ciceronian diction.

Editions: W. HARTEL, CSEL 3, 2 (1871). — L. BAYARD, St. Cyprien, Correspondance. Texte établi et trad. Paris, 1925. — J. VERGÉS-M. T. BELLPUIG, Epistolari. Text rev. and trad. Catalan. Barcelona, 1931, 2 vols.

Translations: English: H. CAREY, The Epistles of St. Cyprian, Bishop of Carthage and Martyr, with the Council of Carthage on the Baptism of Heretics (Library of Fathers 17). Oxford, 1844, 1–316. — R. E. WALLIS, ANL 8; ANF 5, 275–409. — T. A. LACEY, Selected Epistles of St. Cyprian, Treating of the Episcopate. After the translation of N. Marshall, ed. with introduction and notes (SPCK). London, 1922. — *German:* J. BAER, BKV² 60 (1928). — *French:* L. BAYARD, *loc. cit.* — *Spanish:* M. GUALLAR, Cartas selectas. Colección de 30 cartas (Colección Excelsa 27). Madrid, 1946. — *Catalan:* J. VERGÉS-M. T. BELLPUIG, *loc. cit.* — *Dutch:* M. COSTANZA, Cyprianus, Aan de Christenen, die als levende Martelaren werken in de mijnen; aan Successus; aan de Priesters; aan de Diakenen, en aan het Volk (Geert-Groote-Genootschap 573). 's Hertogenbosch, 1939.

Studies: MENDEN, Beiträge zur Geschichte und Lehre der nordafrikanischen Kirche aus den Briefen des hl. Cyprian (Progr.). Bonn, 1878. — O. RITSCHL, De epistulis Cyprianicis. Diss. Halle a. S., 1885; *idem,* Cyprian von Karthago und die Verfassung der Kirche. Göttingen, 1885, 238–250: Die Chronologie der cyprianischen Briefe. — A. HARNACK, Über verlorene Briefe und Aktenstücke, die sich aus der Cyprianischen Briefsammlung ermitteln lassen (TU 23, 2a). Leipzig, 1902. — L. NELKE, Die Chronologie der Korrespondenz Cyprians und der pseudocyprianischen Schriften Ad Novatianum und Liber de rebaptismate. Diss. Thorn, 1902. — H. VON SODEN, Die Cyprianische Briefsammlung. Geschichte ihrer Entstehung und Überlieferung (TU 25, 3). Leipzig, 1904. — G. BONACCORSI, Le lettere di San Cipriano: Rivista stor.-crit. delle scienze teol. 1 (1905) 377–392. — H. VON SODEN, Die Prosopographie des afrikanischen Episkopats zur Zeit Cyprians. Rome, 1909. — F. SCHUBERT, Weidenauer Studien 3 (1909) 235–297. — A. WILMART, La lettre LVIII de Cyprien parmi les lectures non bibliques du Lectionnaire de Luxeuil: RB 28 (1911) 228–233. — J. SAJDAK, De Cypriani Epistularum codice Cracoviensi: Eos 18 (1915) 134–147. — G. RAUSCHEN, Der Ketzertaufstreit zur Zeit des hl. Cyprian: ThGl 8

(1916) 629 ff. — H. K. MENGIS, Ein donatistisches Corpus Cyprianischer Briefe. Diss. Freiburg, 1916. — H. KOCH, IKZ (1920) 229–247 (Epist. 8 and 9). — A. D'ALÈS, RSR (1921) 374–380 (Ep. 59, 14). — F. J. DÖLGER, 'Nihil innovetur nisi quod traditum est'. Ein Grundsatz der Kulttradition in der römischen Kirche: AC 1 (1929) 79 f. (Ep. 74 and 30). — H. LEWY, Sobria ebrietas. Giessen, 1929, 138–146 (Ep. 63). — F. J. DÖLGER, 'Öl der Eucharistie': AC 2 (1930) 184–189 (Ep. 70, 2). — J. LEBRETON, RSR (1930) 160–162 (Ep. 63, 11). — L. PAUCHENNE, Epistola decima et de mortalitate liber. Liège, 1930. — M. DE LA TAILLE, Le sens du mot *passio* dans la lettre 63 de S. Cyprien: RSR 21 (1931) 576–581. — A. GARCÍA DE LA FUENTE, Sobre una nota bibliográfica a el caso del obispo Marcial de Mérida: RC 27 (1934) 123–124 (Ep. 67). Cf. RHE (1934) 877–879. — J. SCHRIJNEN und CHR. MOHRMANN, Studien zur Syntax der Briefe des hl. Cyprians. 2 vols. (Latinitas christianorum primaeva 5/6). Nijmegen, 1936/37. — J. KOEHNE, Die Bußdauer auf Grund der Briefe Cyprians: ThGl 29 (1937) 245–256. — CHR. MOHRMANN, Woordspeling in de brieven van St. Cyprianus: Tijdschrift voor taal en letteren 27 (1939) 163–175. — A. FERRUA, S. Saturnino martire cartaginese-romano (in the letters of St. Cyprian): CC (1939) 436–445. — G. MERCATI, Opere minore 2 (ST 77). Vatican City, 1937, 226–240 (Ep. 49 and 50). — M. BÉVENOT, A New Cyprianic Fragment: BJR 28, 1 (1944) 76–87. — B. MELIN, Studia in Corpus Cyprianeum. Uppsala, 1946. — M. BÉVENOT, A Bishop is Responsible to God Alone (St. Cyprian): RSR 39/40 (1951/52) 397–415.

2. PSEUDO-CYPRIANIC WRITINGS

More numerous than the authentic writings of Cyprian are those which have been attributed to him without sufficient reasons as a result of the high reputation and esteem in which he was universally held.

1. The author of the treatises *De spectaculis* and *De bono pudicitiae* which appear among Cyprian's works, is Novatian (cf. above, pp. 223–226).

2. The *Ad Novatianum* is a polemic against Novatian. The author is not Pope Sixtus II, as A. Harnack (*Chronologie* 2, 387) thought, but some African bishop who shares Cyprian's view on baptism conferred by heretics. It seems to have been written between 253–257.

Edition: W. HARTEL, CSEL 3, 3 (1871) 52–69.

Translations: R. E. WALLIS, ANL 13, 429–445; ANF 5, 657–663.

Studies: A. HARNACK, Eine bisher nicht erkannte Schrift des Papstes Sixtus II. vom Jahre 257/8 (TU 13, 1). Leipzig, 1895. Cf. JÜLICHER, ThLZ (1896) 19–22; F. X. FUNK, ThQ 78 (1896) 691–693. — E. W. BENSON, Cyprian. London, 1897, 557–564. Cf. A. HARNACK, TU 20, 3 (1900) 116–126. — A. ROMBOLD, Über den Verfasser der Schrift Ad Novatianum: ThQ 82 (1900) 546–601. Cf. HAUSSLEITER, ThLB (1900) 221–224. — L. NELKE, Die Chronologie der Korrespondenz Cyprians und der pseudocyprianischen Schriften Ad Novatianum und Liber de rebaptismate. Thorn, 1902, 159–170. — J. GRABISCH, Die pseudo-cyprianische Schrift Ad Novatianum, in: M. SDRALEK, Kirchengeschichtliche Abhandlungen 2. Breslau, 1904, 257–282. Cf. A. HARNACK, Geschichte der altchristlichen Literatur 2, 2, 387 ff, 552 f. — J. ERNST, Die Stellung der römischen Kirche zur Ketzertauffrage vor und unmittelbar nach Papst Stephan I: ZkTh 29 (1905) 274 ff. — H. VOGELS, Untersuchungen zur Geschichte der lateinischen Apokalypse-Übersetzung. Düsseldorf, 1920, 104 f. — B. CAPELLE, RB Suppl. 1 (1921) 114. — A. D'ALÈS, Novatien. Paris, 1925, 25–30. — H. KOCH, Cyprianische Untersuchungen. Bonn, 1926, 358–420.

3. *De rebaptismate*, on the other hand, opposes Cyprian on this issue and defends its validity by a very peculiar and unfortunate distinction between baptism of water and baptism of the spirit to be conferred by the bishop's imposition of hands. The author seems to be an African prelate, who wrote it after A.D. 256, most probably before Cyprian died.

Editions: W. HARTEL, CSEL 3, 3 (1871) 69–92. — G. RAUSCHEN, FP 11. Bonn, 1916. Cf. J. ERNST, ZkTh (1917) 726–741.

Translations: English: R. E. WALLIS, ANL 13; ANF 5, 665–678.

Studies: J. ERNST, Zur handschriftlichen Überlieferung des Liber de rebaptismate: ZkTh 22 (1898) 179 ff. — H. VON SODEN, Eine neue Handschrift des pseudocyprianischen Liber de rebaptismate: Quellen und Forschungen aus italienischen Archiven und Bibliotheken 13 (1910) 217–223. — E. W. BENSON, Cyprian. London, 1897, 390–399. — H. KOCH, Die Tauflehre des Liber de rebaptismate. Braunsberg, 1907; *idem,* Zeit und Heimat des Liber de rebaptismate: ZNW 8 (1907) 190–220. — J. ERNST, Die Tauflehre des Liber de rebaptismate: ZkTh 31 (1907) 648–699; *idem,* Zeit und Heimat des Liber de rebaptismate: ThQ 90 (1908) 579–613; 91 (1909) 20–64; *idem,* Antikritische Glossen zum Liber de rebaptismate: ZkTh 41 (1917) 164–175, 450–471. — G. RAUSCHEN, Die pseudo-cyprianische Schrift de rebaptismate: ZkTh 41 (1917) 83–110. — H. KOCH, IKZ 14 (1924) 134–161. — C. M. EDSMAN, Le baptême de feu. Leipzig-Uppsala, 1940, 142–147.

4. *Adversus aleatores* is a sermon in vulgar Latin against dicethrowers. Harnack (*op. cit.* p. 387) assigns it to Pope Victor (189–199), whereas Koch (*op. cit.* p. 78) holds that it was written by a bishop of North Africa after Cyprian's time, perhaps about A.D. 300.

Editions: W. HARTEL, CSEL 3, 3 (1871) 92–104. — A. HARNACK, Der pseudocyprianische Traktat De aleatoribus, die älteste lateinische christliche Schrift, ein Werk des römischen Bischofs Viktor I (saec. II) (TU 5, 1). Leipzig, 1888. — A. HILGENFELD, Libellum de aleatoribus inter Cypriani scripta conservatum edidit et comm. crit. instr. Freiburg i.B., 1889. — A. MIODOŃSKI, Anonymus adversus aleatores (gegen das Hazardspiel) und die Briefe an Cyprian, Lucian, Celerinus und an den karthaginiensischen Klerus (Cypr. epist. 8; 21–24) kritisch verbessert, erläutert und ins Deutsche übersetzt. Erlangen, 1889. — J. DE LANNOY, Étude critique sur l'opuscule 'De aleatoribus'. Louvain, 1891.

Translations: German: A. MIODOŃSKI, *loc. cit.* — *Dutch:* C. F. M. DEELEMAN, Adversus aleatores: Theol. Studiën 23 (1916) 233–268, 335–353.

Studies: H. J. D. RYDER, Harnack on the 'De aleatoribus': Dublin Review, Ser. 3, 22 (1889) 82–98. — F. X. FUNK, Kirchengeschichtliche Abhandlungen 2. Paderborn, 1899, 209–236. — P. MONCEAUX, Hist. litt. de l'Afrique chrétienne 2. Paris, 1901, 112–118. — A. HARNACK, Geschichte der altchristl. Literatur 2, 2, 370–381. — E. LÖFSTEDT, Eranos 8 (1908) 115. — H. KOCH, Zur Schrift Adversus aleatores: Festgabe K. Müller. Tübingen, 1922, 58–67.

5. *De singularitate clericorum* deals with a practical question. It combats the abuses of certain clerics who lived together with women without being married, describes the dangers of such communal life and the suspicions to which it exposes the priests. Harnack (TU 24, 3) attributed the work to the Donatist bishop Macrobius, following a suggestion of G. Morin. Blacha thought that it was by Novatian. Koch refuted these opinions and proved that an unknown African of the third century must be its author. B. Melin has recently given strong reasons for identifying him with the writer of the pseudo-Cyprianic *Epist.* IV (CSEL 3, 3, 274–282).

Edition: W. HARTEL, CSEL 3, 3 (1871).

Studies: H. ACHELIS, Virgines subintroductae. Leipzig, 1902, 35 ff. — A. HARNACK, Der pseudocyprianische Traktat de singularitate clericorum ein Werk des donatistischen Bischofs Macrobius in Rom (TU 24, 3). Leipzig, 1903. — F. v. BLACHA, Der pseudocyprianische Traktat 'de singularitate clericorum' ein Werk Novatians: Kirchengeschichtliche Abhandlungen, hrsg. von M. Sdralek, 2. Breslau, 1904, 193 ff. — P. SCHEPENS, L'épitre 'De singularitate clericorum' du Ps. Cyprien: RSR 13 (1922) 178–210, 297–327; 14 (1923) 47–65. — H. KOCH, Cyprianische Untersuchungen. Bonn, 1926, 426–472. — TH. BIRT, Marginalien zu lateinischen Prosaikern: Phil (1927) 164–182. — B. MELIN, Studia in Corpus Cyprianeum. Uppsala, 1946, 215–232: De tractatu De singularitate clericorum et epistula quarta pseudocyprianea ab uno atque eodem scriptis.

6. *De pascha computus* intends to correct the Easter cycle of Hippolytus of Rome, the failure of whose computation is imputed to a misinterpretation of Scripture. The improvement proposed therein is based on a different explanation of the same passages with the addition of some other texts. The work was issued in A.D. 243 and the wording of the biblical excerpts suggests Africa as its place of origin.

Edition: W. HARTEL, CSEL 3, 3 (1871) 248-271.

Studies: E. HUFMAYR, Die pseudocyprianische Schrift 'de pascha computus' (Progr.) Augsburg, 1896. — P. MONCEAUX, *loc. cit.* 2, 97-102. — E. SCHWARTZ, Christliche und jüdische Ostertafeln (AGWG Phil.-hist. Kl. N. F. 8, 6). Berlin, 1906, 36-40. — H. VON SODEN, Die cyprianische Briefsammlung (TU 25, 3). Leipzig, 1904, 224 ff. — S. BRANDT, Zu Ps. Cyprian De pascha: PhW (1920) 424-432.

7. *Adversus Judaeos* is a sermon on the ungratefulness of Israel, which persecuted Christ already in the prophets. The Father suffered in the Son and the Son in the prophets. The obduracy of the Jews, especially at Christ's death, was the reason that the Saviour had to turn to the pagans, the poor and the downtrodden, and invite them into His kingdom. Thus Jerusalem ceased to be the city of God and Israel has been made homeless in this world. However, God still exhorts the Jews to do penance and accept eternal salvation through baptism. The sermon is of the third century; most probably it was composed before A.D. 260 (Harnack, *op. cit.* p. 403). E. Peterson has recently shown that it depends to a large degree on Melito's homily *On the Passion*, published by C. Bonner from a papyrus codex of the fourth century. Such is the similarity of expression and theological thought that in some passages the *Adversus Judaeos* appears to be but a translation.

Edition: W. HARTEL, CSEL 3, 3 (1871) 133-144.

Translations: English: S. D. F. SALMOND, ANL 9; ANF 5, 219.

Studies: J. DRÄSEKE, Zu Hippolytos' Demonstratio adversus Judaeos: Jahrbücher für prot. Theologie 12 (1886) 456-461. — G. LANDGRAF, Über den pseudocyprianischen Traktat 'adversus Judaeos': Archiv für lat. Lexikographie u. Gramm. 11, 1 (1898) 87-97. — A. HARNACK, Patristische Miscellen (TU 20, 3). Leipzig, 1900, 126-135. — H. JORDAN, Melito und Novatian: Archiv für lat. Lexikographie u. Gramm. 13, 1 (1902) 59-68. — A. L. WILLIAMS, Adversus Judaeos. A Bird's-Eye View of Christian 'Apologiae'. Cambridge, 1935, 53-55. — E. PETERSON, Ps. Cyprian, Adversus Judaeos und Melito von Sardes: VC 6 (1952) 33-43.

8. *De laude martyrii*, also in the form of a sermon, explains in three parts the meaning (4-12), the greatness (13-18), the advantages of martyrdom (19-24). Among its benefits the author mentions the escape from the universal suffering in Hades after death. He gives on this occasion a description of the tortures of hell, which embodies ancient elements. The sermon is of the third century, but not by Cyprian or Novatian, perhaps by a layman.

Edition: W. HARTEL, CSEL 3, 3 (1871) 26–52.

Translations: English: R. E. WALLIS, ANL 13; ANF 5, 579–587.

Studies: A. HARNACK, Eine bisher nicht erkannte Schrift Novatians 249/50 (TU 13, 4 b). Leipzig, 1895. — H. KOCH, Cyprianische Untersuchungen. Bonn, 1926, 334–357. — G. MERCATI, Opere minore 2 (ST 77). Vatican City, 1937, 184–191.

9. *De montibus Sina et Sion.* The author of this treatise, written in vulgar Latin, regards Mount Sinai as a symbol of the Old, and Mount Sion as a figure of the New Testament. The former has found its spiritual fulfilment in the latter. The date of composition is uncertain. The character of the Latin version of the Scriptural passages points to Africa as place of origin.

Edition: W. HARTEL, CSEL 3, 3 (1871) 104–119.

Studies: A. HARNACK, Zur Schrift Pseudo-Cyprians De montibus Sina et Sion (TU 20, 3). Leipzig, 1900, 135–147; *idem,* Geschichte der altchristl. Literatur 2, 2, 383–386. — C. H. TURNER, The Pseudo-Cyprianic 'De montibus Sina et Sion' written in Rome: JThSt 7 (1906) 597–600. — P. CORSSEN, Ein theologischer Traktat aus der Werdezeit der kirchlichen Literatur des Abendlandes: ZNW 12 (1911) 1–36. — A. SOUTER, The Home of ps.-Cyprian *De montibus Sina et Sion:* JThSt 16 (1915) 554 ff. — V. BULHART, Lexikalische und kritische Beiträge: WSt 48 (1930) 74, n. 7. — G. MERCATI, Opere minore 2 (ST 77). Vatican City, 1937, 195 f.

10. *Exhortatio de paenitentia* is a collection of biblical quotations similar to Cyprian's *Ad Fortunatum* and *Ad Quirinum.* These passages are arranged under the heading: 'That all sins can be forgiven him who has turned to God with his whole heart.' The Latin version is of the African type, but of a more recent edition than that used by Cyprian. The author opposes the Novatians. The treatise has been attributed to the fourth or fifth century, but without convincing reasons.

Editions: ML 4, 863 ff. — A. MIODOŃSKI, Incerti auctoris Exhortatio de paenitentia. Ope codicis Parisini nr. 550 rec. Krakau, 1893 = Rozprawy Akademji Umiejetnosci II, 5, 125–134.

Translations: English: R. E. WALLIS, ANL 13; ANF 5, 592–595.

Studies: C. WUNDERER, Bruchstücke einer afrikanischen Bibelübersetzung in der pseudocyprianischen Schrift Exhortatio de paenitentia (Progr.). Erlangen, 1889. — B. CAPELLE, Le texte du psautier latin en Afrique. Rome, 1913, 51, n. 2.

11. *Caena Cypriani* is the title of a work which describes a supposed banquet at Cana, to which important biblical personalities are invited by a great king, i.e. God. Since the author makes

extensive use of the *Acts of Paul*, we have here a valuable source for one of the most important apocryphal acts of the apostles (cf. vol. I, 130–133). It was written most probably about A.D. 400 in the south of Gaul by the poet Cyprian, the same presbyter Cyprian, it seems, to whom Jerome addressed one of his letters (*Epist.* 140).

Edition: K. STRECKER, Mon. Germ. Hist. Poet. lat. med. aev. IV, 2, 1. Berlin, 1914, 872 ff.

Studies: A. HARNACK, Drei wenig beachtete cyprianische Schriften und die 'Acta Pauli' (TU 19, 3). Leipzig, 1899. — H. BREWER, Über den Heptateuchdichter Cyprian und die Caena Cypriani : ZkTh 28 (1904) 98 ff. — A. LAPÔTRE, La 'Cena Cypriani' et ses énigmes: RSR 3 (1912) 497–596. — W. HASS, Studien zum Heptateuchdichter Cyprian: PhW (1914) 517. — A. WILMART, Le prologue d'Hervé de Bourgdieu pour son commentaire de la Cena Cypriani: RB 35 (1923) 255–263.

12. The *Ad Vigilium episcopum de iudaica incredulitate* is nothing else than the preface to the Latin translation of the *Dialogue* of Aristo of Pella (cf. vol. I, p. 195).

13. *De centesima, sexagesima, tricesima* was most probably composed in the fourth century by an African. It deals with the triple reward which awaits martyrs, ascetics and good Christians. The influence of Cyprian's writings is evident in spirit and language.

Edition: R. REITZENSTEIN, Eine frühchristliche Schrift von den dreierlei Früchten des christlichen Lebens: ZNW 15 (1914) 60–90.

Studies: D. DE BRUYNE, Un traité gnostique sur les trois récompenses: ZNW 15 (1914) 280–284. — E. SEEBERG, Eine neugefundene lateinische Predigt aus dem 3. Jahrhundert: NKZ 25 (1914) 472–544. — G. WOHLENBERG, Eine pseudocyprianische Schrift über dreifach verschiedenen Lohn: ThLB 35 (1914) 169 ff, 193 ff, 217–220. — M. HEER, Pseudo-Cyprian vom Lohn der Frommen und das Evangelium Justins: RQ 28 (1914) 97–186. — E. BUONAIUTI, Un preteso scritto preciprianeo sul diverso fruttato della vita cristiana. Rome, 1914. — J. MARTIN, Zu der ps.-cyprianischen Schrift über den dreifachen Lohn: Woch. klass. Phil. 32 (1915) 141–144. — J. H. SCHMALZ, Syntaktisches (über De fructibus): PhW (1915) 508–511. — H. VON SODEN, Die Erforschung der vornicänischen Kirchengeschichte seit 1914: ZKG 39 (1920) 147–149. — C. WEYMAN, Bemerkungen zu späteren lateinischen Schriftwerken: Münchener Museum 4 (1924) 273. — H. KOCH, Die ps.-cyprianische Schrift De centesima, sexagesima, tricesima in ihrer Abhängigkeit von Cyprian: ZNW 31 (1932) 248–272. — D. NORBERG, Ps.-Cypr. tract. 11 + 26: Eranos 42 (1944) 77.

About *Cyprian of Antioch*, the magicien, with whom Cyprian of Carthage has been erroneously identified, see: H. DELEHAYE, Cyprien d'Antioche et Cyprien de Carthage: AB 39 (1921) 314–332. — F. BILABEL und A. GROHMANN, Griechische, koptische und arabische Texte zur Religion und religiösen Literatur in Ägyptens Spätzeit. 1934.

3. ASPECTS OF CYPRIAN'S THEOLOGY

If Tertullian never tried a systematic presentation of Christian doctrine, Cyprian, the man of action rather than of thought, was even less inclined and equipped for such an attempt. He lacks both the originality of Tertullian and the speculative power of Origen. Still, the fact remains that up to the time of St. Augustine he was the theological authority of the West. His writings were listed side by side with the canonical books of the Old and New Testaments, as the Cheltenham list testifies. Even after Augustine all through the Middle Ages, he was one of the most read Fathers of the Church and his influence on Canon Law was very strong. If popes, bishops and divines refer to him again and again it is especially for his teaching on the nature of the Church, which forms the centre of his thought.

1. *Ecclesiology*

To Cyprian the Church is the only way to salvation. Thus he states simply but clearly *Salus extra ecclesiam non est* (*Epist.* 73, 21). It is impossible to have God as Father except we have her as Mother: *habere non potest deum patrem qui ecclesiam non habet matrem* (*De unit.* 6). For this reason it is of the highest importance to remain within, because nobody can be a Christian except he does so: *christianus non est qui in Christi ecclesia non est* (*Epist.* 55, 24). She is the Bride of Christ and as such she cannot be an adulteress. 'Whosoever separates himself from the Church and attaches himself to an adulteress, separates himself from the promises of the Church, nor will he who leaves the Church attain to the rewards of Christ. He is a stranger, he is unholy, he is an enemy' (*De unit.* 6). Thus the fundamental character of the Church is unity, which Cyprian employs his richest imagery to describe. He sees it typified by the seamless robe of Christ:

> This sacrament of unity, this bond of concord inseparably cohering, is set forth where in the Gospel the coat of the Lord Jesus Christ is not at all divided nor cut, but is received as an entire garment, and is possessed as an uninjured and undivided robe by those who cast lots concerning

Christ's garment, who should rather put on Christ... That coat bore with it an unity that came down from the top, that is, that came down from heaven and the Father, which was not to be at all rent by the receiver and the possessor, but without separation we obtain a whole and substantial entireness. He cannot possess the garment of Christ who parts and divides the Church of Christ (*De unit.* 7 ANF 5).

He compares the Church to the ark of Noah, outside of which no one was saved (*De unit.* 6); to the multitude of grains forming one eucharistic bread (*Epist,* 63, 13); to a ship with the bishop as pilot (*Epist.* 59, 6). But his favorite figure—it occurs more than thirty times—is that of the Mother who joins together all her children in one great family, who is happy to hold in her bosom a people one in body and one in mind (*De unit.* 23). He who severs himself from her womb dooms himself to death (*ibid.*).

To defend ecclesiastical unity, when it was threatened by schisms, Cyprian wrote the *De unitate ecclesiae* and many of his letters, founding it, so far as the members of the Church are concerned, on adherence to the bishop. 'You should understand that the bishop is in the Church and the Church in the bishop and that whoever is not with the bishop is not in the Church' (*Epist.* 66, 8). Thus the ordinary is the visible authority around which the congregation is centered.

The solidarity of the universal Church rests in turn on that of the bishops, who act as a sort of senate. They are the successors of the apostles and the apostles were the bishops of old. 'The Lord chose the apostles, that is, the bishops and rulers' (*Epist.* 3, 3). The Church is built upon them. Thus Cyprian interprets the *Tu es Petrus* as follows:

Our Lord, whose commandment we must fear and obey, establishes the honorable rank of bishop and the constitution of His Church when in the gospel He speaks and says to Peter: 'I say to thee: Thou art Peter and upon this rock I will build my Church and the gates of hell shall not prevail against it. And I will give to thee the keys of the kingdom of heaven. And whatsoever thou shalt bind on earth, it shall be bound also in heaven, and whatsoever thou shalt loose on earth, it shall be loosed also in heaven' (Matth. 16, 18–19). Thence have come down to us in course of time and by due succession the ordained office of the bishop and the constitution of the Church, forasmuch as the Church is founded upon the bishops and every act of the Church is subject to these rulers. Since then this order has been established by divine decree, I am amazed that some individuals have had the bold effrontery to write to me and send letters in the name of the Church, seeing that the Church is composed of the bishop and the clergy and all who are steadfast (*Epist.* 33, 1). Thus he understands Matth. 16, 18 of the whole episcopate, the various members of which, attached to one another by the laws of charity and concord (*Epist.* 54, 1; 68, 5), thus render the Church universal a single body. 'The Church, which is catholic and one, is not split asunder nor divided but is truly bound and joined together by the cement of its priests, who hold fast one to another' (*Epist.* 66, 8).

Studies: O. Ritschl, Cyprian von Karthago und die Verfassung der Kirche. Göttingen, 1885. — E. Michaud, L'ecclésiologie de s. Cyprien: Kirchl. Zeitschr. (1905) 34–54. — B. Poschmann, Die Sichtbarkeit der Kirche nach der Lehre des hl. Cyprian. Paderborn, 1908. — C. A. Kneller, Der hl. Cyprian und das Kennzeichen der Kirche. Freiburg, 1914. — Saltet, BLE (1920) 179–206. — A. d'Alès, Le mysticisme de saint Cyprien: RAM 2 (1921) 256–267; *idem*, La théologie de saint Cyprien. Paris, 1922. — J. C. Navickas, The Doctrine of St. Cyprian on the Sacraments. Diss. Würzburg, 1924. — Nasilkowski, AKK 19 (1927) 32–48, 149–162. — E. Altendorf, Einheit und Heiligkeit der Kirche. 1932, 44–116. — E. Mersch, Le corps mystique du Christ. 2nd ed., vol. 2. Louvain, 1936, 15–34. — G. Bardy, Le sacerdoce chrétien d'après s. Cyprien: VS 60 (1939) Suppl. 87–119. — J. C. Plumpe, Ecclesia mater: TP (1939) 535–555. — G. Nicotra, Dottrina di Cipriano sull' efficacia dei sacramenti: SC (1940) 496–504; *idem*, Alcune osservazioni sulla dottrina sacramentario di Cipriano: SC (1940) 583–587. — H. Rahner, Flumina de ventre Christi: Bibl (1941) 269–302, 367–403. — J. C. Plumpe, Mater Ecclesia (SCA 5). Washington, 1943, 81–108. — G. Bardy, La théologie de l'Église de saint Irénée au concile de Nicée. Paris, 1947, 171–251.

2. The Primacy of Rome

Cyprian is convinced that the bishop answers to God alone. 'So long as the bond of friendship is maintained and the sacred unity of the Catholic Church is preserved, each bishop is master of his own conduct, conscious that he must one day render an account of himself to the Lord' (*Epist.* 55, 21). In his controversy with Pope Stephen on the rebaptism of heretics he voices as the president of the African synod of September 256 his opinion as follows:

No one among us sets himself up as a bishop of bishops, or by tyranny and terror forces his colleagues to compulsory obedience, seeing that every bishop in the freedom of his liberty and power possesses the right to his own mind and can no more be judged by another than he himself can judge another. We must all await the judgment of our Lord Jesus Christ, who singly and alone has power both to appoint us to the government of his Church and to judge our acts therein (CSEL 3, 1, 436).

From these words it is evident that Cyprian does not recognize a primacy of jurisdiction of the bishop of Rome over his colleagues. Nor does he think that Peter was given power over the other apostles because he states: *hoc erant utique et ceteri apostoli quod fuit Petrus, pari consortio praediti et honoris et potestatis* (*De unit.* 4). No more did Peter claim it: 'Even Peter, whom the Lord first chose and upon whom He built His Church, when Paul later disputed with him over circumcision, did not claim insolently any prerogative for himself nor make any arrogant assumptions nor say that he had the primacy and ought to be obeyed' (*Epist.* 71, 3).

On the other hand, it is the same Cyprian who gives the highest praise to the church of Rome on account of its importance for ecclesiastical unity and faith, when he complains of heretics 'who dare to set sail and carry letters from schismatic and blasphemous persons to the see of Peter and the leading church, whence the unity of the priesthood took its rise, not realizing that the Romans, whose faith was proclaimed and praised by the apostle, are men into whose company no perversion of faith can enter' (*Epist.* 59, 14). Thus the *cathedra Petri* is to him the *ecclesia principalis* and the point of origin of the *unitas sacerdotalis*. However, even in this letter he makes it quite clear that he does not concede to Rome any higher right to legislate for other sees because he expects her not to interfere in his own diocese 'since to each separate shepherd has been assigned one portion of the flock to direct and govern and render hereafter an account of his ministry to the Lord' (*Epist.* 59, 14). It is precisely this same idea which led him to oppose Pope Stephen in the question of rebaptism, but it cannot be called his consistent attitude. M. Bévenot has recently and rightly pointed to his reaction to Pope Cornelius' inquiries about the consecration of

Fortunatus, which Cyprian had performed without first consulting Rome. In his reply, the African prelate recognizes his obligation to report to the Pontiff any matter of major importance:

> I did not write you of it at once, dearest brother, for it was not a matter of enough importance or gravity to be reported to you in great haste... Since I supposed that you were aware of these facts and believed that you would certainly be guided by your memory and sense of discipline, I did not consider it necessary to notify you immediately and hurriedly of the heretics' antics... And I did not write you of their performance because we despise all these doings and I was soon to send you the names of the bishops who govern the brethren soundly and correctly in the Catholic Church. It was the judgment of us all in this region that I should send these names to you (*Epist.* 59, 9).

This answer makes no protest about responsibility to God alone but, by actually rendering an account of the incident, recognizes Cornelius' right to expect submission of any 'matter of enough importance or gravity.' The same reason explains exactly the same behaviour when, during the vacancy following the death of Pope Fabian (250), the mere clergy of the capital city expressed their disapproval of Cyprian's going into hiding; in this case also, he yields a report of his conduct, and, over and beyond that, adopts the Roman line of action with regard to the *lapsi*; in short, he feels an obligation, not only to the ordinary, but, in his absence, to the very see.

To return to *De unitate ecclesiae*, we must keep in mind that its primary aim was not to defend the oneness of all the various churches, but of each within itself. Nevertheless, the writer sees in Peter not only the symbol, but also the real reason of unity, which is founded on him: *Primatus Petro datur et una ecclesia et cathedra una monstratur. Et pastores sunt omnes, sed grex unus ostenditur qui ab apostolis omnibus unanimi consensione pascatur. Qui cathedram Petri super quem fundata ecclesia est, deserit, in ecclesia se esse confidit?* (*De unit.* 4). Thus we read in what, according to recent investigations, was the original edition (cf. above, p. 352). If he refuses to the bishop of Rome any higher power to maintain by legislation the solidarity of which he is the centre, it must be because he regards the primacy as one of honor and the bishop of Rome as a *primus inter pares*.

Studies: H. Koch, Cyprian und der römische Primat. Leipzig, 1910. — C. A. Kneller, Römisch-katholisch beim hl. Cyprian: ZkTh (1911) 253–271. — A. Seitz, Cyprian und der römische Primat oder urchristliche Primatsentwicklung. Regensburg, 1911. — C. A. Kneller, Cyprian und die römische Kirche: ZkTh (1911) 674–689. — K. Adam, Cyprians Kommentar zu Mt. 16, 18 in dogmengeschichtlicher Beleuchtung: ThQ (1912) 99–120, 203–244. — J. Ernst, Cyprian und das Papsttum. Mainz, 1912. — Th. Spacil, Die neueste Literatur zur 'Cyprianfrage'. Das Resultat der durch H. Koch veranlaßten Kontroversen: ZkTh 37 (1913) 604–618. — A. d'Alès, Ecclesia principalis: RSR 11 (1921) 374–380. — G. Bardy, L'autorité du Siège Romain et les controverses du IIIe siècle: RSR 14 (1924) 255–272, 385–399. — E. Caspar, Primatus Petri: Zeitschrift der Savigny-Stiftung für Rechtsgeschichte. Kanonistische Abteilung (1927) 253–331. — H. Koch, Die karthagische Ketzertaufsynode vom 1. September 256. Zugleich ein Beitrag zur Primatfrage. Anhang: Die Stellung der Epistula 69 Cyprians im Ketzertaufstreit: IKZ (1923) 73–104. — J. T. Shotwell and L. R. Loomis, The See of Peter. New York, 1927, 322–381, 387–419, 424 ff. — J. Chapman, Studies on the Early Papacy. London, 1928, 28–50. — K. Adam, Neue Untersuchungen über die Ursprünge der kirchlichen Primatslehre: ThQ 109 (1928) 203–256. — H. Koch, Cathedra Petri. Neue Untersuchungen über die Anfänge der Primatslehre. Giessen, 1930. Cf. RHE (1931) 849 ff; RSR (1931) 601 ff. — A. Seitz, Hugo Kochs Cathedra Petri bei Cyprian: ThGl (1931) 42–62. — B. Poschmann, Ecclesia principalis. Ein kritischer Beitrag zur Frage des Primats bei Cyprian. Breslau, 1933. — D. Franses, Cyprianus van Carthago en het primaat van Rome: StC 11 (1933/34) 214–219. — T. Zapelena, Petrus origo unitatis apud S. Cyprianum: Greg (1934) 500–523; (1935) 196–224. — C. Butler, Catholic and Roman. The Witness of St. Cyprian: Downside Review 56 (1938) 127–145. — M. Kuppens, Notes dogmatiques sur l'épiscopat: Revue ecclés. Liége 36 (1949) 355–367; 37 (1950) 9–26, 80–93. — M. Bévenot, A Bishop is Responsible to God Alone: RSR 39/40 (1951/52) 397–415. — J. Ludwig, Die Primatworte Mt 16, 18. 19 in der altkirchlichen Exegese. Münster i. W., 1952, 20–36.

3. *Baptism*

Whereas Cyprian agrees with Tertullian regarding baptism conferred by heretics and rejects it as invalid, he does not share his view on infant baptism. Tertullian recommends its postponement until children are old enough to know Christ (*De bapt.* 18, cf. above, p. 280). Cyprian, on the contrary, wants the sacrament conferred as early as possible and rejects even the custom of waiting eight days after birth. In his letter to Fidus (*Epist.* 64) he speaks of the decision of a synod as follows:

In respect of the case of infants, which you say ought not to be baptized within the second or third day after birth, and

that the law of ancient circumcision should be regarded,
so that you think that one who is just born should not be
baptized and sanctified within the eighth day, we all thought
very differently in our council. For in this course which you
thought was to be taken, no one agreed; but we all rather
judge that the mercy and grace of God is not to be refused
to any one born of man... Spiritual circumcision ought not
to be hindered by carnal circumcision... we ought to shrink
from hindering an infant, who, being lately born, has not
sinned, except in that, being born after the flesh according
to Adam, he has contracted the contagion of the ancient
death at its earliest birth, who approaches the more easily
on this very account to the reception of the forgiveness of
sins—that to him are remitted, not his own sins, but the sins
of another (ANF 5).

Cyprian, like Tertullian, knows of another baptism, richer in
grace, more sublime in power, and more precious in its effects
than that of water, the baptism of blood or martyrdom. Thus he
states in *Epistle* 73 that catechumens who die for the faith would
by no means be deprived of the effects of the sacrament: 'since
the most glorious and the most sublime baptism, the baptism of
blood, is conferred on them, which the Lord had in mind when
He said that He had to be baptized with another baptism' (Luke
12, 50). Comparing the two, he states in the preface to the *Ad
Fortunatum*: 'This is a baptism greater in grace, more sublime in
power, more precious in honor, a baptism which the angels administer, a baptism in which God and His Anointed One rejoice,
a baptism after which one sins no more, a baptism which com-
pletes our growth in faith, a baptism which at our departure
from this world unites us at once to God.' As the last sentence
indicates Cyprian was, with Tertullian, convinced that the martyr
enter the kingdom of heaven immediately after death, while the
others have to wait for the sentence of the Lord on the Day of
Judgment (*De unit.* 14; *Epist.* 55, 17, 20; 58, 3).

Studies: J. ERNST, Die Ketzertaufangelegenheit in der altchristlichen Kirche nach
Cyprian. Mainz, 1901; *idem*, Stephan und der Ketzertaufstreit. Mainz, 1905; *idem*,
Untersuchungen über Cyprian und den Ketzertaufstreit: ThQ (1911) 230–281, 364–
403.—J.B. BORD, L'autorité de S. Cyprien dans la controverse baptismale jugée d'après
S. Augustin: RHE 18 (1922) 445–468. — G. BARDY, RSR (1924) 255–272, 385–399.

— F. J. Dölger, Der Kuß im Tauf- und Firmungsritual nach Cyprian von Karthago
und Hippolyt von Rom: AC 1 (1929) 186–196. — N. Zernov, Saint Stephen and
the Roman Community at the Time of the Baptismal Controversy: ChQ 117 (1934)
304–336. — H. Koch, Gelasius im kirchenpolitischen Dienste seiner Vorgänger, der
Päpste Simplicius und Felix III. Ein Beitrag zur Sprache des Papstes Gelasius I.
und früherer Papstbriefe. Munich, 1935, 79–82. — H. Kayser, Zur marcionitischen
Taufformel (nach Cyprian): ThStKr 108 (1937/38) 370–386. — E. L. Hummel, The
Concept of Martyrdom according to St. Cyprian of Carthage (SCA 9). Washington,
1946, 108–166: Baptism of Blood.

4. Penance

In the question of penitential discipline Cyprian defended
successfully the traditional practice of the early Church against
two extremes, the laxism among his own clergy and the rigorism
of the Novatian party at Rome. His treatise *De lapsis* and his
letters show that the decisions he made do not mark a 'second
departure.' (Those who regard the remission of fornication as the
'first departure'—cf. above, p. 334—hold that of idolatry as the
second). Cyprian gives no indication whatsoever that apostasy had
been considered unpardonable up to that time in the church of
Rome. He never mentions the three 'capital sins' of Tertullian's *De
pudicitia*, nor its distinction between *peccata remissibilia* and *irremissibilia*. On the contrary, in his letter to Bishop Antonianus (*Epist.*
55) he adheres to the principle that 'nobody can be constrained
by us to repentance if the fruit of repentance be taken away' (17).
To make it even clearer, he adds: 'We certainly think that no one
is to be restrained from the fruit of satisfaction and the hope of
peace' (27). It would be a mockery and deception of poor brethren
to exhort them to the act of atonement and then take away its
logical outcome, the healing, to say to them, 'Mourn and shed
tears, and groan day and night, and labor largely and frequently
for the washing away and cleansing of your sin; but after all these
things you shall die without the pale of the Church. Whatsoever
things are necessary to peace, you shall do, but none of that peace
which you seek shall you receive.' This would be to bid the farmer
till his field with all his skill but assure him that he would reap no
harvest (27). *De opere et eleemosynis* (cf. above, p. 358) says explicitly that those who have committed sins after baptism may be
cleansed again (2) and whatever foulness they have contracted,
will be washed away (1), because God seeks to save those whom

He has redeemed at a great cost (2). Nowhere does Cyprian say that the petition of the lapsed for reconciliation goes contrary to the practice maintained up to that time.

According to Cyprian public penance comprises three distinct acts, namely, confession, satisfaction according to the gravity of the sin and reconciliation after its completion. 'I entreat you, beloved brethren, that each one should confess his own sin, while he who has sinned is still in this world, while his confession may be received, while the satisfaction and the remission made by the priests are pleasing to the Lord' (*De laps.* 28; *Epist.* 16, 2). Although, according to Cyprian, the subjective, personal element of doing penance effects the forgiveness of sins (*De laps.* 17; *Epist.* 59, 13), the objective ecclesiastical component of reconciliation is 'the pledge of life' (*pignus vitae; Epist.* 55, 133) because it presupposes the divine pardon. Cyprian emphasizes the healing power and sacramental character of the act of reconciliation more than all his predecessors, even more than later authors up to St. Augustine, who in his controversy with the Donatists developed this doctrine (cf. the bibliography above, p. 335).

5. *The Eucharist*

Cyprian's epistle 63 *On the Sacrament of the Cup of the Lord* (cf. above, p. 365) is the only ante-Nicene writing that deals exclusively with the celebration of the eucharist. Its importance for the history of the dogma consists in the fact that the entire letter is dominated by the idea of sacrifice. The sacrifice of the priest is the repetition of the Lord's Supper, in which Christ offered Himself to the Father (*Patri se ipsum obtulit*):

For if Jesus Christ, our Lord and God, is Himself the chief priest of God the Father, and has first offered Himself a sacrifice to the Father, and has commanded this to be done in commemoration of Himself, certainly that priest truly discharges the office of Christ, who imitates that which Christ did; and he then offers a true and full sacrifice in the Church to God the Father, when he proceeds to offer it according to what he sees Christ Himself to have offered (*Epist.* 63, 14).

Thus Cyprian is the first to testify explicitly to the doctrine that the body and the blood of the Lord are the oblation. Both the Last Supper and the eucharistic sacrifice of the Church are the representation of Christ's sacrifice on the cross. The eucharist is called *dominicae passionis et nostrae redemptionis sacramentum* (*ibid.*). 'We make mention of His passion in all sacrifices because the Lord's passion is the sacrifice which we offer. Therefore we ought to do nothing else than what He did' (17). It is *oblatio* and *sacrificium*: 'It appears that the blood of Christ is not offered if there be no wine in the cup, nor the Lord's sacrifice celebrated with a legitimate consecration unless our oblation and sacrifice respond to His passion' (9).

The objective value of this eucharistic sacrifice is evident from the fact that it is offered for the repose of the souls as a *sacrificium pro dormitione* (*Epist.* 1, 2). It is celebrated for the martyrs, too: *sacrificia pro eis semper... offerimus, quotiens martyrum passiones et dies anniversaria commemoratione celebramus* (*Epist.* 39, 3; 12, 2).

Cyprian sees in the sacramental bread a symbol of the bond between Christ and the faithful and of ecclesiastical unity: 'In this very sacrament our people are shown to be made one, so that in like manner as many grains, collected, and ground, and mixed together into one mass, make one bread, so in Christ, who is the heavenly bread, we may know, that there is one body, with which our number is joined and united' (*Epist.* 63, 13). The mixture of wine and water had the same significance: 'When the water is mingled in the cup with wine, the people is made one with Christ, and the assembly of the believers is associated and conjoined with Him on whom it believes' (*ibid.*). Cyprian regards the eucharist celebrated outside the Catholic Church as invalid just as baptism conferred by heretics. He informs Pope Stephen in a letter (*Epist.* 72) of a resolution to that effect which seventy-one bishops from Africa and Numidia passed in a synod. Such sacrifices are 'false and blasphemous' and 'in opposition to the one divine altar' (*ibid.*). These ideas gained momentum later in the movement of the Donatists, who maintained that the efficacy of the sacrament depended upon the sanctity of the minister.

Texts: J. QUASTEN, Monumenta eucharistica et liturgica vetustissima. Bonn, 1935/37, 356–358.

Studies: PETERS, Cyprians Lehre über die Eucharistie: Katholik 53 (1873) I 669–687; II 25–39. — A. HARNACK, Brot und Wasser die eucharistischen Elemente bei Justin (TU 7, 2). Leipzig, 1891, 120–124. — A. SCHEIWILER, Die Elemente der Eucharistie in den ersten drei Jahrhunderten (FLD 3, 4). Mainz, 1903, 105–119. —

A. STRUCKMANN, Die Gegenwart Christi in der hl. Eucharistie nach den schriftlichen Quellen der vornizänischen Zeit. Vienna, 1905, 306–321. — P. BATIFFOL, L'Eucharistie. 9th ed. Paris, 1930, 226–247. — G. PHILIPS, De Hl. Cyprianus en de Hl. Communie: Algemeen Nederl. Euch. Tijdschrift (1930) 313 ff. — S. SALAVILLE, L'épiclèse africaine (d'après saint Cyprien): EO 39 (1941/42) 268–282.

ARNOBIUS OF SICCA

The pagan habit of blaming all afflictions, disease, famine, war, on Christian infidelity to the gods, which induced Tertullian to write his *Apologeticum* and Cyprian his *Ad Demetrianum*, led another African author of the close of the third century also to compose a refutation of these groundless charges. His name was Arnobius and his work, in seven books, was called *Adversus nationes*. As we learn from Jerome, he taught rhetoric at Sicca in Africa (*Chron.* ad ann. 253–327 A.D.), and had among his pupils Lactantius (*De vir. ill.* 80; *Epist.* 70, 5); he was a pagan and for a long time a vigorous opponent of Christianity until finally won over by dreams to the new religion (*Chron. loc. cit.*). He himself does not mention the motive which led to his conversion, where he speaks of it (1, 39; 3, 24). The peace and happiness of the young convert find utterance in the following words:

Recently, O blindness, I worshipped images drawn from furnaces, gods fashioned on anvils and with hammers, elephant's bones, paintings, ribbons on trees hoary with age. Whenever my gaze fell upon an anointed stone daubed with olive oil, I would, as if there were some power in it, show great respect to it; I would speak to it, and ask blessings of it though it was a block without feeling. And those very gods of whose existence I had convinced myself, I treated with the greatest slanders since I believed that they were sticks of wood, stones, and bones, or that they dwelt in matter of this kind. But now, having been led into the paths of truth by so great a Teacher, I know all those things for what they really are. I have worthy feelings about things that are worthy. I offer no insult to any divine name; and what is owed to each person or head, with clearly understood differences and distinctions, that I grant. Is Christ therefore not to be deemed God by us and should He in no other way be honored with divine worship, from whom for a long time

we have received so many gifts while we live and hope for
more when 'the Day' comes? (1, 39 ACW 7)

Adversus nationes

According to Jerome (*Chron. loc. cit.*) the local bishop was
rather sceptical when Arnobius asked to be received as a Christian
and demanded proof of his change of mind. Thereupon he composed his comprehensive work against the pagans as a pledge of
sincerity. As for its date, it must have been completed before 311
A.D., the end of the persecutions which are mentioned often but
with no hint of the restoration of peace to the Church. In *De vir.
ill.* Jerome places Arnobius twice in the reign of Diocletian (284–
304 A.D.), whereas in his *Chronicon* he lists him under the year
327 A.D. However, the latter must be an error. Thus all we know
is that he wrote during the persecution of Diocletian and prior to
311 A.D. Jerome (*De vir. ill.* 79) reports the title as *Adversus gentes*,
while the unique manuscript (*Codex Paris.* 1661 *saec.* IX) calls it
Adversus nationes. The latter seems to be more correct. The work
bears every mark of hastiness and gives very little evidence of
close acquaintance with the faith. Since the first two books are
devoted to a vindication of Christianity, it is usually classified
among the apologies. However, it is not so much a defense as a
violent attack. McCracken calls it rightly 'the most intense and
most sustained of all extant counterattacks upon the contemporary pagan cults' (p. 4). It is a poor source for Christian teaching
but an extremely rich mine of information on the contemporary
pagan religions.

Book One first refutes the calumny that the Christians caused
all the evils that had afflicted the human race in recent years. He
traces the charge back to the pagan priestlings, who invented it
because their income had been reduced. Such calamities existed
before the Christian faith began. In fact, the new religion reduces
evils like wars, themselves in turn the fount of many others.

If all would for a little while be willing to lend an ear to
His wholesome and peaceful commandments, and would
believe not in their own arrogance and swollen conceit but
rather in His admonitions, the whole world, long since having
diverted the use of iron to more gentle pursuits, would be
passing its days in the most placid tranquillity and would

come together in wholesome harmony, having kept the terms of treaties unbroken (1, 6 ACW 7).

Arnobius next answers the criticism that the Christians worshipped a mere man, even one who was crucified. The pagans are in a very bad position to raise such an objection, seeing that they themselves apotheosized many a hero and emperor. Christ's teaching and miracles witness to a divine nature that is in no way lessened by the mode of His death. The spread of the faith corroborates this testimony. It was necessary for the Saviour to appear in human form, because He came to redeem the human race.

Book Two deals with the pagan hate of the name of Christ, which Arnobius explains by the fact that the Lord drove the heathen cults from the earth. But He brought them the true religion, which the pagans foolishly reject. If they mock at it, they should know that much of its doctrine can be found in the writings of their philosophers, for instance, the immortality of the soul in Plato. However, against this thinker's concept of that truth Arnobius now delivers a lengthy assault, which makes this the most interesting part of the whole work. In the third book, in which he begins his spirited attack upon his opponents, he denounces their anthropomorphism; they attribute to their gods all sorts of base passions, especially sexual, a contradiction to the very idea of God. Book Four ridicules their deification of abstractions, sinister divinities, disgraceful legends of Jupiter's loves attested even by the literature. Book Five censures the myths of Numa and Attis and the Great Mother, excoriates the ceremonies and tales connected with the mystery cults, and rejects any allegorical interpretation of such fables. Book Six is a polemic against pagan temples and images and Book Seven against pagan sacrifices. The cause of all these superstitions is the false concept of divinity to which Arnobius at the end opposes the Christian notion.

As to the style of Arnobius, Jerome thinks him 'uneven and prolix and without clear divisions in his work, resulting in confusion' (*Epist.* 58). The author, it is true, drives home every argument with endless and tiresome repetitions, but the composition as a whole does not lack organic unity. Festugière disagrees with the view that the work is disorderly and badly written; the obscurities come rather from vagueness of ideas. The author shows considerable power of expression and rises at times to genuine eloquence.

Studies: C. STANGE, De Arnobii oratione (Progr.) Saargemünd, 1893. — J. SCHAR-NAGL, De Arnobii Maioris latinitate (Progr.). Görz, 1895. — P. SPINDLER, De Arnobii genere dicendi. Diss. Strasbourg, 1901. — W. TSCHIERSCH, De Arnobii studiis latinis. Jena, 1905. — E. NORDEN, Die antike Kunstprosa 2. Leipzig-Berlin, 1909, 946 f. — T. LORENZ, De clausulis Arnobianis. Diss. Breslau, 1910. — J. H. SCHMALZ, Satzbau und Negationen bei Arnobius: Glotta 5 (1914) 202–208. — K. J. HIDÉN, De casuum syntaxi Arnobii (De Arnobii Adversus nationes libris VII commentationes 3). Helsingfors, 1921. — F. GABARROU, Le latin d'Arnobe. Paris, 1921. — H. KOCH, Zum Ablativgebrauch bei Cyprian von Karthago und andern Schriftstellern: R hM 87 (1929) 427–432. — A. J. FESTUGIÈRE, Mémorial Lagrange. Paris, 1940, 97–132

Mention should be made of the sources which Arnobius employed in the composition of his work. To begin with Greek, he refers fourteen times to Plato or one of his works, twice to Aristotle, Sophocles, Mnaseas of Patara, Myrtillus and Posidippus. There is an excerpt from the *Orphica* and an allusion to Hermes Trismegistus. Festugière has shown that the second book displays considerable familiarity with hermetism, Neo-Platonism, the Chaldaic oracles, Plotinus, Zoroaster, Osthanes and the magical papyri of the Mithriatic liturgies. Of the Latin writers, he relied especially on Varro, of whom there are fifteen citations. He exploited Cicero and Lucretius, but the theory that Cornelius Labeo was among his more important informants has no foundation, as Tullius and Festugière have sufficiently proved.

If we turn to his biblical and Christian sources, it is surprising that he never names a single Christian author, but there is evidence that he read and used Clement of Alexandria's *Protrepticus*, Tertullian's *Apologeticum* and *Ad nationes*, and the *Octavius* of Minucius Felix. The similarities between the *Adversus nationes* and Lactantius' *Divinae institutiones* seem to be based on a common source.

History does not tell us how this work of the African rhetorician was received. Among the Fathers of the fourth century, only Jerome has any acquaintance with it. The *Decretum de libris recipiendis et non recipiendis* of the sixth century lists it among the apocrypha.

Editions: ML 5. — A. REIFFERSCHEID, CSEL 4 (1875). — C. MARCHESI, Corpus script. lat. Paravianum 62. Turin, 1934. Cf. C. MARCHESI, Per una nova edizione di

Arnobio: RFIC 60 (1932) 485-496. — W. KROLL, PhW 55 (1935) 1082-1084. — A. SOUTER, CR 49 (1935) 209.

Translations: English: H. BRYCE and H. CAMPBELL, ANL 19 (1871); ANF 6, 401-572. — G. E. MCCRACKEN, Arnobius of Sicca, The Case Against the Pagans (ACW 7/8). Westminster, Md., 1949. — *German:* F. A. v. BESNARD, Des Afrikaners Arnobius sieben Bücher wider die Heiden, aus dem Lateinischen übersetzt und erläutert. Landshut, 1842. — J. ALLEKER, Arnobius sieben Bücher gegen die Heiden. Trier, 1858. — *Dutch:* J. OUDAAN, Arnobius d'afrikaner tegen de Heydenen vervat in zeven boeken. Harlingen, 1677.

Textual Criticism: F. WASSENBERG, Quaestiones Arnobianae criticae. Diss. Münster i.W., 1877. — M. BASTGEN, Quaestiones de locis ex Arnobii Adversus Nationes opere selectis. Diss. Münster i.W., 1887. — E. LÖFSTEDT, Beiträge zur Kenntnis der späteren Latinität (Diss. Uppsala). Stockholm, 1907; *idem*, Patristische Beiträge: Eranos 10 (1910) 7-29. — C. PASCAL, Emendationes Arnobianae: RFIC 32 (1904) 1-9. — K. MEISER, Studien zu Arnobius: SAM Philos.-hist. Kl. 5 (1908) 19-40. — T. STANGL, Arnobiana: PhW 30 (1910) 126 f, 158 f; *idem*, Bobiensia: RhM 65 (1910) 93. — O. KIRSCHWING, Qua ratione in Arnobii libris ars critica exercenda sit. Diss. Leipzig, 1911. — K. KISTNER, Arnobiana (Progr.). St. Ingebert, 1912. — C. BRAKMAN, Miscella. Leiden, 1912; *idem*, Miscella altera. Leiden, 1913; *idem*, Miscella tertia. Leiden, 1917; *idem*, Arnobiana. Leiden, 1917. — W. KROLL, Arnobiusstudien: RhM 72 (1917) 62-112. — J. S. PHILLIMORE, Arnobiana: Mnem 48 (1920) 388-391. — P. THOMAS, Observationes ad scriptores latinos: ad Arnobium: Mnem 49 (1921) 63 f. — K. J. HIDÉN, Randbemerkungen zu Arnobius Adversus Nationes, in his: De Arnobii Adversus Nationes libri VII commentationes 2. Helsingfors, 1921. — C. WEYMAN, Textkritische Bemerkungen zu Arnobius Adversus nationes: Festschrift S. Merkle. Düsseldorf, 1922, 386-395. — A. THÖRNELL, Patristica: Uppsala Univ. Arsskr. (1923) 1-21. — H. KOCH, Zu Arnobius und Lactantius: Phil 80 (1925) 467-472. — G. WIMAN, Nagra Arnobius-ställen: Eranos 25 (1927) 278-280; *idem*, Textkritiska studier till Arnobius: Svenskt Arkiv för hum. Avhandl. 4. Göteborg, 1931. — T. BIRT, Marginalien zu lateinischen Prosaikern: Phil 83 (1928) 164-182. — H. ARMINI, Textkritiska bidrag: Eranos 28 (1930) 34-39. — K. GUINAGH, Arnobiana: CW 29 (1936) 69-70.—H. HAGENDAHL, La prose métrique d'Arnobe. Contributions à la connaissance de la prose littéraire de l'empire (Göteborgs Högskolas Arsskr. 42, 1936, No. 1). Göteborg, 1937; *idem*, En Ovidiusreminiscens hos Arnobius: Eranos 35 (1937) 36-40. — C. KNAPP, A correction and addendum to Prof. Guinagh's Arnobiana: CW 29 (1936) 152.— B. AXELSON, Zur Emendation älterer Kirchenschriftsteller: Eranos 39 (1941) 74-81; *idem*, Randbemerkungen zu Arnobius: Eranos 40 (1942) 182 f; *idem*, Textkritisches zu Florus, Minucius Felix und Arnobius: K. Humanistiska Vetenskapsamfundets i Lund Arsb. 1944/45 No. 1.— G. WIMAN, Ad Arnobium: Eranos 45 (1947) 129-152.— G. E. MCCRACKEN, Critical Notes to Arnobius Adversus Nationes: VC 3 (1949) 39-49. — J. C. PLUMPE, Some Critical Annotations to Arnobius: VC 3 (1949) 230-236. — A. J. FESTUGIÈRE, Arnobiana: VC 6 (1952) 208-254.

Theological views of Arnobius

There is a beautiful prayer in which Arnobius begs pardon for the persecutors of the Christians in the first book of his *Against the Pagans:*

O Greatest, O Highest Procreator of visible and invisible
things! O Thou who art Thyself invisible and never understood by the things of nature! Worthy, worthy art Thou
truly—if only mortal lips may call Thee worthy—to whom
all breathing and understanding nature should never cease
to be grateful and to give thanks; to whom throughout the
whole of life it should fall on bended knees to pray to Thee
with unending petitions. For Thou art the first cause, the
place and space of things created, the basis of all things
whatsoever they be. Infinite, unbegotten, everlasting, eternal
alone art Thou, whom no shape may represent, no outline of
body define; unlimited in nature and in magnitude unlimited; without seat, motion, and condition, concerning
whom nothing can be said or expressed in the words of
mortals. To understand Thee, we must be silent; and for
fallible conjecture to trace Thee even vaguely, nothing must
even be whispered. Grant pardon, O King Most High, to
those who persecute Thy servants and by reason of the
kindliness which is part of Thy nature, forgive those who flee
from the worship of Thy name and religion (1, 31 ACW 7).

The prayer reveals a lofty concept of God. Arnobius is convinced that the idea of the existence of a First Cause and Foundation of All is innate: 'Is there any human being who has not
entered the day of his nativity with a knowledge of that Beginning? To whom is it not an innate idea; in whom has it not
been impressed, indeed, almost stamped into him in his mother's
womb; in whom is it not deeply implanted that there is a King
and Lord and Regulator of all things which are?' (1, 33 ACW 7)
Thus Arnobius shares Tertullian's opinion of the *anima naturaliter
christiana* (cf. above, p. 265 f). Nevertheless, his notion of the Deity is
far from being clear and certain. He imagined Him entirely
above contact with creatures and thus isolated in grandeur. The
God, in whom he believes, is without feeling and does not care
what happens in the world (1, 17; 6, 2; 7, 5, 36). This idea of
'aloofness' runs through all of *Adversus nationes*, and is really its
central thought, the fountainhead of all its teaching. Thus he
declares anger incompatible with the nature of Divinity. Whereas
Lactantius composed a whole work, *De ira dei*, to prove the
wrath of the Lord, Arnobius throughout warns against such an

association. Whoever is disturbed by any emotion, he reasons, is weak and frail, liable to suffering, and, therefore, necessarily mortal. 'Where there is any affect, there is necessarily also passion; where passion is situated, it is logical that mental disturbance will follow; where there is mental disturbance, there is also anger and grief; where anger and grief are, there the ground is ready for weakness and corruption; and where these two intervene, there close at hand is destruction, there is death ending all' (1, 18). Of course no one could write like this who had even the slightest acquaintance with the Old Testament and its frequent allusions to divine indignation. But he forestalls any attempt to adduce these texts as proof by rashly repudiating their source: 'Let no one bring up against us the fables of the Jews and those of the sect of the Sadducees, as though we also attribute forms to God, for this is thought to be said in their writings and corroborated as if certain and authoritative. These stories have nothing to do with us, absolutely nothing in common with us, or if, as is thought, they do share something with us, you must seek out teachers of higher wisdom and learn from them how you may best remove the clouds that obscure those writings' (3, 12 ACW 7). The real source of this idea of the aloofness of God is Epicurean philosophy and the Stoic concept of passions.

It is significant that Arnobius does not, like the other apologists, identify the pagan gods with demons, nor does he categorically deny their reality. In some passages (3, 28–35; 4, 9; 4, 11; 4, 27; 4, 28; 5, 44; 6, 2; 6, 10) he seems sure that they cannot exist, in others doubtful. Thus he writes: 'We worship their Father by whom, if they really exist, they began to be and have the substance of their power and majesty, their very deity, so to speak, having been allotted by Him' (1, 28). He evinces the same hesitation in another passage, where he rejects the notion that the heathen deities are begotten and born. 'But, we, on the contrary, hold that if they actually are gods and have the authority, the power and the dignity proper to such title, they are either unbegotten— for this our reverence commands us to believe; or if they have a beginning in birth, it is for the Supreme God to know how He has made them or how many ages there are since He made them participants of the eternity of His own divinity' (7, 35 ACW 7). He answers the pagan objection that the Christians do not wor-

ship the gods with the excuse that they receive homage in common
with the Supreme God:

> In attending to the worship of the Godhead, the First God,
> the Father of things and the Lord, the Establisher and
> Governor of all things, is enough for us. In Him we worship
> everything that must be worshipped (3, 32).

And as in earthly kingdoms we are forced by no necessity
to show reverence by name to those who, along with the
sovereigns, compose the royal families, but whatever respect
is attached to them is tacitly understood to be implied in
homage to the kings themselves, so in precisely the same
manner, these gods, whoever they are whom you suggest for
our worship, if they are royal in descent and are sprung from
the primal head, though they receive no worship from us by
name, nevertheless understand that they receive homage in
common with their king and are included in acts of reverence accorded Him (3, 33 ACW 7).

Of course in all these passages it remains doubtful whether the
author expresses his personal conviction or merely concedes
something for the sake of the argument. As a corollary of the
divine 'aloofness'—a theory of Arnobius' set forth above (p. 388)—
he denies the creation of the soul. Its weakness, fickleness and
wickedness are such that God cannot be their author: 'But let the
heinousness of this wicked idea depart far away, that Almighty
God, the Sower and the Founder of great and invisible things, the
Creator, should be thought to have begotten souls so fickle, souls
possessing no seriousness, character, or steadfastness; prone to
slip into vices; with a proclivity for all kinds of sins; and, when
He knew that they were such and of this kind, to have ordered
them to go into bodies' (2, 45 ACW 7). He calls the idea that
'the souls were the Lord's offspring and the descendants of the
Supreme Power' a story (*fama*) (2, 37) and maintains, what he is
convinced is Christ's own doctrine, that they are produced by
some inferior being:

> Hear and learn it from Him who knows and has published
> it abroad—from Christ—namely that the souls are not the
> children of the Supreme King, nor did they, begotten by
> Him, as is stated, begin to identify themselves and speak of
> themselves in terms of their essential origin but they have

some other creator, removed from the Supreme Being by a very great inferiority in rank and power, yet of His court and ennobled by the sublimity of their highborn stations (2, 36 ACW 7).

Here Arnobius implicitly rejects the biblical belief in creation and adopts the myth found in Plato's *Timaeus* as the teaching of Christ. The only positive statement he makes about the essence of the human spirit is that of its *medietas*, of its intermediate character, which he also attributes to Christ: 'They [the souls] are of intermediate character, as is known from Christ's teaching; and they are such as to perish if they fail to know God, but can also be delivered from death to life, if they have given heed to His warnings and graces, and ignorance is cleared up' (2, 14 ACW 7). In other words the soul is not by nature endowed with everlasting life but can attain it by knowledge of the true God. It has thus a conditional immortality.

There is a controversy about the nature of the souls and some say that they are mortal and cannot partake of divine substance, but others that they are everlasting and cannot degenerate into mortal nature. This is the result of the law according to which they have a neutral character: some have arguments ready at hand by which it is found they are subject to suffering and perishable, and others on the contrary have arguments by which it is shown that they are divine and mortal.

Since this is the case and since by the highest authority we have received the view that the souls are established not far from the gaping jaws of death; that, nevertheless, they can be made long-lived (*longaeva fieri*) by the gift and favor of the Supreme Ruler, if only they try and study to understand Him—for knowledge of Him is a sort of leaven of life and a glue to bind together in one elements otherwise not cohesive (2, 31–32, ACW 7).

Most probably we have here the motive for his conversion, the fear of eternal death and the desire for immortality. He says himself: 'On account of these fears we have surrendered and delivered ourselves to God as liberator' (2, 32) and asks: 'Since the fear of death, that is, the destruction of our souls, threatens us, is it not true that we act from an instinct of what is good for us... in embracing Him who promises that He will free us from such danger?' (2, 33 ACW 7)

Studies: K. B. FRANCKE, Die Psychologie und Erkenntnislehre des Arnobius. Diss. Leipzig, 1883. — A. RÖHRICHT, De Clemente in irridendo gentilium cultu auctore. (Diss. Kiel). Hamburg, 1892; idem, Die Seelenlehre des Arnobius nach ihren Quellen und ihrer Entstehung untersucht. Hamburg, 1893. — C. FERRINI, Die juristischen Kenntnisse des Arnobius und Lactantius: Zeitschr. der Savigny-Stiftung. Rom. Abt. 15 (1894) 343–352. — L. ATZBERGER, Geschichte der christlichen Eschatologie innerhalb der vornicänischen Zeit. Freiburg i.B., 1896, 573–582. — E. F. SCHULZE, Das Übel in der Welt nach der Lehre des Arnobius. Diss. Jena, 1896. — P. MONCEAUX, Histoire littéraire de l'Afrique chrétienne 3. Paris, 1905, 241–285. — O. JIRANI, Mythologické prameny Arnobiova spisu Adversus Nationes: Listy Filologické 35 (1908) 1–11, 83–97, 163–188, 323–339, 403–423. — H. C. C. MOULE, Arnobius: Wace and Piercy, A Dictionary of Christian Biography and Literature. Boston, 1911, 49–51. — F. ORSAVAI, Mysterium ok Arnobiusnal. Diss. Budapest, 1914. — C. WEYMAN, Arnobius über das Steinbild der Magna Mater: HJG (1916) 75–76. — W. KROLL, Die Zeit des Cornelius Labeo: RhM (1916) 309–357. — C. J. HIDÉN, Die Erzählung von der Großen Göttermutter bei Arnobius (De Arnobii Adversus Nationes libris VII commentationes 2). Helsingfors, 1921. — F. GABARROU, Arnobe, son œuvre (Diss. Toulouse). Paris, 1921. — E. G. SIHLER, From Augustus to Augustine: Essays and Studies dealing with the contact and conflict of classic paganism and Christianity. Cambridge, 1923, 167–173. — C. MARCHESI, Questioni arnobiane: Atti del R. Ist. Veneto di Scienze, Lettere ed Arti 88 (1929) 1009–1032; idem, Il pessimismo di un apologeta cristiano: Pégaso 2 (1930) 536–550. — P. DE LABRIOLLE, Diction. d'hist. et de géogr. ecclés. 4 (1930) 544. — P. GODET, Arnobe: DTC 1 (1930) 1895 f. — S. COLOMBO, Arnobio Afro e i suoi libri Adversus Nationes: Didaskaleion 9 (1930) 1–124. — A. C. McGIFFERT, A History of Christian Thought 2. New York, 1933, 39–45. — F. TULLIUS, Die Quellen des Arnobius im 4., 5. und 6. Buch seiner Schrift Adversus nationes (Diss. Berlin). Bottrop i.W., 1934. — G. BRUNNER, Arnobius ein Zeuge gegen das Weihnachtsfest: JL 13 (1935) 172–181. — E. RAPISARDA, Clemente fonte di Arnobio. Turin, 1939. — A. J. FESTUGIÈRE, La doctrine des novi viri chez Arnobe II, 16 sqq.: Mémorial Lagrange. Paris, 1940, 97–132. — E. F. MICKA, The Problem of Divine Anger in Arnobius and Lactantius (SCA 4). Washington, 1943. — G. BARDY, RACH 1 (1943) 709–711. — E. RAPISARDA, Arnobio. Catania, 1945. Cf. J. QUISPEL, VC 2 (1948) 123 f. — G. E. McCRACKEN, Arnobius Adversus Genera: CJ 42 (1947) 474–476. — G. L. ELLSPERMANN, The Attitude of the Early Christian Latin Writers Toward Pagan Literature and Learning (PSt 82). Washington, 1949, 54–66. — H. KARPP, Probleme altchristlicher Anthropologie (BFTh 4, 3). Gütersloh, 1950, 171–185.

LACTANTIUS

Arnobius was superseded by his pupil Lucius Caelius Firmianus Lactantius. According to Jerome (*De vir. ill.* 80) Africa was not only the cradle of his rhetorical training but also saw the birth of his first work, now lost, the *Banquet* (*Symposium*), which 'he wrote as a young man.' He left his native province when Diocletian (284–304) summoned him with the grammarian Flavius to Nicomedia in Bithynia, the new capital of the East, to teach Latin rhetoric (*Div. inst.* 5, 2, 2). However, he was not very successful, because Jerome (*De vir. ill.* 80) informs us that 'on account of his lack of pupils, since it was a Greek city, he betook himself to writing.' He was, however, still professor there when in A.D. 303 the persecution forced him, who had become a Christian, to resign his chair. He left Bithynia between A.D. 305 and 306. About 317 the Emperor Constantine summoned the impoverished master in extreme old age to Treves in Gaul to become the tutor of his eldest son Crispus. The date of his death is unknown.

Studies: E. FOULKES, Lactantius: Dictionary of Christian Biography 3 (1882) 613–617. — H. LIETZMANN, Laktantius: PWK 12 (1924) 351–356. — E. AMANN, Lactance: DTC 8 (1925) 2425–2444. — H. LECLERCQ, Lactance: DAL 8 (1928) 1018–1041. S. BRANDT, Über das Leben des Laktantius (SAW 120, Abh. 5). Vienna, 1890. — H. LIMBERG, Quo iure Lactantius appellatur Cicero christianus. Diss. Münster, 1896. — J. MAURICE, La véracité historique de Lactance: Comptes Rendus de l'Académie des Inscriptions et Belles-Lettres (1908) 146–159. — M. GEBHARDT, Das Leben und die Schriften des Laktantius. Diss. Erlangen, 1924. — G. MOLIGNONI, Lattanzio Apologeta: Didaskaleion N.S. 5 (1927) 3, 117–154. — S. COLOMBO, Lattanzio e S. Agostino: Didaskaleion (1931) 2/3, 1–22. — B. ALBAN, The Conscious Rôle of Lactantius: CW 37 (1943/44) 79–81. — M. PELLEGRINO, Studi su l'antica apologetica. Rome, 1947, 151–207.
For *style, language,* and *terminology:* H. GLÄSENER, I. L'emploi des modes chez Lactance, II. La syntaxe des cas, III. Note additionelle, IV. Les changements de signification, V. Les néologismes: Musée Belge (1900) 26–37, 223–235; (1901) 1–27, 293–307, 316–317. — H. HAGENDAHL, Methods of Citation in Post-Classical Latin Prose: Eranos (1947) 114–128. — J. MAROUZEAU, La leçon par l'exemple: RELA (1948) 105–108. — CHR. MOHRMANN, Les éléments vulgaires du latin des chrétiens: VC 2 (1948) 89–101, 162–184.

I. HIS WRITINGS

The humanists called Lactantius the Christian Cicero and he is in fact the most elegant writer of his day. He consciously chose the great Roman orator as his model and in perfection of style approaches him, as already Jerome recognized (*Epist.* 58, 10). He was convinced that, if Christianity was to gain entrance into higher learning, it had to be presented with appeal and charm. Unfortunately, the quality of his thought does not correspond to the excellence of its expression. Most of his work is compilation and evinces shallowness and superficiality. Whatever training in philosophy he boasts, he owes almost entirely to Cicero. His knowledge of Greek authors, pagan as well as Christian, is poor and his theological education insufficient. Well-read, especially in the Latin classics, he had the gift of assimilating the ideas of others and of presenting them clearly and brilliantly. This accounts for the fact that his writings are extant in a great number of manuscripts, some of them of a very early date. The fifteenth century knew fourteen complete editions of them.

Editions: ML 6–7. — S. BRANDT and G. LAUBMANN, CSEL 19, 27 (1890/97).

Translations: English: W. FLETCHER, ANL 21, 22; ANF 7. — *French:* Les Pères de l'Église. Paris, 1837–1843. — *German:* A. HARTL, BKV² 36 (1919).

Studies: H. RÖNSCH, Beiträge zur patristischen Bezeugung der biblischen Textgestalt. II. Aus Lactantius: Zeitschrift für histor. Theologie 150 (1871) 531–629. — S. BRANDT, Lactantius und Lucretius: Neue Jahrbücher für Philologie u. Pädagogik 143 (1891) 225–259. — P. G. FROTSCHER, Der Apologet Lactantius in seinem Verhältnis zur griechischen Philosophie. Diss. Leipzig, 1895. — C. FERRINI, Die juristischen Kenntnisse des Arnobius und Laktantius: Zeitschrift der Savigny-Stiftung für Rechtsgeschichte. Romanist. Abteilung 15 (1894) 343–352. — A. MANCINI, De Varrone Lactantii auctore: Studi Storici 5 (1896) 229–239, 297–316. — B. BARTHEL, Über die Benutzung der philosophischen Schriften Ciceros durch Laktanz, Teil I (Progr. Gymnasium). Strehlen, 1903. — H. JAGIELSKI, De F. Lactantii fontibus quaestiones selectae. Regensburg, 1912. — F. FESSLER, Benutzung der philosophischen Schriften Ciceros durch Laktanz. Leipzig-Berlin, 1913. — A. KURFESS, Laktantius und Plato: Phil (1922) 381–393. — H. KOCH, Zu Arnobius und Lactantius: Phil 80 (1925) 467–472; *idem,* Cyprianische Untersuchungen. Bonn, 1926, 66–73. — L. CASTIGLIONI, Lattanzio e le storie di Seneca padre: RFIC (1928) 454–475. — E. BICKEL, Apollon und Dodona. Ein Beitrag zur Technik und Datierung des Lehrgedichtes Aetna und zur Orakelliteratur bei Laktanz: RhM (1930) 279–302. — H. KOCH, Cipriano e Lattanzio: RR 7 (1931) 122–132. — H. GRÉGOIRE, Les pierres qui crient. Les chrétiens et l'oracle de Didymus: Byz (1939) 318–321. — P. WUILLENMIER, L'influence du Cato maior (sur Lactance): Mélanges Ernout. Paris, 1940, 383–388. — K. VILHELMSON, Laktanz und die Kosmogonie des spätantiken Synkretismus (Acta Univ. Dorpatensis B 49, 4). Tartu, 1940. — B. AXELSON, Quod idola und Laktanz: Eranos (1941) 67–74. — J. NICOLOSI, L'influsso di Lucrezio su Lattanzio. Catania, 1945. — O. TESCARI, Echi di Seneca nel pensiero cristiano e vice versa: Unitas 2 (1947) 171–181. — M. L. CARLSON, Pagan Examples of Fortitude in the Latin Christian Apologists: CPh 43 (1948) 93–104. — G. L. ELLSPERMANN, The Attitude of the Early Christian Writers Toward Pagan Literature and Learning. Washington, 1949, 67–101.

1. *On God's Workmanship*

De opificio dei, addressed to Demetrianus, a former pupil and a well-to-do Christian, is the earliest of his works preserved to us. It shows already the great difference existing between Arnobius and his disciple Lactantius. Whereas the former holds that the soul in the flesh is in prison (2, 45), 'the husk of this petty flesh' (2, 76), and denies that it is a creature of God or by nature immortal, the latter argues to the contrary that the human body in its admirable organization and beauty could have come only from the All-Perfect and is the special care of his providence.

The introduction (2–4) contrasts man with the beasts, and concludes that God instead of arming him with the same physical strength, endowed him with reason, and thus rendered him far superior. 'Our Creator and Parent, God, has given to man perception and reason, that it might be evident from this that we are descended from Him, because He Himself is intelligence, He Himself is perception and reason... He did not place his protection in the body, but in the soul: since it would have been superfluous, when He had given him that which was of the greatest value, to cover him with bodily defences, especially when they hindered the beauty of the human body. On which account I am accustomed to wonder at the senselessness of the philosophers who follow Epicurus, who blame the works of nature, in order to show that the world is prepared and governed by no providence' (2 ANF). To confound these theorists and to demonstrate divine providence even more triumphantly, he begins a treatise on anatomy and physiology. There follows (16–19) a psychology, which is rather abbreviated. The last chapter (20) promises a more comprehensive exposition of the true learning against the pernicious disturbers of the truth, the philosophers. He alludes here to the *Divinae institutiones*.

The study fails of distinctively Christian ideas and has a purely rational character. The author himself declares that he intended only to follow up the fourth book of Cicero's *Republic* with a more thorough treatment of the subject. His main sources are Cicero and Varro. The date of composition seems to be the end of A.D. 303 or the beginning of 304, as indicated by several references to the Diocletian persecution (1, 1; 1, 7; 20, 1).

Edition: S. BRANDT, CSEL 27 (1893) 3–64.

Translations: English: W. FLETCHER, ANL 22, 49–91; ANF 7, 281–300. — *German:*

A. Knappitsch, Gottes Schöpfung von L. C. F. Laktantius aus dem Lateinischen übertragen und mit sachlichen und sprachlichen Bemerkungen versehen. Graz, 1898. *Studies:* S. Brandt, Über die Quellen von Laktanz' Schrift 'De opificio dei': WSt 13 (1891) 2, 255–292. — A. Harnack, Medizinisches aus der ältesten Kirchengeschichte (TU 8, 4). Leipzig, 1892, 88–92. — L. Rosetti, 'De Opificio Dei' di Lattanzio e le sue fonti: Didaskaleion 6 (1928) 115–200. — J. Svennung, Untersuchungen zu Palladius. Uppsala, 1935, 507. — A. S. Pease, Caeli enarrant: HThR (1941) 163–200.

2. *The Divine Institutes*

Divinae institutiones in seven books constitutes the main work of Lactantius. It represents in spite of all its shortcomings the first attempt at a Latin summa of Christian thought. It has a double purpose, to demonstrate the falsehood of pagan religion and speculation and set forth the true doctrine and worship. The title of the work is borrowed from the manuals of jurisprudence, the *Institutiones juris civilis* (1, 1, 12). Answering in particular two recent philosophical attacks, one of them by Hierocles, the governor of Bithynia and instigator of Diocletian's persecution (5, 2–4; *De mort. pers.* 16, 4), Lactantius intended to refute at the same time all past and future opponents of Christianity, 'in order to overthrow once and for all by one attack all who everywhere effect, or have effected, the same work... and cut off from future writers the whole power of writing and of replying' (5, 4, 1). The first book, entitled 'The False Worship of the Gods', and the second, 'The Origin of Error', disprove polytheism, the prime source of error. The author demonstrates that those whom the Greeks and Romans worshipped had at first been simple men and had later been apotheosized. The very concept of deity necessitates that there should be but one. The third book 'The False Wisdom of Philosophers' points to philosophy as the secondary source of all error. There are so many contradictions in the different systems regarding the essential questions of human life that nothing remains of any value. Correct knowledge is given only by revelation. Book Four demonstrates against this background under the heading 'True Wisdom and Religion' that Christ, the Son of God, brought the true insight, i.e. the right idea of the Divinity to men. Wisdom and religion are inseparable and thus the Saviour is also our infallible source for the latter. The prophets of the Old Testament, the Sibylline oracles, and Hermes Trismegistos testify to His divine sonship. His incarnation

and His crucifixion are defended against the arguments of unbelievers. Book Five deals with 'Justice', that virtue which is most
important for human society. Banished by idolatry, it was
reintroduced by Christ coming down from heaven. It is based on
piety and consists in the knowledge and worship of the true God.
It is based essentially on equity, which regards all men as equal:
'God who produces and gives breath to men, willed that all
should be equal, that is, equally matched. He has imposed on all
the same condition of living; He has produced all to wisdom; He
has promised immortality to all; no one is cut off from His
heavenly benefits. For as He distributes to all alike His one light,
sends forth His fountains to all, supplies food, and gives the most
pleasant rest of sleep; so He bestows on all equity and virtue. In
His sight no one is a slave, no one a master; for if all have the
same Father, by an equal right we are all His children' (5, 15
ANF 7). Book Six, 'True Worship', continues this topic, showing
that religion towards God and mercy towards men are the pre-
requisites of justice and of true worship. 'The first function of this
virtue is union with our Maker, the second, union with our
fellows. The former is called religion, the second is named mercy
or kindness (*humanitas*); which virtue is peculiar to the just, and
to the worshippers of God' (6, 10 ANF 7). Books Five and Six
form by far the best part of the entire work in content and style.
The last of the seven, entitled 'On the Happy Life', offers a kind
of chiliastic eschatology with a detailed description of the reward
of those who have adored the one God, the devastation of the
world, the advent of Christ to judgment and the damnation of the
wicked.

The *Divine Institutes* was begun about A.D. 304, shortly after
the *De opificio dei*, to which the author refers (2, 10, 15) as recently
written. The sixth book must have been composed before Galerius' edict of toleration in 311. The dedication to Constantine in
Book Seven presupposes the edict of Milan in 313. There are a
number of additions to the text in a rather small group of manuscripts. Some of them have dualistic, others panegyrical content.
The former (2, 8, 6; 7, 5, 27) deal with the origin of evil and
defend the doctrine that God intended and created it, *De opificio
dei* 19, 8, being a variant of the same sort. The latter are addressed
to the Emperor Constantine (1, 1, 12; 7, 27, 2; 2, 1, 2; 3, 1, 1;

4, 1, 1; 5, 1, 1; 6, 3, 1). All of these passages seem to have come from Lactantius himself; most probably the dualistic were subsequently deleted as offensive to faith, the panegyrical as superfluous. This solution seems to be more convincing than Brandt's idea of later interpolation.

As the first systematic presentation of the main Christian doctrines in the Latin language, the *Divine Institutes* is much inferior to its Greek counterpart, Origen's *De principiis* (cf. above, p. 57 ff). It lacks theological demonstration and metaphysical depth. As for its sources, the work abounds in quotations from classical authors, especially Cicero and Vergil. The author utilizes the Sibylline oracles as well as the writings of the *Corpus Hermeticum*. He is very sparing in his use of the Bible. Most of his Scriptural quotations are taken from Cyprian's work *Ad Quirinum* (cf. above, p. 362). Where he speaks of the first advocates of the Christian religion (5, 1) he mentions as 'those who are known to him' Minucius Felix, Tertullian and Cyprian, without the slightest reference to any of the Greek Christian authors. Moreover, it is surprising that Arnobius does not appear among his predecessors, since he was his teacher. The explanation may be found in the fact that Lactantius, far away at Nicodemia in Bithynia, may never have heard of his former preceptor's work *Against the Pagans*.

Editions: S. BRANDT, CSEL 19 (1890) 1–672; S. BRANDT-G. LAUBMANN, CSEL 27 (1897) 30–32. — C. JORDACHESCU-TH. SIMENSCHY, Lactantius, Institutiones divinae. Liber VI: De Vero Cultu. Chisinau, 1938.

Translations: English: W. FLETCHER, ANL 21; ANF 7, 9–223. — *Italian:* G. MAZZONI, Le divine istitutioni. Trad. e note (I classici cristiani 63). Siena, 1937.

Studies: J. G. TH. MÜLLER, Quaestiones Lactantianae. Diss. Göttingen, 1875. — S. BRANDT, Der St. Galler Palimpsest der divinae inst. des Laktantius: SAW 108 (1884) 231 ff.; *idem*, Über die dualistischen Zusätze und die Kaiseranreden bei Lactantius. I. Die dualistischen Zusätze : SAW 118, Abhandlung 8; II. Die Kaiseranreden: SAW 119, Abhandlung 1. Vienna, 1889. — LOBMÜLLER, Die Entstehungszeit der Institutionen des Laktanz: Katholik (1898) 2, 1–23. — R. PICHON, Lactance. Paris, 1901, 6 ff.; *idem*, Note sur un vers des Oracles Sibyllins: RPh (1904) 41 (Inst. div. 4, 17, 4). — W. HARLOFF, Untersuchungen zu Laktantius. Diss. Borna.Leipzig, 1911. — TH. STANGL, Lactantiana: RhM 70 (1915) 224–252, 441–471. — H. WINDISCH, Das Orakel des Hystaspes (Verh. Ak . Amsterdam N.F. 28). Amsterdam, 1929. — P. FABBRI, Perché Lattanzio in Div. Inst. I, 5, 11–12 non cita la IV egloga di Virgilio: BFC 36 (1930) 274. — A. PIGANIOL, Dates Constantiniennes: RHPR 12 (1932) 360–372. — F. CUMONT, La fin du monde selon les mages occidentaux: RHR

103 (1931) 68 ff. — H. Emonds, Zweite Auflage im Altertum. Leipzig, 1941, 55–72.
— J. C. Plumpe, Mors Secunda: Mélanges de Ghellinck. Gembloux, 1951, 387–403.

3. The Epitome

In many manuscripts there is an *Epitome* appended to the *Divine Institutes*, which Lactantius prepared for a certain 'brother Pentadius.' To judge from its contents, it is not an excerpt of the main work but an abridged re-edition. There are not only omissions but also additions, changes and corrections. Thus it has a certain independent value. Lactantius must have written it after 314. It was not until the beginning of the eighteenth century that the entire text was discovered in a seventh century manuscript of Turin (*Cod. Taurinensis* I b VI 28 *saec.* VII). All other copies contain only a mutilated version to which St. Jerome refers (*De vir. ill.* 80) as 'the book without a head.'

Editions: S. Brandt, CSEL 19 (1890) 675–761. — H. Blakeney, Lactantius' Epitome of the Divine Institutes. Edited and translated (SPCK). London, 1950.

Translations: English: W. Fletcher, ANL 22, 92–160; ANF 7, 224–255. — H. Blakeney, *loc. cit.* — *German:* A. Hartl, BKV² 36 (1919).

Studies: S. Brandt, Über die Entstehungsverhältnisse der Prosaschriften des Lactantius: SAW 1225, Abh. 6. Vienna, 1892, 2–10. — J. Belser, Echtheit und Entstehungszeit der Epitome: ThQ 74 (1892) 256–271. — J. W. Ph. Borleffs, De Lactantio in Epitome Minucii imitatore: Mnem 57 (1929) 415–426.

4. The Anger of God

The Epicureans imagined God as entirely inert. His happiness demands that He remain aloof from the world, without anger or kindness, because these emotions are inconsistent with His nature. Arnobius shared this view, as we saw (above, p. 388 f). Lactantius devotes an entire treatise to its refutation, *De ira dei*, written in A.D. 313 or 314. The theory, he insists, implies a denial of divine providence and even of God's existence. For if He exists, He cannot be inoperative, since to live is to function. He must engage in action and 'what can this action of God be, except the administration of the world?' (17, 4). Nor can the Stoics' concept of the Deity be accepted, that God is kind but not angry. If God is not angry, there can be no providence, since God's care of man demands that He be moved to anger against those who do evil. 'In opposite things, it is necessary to be moved to both parts or to

neither. Thus he who loves those who do good also hates those
who do evil. The reason is that the loving of the good comes from
hatred of evil and the hatred of evil from the love of the good...
These things are so connected by nature, that the one cannot
exist without the other' (5, 9). If kindness and anger are removed
from God, it follows that religion must also be taken away, since
salutary fear vanishes. Thus man's greatest dignity, his very purpose in life, is destroyed. The author refers on several occasions
to the *Divine Institutes* (2, 4, 6; 11, 2), and addresses his work to
a certain Donatus.

Edition: S. BRANDT, CSEL 27 (1893) 67-132.

Translations: English: W. FLETCHER, ANL 22, 1-48; ANF 7, 259-280. — *German:*
A. HARTL, BKV² 36 (1919).

Studies: M. POHLENZ, Vom Zorne Gottes (FRL 12). Göttingen, 1909. — G. KUTSCH,
In Lactantii De ira Dei librum quaestiones philologicae (Klassisch-philolog. Studien
6). Leipzig, 1933. — E. F. MICKA, The Problem of Divine Anger in Arnobius and
Lactantius (SCA 4). Washington, 1943. — E. RAPISARDA, La polemica di Lattanzio
contro l'epicureismo: Misc. di Studi di Lett. Crist. antica 1 (1947) 5-20.

5. *The Death of the Persecutors*

De mortibus persecutorum sets forth the tremendous effects of
divine anger and the punishment of the wicked persecutors. It
was written after peace had been granted the Church and intends to prove that all its oppressors met with a terrible end. Since
Licinius is depicted, along with Constantine, as the protector of
the faith, the treatise must have been composed before the beginning of his attack on it, at the latest before A.D. 321. On the
other hand, the death of Maximinus Daia (313) and of Diocletian
(about 316) is recorded, affording a *terminus post quem*.

The introduction deals with the origin of Christianity and the
fate of Nero, Domitian, Decius, Valerian and Aurelian (2-6).
The author then turns to the persecutions of his own times and
gives a vivid description of Diocletian, Maximian, Galerius,
Severus and Maximinus, their crimes against the churches and
their destruction, up to Licinius' victory in 313. Addressed to
Donatus who had himself 'displayed to mankind a pattern of
invincible magnanimity' during the troubles (16, 35), the treatise
sparkles with joy that Christ has been victorious and His enemies
are annihilated:

Behold, all the adversaries are destroyed; tranquillity has been re-established throughout the Roman empire, the late-oppressed Church arises again, and the temple of God, overthrown by the hands of the wicked, is built with more glory than before... And after the furious whirlwind and black tempest, the heavens are now become calm, and the wished-for light has shone forth; and now God, the hearer of prayer, by His divine aid has lifted His prostrate and afflicted servants from the ground, has brought to an end the united devices of the wicked, and wiped off the tears from the faces of those who mourned. They who attacked the divinity, lie low; they who cast down the holy temple, are fallen with more tremendous ruin; and the tormentors of the just have poured out their guilty souls amidst plagues inflicted by Heaven, and amidst deserved tortures. For God delayed to punish them, that by great and marvellous examples, He might teach posterity that He alone is God, and that with fit vengeance He executes judgment on the proud, the impious, and the persecutors (1 ANF 7).

As a source for Diocletian's persecution the work remains, despite certain exaggerations, of the greatest importance. The author writes as an eyewitness and from first-hand information. The authenticity has been doubted, but there seems to be nothing either in matter, form, or historical circumstances that forbids one to attribute the work to Lactantius. The strongest argument in favor is the testimony of St. Jerome (*De vir. ill.* 80). The text survives in a single manuscript of the eleventh century, *Codex Paris.* 2627 (ol. *Colbertinus* 1297).

Editions: S. BRANDT.-G. LAUBMANN, CSEL 27, 2 (1897) 171 ff. — J. B. PESENTI, Corpus script. lat. Parav. 40. Turin, 1922. — A. DE REGIBUS, De mortibus persecutorum, ed. et comm. Turin, 1931. — G. MAZZONI, Siena, 1930. — U. MORICCA, Milan, 1933. — J. B. PESENTI, Turin, 1934.

Translations: English: G. BURNET, A Relation of the Death of the Primitive Persecutors. Amsterdam, 1687, 2nd ed. 1715. — W. FLETCHER, ANL 22, 164–210; ANF 7, 301–322. — *German:* A. HARTL, BKV² 36 (1919). — E. FAESSLER, So starben die Tyrannen. Des Laktantius Schrift über die Todesaten der Verfolger. Luzesrn, 1946. — *Dutch:* D. FRANSES, Over den dood der vervolgers (Getuigen) 1e reeks, dl. 7). Amsterdam, 1941. — *Italian:* F. SCIVATTARO, Lattanzio, La Morte dei persecutori. Rome, 1923. — G. MAZZONI, Siena, 1930. — *Spanish:* G. SÁNCHEZ ALISEDA, Sobre la muerte de los perseguidores (Colección Exelsa 23). Madrid, 1947.

402

Studies: S. Brandt, Über die Entstehungsverhältnisse der Prosaschriften des Lactantius: SAW 1225, Abh. 6. Vienna, 1892, 22–122. — J. Belser, Über den Verfasser des Buches De mortibus persecutorum: ThQ 74 (1892) 246–293, 439–464. — A. Mancini, La Storia Ecclesiastica di Eusebio e il De mortibus persecutorum: Studi Storici (1897) 125–135. — S. Brandt, Über den Verfasser des Buches De mort. persec.: Neue Jahrbüch. für Philol. und Paed. 147 (1893) 121–138, 203–223. — O. Seeck, Geschichte des Unterganges der antiken Welt 1. Berlin, 1895, 426–430. — J. Belser, Der Verfasser des Buches De mortibus persecutorum: Th 80 (1898) 547–596. — M. Petschenig, Zur Kritik der Schrift De mort. persec.: Phil (1898) 191–192. — J. Kopp, Über den Verfasser des Buches De mort. persec. Diss. St. Ingbert, 1902. — R. Pichon, Sur un passage du De mort. persec. (14, 4–5): RPh (1904) 60. — P. Monceaux, Études critiques: RPh (1905) 104–139. — K. Jagelitz, Über den Verfasser der Schrift De mortibus persecutorum. Berlin, 1910. — W. A. Baehrens, Zum Liber De mortibus persecutorum: Hermes (1912) 635–636. — K. Bihlmeyer, Das Toleranzedikt des Galerius von 311 (De mort. persec. 34): ThQ (1912) 411–427, 527–589. — H. Silomon, Laktanz De mortibus persecutorum: Hermes 47 (1912) 250–275. — C. Weyman, Zur Schrift De mortibus persecutorum: HJG (1916) 76–77. — H. Koch, ZNW (1918) 196–201. — R. Graszynski, Quaestiones in aliquot locos commentarii De mortibus persecutorum: Eos (1919/20) 24 ff. — S. Anfuso, Lattanzio autore del 'De mortibus persecutorum': Didaskaleion 3 (1925) 31–88. — K. Roller, Die Kaisergeschichte in Laktanz 'De mortibus persecutorum'. Diss. Giessen, 1927. — A. Giusti, La malattia dell' imperatore Galerio nel racconto di Lattanzio: Bilychnis 32 (1928) 85–98. — A. Müller, Lactantius 'De mortibus persecutorum' oder die Beurteilung der Christenverfolgungen im Lichte des Mailänder Toleranzreskripts vom Jahre 313: F. J. Dölger, Konstantin der Große und seine Zeit. Gesammelte Studien. Freiburg, 1913, 66–88. — F. Martroye, Différences de texte entre Lactance et Eusèbe sur l'édit de Milan: Bull. de la Soc. nat. des Antiquaires de France (1915) 105–107. — J. W. Ph. Borleffs, Mnem 57 (1929) 427–436; *idem*, An scripserit Lactantius libellum qui est de mortibus persecutorum: Mnem 58 (1930) 223–292. — K. Guinagh, The Vicennalia in Lactantius: CJ 28 (1933) 449 f. — G. Billiet, De authenticiteit van De mortibus persecutorum: Philologische Studiën 5 (1933/34) 117–121, 198–214. — A. Maddalena, Per la definizione storica del *De mortibus persecutorum:* Atti del R. Istituto Veneto di scienze, lettere ed arti 94 (1934/35) 557–588. — G. Gonella, La critica dell'autorità delle leggi secondo Tertulliano e Lattanzio: Rivista Internazionale di Filosofia del Diritto (1937) 23–37. — H. Grégoire, About Licinius' Fiscal and Religious Policy: Byz (1938) 551–560; *idem*, La vision de Constantin 'liquidée' (sur le récit de Lactance): Byz (1939) 341–351. — J. Zeiller, Quelques remarques sur la 'vision' de Constantin (et le récit de Lactance): Byz (1939) 329–339. — A. Alföldi, Hoc signo victor eris. Beiträge zur Geschichte der Bekehrung Konstantins des Großen: Pisciculi (AC Ergänzungsband I). Münster, 1939, 1–18. — W. Seston, Dioclétien et la tétrarchie. Paris, 1946, 26 f. — A. d'Accinni, La data della salita al trono di Diocleziano: RFIC (1948) 244–256. — G. Bovini, La proprietà ecclesiastica e la condizione giuridica della Chiesa in età preconstantiniana. Milan, 1949. — E. Galletier, La mort de Maximien d'après le panégyrique de 310 et la vision de Constantin au temple d'Apollon: REAN (1950) 288–299.

6. *The Bird Phoenix*

The poem *De ave Phoenice* gives the well-known story of the phoenix in 85 distichs. Herodotus is the first to narrate it (11, 73), and Clement of Rome (25; cf. vol. I, p. 47) the earliest Christian author to make it a symbol of the resurrection. Thus it appears also in Tertullian, *De resurrectione carnis* 13, and in later writers as well as in the art of the early Church. According to *De ave Phoenice* there is a happy country in the Far East, where the great gate of heaven opens and the sun pours its light of spring. It rises above the highest mountains. A wood stands planted there perpetually verdant. No disease, no old age, no cruel death, no dreadful crime, no fear or grief ever enters. A fountain plays in the midst, which is called 'the living.' A wondrous tree bears mellow fruits that do not fall to the ground. This grove a single bird, the phoenix, inhabits—unique and eternal. When at its first rising the saffron morn grows red, she takes her seat on the highest top of the lofty tree, and begins to pour strains of sacred song and to hail the new light with wondrous voice and thrice adores the fire-bearing head of the sun with quivering of her wings. After she has spent a thousand years of her life, she desires to be reborn. She leaves the hallowed precinct and seeks this world, where death reigns. She directs her swift flight to Syria (Phoenicia). She chooses a lofty palm, with top reaching to the heavens, which has the pleasing name phoenix from the bird. There she builds for herself a nest or a tomb, for she perishes that she may live. She commends her soul (*animam commendat* v. 93) and dissolves in fire. From the ashes an animal is said to arise without limbs, a worm of a milky color, which develops into a cocoon. A new phoenix bursts out of it like a butterfly and flies forth about to return to her native abode. She carries all the remains of her old body to the altar of the sun, at Heliopolis in Egypt and presents herself an object of admiration to the beholder. The exulting crowd of Egypt salutes this wondrous bird. Then she returns to her country in the East. The poem closes with praise: 'O bird of happy lot and fate, to whom God himself granted to be born from herself... her only pleasure is in death: that she may be born, she desires previously to die... having gained eternal life by the blessing of death' (165-170 ANF 7).

Although there is an ancient myth behind this story, there are a number of features which are of Christian origin. The entire symbolism points to Christ, who comes from the country in the East, i.e. paradise, to the country where death reigns and dies there, but returns after His resurrection to His home. The words *animam commendat* actually remind one of Jesus saying: *In manus tuas commendo spiritum meum* (Luke 23, 46). Thus the phoenix is the symbol of the risen and glorified Saviour. The idea of death as a rebirth and beginning of a new life is well known in early Christianity (cf. vol. I, p. 47). Gregory of Tours (*De cursu stell.* 12) mentions Lactantius as the author of the poem and sees in the phoenix a symbol of resurrection. This view is not universally received and some think the work pagan. The similarities of thought, language and style existing between the poem and Lactantius' authentic works favor his authorship.

Editions: S. BRANDT, CSEL 27 (1897) 135–147. — M. C. FITZPATRICK, Lactantius' De ave Phoenice, with a translation. Diss. Philadelphia, 1933.

Translations: English: W. FLETCHER, ANL 22, 214–219; ANF 7, 324–326. — M. C. FITZPATRICK, *loc. cit.* — *German:* A. KNAPPITSCH, De L. Caeli Firmiani Lactantii 'ave Phoenice'. Progr. Graz, 1896.

Studies: S. BRANDT, Zum Phoenix des Laktantius: RhM 47 (1892) 390–403. — P. DE WINTERFELD, Coniectanea, 4–5: Hermes (1898) 168; *idem,* Ad Lactantium de ave Phoenice: Phil 62 (1903) 478–480. — A. RIESE, Zu dem Phoenix des Laktantius: RhM (1900) 316–318. — C. PASCAL, Sul carme De ave Phoenice attribuito a Lattanzio, con un appendice contenente le lezioni di due codici Ambrosiani. Naples, 1904. — P. MONCEAUX, Études critiques: RPh (1905) 104–139. — C. LANDI, Il carme 'de ave phoenicae' e il suo autore: Atti e Memorie della R. Academia Padua 31 (1915) 33–74. — H. BREWER, Die dem Laktantius beigelegte Dichtung 'De ave Phoenice', ein Werk aus dem Ende des 4. Jahrh.: ZkTh 46 (1922) 163–165. — F. J. DÖLGER, Sol salutis. 2nd ed. Münster, 1925, 222 f. — M. MASANTE, Lattanzio Firminiano o Lattanzio Placido autore del 'De ave Phoenice'?: Didaskaleion N.S. 3 (1925) I, 105–110. — B. BIANCO, Il carme 'De ave Phoenice' di Lattanzio Firminiano. Chieri, 1931. — M. LEROY, Le Chant du Phénix. L'ordre des vers dans le Carmen de ave Phoenice: ACL I (1932) 213–231. — M. SCHUSTER, Der Phönix und der Phönixmythos in der Dichtung des Lactantius: Commentationes Vindobonenses (1936) 55–69; *idem,* Zur Echtheitsfrage und Abfassungszeit von Lactantius' Dichtung *De ave Phoenice:* WSt 54 (1936) 118–128. — BLOCHET, Mus (1937) 123–129. — C. BRAKMAN, Opstellen en Vertalingen betreffende de Latijnse letterkunde 4. Leiden, 1934, 247–251.— J. HUBEAUX - M. LEROY, Le mythe du Phénix dans les littératures grecque et latine. 1939. — E. RAPISARDA, De ave Phoenice di L. Cecilio Firmiano Lattanzio (Raccolta di Studi di lett. crist. ant. 4). Catania, 1946. — C. M. EDSMAN, Ignis divinus. 1949, 127–203.

2. LOST WRITINGS

1. The *Symposion*, or *Banquet*, the first of Lactantius' works, has been mentioned above (p. 393).

2. The *Hodoeporicum* or *Itinerary* mentioned by Jerome (*De vir. ill.* 80) is a description of his journey from Africa to Nicomedia in hexameters.

3. Jerome refers in the same place to a treatise *Grammaticus*, of which nothing else is known.

4. He also speaks of two books *To Asclepiades*, four books of *Epistles to Probus*, two books of *Epistles to Severus* and two books of *Epistles to his Pupil Demetrianus*. This pupil was the one to whom he addressed his *De opificio dei*.

5. A manuscript at Milan (*Codex Ambrosianus* F 60 *sup. saec.* VIII–IX) contains a small fragment with the marginal note *Lactantius de motibus animi*. Consisting of a few lines only, it deals with the affections of the soul and explains their origin. They have been implanted by God, to help man in the practice of virtue. If they are kept within limits they lead to righteousness and eternal life, otherwise to vice and everlasting damnation. Form and content make it probable that the fragment is really Lactantius'.

Editions: S. BRANDT, CSEL 27 (1893) 157. — J. B. PESENTI, *op. cit.* 64 f.

Study: S. BRANDT, Über das in dem patristischen Exzerptencodex F. 60. Sup. der Ambrosiana enthaltene Fragment des Laktantius De motibus animi (Progr.). Leipzig, 1891.

Some of the manuscripts attribute the poems *De resurrectione* and *De pascha* to him. But the oldest manuscripts testify to their belonging to Venantius Fortunatus. Nor is the poem *De passione Domini* by Lactantius.

Edition: S. BRANDT, CSEL 27, I (1893) 148–151.

Translations: English: W. FLETCHER, ANL 22; ANF 7, 327–328.

Study: J. MARTIN, Ein frühchristliches Kreuzigungsbild? Würzburger Festgabe für H. Bulle. Würzburg, 1938, 151–168.

3. THEOLOGICAL VIEWS

Although Lactantius was the first Latin writer to attempt a systematic presentation of the Christian faith, he is not a genuine theologian; he lacks both the knowledge and the capacity. Even in his main work, the *Divine Institutes*, he defines Christianity only as a kind of popular morality. Of course, he is quite enthusiastic about martyrdom, the love of God and of neighbour, the virtues of humility and chastity, but he hardly mentions the supernatural gift of grace, that enables man to live up to this ideal. He speaks of the transformation wrought by the new faith without giving enough attention to the redeeming of mankind by a divine Saviour. His ethical demands are based more on philosophy than on religion. Deeply convinced of the absolute superiority of the faith, he is better in his devastating criticism of paganism than in his positive presentation of Christianity. Jerome already felt this keenly, exclaiming: *Utinam tam nostra confirmare potuisset quam facile aliena destruxit* (*Epist.* 58, 10). If there is one central thought that inspires all his work it is the idea of divine providence, to which he returns again and again.

1. *Dualism*

Mention has been made of dualistic passages occuring in some manuscripts, omitted in others. There is no need of these to prove Lactantius' dualism. According to him, before the creation of the world, God produced a Spirit, His Son, like to Himself, whom He endowed with all the divine perfections. Then He generated a second being, good in himself, but who did not remain true to his divine origin. He envied the Son and of his own free will he passed from good to evil and was called the devil (*Div. inst.* 2, 8). He became the source of wrong and the archenemy of God, in fact an anti-god (*antitheus* 2, 9, 13). Consequently, Lactantius speaks of two principles (*duo principia* 6, 6, 3). The enmity between them found expression in the universe at its creation, for it consists of two opposing elements, the heavens and the earth. The former is the abode of God, the place of light; the latter, the abode of men, the place of darkness and of death. Even the earth itself was set at odds. The east and south were assigned to God; the west and north to the evil spirit (*Div. inst.* 2, 9, 5–10). In this world God placed man, in himself an image of the cosmos because made up of soul and body, of elements hostile to, and at war with, each other: the soul being from heaven and belonging to God, the body being from the earth and belonging to the devil (*Div. inst.*

2, 12, 10). In the one good inheres; in the other evil (*De ira dei* 16, 3). According as spirit or flesh, right or wrong, is victorious in the lifelong conflict, man receives an eternal reward or eternal punishment (*Div. inst.* 2, 12, 7). In this dualism, which seems to be derived from Stoicism, in this enmity between the devil and God, Lactantius sees the origin of all morality as well as of all immorality. God, in His almighty power, can take away the bad but He does not wish to do so. 'With the greatest prudence God placed in evil the material cause of virtue' (*Epitome* 24). He intended that there should exist this great distinction between good and evil, so that from evil the nature of good might be known and understood (*Div. inst.* 5, 7, 5). Just as there can be no light without darkness, no war without an enemy, so there can be no virtue unless vice exists (*Div. inst.* 3, 29, 16). For if vice is an evil because it is opposed to virtue, and virtue is a good because it overthrows vice, then both are necessary to each other. To exclude evil is to eliminate virtue (*Epitome* 24).

2. *The Holy Spirit*

Since the second being generated by God the Father became the archenemy of God, the question is, what place the Holy Spirit occupies in the theology of Lactantius. Jerome (*Epist.* 84, 7; *Comm. in Gal. ad* 4, 6) testifies that he denied, especially in the two books of his *Letters to Demetrianus*, now lost, the existence of a third member of the Trinity or the divine personality of the Holy Spirit, identifying Him sometimes with the Father, sometimes with the Son.

3. *The Creation and Immortality of the Soul*

Lactantius does not share the opinion of his teacher Arnobius regarding creation by subordinate powers. He is, on the contrary, convinced that 'the same God who made the world also created man from the beginning' (*Div. inst.* 2, 5, 31). He personally fashioned both Spirit and flesh infusing the one into the other so that the product is entirely His (*Div. inst.* 2, 11, 19; *ipse animam qua spiramus infudit*). Lactantius rejects all traducianism, for the soul is begotten through the efforts of neither the father nor the mother nor both together.

For a body may be produced from a body, since something

is contributed from both; but a soul cannot be produced from souls, because nothing can depart from a slight and incomprehensible subject. Therefore the manner of the production of souls belongs entirely to God alone... For nothing but what is mortal can be generated from mortals. Nor ought he to be deemed a father who in no way perceives that he has transmitted or breathed a soul from his own; nor, if he perceives it, comprehends in his mind when or in what manner that effect is produced. From this it is evident that souls are not given by parents, but by one and the same God and Father of all, who alone has the law and method of their birth, since He alone produces them (*De opif.* 19, 1 ff; ANF 7).

Lactantius thus believes in creationism. As to the exact moment, he states: 'It is not introduced into the body after birth, as it appears to some philosophers, but immediately after conception, when the divine necessity has formed the offspring in the womb' (*De opif.* 17, 7).

He also differs from Arnobius regarding immortality. Whereas his teacher held the view that the soul was not of itself endowed with deathlessness but could achieve it by a Christian life, Lactantius says explicitly that it possesses this property by nature. Just as God lives always, so He made the spirit of man (*Div. inst.* 3, 9, 7). Further evidence of the writer's view is to be found in his belief that the wicked are not annihilated but subject to eternal punishment (*Div. inst.* 2, 12, 7–9). 'Since wisdom, which is given to man alone, is nothing else than a knowledge of God, it is evident that the soul does not die nor is it annihilated, but rather remains forever, because it seeks and loves God who is eternal' (*Div. inst.* 7, 9, 12). Thus man is in essence everlasting, but does not experience the full effects and purpose of this gift unless by the sincere practice of true religion he attains to heaven and a life of unending happiness with God.

4. *Eschatology*

Chapters 14–26 of the seventh book of the *Divine Institutes* present an eschatology of definitely chiliastic color:

Since all the works of God were completed in six days, the world must continue in its present state through six ages, that is, six thousand years. For the great day of God is limited by a circle of a thousand years, as the prophet shows, who says (Ps. 89, 4), 'In Thy sight, O Lord, a thousand years are as one day.' And as God laboured during those six days in creating such great works, so His religion and truth must labour during these six thousand years, while wickedness prevails and bears rule. And again, since God, having finished His works, rested on the seventh day and blessed it, at the end of the six thousandth year all wickedness must be abolished from the earth, and righteousness reign for a thousand years; and there must be tranquillity and rest from the labours which the world now long has endured (7, 14 ANF 7).

Lactantius is convinced that there are at the most only two hundred years left of the six thousand. Then 'the Son of the most high and mighty God shall come to judge the living and the dead... When He shall have destroyed unrighteousness, and executed His great judgment, and shall have recalled to life the righteous, who have lived from the beginning, He will be engaged among men a thousand years, and will rule them with most just command... About the same time also the prince of the devils, who is the contriver of all evils, shall be bound with chains, and shall be imprisoned during the thousand years of the heavenly rule in which righteousness shall reign in the world, so that he may contrive no evil against the people of God. After His coming the righteous shall be collected from all the earth, and, the judgment being completed, the sacred city shall be planted in the middle of the earth, in which God Himself the builder may dwell together with the righteous, bearing rule in it... the sun will become seven times brighter than it is now; the earth will open its fruitfulness and bring forth most abundant fruits of its own accord; the rocky mountains shall drop with honey; streams of wine shall run down, and rivers flow with milk; in short the world itself shall rejoice, and all nature exult, being rescued and set free from the dominion of evil and impiety and guilt and error' (7, 24 ANF 7). Before the end of the thousand years the devil shall be loosed afresh and shall assemble all the pagan nations to make war against the holy city. He shall besiege and surround it. 'Then the last anger of God shall come upon the nations, and shall utterly destroy them' (7, 26) and the world shall go down in a great conflagration. The people of God will be concealed in the caves of the earth during the three days of destruction, until the anger of God against the nations and the last judgment shall be ended. 'Then the righteous shall go forth from their hiding-places, and shall find all things covered with carcasses and bones... But when the thousand years shall be completed, the world shall be renewed by God, and the heavens shall be folded together, and the earth shall be changed, and God shall transform men into the similitude of angels... At the same time shall take place that second and public resurrection of all, in which the un-righteous shall be raised to everlasting punishment' (7, 26 ANF 7).

Studies: E. OVERLACH, Die Theologie des Lactantius. Schwerin, 1858. — M. HEINIG, Die Ethik des Lactantius. Grimma, 1887. — MARTENS, Das dualistische System des Laktanz: Der Beweis des Glaubens 24 (1888) 14–25, 48–70, 114–119, 138–153, 181–193. — F. MARBACH, Die Psychologie des Firmianus Laktantius. Diss. Halle a.S., 1889. — F. W. BUSSEL, The Purpose of the World-Process and the Problem of Evil as Explained in the Clementine and Lactantian Writings in a System of Subordinate Dualism: Studia Biblica et Ecclesiastica 4. Oxford, 1896, 177–187. — L. ATZBERGER, Geschichte der christlichen Eschatologie innerhalb der vornicänischen Zeit. Freiburg i.B., 1896, 583–611. — R. PICHON, Lactance. Étude sur le mouvement philosophique et religieuse sous le règne de Constantine. Paris, 1901. — J. SIEGERT, Die Theologie des Laktantius in ihrem Verhältnis zur Stoa. Diss. Bonn, 1919. — H. KOCH, Der 'Tempel Gottes' bei Laktantius: Phil (1920) 235–238. — K. E. HARTWELL, Lactantius and Milton. London, 1929. — J. STELZENBERGER, Die Beziehungen der früh-christlichen Sittenlehre zur Ethik der Stoa. Munich, 1933, 83–86, 125–128. — H. BOLKESTEIN, Humanitas bei Laktantius. Christlich oder orientalisch?: Pisciculi. Franz J. Dölger dargeboten. Münster, 1939, 62–65. — G. RICHARD, Les obstacles à la liberté de conscience au IVe siècle de l'ère chrétienne (et la notion de liberté de conscience chez Lactance): Mélanges Radet: REAN (1940) 498–507. — J. BARBEL, Christos Angelos. Bonn, 1941, 188–192. — A. VASILEV, Medieval Ideas of the End of the World, West and East: Byz 16 (1942/43) 462–502. — E. SCHNEWEIS, Angels and Demons according to Lactantius (SCA 3). Washington, 1943. — E. RAPISARDA, L'epi-cureismo nei primi scrittori cristiani: Antiquitas 1, 1 (1946) 49–54. — P. J. COUVÉE, Vita beata en vita aeterna. Een onderzoek naar de ontwikkeling van het begrip vita beata naast en tegenover vita aeterna bij Lactantius, Ambrosius en Augustinus, onder invloed van de romeinsche Stoa. (Diss.). Baarn, 1947. — J. DANIÉLOU, La typologie millénariste de la semaine dans le christianisme primitif: VC 2 (1948) 1–16. — G. L. ELLSPERMANN, The Attitude of the Early Christian Writers Toward Pagan Literature and Learning (PSt 82). Washington, 1949. — A. HUDSON-WILLIAMS, Orientius and Lactantius: VC 3 (1949) 237–243. — R. M. GRANT, Patristica (Lactantius and Irenaeus): VC 3 (1949) 225–229. — H. KARPP, Probleme altchristlicher Anthro-pologie (BFTh 44, 3). Gütersloh, 1950, 132–171. — J. FISCHER, Die Einheit der bei-den Testamente bei Laktanz, Victorin von Pettau und deren Quellen: Münchener Theol. Zeitschr. 1 (1950) 96–101.

CHAPTER V

THE OTHER WRITERS OF THE WEST

VICTORINUS OF PETTAU

The first exegete to write in Latin was Victorinus, bishop of
Petabio in Pannonia Superior, the modern Pettau in Styria. He
died as a martyr, most probably in A.D. 304, a victim of Diocletian's persecution. Jerome (*De vir. ill.* 74) gives the following
information about him:

> Victorinus, bishop of Pettau, was not equally as familiar
> with Latin as with Greek. On this account his works, though
> noble in thought, are inferior in style. They are the follow-
> ing: Commentaries on Genesis, On Exodus, On Leviticus,
> On Isaias, On Ezechiel, On Habakkuk, On Ecclesiastes, On
> the Canticle of Canticles, On the Apocalypse of John,
> Against all Heresies and many others. At the last he received
> the crown of martyrdom.

The fact that his Greek was better than his Latin does not
necessarily imply that he was a Greek by birth, because of the
well-known mixture of languages in his native Pannonia.

HIS WRITINGS

His works do not reveal much scholarship. Jerome pronounces
erudition lacking, but not goodwill: *licet desit eruditio, tamen non
deest eruditionis voluntas* (*Epist.* 70, 5). He had difficulty in expressing
himself in Latin and his style suffers from a lack of versatility and
skill: *Quod intelligit eloqui non potest* (Jerome, *Epist.* 58, 10).

1. *The Commentary on the Apocalypse*

Of all the commentaries mentioned by Jerome, only one is
extant, that on the Apocalypse. Its original text, preserved in
Codex Ottobon. lat. 3288 A *saec.* XV, was not published until 1916
(CSEL 49). It testifies to the chiliastic view of its author. Before the
discovery of this manuscript, the work was known only in Jerome's edition, which omits the unmistakable milleniarism of the

conclusion and several valuable references to earlier writers, for instance to Papias, but adds sections from his contemporary Tyconius. Jerome's edition was later on enlarged. In the eighth century it was used by the Spanish priest Beatus in his great commentary on the Apocalypse.

Edition: J. HAUSSLEITER, CSEL 49 (1916) 11–154.

Translations: English: R. E. WALLIS, ANL 18, 394–433; ANF 7, 344–360.

Studies: J. HAUSSLEITER, Die Kommentare des Victorinus, Ticonius und Hieronymus zur Apokalypse: Zeitschr. f. kirchl. Wiss. u. kirchl. Leben 7 (1886) 239 ff. — J. R. HARRIS, A New Patristic Fragment: Expositor (1895) 448 ff. — L. ATZBERGER, Geschichte der christlichen Eschatologie innerhalb der vornicänischen Zeit. Freiburg i.B., 1896, 566–573. — J. HAUSSLEITER, Beiträge zur Würdigung der Offenbarung des Johannes und ihres ältesten lateinischen Auslegers, Victorinus von Pettau. Greifswald, 1901. — H. J. VOGELS, Untersuchungen zur Geschichte der lateinischen Apokalypse-Übersetzung. Düsseldorf, 1920, 48–55. — H. KOCH, Cyprianische Untersuchungen, Bonn, 1926, 473 f. — J. BARBEL, Christos Angelos. Bonn, 1941, 79–80. — J. FISCHER, Die Einheit der beiden Testamente bei Laktanz, Victorin von Pettau und deren Quellen: Münchener Theol. Zeitschrift 1 (1950) 96–101.

2. *De fabrica mundi*

The chiliastic tendency that we notice in the *Commentary on the Apocalypse* appears clearly in the fragment *De fabrica mundi*, preserved in a single manuscript, *Codex Lambethanus 414 saec.* IX, from which it was published by W. Cave in 1688. It must be one of the 'many other' works to which Jerome refers without giving their titles. Style and thought are those of Victorinus.

Edition: J. HAUSSLEITER, CSEL 49 (1916) 3–9.

Translations: English: R. E. WALLIS, ANL 18, 388–393; ANF 7, 341–343.

Studies: W. MACHOLZ, Spuren binitarischer Denkweise im Abendlande seit Tertullian. Jena, 1902, 16 ff. — C. WEYMAN, Wochenschrift f. klass. Philologie 34 (1917) 1103 ff. — A. JÜLICHER, GGA (1919) 46–49.

3. *Against All Heresies*

It is possible that this work, mentioned by Jerome, is identical with the pamphlet of the same name appended to Tertullian's *Prescription of Heretics* (46–53) which, originally published in Greek, is believed to have been translated by Victorinus (cf. above, p. 272).

Edition: A. KROYMANN, CSEL 47 (1906) 213–226.

Translations: English: S. THELWALL, ANL 18, 259–273; ANF 3, 649–654.

Studies: A. HARNACK, Geschichte der marcionitischen Kirchen: Zeitschr. f. wissen-schaftl. Theologie 19 (1875) 115 ff.; *idem*, Geschichte der altchristl. Literatur 2, 2, 430 ff. — E. SCHWARTZ, Zwei Predigten Hippolyts (SAM Philos.-hist. Abt. Fasc. 3). Munich, 1936.

The exegesis of Victorinus is based on Greek authors, on Papias, Irenaeus, Hippolytus, and especially on Origen. It seems that he did not give a running commentary on the entire text but contented himself with a paraphrase of selected passages. Thus Cassiodorus is more exact than Jerome, when he avoids the term commentary and states that Victorinus dealt briefly with some difficult places in the Apocalypse (*Inst.* 1, 9). The so-called *Decretum Gelasianum de libris recipiendis et non recipiendis* declared the works of Victorinus 'apocryphal,' most probably on account of their chiliastic tendencies.

Studies: J. HAUSSLEITER, Realencykl. f. protest. Theol. 20, 614–619. — F. KATTEN-BUSCH, Das apostolische Symbol 1. Leipzig, 1894, 212 ff. — G. MERCATI, Varia Sacra 1 (ST 11). Rome, 1903, 1–49. — C. H. TURNER, An Exegetical Fragment of the Third Century: JThSt 5 (1904) 218–241. — A. SOUTER, Reasons for regarding Hilarius (Ambrosiaster) as the Author of the Mercati-Turner Anecdoton: JThSt 5 (1904) 608–621. — TH. ZAHN, Neue Funde aus der alten Kirche: NKZ 16 (1905) 419–427. — A. WILMART, Un Anonyme ancien de decem virginibus: Bull. d'anc. litt. et d'archéol. chrét. 1 (1911) 35–50, 88–103. — J. WÖHRER, Eine kleine Schrift, die vielleicht dem hl. Märtyrerbischof Victorin von Pettau angehört: Jahresbericht des Privatgymnasiums Wilhering 1927, 3–8; *idem*, Victorini ep. Petav. (?) ad Justinum Manichaeum: *ibid.* 1928, 3–7; cf. RB Bull. 2 n. 44 f (1929). — F. LOOFS, Theophilus von Antiochien Adv. Marcionem und die andern theol. Quellen bei Irenaeus (TU 46, 2). Leipzig, 1930, 126–130, 232 f. — E. BENZ, Marius Victorinus. Stuttgart, 1932, 23–30. — N. J. HOMMES, Het Testimoniaalboek. 1935, 225–230. — L. BIELER, The 'Creeds' of St. Victorinus and of St. Patrick: TS 9 (1948) 121–124.

RETICIUS OF AUTUN

Among the bishops of the Constantinian period there is hardly anyone who had a greater reputation in Gaul than Reticius, bishop of Autun. The Emperor sent him to Rome to attend the synods of 313 and 314, which dealt with the Donatist controversy. Jerome mentions that he had read his commentary *On the Canticle of Canticles* and 'his great volume' *Against Novatian* (*De vir. ill.* 82). He passes a severe criticism on the first because he found many absurdities in it (*Epist.* 37; *Epist.* 5, 2). Neither of the two works known to Jerome survives. The exegetical study of the Canticle of Canticles was used in the twelfth century by Berenger of Poitiers, whose *Apology for Abelard*, written against Bernard of Clairvaux, contains a passage from the introduction. Augustine quotes an interesting sentence regarding original sin which seems to be from the *Against Novatian* (*Contra Julianum* 1, 3, 7; *Opus imperf. c. Jul.* 1, 55).

Editions: Contra Novatianos (Fragment in: Augustine, *Contra Julianum* 1, 3, 7 or *Opus imperfectum* 1, 55): ML 44, 644. — *Commentarius in Canticum Canticorum* (Fragment in Peter Berengar of Poitiers, *Liber apologeticus pro Abaelardo*): ML 178, 1864.

Studies: H. WRIGHT PHILLOT, in: Smith and Wace, Dictionary of Christian Biography 4 (1887) 544 f. — A. HARNACK, Geschichte der altchristlich. Literatur 1, 751 f.; 2, 2, 433. — G. BARDY, DTC 13, 2571 f. — G. MORIN, Reticius d'Autun et 'Beringer': RB 13 (1896) 340 f.

INDEXES

I. REFERENCES

1. OLD AND NEW TESTAMENT

2. ANCIENT CHRISTIAN WRITERS

(Brackets enclosing the name or the passage = Pseudo-)

3. MODERN AUTHORS

Aalders, G. J. D., 244, 275
Aall, A., 79
Accini, A. d', 402
Achelis, H., 151, 166, 171, 175, 176, 182,
    186, 197, 198, 369
Adam, K., 234, 314, 327, 330, 331, 378
Agius, A., 82
Akermann, M., 269
Alban, B., 393
Albizzati, C., 317
Alès, A. d', 41, 42, 69, 79, 143, 165, 169,
    216, 233, 244, 248, 249, 250, 273, 275,
    278, 280, 281, 301, 314, 315, 320, 324,
    341, 349, 367, 375, 378
Alföldi, A., 402
Alfonsi, L., 9, 19, 163, 264
Allcker, J., 387
Allevi, L., 2
Allgeier, A., 244
Allie, J. L., 273
Almen, I. J. von, 84
Altaner, B., 43, 139
Altendorf, E., 332, 375
Amann, E., 117, 129, 138, 142, 165, 185,
    216, 281, 393
Amelli, A., 345
Ammundsen, V., 216
Anderson, J. O., 216
Andres, F., 27
Andriessen, P., 173
Anfuso, S., 402
Anglus, Joh. Clem., 253
Anrich, G., 90
Antweiler, A., 41
Arbesmann, R., 159, 266, 268
Arbez, E. P., 123
Arendzen, J. P., 14, 49, 185
Armini, H., 387
Arnold, A., 190
Arnou, R., 2, 41, 91
Arpe, C., 250
Athenagoras, M., 103, 185
Atzberger, L., 90, 136, 284, 340, 392,
    410, 412
Axelson, B., 160, 161, 162, 364, 387,
    394

Babut, E. Ch., 211
Backer, E. de, 250
Bacon, B. W., 211
Bader, R., 57
Badurina, F., 130

Baehrens, W. A., 43, 47, 48, 50, 161, 402
Baer, J., 129, 226, 340, 346, 347, 348,
    349, 352, 354, 356, 357, 359, 361, 362,
    363, 366
Bainton, R. H., 309
Bakhuizen van den Brink, J. N., 272,
    332, 347, 349, 352
Balanos, D. S., 143
Ball, M. T., 345
Balogh, J., 36
Balsamo, M., 255, 263
Balthasar, H. U. von, 44, 51, 100
Bancy, M. M., 249
Bannier, W., 177
Barbel, J., 81, 202, 233, 286, 410, 412
Barclay, W., 57
Bardenhewer, O., 138, 173, 175
Bardon, H., 154
Bardy, G., 3, 5, 6, 7, 27, 35, 40, 41, 43,
    44, 48, 50, 57, 61, 62, 69, 72, 79, 83,
    93, 100, 123, 130, 138, 142, 143, 144,
    146, 154, 155, 165, 169, 173, 204, 212,
    235, 239, 243, 244, 245, 286, 314, 322,
    332, 375, 378, 379, 392, 414
Barjeau, J. Philip de, 122
Barnard, P. M., 16
Barnes, W. E., 41
Barre, A. de la, 6
Barth, F., 47
Barthel, B., 394
Bartlet, J. V., 152, 190
Bassi, D., 160
Bastgen, M., 387
Batiffol, P., 31, 108, 117, 190, 235, 314,
    337, 383
Bauer, A., 166, 177
Bauer, C., 122
Bauer, W., 139
Bauernfeind, O., 50
Baumstark, A., 119, 120, 183, 184, 211,
    216
Baus, K., 309
Bayard, L., 129, 226, 248, 340, 344, 347,
    348, 364, 366
Baylis, H. J., 162
Beaucamp, P., 152
Beck, A., 289, 323, 345
Becker, C., 262, 263
Bedard, W., 281
Bedjan, P., 118, 124
Behr, E., 160
Beïs, N., 175

Buonaiuti, E., 6, 129, 143, 161, 243, 249, 282, 372
Burel, J., 103
Burger, F. X., 160
Burghardt, W. J., 4, 26
Burgon, J. W., 101
Buri, F., 26
Burke, G., 84
Burkitt, F. C., 2, 152, 250
Burmester, O. H. E., 114, 186
Burnet, G., 401
Busch, B., 343
Bussel, F. W., 410
Butler, C., 353, 378
Butterworth, G. W., 8, 9, 16, 18, 35, 61

Cabrol, F., 243
Cadiou, R., 3, 41, 43, 51, 79, 100, 121
Cagnat, P., 243
Cairns, W. H., 56
Callewaert, C., 190, 261, 263
Camelot, Th., 21, 26, 36, 286, 327
Camino y Orella, J. A. del, 346
Campbell, H., 387
Campenhausen, H. v., 292
Capelle, B., 64, 142, 165, 194, 202, 244, 269, 349, 368, 371
Capitaine, W., 11
Capua, F. di, 160, 162, 263
Carcopino, J., 264
Carey, H., 226, 346, 366
Carlier, V., 160
Carlson, M. L., 299, 394
Carpenter, H. J., 194
Casel, O., 4, 36, 87, 100, 179, 183, 352
Casey, R. P., 15, 21, 23
Caspar, E., 235, 237, 378
Caspari, C. P., 28, 126, 237, 242
Caster, M., 14
Castiglioni, L., 248, 256, 282, 310, 316, 349, 355, 394
Catalfamo, G., 6
Cataudella, Q., 8, 9, 19, 21, 57, 161, 316
Cavallera, F., 41, 57, 314
Cave, W., 412
Cecchielli, C., 244
Cerfaux, L., 2
Chadwick, H., 56, 57, 64, 65, 91, 130, 136
Champonier, J., 6, 41
Chapman, J., 211, 349, 352, 378
Charlier, G., 162
Chartier, C., 302, 335, 349
Chase, F. H., 69

Chase, R. M., 293
Cherniss, H., 196
Ciceri, P. L., 160
Ciganotto, L., 69
Claesson, Gösta, 252
Clark, F. L., 21
Clark, W. R., 129, 133, 134, 136
Colombo, S., 160, 161, 250, 262, 263, 343, 345, 346, 347, 348, 349, 352, 355, 356, 357, 359, 361, 392, 393
Colon, J. B., 93
Colson, F. H., 14, 105, 275
Concasty, M. L., 176
Connolly, R. H., 151, 179, 181, 182, 183, 186, 190, 194, 196
Conybeare, F. C., 102, 239
Combe, E., 159
Combefis, F., 117
Cooper, J., 185
Corssen, P., 211, 212, 275, 340, 371
Cortelezzi, G., 296
Costanza, M., 366
Couratin, A. H., 293
Courcelle, P., 48
Coustant, P., 237, 239, 241, 242
Couvée, P. J., 410
Cramer, J. A., 46, 65
Crehan, J. H., 64, 183, 194, 324
Cresswell, R. H., 184
Crombie, F., 43, 56, 61, 75, 139
Cruice, P., 168
Crum, W. E., 114, 117
Cuesta, J. J., 152
Cullmann, O., 50, 57, 64, 190
Cumont, F., 273, 398

Dahl, N. A., 190
Dale, A., 69
Dalmasso, L., 162
Dalrymple, D., 159
Daly, C. B., 226, 335
Daly, E. J., 262
Damsté, P. H., 159, 160
Daniélou, J., 4, 36, 41, 43, 93, 101, 169, 179, 340, 410
Decker, A., 11
Deeleman, C. F. M., 369
Dekkers, E., 253, 298, 324, 337
Delatti, A., 162
Delazer, J., 306
Delehaye, H., 341, 372
Demmel, J. A., 250
Demmler, A., 224, 226
Dennefeld, L., 122

Mengis, H. K., 344, 346, 367
Menoud, Ph., 84, 194
Menzies, A., 43, 44, 49
Mercati, G., 17, 45, 57, 114, 133, 144, 146, 184, 185, 237, 245, 344, 363, 367, 371, 413
Mercer, E., 243
Merkx, P. A. H. J., 345
Merrill, E. T., 263
Mersch, E., 83, 130, 332, 375
Mesnage, J., 243
Mesnard, M., 219, 251, 254
Metcalfe, M., 72, 75, 125
Meunier, A., 48
Meyboom, H. U., 7, 9, 11, 14, 16, 44, 56, 61, 69, 72, 75, 93, 159, 168, 254, 255, 266, 268, 269, 272, 275, 276, 277, 281, 282, 283, 286, 289, 292, 293, 296, 297, 299, 301, 304, 305, 306, 307, 309, 310, 311, 312, 314, 316
Meyer, H., 90
Meyer, W., 358
Michaud, E., 331, 375
Michels, Th., 354
Michiels, E., 251
Micka, E. F., 392, 400
Milburn, R. L. P., 142
Miller, E., 166, 168
Miller, P. S., 103
Millosevich, F., 356
Minn, H. R., 309
Miodoński, A., 266, 368, 369, 371
Miura Stange, A., 57
Modius, Fr., 261
Moffat, J., 297, 355
Mohlberg, L. C., 216
Mohrmann, Chr., 155, 162, 209, 233, 249, 251, 253, 262, 273, 281, 292, 293, 299, 301, 304, 345, 367, 393
Moingt, J., 21
Molignoni, G., 393
Molland, E., 21, 26
Mommsen, H., 345
Monceaux, P., 243, 248, 343, 369, 370, 392, 402, 404
Mondésert, C., 8, 9, 14, 18, 26, 36
Montfaucon, B. de, 45
Montgomery, J. A., 174
Moore, H., 219
Morel, V., 250, 332
Morgan, J., 320
Moricca, U., 160, 296, 345, 347, 401
Morin, G., 44, 48, 154, 165, 183, 185, 345, 369, 414

Morize, P., 103
Mossbacher, H., 36
Motherway, T. J., 330
Moule, H. C. C., 392
Mras, K., 9, 177
Muir, W., 343
Müller, A., 159, 402
Müller, J. G. Th., 398
Müller, K., 62, 165, 169, 183, 186, 235
Müller, M., 154, 233, 319
Muncey, R. W., 297
Munck, J., 2, 3, 5
Mundle, W., 212
Muratori, L. A., 207, 209
Murray, J., 41
Murphy, F. X., 43, 48, 50, 51, 62, 147
Murphy, M. G., 36

Nairne, A., 190
Nasilowski, 375
Nau, F., 109, 118, 151, 184, 185
Naumann, J., 275
Nautin, P., 165, 166, 169, 170, 194
Navickas, J. C., 375
Nelke, L., 366, 367
Nelz, H. R., 3, 121, 122
Nemes, V., 248
Nero, E., 11
Neumann, K. J., 165, 171
Nicolesi, J., 394
Nicotra, G., 375
Niemer, G., 343
Nihard, R., 160
Nilsson, M., 2
Nisters, R., 249
Niven, W. D., 343
Nock, A. D., 2, 62, 64, 281, 290, 315, 343
Nöldechen, E., 248, 269, 293
Norberg, D., 372
Norden, E., 162, 250, 386
Norwood, P. O., 183

Oehler, F., 254, 261, 262, 306, 307
Oepke, A., 28
Ogg, G., 15, 173, 177
Oggioni, G., 165
Öhlander, C. J., 186
Oldfather, W. A., 139
O'Leary, D. L., 184
O'Meara, J. J., 69, 72
Opitz, H. G., 103, 162
Orlinsky, H. M., 45
Orsavai, F., 392
Orth, E., 160

Regibus, A. de, 401
Reichardt, W., 74, 139
Reifferscheid, A., 254, 255, 266, 280, 282, 289, 293, 297, 311, 312, 314, 386
Reinach, Th., 161
Reinhardt, K., 21, 169
Reitzenstein, R., 43, 160, 340, 344, 372
Régnon, T. de, 77, 79
Rendall, G. H., 159, 163
Restrepo-Jaramillo, J. M., 324
Reuss, J., 49
Révay, G., 160
Revel, G., 169
Rhenanus, Beatus, 253
Richard, G., 410
Richard, M., 46, 62, 109, 114, 169, 177, 178
Richardson, C. C., 42, 183, 190
Riedel, W., 51, 174, 186
Riedmatten, H. de, 142
Riese, A., 404
Riessler, R., 143
Rietz, G., 51
Rigaltius, Nic., 254
Rist, M., 275
Ritschl, O., 366, 375
Ritter, S., 210
Rivière, J., 81, 328
Roberts, R. E., 320
Robertson, D. S., 316
Robinson, J. A., 43, 57
Robinson, Th. H., 209
Roch, G., 103
Roethe, G., 210, 237
Röhricht, A., 392
Rolffs, E., 207, 314, 332
Roller, K., 402
Rombold, A., 367
Rönsch, H., 275, 394
Rosenmeyer, L., 286
Rosetti, L., 396
Rossi, G., 41, 90, 91
Rossi, G. B. de, 234
Rost, H., 245
Rougier, L., 57
Routh, M. J., 110, 113, 114, 127, 138, 141, 143, 237, 241
Rücker, A., 186
Rucker, I., 242
Rue, C. de la, 43
Rush, A. C., 358
Rüsche, F., 92
Rüther, Th., 7, 23, 33, 36

Ruwet, J., 26, 93
Ryan, E. A., 309
Ryba, B., 160
Ryder, H. J. D., 369
Ryssel, V., 124, 125, 127

Sagarda, N. J., 125
Sagnard, F., 15
Saint, W. P. le, 304, 305, 306
Saitta, A., 21
Sajdak, J., 263, 366
Salaverri, J., 3
Salaville, S., 190, 383
Salmon, G., 129, 168
Salmond, S. D. F., 102, 103, 104, 106, 107, 108, 110, 113, 125, 126, 127, 138, 139, 166, 171, 173, 174, 175, 176, 180, 196, 197, 370
Saltet, 375
Sánchez Aliseda, C., 401
Sanctis, G. de, 161
Sanday, W., 244, 345
Sande Bakhuyzen, W. H. van de, 147
Sargisean, B., 177
Savio, C. F., 273
Schaefer, A., 209
Schäfer, K. Th., 211, 212, 244, 245
Schäfer, O., 298
Scham, J., 36
Scharnagl, J., 386
Scharsch, P., 337
Scheiwiler, A., 31, 382
Schepens, P., 281, 353, 369
Scherer, J., 50, 64
Schermann, Th., 119, 182, 183, 184
Schildenberger, J. P., 245
Schilfgaarde, A. P. van, 253
Schilling, O., 16
Schindler, J., 355
Schlegel, G. D., 292
Schmalz, J. H., 372, 386
Schmaus, M., 34, 85
Schmidt, A., 250
Schmidt, C., 186
Schmidt, J., 161, 210, 268
Schmidt, K. L., 41
Schmidt, P. J., 21
Schneider, A. M., 182, 244, 357
Schneider, H., 245
Schneider, D., 169
Schneidewind, F. G., 166, 168
Schneweis, E., 410
Schnitzer, C. F., 61
Schnitzer, J., 162

4. GREEK WORDS

IMPRIMATUR

Driebergen, d. 22 m. dec. A. D. 1952

J. A. PREIN, cens. a.h.d.

34031

2005 Keep

Date Due

3-4 9AM			
3-5-2PM			
3-6-9AM			
3-10-9am			
3-13-9AM			
3-14-9PM			
3-16-9AM			
AP 3'63			
NOV 15 1963			
OC 22'68			

Demco 293-5